Emotion

Emotion

Annett Schirmer

National University of Singapore

Los Angeles | London | New Delhi
Singapore | Washington DC

Los Angeles | London | New Delhi
Singapore | Washington DC

FOR INFORMATION:

SAGE Publications, Inc.
2455 Teller Road
Thousand Oaks, California 91320
E-mail: order@sagepub.com

SAGE Publications Ltd.
1 Oliver's Yard
55 City Road
London EC1Y 1SP
United Kingdom

SAGE Publications India Pvt. Ltd.
B 1/I 1 Mohan Cooperative Industrial Area
Mathura Road, New Delhi 110 044
India

SAGE Publications Asia-Pacific Pte. Ltd.
3 Church Street
#10-04 Samsung Hub
Singapore 049483

Acquisitions Editor: Reid Hester
Editorial Assistant: Lucy Berbeo
Production Editor: David C. Felts
Copy Editor: Talia Greenberg
Typesetter: C&M Digitals (P) Ltd.
Proofreader: Wendy Jo Dymond
Indexer: Scott Smiley
Cover Designer: Anupama Krishnan
Marketing Manager: Shari Countryman

Printed in the United States of America

Library of Congress Cataloging-in-Publication Data

Schirmer, Annett.

Emotion / Annett Schirmer, National University of Singapore.

pages cm
Includes index.

ISBN 978-1-4522-2625-5 (pbk. : alk. paper)

1. Emotions. 2. Emotions and cognition. 3. Cognition. 4. Neurosciences. I. Title.

BF531.S353 2015
152.4—dc23   2014006257

This book is printed on acid-free paper.

SUSTAINABLE FORESTRY INITIATIVE
Certified Chain of Custody
Promoting Sustainable Forestry
www.sfiprogram.org
SFI-01268
SFI label applies to text stock

14 15 16 17 18 10 9 8 7 6 5 4 3 2 1

Brief Contents

Preface   xv

About the Author   xvii

PART 1: EMOTION THEORIES FROM ANTIQUITY TO MODERNITY   1

1. The Passions of the Soul: Early Emotion Theories   2
2. Brain and Thought Processes as Antecedents to Emotion: Emotion Theories of the 20th Century   20
3. What Is an Emotion? Modern Thoughts and Concepts   42

PART 2: FOUNDATIONS FOR EMOTION RESEARCH   71

4. Biological Foundations   73
5. Methodological Foundations I: Eliciting Emotions   102
6. Methodological Foundations II: Exploring Emotions   125

PART 3: EMOTIONS   151

7. Joy and Positive Emotions   152
8. Sadness   178
9. Fear   204

PART 4: EMOTIONS AND OTHER MENTAL PROCESSES   231

10. Emotion Effects on Cognition   233
11. Emotion Regulation   263

PART 5: INTRA- AND INTER-INDIVIDUAL DIFFERENCES IN EMOTION   287

12. Emotions Across the Life Span   289

13. Emotions and Sex Differences   320

14. Emotions and Culture   355

References   385

Glossary   446

Author Index   461

Subject Index   493

Detailed Contents

Preface   xv

About the Author   xvii

PART 1: EMOTION THEORIES FROM ANTIQUITY TO MODERNITY   1

1 The Passions of the Soul: Early Emotion Theories   2

Ancient Greece and the Early Roman Empire   2
    The Classical Period   3
    The Hellenistic Period   5
    The Roman Period   6
    Greek Ideas Still Reflected in Modern Thinking   6
The Renaissance and Post-Renaissance Period   7
(R)evolutionary Ideas of the 19th Century   11
Establishment of Psychology as a Discipline and Emotions as a
    Topic for Psychological Inquiry   15
Summary   18
Thinking Critically About "Early Emotion Theories"   18

2 Brain and Thought Processes as Antecedents to Emotion: Emotion Theories of the 20th Century   20

Brain Processes as the Basis for Emotions   20
    Cannon's Emotion Theory   20
    The Papez Circuit   21
    The Limbic System Theory   24
        Theory Development   24
        Theory Application   27
    Critique of the Limbic System Theory and Recent Developments 28
        Neuroanatomical Issues   28
        Neurofunctional Issues   28
        Conceptual Issues   31
Thoughts as the Basis for Emotions   32
    Historical Background   32
    Thoughts Disambiguate Unspecific Bodily Arousal   32

Thoughts Create Bodily Arousal	35
Defying Thought	38
Merging Brain and Thought	39
Summary	40
Thinking Critically About "Emotion Theories of the 20th Century"	41

3   What Is an Emotion? Modern Thoughts and Concepts — 42

The Categorical Approach—Emotions as Discrete Entities	42
Historical Background	42
An Example—Ekman's Basic Emotions	43
Support for the Categorical Approach	47
Limitations of the Categorical Approach	48
The Dimensional Approach—Emotions as Instances in a Multidimensional Space	50
Historical Background	50
An Example—Circumplex Model and Core Affect	53
Support for the Dimensional Approach	55
Limitations of the Dimensional Approach	57
The Appraisal Approach—Emotions as a Result of Appraisal Processes	58
Historical Background	58
An Example—Component Process Model of Appraisal	59
Support for the Appraisal Approach	62
Limitations of the Appraisal Approach	65
Summary and Outlook	68
Thinking Critically About "What Is an Emotion?"	69

PART 2: FOUNDATIONS FOR EMOTION RESEARCH — 71

4   Biological Foundations — 73

Nervous System	74
Cell Types and Their Function	74
Neurons	74
Glia	77
Central Nervous System	78
Spinal Cord	79
Brain	79
Peripheral Nervous System	83
Autonomic Nervous System	83
Genetic and Epigenetic Regulation of Brain Structure and Function	85
A Biological Basis for Emotions	87
Important Brain Structures	87
Amygdala	87
Insula	89

Anterior Cingulate   90
Medial Prefrontal Cortex   93
Stimulus and Task-Dependent Emotional Processing   93
Important Chemical Messengers   94
Oxytocin   95
Monoamines   96
Opioids   99
Summary   99
Thinking Critically About "Biological Foundations of Emotions"   100

5   Methodological Foundations I: Eliciting Emotions   102

Laboratory Constraints on Emotion Elicitation   102
Popular Methods of Emotion Elicitation   105
Unconditioned and Conditioned Stimuli   105
On the Nature of Unconditioned Stimuli   105
On the Nature of Conditioned Stimuli   107
Typical Unconditioned and Conditioned
Stimuli Used in Human Research   110
Autobiographical Memories   116
Behavioral Responses as Emotion Stimuli   118
Electrical Brain Stimulation   120
Emotion Elicitation in the Context of Current Emotion Theories   122
Summary   122
Thinking Critically About "Eliciting Emotions"   123

6   Methodological Foundations II: Exploring Emotions   125

Behavioral Correlates of Emotions   125
Implicit Explorations of Behavior   126
Gross Behaviors   126
Nonverbal Expression   127
Psychological Tasks   129
Explicit Explorations of Behavior   131
Pros and Cons of Implicit and Explicit Exploration Techniques   133
Peripheral Correlates of Emotions   134
Heart Rate   134
Electrodermal Activity   137
Brain Correlates of Emotions   138
Lesion Studies   138
Techniques to Influence Brain Function   141
Techniques to Assess Electrical Brain Activity   142
Techniques to Assess Brain Metabolism   145
Summary   149
Thinking Critically About "Exploring Emotions"   150

PART 3: EMOTIONS 151

7   Joy and Positive Emotions 152

How Many Positive Emotions Are There? 154
What Triggers Joy? 155
Feeling Joy—Behavioral Tendencies, Mental Processes, and Bodily Correlates 157
    Behavioral Tendencies 158
    Mental Processes 160
    Bodily Correlates 163
        Peripheral Correlates 163
        Central Nervous System Correlates 164
    Mechanisms 169
Why Do We Feel Joy? 172
Can Feeling Good Be Bad? 174
Summary 176
Thinking Critically About "Joy" 177

8   Sadness 178

What Triggers Sadness? 178
Feeling Sad—Behavioral Tendencies, Mental Processes, and Bodily Correlates 179
    Behavioral Tendencies 180
    Mental Processes 183
    Bodily Correlates 184
        Peripheral Correlates 185
        Central Nervous System Correlates 185
    Mechanisms 192
Why Do We Feel Sad? 195
When Sadness Becomes a Problem 197
    Depression 197
    Treatment Approaches for Depression 198
Summary 201
Thinking Critically About "Sadness" 202

9   Fear 204

What Triggers Fear? 204
Feeling Fearful—Behavioral Tendencies, Mental Processes, and Bodily Correlates 205
    Behavioral Tendencies 206
    Mental Processes 209
    Bodily Correlates 213
        Peripheral Correlates 213
        Central Nervous System Correlates 216
    Mechanisms 220

Why Do We Feel Fear? 222
When Fear Becomes a Problem 222
    Anxiety Disorders 222
    Treatment Approaches for Phobias 223
Summary 227
Thinking Critically About "Fear" 228

PART 4: EMOTIONS AND OTHER MENTAL PROCESSES 231

10 Emotion Effects on Cognition 233

How Emotional Events Modulate Attention 234
    Attentional Mechanisms 234
    Emotions and Attention 237
        Behavioral Insights 237
        Insights From Brain Research 238
        Mechanisms 240
How Emotional Events Modulate Memory 242
    Memory Processes and Types 242
    Emotions and Memory 243
        Behavioral Insights 243
        Insights From Brain Research 245
        Mechanisms 247
How Emotional Events Modulate Higher-Order Cognitive Processes 251
    Language and Categorization 251
        Behavioral Observations 251
        Mechanisms 252
    Time Perception 254
        Behavioral Observations 254
        Mechanisms 255
    Decision Making 257
        Behavioral Observations 257
        Mechanisms 258
Summary 261
Thinking Critically About "Emotion Effects on Cognition" 262

11 Emotion Regulation 263

Why Regulate? The Functions of Emotion Regulation 264
Emotion Regulation Strategies 265
    Attentional Deployment 265
    Cognitive Change 268
    Response Modulation 270

Principles That Govern the Use and Usefulness of Emotion Regulation   272
    Factors Associated With the Event   272
    Factors Associated With the Individual   274
Brain Mechanisms That Support Emotion Regulation   276
Emotion Regulation and Mental Health   279
    Why Do Depressed Individuals Regulate Differently?   279
    Are Differences in Emotion Regulation Cause or Consequence of Depression?   280
Challenges and Future Directions of Emotion Regulation Research   281
    Conceptual Challenges   281
        Strategy Terminology   281
        Strategy Categorization   281
        What Is Emotion Regulation?   282
    Methodological Challenges   283
        What Strategy?   283
        Emotion Regulation in Other Species   283
Summary   285
Thinking Critically About "Emotion Regulation"   286

PART 5: INTRA- AND INTER-INDIVIDUAL DIFFERENCES IN EMOTION 287

12 Emotions Across the Life Span 289

Early Infancy and Childhood   290
    Attachment   290
        Caring About Mother   290
        Making Mother Care   292
    Exploration   298
    Emotion Regulation   300
        Attentional Deployment   300
        Response Modulation   301
        Getting Help   302
Adolescence and Young Adulthood   303
    Gaining Independence   303
        Bonding—From Parents to Peers   303
        More Exploration—A Risky Business   305
    Finding Love   306
        Mate Choice   306
        Mate Attachment   309
Late Adulthood and Aging   311
    Socioemotional Selectivity Theory   312
        Caring About the "Here and Now"   313
        The Positivity Effect   313
    Functional Decline Affects Emotions   316
Summary   317
Thinking Critically About "Emotions Across the Life Span"   318

13 Emotions and Sex Differences 320

What Is Sex? The Origins of Sexual Differentiation 321
Does Sex Matter for Emotions? 323
   Theoretical Positions 323
      Gendered Minds Position 323
      Sex-Typed Minds Position 326
      Merging Positions 328
   Factors Relevant for Sex Differences in Emotion 328
      Environment 328
      Genes 330
   Sex and the Brain 331
Sex Differences in Emotion 334
   Emotion Elicitation—How Sex Shapes the Appraisal of Emotion Antecedents 334
   Emotional Response—How Sex Shapes Emotions in Mind, Body, and Behavior 339
      Mental Responses 339
      Bodily Responses 342
      Behavioral Responses 345
   Emotion Regulation—How Sex Shapes an
      Individual's Attempts to Manage Emotions 348
Challenges for Research on Sex Differences in Emotion 349
Summary 353
Thinking Critically About "Emotions and Sex Differences" 354

14 Emotions and Culture 355

What Is Culture? 355
   Answers From Cultural and Evolutionary Anthropology 355
   Issues With Accepting the Evolutionary Approach 356
   A Holistic Definition of Culture 357
Does Culture Matter for Emotions? 359
   Theoretical Positions 359
   Some Environmental Conditions Relevant to Culture and Cultured Emotions 360
   The Cultured Brain 367
Psychological Dimensions of Culture 369
   Independence and Interdependence as Cultural Characteristics 369
   Caveats of the Independence–Interdependence Dimension 371
Cultural Differences in Emotion 371
   Emotion Elicitation—How Culture Shapes the Appraisal of
      Emotion Antecedents 372
      Novelty 373
      Goal Conduciveness 376
      Causality and Other Appraisals 377
   Emotional Response—How Culture Shapes Emotions in Mind, Body, and Behavior 377
      Mental Responses 378

Bodily Responses 380
Behavioral Responses 380
Emotion Regulation—How Culture Shapes an
Individual's Attempts to Manage Emotions 382
Summary 383
Thinking Critically About "Emotions and Culture" 384

References   **385**

Glossary   **446**

Author Index   **461**

Subject Index   **493**

Preface

Emotions involve basic bodily mechanisms that motivate behavior. They are present in all living and independently moving organisms, where they serve to ensure survival and successful reproduction. In humans, as in other animals, emotions are fundamental in determining what individuals attend to, what they store and recall from memory, and what behaviors they initiate (e.g., approach versus avoidance). Because of their ubiquitous significance, emotions play a central role in a wide range of mental dysfunctions.

Given psychology's goals of explaining and predicting behavior and of treating mental dysfunctions, understanding emotions is of paramount interest. As such, the topic of emotions has garnered an increasing role in most undergraduate psychology programs. Additionally, it has received growing attention as an area of research. A quick Web search suggests a sevenfold growth in the number of published emotion articles over the last 50 years. During this time, the proportion of emotion articles relative to all scientific publications doubled, indicating that emotions gained significantly relative to other fields.

Notably, this gain was not restricted to psychology. Publications in areas as diverse as computer science, engineering, medicine, neuroscience, biology, anthropology, philosophy, business, and economics indicate that interest in emotions has diversified and that emotion research has become a multidisciplinary endeavor. This diversification has greatly benefited our understanding of emotions. For example, advances in engineering and computer science provided tools and techniques to study emotions; the life sciences shed light on biological aspects of emotion; and business and economics uncovered human emotional behaviors in real-life settings, with real-life consequences.

The goal of this book is to explore human emotions against the backdrop of these developments. To this end, relevant human research takes center stage. However, it is complemented by research in nonhuman animals elucidating basic emotion mechanisms—many of which are shared across a wide range of species, including humans. Additionally, classical psychological theories are reviewed against evidence from new imaging technologies revealing electrical, metabolic, and structural aspects of emotions. Thus, social and cognitive perspectives anchored within traditional psychology are married with biological perspectives of the brain and the functioning of the body.

The ambitions of this book may daunt a reader without much knowledge of the academic disciplines mentioned here. Yet the author hopes that reading a few pages will dispel any apprehension. Being targeted at psychology undergraduates, the book approaches "difficult" topics slowly and offers much guidance along the way. Thus, the book should be accessible to motivated students of emotions with little or no background in the topic. However, it should also be interesting to more advanced students in the context of graduate training.

In either case, instructors working with students are encouraged to select relevant content and to facilitate student learning with questions and discussion.

The structure of this book is arranged along five major themes. The first theme concerns the history of emotion theory and research. It includes chapters covering philosophical origins in antiquity, more recent empirical efforts arising from the industrial and digital revolutions, and present-day approaches or "emotion schools." The second theme addresses the necessary foundations for understanding and pursuing modern emotion research. On one hand, it provides an introduction to the biological underpinnings of the mind. On the other hand, it reviews and contrasts the methods by which researchers elicit and measure emotions. The third theme outlines emotions in more detail. Due to space constraints, emphasis is placed on three exemplary emotions—joy, sadness, and fear—which are each covered in separate chapters. The fourth theme tackles the intricate relationship between emotion and thought. One chapter details basic cognitive processes, such as attention and memory, and explores how they vary as a function of emotions. Another chapter examines the opposite—namely, how emotions vary as a function of thought. It is concerned with the mechanisms we use to regulate emotions. Finally, a last theme is dedicated to individual differences in emotions. Drawing on what went before, chapters provide insights into how emotions change throughout development, how they differ between the sexes, and how human culture shapes emotions. Because later chapters build on previous chapters, it is advisable to adhere to their order when exploring the contents of this book.

Apart from providing content, the book offers a number of features that are aimed at facilitating comprehension. A first feature is that chapters, where possible, are similarly structured. For example, the three chapters covering joy, sadness, and fear have comparable outlines that help establish links and cross-chapter integration. A second feature is an extensive use of cross-chapter referencing. Thus, additional content or previous explanations are made readily accessible. A third feature is that all technical terms relevant for understanding chapter content are highlighted and specifically defined. In most cases, a short definition is provided immediately in the text. Additionally, each term is defined in a glossary, often with additional facts. Chapter summaries with thinking questions comprise the fourth feature. Summaries should help students identify and connect key points or "take home messages." Thinking questions should spark discussions of chapter content and encourage students to critically evaluate what they read. A fifth feature is a media library including Web links that students can use to explore chapter content more deeply and that instructors can use to augment their teaching. Last, each chapter contains outstanding and fascinating facts that go beyond the primary text and that are presented in separate sections entitled "A Closer Look." These sections serve to capture the students' interest and to inspire a greater engagement with the topic.

In sum, this book samples the most important and interesting emotion research done in past decades and centuries and presents this research in a carefully developed and pedagogical way. As such, the book opens a window through which emotions can be studied and recognized for what they are—a principal force of human (and animal) life.

ACKNOWLEDGMENTS

The author would like to thank her students for providing the incentive, her publisher for providing the opportunity, and her husband for providing the advice, encouragement, and distraction necessary to write this book.

About the Author

Annett Schirmer completed an undergraduate degree in psychology in 1999 at Leipzig University, Germany's second-oldest university and where psychology was first established as an academic discipline. She obtained her doctorate in life sciences from Leipzig University in 2002 for research she completed at the Max Planck Institute for Human Cognitive and Brain Sciences. Dr. Schirmer's subsequent professional career took her to the United States and later to Singapore, where she is now an associate professor of psychology at the National University of Singapore (NUS). At NUS, she directs an active lab in which undergraduate, graduate, and postgraduate students conduct research in the area of affective and social neuroscience. More specifically, Dr. Schirmer and her students address questions about the mental and neural underpinnings of emotional communication. Dr. Schirmer teaches a wide range of topics including emotions, cognition, communication, and neuroscience. She has won teaching awards for both undergraduate and graduate teaching.

PART 1

Emotion Theories From Antiquity to Modernity

Everyone knows what an emotion is, until asked to give a definition.

—Beverley Fehr and
James A. Russell (1984, p. 464)

Most of us probably have an intuitive understanding of what emotions are. Yet do we really know them? Can we explain whether and how emotions are different from thoughts, how they come about, why we feel them, and why our feelings are never quite the same? Emotions are like constant companions that are sometimes welcome, sometimes disagreeable, and often inexplicable. Although always on our side, they easily elude our attempts to apprehend them.

The scrutiny of emotion science, however, is not as easily eluded. Grounded in theoretical and empirical efforts, this science could capture and characterize important aspects of emotions. Here, we will consider the emergence of this science in antiquity and explore the chain of ideas that led to modern thinking about emotions. Specifically, we will look at early explanations or theories and track their evolution across history, considering political as well as technical constraints. We will see that progress was not strictly linear. Existing constraints often led thinkers astray; many of their efforts resulted in setbacks, mixed in with the occasional advance.

Given the back and forth of this process, you may ask yourself whether studying it is worthwhile. In a world where time is limited, should we not focus on what we know *now* to be true? Although such a focus may be tempting, it would be too narrow for us to comprehend emotions. When considering where we are and where to go next, it is always good to look back at where we came from. The past has clues for us to understand the present and to predict the future. Thus, let's keep our minds open as we explore the interesting and multifaceted history of emotion theory—a scientific quest that unravels a central aspect of who we are.

CHAPTER 1

The Passions of the Soul

Early Emotion Theories

Western thinking about emotions has a long history. For the purpose of this book, this history is divided into three chapters. Because initial theoretical development was quite slow, the first chapter spans across many centuries, from antiquity to the inception of biological science and psychology in the 19th century. Across these centuries, emotion theory developed in tandem with political, religious, and technical change.

Although derived primarily on chance observation and philosophical musing, early emotion theory has shaped later emotion research and is still reflected in current thinking about emotions. It is thus relevant for Chapter 2, which details emotion theories of the 20th century leading up to today. In this epoch, the role of political and religious ideas became less prominent and was overshadowed by methodological advances that boosted experimental work including the study of the brain.

Chapter 3, the last chapter in this series, is dedicated to three schools of thought that developed out of traditional emotion theory and the new insights gained from the 20th-century experimental approach. These schools will be introduced and evaluated based on empirical evidence from psychology and neuroscience. They will form the theoretical basis for the remainder of this book.

ANCIENT GREECE AND THE EARLY ROMAN EMPIRE

Many aspects of Western civilization, including modern medical and psychological theories, have their roots in the flourishing cultural and intellectual climate of ancient Greece. After defeating Persian invasion at the beginning of the 5th century BC, Greece developed into a rich and influential political power, with Athens at its center. Its wealth enabled remarkable technical, artistic, and scientific advancements, and it generated a climate in which knowledge was highly esteemed. It was during this time that one of the first learning institutes, Plato's Academy, was founded and that thinkers started to document scientific and philosophical progress. Although much of the original documentation is lost, Greek ideas about the human mind and emotions can be gleaned from a few surviving scripts and from the writing of following generations of thinkers.

From these documents it seems that the mind—also referred to as the psyche, or the soul—was a topic of vivid interest. The soul was held as a source of life separate from the body and responsible for humans' ability to feel, behave, and reason. Reason was perceived as humans' greatest gift and the means by which we can lead a life of virtue. As such, reason was of primary interest to the Greeks, and relatively little attention was paid to other aspects of the soul—including emotions. No treatise is known that specifically discusses emotions. Instead, propositions about emotions surface in the context of other topics and often are ambiguous and contradictory. They contradict across the writings of different authors, but also within the writings of a single author. Moreover, their direct meaning is often difficult to assess. Ancient Greek differs substantially from modern European languages, and many of the terms used by the ancient philosophers have no literal translation. Despite these challenges, however, modern historians and philosophers have formulated ideas about what the ancient Greeks thought about emotions—ideas that will be reviewed next.

The Classical Period

In general, emotions were not highly esteemed during the classical period. Greek society was what we would call today interdependent, with individuals having great concern for others and the orderly workings of their social group. As such, showing emotions was frowned upon and considered shameful and weak. This is evident from the art that originated during the classical period and that is characterized by a perfect human image whose bodily and facial expressions are seemingly affectless (Figure 1.1). It is also evident from the writings of three key figures in classical philosophy: Democritus, Plato, and Aristotle.

Democritus. Democritus lived around 460 to 370 BC and is today best known for his *átomos* theory, which holds that the things we see are made up of small, indivisible parts. He also believed that the soul was made up of these indivisible parts, called atoms, and like others at the time assumed that the soul is responsible for human intellect (Crivellato & Ribatti, 2007). His attitude toward emotions can be inferred from his notion that a pleasant life presupposes little "movement of the soul" and a satisfaction with one's own achievements (as cited by Kahn, 1985). This suggests that he viewed both too positive and too negative emotions as unsettling and therefore bad. This negative view toward emotions is even more evident from his statement that "wisdom frees the soul from emotions" (as cited by Sorabji, 2002), which implies that emotions are like a disease that needs curing. Apart from these propositions, however, we know little about what Democritus thought emotions are, how they are related to reason, and where they are located in the body.

Plato. Plato lived from 427 to 347 BC and was a younger contemporary of Democritus. Plato is credited with making Socratic thinking available to posterity. He documented his teacher

FIGURE 1.1   Venus de Milo

This ancient Greek sculpture was created between 130 and 100 BC. It is believed to depict the Greek goddess of love and beauty. It is currently on display at the Louvre Museum in Paris, France.

Source: © Mrakor—Fotolia.com.

Socrates in written dialogues, which illustrate the Socratic approach to insight (Hunt, 1994). Like Democritus, Plato assumed the soul to be a special entity, separate from the body (Crivellato & Ribatti, 2007). One part of this soul he called *logos* (Greek, "reason") and argued that it was divine and immortal. Because logos enabled humans to think, it dominated other aspects of the soul and the body. Given its hierarchical position, Plato thought logos to be situated in the head. As a second part of the psyche, Plato named the *thymos* (Greek, "spirited"), situated in the chest and responsible for feelings or emotions (e.g., courage, rage). Because to Plato emotions had a better and a worse side, he thought thymos to comprise two divisions, with the better division being located closer to the head. As a third part of the soul, Plato named the *epithymētikon* (Greek, "desire"), which he thought was responsible for the body's appetites. As it was the least "worthy" of the three parts, it was located near the liver, furthest away from the head. Thus, like Democritus, Plato separated reason from emotion and elevated the former over the latter. Moreover, he made reason immortal and potentially independent from the body, while tying emotions to perishable internal organs whose action was known to change with extreme "movements of the soul."

Aristotle. Aristotle lived from 384 to 322 BC and was a student of Plato (Figure 1.2). He joined him at the age of 18 at the Academy in Athens and remained there for about 20 years, after which he spent some time traveling and tutoring Alexander the Great (Hunt, 1994). Although a devoted student, Aristotle disagreed in many ways with his teacher Plato. For example, he not only relied on deductive reasoning like Plato, but included observation and investigation in his modes of inquiry. He therefore is conceived as the founder of modern empirical science. Aristotle also differed from Plato in his definition of the soul. This comprised a vegetative or nourishing part, present in plants and animals; a sensing and motor part, present in animals only; and an intellectual part, present in humans only. Moreover, he held that, in humans, all parts are connected with or housed in the heart because the heart is what gives life to a body (Crivellato & Ribatti, 2007).

Although Aristotle never wrote a treatise on emotions that we know of, he mentioned them in several of his writings. In *On the Soul* he defined emotional events as "things on account of which people change and differ in regard to their judgments, and upon which attend pain and pleasure, for example anger, pity, fear, and all other such things and their opposites" (as cited by Konstan, 2006). He tied emotions to reason by assuming that emotions arise from our reflection of events. Moreover, he purported that the same event may trigger different emotions depending on how we think about it. Thus, he believed that only adult humans, but not children and animals, have emotions, as the latter were believed incapable of reason (Konstan, 2006). Finally, some reviewers of

FIGURE 1.2   Plato and Aristotle

Section of the fresco "School of Athens," which Raffaello Sanzio created around 1509 for the Vatican in Rome, Italy. The section shows Plato on the left and Aristotle on the right.

Source: Wikimedia Commons.

his work speculate that Aristotle viewed emotions as arising primarily from our interactions with other humans (Konstan, 2006; Nussbaum 2001). This is because he only mentioned them at length in his treatise *Rhetoric* (Greek, "oratorical"), where he outlined the art of persuasion and where all his emotion examples referred to human dialogue.

The Hellenistic Period

Toward the end of the classical period, political influence shifted from Athens to Macedonia, which became the new center from where Alexander the Great expanded Greek rule to Persia and beyond. The era after this change in power, the Hellenistic period, is marked by a diversification of philosophic schools. One of these schools, the **Stoic school**, further developed emotion theory. It reinforced the old idea that the mind should control emotions and subdue desires because gratifying them could cause a person harm.

Chrysippus (280–206 BC), one of the Stoics' more prominent thinkers, elaborated on the Aristotelian idea of emotions presupposing reason or judgment. He suggested that emotions consist of two judgments. The first one decides whether an event is good or bad, whereas the second one decides what can be done about it. The types of emotions produced by these judgments were classified based on their **valence** and their temporal relation to the event. Desire and fear were conceived as positive and negative emotions, respectively, and associated with a future event. Pleasure and pain were conceived as positive and negative emotions, respectively, and were associated with a present event (Brennan, 2007; Sorabji, 2002).

This emotion conceptualization differs greatly from present conceptualizations, where "desire" and "pain" would be excluded because they refer to a motivation and a sensation, respectively. Nevertheless, it was useful, as it represented a first attempt at organizing emotions on more than one continuum and thus facilitated later attempts at characterizing what is and is not an emotion. Another Stoic proposal that was revisited about 2,000 years later concerned the distinction between emotions and bodily changes. Here, the Stoics argued that emotions do not arise from bodily changes, but rather that emotions may eventually cause bodily changes (Sorabji, 2002).

The Roman Period

The last two centuries BC saw again a shift in power. The Romans gained influence and eventually took over the Macedonian Empire. Yet the only significant contribution to the development of emotion theory came again from a Greek mind, Galen. Galen was a Roman citizen of Greek ethnicity who lived from about 130 to 200 AD (Watson & Evans, 1991). He worked as a personal physician at the Roman court and is best known for his contributions to medicine. Yet he also was a philosopher and interested in matters of the mind. For example, he further developed Plato's division of emotions into those arising from insult and those arising from desire (Hunt, 1994). He also extended an ancient Greek theory that posited the existence of four basic bodily fluids, or **humors** (Latin root humor = fluid), the balance of which was critical for a person's physical and mental health. Galen extended these ideas by linking humors to a person's temperament, which he saw as one possible contributor to illness (Watson & Evans, 1991; Figure 1.3). Later, medical doctors would take Galen's theory further by assuming that a person with a dominance of blood was warmhearted, a person with a dominance of black bile was melancholic, a person with a dominance of yellow bile was choleric, and a person with a dominance of phlegm was phlegmatic (Watson & Evans, 1991). Needless to say, these ideas were wrong, and they did a lot of damage to patients throughout history. Yet they established a link between a person's organic makeup and his or her emotional life, and thus advanced the notion that emotions have a biological basis.

Greek Ideas Still Reflected in Modern Thinking

When considering the contributions of ancient Greeks to our understanding of emotions, at least four principal ideas stand out. The first idea is that reason is separate from emotions. This divide remains with us to the present day, and researchers are just now beginning to challenge it. The second idea is that emotions presuppose reason, and here the

Greeks anticipated modern insights regarding the role of cognition. Third, the Greeks introduced emotions as faceted experiences that can take many shapes and forms and that can be categorized or organized along different dimensions. As such, they formulated the foundation for present emotion theories, which we discuss in Chapter 3. Finally, the Greeks held that emotions rest in the human body rather than in the brain. In subsequent centuries, this notion was empirically tested and at the same time permeated popular conceptions and language. For example, English idioms such as "breaking your heart" or "pouring your heart out" still bear the voice of Plato, Aristotle, and Galen. Will they have the last say? The answer is both yes and no. Yes, because the body clearly contributes to emotions, and we explore these contributions in later chapters. No, because we now know for certain that the brain contributes as well.

FIGURE 1.3   Galen and the Four Temperaments

Galen's theory remained popular for centuries to come. Illustrated here is its application to human physiognomy, by Johann Kaspar Lavater. The latter believed that the four temperaments find expression in different facial features. The etching is taken from Lavater's "Essai sur la physiognomonie destiné à faire connoître l'homme et à le faire aimer," published by Jacques Van Karnebeek at The Hague in 1781. Sanguine (top left), Phlegmatic (top right), Choleric (bottom left), and Melancholic (bottom right).

Source: Courtesy of Jean-Marie Bertin, La Meignanne, France.

THE RENAISSANCE AND POST-RENAISSANCE PERIOD

After the initial growth of interest in matters of the mind, there came a long period during which this interest was subdued. First, there was a change in Europe's political climate that dampened the Greeks' intellectual spirit. With the ascent of the Roman Empire, a lesser emphasis was placed on scientific advancement, and changes were introduced that specifically impeded medical and psychological discovery such as the prohibition of human dissection. Second, with the establishment of Christianity, philosophy and science were directed toward justifying and defending Christian ideology. Thus, deliberations on the soul concerned primarily its spiritual nature rather than its functioning in the here and now or its relationship to biological matter. Only in the Renaissance, with the introduction of print and a revival of the arts and sciences, do we see fresh contributions to psychological and emotion theory.

These contributions came first and foremost from René Descartes (1596–1650), the famous French scientist and philosopher. Descartes benefited from a range of scientific and technological advances made before his time, since the beginning of the Renaissance in the 15th century. Like his predecessors, Descartes believed in a distinction between body and soul and assumed that the soul exists in a form that cannot be described by common physical laws. His assertions on the soul and the soul's relationship to emotions are elaborated in great detail in *The Passions of the Soul,* a treatise he published shortly before his death (Descartes, 1649/1989; A Closer Look 1.1).

As the soul could move the body, it needed a point of contact. Descartes assumed this contact to occur in the pineal gland, a small endocrine structure located in the middle of the brain (Figure 1.4). He reasoned that although we see with two eyes and hear with two ears, our sensory impressions are united in that they reflect only one rather than two sensory sources. Moreover, he speculated that the soul can behold only one thing at a time, and that therefore it would need to contact a part of the brain that is not dually represented.

FIGURE 1.4   Pineal Gland

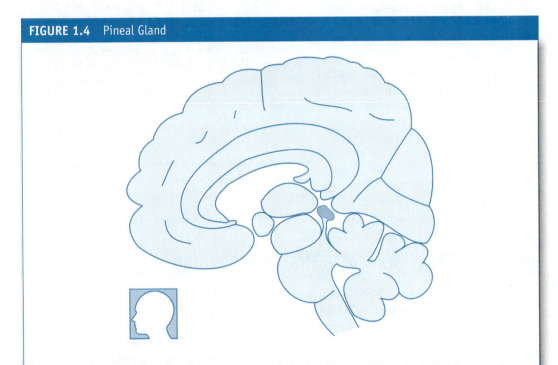

A sagittal slice of a human brain illustrating the pineal gland in blue. The icon in the lower-left corner shows the position of this slice relative to an individual's head.

A CLOSER LOOK 1.1

Selected Quotes From *The Passions of the Soul*

On the value of Greek philosophy: "There is nothing more clearly evinces the learning which we receive from the ancients to be defective, than what they have written concerning the passions. For although it be a matter the understanding whereof has even been hunted after; and that it seems to be none of the hardest, because every one feeling them in himself, need not borrow foreign observations to discover their nature. Yet what the Ancients have taught concerning them, is so little, and for the most part so little credible that I cannot hope to draw nigh truth, but by keeping aloof off from those roads which they followed. Wherefore I shall here be forced to write in such a sort, as if I treated of a matter never before handled" (*The Passions of the Soul,* Article 1).

On the role of the soul in emotions: "Our passions also cannot be directly excited or taken away by the action of our will, but they may indirectly, by the representation of things which use[d] to be joined with the passions which we will have, and which are contrary to these we will reject. Thus, to excite in oneself boldness, and remove fear, it is not enough to have a will to do so, but reasons, objects and examples are to be considered of, that persuade the danger is not great, that there is ever more security in defense than flight, that there is glory and joy in vanquishing, whereas there is nothing to be expected but grief and dishonor in flying and the like" (*The Passions of the Soul,* Article 45).

On the differences between sensation and emotion: "[O]ne may distinguish two kinds of movements excited by the [animal] spirits on the [pineal] gland: the one [kind] represent to the soul the objects that move the senses . . . and do not have any effect on the will; the other [kind] does have some effect on the will, namely those that cause the passions or the movements of the body that accompany them" (*The Passions of the Soul,* Article 47).

On the generally positive nature of emotions: "And now we know them all [the emotions], we have less reason to fear them than we had before. For we see that naturally they are all good, and that we ought to avoid only the ill use of them, or their excesses, for which the remedies I have laid down may suffice, if every man were careful enough to practice them" (*The Passions of the Soul,* Article 211).

FIGURE 1.5   René Descartes

Source: © Georgios Kollidas—Fotolia.com.

As, apart from the pineal gland, all brain structures are more or less symmetrically represented in the two brain hemispheres, he inferred that the pineal gland—being a central, unreplicated structure—must be where the soul and the body meet.

Importantly, Descartes held that the soul was unnecessary to move the body. Some bodily actions such as breathing or walking could be performed without thinking about them and thus were likely the result of automatic, inbuilt mechanisms, which he attributed to the action of spirits—fluid-like substances that move through the body. These spirits were shared between humans and animals, whereas the soul was not.

In keeping with Greek tradition, Descartes tied emotions to the existence of a soul. However, rather than making emotions a direct part of the soul, he let them arise from the soul's contact with the body. Specifically, he defined them as "caused, fomented, and fortified by some motion of the spirits" (*The Passions of the Soul,* Article 27). To illustrate this, he suggested that we flee automatically from a predator simply through the sensation of an external threat, which activates the spirits. We only experience fear because our soul is sensitive to the body's mechanical action that was caused by the spirits. This action stirs the pineal gland and thereby moves the soul.

Although Descartes assumed that emotions are chiefly caused by external events and are passively experienced by the soul, he made room for instances in which the soul can moderate or create emotions. This, he argued, could be achieved if one were to differently evaluate the events that triggered one's current emotion or if one were to conjure memories of events that previously evoked the emotion one wishes to feel. For example, if you were sad and wanted to "will" your emotions to become more positive, you could reinterpret the event you thought was sad as one of opportunity for change, or you could think of previous events that made you happy. Thus, your will would have an impact on the spirits in your body whose action would be perceived as an emotional change by the pineal gland. To date, these two emotion-regulation mechanisms are referred to as reinterpretation and distraction, and are a lively area of research.

The emotions that Descartes recognized are divided into a set of primary emotions and a set of secondary emotions, which are variants of a single primary emotion or combinations of different primary or secondary emotions. In the primary set he included admiration, love, hatred, desire, joy, and sadness. Examples of secondary emotions are estimation, contempt, generosity, pride, humility, or dejection—all of which Descartes presumed to be related to the primary emotion of admiration. With the proposition of primary and secondary emotion states, Descartes foreshadowed what was to become our present conceptualization of basic emotions. Descartes also formulated the hypothesis that emotions have sensory precursors. Specifically, he held that pleasure and pain are precursors in the experience of joy and sadness. The presumed relationship between pain and sadness is particularly interesting, as it was proved correct by present-day neurophysiological and neuroimaging research.

Last, an important contribution of Descartes was that he improved the negative image emotions had since antiquity. Rather than viewing them as experiences that compromise rational thought and that therefore should be avoided, he assigned them a functional significance. With a surprisingly Darwinian spirit, he postulated that emotions "dispose the soul to will the things nature tells us are useful and to persist in that volition"

(*The Passions of the Soul,* Article 52). If we feel fear, it is likely because flight is a beneficial action in that circumstance. If we feel anger, it is likely because confrontation or fight is a beneficial action in that circumstance. Thus, emotions bias us to behave in a self-serving manner. Despite their having an obvious function, however, Descartes warns that excessive emotions may be bad for a person and suggests ways in which such excess may be prevented.

In sum, with his treatise *The Passions of the Soul,* Descartes introduced a range of ideas that shaped the thinking of both laypeople and scientists for several generations to come. First, he recognized both the body and the brain as being important for emotions. Moreover, he argued that the experience of emotions depends on a center in the brain. Although this center was anatomically misplaced, it pointed subsequent inquiries in the right direction. Second, unlike the ancient Greeks, who attributed emotions chiefly to cognitive reflection about external events, Descartes rightly recognized that many emotional responses are highly automatic and may occur in the absence of deliberate thought. Thus, he acknowledged the existence of both bottom-up and top-down emotional responses and introduced the idea of emotion regulation. Finally, he made an attempt at identifying basic emotion states and assigned these states a functionality. Unfortunately, he failed to recognize that such attributed functionality should hold for both human and nonhuman animals and that therefore both should have emotions. He also had some curious notions about the relationship of body and mind, which misdirected our thinking about emotions to the present day. He assumed the body to be nothing more than an automaton, a biological machine that in the case of nonhuman animals can function without the mind. The mind he assumed to be an immaterial substance that perceives and acts through the body. Although he connected body and mind through the brain, there still remained a sharp divide that discouraged the physical study of mental phenomena, such as emotions.

Although it is difficult to pinpoint the reasons for these misconceptions, one possibility is that they grew out of contemporary religious pressures (Descartes, 1649/1989). Descartes was aware of religious censorship, which banned many important works such as Copernicus's heliocentric theory and not infrequently led to arrests, as in the case of Galileo. Undoubtedly, Descartes was motivated to evade such treatment and may thus have aligned his philosophy with Christian doctrine.

(R)EVOLUTIONARY IDEAS OF THE 19TH CENTURY

After Descartes, there came a long period during which emotion theory more or less stagnated. New insights required a big shift in how people thought about themselves and their role on Earth. This shift depended on a range of developments in the 18th century. One of these developments was again a change in Europe's political structure introduced by the French Revolution and the downfall of the aristocracy. Another development was the industrial revolution, brought on by significant technological advances (e.g., the steam engine) that changed existing agricultural and manufacturing modes. Production now moved to a larger scale, leading to higher living standards and an increase in Europe's population. During this time, economic powers established themselves independently from the Church and the nobility. This allowed the political climate to become more secular and enabled scientists to pursue their discoveries with less of a fear of religious censorship.

In the wake of this, we see a renewed interest in the study of human life and nonhuman life-forms as evidenced by the establishment of biology as an academic discipline at the beginning of the 19th century. An important task of this new scholarship was to develop taxonomies to organize the different life-forms and to identify their relationships. One man who famously contributed to this task was the Englishman Charles Darwin. Freshly graduated from a Christian college in 1831, Darwin set sail for a five-year journey around the world. On this journey, he made geological observations and collected numerous specimens of living and already extinct animals. On various points during this journey, Darwin sent home written reports of his observations together with some specimens. Because his communications were well received, Darwin quickly achieved scientific recognition and was treated as an authority upon his return to England in 1836. Back home, Darwin sought the help of other experts to categorize his collection. Together, they identified individual species and tracked their existence across different geographical regions. Thus, Darwin observed that individuals from the same species but different origins sometimes showed small physical variations. This observation made Darwin think about the forces that created variations among species and made him pursue the possibility that one species could merge into another. Darwin first published the results of this pursuit in *The Origin of Species* (Darwin, 1864), where he formulated his theory of evolution based on natural selection.

The crux of his theory is thus: Although a species is defined by a set of characteristics, individuals within that species show considerable variation. For example, giraffes vary in the lengths of their necks. Due to the variation within a species, some individuals are better equipped to face nature's challenges than are others. In an environment where food hangs high, giraffes with longer necks would be more likely to sustain themselves than would giraffes with shorter necks. As a consequence, long-necked giraffes would be better able to reproduce and raise offspring, thereby passing on their long necks to future generations of giraffes. Over time, we would see an increase in the average neck length of giraffes and thus a change in the morphology of this species. As there are many ways in which a species could adapt to its environment, there are many possibilities for change. Thus, the changes that occur within one species may result in a multitude of related species, as in the case of mammals and primates.

Darwin's evolutionary theory summarized what humans knew implicitly since they started to purposefully domesticate animals such as dogs, cattle, and poultry about 12,000 years ago (Driscoll, Macdonald, & O'Brien, 2009). Yet the deep-seated belief in an Earth designed by God with humans as a special kind of creature, a master over all others, was difficult to overthrow. Therefore, Darwin's theory, although ingeniously making sense of hitherto conflicting observations, created a raging controversy. This controversy was fought publicly by Darwin's friends and colleagues, who defended natural selection as the principle for evolution. Darwin himself, however, withdrew from the public to live, study, and write in relative seclusion. He wrote several important works during this time, one of which is particularly relevant for the study of emotions.

The work in question is a book entitled *The Expression of the Emotions in Man and Animals* (Darwin, 1872). First published in 1872, it was Darwin's last big treatise and the one where he was most careful not to offend his audience and to keep references to natural selection at a minimum. Yet he wrote his emotions book in an evolutionary spirit and, for the first time, drew a clear parallel between the emotional life of nonhuman animals and humans. Perhaps surprisingly, Darwin never raised the issue of whether nonhuman animals have emotions but simply took for granted that they do. Moreover, he held that certain principles govern emotion and emotional expression, and that these principles apply similarly irrespective of species. In the following section, we review Darwin's principles and also touch on other contents of his book.

The first principle Darwin called "the principle of serviceable associated habits." It expressed the idea that animals, humans included, perform certain voluntary actions because they are useful in a given context. For example, you might avert your face and cover your nose and mouth at the sight of rotten food or a cadaver.

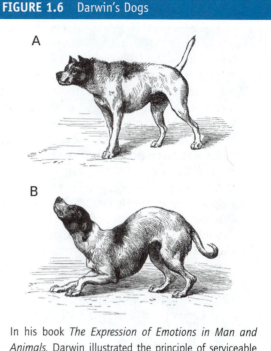

FIGURE 1.6   Darwin's Dogs

A

B

In his book *The Expression of Emotions in Man and Animals*, Darwin illustrated the principle of serviceable associated habits by displaying a hostile-aggressive dog with an erect body frame (A). He illustrated the principle of antithesis by displaying an affectionate dog with a lowered body frame (B).

Source: Charles Darwin, *The Expression of Emotion in Men and Animal* (1872).

Over time, such actions become a habit that is then not just associated with a specific context but also with a specific mental state, or emotion. Thus, any time you experience that emotion, you feel the urge to move according to the acquired habit. Darwin suggested that habitual expression is passed on to offspring; he thus made reference to Lamarckian theory on the inheritance of acquired characteristics rather than his own ideas about natural selection to explain continuity in emotion expression across successive generations.

Darwin's second principle was called "the principle of antithesis," and it derived from his first principle. It held that certain expressions emerged because they came to represent the opposite of serviceable habits. As an example he mentioned the dog, which in a hostile state of mind is stiffly erect, its fur raised, eyes glaring, and teeth exposed (Figure 1.6). This expression, so Darwin argued, is a serviceable habit, associated with the action of fighting. A dog falls into the opposite behavioral display when it is in an affectionate state of mind. Here, the body is fluid, the fur flat, the eyes partially closed, and the frame lowered, making

FIGURE 1.7   Duchenne's Expressions

In his writings on human facial expressions, Darwin referred to the work of Duchenne de Boulogne, who had studied human facial expressions and their muscular underpinnings. By electrically stimulating individual facial muscles, Duchenne had shown that different muscle groups contribute to different facial expressions. The picture is taken from Duchenne's monograph "Mécanisme de la physionomie humaine," first published in 1862.

Source: Wikimedia Commons.

the dog appear smaller than it is (Figure 1.6). Darwin believed that the latter display simply arose from being the practical opposite of the former, and he did not assume it to be functional. However, one can make a case that these and other expressions, which fall under Darwin's second principle, are useful in their own right. For example, the dog's affectionate behavior may effectively signal submissiveness toward or dependency on a higher-ranked animal or its master.

The third and last basic principle of emotion expression was "the principle of actions due to the constitution of the nervous system, independently from the first of the will and independently to a certain extent of habit." He called this principle more "obscure" than the others—and so it is. Darwin assumed that not all expressions are serviceable habits or their opposites. He argued that some expressions are chiefly due to changes in the nervous system under certain mental states. As an example he gave trembling, which "is of no service, often of much disservice, and cannot have been at first acquired through the will and then rendered habitual in association with any emotion."

In the remainder of his book, Darwin described emotional expressions of many species, including reptiles, birds, and mammals. When turning to humans, he paid particular attention to facial expressions (Figure 1.7) and explored their characteristics and causes for different emotion groups, reminiscent of Descartes' primary and secondary emotions. Moreover, like Descartes, he linked emotions to bodily changes (e.g., heart rate) and behavior. Although he made no formal attempt to define emotions, his thinking is evident from statements such as, "Anger and joy are from the first exciting emotions and they naturally lead, more especially the former, to energetic movement, which react on the heart and this again on the brain" (p. 84). Darwin thought that the experience of emotions results in some excitation of the nervous system and the release of "nerve-force." However, it is unclear what exactly he meant by nerve-force and how an emotional state differs from any other mental state. In fact, he included a range of mental states in his discussion (e.g., reflection, pain) that by present definitions would not be considered emotions.

ESTABLISHMENT OF PSYCHOLOGY AS A DISCIPLINE AND EMOTIONS AS A TOPIC FOR PSYCHOLOGICAL INQUIRY

Darwin's biological perspective on mental processes as well as new insights on the workings of the brain produced changes in the way scientists and philosophers approached matters of the mind. Some no longer considered the mind as something accessible through philosophical insight only, but as something measurable and quantifiable. These individuals departed from philosophy and established a new discipline called psychology. In Europe, this movement was headed by Wilhelm Wundt, who set up the first experimental psychology laboratory in 1879. At around the same time, William James established psychology as a discipline in the United States. Although both individuals discussed emotions in their writings, we will now turn to James, as his contributions to emotion theory were more significant.

James criticized previous work on emotion, suggesting that it was mostly concerned with classifying different emotion states. Moreover, unlike his predecessors, he assumed that everyone feels something akin to grief, fear, rage, or love and that most other emotion terms (e.g., malice, spite) simply reflect differences in the eliciting object, not the underlying emotion. Thus, rather than worrying about emotion terms, James was interested in identifying general principles that apply to all emotions.

One of these principles was what exactly constitutes an emotion. To this end, he made a proposal that, although anticipated by René Descartes, turned contemporary notions upside-down. Specifically, he proposed that emotions arise from one's perception of bodily changes induced by emotion-provoking situations (James, 1884). According to James, emotional situations elicit brain representations of external events, which trigger emotion-specific bodily changes, specifically in the viscera—defined as the internal organs such as the stomach, heart, or liver. For example, the visual perception of a dangerous animal such as a snake or bear, he thought, affects the viscera as well as other bodily aspects (e.g., muscular tension) and moves an individual to flight. James held that this happens instinctively or reflex-like and that bodily consequences are relayed back to the brain (A Closer Look 1.2), which then gives rise to what we call an emotion (Figure 1.8).

Shortly after James published his thoughts on emotions in 1884, Carl Lange incidentally put forth a similar set of ideas, which are now referred to as the James-Lange theory. However, as this theory contradicted the common belief that bodily changes result from emotions—and not the other way around—it met with a lot of criticism. Its opponents, including Wundt, contended that bodily changes occur at a slower rate than does the experience of an emotion, that they are not specific enough to possibly enable different emotions, and that situational factors are often more important than the emotional object itself in influencing states of feeling. James addressed some of these and other criticisms in an 1894 publication (James, 1894). For example, he stressed that it is the perception of the situation as a whole rather than an individual object that triggers bodily changes. However, as he had no experimental data to support his theory, and exact information about the temporal course and specificity of bodily changes was unavailable, no definite conclusions could be drawn. James acknowledged this to be the case and encouraged other researchers and physicians to put his ideas to the test.

FIGURE 1.8 The James-Lange Theory of Emotion

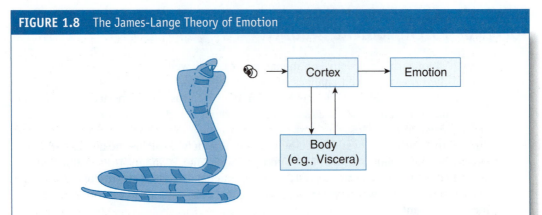

According to James and a contemporary Danish physician, Carl Lange, the perception of an emotional object (e.g., a snake) at the level of the cortex triggers bodily responses. For example, it might increase an individual's heart rate and change the activity of other bodily organs. These changes were presumed to feed back to the brain, where they are experienced as an emotion.

A CLOSER LOOK 1.2

FIGURE 1.9 William James

Harvard University, Harvard University Archives, W279404_1

Source: Harvard University Archives, HUP James, William (5).

William James and the Brain

William James (1842–1910) was born into a wealthy, cosmopolitan New York family. He went to medical school at Harvard University and stayed there as a lecturer and professor for most of his career. Although he started off as a medical doctor, James achieved his greatest fame through work he conducted in psychology and his efforts to establish psychology as a discipline in the United States. In his writings, James approached a wide range of psychological topics, including consciousness, attention, memory, and perception of time.

Perhaps due to his medical background, James was genuinely interested in the brain and looked at brain evidence to inform his psychological theories. For example, he held that evolution modified the brain and that it enabled more advanced processing in species more closely related to humans. Moreover, he distinguished between lower and higher brain centers responsible for more reflex-like and deliberate actions, respectively. During James's lifetime, however, neuroscience was still in its infancy, and detailed models about brain function were lacking. For example, the brain was held as a sensory-motor device specifically dedicated for perception and volition. Many thinkers, including James, still viewed the mind or soul as a separate entity that moved independently and possibly in parallel with what was going on in the brain.

Nevertheless, James considered the brain of importance for all mental processes—including emotions. In *The Principles of Psychology* (James, 1890, p. 17), he examined how frog behavior is affected by the removal of different parts of the central nervous system. After removing the two cerebral hemispheres, James observed, "Fear . . . seems to have deserted him [the frog]. In a word, he is an extremely complex machine whose actions, so far as they go, tend to self-preservation; but still a machine. . . . " Thus, he believed the two cerebral hemispheres to be important for emotions. While James assumed the hemispheres to be largely unorganized at birth and to become organized during an individual's lifetime, he also held that they possess "native tendencies," which he called instincts and emotions. The following quote illustrates how he conceived emotions to occur (James, 1890, pp. 473–474):

> Supposing the cortex to contain parts, liable to be excited by changes in each special sense-organ, in each portion of the skin, in each muscle, each joint, and each viscus, and to contain absolutely nothing else, we still have a scheme capable of representing the process of the emotions. An object falls on a sense-organ, affects a cortical part, and is perceived; or else the latter, excited inwardly, gives rise to an idea of the same object. Quick as a flash, the reflex currents pass down through their preordained channels, alter the condition of muscle, skin, and viscus; and these alterations, perceived, like the original object, in as many portions of the cortex, combine with it in consciousness and transform it from an object-simply-apprehended into an object-emotionally-felt. No new principles have to be invoked, nothing postulated beyond the ordinary reflex circuits, and the local centers admitted in one shape or another by all to exist.

During the 19th century, emotion theory matured from a topic of philosophical interest to a psychobiological framework that was directional for much of the research conducted since then. The inception of biology as a discipline, as well as contemporary developments in medicine, highlighted both body and brain processes as important and encouraged cross-species comparisons that identified basic aspects of emotions that are preserved across species. Furthermore, the inception of psychology as a discipline formalized the scientific inquiry into mental processes and led to the development of testable emotion theories. Prominent among them was the James-Lange theory, which integrated contemporary biological, medical, and psychological insights. The debate and interest ignited by this theory fueled subsequent emotion research, which confirmed some but not all of its claims. One of the claims that stood the test of time is that bodily changes feed back to the brain. Although this feedback is not necessary, as suggested by James, it was found to critically modulate and potentially trigger emotions. Therefore, contemporary writing still reminds us of James and his important contributions to emotion theory.

SUMMARY

Many generations of thinkers were intrigued by the feeling states called emotions and aimed to understand their nature and function. Philosophers of ancient Greece laid the foundation for subsequent views on emotions. For example, they drew a divide between thinking and feeling, introduced the role of both intellect and body in emotions, and established key concepts such as that of emotional valence. During the post-Renaissance period, these ideas were augmented by a first comprehensive theory of emotions put forth by René Descartes. Among other things, he linked emotions to the brain, differentiated between primary and secondary emotions, and made a case for their usefulness or functional significance.

Descartes' ideas and those of earlier philosophers made an important mark. However, due to the nature of philosophical inquiry and information exchange at that time, this mark was temporarily not well recognized and often remained uncredited. During the course of the 19th century, the nature of inquiry became more scientific or evidence-based, and information exchange became more formalized through the establishment of new disciplines, international conferences, scientific journals, and **peer review**. Together, these developments facilitated the integration of knowledge and prompted empirical research that systematically tested predictions derived from existing theoretical frameworks. Moreover, existing theories were pushed to the next level by new insights about the evolution of physical and mental traits, nonhuman animal emotions, and the triangular relationship between emotions, body, and brain. Thus, 19th-century science, spearheaded by scholars such as Darwin or James, set an agenda for emotion research that motivated a growth of the field in the 20th century and enabled many key discoveries.

THINKING CRITICALLY ABOUT "EARLY EMOTION THEORIES"

1. How did ancient philosophy conceptualize emotions? Discuss whether and in what way this changed throughout history.

2. For much of history, emotion theory developed quite slowly. This changed toward the end of the 19th century, when we see an increased interest in the topic. Why did this increase not occur earlier?

3. Many scholars postulated supposedly new ideas that others had already introduced. Identify some of these ideas and think of why older scholars were not always recognized.

MEDIA LIBRARY

Aristotle's *Rhetoric:* http://classics.mit.edu/Aristotle/rhetoric.html

René Descartes' *The Passions of the Soul:* http://net.cgu.edu/philosophy/descartes/index .html

Charles Darwin's complete published work as well as a collection of private writing and unpublished manuscripts: http://darwin-online.org.uk

William James's published work: http://www.uky.edu/ ~ eushe2/Pajares/james.html

CHAPTER 2

Brain and Thought Processes as Antecedents to Emotion

Emotion Theories of the 20th Century

The drive for evidence-based research and scientific exchange, which became dominant toward the late 19th century, inspired a burst of activity in the 20th century. This was supported by technical advances that turned electricity from a curiosity into a useful tool and kick-started what is called the second industrial revolution. Due to emerging specializations and the segregation into different disciplines, medicine and psychology initially pursued emotion research independently of each other. The former focused on the brain processes, whereas the latter aimed at discovering general psychological laws or mental operations that underpin emotions. This chapter reviews both lines of discovery and shows how they eventually merged into a collaborative and cross-disciplinary approach.

BRAIN PROCESSES AS THE BASIS FOR EMOTIONS

Cannon's Emotion Theory

In the early 20th century, psychologists began to quibble with the methods of William James and Wilhelm Wundt. They thought these methods too subjective and not scientific enough. Among other things, they criticized the reliance on phenomenological evidence or introspection and started to place more emphasis on the study of observable and quantifiable behavior. In the wake of this, behaviorism developed as new psychological approach, focusing on stimulus-response patterns and banning mind-related topics of inquiry. Not surprisingly, emotions were also banned and more or less disappeared from psychological research until the dogmas of behaviorism began to weaken in the 1950s.

Fortunately, the temporary restraint of behaviorism was limited only to psychology. Other fields, such as physiology or neurology, paid steady attention to matters of the mind and continued to pursue emotion research. One individual whose research stands out in this regard was Walter Cannon (1871–1945), a professor of physiology at Harvard University. His main interest lay with the sympathetic nervous system and the bodily changes incurred by sympathetic activation (Cannon, 1915; Chapter 4). The work that he completed on this topic, as well as the knowledge gained from the research of others, made him question the James-Lange theory mentioned in Chapter 1 (Cannon, 1927, 1931).

Specifically, Cannon saw a range of problems with the assumption that bodily feedback produces emotional feelings. For one thing, Cannon felt that James's emphasis on feedback from the viscera was unjustified. He had investigated the effect of removing the sympathetic aspects of the autonomous nervous system in cats and found that these cats still hissed and showed their teeth when confronted by a dog. Thus, he argued, they still experienced emotions despite the fact that the sympathetic system could no longer affect the viscera. Cannon also held that the same visceral changes may be linked to different emotions as well as nonemotional states. Sympathetic activation associated with a discharge of adrenaline was known to produce heart-rate acceleration, a constriction of blood vessels, sweating, and a widening of the pupils, among other things. Moreover, these effects seemed comparable, for the emotions of fear and anger and were observed in nonemotional states provoked by fever or the injection of adrenaline into the bloodstream. Thus, processes, apart from visceral changes, must produce specific emotions. Finally, Cannon was convinced that changes in the viscera were not readily felt by an individual and that they were too slow to account for the rapidity with which we experience emotions.

Together, these points led Cannon to refute the James-Lange theory and to offer an alternative brain-based emotion theory instead (Cannon, 1927, 1931). The latter theory builds on the observation that certain emotional expressions are preserved in animals with an ablated cortex. Upon trifling stimulation (e.g., handling), such animals could break into aggressive fits, termed sham-rage, suggesting that the brain center for emotional expression was located subcortically. Cannon believed this brain center to be the thalamus, a structure situated above the brainstem that forms part of the diencephalon and that serves as a processing hub for all senses except olfaction (Chapter 4). Moreover, he speculated that sensory information processed at the level of the thalamus or the cortical signals projected to the thalamus trigger bodily responses to emotional challenges. Cannon conceptualized these responses as mere emotional expressions and distinguished them from emotional feelings or emotional consciousness, which he believed to depend on the cerebral cortex. A diagram elaborating his ideas is presented in Figure 2.1.

The Papez Circuit

Cannon's theory attracted attention and inspired further inquiries into the brain basis for emotions. Worth mentioning here is a subsequent proposal by James Papez (1937), an American neurologist at Cornell University. He incorporated Cannon's ideas as well as those of James Bard, a PhD student of Cannon's who had isolated parts of the thalamus and the posterior hypothalamus as the diencephalic structures responsible for the sham-rage of decorticated animals and the potential seat for emotional expression (Bard, 1928, 1934). Accordingly, the thalamus and the hypothalamus became key structures in Papez's

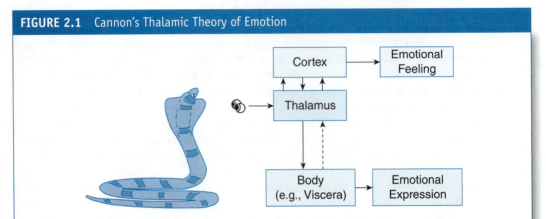

FIGURE 2.1 Cannon's Thalamic Theory of Emotion

According to Cannon, all sensory information (except olfaction) is first processed by the thalamus and then relayed to the cortex. In some instances, perceptual computations at the level of the thalamus (e.g., loud noise) would suffice to excite thalamic activity relevant for emotions. However, in most cases, perceptual computations at the level of the cortex would be necessary. Those, Cannon argued, would release the thalamus from cortical inhibition. The resulting thalamic activity could then trigger sympathetic activation and bodily changes. At the same time, thalamic activity would feed back to the cortex and there produce conscious feelings of emotion. Although Cannon mentioned the possibility of bodily feedback to the brain, he assumed this feedback to be irrelevant for emotions.

emotion theory. He included two more structures based on their neuroanatomical connections with the diencephalon, as well as evidence from patients with damage to these structures that appeared to affect their emotions. These structures comprised the **cingulate gyrus** and the **hippocampus**, which are situated along the interior walls of the two cortical hemispheres (Figure 2.2).

Papez envisioned the information flow between these structures as follows. In line with Cannon and Bard, he assumed that most sensory information first passes from the sensory receptors to the thalamus. From there it could take one of three specialized processing streams. The "stream of thought" entailed projections to the lateral cortex, the "stream of movement" entailed projections to the basal ganglia, and the "stream of feeling" entailed projections to the hypothalamus. Like Cannon and Bard, Papez believed the activation of the hypothalamus to be critical for the bodily responses that accompany an emotion, and projections from the hypothalamus to the cortex to be critical for the conscious feeling of an emotion. According to Papez, the latter proceeded from the hypothalamus to the cingulate cortex via the anterior thalamus. He presumed the cingulate cortex to be a receptive structure for emotions, just like the occipital cortex is a receptive structure for vision or the temporal cortex for audition. Moreover, he thought that activation of the cingulate cortex bestowed perceptual representations in the occipital or temporal cortex with an emotional tone.

To account for the fact that emotions may arise from basic percepts (e.g., loud noise) available at the level of the thalamus as well as from thoughts or memories, Papez envisioned two modes of hypothalamic activation. The first, as described earlier, would be via

FIGURE 2.2 Structures of the Papez Circuit

Shaded in blue are the cingulate gyrus (CG), the thalamus (TH), the hypothalamus (HT), and the hippocampus (Hip). The top of this figure presents a sagittal view of the brain; the bottom presents a coronal view of the brain.

the "stream of feeling." The second would be via cortical projections to the hippocampus, which could then enter the stream of feeling. Together, these two modes form a circuit, which is now known as the Papez circuit (Figure 2.3).

The Papez circuit integrated experimental and neuroanatomical discoveries of the early 20th century and was thus a very modern way of looking at emotions. After the rather general convictions of the 19th century that the brain was important for emotions, researchers like Cannon and Papez finally arrived at a set of brain structures that ostensibly contributed

FIGURE 2.3   The Papez Circuit

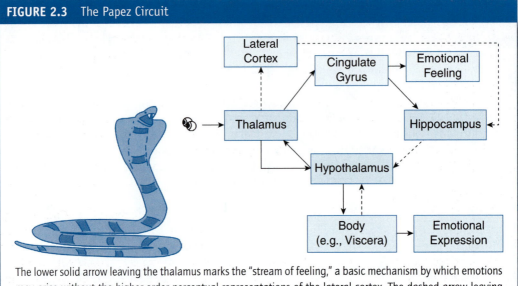

The lower solid arrow leaving the thalamus marks the "stream of feeling," a basic mechanism by which emotions may arise without the higher-order perceptual representations of the lateral cortex. The dashed arrow leaving the thalamus shows how emotions may arise from the "stream of thought." Papez proposed that the latter could access the "stream of feeling" via the hippocampus.

to the feeling and behavioral aspects of emotion. Moreover, they pointed to a mechanism by which emotional experiences could affect the body, and vice versa. Thus, the Papez circuit provided clinicians with a better understanding of certain organic disorders.

For example, as the relationship between emotions and the autonomic nervous system became better known, clinicians could explain why individuals after extreme and sustained exposure to threat (e.g., war) presented with somatic complaints as related to digestion or sleep. They now understood that a chronic activation of the sympathetic nervous system impaired these life-sustaining processes and could lead to organic damage. Additionally, the Papez circuit enabled clinicians to appreciate why certain neurological conditions produced emotional symptoms. For example, it was now apparent that tumors or damage to certain brain areas could change an individual's mood or leave him or her without apparent emotions. Thus, observations of emotional change could alert clinicians about a possible neurological impairment.

The Limbic System Theory

Theory Development

One individual who was particularly intrigued by the clinical applications of the Papez circuit was Paul MacLean (1913–2007). MacLean was interested in emotions as the principal cause for the behaviors in which humans engage, and he was able to pursue this interest as a research fellow at Massachusetts General Hospital. Here, he was introduced to a range of patients with epilepsy, some of whom reported emotional auras preceding an epileptic seizure. An investigation of these patients using electroencephalography (EEG; Chapter 6) indicated abnormal electrical activity primarily at electrodes placed close to the hippocampus. (These recordings were made with electrodes inserted through the nose and positioned at the base of the brain.)

In search for a link between the patients' emotional auras and an epileptogenic focus in the hippocampus, MacLean came across the Papez circuit. As its implication of the hippocampus in emotions seemed promising, MacLean sought a direct discussion of his work with Papez. After this discussion, which comprised a several-day-long visit to the Papez lab, MacLean set to writing a paper that explained how the Papez circuit bore significance both for his epileptic patients and patients with psychosomatic complaints (MacLean, 1949).

Apart from highlighting the work of Papez, MacLean's paper made a number of original contributions. First, it reintroduced the term limbic to refer to the structures of the Papez circuit. The term derived from the Latin word *limbus,* which means "rim" or "edge." It was first used by the French neurologist Paul Broca (1824–1880) as a name for the cortical regions that surround the basal ganglia and that were thought to support olfactory perception. Subsequently, these regions became known as the rhinencephalon, or smell-brain. MacLean argued that smell governs the behavior of lower animals and that, with the emergence of higher animals, other sensory modalities gained greater importance. Moreover, because visual, auditory, and somatosensory impressions critically added to the processes in the rhinencephalon, he thought that its name was no longer appropriate and used the nonfunctional and anatomically descriptive term limbic instead.

MacLean's second contribution is that he included the amygdala in the discussion of emotions and gave the hippocampus a more central role. The latter he presumed to support the forming of associations between different percepts or events. For example, he thought that the hippocampus could link the color red with negative experiences such as injury and fainting and thus provoke negative emotions on subsequently seeing something red.

Finally, MacLean linked the proposed limbic processes with psychoanalytic theory, as formulated by Sigmund Freud (1856–1939). Freud had postulated that a person's psychosexual development undergoes a series of stages and that the human mind can be divided into id, ego, and superego. MacLean saw these ideas reflected in the organization and functioning of the human brain. For example, he identified the Freudian id, an animalistic drive for the satisfaction of basic needs, with the limbic structures, particularly with the hippocampus. Moreover, he thought that childhood experiences shape the functioning of these structures and may be responsible for an individual's fixation on an early psychosexual stage and the development of psychological problems in adulthood.

In later publications, MacLean elaborated on these propositions. He defined a limbic system, which included the structures of Broca's limbic lobe (i.e., cortex adjacent to the olfactory striae; the pyriform area; the hippocampal complex; and parasplenial, cingulate, and subcallosal gyri) as well as associated subcortical structures such as the amygdala, the hypothalamus, and the anterior thalamus (MacLean, 1952). These structures were thought to make up a paleomammalian brain, which with the Greek prefix *paleo* means ancient mammalian brain or a brain shared among all mammals. MacLean postulated that, in higher mammals such as primates, the paleomammalian brain was sandwiched between a phylogenetically older and a phylogenetically newer system (MacLean, 1972; Figure 2.4), which together formed a triune brain.

The phylogenetically older system comprised the striatum and the globus pallidus, and it was named the reptilian brain. As the name suggests, MacLean thought this system to be largely equivalent to the brain of the reptile—an evolutionarily ancient vertebrate. According to his theory, it supported basic self-preserving behaviors such as hunting and territorial marking.

FIGURE 2.4   The Triune Brain

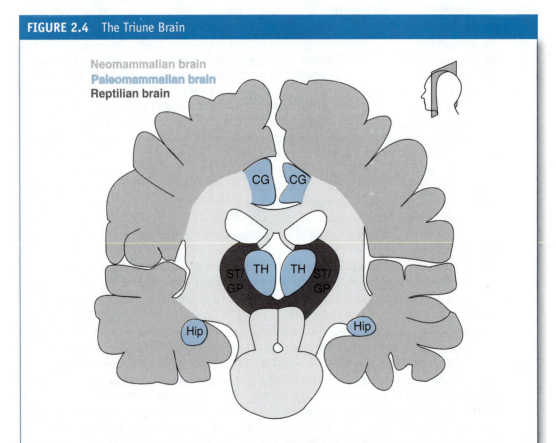

This figure shows a coronal view of the human brain and outlines some of the structures that Paul MacLean associated with the reptilian (dark gray), the paleomammalian (blue), and the neomammalian brain (light gray). They include the anterior thalamus (TH), the corpus striatum and globus pallidus (ST/GP), the hippocampus (Hip), and the neocortex. With the exception of the thalamus, structures believed to be evolutionarily newer wrap around structures believed to be evolutionarily older.

The phylogenetically newer system comprised the neocortex, the six-layered gray mass that folds around the surface of the two hemispheres. It was named the neomammalian brain. This system, MacLean argued, existed in higher mammals only, and there supported cognitive processes such as language, problem solving, and decision making. MacLean thought that most of the neocortex operated like "a giant heartless computer" (MacLean, 1977, p. 216), with the exception of the prefrontal cortex. The latter grew most in the course of mammalian evolution, and by "looking inward" where the cortex lies between the two hemispheres (MacLean, 1977, p. 217) formed connections with the limbic system. This he believed allowed communication with emotional processes and enabled humans, more than any other species, to empathize with the feelings of others.

Theory Application

MacLean's limbic system theory was well received and quickly became the golden standard for understanding emotions. It made its way into teaching materials and instructional texts and has remained there uncriticized up to the beginning of the 21st century. The limbic system theory also shaped the clinical diagnosis and treatment of psychological, psychiatric, and neurological disorders. By linking emotions to a dedicated set of brain structures, it enabled inferences about localized neurological dysfunction in patients with emotional symptoms and pointed to treatment targets.

Prior to the limbic system theory, medical treatments of mental illness had been very crude. These largely comprised the destruction of frontal lobe tissue deemed responsible for negative emotion states. Such destruction was first attempted by Egas Moniz (1874–1955) based on experiments by John Fulton and Carlyle Jacobsen (1935, as cited in Kopell, Machado, & Rezai, 2005). The latter two had lesioned the frontal lobe of chimpanzees and observed that, while no apparent cognitive deficits ensued, these animals were less prone to frustration or what they called "experimental neurosis." Thus, Moniz attempted the treatment of mental illness by severing the white-matter tracts that connected the frontal lobe to other parts of the brain.

Despite the lack of objective tests, Moniz considered his technique successful and recommended it to colleagues, who, given the lack of alternatives, readily followed his lead. Infamous among them was the neurologist Walter Freeman (1895–1972), who adapted and popularized the technique in the United States (Freeman & Watts, 1950). While initially working together with a proper neurosurgeon, James Watts, Freeman later worked by himself, using a simplified technique by which he inserted an icepick-like device through the thin, bony orbit above the eyes. Freeman held that any regular physician could perform this procedure after minimal instruction.

That Freeman placed neurosurgery into the hands of untrained individuals caused an outcry among the medical profession. This, coupled with the inception of psychopharmaca and the increasingly negative reports concerning the outcomes of frontolobotomies, greatly reduced their popularity. Yet the general interest in neurosurgery as a treatment for mental illness remained, and with the limbic system theory took on a new direction. Now, instead of blindly ablating frontal lobe tissue, neurosurgeons would carefully target limbic structures such as the anterior cingulate, connections between the frontal lobe and subcortical structures, or tissue in and around the amygdala (Kelly, 1973; Mashour, Walker,

& Martuza, 2005). Some of these treatments are still practiced today in patients that combine a severe psychological dysfunction with a resistance to other, less invasive approaches. However, due to their infrequency and irreversible nature, these treatments were never properly compared to sham surgeries; therefore, their efficacy is still a matter of debate (Mashour et al., 2005).

Critique of the Limbic System Theory and Recent Developments

The numerous technical advances introduced in the second half of the 20th century brought forth a range of new methodologies that benefited neuroscience and that helped shed light on the brain basis for emotions. The ensuing discoveries supported some of the assumptions put forth by MacLean. For example, they proved that some of the "limbic" structures, such as the amygdala and the cingulate gyrus, indeed mediate emotions. However, they also indicated that many of the neuroanatomical, neurofunctional, and conceptual assumptions of MacLean were incorrect.

Neuroanantomical Issues

Specifically, neuroanatomical knowledge emerged that contradicted the notion of there being a reptilian, a paleomammalian, and a neomammalian brain, and that showed that evolution did not simply add new brain layers onto older ones (A Closer Look 2.1). Microscopic examinations of the brains of present-day reptiles revealed them to possess tissue homologous to the human amygdala, the hippocampus, and even the neocortex (Kaas, 2011).

For example, reptiles were found to possess a structure called the dorsal cortex, which has some of the properties that we associate with the neocortex, such as a layer of pyramidal cells that receive input from the thalamus. Moreover, the actual neocortex, with up to 20 subdivisions, seems to have existed already in the earliest mammals (Kaas, 2011), which, according to MacLean, should have possessed no more than a limbic system and its reptilian predecessor. Finally, there is evidence for evolutionary modifications and even additions to limbic structures in some more recent mammals. Comparative brain investigation revealed a class of neurons, called von Economo neurons, in great apes and humans, that are absent in most other primates and mammals (Allman et al., 2011). They are large, bipolar neurons situated in the anterior insula and anterior cingulate, which presumably support fast communication between these and more distant brain regions (Chapter 4).

Thus, this evidence indicates that "limbic" or neocortical structures did not suddenly emerge as new layers on top of evolutionarily older structures. Instead, they seem to have developed from tissue specializations that led both to the expansion and shrinkage of some areas relative to others and that resulted in brains that comprise a patchwork of evolutionarily older and younger components.

Neurofunctional Issues

A second line of evidence in contradiction of the limbic system theory comes from modern research on brain function. This research indicated that some of the structures that MacLean associated with emotions serve functions typically associated with cognition. For example, the hippocampus, which MacLean thought to represent the beast in man and to

A CLOSER LOOK 2.1

Brain Evolution

Charles Darwin's theory of evolution provided neurologists with a framework for understanding species differences in brain structure and function. Traditionally, these differences were conceptualized as signifying a linear process, with the lowest animal at the beginning and humans, as the most intelligent and therefore most evolved animal, at the end. Furthermore, the process was envisioned as tissue growth whereby new and more complex tissue emerged on top of evolutionarily older and simpler tissue.

Although largely incorrect, these ideas gained much popularity and are still reflected in the scientific literature of today. This is because actual insights into brain evolution are inherently difficult. Brains, unlike other animal artifacts such as bones or teeth, do not fossilize. Therefore, many inferences regarding the brains of our ancestors must be speculative. Researchers try to get around this by comparing the brains of humans to those of other animals of today. However, these animals

FIGURE 2.5   Amniote Evolution

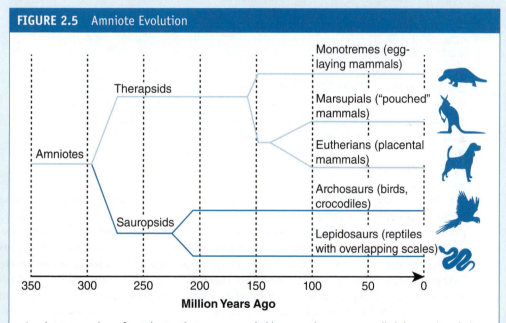

Amniotes are a class of vertebrates that are surrounded by a membranous sac, called the amnion, during embryonic development. About 300 million years ago, they split into therapsids, reptile-like mammals that were the ancestor of modern mammals, and sauropsids, the ancestor of birds and reptiles.

(Continued)

(Continued)

likely differ from the ancestor they share with humans, as they would have continued to evolve in the intervening time. Nevertheless, some of this evidence—as well as evidence from DNA and skulls, fossilized and modern—can provide valuable insights.

So far, these insights revealed that brain evolution was not linear. Like the evolution of other bodily features, it was a multipronged process that enabled animals to adapt to different environmental niches. Thus, depending on the niche, different mental operations were more or less important for survival such that animals evolved the former and dispensed with the latter. Moreover, this evolution proceeded in parallel and convergent manner.

Parallel evolution refers to a characteristic that is shared between two species and that can be traced back to a common ancestor. For example, the neocortex evolved in parallel in humans and other primates and can be traced back to the earliest mammals.

Convergent evolution refers to a characteristic that is shared between two species but was absent in a common ancestor. For example, brain structures that support complex social behaviors and abstract thought appear to be present in both primates and certain birds yet were most likely absent in the ancient amniotes, the ancestor primates and birds shared more than 300 million years ago (Figure 2.5). Moreover, complex social behaviors and abstract thought seem to be supported by different structures in the primate and the avian brain. In the primate brain they rely on the six-layered neocortex, whereas in the avian brain they rely on a forebrain structure made up of several nuclei (Güntürkün, 2012).

Together, these insights make it futile to refer to one brain as better or worse, more or less evolved than another. The brains of today's animals are adapted to enable behaviors relevant for survival in the animals' respective environmental niche. As the niche of humans differs from that of other species, so do their brains. Thus, we may be capable of doing things that other species are incapable of, and vice versa.

support exclusively emotional associations of a preverbal nature, was shown to be a key structure for explicit or **declarative memory.**

Lesion studies indicated that damage to the hippocampus leaves recall and verbalization of memories formed prior to the damage intact. However, it compromises the long-term storage of events that occurred after the lesion so that these events can later not be recalled (Corkin, 2002; Kennedy & Shapiro, 2004; Scoville & Milner, 1957). Thus, an individual who incurred hippocampal damage in adulthood would be able to recall his or her parents and world events that happened during childhood such as the end of the Cold War. However, that individual may not recall any of the doctors that provided treatment after the brain damage or subsequent world events such as the terrorist attack on the World Trade Center in 2001.

A further neurofunctional error of the limbic system theory is that structures excluded from the limbic system because they were presumably irrelevant for emotions have been shown to support important aspects of emotional experiences. For example, the corpus striatum, thought to be part of the reptilian brain, proved to support the experience of pleasure from reward (Burgdorf & Panksepp, 2006). Likewise, the insula, originally part of the "heartless" neomammalian brain, was found to support the representation of emotion-induced bodily changes and thus to enable bodily changes to affect ongoing mental processes and decision making (Craig, 2009).

Conceptual Issues

Finally, advances in our understanding of emotions suggest a range of conceptual problems with the limbic system theory. First, this theory places a sharp divide between emotion and cognition. Emotions are assigned strictly to the limbic system, whereas cognition or symbolic thought are assigned to a heartless computer in the neocortex. Recent insights suggest that this divide is inappropriate. Although many researchers still use the words *emotion* and *cognition* to refer to feeling and thinking separately, there is now a universal recognition that both are intimately linked. Moreover, the difficulty in differentiating these two concepts has been acknowledged (Chapter 11).

A second conceptual problem associated with the limbic system theory arises from its definition of emotions. Today, we define emotions as mental states that motivate behaviors relevant for survival. For example, we assume that positive emotions govern consummatory behaviors associated with foraging, hunting, or mating. Moreover, we assume that negative emotions govern, among other things, aggressive behaviors associated with territorial defense. In accord with these present-day conceptions, MacLean linked a range of survival behaviors to emotions in mammals. However, he linked these same behaviors to simple, nonemotional programs in reptiles and thus failed to see evolutionary continuity in the function of emotions.

Last, the realization that different emotions motivate different behaviors led researchers to see the futility of trying to explain all emotional experiences with only one brain system (LeDoux, 2001). Moreover, they began to use a more differentiated approach by looking at different emotions separately. This in turn revealed evidence for emotion-specific neural networks, proving MacLean's "one-system-serves-all" approach to be incorrect.

The shortcomings of the limbic system theory reviewed here started to become apparent almost immediately after its original inception. Moreover, they became increasingly pressing toward the end of the 20th century, leading many researchers to discard the limbic system as a theoretical framework in favor of a data-driven or theoretically more differentiated approach (Kötter & Meyer, 1992; LeDoux, 2001). Nevertheless the notion of an emotional or "limbic" brain remained popular, and we thus see a continued use of this term in reference to brain regions that support emotions. However, as the original definition of the limbic system is neuroanatomically, neurofunctionally, and conceptually flawed, the use of this term has incorrect theoretical implications. Neuroanatomical terms that bear no reference to underlying function are a better choice when describing the structures implicated in emotions.

THOUGHTS AS THE BASIS FOR EMOTIONS

Historical Background

The close of the 19th century and the beginning of the 20th century brought on two developments that excited a new theoretical approach to emotions. The first development arose from general insights into brain function. Based on the microscopic observations of anatomists such as Camillo Golgi and Santiago Ramón y Cajal, it became apparent that the cells of the central nervous system differ in many respects from the cells of other bodily organs, and that these differences are essential for the workings of the mind. Moreover, the comparison of cell types and their architecture across different parts of the central nervous system suggested regional specialization and cross-regional communication. Thus, individuals like Korbinian Brodmann developed anatomical maps that outlined areas of a particular cellular organization and that enabled a range of neurofunctional inferences, such as those linked to emotions (Chapter 4, Figure 4.6).

The second development critical for emotion theory concerned the automatization of industrial processes. By the beginning of the 20th century, this development had reached a point where engineers were able to implement formally derived concepts of "algorithm" and "computation" to produce "intelligent machines." Over time, these machines became increasingly sophisticated, culminating in the modern computer. While it was the nature of intelligent thought that had inspired this development, its result then inspired theories about intelligent thought and mental processes in general (Gigerenzer & Goldstein, 1996). Moreover, together with the modular perception of brain function as suggested by contemporary neuroscience, this helped overcome the dogmas of behaviorism and led to a renewed interest in the mind.

In the 1950s, this culminated in a paradigm shift for psychology—a shift away from behavior toward thought and cognition. The then-fashionable notion of the mind as a computer or "thought machine" was applied to many mental phenomena, including those linked to emotions. Moreover, some psychologists ventured that even the very subjective experiences of emotions could be ascribed to simple mental algorithms, and they set out to identify them.

Thoughts Disambiguate Unspecific Bodily Arousal

Among the cognitive pioneers were Stanley Schachter and Jerome Singer of Columbia University in the United States. They revisited the James-Lange theory and tried to address one of its weaknesses. Physiological research conducted in the intervening years negated the idea of bodily feedback differing among various emotions. Thus, it was unclear how this feedback could produce the range of emotions we feel. Schachter and Singer set out to address this issue and hypothesized that cognition or thought could act as a mediator. Furthermore, they speculated that bodily change triggered by an emotional event forces itself into awareness and makes an individual wonder what caused the change. If the individual can attribute the change to an event that seems emotionally salient, he or she will feel an emotion.

To test this notion, Schachter and Singer (1962) performed a now-classic study. In this study, participants were invited to help examine the effect of a new vitamin compound on visual acuity. Unbeknownst to the participants, no vitamin but adrenaline or a placebo were given. One participant group received adrenaline and was told about its actual sympathetic effects (e.g., increased heart rate and body temperature). A second group received adrenaline and was told about side effects such as numb feet or a slight headache, which are not actually caused by the drug. A third and a fourth group received adrenaline and placebo, respectively, without any mention of side effects.

After the application of the drug, participants were asked to wait 20 minutes for a vision test with the explanation that the drug first needed to become active. Participants were thus brought to a waiting room and introduced to another participant, who in reality was a confederate of the experimenter. For half the participants in each group, the confederate was instructed to exude a positive mood. For the other half, he was instructed to exude a negative mood. In the former instance, the confederate was an altogether happy companion and engrossed the participant in funny games. In the latter instance, the experimenter left confederate and participant with a long and boring questionnaire to complete, about which the confederate complained excessively. After 20 minutes, the experimenter returned and asked participants to give a short self-report concerning their present emotional state, as this could impact their vision. After the participants provided this report, they were debriefed and dismissed.

In accord with their predictions, Schachter and Singer found that participants in the three adrenaline groups felt differently. Those who had been correctly informed about the effects of the drug were least influenced by the activity of the confederate. Their reported emotions stayed relatively neutral. In contrast, individuals who were un- or misinformed were greatly affected by the confederate. If placed in the positive condition, their emotions were more positive, and if placed in the negative condition, their emotions were less positive than those of participants who had been correctly warned about side effects. The emotions of the placebo group ranked in between (Figure 2.6).

Together, these results formed the basis for what is now known as Schachter and Singer's cognitive arousal theory. According to this theory, two things are necessary for an emotion: thought and bodily arousal. Moreover, individuals are proposed to "label" the bodily arousal triggered by an emotional event based on their evaluation of the event. If that evaluation is positive, then a positive emotion ensues; if it is negative, then a negative emotion ensues.

Although subsequent research failed to replicate the study that formed the basis for this theory (Reisenzein, 1983), enough related evidence accumulated to secure its impact (Lindquist & Barrett, 2008; Nisbett & Schachter, 1966; Valins, 1966; Zillmann & Bryant, 1974). For example, it was found that mock psychophysiological feedback in the form of an audible heartbeat influenced male participants in their liking of concurrently viewed nude female photographs. Nudes viewed in the context of an accelerated heartbeat were subsequently rated more favorably than were nudes viewed in the context of a normal heartbeat (Valins, 1966). Physical exercise, presumably leading to emotion-unspecific arousal, was found to facilitate emotional responses to both negative and positive stimuli (Zillmann & Bryant, 1974). Moreover, a placebo given to participants in the disguise of an arousal-inducing drug was found to reduce the apparent impact of emotion-provoking stimuli on participants (Nisbett & Schachter, 1966).

FIGURE 2.6   Methods and Results of a Study by Schachter and Singer (1962)

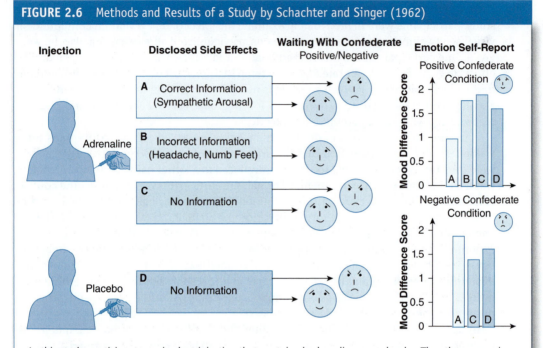

In this study, participants received an injection that contained adrenaline or a placebo. They then were given correct information about to-be-expected side effects, incorrect information, or no information. Subsequently, groups were asked to wait in the company of a confederate who created a positive or negative atmosphere. Schachter and Singer measured the participants' pulse, observed their behavior during the waiting period, and obtained mood ratings at the end of this period. The mood ratings were obtained on a positive and a negative mood scale. The difference scores illustrated here were derived by subtracting the negative from the positive scale results. Thus, the greater the score, the lesser the participants' negative mood and/or the greater their positive mood.

Source: "Cognitive, Social, and Physiological Determinants of Emotional State," by S. Schachter and J. Singer, 1962, *Psychological Review, 69,* pp. 379–399.

Together, this and other evidence supported the notion that cognitive evaluations are relevant in the relationship between bodily arousal and emotions. Thus, it usefully extended the original ideas of James and Lange by offering a mechanism through which unspecific bodily arousal could produce the various emotions we feel. Yet some of the core problems of the James-Lange theory remained. First, there was still no evidence to suggest that bodily feedback was indeed necessary for an emotion. What research hitherto had shown was simply that bodily feedback could influence what people felt. Moreover, accounts of individuals with impaired bodily feedback and a purportedly intact emotional life suggested to many that emotions can occur based on mental processes alone. Second, the reliance of emotion on bodily responses and the deliberate evaluation of their relationship to the emotional event introduced a temporal delay that contradicted the commonsense notion that emotions occur very rapidly. Third, and perhaps most important, researchers had ignored the issue of how bodily changes occur in the first place. Both the James-Lange and the Schachter-Singer theories stipulated that the perception of an emotional stimulus triggered bodily reactions. Yet the mechanism by which this occurs was left unspecified.

Thoughts Create Bodily Arousal

The psychologist Magda Arnold (A Closer Look 2.2) tackled these issues head on. However, rather than conducting her own empirical work, Arnold reviewed the extant literature and integrated insights from different researchers and disciplines with a phenomenological approach. The result was a manifesto titled *Emotion and Personality* (Arnold, 1961), which laid out a theory of emotion and was trend-setting for future research. Notably, this theory was not entirely new but already anticipated by Aristotle, who declared thought a precedent to emotions. It also had more recent predecessors in contemporary philosophy (e.g., Franz Brentano, Alexius Meinong, and Jean-Paul Sartre). Nevertheless, Arnold is now considered the "pioneer of cognitive emotion theory in modern (i.e., post-behaviourist) psychology" (Reisenzein, 2006).

Arnold's theory built on the notion that emotions, like sensory percepts, have an object. If we feel happy, there is something to be happy about, such as a meeting with a friend or an unexpected financial reward. If we feel sad, it is because we have lost something valued, such as a friend or a loved one. Therefore, Arnold thought, the primary source of an emotion must be the evaluation of its eliciting object. Moreover, she defined this evaluation in the following way.

First, she argued, we must hold a belief that something is true. For example, that belief might be that an old friend, whom we have not seen for many years, is coming for a visit. Second, Arnold postulated, we must evaluate whether and how the belief or emotion object could affect us and our goals. This evaluation extends along three dimensions. One is a valence dimension, on which we locate the emotion object as being positive or negative. One is an existence dimension, on which we locate the emotion object as being present or absent. The third is a coping dimension, on which we evaluate whether we can manage the emotion object: In other words, whether we feel that this object is attainable versus unattainable or avoidable versus unavoidable.

To revisit our example, we might now evaluate whether we perceive the visit of our friend to be something good or bad. The visit might be good if we parted amicably but bad if there was some dispute. We might also evaluate the temporal proximity or acuteness of the visit and whether we will be around at the time. After we have evaluated both the emotion object and its impact on us, we experience a mental bias or tendency to behave in a certain way. For example, we may be biased to act in a warm, welcoming way. This action tendency was what Arnold believed is felt as an emotion. According to her it is accompanied by physiological responses, which prepare the body for action but are unnecessary for the emotion itself. The key points of her theory are illustrated in Figure 2.7.

FIGURE 2.7   Magda Arnold's Appraisal Theory

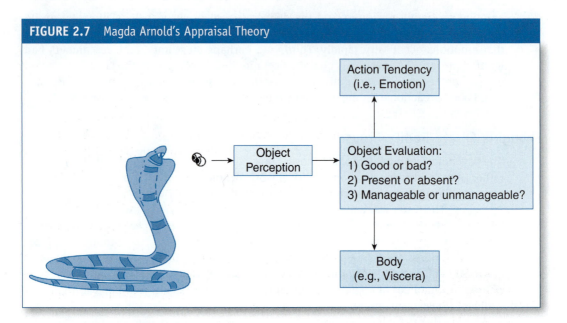

Arnold referred to the cognitions that precede an emotion (i.e., the evaluations of emotion object and its impact on us) as appraisals and used them to explain the many emotions we feel as well as why humans differ so greatly in their emotions. Although these appraisals are cognitive in nature, Arnold did not imply that they are restricted to humans or that they have to be conscious. In fact, she held that immediate and intuitive appraisals are more important than deliberate and reflective appraisals. The former we may conceive of as "automatic" cognitive programs that can occur outside of consciousness (Kappas, 2006). The latter we may conceive of as "controlled" cognitive processes that depend on consciousness.

According to Arnold, all emotions are based on the automatic appraisal, whereas controlled appraisal may contribute to only some emotions by moderating automatic appraisal. Arnold derived the notion of automatic appraisal from the fact that nonhuman animals and infants are capable of experiencing emotions and that therefore some appraisal mechanisms must be supported by innate, biological systems. She was keenly interested in these systems and followed the relevant neuroscientific research published at that time.

Arnold communicated her notions through publications and participation in scientific meetings. In the latter context, she met the psychologist Richard Lazarus, who helped Arnold's theory gain popularity and garnered the research interest that was necessary to test her predictions empirically. Lazarus also conducted a number of studies himself that led him to develop his own appraisal theory. Nevertheless, he was always careful to acknowledge his intellectual debt to Arnold.

Among the differences between his and Arnold's theory was the emphasis on the role of automatic versus controlled appraisal. Arnold emphasized that appraisals can and do occur automatically. According to her, we need no conscious reflection to represent an event and its importance to us. The reward felt from a friend's visit can embrace us without our being aware of it. In contrast, Lazarus thought this impossible and posited instead that

A CLOSER LOOK 2.2

Magda Arnold—A Female Psychologist Breaking Through Male-Dominated Behaviorism

FIGURE 2.8   Magda Arnold

Source: Courtesy of Loyola University Chicago Archives and Special Collections.

We can now define emotion as the felt tendency toward anything intuitively appraised as good (beneficial), or away from anything intuitively appraised as bad (harmful). This attraction or aversion is accompanied by a pattern of physiological changes organized toward approach or withdrawal. The patterns differ for different emotions.

—Magda Arnold (1961, p. 182)

Magda Arnold was born in 1903 in a German-speaking part of today's Czech Republic. Her parents worked in a traveling theater. Thus, although she was interested in psychology from her teens, a career in psychology seemed unlikely. In her 20s, Arnold married a fresh PhD in Slavic languages who urged her to leave prewar Europe for the safer havens of Canada. Here, Arnold started to pursue her interest in psychology both as an undergraduate and a graduate student. Unhappy with its impact on their family life, Arnold's husband separated from her during this time.

In 1942, Arnold received her PhD from the University of Toronto and stayed on as a lecturer. Some years later, she moved to the United States, where she held faculty positions at Bryn Mawr College, Barat College, and Loyola University. Once in the United States, Arnold established links with America's psychologists and participated in an international emotion meeting in 1948 as one of only 3 females among 50 presenters. In 1968, she organized her own emotion meeting, which brought on a renaissance for emotion research and let the shadows of behaviorism slowly disappear. Arnold invited individuals such as Nico Frijda, Richard Lazarus, Stanley Schachter, and Silvan Tomkins, who contributed to making appraisal theory a dominant paradigm for the psychology of emotions.

Supported through various grants, Arnold embarked on writing *Emotion and Personality* in the 1950s. Her goal for this book is expressed in the following quote: "What is needed, I thought, is a theory that will encompass not only psychological but physiological and neurological research results. In fact, without a comprehensive theory integrating psychological phenomena with brain function, research is bound to be haphazard" (as cited by Shields, 2006, p. 914). The book was well received, and her theory enticed several generations of psychologists to study appraisal mechanisms and to find support for her proposition of what emotions are. Arnold remained interested in emotions and academically active into old age. She died in 2002.

feelings of any kind require effortful thought. This and the fact that many appraisal researchers use self-report measures in their work generated the misconception that appraisal theory in general considers appraisals as conscious, cognitive processes. Moreover, researchers that were not of the "appraisal tradition" started to disregard appraisal theory because they felt that it did not adequately account for the automaticity with which emotions occur (Kappas, 2006).

Defying Thought

Exemplary for the growing disregard of appraisal theory stands Robert Zajonc, a major figure in social psychology. He held that much of our behavior is influenced by mental processes that are not subject to consciousness or awareness, and he proved this point in a seminal experiment (Kunst-Wilson & Zajonc, 1980). In this experiment, he and his coworker Kunst-Wilson presented participants with a series of octagons that appeared for only one millisecond on a computer screen. With such a short presentation, the participants only noticed a flash of light and were unable to clearly see or recognize the images. After an initial passive exposure block, participants were then presented with these octagons again. However, this time they appeared for one second and were thus clearly visible. Moreover, they were presented side by side with new octagons, and participants were asked to guess which one they had previously seen and which one they liked better. For the former decision, accuracy was no better than chance (Figure 2.9). Participants were as likely to indicate the old octagon as they were to indicate the new octagon, verifying that they had been unable to properly process the octagons presented in the passive exposure phase. Interestingly, however, the latter decision revealed results that differed from chance. Participants were more likely to "like" an octagon to which they had previously been exposed than they were to like a new octagon. This suggested to Zajonc that humans are capable of "making affective discriminations without extensive participation of the cognitive system" (Kunst-Wilson & Zajonc, 1980, p. 558). Moreover, he reinforced his stand in a subsequent article titled "The Primacy of Affect" (Zajonc, 1984).

Zajonc's writings were answered by Richard Lazarus with a competing article titled "On the Primacy of Cognition" (Lazarus, 1984). In this article, he criticized Zajonc for failing to define what an emotion is and rejected that preferences expressed in "liking" can be regarded as emotion. He argued that such preferences simply reflect what is perceived as good or bad in one's environment. Such preferences would not entail all relevant information in relation to the person and his or her goals. In other words, they would lack some of the appraisal dimensions postulated by Magda Arnold as a precondition for emotions. Furthermore, Lazarus countered Zajonc's criticism that there is no evidence that cognition is necessary for an emotion with the observation that there likewise is no evidence to the contrary.

As may be apparent from this debate, the crux of the problem was definitional in nature. Neither Zajonc nor Lazarus could put forward an emotion definition that the other was ready to accept. Moreover, Zajonc and other opponents of appraisal theory assumed a clear divide between emotion and cognition—a divide as old as ancient Greek philosophy, which attributed thinking and feeling to different bodily organs. In contrast, Lazarus and other appraisal theorists saw emotion and cognition as being intimately linked. They considered

FIGURE 2.9   Methodological Descriptions and Results From a Study by Kunst-Wilson and Zajonc (1980) Showing "the Primacy of Affect"

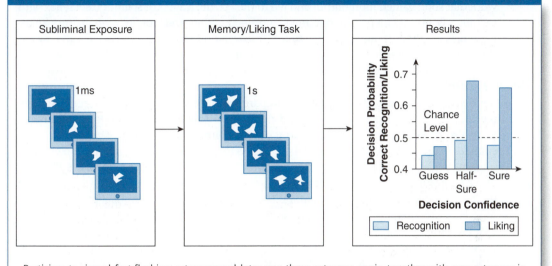

Participants viewed fast-flashing octagons and later saw these octagons again together with new octagons in paired presentations. They indicated for each pair whether the old octagon was left or right and which octagon they liked better. For each decision they reported whether they were guessing, half-sure, or sure. Recognition accuracy was no better than chance irrespective of whether participants considered themselves guessing, half-sure, or sure. However, half-sure and sure liking decisions were more frequently in favor of the old as compared with the new octagon in each pair.

Source: "Affective Discrimination of Stimuli That Cannot Be Recognized," by W. R. Kunst-Wilson and R. B. Zajonc, 1980, *Science, 207,* pp. 557–558.

the mental processes that trigger and sustain emotions as cognitive processes, and although they included automatic and potentially hardwired mechanisms into these considerations, that was lost in the debate. Therefore, emotion researchers became divided into those who saw emotions as independent and primary to cognition and those who saw emotions as dependent on cognition.

MERGING BRAIN AND THOUGHT

In the second half of the last century, new research methodologies became available that eventually united medical and psychological pursuits of emotion (Chapter 6). For example, the electroencephalogram (EEG), first recorded from a human in 1924, matured into an easily and relatively cheaply applied research tool that found its way into many psychology and medical research laboratories (Wiedemann, 1994). It enabled the noninvasive investigation of mental processes as they unfold in time. Furthermore, magnetic resonance imaging (MRI) became available, which allowed researchers to display both the brain and its metabolic activity in healthy individuals.

Readily accessible to different fields, these methodologies inspired cross-disciplinary work that soon gained momentum and led to the establishment of scientific societies with members coming from psychology, medicine, engineering, and biology, among other areas. Examples are the International Society for Research on Emotions, founded in 1984, or the Cognitive Neuroscience Society, which held its first meeting in 1994.

The ensuing dialogue between disciplines benefited emotion research. Brain evidence started to play a greater role in psychological theory, which in turn was more likely to guide neuroscientific inquiry. For example, comparative neuroanatomy and neurophysiology revealed that some brain structures and neurochemicals linked to emotions in humans were also present in other, evolutionarily distant animals, such as fish. This opened possibilities to use these animals as model organisms for understanding emotions and enabled inferences about evolutionarily preserved emotion mechanisms. In humans, the EEG and other neuroimaging tools were used to test different types of appraisals and to examine their neural underpinnings and temporal course. Moreover, the theoretical conviction that different emotions serve different functions led researchers to explore emotions individually and promoted the discovery of emotion-specific brain processes.

As will be apparent from the remainder of this book, the cross-disciplinary approach produced a tremendous amount of empirical work and many insights into human emotions. Nevertheless, important questions remain, and whether they will be answered depends on whether and how existing research challenges can be addressed.

Some of these challenges arise from technical or methodological limitations. For example, current neuroimaging techniques, although providing a window into the brain, are limited in what they reveal about brain function. They illustrate only a small aspect of a complex organ (e.g., metabolism) that needs to be understood in its entirety. Other challenges are ethical in nature. For example, many emotions are unpleasant and thus cannot be elicited or can be elicited only weakly in the laboratory setting.

Finally, existing concepts about emotions challenge emotion inquiry. These concepts determine how research is approached, which, if done wrongly, must lead to wrong conclusions. An example here is the conceptualization of emotion and cognition as different mental faculties. This conceptualization, rooted in Greek philosophy, led researchers to look and purportedly find evidence for separate brain systems. That this evidence was flawed became apparent only after some started to challenge the divide between feeling and thinking and began to explore their confluence in the brain. This illustrates that our understanding of emotions is limited by how we think about them and that we have to remain open to reconsider accepted truths in order for emotion theory to progress.

SUMMARY

Efforts directed at understanding emotions were divided for most of the 20th century into those targeted at brain anatomy and function and those targeted at psychological processes. The former efforts culminated in the limbic system theory, which dominated medical thinking about emotions for most of the 20th century. This theory saw emotions as separate from thought or intellect and proposed a special neural substrate called the limbic system that is sandwiched between an evolutionarily older system implicated in movement and basic bodily needs and an evolutionarily younger system that separates humans from other species and allows us to subdue "animal instincts."

Psychological inquiries into emotions were inspired by the notion of computing and focused on identifying underlying mental operations. One such operation was termed *appraisal* and proposed to involve both automatic and reflective thought processes. Appraisal was postulated to affect behavior by generating action tendencies, as in the tendency to approach or avoid something. While psychological theories were relatively silent on a potential role of the brain, this role was taken for granted. Moreover, psychological theories eventually helped to specify the brain's role by clarifying that emotions are highly differentiated experiences that are unlikely to be served by a single system segregated from thought. Additionally, they outlined a set of mental operations or modules that could serve as a framework to explore the neural substrates of emotions.

The integration of the medical and the psychological approach was facilitated by the introduction of research tools such as the EEG and MRI, which enabled physiologists and neurologists to study emotions noninvasively in healthy human participants. At the same time, these tools enabled psychologists to probe the neural underpinnings of mental operations. The ensuing cross-talk among disciplines proved extremely fruitful and led to the establishment of cross-disciplinary research platforms in the shape of societies, conferences, and journals. The results and insights from this work form the remainder of this book.

THINKING CRITICALLY ABOUT "EMOTION THEORIES OF THE 20TH CENTURY"

1. Why was the limbic system theory so successful, and why is it no longer an appropriate model for understanding emotions?

2. Since antiquity, many theories have been postulated regarding the causes and nature of emotions. We now know that most of these theories were wrong. Did these "wrong" theories have positive, negative, or no consequences for humankind?

3. How could the brain-based approach benefit from the thought-based approach, and vice versa?

MEDIA LIBRARY

Walter Cannon biography: http://www.harvardsquarelibrary.org/unitarians/cannon_walter.html

Paul MacLean biography and theory: http://www.nytimes.com/2008/01/10/science/10maclean.html?_r=0

PBS documentary on Walter Freeman and the development of lobotomies: http://www.pbs.org/wgbh/americanexperience/films/lobotomist

What Is an Emotion?

Modern Thoughts and Concepts

Across many centuries, philosophers and scientists asked what emotions are. Despite a tremendous amount of theoretical and empirical work, however, we have as yet no unequivocal answer. Instead, a range of answers emerged that can be grossly attributed to three theoretical schools or approaches. Because these schools differ in what they consider to be an emotion, they also differ in the types of research questions they ask and in what their research reveals about emotions. Thus, although different and potentially conflicting, it is useful for us to review these schools, as their insights are complementary and together can bring us one step closer to understanding why and how we feel.

THE CATEGORICAL APPROACH—EMOTIONS AS DISCRETE ENTITIES

Historical Background

When considering the range of events that produce emotions, it seems obvious that these events are more varied than the feelings they excite. For example, winning at a game and scoring an A on an exam both elicit the same or very similar feelings of joy. Therefore, some argued that it makes sense to view emotions as discrete mental states that are linked to a range of situations that, although different on the surface, share some basic commonalities. For example, winning at a game and scoring an A are similar in that both times the individual distinguishes him- or herself from among peers.

The idea of discrete emotion categories was already proposed centuries ago in the writings of René Descartes and Charles Darwin (Chapter 1). A person who followed their steps more recently was Sylvan Tomkins, a philosopher of psychology. In 1962, he published the first volume of an emotions book that outlined and discussed eight primary affects conceptualized as separate programs or programmatic responses to an environmental event

(Tomkins, 1962, 2008). These affects included interest-excitement, enjoyment-joy, sur-prise-startle, distress-anguish, fear-terror, shame-humiliation, contempt-disgust, and anger-rage. The former state in each pair was conceived as a weaker variant of the latter state. Tomkins referred to these variant states as affect or affect programs rather than emotions because he believed emotions to be more complex phenomena that are derived from affect but that comprise additional components such as memories of former affective experiences (A Closer Look 3.1). In the spirit of Descartes and Darwin, Tomkins held that affects are functional and that they evolved through natural selection. Because affects motivate self-preserving behaviors such as feeding or territorial defense, they benefit individuals by increasing their potential to successfully reproduce.

Tomkins linked affect-associated behaviors to bodily organs, which he believed to form different "assemblies" for the eight innate affect programs and that thus promote affect-specific responses. Like Darwin, Tomkins showed particular interest in the face, which he identified as the "prime organ of affect." Due to its sophisticated expressive and perceptual properties, he presumed the face to support both behaviors (e.g., feeding, biting) and associated affective feelings. Facial blood flow and muscle tension would promote a particular action, while at the same time providing critical feedback about a person's affective state. Together, these and other ideas of Tomkins inspired emotion researchers of the 20th and the 21st centuries, who went on to test, develop, and popularize them.

An Example—Ekman's Basic Emotions

The dominant categorical approach of today postulates the existence of basic emotions. A leading proponent of this approach is the psychologist Paul Ekman, who, inspired by

A CLOSER LOOK 3.1

Emotions and Other Feeling States

Many emotion theorists distinguish emotions from other feeling states such as affects and moods. Affects are typically considered more basic feeling states than emotions. Some theorists conceive them simply to represent valence or feelings of pleasure and displeasure (Bradley, Codispoti, Cuthbert, & Lang, 2001; Scherer, 2001). Others conceive affects to be more differentiated than that but to lack other aspects of an emotion such as their subjective feeling characteristics, emotion-related cognitions, or physiological and behavioral responses (Feldman-Barrett et al., 2007; Russell, 2003; Tomkins, 2008).

(Continued)

(Continued)

Moods are typically differentiated from emotions in that they have no specific object or in that their object is temporally removed (Russell, 2003). In other words, the cause for a mood is less circumscribed or more distant than that for an emotion. A mood may arise from a combination of factors internal (e.g., hormones) and external (e.g., cumulative history of life events) to the individual. Moods may also arise from a particular event, if this event caused a strong emotional response. Regardless of their cause, moods are defined as lasting longer than emotions, which many (but not all; Panksepp, 1992) believe to subside after the eliciting event has passed.

Some have likened moods with affects by assuming that affects can exist without a specific object (Russell, 2003). According to this view, individuals maintain a core affective tone that undergoes dynamic changes, which may be attributed to an object or event but not necessarily caused by it. Others, however, conceptualize affect as a response to an affective or emotional

FIGURE 3.1   Moody and Sad

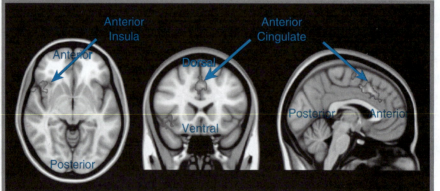

The figure illustrates the results from a mood induction study (Harrison et al., 2008). In separate sessions, participants were asked to recall sad (e.g., death of a loved one) or neutral (e.g., typical working day) memories and to attempt feeling the associated emotions so as to produce a more lasting sad or neutral mood. Subsequently, they underwent a functional magnetic resonance imaging scan that investigated their resting-state brain activity. Areas highlighted by arrows mark regions whose activity was more strongly functionally coupled when participants were in a sad as compared to a neutral mood. Notably, these same areas are also active when participants experience a sad emotion from being socially excluded (Eisenberger, Lieberman, & Williams, 2003).

Source: "Modulation of Brain Resting-State Networks by Sad Mood Induction," by B. J. Harrison, J. Pujol, H. Ortiz, A. Fornito, C. Pantelis, and M. Yücel, 2008, PLoS ONE 3:e1794.10.1371/journal.pone.0001794.

stimulus and thus as something that emerges rather than exists (Bradley et al., 2001; Scherer, 2001; Tomkins, 2008).

As may be apparent from these definitions, theoretical differentiations between emotions, affects, and moods are still quite vague. The boundaries are poorly defined and not unanimously agreed on. Moreover, insights into the brain basis for emotions suggest great overlap among the three constructs under discussion here. For example, negative affect as evoked by a subliminally presented fear stimulus involves similar brain mechanisms as are involved in the conscious feeling of the emotion fear (Liddell et al., 2005). Likewise, similar brain mechanisms seem to underpin moods and emotions (Harrison et al., 2008) and mediate apparent interactions between the two (Figure 3.1). From your own experience, you may recall that it is easier to find something positive and thus to feel a positive emotion when you are already in a happy mood than when you are in a sad or fearful mood (Becker & Leinenger, 2011).

For the purpose of this book, we will make no differentiation between affects and emotions; both can be defined in reference to an object or event, and it is at present impossible to say where affect ends and an emotion begins. We will subsume affects under the term *emotions*. However, we will, for the purpose of this book, differentiate between moods and emotions. The former we will conceptualize as sustained mental states that can be characterized by an emotional tone and that form the backdrop for our stimulus-bound and more transient emotional experiences.

Darwin and Tomkins, put forth a number of criteria that define basic emotions and that discriminate them from other mental states (Ekman, 1999).

The first of these criteria holds that basic emotions have distinct universal signals. In other words, they have a specific form of bodily expression, and although this expression can be suppressed, modified, or faked, it is innately linked to its emotion. If true, there should be expressions that individuals display and recognize regardless of their ethnicity and cultural background, and that are thus universal.

Ekman and colleagues found such expressions in a study that examined face emotion recognition in six different cultures, some of which were preliterate and had not yet been exposed to television and electronic media (Ekman, Sorenson, & Friesen, 1969). For this study, the researchers selected a set of photographs from a range of sources that they perceived to display facial expressions of happiness, fear, disgust/contempt, anger, surprise, and sadness. Although participants from preliterate cultures performed worse than participants from literate cultures, who were more familiar with the face material, all cultures recognized the target emotions significantly above chance. Specifically, their judgments of the facial displays were not random but more often than not accorded with those of the researchers. When visiting the preliterate cultures, Ekman also studied the facial expressions he found there. Among other things, he gave individuals an emotional scenario (e.g., "Your friend has come and you are happy") and asked them to portray the emotion with their face. He found that preliterate and culturally isolated individuals produced expressions that individuals from literate cultures readily identified as happy, angry, fearful, and so forth (Ekman & Friesen, 2003).

As a second defining principle for basic emotions, Ekman proposed emotion-specific physiological profiles. Like his intellectual predecessors, he argued that emotions are functional in dealing with important life tasks and that they evolved via natural selection. He presumed that the functionality of emotions rests in the preparation of the body for action via emotion-specific modulations of the autonomic nervous system. According to Ekman, anger, for example, would lead to an autonomic pattern associated with the fight-or-flight response, including an increase in breathing and heart rate.

Ekman and his colleagues tested the supposition of emotion-specific physiological profiles in several studies. In one of them, they instructed participants to pose a certain facial expression or simply to relive an emotional episode (Ekman, Levenson, & Friesen, 1983). While a single physiological measure could not differentiate between the six target emotions in the experiment, several measures including heart rate, finger temperature, skin conductance, and forearm muscle tension could—thereby suggesting that each emotion has its specific physiological profile.

Ekman's third defining principle for basic emotions stipulates the existence of an automatic appraisal mechanism. Like others, he assumes that because of their evolutionary significance, certain sensory impressions can activate emotion representations and associated behaviors without the contribution of higher-order cognitive processes. Support for this comes from a range of human and nonhuman animal studies that have identified pre- or subconscious emotional responses. For example, humans show signs of fear to conditioned stimuli such as a tone that was previously paired with unpleasant noise (Knight, Nguyen, & Bandettini, 2003). Moreover, their fear persists even when the tone is played subliminally and therefore cannot be consciously perceived; it then nevertheless excites the sympathetic nervous system.

As a fourth principle in the definition of basic emotions, Ekman formulates that each basic emotion has a universal antecedent—an event or event type that reliably triggers this emotion regardless of a person's upbringing or cultural background. This principle is a logical extension of the preceding principle in that emotion-specific antecedents enable the activation of emotion-specific appraisals. Moreover, both may be seen to operate on a key-lock basis. However, as both serve to help an individual survive in a dynamic environment, their fit cannot be expected to be perfect. Just imagine that evolution endowed a prey animal such as a mouse with a fear appraisal mechanism that is activated only by a certain predator, such as a gray cat. If a brown cat moves into the mouse's territory, it would have no warning mechanism to stay away from it. Of course, one could speculate that over time another appraisal mechanism evolves that motivates later generations of mice to avoid both gray and brown cats. More probable, however, is that rather than being so differentiated and specific, appraisal mechanisms and their universal antecedents are abstract and enable the identification of predators by more general characteristics, such as predatory odor, that are potentially shared across species (Takahashi, Nakashima, Hong, & Watanabe, 2005).

Apart from these four main principles, Ekman postulates several other characteristics of basic emotions. For example, he suggests that basic emotions need not be present or fully differentiated at birth (Ekman, 2005). Although they may be innate, they are bound to emerge developmentally only once they are needed to motivate self-sustaining behaviors. Given an infant's limited behavioral repertoire, highly differentiated negative emotions (e.g., anger, fear, disgust) may not be useful and only become so later in life. Ekman also suggests that basic emotions are shared between humans and other primates. With evidence for fear conditioning in invertebrates (Quinn, Harris, & Benzer, 1974), others have gone even further to suggest their existence in so-called lower animals (Panksepp, 1992). Ekman also believes basic emotions to be characterized by a sudden onset, a short duration, and an unbidden occurrence. Thus, they may surprise and influence us despite our better judgment. Moreover, Ekman links basic emotions to specific thoughts or memories and supposes that they arouse a distinct subjective experience.

With these defining principles in mind, Ekman recognizes a number of basic emotions including amusement, anger, contempt, contentment, disgust, embarrassment, excitement, fear, guilt, pride in achievement, relief, sadness/distress, satisfaction, sensory pleasure, and shame (Ekman, 2005). He conceives these basic emotions as emotion families—meaning that there are a number of related states that fall under each of the listed emotion terms. When considering the listed terms together with Ekman's many defining principles, you may wonder how basic emotions differ from nonbasic ones. According to Ekman, they do not differ, because he thinks nonbasic emotions do not exist. Anything that deserves to be called an emotion should be considered basic (Ekman & Davidson, 1994).

The basic emotions approach put forth by Ekman and others became a dominant paradigm for emotion research. It allowed the field to move forward by making emotions more accessible to examination. Researchers could use the idea of universal antecedents to develop experimental conditions that provoked specific emotions in their participants. Moreover, they could study their participants' emotional response by examining universal signals such as facial expressions and the activity of the autonomous nervous system. Finally, by considering different emotions as discrete states and examining them separately, they were more likely to uncover the differentiated mental processes or appraisals that enable varied emotional experiences.

Support for the Categorical Approach

The research that probed the categorical approach produced empirical evidence that supported the notion of emotions being discrete mental states with specific survival function. Part of this evidence comes from studies that examined emotional expressions and behavior. For example, a closer look at how emotions are reflected in the voice suggested emotion-specific universal signals similar to what has been found for the face. The first to identify these signals were Klaus Scherer and colleagues. They examined emotion-related vocal changes by measuring a range of parameters including mean pitch, pitch range, speech rate, mean intensity, spectral noise, and so forth. They found that different emotions have characteristic vocal profiles. Joy, for example, is linked to an increase, whereas sadness is linked to a decrease in mean pitch and pitch range (Banse & Scherer, 1996). Listeners are sensitive to these acoustic variations and can guess a speaker's emotions simply from hearing his or her voice. As for facial expressions, their recognition performance is significantly better than would be expected when guessing randomly, even if the listeners are unfamiliar with the speaker's language and cultural background (Min & Schirmer, 2011; Pell & Skorup, 2008; Scherer, Banse, & Wallbott, 2001).

Apart from the voice, emotion-expression categories have been identified for body movements or posture (Kleinsmith, De Silva, & Bianchi-Berthouze, 2006), interpersonal touch (Hertenstein, Keltner, App, Bulleit, & Jaskolka, 2006), and the secretion of bodily substances. For example, researchers discovered the existence of chemical communication signals called pheromones, which are contained in sweat, urine, or feces and are perceived via the olfactory system or the vomeronasal organ (Matsunami & Amrein, 2003). Some emotions have been linked to specific pheromones. For example, researchers have found a pheromone that some animals, including humans, release in the face of threat or danger and that helps to warn conspecifics (Haegler et al., 2010; Mathuru et al., 2012).

Although not explicitly stated by Ekman, emotion-specific mental, physiological, and expressive responses presuppose emotion-specific neural processes. Thus, evidence for the latter would further substantiate the basic emotions concept. Work that pursued such evidence has met a number of challenges including the complexity of the brain, which makes it impossible to pin down mental states to individual structures or the action of individual neurotransmitters. Nevertheless, some evidence has emerged that aligns with the basic emotions concept. For example, positive emotions elicited by rewarding stimuli have been linked to the ventral striatum. This brain region is activated when participants are enjoying a joke or when they receive a monetary reward. Conversely, electrical stimulation of this structure will elicit positive feelings in the absence of any external rewards. These and other findings have been summarized in reviews (Arias-Carrión, Stamelou, Murillo-Rodríguez, Menéndez-González, & Pöppel, 2010) and meta-analyses (Cauda et al., 2011; Vytal & Hamann, 2010) and are explored in more detail when we discuss specific emotions in Part 3 of this book.

Limitations of the Categorical Approach

Despite many conceptual benefits and much supporting evidence, the categorical approach is not without limitations. The first and probably most significant limitation is that the presumed emotion categories may be produced artificially through methodological choices made by researchers (Russell, 1994). Researchers would typically preselect stimuli into neat emotion categories and provide their participants with category labels. Thus, they would set themselves up to find emotion categories while being blind to potentially graded changes in emotional responses and potential relationships among the emotions tested.

A second concern is the lack of agreement regarding the exact number and types of categories or basic emotions. Although many researchers believe, like Ekman, in the concept of basic emotions, they disagree with his defining principles and thus in what they consider a basic emotion. Jaak Panksepp (1992, 2004), for example, proposed a set of neural criteria. Among other things, he postulated basic emotions to be characterized by inborn and emotion-specific neuronal systems that are capable of activating relevant sensory and behavioral processes that proved adaptive in a species' evolutionary past. Unlike Ekman (2005), Panksepp (2005a) does not consider emotional expressions as important and recognizes only 7 rather than 15 or more basic emotions. His neural systems represent appetitive states such as (1) seeking, which motivates foraging; (2) lust, which motivates sexual behaviors; (3) play, which helps in the development of social skills and social bonds; and (4) care, which triggers and sustains nurturing behaviors directed toward needy, socially bonded individuals. They also include aversive states such as (5) panic, associated with separation in social animals; (6) rage, associated with resource competition and aggression; and (7) fear, experienced in response to threat to motivate self-protective behaviors.

The lack of agreement among basic emotion theorists regarding the concept of basic emotions has been a main point of critique from individuals who oppose the notion of basic emotions (Feldman-Barrett, 2006a; Ortony & Turner, 1990). In their defense, basic emotion theorists have argued that there is some agreement concerning certain defining principles and emotions. For example, most would accept that basic emotions played an important role in evolution by promoting behaviors that were relevant for survival (Ekman, 1992; Izard, 1992; Panksepp, 1992). Moreover, there are certain emotions that are recognized by the majority of basic emotion theorists. For example, in a review by Ortony and Turner (1990), 11 out of 14 theorists recognized anger or rage, 12 recognized fear or anxiety, and 9 recognized an emotion akin to sadness. With this in mind, one may speculate that basic emotion theorists may eventually sort out their differences.

A third weakness raised against the basic emotions approach is the absence of support for emotion-specific physiological and behavioral responses (Feldman-Barrett, 2006a; Feldman-Barrett, 2006b; Ortony & Turner, 1990). Being grounded in Darwin's theory of evolution, the basic emotions approach sees emotions as mental states that motivate certain adaptive behaviors that are mapped via specific physiological profiles. However, research suggests this mapping to be more complex and diversified. Specifically, the initial work by Ekman and colleagues that highlighted emotion-specific responses failed to be replicated (Cacioppo, Berntson, Larsen, Poehlmann, & Ito, 1993). Subsequent work found emotions linked to several physiological profiles as well as physiologically opposing behaviors. Fear, for example, was found to elicit different behaviors in different contexts. In some contexts, an animal may inhibit all behaviors and freeze, whereas in other contexts it may aggressively defend itself or run away. Thus, critics have argued that the situation or context of an emotion is more important for physiology and behavior than the emotion itself (Feldman-Barrett, 2006b).

Yet basic emotion theorists also counter this second weakness. They hold that past difficulties in the replication of emotion-specific physiological profiles resulted from methodological and conceptual differences among studies. Moreover, they point out that despite these differences, a subset of emotion-induced physiological changes could be replicated (Kreibig, 2010). For example, physiological changes in fear, although largely comparable to those of anger, relatively consistently differed with respect to total peripheral resistance, a blood pressure measure that takes into account both arterial and venous pressure and divides them by the amount of blood pumped by the heart. While fear typically produces a reduction in total peripheral resistance, anger produces an increase in total peripheral resistance presumably through a constriction of blood vessels mediated by adrenaline and noradrenaline (Kreibig, 2010; Stemmler, 2004).

Furthermore, proposals have been made as to why the mapping between emotion, physiology, and behavior is more differentiated than initially suspected. For example, Stemmler and colleagues (Stemmler, 2004; Stemmler, Heldmann, Pauls, & Scherer, 2001) argue that emotion-specific physiological responses are embedded into a wider physiological context that is subject to preemotional factors (e.g., body posture, room temperature) as well as more general situational factors that dictate the ways in which an individual can respond (e.g., whether escape is possible). Thus, the immediate emotion-induced physiological changes may be masked. Moreover, they may not always be linked to a specific behavior but instead prepare for more general outcomes associated with an emotion. For example, the likelihood of physical injury in the face of fear may have led to the emergence of a physiological profile that reduces the chance of succumbing to injury. Thus, blood flow to the extremities may be reduced in favor of internal organs and the brain (Stemmler, 2004). A reconsideration of the link between emotions, physiology, and behavior as well as a look at physiology beyond simple changes in heart rate or breathing may therefore be necessary to better test the assumptions underlying the basic emotions approach.

A fourth and last concern to be mentioned here is that evidence in support of the basic emotions approach does not rule out alternative interpretations. Specifically, proponents of competing conceptual approaches insist that the emotions listed by the basic emotions approach together with their physiology and behavior may be explained by fewer and psychologically simpler underlying processes. For example, some researchers have looked at the facial emotion expressions that Ekman takes as proof for basic emotions (Ortony & Turner, 1990). These expressions are composed of a set of muscle actions such as opening the mouth or furrowing the brows. Some of these actions are implicated in other emotional as well as nonemotional states. For example, individuals may furrow their brows when angry but also when concentrating or trying to solve a problem. Thus, it has been called into question whether facial expressions reflect basic emotions or whether they reflect a combination of more basic mental states that give rise to a particular feeling we may refer to as anger, fear, and so forth. We will revisit this and other points of contention at the end of this chapter, after due consideration of two other approaches to define emotions.

THE DIMENSIONAL APPROACH—EMOTIONS AS INSTANCES IN A MULTIDIMENSIONAL SPACE

Historical Background

An alternative to considering emotions as discrete entities is to consider them as graded experiences that vary along one or more continuous dimensions. For example, one may envision emotions to vary along a valence dimension that ranges from good to bad or from positive to negative. Proposals to this effect have existed since antiquity and remained popular to the present day. They outline a range of possible emotion dimensions and the relationship of these dimensions to individual emotions such as fear or sadness.

Of interest to us is a proposal developed by Robert Woodworth, an influential American psychologist of the last century. He sought insights into the underlying dimensions of emotions by examining human facial expressions and the errors that observers make in emotion judgments (Woodworth, 1938, as cited in Schlosberg, 1941). He found that such errors were not equally distributed across available judgment options, but tended to cluster on a couple of options that differed for each expression. Woodworth sorted these options to derive a linear scale that ranged from (1) happiness to (2) surprise, (3) fear, (4) anger, (5) disgust, and (6) contempt, with errors for

FIGURE 3.2   Woodworth Emotion Scale

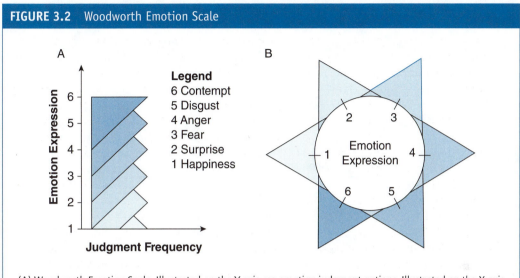

(A) Woodworth Emotion Scale. Illustrated on the Y-axis are emotion judgment options. Illustrated on the X-axis is the frequency with which participants associated a given emotional expression (indicated by the different colors) with a particular emotion. For example, angry faces were most often judged to express anger (4) followed by fear (3) and disgust (5). (B) Revised Woodworth Emotion Scale based on the findings of Schlosberg (1941).

a given facial expression being most frequent for neighboring judgment options (Figure 3.2a). For example, angry faces were most frequently misjudged as portraying fear or disgust, which were the judgment options that framed anger on the Woodworth scale. Moreover, they were less likely to be mistaken for more distant emotions, such as happiness or contempt.

To further explore the Woodworth scale, Harold Schlosberg, a colleague of Woodworth's, conducted an experiment in which he asked participants to sort 200 facial expressions into six bins so that expressions in a given bin were more similar than expressions from different bins (Schlosberg, 1941). In accordance with Woodworth, Schlosberg observed that the sorted expressions fell along an emotion scale whereby most expressions were more likely to be confused with neighboring as opposed to distant emotions. Interestingly, Schlosberg also noted that expressions representing the two endpoints of the Woodworth scale did not follow this principle. Being maximally apart, the two endpoints should be unlikely to be confused. However, they were as likely to be confused as they were to be confused with their immediate neighbors. Thus, Schlosberg concluded that the scale must be circular instead of linear (Figure 3.2b) and be two- rather than one-dimensional in nature. As a first dimension, he postulated pleasantness/unpleasantness, which he presumed to span from happiness to anger. As a second dimension, he postulated attention/rejection. Attention, he thought, is maximal for expressions that fall between fear and surprise, and rejection, he thought, is maximal for expressions that fall between disgust and contempt. In a later publication, Schlosberg suggested a third dimension that could deal with some of the expressions that did not perfectly fit his circular model (Schlosberg, 1954). This third dimension presumably

FIGURE 3.3 Schlosberg Three-Dimensional Model

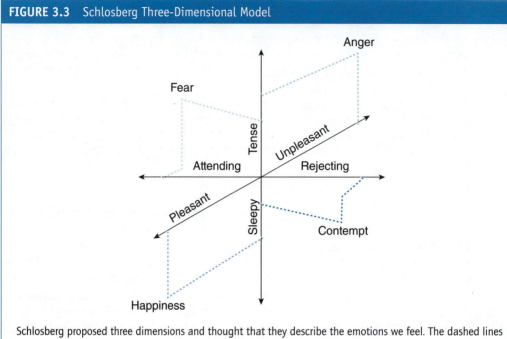

Schlosberg proposed three dimensions and thought that they describe the emotions we feel. The dashed lines mark the approximate points in this space for the emotions happiness, fear, anger, and contempt. Other emotions would fall somewhere in between these points.

reflected a person's level of activation, ranging from sleep to tension. Together with the former two dimensions, it described a three-dimensional space that could capture any kind of emotional expression and, by inference, its underlying emotion (Figure 3.3). Thus, it reduced the complexity of the basic emotions approach to only three dimensions or mental systems that together might suffice to account for the multitude of emotions we feel.

Although the dimensions postulated by Schlosberg seem sensible, they were only guesses. He simply used his intuition to describe the sorting results of his participants. By the 1960s and 1970s, intuition alone was no longer necessary. New statistical tools became available, including factor analysis and multidimensional scaling, which enabled a more objective identification of dimensions in a given data set and thus provided a better test for the dimensional approach.

In addition to methodology, philosophical and psychological theory advanced our understanding of the nature of mental concepts or categories. For example, the philosopher Ludwig Wittgenstein (1953) had highlighted the fact that what we consider as categories in the real world are not necessarily discrete kinds that all share the same number of features. Instead, they may be understood as a family of kinds that differ in the number of features they have in common and thus in how they differentiate themselves from other categories. This idea inspired psychologists Carolyn Mervis and Eleanor Rosch (1981), who put forth a theory according to which categories derive from similarity assessments. Such assessments are thought to result in the identification of a best exemplar or prototype that defines a category. Other exemplars are included into a category depending on their degree of similarity to the category prototype. For example, a good prototype for the category *emotion* may be anger, and individuals may consider something an emotion if it bears some minimum resemblance to what they feel when they are angry.

Together, these theoretical advances helped researchers realize that the language we use to refer to emotions may be discrete but that the underlying phenomena may nevertheless be graded or have fuzzy boundaries. Moreover, with the new methodological and statistical procedures, researchers now had the means to further scrutinize these boundaries.

An Example—Circumplex Model and Core Affect

The circumplex model of emotions is one of the most influential dimensional models that emerged in the second half of the 19th century. Its inventor, the American psychologist James Russell, was inspired by theoretical insights into categorization and applied these insights to the topic of emotions. He found that, like other categories, the category of emotions was lacking clear boundaries (Fehr & Russell, 1984). For example, certain emotions were almost always mentioned by participants asked to name emotions, whereas other emotions were only rarely mentioned. Moreover, many emotions fell in between these two extremes in a graded fashion. Further investigation into individual emotions also suggested a graded rather than a discrete organization (Russell, 1980).

Using a similar method as that introduced by Woodworth and Schlosberg (Schlosberg, 1952), Russell asked his participants to sort 28 emotion words into categories based on their perceived similarity. He then subjected the sorting results to a multidimensional scaling procedure, which returned the relationship between the words in a space defined by the experimenter. The fit for this procedure was relatively poor for a one-dimensional space but improved dramatically for a two-dimensional space (Figure 3.4). As the addition of further dimensions failed to further increase the fit, Russell concluded that emotion words are best represented by two dimensions. Moreover, he found that they fall along the edge of a circle in a manner formerly proposed by Schlosberg (1952). Based on this and similar results obtained from other studies, Russell then formulated his circumplex model of affect.

At the crux of his model is the assumption that all emotions can be described by two dimensions. One dimension reflects the pleasure or displeasure associated with an affective experience, and we will henceforth refer to this dimension as valence. The other dimension reflects the degree to which an individual is aroused or physiologically excited, and we henceforth refer to this dimension as arousal. At the most basic level, these two dimensions describe what Russell terms core affect, a basic affective experience linked to a current neurophysiological state (Russell, 2003; Yik, Russell, & Steiger, 2011). According to Russell, core affect is experienced continuously throughout an individual's lifetime and changes as a function of internal (e.g., circadian rhythm) and external (e.g., change in temperature, frightening image) events, which may or may not be considered emotional. When changes in core affect become apparent, an individual is bound to feel an emotion.

FIGURE 3.4 Multidimensional Scaling Solution for 28 Emotion Terms

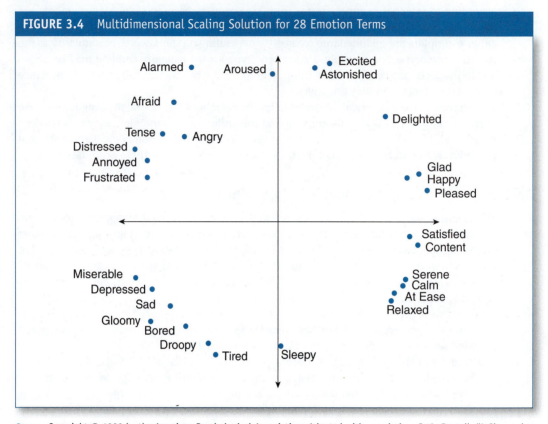

Source: Copyright © 1980 by the American Psychological Association. Adapted with permission. J. A. Russell, "A Circumplex Model of Affect," *Journal of Personality and Social Psychology, 39,* pp. 1161–1178, 1980, APA. The use of APA information does not imply endorsement by APA.

An emotion, however, is more than a perceived change in core affect. Russell's theory, as well as related dimensional proposals, view emotions as "constructions" resulting from a transformational process (Feldman-Barrett, 2006b; Russell, 2003). Specifically, changes in core affect, the attribution of core affect to a given internal or external event, situational appraisal, autonomic responses, and other aspects of an emotional episode are mapped onto existing knowledge about what emotions are like. Activation of this knowledge, which is organized by emotion prototypes resembling basic emotions, then enables an individual to experience an emotion. According to Russell, emotion prototypes are related by degrees, in a circular fashion. This circular fashion arises from his multidimensional scaling research on affect terms, as explained earlier (Figure 3.4). It reflects an underlying affective organization along the two identified dimensions, valence and arousal. The hypothesized relationship between emotion prototypes is illustrated in Figure 3.5.

FIGURE 3.5   Circumplex Model of Yik, Russell, and Steiger (2011)

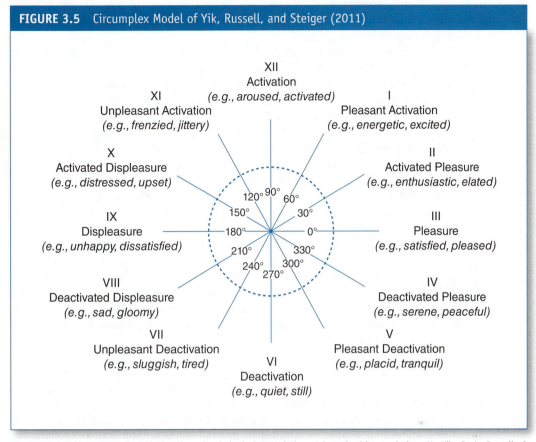

Source: Copyright © 2011 by the American Psychological Association. Adapted with permission. M. Yik, J. A. Russell, & J. H. Steiger, "A 12-Point Circumplex Structure of Core Affect," by 2011, *Emotion, 11,* pp. 705–731, 2011, APA. The use of APA information does not imply endorsement by APA.

Support for the Dimensional Approach

The dimensional approach enjoys great popularity among emotion researchers. It has been applied to a wide range of stimuli, including linguistic corpora, facial expressions, and emotional scenes, responses to which have been examined with various statistical tools including uni- and multidimensional scaling and factor analysis. Across these stimuli and statistical techniques, a similar set of dimensions emerged that can largely be conceived of as representing valence and arousal. For example, the linguist Charles Osgood and colleagues examined a large corpus of words that participants rated on a number of scales (Osgood, 1969; Osgood, May, & Miron, 1975). They subjected the participants' word ratings to a factor analysis, which revealed four significant factors. Osgood and colleagues referred to the first factor as evaluation, as it derived from rating scales such as "good-bad" or "true-false." They referred to the third factor as activity, as it derived from rating scales such as "excitable-calm" or "hot-cold." Thus, at least two of the four factors were comparable to the findings of Schlosberg and Russell.

Valence and arousal were also identified as key dimensions in the work of Margaret Bradley and Peter Lang. These two psychologists developed an affective picture system, which they subjected to a number of investigations. Among other things, they presented the pictures to participants who rated them on the dimensions of valence and arousal. When analyzing the rating results, Bradley and Lang found that the two ratings were not independent. In line with previous work, the picture ratings formed a continuous shape within a two-dimensional space, indicating that the emotions we experience from viewing pictures vary in a graded fashion (Bradley et al., 2001; Lang, Greenwald, Bradley, & Hamm, 1993).

Lang and Bradley also explored whether autonomic responses to emotions are continuous and can be explained by the dimensions valence and arousal. To this effect, they presented their pictures to participants and measured a range of physiological markers, including heart rate, skin conductance, and startle propensity. Interestingly, some markers reflected valence in that they showed differential responses to positive and negative pictures. For example, the propensity to startle was increased with increasingly negative picture valence (Bradley et al., 2001), but decreased with increasingly positive picture valence. There were also physiological markers that varied continuously with picture arousal. For example, skin conductance was greater the more arousing the pictures were, irrespective of picture valence (Lang et al., 1993). Thus, autonomic responses to emotional events seem to vary continuously as a function of event valence and arousal.

Another line of support for the dimensional approach comes from the neuroimaging literature. Here, some researchers have used emotion words and asked participants to rate these words with respect to valence and arousal (Posner et al., 2009). They found that the ratings on both dimensions correlated with neuronal activity in separate brain systems. Valence positively correlated with activity in a part of the insular cortex associated with the regulation of autonomic responses. Arousal positively correlated with activity in the para-hippocampal gyrus, a region typically associated with memory, as well as the anterior cingulate, a structure implicated in the perception of conflict and pain.

Other studies also explored the brain systems mediating valence and arousal (Colibazzi et al., 2010; Gerdes et al., 2010; Wilson-Mendenhall, Feldman-Barrett, & Barsalou, 2013). For example, Colibazzi and colleagues presented participants with sentences that described a range of emotional experiences and asked participants to rate these experiences with respect to valence and arousal. They then correlated participant ratings with brain activity recorded while participants were reading the sentences (Colibazzi et al., 2010).

Wilson-Mendenhall and colleagues conducted a similar study, in which they used short verbal scenarios that varied with respect to both core affect and the constructed emotion. Again, participants rated their experiences of core affect and the researchers correlated these ratings with brain activity (Wilson-Mendenhall et al., 2013).

Both research teams could identify brain structures that responded to valence and arousal, respectively, suggesting that the two are supported by separate mental systems that might form the basis for human emotional experiences. Additionally, Wilson-Mendenhall and colleagues could show that apart from areas shared across emotions and involved in the processing of core affect, there were areas that seemed emotion-specific. Thus, the researchers could support the idea that different emotions are constructed from core affect.

Limitations of the Dimensional Approach

Like the categorical approach, the dimensional approach has much merit. Yet a critical look at the extant literature also suggests limitations. One such limitation is that the primary evidence for this approach comes from self-report data. Across the many studies reviewed above, valence, arousal, and other dimensions were derived from participants' explicit evaluation of emotional stimuli. As will be reviewed later in this book (Chapter 6), some aspects of an emotion are not accessible to explicit evaluation and thus would not factor or factor incorrectly in the participants' response (Sander, Grandjean, & Scherer, 2005). As a result, the dimensions obtained with the self-report data may misrepresent true emotional experiences.

To tackle this limitation, researchers began to validate the dimensional approach by using implicit measures, such as physiological recordings and neuroimaging (Bradley et al., 2001; Colibazzi et al., 2010; Gerdes et al., 2010; Posner et al., 2009). However, at present these validations are based on the dimensions established with self-reports and are thus potentially biased. Moreover, other dimensions could not be discovered and compared with respect to their utility. What is needed to address this problem is a data-driven approach using implicit measures recorded from a wide range of emotional scenarios. A classification of the obtained data, similar to the multidimensional scaling applied previously to self-reports, should then determine whether the postulated dimensions hold.

A second limitation of the dimensional approach concerns disagreement in the number and nature of proposed dimensions. Some researchers proposed only one dimension (Woodworth, as cited in Schlosberg, 1941), whereas others proposed four or more (Osgood et al., 1975). Moreover, proposals differ with respect to the function and interrelationship between dimensions. These differences arise from a range of methodological factors, including the statistical analysis tools and the type of stimuli that were selected for the research. For example, Schlosberg in his seminal study (Schlosberg, 1941) included more than 200 facial expressions, some of which displayed disgust and contempt. Russell, on the other hand, investigated only a limited number of emotion terms, none of which referred to feelings of disgust or contempt (Russell, 1980). Thus, although both researchers identified two dimensions in their data, they differ in their interpretation of the second dimension. While Schlosberg assumed this dimension reflects the level of attention to or rejection of an emotional event, Russell assumed this dimension reflects arousal.

There is also discord with respect to the relationship of emotions in a two-dimensional space. While work by Schlosberg and Russell suggests a circular relationship, Bradley and Lang identified a boomerang shape, or a half-circle (Bradley et al., 2001). Moreover, the latter research group found that arousal ratings correlated linearly rather than curvilinearly, with valence ratings for positive and negative stimuli. Thus, similar to basic emotion researchers, dimensional researchers still need to agree on the number, type, and interdimensional relationships that best describe emotional states.

A third limitation of the dimensional approach is that it seems to strip emotions of essential qualitative differences. Placing them on one or more continua makes emotion aspects, which cannot be quantified on the proposed dimensions, appear irrelevant. The circumplex model of affect, for example, has afraid and angry states as direct neighbors on the circle (Figure 3.4). Thus, when interpreting the model, one may think that the two differ only by degrees. However, most would agree that fear and anger feel qualitatively different and bias different behaviors. Fear is associated with vulnerability and uncertainty and motivates self-protective behaviors such as flight or withdrawal. Anger, on the other hand, is associated with dominance and self-righteousness and motivates direct or indirect forms of aggression. To address this issue, Russell and others concede that the graded relationship among emotions is a basic structural or functional property that does not necessarily reflect associated subjective feelings (Bradley et al., 2001; Feldman-Barrett, 2006b; Russell, 2003).

Finally, some discrepancies in the neuroimaging literature cast doubt on the dimensional approach. While there are a number of studies that find correlations between brain activity and subjective dimensions of valence and arousal, the locus of these correlations differs between studies. For example, Posner and colleagues found that arousal correlated with activity in the left parahippocampal gyrus and the anterior cingulate (Posner et al., 2009). Another study from that group found that arousal correlated with activity in the left thalamus, globus pallidus, caudate, parahippocampal gyrus, amygdala, **premotor cortex**, and the **cerebellum** (Colibazzi et al., 2010). Last, a study by Wilson-Mendenhall and colleagues linked positive and negative arousal to activity in the left amygdala (Wilson-Mendenhall et al., 2013), whereas a German research team linked arousal to activity in the right amygdala and the left caudate, but only for items of negative valence (Gerdes et al., 2010).

Thus, it remains unclear whether valence and arousal are indeed useful parameters to describe the neural systems underlying emotions (but see Lindquist, Wager, Kober, Bliss-Moreau, & Feldman-Barrett, 2012). Moreover, as few neuroimaging studies have hitherto examined these parameters, more research is needed to confidently answer this question.

THE APPRAISAL APPROACH—EMOTIONS AS A RESULT OF APPRAISAL PROCESSES

Historical Background

Appraisal theory addresses some of the weaknesses of the categorical and the dimensional approach and is, therefore, often considered a compromise between them. For example, appraisal theory allows for a multitude of emotion states and thus overcomes the problem of the categorical approach, which limits emotions to only a few types. Moreover, like the dimensional approach, it assumes the existence of critical evaluative dimensions but is much more generous in the number of dimensions it allows. It can thus explain emotions without reference to nonaffective processes.

Nevertheless, appraisal theory is not simply a conceptual middle ground or neutral territory. Instead, it has to be understood as a qualitatively different approach, with a historical background that is largely independent from that of both the categorical and the dimensional approach. Like most Western thoughts about emotions, the idea of appraisal as a mechanism underlying emotions was already conceived of in Greek antiquity. Aristotle, the famous Greek philosopher, had postulated that emotions presuppose reason or the reflection about an event (Konstan, 2006; Chapter 1).

This idea revived during the cognitive revolution, when psychologists began to formally describe mental processes. Advances were made with regard to psychological measurement tools. Additionally, cognitive functions were increasingly understood as resulting from simpler building blocks or subprocesses. Together, this progress inspired researchers to approach the seemingly evasive topic of emotions experimentally and to dissect emotions into measurable subprocesses.

According to appraisal theory, these subprocesses are evaluations or **appraisals**. First formalized in the writings of Magda Arnold (1961; Chapter 2), the notion of appraisals as building blocks for emotions fell on fertile soil. Many contemporary psychologists embraced and further developed Arnold's theory. As a result, a number of appraisal models emerged during the end of the last and the beginning of this century (Roseman & Smith, 2001). In the following section, we examine one of these models in greater detail. This model makes specific predictions about the temporal course of appraisals and has been tested with behavioral "offline" measures as well as with neurophysiological **online measures**.

An Example—Component Process Model of Appraisal

The **component process model** of appraisal was developed by Klaus Scherer (Sander et al., 2005; Scherer, 2001), a German psychologist who spent most of his career at the University of Geneva in Switzerland. Like other appraisal theorists, Scherer assumed that emotions result from a set of mental operations that serve to prepare the body for action. Scherer postulated four such operations or appraisals, including (1) a relevance check, (2) a check of event implications, (3) a check of the individual's coping potential, and (4) a check of the normative significance of the event (Figure 3.6). In the following section, we review these checks and their interrelationship in more detail.

As a first step toward feeling an emotion, Scherer proposes a relevance check. During this check, an event is assessed on a number of dimensions that together determine relevance. At the most basic level, events are assessed for their novelty or expectancy. Events that are highly familiar and expected do not warrant as extensive a response as events that are novel and unexpected. Just imagine yourself getting on a bus where you can hear the conversations of other passengers, the noise of the engine, and the traffic on the road. With time, you adapt to these auditory impressions so that they no longer hold your attention and your thoughts move elsewhere. If now, all of a sudden, you hear screeching tires, a sound both relatively novel and unexpected, your thoughts quickly return to the here and now because there is something relevant for you to attend.

A second level of relevance checking comprises the evaluation of an event's intrinsic pleasantness. This may or may not be associated with how much an event is desired or wished for. For example, you may find chocolate intrinsically pleasant, and nevertheless wish it away as you are aiming to lose a few pounds. Scherer links intrinsic pleasantness evaluation to two basic affective states—pleasure and pain—that he assumes fundamental to all emotions. Like some of the dimensional approaches, Scherer's model associates pleasantness with approach and unpleasantness with avoidance motivation, and thus makes pleasantness appraisal critical for differentiating between these primary motivational tendencies. Finally, relevance is influenced by an individual's evaluation of the relationship between the event and his or her goals. Events with a close relationship to one's goals are deemed more relevant than are events with a loose relationship to one's goals. To return to our example, the sound of screeching tires will be perceived as relevant, not only because it seems novel and unexpected but also because it is an intrinsically unpleasant stimulus that is closely linked to the goal of staying unharmed or reaching one's target destination on time.

Following the relevance check, Scherer posits an implications check, which again occurs along several dimensions. This latter check includes inferences about the causality of the event and the likelihood of possible outcomes. For example, what caused the screeching tires, and will the screeching tires result in a car accident and damage to one's person? The implications check also includes inferences about event urgency and goal conduciveness. Screeching tires and a potential car accident could be considered urgent events because they affect a very important goal—that is, staying alive. Moreover, they affect this goal by obstructing it rather than furthering it, and thus would elicit a negative emotion.

Following the implications check, individuals purportedly assess their coping potential. To this end, they determine whether the event can be controlled in some way, what resources are available to exert control, and whether they could adjust to or "live with" potential event consequences. In the case of the screeching tires, one would infer that control rests with the vehicle driver, that as a passenger one has no resources to reasonably influence the course of events, and that some outcomes, such as a delay in the journey, are more easily coped with than others, such as hospitalization.

Finally, the component process model posits an evaluation of an event's normative significance. In other words, it postulates a process by which an individual relates the event to personal and societal norms and expectations. For example, individuals who consider themselves lucky may perceive a potential car accident differently from individuals who consider themselves unlucky. The former may feel less threatened by the incident than the latter. Individuals will also show different emotions depending on the norms and expectations of their peers, family, and society at large. For example, screeching tires and risky driving are more acceptable in some cultures than others and thus are variably linked to negative emotions, such as fear or anger, and possibly positive emotions, such as joy or exhilaration.

As may be apparent from the preceding discussion, the four appraisal types are presumed to operate in sequential order. The appraisal of relevance is a prerequisite for the appraisal of event implications, which is a prerequisite for the appraisal of coping potentials, which in turn is a prerequisite for the appraisal of normative significance. In other words, unless you recognize an event as relevant, you will not ponder its implications. Moreover, unless you have identified event implications, you will not know whether and in what way you might cope with the event. Finally, it is difficult for you to accurately assess the significance of the event with respect to your personal norms and the norms of others unless you understand the event in its entirety—that means you understand its relevance, implications, and coping potentials.

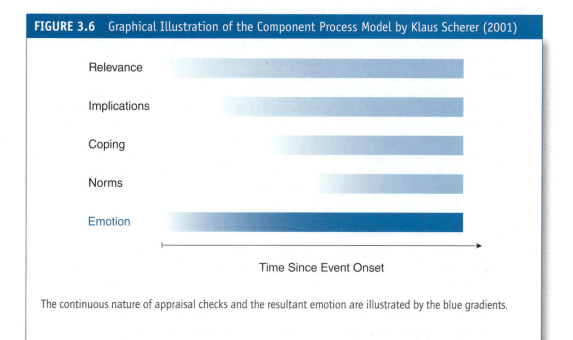

FIGURE 3.6   Graphical Illustration of the Component Process Model by Klaus Scherer (2001)

Relevance

Implications

Coping

Norms

Emotion

Time Since Event Onset

The continuous nature of appraisal checks and the resultant emotion are illustrated by the blue gradients.

The sequential model does not assume that sequential checks presuppose the closure of preceding checks. Rather, it assumes that all checks operate continuously and thus influence each other even after initial results have been passed on to subsequent checks (Figure 3.6). While the checks are performed, an emotion emerges incrementally and is maximally felt following the last check. This emotion is not a discrete entity as proposed by the categorical approach, but instead a graded experience that may be represented in a multidimensional space. Thus, the model potentially describes a multitude of feelings—each with a different pattern of appraisal results. Because some appraisal patterns are more probable than others, certain emotions occur relatively more frequently and thus have names like fear, anger, or joy. Other emotions that result from less probable appraisal patterns may be felt but cannot be verbalized.

A last assumption of the component process model to be mentioned here is that appraisals occur on multiple levels of processing. The idea of **level of processing** derives from seminal research in cognitive psychology, suggesting that we process information at different depths (Craik & Lockhart, 1972). For example, if asked to indicate as fast and accurately as possible whether a written word is printed in upper or lower case, people tend to "block out" the word's semantic content and focus entirely on visual form. Thus, they will do relatively poorly in a surprise recall test. However, if asked to indicate whether a word represents a living or a nonliving thing, people process the words in greater depth, thus remembering them better later on.

In line with this, Scherer and colleagues propose that, like words, emotional events are processed at different levels, and he roughly classifies these levels as sensory-motor, schematic, and conceptual (Grandjean, Sander, & Scherer, 2008). According to this classification, screeching tires may be initially appraised only at the sensory-motor or the schematic level, as our attention is directed elsewhere. The sensory-motor level relies on mostly genetically prepared emotion programs, whereas the schematic level comprises learned programs, which chiefly classify events based on familiarity. Both the sensory-motor and the schematic level operate automatically and mostly outside of consciousness. After the sound of the screeching tires has been processed at these lower levels, it will likely alert us and call our attention to the here and now. We may then engage the highest level of appraisal, referred to as the conceptual level. This higher level uses more sophisticated analysis and thus relies on conscious cognition. It is recruited if appraisals at lower levels are unsuccessful, and it is believed to operate with them in a synchronized fashion (Grandjean et al., 2008). While the conceptual level offers greater processing resources, it also requires more effort and time.

Support for the Appraisal Approach

The appraisal approach taken by Scherer and others offers a sophisticated perspective on emotion processes. Unlike other approaches, it explains the broad spectrum of emotional experiences, including nonprototypical experiences for which we do not have a proper emotion name. It also is the only current approach that explicitly specifies why two individuals confronted with the same event may feel differently or why two seemingly different events may cause the same emotion. For example, an encounter with a snake may cause very different emotions in a snake expert and an individual who is inexperienced with snakes. The former may appraise the snake as harmless and himself or herself as lucky to encounter such a rare animal in the wild, whereas the latter may appraise the snake as dangerous. Thus, the expert may feel joy, whereas the layperson may feel fear. Appraisals also explain why an emotion such as fear may result from a diverse set of events including a simple tone, the sight of another human, or a boat ride on the ocean. Fear results from any event that is appraised as dangerous and uncontrollable.

The theoretical sophistication of the appraisal approach was and is helpful in directing empirical research because it allows for concrete hypotheses to be formulated and tested. Efforts to this effect provided support for the appraisal approach and highlighted the need to consider emotions as the product of multiple subprocesses. Specifically, experiments designed to identify emotion subprocesses suggest that the different emotions are not unrelated but result from a common set of mental operations that are characterized by more than two dimensions.

One of the studies demonstrating this required participants to rate 28 emotion words (e.g., "hate") with respect to 144 emotional features that tapped cognitive reflections (e.g., "incongruent with own standards and ideals"), psychophysiological changes (e.g., "muscle tensing"), motor expressions (e.g., "frown"), action tendencies (e.g., "want to oppose"), subjective feelings (e.g., "felt negative"), and emotion regulation (e.g., "tried to control the intensity of the emotional feeling"; Fontaine, Scherer, Roesch, & Ellsworth, 2007). The rating results were subjected to a principal component analysis that revealed four components or dimensions consistently across three different languages or cultures. The first component was interpreted as evaluation-pleasantness dimension. It derived from emotional features associated with pleasantness, goal conduciveness, and the tendency to approach. The second component was interpreted as control dimension and linked to emotional features associated with power and dominance. The third component was interpreted as activation dimension and was mainly characterized by sympathetic arousal. The fourth and last component was interpreted as novelty and unpredictability dimension and linked to motor expressions such as jaw dropping or eyebrow raising.

The findings of Fontaine and colleagues are in line with other studies that examined multiple aspects of an emotional experience and/or that derived emotion measures from appraisal theory by specifying appraisal relevant rating dimensions. All of them found evidence for multiple appraisal dimensions (Scherer, 1988; Scherer & Ellgring, 2007; Smith & Ellsworth, 1985). Moreover, some make explicit connections to existing appraisal models, such as Scherer's component process model, and support more specific theoretical assumptions. For example, Scherer and Ceschi tested the presumed relationship between appraisals and prototype emotions (Scherer & Ceschi, 1997). At an airport, they interviewed travelers whose luggage had gone missing. Based on the travelers' answers, the researchers could partially confirm the hypothesized appraisal pattern for anger. Travelers who reportedly felt angry also appraised the loss of their luggage as highly obstructive and norm-incongruous.

Further support for the theoretical assumptions made by appraisal theory comes from studies that used neuroimaging techniques such as event-related potentials or functional magnetic resonance imaging. These techniques, which are discussed in more detail in Chapter 6, enable the investigation of mental processes with respect to their temporal and spatial organization and thus help probe the proposed sequential and componential nature of appraisal.

Event-related potentials provided evidence for the sequential nature of appraisal (Grandjean & Scherer, 2008). Here, investigators presented individual images to participants on a computer screen using an oddball procedure. The stimuli for this procedure comprised a small set of positive, neutral, and negative target images to which participants should respond, as well as a large set of neutral standard images. Thus, target images were rare "oddballs" among neutral standards. Both targets and standards were repeated and thus familiar to the participants. Intermixed with targets and standards was a small set of novel images, which, like the targets, varied in valence, but were never repeated and were task-irrelevant. Thus, the investigators could explore novelty appraisal by comparing novel images with the other conditions. They could explore intrinsic pleasantness appraisal by comparing the three image valences of the novel and target stimuli, and they could investigate goal relevance appraisal by comparing targets to the other two conditions. In line with Scherer's component process model, they found a novelty effect prior to an intrinsic pleasantness effect, which in turn occurred prior to a goal relevance effect. Interestingly, all these effects were very fast in that they had a latency of less than 200 milliseconds from the onset of image exposure.

Functional magnetic resonance imaging work supported the componential nature of appraisal by revealing information about the brain structures that contribute to emotional processing. One of the structures identified most reliably is the amygdala. The amygdala is more strongly activated when participants encounter emotional stimuli as compared to neutral stimuli. Notably, however, there is evidence to suggest that rather than simply representing intrinsic pleasantness or unpleasantness, amygdala activation represents the relevance of an event for the individual, which derives from novelty, intrinsic pleasantness, and goal relevance according to the Scherer model (Sander, Grafman, & Zalla, 2003).

Researchers found the amygdala activated not only to emotional stimuli but also to seemingly neutral stimuli such as a person's own name or unfamiliar neutral faces, which bear a certain relevance for a person's life. Moreover, experimental manipulations of stimulus relevance that were seemingly independent of intrinsic pleasantness also affected the amygdala (N'Diaye, Sander, & Vuilleumier, 2009; A Closer Look 3.2). Together, these data support the idea that emotions derive from a combination of emotion-unspecific subprocesses or processing components.

A CLOSER LOOK 3.2

Relevance Versus Intrinsic Pleasantness

We often associate strong emotional reactions with events of strong intrinsic pleasantness or unpleasantness. In other words, we link them to specific stimuli such as a delicious meal or an angry face. However, the emotions we feel in response to such stimuli depend on other contextual factors such as whether we are hungry or whether anger is directed at us. Appraisal theory aims to account for this by proposing a number of appraisals that deal with contextual factors.

FIGURE 3.7   Snapshots of Mild Emotional Expressions Generated With FACSGen

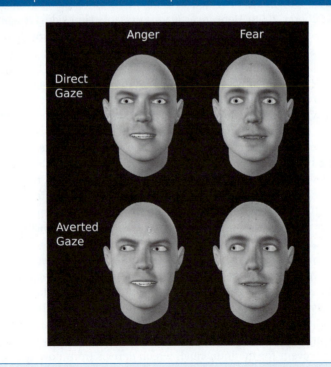

Source: Courtesy of Karim N'Diaye, Swiss Center of Affective Sciences.

An example is the appraisal of goal relevance. It concerns the assessment of how important a particular stimulus is for one's goals. Such goals include long-term interests like staying healthy and unharmed as well as short-term interests like appeasing one's hunger or avoiding blame. Thus, a delicious meal is of greater goal relevance when you are hungry as compared to satiated. Moreover, an angry face is of greater goal relevance when it is looking at you as compared to someone else.

That such differences in goal relevance affect a person's overall emotional response has been shown in a number of behavioral and neuroimaging studies (Sander et al., 2003). One such study presented participants with angry and fearful faces that either looked directly at the participant or that looked toward the side (N'Diaye et al., 2009). If expressions of anger and fear were mild, the participants' rating of these stimuli was significantly influenced by gaze direction. They rated angry faces that looked back at them as more angry than angry faces that looked to the side. Furthermore, they rated fearful faces that looked to the side as more fearful than fearful faces that looked back at them. Thus, in both cases the more relevant stimulus was perceived as more emotional. Angry faces are more relevant with direct as compared to averted gaze, whereas fearful faces are more relevant with averted as compared to direct gaze, because gaze direction automatically informs about the cause of the expressed emotion. Example faces are presented in Figure 3.7. Does the person's gaze influence your emotion judgment?

In addition to eliciting behavioral effects, goal relevance also influenced participants' brain activity. Specifically, the amygdala, a structure linked to the detection of relevance, showed an interaction between emotion and gaze direction. Like the emotion ratings, activity in this region was stronger for angry faces with direct as compared to averted gaze and fearful faces with averted as compared to direct gaze. Thus, we can conclude that apart from intrinsic pleasantness or unpleasantness, contextual factors such as the relevance of a stimulus for an individual's goals modulate emotional experiences.

Limitations of the Appraisal Approach

Despite a long history and substantial empirical support, appraisal theory has attracted only limited enthusiasm. Its opponents consider it computationally too demanding to provide a useful explanation for emotions. Additionally, many view it as an inappropriate explanation for emotions because they perceive the heavy reliance on self-report as an indicator that appraisal theory conceptualizes appraisals as conscious cognitions. However, not all appraisal models are as computationally demanding as the one introduced here, and most of them recognize the existence of automatic and potentially unconscious appraisals. Thus, at least some reservations against the appraisal approach are clearly misinformed.

Nevertheless, there exist reservations that rest on more solid ground. Foremost among them is the reservation that emotions may be experienced without appraisal or the evaluation of an emotional event (Izard, 1993; Parkinson, 2007). For example, there is evidence that simple changes in body position or muscle activity can affect emotions. Individuals asked to rate the funniness of cartoons will give higher ratings when holding a pen with their teeth as compared to their lips or their hands (Strack, Martin, & Stepper, 1988). The former creates an artificial smile, which seems to improve the participants' affect relative to the two latter conditions (Figure 3.8). Furthermore, emotions may be induced by the application of drugs or the electrical stimulation of certain brain areas. It is well known that drugs that increase the level of dopamine in the brain (e.g., cocaine) also increase subjective well-being and may cause strong feelings of pleasure. Similar effects can be evoked by electrically stimulating dopaminergic structures such as the medial forebrain bundle (Arias-Carrión et al., 2010). The pleasure associated with dopaminergic drugs or electrical stimulation can be so great that nonhuman animals and humans pursue them at the expense of other, more meaningful rewards (e.g., food) or their physical well-being.

Thus, one might argue that event appraisals are not necessary for an emotion and may instead be a mere afterthought by which an individual explains or attributes appraisal-independent brain states. Appraisal theorists counter such argumentation by saying that nonappraisal mechanisms may facilitate or provoke emotions but that their contribution to emotions in everyday life is negligible (Roseman & Smith, 2001). This is because in everyday life, emotions are naturally tied to an event or stimulus that must be evaluated.

A second point raised against appraisal theory is that appraisals may not be sufficient for feeling an emotion or changing one's emotional state. We can probably all recount events

---

FIGURE 3.8   Putting on a Smile

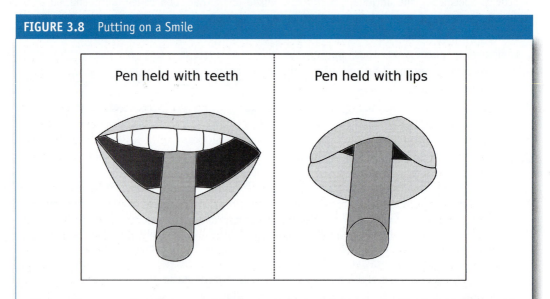

Illustrated is a cartoon face of a person holding a pen with her teeth (left) or her lips (right). Holding a pen with one's teeth mimics the facial features of a smile and helps to improve one's mood.

that we evaluated similarly to events that would typically make us angry. Yet we failed to experience anger because at the time we were simply in a good mood (Parkinson, 1999). On the other hand, we probably all remember feelings of anger that were unreasonable and yet difficult to inhibit or control (Parkinson, 1999). Thus, some hold that appraisals may not be sufficient to provoke or change emotions.

To counter this criticism, appraisal theorists refer to appraisal patterns as well as differences between initial and retrospective appraisals. Specifically, they argue that although two event evaluations may differ with respect to a particular appraisal (e.g., relevance), the overall appraisal pattern across the various appraisal dimensions may be similar and thus elicit a similar emotion (Roseman & Smith, 2001). Moreover, initial appraisals on the various appraisal dimensions may be different from retrospective appraisals that we employ when recalling an emotional event. Then, additional information may be available that makes events seem similar that were formerly perceived as different or emotions unreasonable that based on initial information may have been perfectly reasonable (Siemer & Reisenzein, 2007).

Another problem of appraisal theory concerns its evolutionary feasibility. Like the categorical and the dimensional approach, it assumes that emotions were adaptive during evolution. Yet how the different appraisals would have evolved to support emotions is not intuitive. One possibility is that the different appraisal dimensions evolved independently, with earlier appraisals related to event relevance being phylogenetically older than later appraisals related to event implications, coping, or norms. However, upon closer inspection, this possibility seems implausible. Simply knowing whether an event is relevant would do little toward biasing appropriate behavioral responses. Nevertheless, such responses can be seen in evolutionarily ancient species such as fish, which may evade a predator, attack a competitor, or pursue a mate. Another, perhaps more plausible, possibility is that appraisals evolved in an emotion-specific way, whereby stimulus-processing modes leading up to a particular emotion were selected for. For example, appraising threats as relevant, goal impeding, and beyond one's coping potential may have conferred a benefit, allowing these appraisals to emerge in conjunction so as to produce fear. If true, however, then appraisal theory would be little different from the categorical or dimensional accounts that argue for the evolution of specific emotions or affect states.

Last, appraisal theory suffers from the same lack of consensus that gnaws on the other theoretical approaches. Different researchers proposed different appraisal models that vary with respect to the number and nature of appraisal dimensions. As with the dimensional models, these dimensions are largely determined by the researchers' theoretical framework and the methods they choose to test them. Consensus also lacks with regard to the process of appraisal (Sander et al., 2005). Some theorists assume that appraisals unfold in a fixed order (Scherer, 2001), whereas others assume this order to be flexible (Smith & Lazarus, 1990). Finally, there is disagreement as to whether the emotions that result from appraisals are continuous (Scherer, 2001) or discrete (Roseman, Wiest, & Swartz, 1994). Thus, some appraisal models are more similar to the dimensional approach, whereas others are more similar to the categorical approach.

SUMMARY AND OUTLOOK

The three theoretical approaches introduced here differ in a number of ways. For example, they differ in the type of processes that presumably elicit emotions. The categorical approach assumes an automatic mapping between certain stimulus characteristics and the brain mechanisms underlying a specific emotion. The dimensional and appraisal approaches assume an automatic as well as a more effortful mapping of stimulus characteristics along several dimensions such as valence, arousal, goal conduciveness, and so forth. Moreover, rather than considering emotion-specific processing mechanisms, dimensional and appraisal approaches hold that all emotions engage a similar set of mechanisms but that they engage these mechanisms to different degrees or with different outcomes. As a consequence, the various approaches differ in whether they conceive emotions to be related or unrelated.

Given this theoretical discord, one may wish to know which of the above approaches is most appropriate. Which of them receives most empirical support and thus is most likely to accurately reflect the nature of emotions? Unfortunately, we currently have no answer to this question. Each approach has its own merits as well as a number of shortcomings that arise from the nature of the predictions (e.g., emotion-specific physiological profiles) and the way these predictions are tested. Additionally, some shortcomings arise from more general constraints of emotion research and are thus common to all approaches. The first such shortcoming is that neither of the approaches can boast a unanimously agreed-on model. Rather, each approach is fragmented, with different researchers proposing different models and emotion criteria. While for the categorical approach disagreement concerns the number and nature of basic emotions, for the dimensional and appraisal approach disagreement concerns the number and nature of affective or appraisal dimensions, respectively. Second, albeit all are useful in explaining emotion-related phenomena, none can rule out other approaches as less plausible explanations.

Despite this apparent discord, however, we can use the three approaches to make sense of emotions. Although they differ in some of their assumptions, certain ideas recur and are thus potentially useful. The first recurrent idea is that of appraisal. Categorical, dimensional, and appraisal theorists assume that emotions result from the evaluation of an event or a stimulus. They may differ in how they define this evaluation process, yet they agree that some sort of evaluation must take place. Second, all current theories acknowledge that emotions motivate behaviors that proved beneficial during the course of evolution. Moreover, they see emotions as useful adaptations that help individuals interact with their environment so as to successfully reproduce their kind. Third, many—albeit not all—researchers recognize the importance of current states for the probability of experiencing a certain emotion. For example, Russell proposed that core affect, or an individual's current disposition to feel positive or negative, determines the elicitation of an emotion. Events that match with an individual's core affect trigger emotions more readily than do events that do not match. Positive emotions are experienced more readily when a person is already in a positive mood, whereas negative emotions are experienced more readily when a person is already in a negative mood. A related notion is postulated by appraisal theory, which considers current goals or needs as determining factors in the elicitation of an emotion.

Together, these commonalities provide us with the means for a relatively succinct working definition of emotions. Specifically, we may define emotions as conscious or unconscious mental states elicited by events that we appraise as relevant for our needs and that motivate behaviors to fulfill these needs. Thus, needs and their fulfillment are at the core of an emotion. Such needs may be basic physiological ones or needs that concern personal safety, social belonging, self-esteem, and even personal fulfillment, also referred to as self-actualization (Maslow, 1943). They develop and exist throughout a person's lifetime and show some periodic variation. For example, physiological needs typically vary with the circadian cycle. Thus, most individuals feel hungry in the morning and sleepy in the evening. Events are need relevant, if they are appraised to increase or decrease a need. For example, a snake may be appraised to increase one's need for personal safety. It may elicit fear, which motivates us to move away from the snake. Likewise, a good grade may be appraised to decrease one's need for self-esteem and self-actualization. It may thus elicit joy, which motivates us to repeat the efforts that led up to the good grade. Events that address needs that are fully satisfied have little or no power to evoke emotions. For example, a delicious meal may evoke no joy in someone who just filled his or her stomach. A poor grade may be undisturbing, if such a grade is the exception rather than the norm and does not jeopardize one's degree.

Thus, despite the diversity in conceptual approaches, researchers have come to agree on a few basic points that enable a working definition of emotions, which for a long time seemed elusive (Fehr & Russell, 1984). This working definition, as well as the theoretical perspectives offered by the categorical, dimensional, and appraisal approach, form the basis for our current understanding of emotions and are the guiding principles of this book.

THINKING CRITICALLY ABOUT "WHAT IS AN EMOTION?"

1. Which of the three theoretical approaches do you find most convincing, and why?

2. When examining existing emotion research, the categorical approach is more prevalent than the other two approaches. What might be the reason(s) for this?

3. In the summary section, we reviewed a number of similarities among the different theoretical approaches. Can you think of additional similarities? Why is it important to identify and highlight such similarities?

MEDIA LIBRARY

Instructional videos on human emotions and video interviews with emotion experts: http://www.yalepeplab.com/teaching/psych131_summer2013/materials.php. Relevant for this chapter are interviews with Paul Ekman, Lisa Feldman-Barrett, and Jaak Panksepp.

PART 2

Foundations for Emotion Research

An experiment is a question which science poses to Nature, and a measurement is the recording of Nature's answer.

—Max Planck and
Max von Laue (1949, p. 110)

For much of history, insights into the nature of human emotions were sought exclusively through introspection and philosophical musing and were thus quite limited. This changed during the 19th century with the emergence of new scientific disciplines such as biology and psychology. During this time, researchers began to apply scientific methods to study the mind and to quantify mental processes, including those that underlie emotions. When comparing resulting discoveries from humans and nonhuman animals, researchers noted a range of similarities and thus began to add nonhuman animals as model organisms to their pursuit of human emotions.

This part of the book gives an overview of the biological and methodological foundations that researchers established along the way. With respect to the biological foundations (Chapter 4), it provides basic insights into what is known about the nervous system. It shows how nervous system structure and function depend on genes and the environment, and it gives a rough summary of the nervous system aspects that are particularly important for emotions.

With respect to the methodological foundations, this section of the book details emotion elicitation techniques (Chapter 5) and techniques to characterize the various aspects of an emotion (Chapter 6). Being able to successfully elicit an emotion in the lab is a necessary precondition to studying that emotion, and researchers have developed different means to achieve this end. These means have different advantages and disadvantages, and understanding both is critical for evaluating the resulting research findings.

Likewise critical is an understanding of how emotions can be measured or delineated (Chapter 6). Relevant techniques range from verbal self-reports to behavioral and autonomic markers to approaches that reveal an emotion's substrate in the brain. Different techniques are more or less appropriate for different subject populations and research questions. They also enable different inferences, as each technique speaks to a specific aspect of an emotion rather than to emotions as a whole.

By detailing this and by providing basic facts about bodily processes and emotion methods, the following three chapters will be a useful guide for understanding and evaluating emotion research.

Biological Foundations
for Emotions

Since antiquity, humans have debated the nature of the mind and how the mind relates to the body. Unlike the body, the mind is seemingly elusive. Thoughts and feelings cannot be sensed or held onto in the way one can sense or hold onto physical matter. Yet the mind depends on physical matter for its interactions with the world, and as such must have some sort of physical representation.

For a long time, religious and philosophical convictions, rather than scientific evidence, formed the basis for how humans thought about the relation between mind and body. During this time, many ideas emerged that, retrospectively, may be classified into dualist, idealist, and materialist positions. The dualist position traces back to Plato, who claimed that mind and body are dissociable in that the mind is immaterial and can live on after the body perishes (Bennett, 2007). The idealist position holds that there is only mind, and that what we perceive as impressions from the physical world are in reality mental constructions. George Berkeley was a famous proponent of this position who is often quoted with the phrase "to be is to be perceived (or to perceive)" (Downing, 2013). Last, the materialist position maintains that mind is matter. Mental processes are thought to arise from physical processes within the body. Although this position was traditionally less popular than the dualist and the idealist positions, it was supported by some thinkers including the English philosopher Thomas Hobbes (Duncan, 2013). Moreover, it grew in strength during and after the Enlightenment period and eventually came to dominate modern conceptions of the mind.

This chapter deals with the bodily substrates that underpin emotions, and as such takes a materialist perspective onto the mind-body problem. It reviews the workings of two bodily systems, called the central and the peripheral nervous system, that have been implicated in mental phenomena in general and emotions in particular. Additionally, this chapter describes the biological mechanisms that create these systems, that adjust them to environmental challenges, and that enable between-system interactions. Last, this chapter reports some basic discoveries regarding how emotions "materialize" in the body.

NERVOUS SYSTEM

Almost all multicellular animals have a nervous system that enables them to receive information from both their body and their environment and to coordinate their behavior based on that information. Microscopically, nervous systems are characterized by a particular type of cell called a nerve cell or neuron. Macroscopically, the nervous systems of many animals, including those of humans, additionally comprise functionally different components referred to as the central and the peripheral nervous systems. In the following paragraphs, we will take a look at both micro- and macroscopic aspects.

Cell Types and Their Function

Neurons

For a cell structure to be considered a nervous system, it needs to contain nerve cells or neurons, which form a computational basis for mental processes such as emotions. Neurons differ from other cells in that they employ fast, electrochemical mechanisms and membrane junctions called synapses to communicate with neighboring neurons. To accomplish this, most neurons comprise three components—a soma, dendrites, and an axon (Figure 4.1).

As in any other cell, the soma—or, more simply, the cell body—contains cytoplasm, a watery substance that protects and supports the cell and that holds important cellular contents such as the nucleus with the cell's building instructions, called deoxyribonucleic

FIGURE 4.1   Schematic Illustration of a Neuron

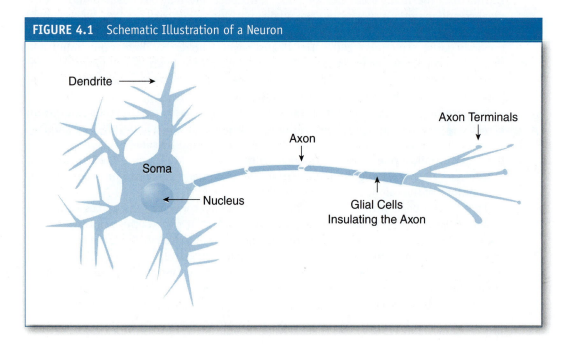

acid or DNA. Dendrites are tree-like extensions branching off from the soma and forming a neuron's primary input site. Last, the axon is a long, arm-like extension that reaches out from the soma and that enables the cell to send information to another neuron close or far. In humans, such axons can be very short as well as long, ranging from one millimeter to a meter.

Although soma, dendrites, and axon are all part of a neuron, they look different and are differently located in the brain. Somas and their dendrites look gray and are therefore referred to as "gray matter." Within the brain, they can be found in the cerebral folding, termed *cortex,* as well as in centrally situated nuclei. Most axons have a white appearance (see glia, further below) and are therefore referred to as "white matter." Within the brain, their large majority is situated between the cortex and the central nuclei (Figure 4.2).

Given the typical structure of a neuron, most neuronal communication flows from the axon of one neuron to the dendrite of another neuron via membrane junctions called syn-apses (Figure 4.2). These synapses comprise two terminals, one of which is situated at the end of the axon in the presynaptic neuron and the other of which is situated somewhere on the dendrite of the postsynaptic neuron. The extracellular space between both synaptic terminals is called the synaptic cleft.

The code or currency of neuronal exchange is a class of chemicals called neurotrans-mitters. These chemicals are produced based on instructions from the cell's nucleus, they travel to the axon terminal, and there are packaged into vesicles ready for use. At the axon terminal, the vesicles enable interneuronal communication by fusing with the axon's membrane and thus releasing neurotransmitters into the synaptic cleft. Once in the syn-aptic cleft, neurotransmitters attach themselves to receptors located on the postsynaptic terminal and thus influence activity in the postsynaptic neuron. As we will learn soon, neurotransmitters can excite or inhibit postsynaptic neurons, thereby furthering or sub-duing the emergence of an emotion.

The cellular process that triggers vesicle fusion and enables interneuronal communica-tion is called an action potential and depends on the cell's membrane potential. The membrane potential, defined as the voltage difference between the cell's interior and

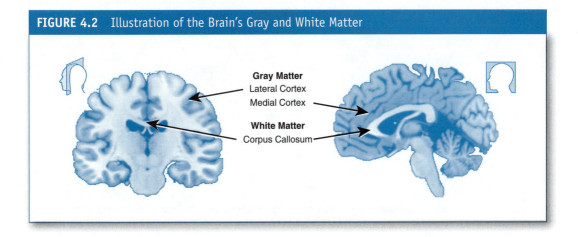

FIGURE 4.2   Illustration of the Brain's Gray and White Matter

Gray Matter
Lateral Cortex
Medial Cortex

White Matter
Corpus Callosum

exterior space, is constant as long as the cell remains unperturbed or at rest. However, based on the instructions from other cells, the membrane potential may rise through an influx of positively charged ions. If this rise exceeds a certain threshold, membrane processes now dramatically enhance the ion influx leading to a rapid, spike-like escalation of the membrane potential. Moreover, this escalation travels along the cell's axon to the axon terminal where it triggers the release of neurotransmitters. A colloquial expression for this process is that the neuron "fires." After firing, ion pumps within the membrane help restore the membrane potential to its resting state by moving positive ions out of the cell (Figure 4.3).

FIGURE 4.3 Neuronal Signaling

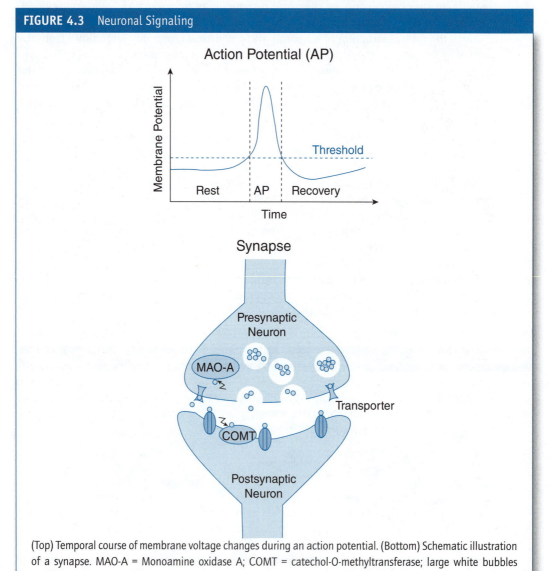

(Top) Temporal course of membrane voltage changes during an action potential. (Bottom) Schematic illustration of a synapse. MAO-A = Monoamine oxidase A; COMT = catechol-O-methyltransferase; large white bubbles indicate vesicles.

As already hinted, the neurotransmitters released in the course of an action potential may have an excitatory or inhibitory effect on the postsynaptic neuron. Which it is depends on the transmitters' chemical composition and the functionality of the receptors to which they bind. Glutamate is a common excitatory neurotransmitter that exerts its effect by binding to glutamate receptors in the postsynaptic terminal (Nedergaard, Takano, & Hansen, 2002). This process increases the membrane potential of the postsynaptic neuron and thus the likelihood that this neuron responds with an action potential. Gamma-aminobutyric-acid, or GABA, is a common inhibitory neurotransmitter that acts by binding to GABA receptors (Farrant & Nusser, 2005). Its binding decreases the postsynaptic membrane potential, and with this the likelihood that the postsynaptic neuron will fire. Together, glutamate and GABA have antagonistic effects on brain activity and play an important role in the regulation of excitatory and inhibitory states such as fear or sadness. For example, drugs that further GABAergic activity are often prescribed when ordinary fear turns into anxiety (Chapter 9). Conversely, drugs that inhibit GABAergic activity appear useful in the context of depression (Cryan & Slattery, 2010).

Neurotransmitters that are released into the synaptic cleft and that do not immediately bind to the postsynaptic neuron could, in principle, affect postsynaptic processes later, when postsynaptic receptors become available to them. While such delayed effects may be beneficial, they may also be a problem, as they would reduce the temporal precision with which neural communication occurs. Thus, several mechanisms exist that help "clean up" extraneous neurotransmitters that are not immediately binding to postsynaptic receptors (Figure 4.3).

One of these "clean up" mechanisms involves so-called **transporters** sitting in the presynaptic membrane (Figure 4.3). These transporters move extraneous neurotransmitters back into the presynaptic neuron where they can be recycled. Other mechanisms rely on **enzymes** available in both neurons and surrounding glial cells that degrade neutransmitters so that they are no longer functional (Figure 4.3). One example of such an enzyme is monoamine oxidase (MAO), which specifically targets monoamines, a class of neurotransmitters introduced further later. Another example is catechol-O-methyltransferase (COMT), an enzyme that degrades a specific type of monoamines called catecholamines.

Given the importance of neurotransmitter levels for emotions, these cleanup processes contribute to the likelihood and strength with which emotions are felt. Thus, besides targeting the release of neurotransmitters, some psychoactive drugs target the mechanisms that remove neurotransmitters from the synaptic cleft. These drugs include selective serotonin reuptake inhibitors (SSRIs), which target the transporters of the neurotransmitter serotonin, and MAO-inhibitors, which inhibit the activity of MAO enzymes. Both types of drug play an important role in the treatment of depression (Chapter 8).

Glia

Although neurons are important, they are not the only kind of nervous system cell. Other, even more numerous cell types are the **glial cells** (Pelvig, Pakkenberg, Stark, & Pakkenberg, 2008). Their name is of Greek origin and stands for "glue." It reflects the long-standing belief that glial cells hold the nervous system together by providing structural and functional support (Kettenmann & Verkhratsky, 2008). In line with this belief, many types of glial cells were discovered that cluster around neurons. For example, oligodendrocytes and Schwann cells were found that insulate axons, thus enhancing the speed at which action potentials travel to the axon terminal. Their shielding gives axons the white color that we see in the brain's white matter. Astrocytes, another common type of glia, are important in regulating the extracellular environment of neurons, including blood flow and the supply of energy and building materials.

Toward the end of the last century, it became clear that glial cells perform more than just a backstage role within the nervous system (Kettenmann & Verkhratsky, 2008). The development of new technologies enabled researchers to see glia in a new light and to realize that they are signaling agents in their own right. Although they do not generate action potentials like neurons do, they synthesize chemicals called gliotransmitters that, if released into extracellular space, can modulate neuronal function (Perea & Araque, 2010). One such gliotransmitter is glutamate, and like its neural counterpart it increases the excitability of target neurons. Other gliotransmitters may have similar or opposite effects.

In addition to modulating neuronal excitability, glial cells shape synaptic connections between neurons (Eroglu & Barres, 2010). Through a range of mechanisms, they can influence the formation of a synapse and determine whether and to what extent this synapse is likely to produce a postsynaptic action potential. Additionally, glial cells prune axons and eliminate existing synapses. Thus, they are far more important for mental processes than their somewhat outmoded name suggests.

Together, the various functions of glial cells make them indispensable for nervous systems. Their disintegration as seen in a disorder called multiple sclerosis (MS) has numerous consequences for the individual including fatigue, impaired movement, sensory problems, dizziness, pain, cognitive dysfunctions, and emotional perturbations (http://www.nationalmssociety.org). Notably, there is research in nonhuman animals suggesting an active role of glial cells for a number of mental processes. This research highlights that MS symptoms arise not simply from a lack of neuronal support but also from a direct loss of glial computations (Han et al., 2013).

Central Nervous System

A typical human nervous system comprises many billions of neurons and even more glial cells (Pakkenberg & Gundersen, 1997; Pelvig et al., 2008). Most of these cells contribute to what is called the central nervous system (CNS). As the name suggests, this part of the nervous system has a central processing role. It comprises a critical number of nerve and glial cells that are organized in tissue formations. These cells receive distributed information from the sense organs and from within the body, they integrate this information, and they issue instructions that are sent back to the periphery. In humans and many other animals, CNS tissue formations are found in two structures referred to as the spinal cord and the brain.

Before we explore these structures, however, we need to familiarize ourselves with the terminology used to spatially orient within the body. For this purpose, medical professionals have introduced terms with Latin roots. Anterior derives from *ante,* which means "before" or "in front." Posterior derives from *post,* meaning "after." Together, these terms are used to refer to the front and back of a structure, respectively. Ventral derives from *venter,* which means "belly" or "abdomen." Dorsal derives from *dorsum,* which means "back." They are used similarly to the English terms *inferior* and *superior,* and refer to the lower and upper side of a structure, respectively (Figure 4.4). Note that the meaning of

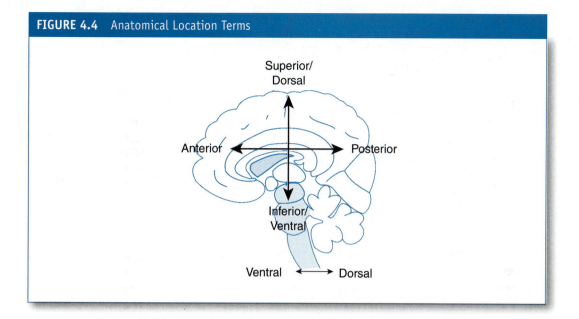

FIGURE 4.4 Anatomical Location Terms

ventral and dorsal differs somewhat between the brain and the rest of the body. Moving from the head downward, ventral is no longer below but forward, and dorsal is no longer on top but backward. This difference relates to the angular orientation between brain and spinal cord. In addition to the terms mentioned so far, the terms medial and lateral are used to refer to the interior of a structure and to its outer walls, respectively (Figure 4.6).

Spinal Cord

The spinal cord is a longitudinal structure. Like the brain, it is protected by surrounding membranic structures called meninges. Its core has a grayish color and contains the cell bodies of neurons. Centered within the core is a small canal, an extension of the brain's ventricular system that contains cerebrospinal fluid. This fluid offers structural support, buffers against concussions, and helps maintain a healthy chemical balance by removing superfluous substances that could potentially harm neuronal function.

Around its center of gray matter, the spinal cord is filled with nerve axons that form bundles, or fiber tracts. Some of these bundles are afferent in nature—meaning that they relay information from the periphery to the brain. These bundles include somatosensory fibers that project temperature, pain, or mechanosensation. The remaining bundles within the spinal cord are efferent in nature. They project information from the brain to some of the brain's efferent or executing systems, such as the muscles and the internal organs.

Brain

Situated at the spinal cord's upper end is the brain consisting of brainstem, diencephalon, cerebrum, and cerebellum (Figure 4.5).

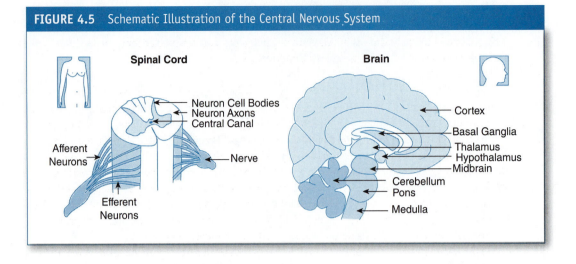

FIGURE 4.5 Schematic Illustration of the Central Nervous System

Spinal Cord

- Neuron Cell Bodies
- Neuron Axons
- Central Canal
- Afferent Neurons
- Nerve
- Efferent Neurons

Brain

- Cortex
- Basal Ganglia
- Thalamus
- Hypothalamus
- Midbrain
- Cerebellum
- Pons
- Medulla

Brainstem. The brainstem connects to the last spinal segment and is composed of *medulla oblongata* (Latin, "elongated mark"), *pons* (Latin, "bridge"), and *mesencephalon* (Greek, *mes* = middle, *enkephalon* = in the head), also called midbrain. The brainstem conveys most cranial nerves and is hence responsible for the sense and innervation of the face. Despite their name, however, not all cranial nerves are specific to the cranium or head. The vagus nerve in particular sends and receives information to and from the internal organs of the body and is, as we will see later, a major player in the peripheral nervous system. Apart from simply relaying information, the brainstem already comprises tissue involved in signal processing and in the issuing of bodily responses. One example is the startle reflex, a quick protective response to sudden physical changes in the environment (Lang, Davis, & Öhman, 2000; Chapter 9). It is evoked based on sensory processes in the brainstem.

Diencephalon. The diencephalon (Greek, *di-* = double; *enkephalon* = in the head) sits between the brainstem and the cerebrum and comprises thalamus and hypothalamus—two structures implicated in early brain-based theories of emotion (Chapter 2). The *thalamus* (Latin, "inner chamber") is an important sensory gateway. With the exception of the olfactory sense, all other senses project to the cerebrum via the thalamus. Again, these projections are not passive in nature. Different nuclei within the thalamus perform crude sensory analyses, which some researchers have postulated to form the basis for very fast emotional responses (Chapter 9). Specifically, although the senses project from the thalamus to so-called primary sensory areas in the cerebrum, there appear to be some exceptions, where crude thalamic computations reach cerebral emotion structures such as the insula (Olausson et al., 2002) or amygdala (LeDoux, Sakaguchi, & Reis, 1984) directly, bypassing primary sensory areas.

The *hypothalamus* (Greek, "below the thalamus") is another important diencepalic structure. It regulates basic processes related to the intake of food and water (Grossman, 1975), sexual attraction, and sexual consummatory behaviors (Garcia-Falgueras & Swaab, 2008; Swaab & Hofman,

1995). Additionally, it plays a role in stress. As part of the hypothalamic-pituitary-adrenal (HPA) axis as well as the sympathetic adrenal medullary system, further detailed below, it serves as a main site within the brain that initiates the physiological changes needed for an individual to cope with stress (Cannon, 1931; Foley & Kirschbaum, 2010).

Cerebrum. The cerebrum makes up the largest part of the brain and is comprised of subcortical nuclei, white matter, and cortex. Encasing the diencephalon are the subcortical nuclei, also referred to as the basal ganglia (Greek, *ganglia* = gathered into a ball; Chapter 6, Figure 6.7). The basal ganglia's major nuclei include the *globus pallidus* (Latin, "pale globe"), the *substantia nigra* (Latin, "black substance"), and the *nucleus accumbens* (formerly known as the *nucleus accumbens septi;* Latin, "nucleus adjacent to the septum"). Additionally, the striatum forms a major part of the basal ganglia. The striatum is a structural organization made up of the *caudate nucleus* (Latin, "tailed nucleus") and the *putamen* (Latin, "shell"), which are divided by a white fiber tract. This division gives the striatum a striped appearance and accounts for its name, which derives from a similar Latin word for wrinkles, or ribs.

The basal ganglia are often considered a dopaminergic region because they receive input from neurons that release a neurotransmitter called dopamine and because they are a primary site for receptors that bind dopamine. Although the basal ganglia are known for their role in movement disorders such as Parkinson's disease, they do more than just regulate movements. Their dopaminergic activity in particular makes them highly relevant for approach-related emotions such as joy and anger.

Surrounding the basal ganglia are billions of axons that also go by the name of white matter. These axons are not organized randomly but along fiber bundles that connect certain areas of the brain. One prominent structure arising from such bundles is the *corpus callosum* (Latin, "tough body"), which conveys axons from the left to the right cerebral hemisphere, and vice versa. For example, corresponding frontal or anterior regions in both hemispheres exchange

FIGURE 4.6   Major Lobes

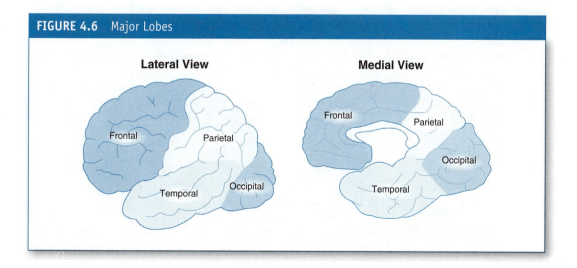

fibers through the anterior aspect of the corpus callosum, whereas corresponding rear or posterior regions exchange fibers through the posterior aspect of the corpus callosum (Fabri, Polonara, Mascioli, Salvolini, & Manzoni, 2011; Phillips & Hopkins, 2012).

Folding around the brain's white matter are multiple layers containing neuronal somas and dendrites that go by the name cortex, which is Latin for "rind" or "bark." With the naked eye, one can see major fissures running through the cortex; these have been used as landmarks for division into frontal, parietal, occipital, and temporal lobes (Figure 4.6).

Looked at through the microscope, however, the cortex reveals further differentiation. Its various parts differ in their cytoarchitechture—meaning that their cellular composition and layering vary. Some areas—for example, within the insula and anterior cingulate—have only four cortical layers, whereas most other areas have six layers. Moreover, there are regional differences within each layer concerning the density with which certain types of neuronal or glial cells occur. Based on these differences, cytoarchotetonical maps have been developed, the most famous of which was published by Korbinian Brodmann in 1909 (for a more recent translation, see Brodmann, 2006).

The cortical subdivisions identified by Brodmann and others differ not only structurally but also functionally. As such, they are often used as nomenclature to report and discuss the localization of certain mental processes. For example, primary somatosensory cortex, the region that does basic tactile and proprioceptive analysis, was found to be located in Brodmann areas 1, 2, and 3; the primary visual cortex, the brain structure required for one's ability to see, has been linked to Brodmann area 17; and the primary auditory cortex, the main site of auditory analysis, was traced to Brodmann areas 41 and 42. These and other functional divisions are illustrated in Figure 4.7.

Although some mental processes, such as those associated with the senses, can be neatly pinned to certain parts of the brain, this does not work for higher-order functions, such as attention or emotion. Because the latter functions typically involve a range of subfunctions and processes, they are not housed within a single brain region. Instead, they

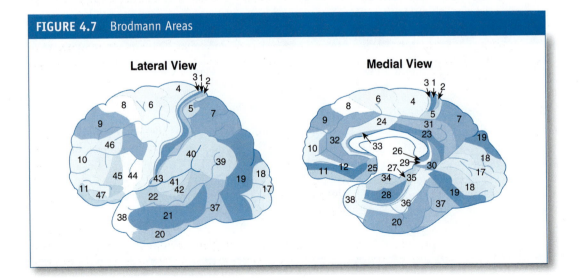

FIGURE 4.7   Brodmann Areas

draw on multiple regions, and researchers are currently characterizing their distribution across networks. Notably, different mental processes can engage overlapping networks. Or, phrased differently, the same brain region can contribute to multiple mental processes by being part of multiple networks. This makes the investigation of higher-order mental processes particularly challenging and ensures that their investigation will remain on the agenda of generations of scientists to come.

Cerebellum. A last part of the brain that shall be discussed here is the cerebellum (Latin, "small brain"). It is tucked away behind the brainstem and below the occipito-temporal aspects of the cerebrum. In its composition, the cerebellum looks like a mini variant of the cerebrum. It has an interior set of core nuclei that is surrounded by white matter, which in turn is encased by cortical folding. However, this folding is more minute than that of the cerebral cortex and, in contrast to its smaller size, contains many more neurons. The cerebellum communicates with the rest of the brain via projections through the brainstem. For a long time, it was considered to contribute primarily to motor function. However, recent findings implicate the cerebellum also in a range of emotional and cognitive phenomena, although its exact role in these phenomena is still debated (Ito, 2008; Leiner, 2010).

Peripheral Nervous System

Nerve cells outside the central nervous system, which are hence not part of the brain and the spinal cord, are considered part of the peripheral nervous system (PNS). These nerve cells sit in the skin, muscles, and other organic tissue, where they gather information to be sent to the CNS or where they can affect tissue function based on local signaling or on CNS instructions. Depending on how peripheral nerve cells operate, they are classified as sensory, somatic, or autonomic. Afferent cells that convey somatosensory and other kinds of sense information are classified as sensory. Efferent cells that are situated in the body's muscle tissue and enable the production of voluntary movements such as grasping or walking are considered to make up the somatic nervous system. Finally, efferent cells that send instructions from the CNS to the body's organs and that underpin certain involuntary movements (e.g., the erection of body hair) are considered part of the autonomic nervous system. Because the latter play a significant role in emotions, we'll examine their workings in a little more detail.

Autonomic Nervous System

The autonomic nervous system (ANS) is responsible for monitoring activity within the body and for affecting bodily changes that optimize an individual's ability to function in the face of ever-changing environmental conditions. As such, ANS neurons target a wide array of structures, including the pupils, skin, heart, lungs, adrenal gland, and intestinal tract. They relay input from the CNS to these structures, which in turn provide the CNS with feedback via afferent visceral and endocrine mechanisms.

The efferent arm of the ANS divides into two strands, the sympathetic and the parasympathetic nervous system. These strands perform antagonistic but complementary roles. Although active at all times, they differ in their relative involvement across different

FIGURE 4.8 Schematic Illustration of the Autonomic Nervous System

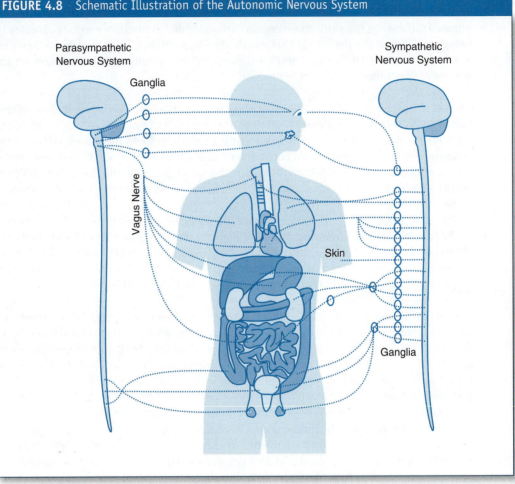

contexts. The sympathetic system becomes relatively more engaged than the parasympathetic system when resources are needed for instantaneous action. An example is the fight-or-flight response, during which the heart beats faster, blood pressure rises, and stored nutrients are turned into energy (Chapter 9). In contrast, the parasympathetic system is more active than the sympathetic system when there are no urgent concerns and the individual is resting. It is responsible for charging the body's batteries and ensuring the body's long-term endurance. To this end it serves functions such as the stimulation of appetite for food (Kral, Paez, & Wolfe, 2009), salivation (Proctor & Carpenter, 2007), digestion (Ramsay & Carr, 2011), and sleeping (Trinder, 2007).

Nerves of the sympathetic nervous system leave the spinal cord close to their target organs (Figure 4.8). Before they reach these organs, however, they enter nerve tissue formations called ganglia. These ganglia are often located more closely to the spinal cord than the target organ so that together with the spinal cord they form a ladder-like construction.

One target organ innervated by the sympathetic nervous system is the adrenal gland. It deserves special mention as it is central to the body's fight-or-flight response. Hypothalamic input travels via the brainstem and the spinal cord to the adrenal medulla. This projection, also termed the sympathetic adrenal medullary (SAM) system, is responsible for the release of adrenaline and noradrenaline—two activating neurochemicals. As such, it enables the quick mobilization of bodily resources (Chapter 9, Figure 9.7).

Apart from this direct sympathetic route, there exists a nonsympathetic route to the adrenal gland. This route is called the hypothalamic-pituitary-adrenal (HPA) axis. Instead of engaging peripheral nerve fibers, it involves the endocrine system. Specifically, hypothalamic input is relayed to the *pituitary* (Latin, "secreting phlegm"), which releases hormones into the bloodstream that activate the adrenal cortex and there release stress hormones such as cortisol. Being dependent on blood flow and diffusion, this release is necessarily sluggish and hence plays no role in the initial reaction to stress. Instead, it helps sustain this reaction.

The parasympathetic nervous system has target organs that largely overlap with those of the sympathetic system (Figure 4.8). However, most of these organs are innervated by nerves leaving the CNS at the level of the brainstem. Moreover, only a few organs receive innervation via nerves leaving from the lower spinal cord. Thus, parasympathetic nerves appear not as neatly organized and more distributed across the body than sympathetic nerves.

One example is the vagus nerve (Latin, "wandering nerve"), which leaves the CNS at the level of the brainstem and sends CNS input to many internal organs, including heart, lungs, stomach, liver, and kidneys (Figure 4.8). Additionally, the vagus nerve carries afferent fibers with receptors for hormones such as adrenaline. It can hence measure hormonal levels in the blood (Miyashita & Williams, 2006) and provide the brain with indirect feedback about ongoing peripheral activity. Direct feedback about the blood's hormonal concentrations is naturally hampered by a close arrangement of endothelial cells around blood vessels in the brain that create a "blood-brain barrier."

GENETIC AND EPIGENETIC REGULATION OF BRAIN STRUCTURE AND FUNCTION

There is great structural variation among the nervous systems of different species. For example, a nematode, which is a tiny, earth-dwelling worm, has only 302 neurons (White, Southgate, Thomson, & Brenner, 1986), whereas a human has several billions (Pakkenberg & Gundersen, 1997; Pelvig et al., 2008). Yet, whether worm or human, each nervous system is a complex machinery that operates on a common set of principles. These principles concern the cell types and modes of information exchange discussed earlier. Additionally, they concern the processes that create and sustain nervous systems.

The development of a nervous system in any organism depends on the genetic instructions that the organism receives from its parent(s). These instructions are contained within the parents' sex cell(s) from which the organism develops (Figure 4.9). More specifically, they are contained within the cellular nucleus, where they take the shape of chromosomes made up of nucleotides that are arranged in a double-stranded structure called deoxyribonucleic acid (DNA). Genes are defined as sections of DNA that form functional units responsible for a particular aspect of the body. With respect to the nervous system, different genes are responsible for the production of different substances such as neurotransmitters, receptors, or enzymes. For example, the human gene responsible for producing the enzyme COMT is located on chromosome 22 and comes in slightly different variants across the human population (Dickinson & Elvevåg, 2009; Chapters 7 and 8). At present, researchers estimate that humans have about 30,000 genes and thus only one third more than nematodes (Claverie, 2001; Venter et al., 2001).

As the organism develops, the initial parent cell or cells divide, thereby increasing in number. However, not every cell is going to be exactly like every other cell. Moreover, despite a more or less identical DNA, different cells will take on different shapes and functions. Some will become nerve cells, whereas others may turn into glia, skin, or bone. Some will produce COMT, whereas others will produce other substances. This structural and functional differentiation is enabled through so-called **epigenetic mechanisms** that operate on the DNA surface and that result in cell-specific DNA transcription. In other words, these mechanisms ensure that only those genes are translated and expressed that are relevant for a cell's purpose. Although many aspects of epigenetic mechanisms are still unknown, some have been identified and will shortly be described here.

The DNA contained in a cell's nucleus is not always accessible for gene transcription. During inactivity, it forms a ball-like structure that is held in place by histones, a kind of protein that specifically serves the DNA (Figure 4.9). Histones have tails protruding from the DNA ball with binding sites for other cell particles. Binding of such particles kick-starts processes that remove the histones from the DNA and allow the DNA to unfold for transcription. Once this happens, a class of proteins called transcription factors moves in, ready to read the DNA code. However, they can do this only if the relevant part of the code is clear for reading, which may or may not be the case. What may block this code and prevent transcription factors from binding are methyl groups. Thus, these methyl groups determine whether and to what extent genes along the DNA are expressed or remain silent.

FIGURE 4.9   Cellular Storage of Genetic Instructions

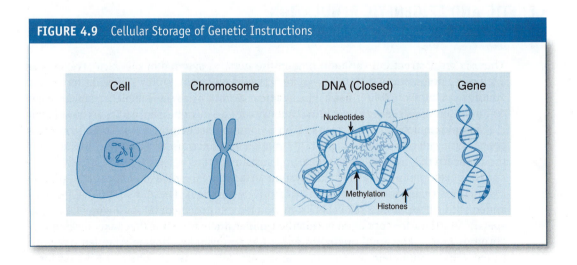

What exactly determines the presence of a methyl group on DNA, and how DNA can be demethylized, are still open issues. However, what is clear already is that the cell's environment plays a role in this. Neighboring cells, as well as the organism's more general living conditions, alter DNA methylation.

Relevant insights come from developmental research in nonhuman animals (Chapter 14, Figure 14.4). Specifically in rodents, epigenetic mechanisms were identified that depend on parental care. Compared to offspring with little parental care, offspring with much parental care in the form of licking and grooming had fewer methyl groups sitting on their cortisol receptor gene in a brain structure called the hippocampus (Liu et al., 1997). As a consequence, this gene was transcribed more actively in offspring with more parental care leading to more cortisol receptors in the hippocampus. That this effect was indeed due to an epigenetic mechanism triggered by offspring care rather than to heredity or the DNA itself was evident from the fact that the research results were obtained irrespective of whether offspring were reared by their biological parents or given into unrelated foster care. The only thing that mattered was how much care they got.

A BIOLOGICAL BASIS FOR EMOTIONS

With the limbic system theory crumbling, researchers made efforts to explore and identify emotion-specific brain structures, networks, and neurochemical signatures. However, several decades of experimentation provided only limited insights and have left our understanding of the relationship between emotions and the body's physical matter fairly incomplete. Moreover, rather than answering fundamental questions, empirical work has opened windows through which emotions' neural basis looks surprisingly complex. The following paragraphs represent an attempt to condense this complexity into a few major insights that should prove helpful in understanding the more detailed discussions of specific emotion aspects that form the remainder of this book.

Important Brain Structures

Amygdala

One of the brain structures first suspected to perform an emotion-specific function goes by the name amygdala, which is Latin for "almond" (Figure 4.10). As part of the traditional limbic system, the amygdala was an obvious starting point from which to explore the brain's involvement in emotions. Situated in the anterior part of the medial temporal lobe, the amygdala connects with regions that regulate the activity of the autonomic nervous system and regions involved in perception, memory, and cognitive control.

Initial research on the amygdala implied a role in fear. Nonhuman animals were found to become fearless when their amygdalae were lesioned. They no longer showed the typical avoidance responses toward dangerous objects such as snakes (Klüver & Bucy, 1939). They also proved incapable of learning to fear a neutral object that was paired with an emotional event such as a painful electric shock (LeDoux, Sakaguchi, Iwata, & Reis, 1985). Later research in humans corroborated these findings. Although

FIGURE 4.10   Amygdala

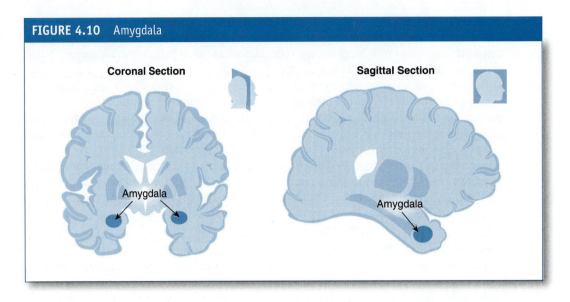

human patients with damaged amygdalae were found to retain explicit knowledge about what was dangerous and could still learn about dangers, their peripheral physiology would reflect none of this. For them, fear became an abstract mental state that was no longer exciting (Buchanan, Tranel, & Adolphs, 2004; LaBar, LeDoux, Spencer, & Phelps, 1995; Weike et al., 2005).

While initial research implicated the amygdala in fear, subsequent studies established links to other emotions. For example, neuroimaging studies found that the amygdala activates when participants smell disgusting and pleasurable odors (Wicker et al., 2003), when they view comedies or cartoons (Aalto et al., 2002; Bartolo, Benuzzi, Nocetti, Baraldi, & Nichelli, 2006), and when they see sexually arousing images (Hamann, Herman, Nolan, & Wallen, 2004). Thus, albeit critical for fear, the amygdala seems to contribute to other emotions as well.

Based on this, some researchers dispute the amygdala's specificity for fear and argue instead that it serves as a relevance detector that issues enhanced bodily and mental responses whenever the senses behold something of importance (Sander, Grafman, & Zalla, 2003). Moreover, the fact that threats more than other emotional events excite the amygdala is explained by their greater importance or urgency for the individual. Missing a threat in one's environment can cause immediate death, whereas the same does not hold for events that provoke anger, joy, or sadness.

Other researchers, however, hold onto the notion that the amygdala performs a fear-specific function. They point to the amygdala's structural complexity that likely supports multiple roles. Moreover, they argue that this structural complexity allows the amygdala to contribute to fear-specific processes alongside more general emotion processes, including the computation of stimulus relevance (Palomares-Castillo et al., 2012; Paré & Duvarci, 2012).

Insula

Another structure that is often cited as an example of emotion-specific processing within the brain is the insula (Figure 4.11). The term *insula,* which is Latin for "island," refers to a stretch of cortical tissue that rests below frontal, temporal, and parietal cortex in immediate proximity to the sylvian fissure. As such, the insula is not visible from an outside view of the brain, but only emerges once cortex around the sylvian fissure is removed.

Given its relatively large size and cytoarchitectonic diversity (A Closer Look 4.1), it is not surprising that the insula serves multiple functions (Chikama, McFarland, Amaral, & Haber, 1997). Its antero-ventral aspect is referred to as agranular insula because the two granule cell layers that are present in ordinary six-layered cortex are absent here. This part of the insula plays a role in olfactory and autonomic function. The antero-dorsal and middle aspects of the insula have weakly developed granule cell layers and are therefore referred to as dysgranular. They support our sense of taste by forming primary gustatory cortex. Last, the most posterior aspect of the insula has fully developed six-layered cortex and goes by the name granular insula. It forms a multisensory hub that receives somatosensory, visual, and auditory information.

Many studies using a brain lesion approach or functional imaging (Chapter 6) have implicated the insula in emotion. Stimuli that excite this structure most consistently are those associated with disgust. Thus, comparing disgust relevant with neutral events typically isolates insula activation (Wicker et al., 2003). Notably, this activation tends to fall within the part of the insula that contains gustatory cortex, suggesting a link between the emotion of disgust and our sense of taste.

However, as for the amygdala, there is evidence that implicates the insula in emotions other than disgust (Phan, Wager, Taylor, & Liberzon, 2004). For example, studies found the insula activated when comparing fear-inducing with neutral stimuli (Schienle et al., 2002),

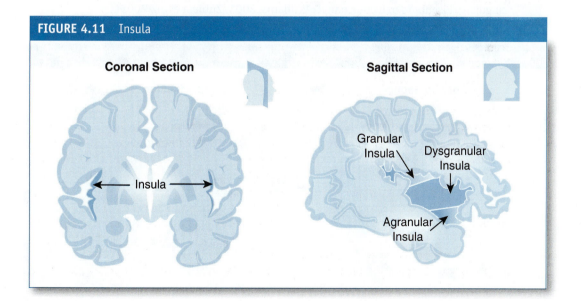

FIGURE 4.11 Insula

Coronal Section

Sagittal Section

Insula

Granular Insula

Dysgranular Insula

Agranular Insula

or when presenting participants with unexpected rewards (Sescousse, Redouté, & Dreher, 2010). In each of these cases, however, insula activations clustered in the agranular part involved in autonomic function, rather than in the dysgranular part involved in taste. As such, these results seem to tap on more general aspects of emotions that relate to bodily changes.

Anterior Cingulate

The anterior cingulate forms part of the cingulate gyrus that sits in the medial walls of the two hemispheres, surrounding the corpus callosum (Figure 4.12). Its name again has a Latin origin, where *cingulum* means "belt." The anterior cingulate divides from the posterior cingulate at the central fissure that runs between frontal and parietal lobe. Similar to the anterior and posterior aspects of the insula, the anterior cingulate is agranular, whereas the posterior cingulate is granular (Vogt, Nimchinsky, Vogt, & Hof, 1995). Thus, again, a lack of granule cells seems associated with emotional function.

Within the anterior cingulate there are cytoarchitectonically different subregions that appear also to be functionally different. On a large scale, they may be categorized into a dorsal and ventral component, with the former extending from the central fissure anteriorly and meeting the latter, where the cortex begins to bend downward (Etkin, Egner, & Kalisch, 2011; Figure 4.12).

The dorsal anterior cingulate receives pain-related somatosensory information and is hence a target for surgery in patients with severe chronic pain that is unresponsive to other, less invasive treatments. In line with theoretical speculations that sadness grew out of an evolutionarily older pain system (Chapter 8), researchers found this emotion taps on the same areas that support physical pain. Specifically, they now suggest that aspects of sadness, namely, the initial distress experienced from social separation or the severance of important relationships, recruit neuronal processes located within the dorsal anterior cingulate (Eisenberger, Lieberman, & Williams, 2003; Zubieta et al., 2003).

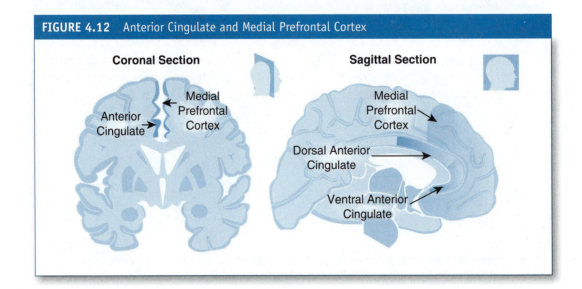

FIGURE 4.12 Anterior Cingulate and Medial Prefrontal Cortex

Coronal Section

Medial Prefrontal Cortex

Anterior Cingulate

Sagittal Section

Medial Prefrontal Cortex

Dorsal Anterior Cingulate

Ventral Anterior Cingulate

Yet, as for other structures mentioned above, the dorsal anterior cingulate seems relevant for emotions other than sadness. One that was frequently brought in connection with this structure is fear. Specifically, in the context of fear conditioning or experiments that expose participants to otherwise threatening stimuli, researchers often observe activation within the dorsal anterior cingulate (Etkin et al., 2011).

Again, one possibility to reconcile these divergent reports is to assume that sadness and fear activate different parts of the dorsal anterior cingulate or that they recruit this region within different neuronal networks. Another possibility is that sadness and fear share pain-related processes. Specifically, fear, resulting from a perceived danger to one's physical integrity, may involve the anticipation of pain.

Last, there is a substantial body of research linking the dorsal anterior cingulate to cognitive conflict (Etkin et al., 2011; Gasquoine, 2013). For example, Stroop-like tasks in which participants have to suppress a more automatic response (e.g., reading) to perform a less automatic one (e.g., naming print color) recruit aspects of the dorsal anterior cingulate. Hence, this structure may perform some very basic processes related to detecting and monitoring experience-based incongruities.

A CLOSER LOOK 4.1

Big Neurons in Emotion Hotspots

Not all neurons are equal. Under the microscope, structural differences become evident that point to functional differences and that raise the possibility of some neurons being more important for emotions than others. Von Economo neurons are an example of this. They were discovered by Constantin von Economo and Georg N. Koskinas in the first half of the last century, and they stand out from other neurons in a number of ways (Seeley et al., 2012).

First, they are large and have a sparse dendritic structure, with only two dendrites protruding from opposite sides of a spindle-shaped soma (Figure 4.13). Second, and probably related to this, they are found only in large-brained species such as humans, apes, whales, and elephants. Incidentally, these species are also recognized for their complex social behavior. Third, von Economo neurons appear during the first months after birth within two emotion hotspots, the antero-ventral insula and the anterior cingulate, both of which are characterized by four-layered cortex. Moreover, their appearance in these regions is lateralized to the right hemisphere, which many consider to be more important for emotions than the left hemisphere.

Together, these properties suggest a role for von Economo neurons in emotions. Their large size is suspected to enhance transmission speed relative to smaller neurons that need to form multiple synapses in order to cover a comparable distance (Allman et al., 2011). This could support the immediacy of emotional evaluations. Furthermore, the presence of von Economo neurons in

(Continued)

(Continued)

FIGURE 4.13   Von Economo Neuron

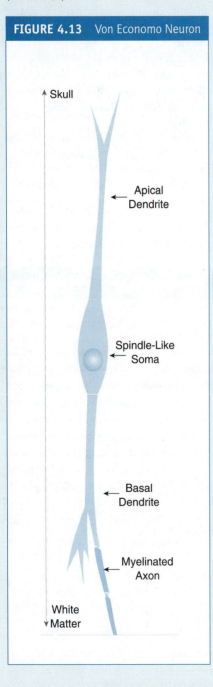

↑ Skull

← Apical
   Dendrite

Spindle-Like
← Soma

← Basal
   Dendrite

Myelinated
← Axon

White
↓ Matter

large-brained animals with complex social behaviors suggests that they are crucial to the emotions that underpin these behaviors. Last, their postnatal emergence in emotion regions suggests that they develop with exposure to social interactions and as social emotions become relevant.

Based on such reasoning, it has been argued that von Economo neurons support the monitoring of one's own emotions in relation to environmental conditions (Allman et al., 2011). Additionally, it has been suggested that they underlie the monitoring of another person's emotions and that they are critical for empathy (Allman et al., 2011). Evidence in line with these propositions comes from neurological disorders that affect von Economo neurons.

For example, a condition called frontotemporal dementia is characterized by initial morphological changes to and loss of von Econonomo neurons, which is followed by more general neuronal decline in both frontal and temporal regions (Seeley et al., 2006). These changes are accompanied by behavioral changes that imply emotional blunting and a loss of empathy (Neary et al., 1998).

Another neurological condition characterized by emotional impairments especially in the context of social interactions is autism. Like frontotemporal dementia, autism involves von Economo neurons. However, rather than being damaged or too few, here von Economo neurons exceed ordinary numbers. Presumably, this compromises their ability to function normally and impedes the functioning of other, surrounding neurons.

Taken together, some of the brain's emotion hotspots are characterized by von Economo neurons, which presumably support the monitoring of one's own emotions and the emotions of others. Changes in the morphology and number of von Economo neurons are associated with emotion impairments. Both too few and too many of them can compromise healthy mental processing and an individual's chance of leading an ordinary emotional life.

Medial Prefrontal Cortex

The medial prefrontal cortex is the last structure that shall be mentioned here as an important contributor to emotions. It surrounds the anterior cingulate dorsally and is thus its immediate anatomical neighbor (Figure 4.12). Unlike the structures discussed so far, the medial prefrontal cortex seems fairly emotion-unspecific. In other words, it has not been linked to a particular emotion. Instead, it emerges in many emotion studies irrespective of the states that are being investigated (Etkin et al., 2011; Phan et al., 2004).

First evidence for a role of medial prefrontal cortex in emotions came from a man named Phineas Gage who, due to a work accident, suffered brain damage. During the preparation of explosives, a large piece of metal propelled through Gage's head, damaging primarily medial frontal aspects of his brain. Although Gage recovered fairly well from this accident, his personality changed. While reliable and considerate before the accident, he was now driven by his immediate emotional impulses, irrespective of impending consequences (Harlow, 1993; Chapter 5).

More recent neuroimaging work further specified the contributions of medial prefrontal cortex to emotions. One line of research that is relevant here tackled the neural mechanisms involved in mentalizing. Specifically, studies in which participants were asked to attribute certain personal characteristics (e.g., intelligence), thoughts, and beliefs either to themselves or to others typically recruited the medial prefrontal cortex (Denny, Kober, Wager, & Ochsner, 2012).

Interestingly, medial prefrontal cortex is also active when research participants seemingly do nothing. When brain scans of so-called resting periods are compared with those of task periods, medial prefrontal cortex emerges as more active in the former relative to the latter condition (Di & Biswal, 2014; Raichle et al., 2001; Shulman et al., 1997). Because while resting, participants are suspected of engaging in self-referential processing, or "mind wandering," these findings corroborate research on mentalizing. Moreover, together they suggest that the medial prefrontal cortex supports processes that track one's own mental state—including one's emotions—and that help emulate the state of others.

Given these findings, it is not surprising that emotion studies with involvement of medial prefrontal cortex often require participants to judge their own emotions, to judge the emotions of others (Escoffier, Zhong, Schirmer, & Qiu, 2013; Schirmer & Kotz, 2006), or to regulate emotions that were evoked by an experimental stimulus (Phan et al., 2004; Chapter 11). Presumably, the emotion tracking that is necessary in these conditions depends on medial prefrontal cortex and its connections with some of the aforementioned brain regions that are relevant for emotions more specifically.

Stimulus and Task-Dependent Emotional Processing

One caveat of studies exploring the brain basis for emotions is that their findings depend not only on *what* emotion they investigate but also on *how* they investigate that emotion. For example, there are considerable differences in the neuronal activation patterns observed when researchers employ visual scenes to elicit emotions as compared to when they employ facial expressions (Sabatinelli et al., 2011). Although both are visual stimuli, the former activate specific regions in the thalamus and occipital cortex, whereas the latter activate specific regions in inferior and middle temporal gyrus (Sabatinelli et al., 2011).

Thus, the social relevance of a stimulus and associated opportunities for empathy seem to modulate neural aspects of emotions.

Another factor that has proven critical is the participants' task or mental set when encountering emotion stimuli. For one thing, different brain networks are engaged when participants attend to emotional as compared to nonemotional aspects of the experiment. Focusing on emotional aspects is often referred to as explicit emotion processing; it preferentially activates structures such as the amygdala, the anterior cingulate, and the medial prefrontal cortex (Cunningham, Raye, & Johnson, 2004; Frühholz, Ceravolo, & Grandjean, 2012). Focusing on nonemotional aspects while passively perceiving emotional ones is often referred to as implicit emotion processing; it preferentially activates the inferior frontal gyrus, the globus pallidus, and the planum polare (Frühholz et al., 2012). Thus, asking one's participants to process emotions explicitly increases the likelihood of detecting activity in the brain structures that were discussed above and that are typically highlighted in meta-analyses (Denny et al., 2012; Phan, Wager, Taylor, & Liberzon, 2002).

Related to the issue of whether participants engage in implicit or explicit emotion processing is the issue of what kind of emotion judgment they perform. Judgments of the participants' own emotions are arguably different from judgments of the evoking stimulus or another person's emotions. For example, listening to a particular piece of music can make you happy because it revives fond memories. However, if it carries a minor tune, the piece itself might be sad, and you might expect some other person listening to it to feel sad rather than happy.

Research contrasting these different kinds of explicit emotion judgments suggests that they engage the brain differently (Lee & Siegle, 2012). Moreover, while some activations are shared, other activations seem specific to judgment type. Such specific activations include the posterior insula and the dorsal anterior cingulate for judging one's own emotions; sensory and ventrolateral prefrontal cortex for judging the emotion-provoking situation; and lateral temporal lobe, including the superior temporal sulcus and the temporo-parietal junction, for judging another person's emotions. Thus, the representation of emotions in the brain and associated subjective feelings depend on a number of factors, including the eliciting stimulus, whether emotion aspects are processed implicitly or explicitly, and whether these aspects concern self, the emotion stimulus, or another individual. This issue receives special attention in the following two chapters.

Important Chemical Messengers

As mentioned earlier, the gathering and processing of information within the nervous system depend on chemical messengers that are released by one cell and that affect the functioning of another cell. Depending on where in the body these messengers are released, they go by different names. Specifically, messengers that are released into the bloodstream and that act diffusely and distantly are referred to as hormones. Examples include cortisol and adrenaline, the stress hormones released by the adrenal gland. Messengers that are released by nerve or glial cells and that affect other nerve or glial cells so that information transmission is maintained within the nervous system are called neuro- and gliotransmitters, respectively.

Because some messengers act within both the body and the nervous system, they are referred to by multiple names. For example, the messenger oxytocin is referred to as a hormone when it is released and active within the body (e.g., mammary glands) and is referred to as a neurotransmitter when it is released and active within the brain (Meyer-Lindenberg, Domes, Kirsch, & Heinrichs, 2011).

To make matters more complicated, hormones or transmitters differ in their chemical composition, and this chemical composition is sometimes used to label a messenger more specifically. Those that contain a protein may be referred to as peptides when encountered in the body's viscera and as neuropeptides when encountered within the nervous system. Again, oxytocin is an example of this. In the following section, we explore a few chemical messengers that appear particularly relevant for emotions.

Oxytocin

The chemical messenger oxytocin is produced by neurons in the hypothalamus. Some of these neurons project axons to the pituitary, where they release oxytocin into the bloodstream so that it can act as a hormone or peptide. Other neurons send axons to other brain regions, including the amygdala, the hippocampus, the striatum, and the ventral aspect of the anterior cingulate. When released from these latter neurons, oxytocin acts as a neurotransmitter or neuropeptide.

Although there is evidence that the release of oxytocin into the bloodstream and into the brain may be temporally coupled, both processes serve different functions and require different oxytocin amounts. Thus, bodily and central oxytocin are largely kept separate thanks to the blood-brain barrier (Neumann & Landgraf, 2012). However, because the blood-brain barrier is not perfect, some amount of bodily oxytocin may cross over to the brain.

Although oxytocin crossover is minimal, it can nevertheless be leveraged in pharmacological research and clinical therapy. One popular approach here has been the application of oxytocin using nasal spray, which presumably passes the blood-brain barrier and influences central function.

As a hormone, oxytocin is important for regulating female reproductive functions, such as the dilation of the cervix during birth and the production of milk during breast-feeding (Matthiesen, Ransjö-Arvidson, Nissen, & Uvnäs-Moberg, 2001). Additionally, peripheral oxytocin appears to play a role in regulating stress (Parker, Buckmaster, Schatzberg, & Lyons, 2005) and in combating inflammation and disease (Szeto et al., 2013).

As a neurotransmitter, oxytocin has been implicated primarily in the promotion of the kind of "friendly feelings" or love that underpin the formation of social bonds (Chapter 12). For example, there is evidence that the intranasal application of oxytocin affects emotion recognition and empathy. Compared to a placebo, oxytocin spray was shown to make participants more sensitive toward others' emotional expressions (Schulze et al., 2011) and more emotionally affected or aroused by others' misfortunes (Hurlemann et al., 2010). Participants who took intranasal oxytocin as compared to a placebo were also found to be more trusting. It increased their readiness to endow investment funds to an unknown person but left their readiness to invest in a lottery unaffected (Kosfeld, Heinrichs, Zak, Fischbacher, & Fehr, 2005). Thus, it seems that oxcytocin alters emotions specifically in response to socially relevant stimuli and situations.

In an effort to better understand the functional significance of oxytocin and its effect on body and mind, researchers began to explore oxytocin's genetic basis. In this context, they discovered a gene responsible for the production of oxytocin receptors that varies considerably within the human population (Ebstein, Israel, Chew, Zhong, & Knafo, 2010; Israel et al., 2009). This gene is located on chromosome 3 and is called the oxytocin receptor (OXTR) gene. Some of its individual nucleotide pairs are polymorphic—meaning they are different for different people. For example, a nucleotide pair with the number rs53576 on the OXTR gene may contain Guanine in some and Adenine in other individuals and is hence referred to as a single nucleotide polymorphism or SNP (pronounced *snip;* Figure 4.14).

Notably, these SNPs appear to have functional consequences. In the case of rs53576, research suggests an association between the Adenine variant and autism, a neurodevelopmental disorder that impairs social functioning (Wu et al., 2005; A Closer Look 4.1). Additionally, healthy individuals who inherited the Adenine variant from both their mother and their father, and who are thus Adenine homozygous, have smaller hypothalami and ventral anterior cingulate gyri than do individuals who are Guanine homozygous (Tost et al., 2010). Compared to the latter group, the former group also has reduced amygdala activation in response to emotional faces (Tost et al., 2010). This and similar genetic work highlights a role for oxytocin in emotion and social function and nicely complements related pharmacological research (e.g., nasal spray manipulations).

Monoamines

Monoamines are another group of chemical messengers with a particular relevance for emotions. They are named based on a prominent structural characteristic, which is that they have one—and only one—amino group. Different types of monoamines fulfill different roles within the body, and we will now take a look at two types that have garnered much scientific interest and that will play a role in the chapters to come.

Catecholamines. The first type of monoamines are called catecholamines. Catecholamines are derived from the amino acid tyrosine, which is either ingested directly from protein-rich food or synthesized from phenylalanine that is already available in the body (Fernstrom, 1977). A chain of chemical processes converts tyrosine into dopamine, dopamine into norepinephrine, and norepinephrine into epinephrine.

The first of these catecholamines, dopamine, is an ancient neurochemical that has been identified in a wide range of species including plants, invertebrates such as nematodes and flies (Barron, Søvik, & Cornish, 2010), vertebrates such as fish, and, of course, mammals. In mammals, brain foci of dopamine synthesis were found in the substantia nigra and the ventral tegmental area. Initial attempts to characterize the neural targets of these areas resulted in the conceptualization of three dopaminergic pathways (Björklund & Dunnett, 2007; Dahlstroem & Fuxe, 1964): (1) the mesostriatal pathway projecting from the substantia nigra to the dorsal striatum (i.e., caudate, putamen, and globus pallidus), (2) the mesolimbic pathway projecting from the ventral tegmental area to the ventral striatum (i.e., nucleus accumbens and olfactory tubercle), and (3) the mesocortical pathway projecting from the ventral tegmental area to the prefrontal cortex (Chapter 7, Figure 7.6).

FIGURE 4.14 Single Nucleotide Polymorphism (SNP)

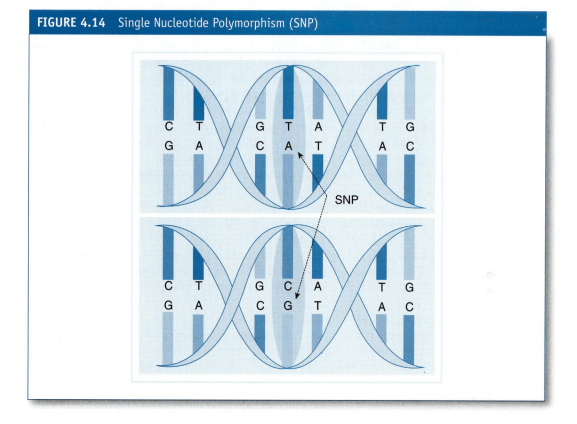

Today, these pathways are still used to study and describe dopamine function, even though their strict differentiation has been called into question (Björklund & Dunnett, 2007). Specifically, there is now evidence for the intermixing of neuronal projections according to which all of the previously mentioned subcortical and cortical targets receive input from both the substantia nigra and the ventral tegmental area. Moreover, additional targets including the amygdala have been identified.

Given the diversity of projection targets, dopamine's functions are also diverse, involving motor, cognitive, and emotion aspects (Roeper, 2013). In the context of motor aspects, dopamine plays a role in the initiation, coordination, and inhibition of movement, and is thus implicated in movement disorders such as Parkinson's disease. In the context of cognitive aspects, dopamine was found to support the ability to select information for attention and to keep this information in working memory. Last, in the context of emotion, dopamine has been implicated in the appreciation of positive stimuli or rewards as well as approach-related motivational tendencies. These latter functions will be explored in detail in Chapter 7.

Not all bodily dopamine is meant for neural transmission, but instead may undergo further synthesis into norepinephrine and epinephrine. In contrast to dopamine, these latter derivatives are not as widely present across the animal taxa (Barron et al., 2010). Their more popular names, noradrenaline and adrenaline, point to an origin within the adrenal gland. Importantly, however, they are not only synthesized within this peripheral organ but also within the brain. Similar to dopamine, brain synthesis of noradrenaline and adrenaline happens primarily in brainstem nuclei such as the locus coeruleus (Smythies, 2005; Tsai, Shih, & Lin, 1985). From there, neurons project to widespread targets including other parts of the brainstem and the spinal cord, parts of the diencephalon, subcortical structures such as amygdala and hippocampus, as well as cortical regions.

As hormones, noradrenaline and adrenaline are important in preparing bodily organs for action, and this preparation is initiated via the sympathetic adrenal medullary system. As neurotransmitters, they have an equally activating effect and are involved in sympathetic mobilization (Smythies, 2005; Tsai et al., 1985). Additionally, however, they impact on cognition and emotion (Sara, 2009). Research on attention and learning provides a demonstration of this. In the context of attention, noradrenaline was shown to enhance brain responses to sensory stimulation (Bouret & Sara, 2002). In the context of learning, noradrenaline was found to play a role in the formation of long-term memories by facilitating the storage specifically of emotional information (Sterpenich et al., 2006). Related to this, emotion disorders such as anxiety and depression have been linked to abnormalities in noradrenaline function (Dremencov, Mansari, & Blier, 2009). Whether and in what way central adrenaline contributes to these effects is at present unknown.

Tryptamines. A second class of monoamines are called tryptamines. Again, one of its members, serotonin, appears relevant for emotions and will be discussed in more detail here. Serotonin, like dopamine, existed in plants long before the evolution of animals (Azmitia, 2001). It is synthesized from tryptophan, an essential amino acid, which in many animals including humans is ingested with food. Although protein-rich foods represent the main source for tryptophan, meals without proteins but rich in carbohydrates are more effective in moving tryptophan across the blood-brain barrier and thus in providing for central serotonin production (van Donkelaar et al., 2011). Researchers speculate that it is partly because of this effect that the consumption of sweets and french fries is so appealing.

Serotonin was first discovered as a peripheral messenger in muscle tissue, where it was found to modulate muscle tone (Rapport, Green, & Page, 1948). Subsequently, it was identified as a modulator in other bodily organs including the kidneys, the adrenal gland, and of course the brain (Watts, Morrison, Davis, & Barman, 2012). Within the brain, serotonin is synthesized primarily by brainstem neurons located in the raphe nucleus. These neurons send axons to multiple cortical and subcortical regions including prefrontal cortex, hypothalamus, amygdala, and hippocampus (Azmitia & Segal, 1978; Moore, Halaris, & Jones, 1978; Vertes, 1991). Its wide distribution, coupled with the existence of several types of serotonin receptors, makes serotonin a complex neural messenger with multiple functional roles.

The functions in which serotonin has been implicated include the regulation of appetite (Halford, Harrold, Lawton, & Blundell, 2005), sleep and wakefulness (Monti, 2011), and emotions. In the context of emotions, clinical research found a relationship between serotonergic transmission and depression. Specifically, drugs that reduce the reuptake of serotonin into the presynaptic neuron and thus increase the potential of serotonin binding to the postsynaptic neuron were found to improve negative mood. Nonclinical research has extended these findings by modulating serotonin levels in healthy individuals (van Donkelaar et al., 2011) and by exploring serotonin-related genetic variations (Homberg & Lesch, 2011). Together, this research paints a fairly complex picture, according to which serotonin modulates interest in and responses to both positive and negative stimuli (Chapter 8).

Opioids

Opioids are another group of chemical messengers that is ancient and that can be found in both simple and complex life forms ranging from single-cellular organisms such as protozoa (Renaud et al., 1995) to multicellular organisms such as humans. In humans, opioids are produced by a variety of cells, including immune-cells that are distributed within the blood (Mousa, Shakibaei, Sitte, Schäfer, & Stein, 2004) and neurons located throughout the peripheral and central nervous system (Merrer, Becker, Befort, & Kieffer, 2009). Moreover, the opioids produced by these cells come in different variants that are referred to as β-endorphins, enkephalins, and dynorphins and that bind to mu, delta, and kappa opioid receptors, respectively.

Opioids are commonly known for their analgesic effects within the body. They are released when organisms experience events causing injury, pain, or stress. By binding to opioid receptors, they reduce the negative impact of these events and enable organisms to remain active in adverse circumstances. Apart from their analgesic properties, however, opioids perform other bodily functions, some of which have been linked to respiration, digestion, and the activity of the immune system (Bodnar, 2011; Merrer et al., 2009).

Within the brain, opioid signaling produces changes in emotion (Lutz & Kieffer, 2013). In this regard, beta-endorphins and their activation of mu-opioid receptors have been extensively investigated. Results indicate a role in the appreciation of rewards—especially social ones like play (Trezza, Damsteegt, Achterberg, & Vanderschuren, 2011) or the presence of a bonded partner (Machin & Dunbar, 2011). In line with this, the application of exogenous endorphins such as opium or morphine is typically experienced as pleasurable and may curb feelings of distress from being socially isolated (Herman & Panksepp, 1978).

The kappa and delta opioid systems are relatively less explored. While they also appear relevant in the context of rewards, their individual contributions to hedonic feelings and approach behaviors seem somewhat different from each other and from those of the mu-opioid system (Lutz & Kieffer, 2013). However, clearly delineating these differences is challenging because the effect of opioid signaling depends not only on the kind of opioid and the receptor that is engaged but also on where that receptor is located. Complex interactions emerge from opioid receptors being situated on dopaminergic, noradrenergic, or serotonergic neurons (Lutz & Kieffer, 2013).

SUMMARY

Modern science has identified the nervous system as the physical substrate for the mind and elucidated its structure and function.

At a microscopic level, the nervous system is characterized by neurons that communicate with one another via fast action potentials and the release of neurotransmitters. Glial cells support neuronal function as relates to communication and cell metabolism. Additionally, they release substances akin to neurotransmitters that enable slow intercellular exchange.

At a macroscopic level, the nervous system of humans and many other animals can be divided into a central part comprising the brain and the spinal cord and a peripheral part comprising nervous tissue elsewhere in the body. The central part serves as a computational hub. It receives sensory information from the body and the environment; it computes the relevance of this information for the organism; and it plans and issues behavioral and bodily responses. The peripheral part of the nervous system serves as an information-gathering and response system. One of its components, the autonomic nervous system, relays information that is particularly relevant for emotions. Among other things, parasympathetic and sympathetic autonomic pathways are involved in adapting bodily processes to periods of contented rest and periods of challenge and stress.

The DNA inherited from an individual's parent(s) forms the basis for the development and function of the nervous system. Each cell of the individual, including those that make up the nervous system, contains DNA and thus the instructions that regulate cellular activity. Epigenetic information (e.g., methylation) stored with the DNA enables cells to specialize both structurally and functionally. Thus, some cells become nerve cells and serve mental processes such as emotions, whereas others turn into immune cells, muscle cells, skin, or bone. Epigenetic mechanisms are also at the heart of processes that allow organisms to adapt to environmental conditions such as the availability of parental care.

Because different emotions serve different functions, they depend on separate brain structures or systems. For example, the amygdala seems important for representing the personal significance of an event, especially in the context of threat; the insula appears to support disgust; and the dorsal anterior cingulate contributes to experiences of social distress. However, not all emotions can be mapped onto a specific structure, and not all structures implicated in emotions perform emotion-specific functions. Moreover, the relationship between an emotion and the brain's physical matter is highly complex. It depends on a number of things, including the networks formed by individual regions, the engagement of autonomic pathways, and the type of chemical messengers that are being used (e.g., oxytocin, monoamines, opioids). In the remainder of this book, we explore this complexity further by taking a look at specific emotions and by drawing a link between these emotions and the mental processes we call thought.

THINKING CRITICALLY ABOUT "BIOLOGICAL FOUNDATIONS OF EMOTIONS"

1. Based on the research reviewed in this chapter, which philosophical tradition seems more appropriate for understanding emotions, and why—the dualist, the mentalist, or the physicalist tradition?

2. Humans share neurotransmitters implicated in emotions with a wide range of species including single-cellular organisms. What if any implications might this have for the evolution of emotions?

3. Why do some emotions appear to converge on a specific brain substrate (e.g., fear, disgust), whereas other emotions appear physically more elusive (e.g., jealousy, regret)?

MEDIA LIBRARY

DNA teaching materials: http://www.nobelprize.org/educational/medicine/dna

Instructional videos for brain anatomy and function: http://www.interactive-biology.com/category/ibtv/human-anatomy-ibtv

Interactive 3-D brain visualization: http://www.dnalc.org/resources/3dbrain.html

Nervous system teaching materials: http://www.brainfacts.org/about-neuroscience/core-concepts

CHAPTER 5

Methodological Foundations I

Eliciting Emotions

Compared with the study of other mental phenomena, the study of emotions is a relatively challenging process. While it is easy to make individuals engage their attention, commit information to memory, or solve a problem at hand, it is not as easy to make them feel happy, angry, or sad. Most would find it hard to generate such feelings at will because they require certain eliciting conditions or stimuli. Moreover, the truthful recreation of such conditions in the laboratory is often limited by a number of ethical and practical constraints. In this chapter, we review these constraints and take a look at the ways in which emotions may nevertheless be evoked and studied.

LABORATORY CONSTRAINTS ON EMOTION ELICITATION

Most natural phenomena are governed by complex laws and thus are difficult to understand. Their simple observation often provides limited insights and needs to be complemented by laboratory research. Natural phenomena need to be taken from their environment into a controlled setting, where they can be subjected to careful manipulations. Although laboratory research meaningfully adds to observational methods, it nevertheless poses potential limitations. One of these limitations is that one can never be certain whether a phenomenon brought into the laboratory remains authentic. Ethical and practical constraints on what can be done in the laboratory often compromise authenticity and thus limit our understanding of the phenomenon under study. In the following section, we look at both ethical and practical constraints as they are relevant for emotion research.

In former days, considerations about ethical constraints were left entirely to experimenters, who, due to limited insights into the human or animal mind, had a relatively low awareness of potential issues. Thus, many historical studies are now considered unethical. Today, professional bodies such as the World Medical Association or the American Psychological Association set the standards for ethics in research. They lay out guidelines that are recognized by most academic research institutes around the world. Moreover, these institutes typically have ethical committees themselves, which evaluate the compliance of research projects with international and local regulations.

One thing these regulations have in common is that they seek to minimize discomfort of both human and nonhuman research subjects and limit the elicitation of strong negative emotions. Thus, researchers typically evoke only mild emotion states. Moreover, researchers often only approximate the stimuli that elicit emotions in real life and present those approximations for only a short period of time. For example, instead of exposing subjects to a freely moving poisonous scorpion they may simply flash a photograph of a scorpion (Figure 5.1).

Apart from ethical considerations, there are a number of practical issues that constrain emotion elicitation in the lab. Some of these issues arise necessarily from the nature of experimental research. This research typically aims to create two conditions that differ in only one aspect, such as emotional significance, while keeping other aspects comparable. Moreover, to ensure that results are not subject to chance, researchers repeat each condition multiple times. For example, they may present participants with 30 or more threat-related pictures and an equal number of neutral pictures. Thus, it is hoped that true condition differences, also termed *signal*, can be distinguished from random condition

FIGURE 5.1   Images of Emotionally Charged Stimuli

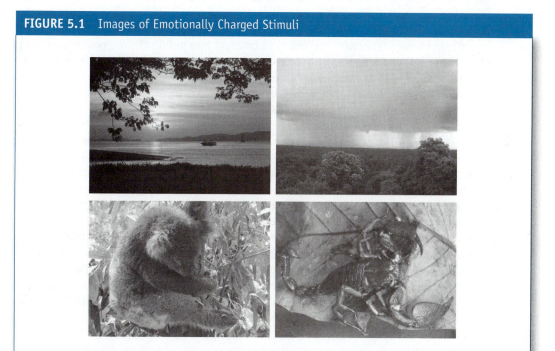

Emotion research often relies on images such as these rather than the actual stimuli themselves for emotion elicitation. The images on the left are affectively positive. The images on the right are affectively negative.

differences, or "noise." Unfortunately, however, the short-term repetition and intermixing of emotional and neutral stimuli limit the authenticity of emotion effects. In real life, we rarely experience emotional and neutral events in that way. Emotional events often stand out and are comparatively rarer than are neutral events. Moreover, the condition repetitions in a typical experiment likely induce habituation and change the nature and/or reduce the size of potential emotion effects.

Other practical constraints on emotion elicitation are largely emotion-specific and arise from what is feasible in the lab. While certain emotions can be induced relatively easily and with little cost, the elicitation of other emotions is a much more involved process. For example, researchers have faced little trouble evoking fear in human and nonhuman subjects. This emotion occurs in response to a range of stimuli that are naturally threatening (e.g., sudden loud noise, pain) and that are easily created in the lab. Additionally, both human and nonhuman subjects readily learn to fear neutral stimuli that are temporarily associated with such threats and that therefore can be used to design well-controlled studies.

Unlike fear, however, many other emotions are challenging to evoke in the lab. An example of this is sadness, which is not triggered by a set of stimuli that are inherently threatening. Instead, it is felt when individuals lose someone dear to them. Thus, the scientific study of sadness necessitates that participants are reminded of lost relationships or that they experience such a loss in the lab. Both methods have their problems. The utility of loss reminders depends on the ability and willingness of participants to actively retrieve sad memories. It also assumes that these memories compare to what participants experienced at the time of the loss. The utility of creating loss within the lab presupposes that participants did form a relationship or social bond that can be severed. While this may be done relatively easily in nonhuman animals, it is harder and ethically more sensitive in human participants. Additionally, it does not allow for easy repetition and thus has negative consequences for the study's signal to noise ratio.

Finally, laboratory research on emotions is constrained by the subjects' expectations. Ethical guidelines dictate that human participants are to be informed of major components of an experiment. They have to consent to anything that experimenters have planned for them. Thus, emotional challenges are not surprising, and participants may engage in prospective coping strategies that alter their emotional response (Chapter 11). Moreover, they may appraise emotional challenges as artificial and of little consequence to their lives.

Nonhuman research animals also have expectations. Many of them are reared and housed in research laboratories and participate in a number of studies for which they may be specifically trained. For example, they may be trained to discriminate between different sets of stimuli or to perform arbitrary behaviors such as touching a screen or pushing a lever. In this context, some stimuli and behaviors would be rewarded, whereas others might be punished. If an animal then participates in a new research project, previously learned stimulus or behavioral associations will influence its mental state and potentially confound the researchers' results.

In sum, there are many constraints that impede on laboratory research. Here, we reviewed the constraints that are particularly relevant for emotion research and that need to concern us when we interpret research findings. From this review it is apparent that the study of emotions is quite challenging, and potentially more so than the study of other mental phenomena such as attention or memory. Nevertheless, if done with care, the study of emotions can be a fruitful endeavor that provides important insights not only to the field of emotions but to a range of related fields within psychology, philosophy, or neuroscience.

POPULAR METHODS OF EMOTION ELICITATION

Unconditioned and Conditioned Stimuli

The most popular means for eliciting emotions in research subjects has been the presentation of emotionally significant stimuli. For the most part, these stimuli can be differentiated into those that have a natural emotional significance and those that acquired emotional significance through learning. In the remainder of this book, they are referred to as unconditioned and conditioned stimuli, respectively.

On the Nature of Unconditioned Stimuli

Unconditioned stimuli comprise a large variety of events, some of which are shared across a wide range of species. The reason why these events are shared is that they have universal significance for basic physical needs. Specifically, all animal species have to feed themselves and maintain physical integrity. Thus, food and bodily injuries evoke affective or emotional states that motivate approach and avoidance behaviors, respectively. Apart from food and pain, many animals show an emotional response to unexpected sharp, physical contrasts. For example, they may withdraw from steep drops in altitude, erratically moving objects, or the source of a sudden loud noise. Because these stimuli are easily produced in the lab, they can and do have wide application in emotion research.

Although some needs are shared across all animals, there are also needs that are shared within only a subset of species and some that are species specific. This is because each species evolved for a particular environmental niche that required a specific set of physical, mental, and behavioral characteristics. For example, some species such as rats adapted to life in burrows and are largely active at night, when they forage for food. Part and parcel of this lifestyle is an avoidance of bright open spaces, which would easily expose them to predators. Thus, bright open spaces can be used to evoke fear in rats but may not be as useful for emotion research in humans.

Other needs that differ across species concern the care for offspring or the belonging to an individual or group of conspecifics. For species with such needs, researchers can use the presence of offspring or companions as well as species-specific communication signals as unconditioned stimuli. Communication signals may reflect both neutral and emotional states in the sender, either of which could produce an emotion in the receiver. If reflective of a neutral state, communication signals may be rewarding because they suggest the presence of another individual or punishing if the sender is perceived as being untrustworthy (Kleinhans et al., 2007; Winston, Strange, O'Doherty, & Dolan, 2002). If reflective of an emotional state, the communication signal may evoke a range of emotions depending on

FIGURE 5.2 Illustrative Images of Human Facial Expressions

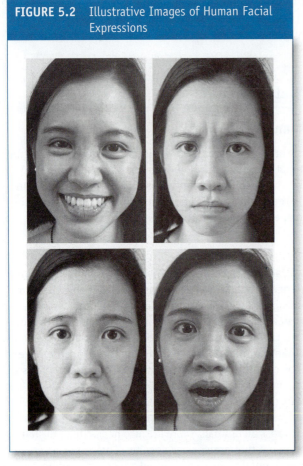

the emotional message that is encoded in the signal. While some communicative signals evoke a similar emotion in the subject as is expressed by the sender, this is not always the case. Specifically, some signals elicit more varied responses that depend on the subject and its relationship to the sender. For example, threatening gestures may provoke fear in a low-ranked individual but indifference or anger in an individual of high rank (de Waal, 1990). A female's sexual pheromones may produce a positive state in a male who has successfully secured her, whereas it may trigger aggression in a male who still competes with other males for the female's attention (Fischer & Brown, 1993; Stowers & Logan, 2010). In humans, happy expressions in a competitor may evoke envy, whereas sad expressions may evoke joy (Smith & Kim, 2007; Figure 5.2). Thus, although species-specific communication signals can be used as unconditioned stimuli in emotion research, their effects are potentially complex, and the relationship between sender and receiver has to be carefully considered.

Another relevant factor in the use of unconditioned stimuli for emotion research concerns the matching of such stimuli with the subjects' age. Because individuals face different evolutionary tasks at different points in life, what they like and dislike changes (Chapter 12). As an example, take the young offspring of species that engage in parenting, such as birds. These offspring have to form some sort of attachment to their parents to ensure that they remain within the reach of their parents' care and protection (Figure 5.3). Thus, they must find the company of their parents rewarding and a temporary separation as unpleasant and distressing (Lorenz, 1935). As they grow older, however, the offspring's emotional response to the presence or absence of their parents must change. Eventually, they must prefer to explore the unknown over parental safety so that they can find a mate and reproduce themselves.

Like birds, humans and other animals undergo different developmental stages in which they need to demonstrate stage-specific behaviors that are motivated by respective emotions. In order to successfully induce emotions, researchers need to consider a subject's current age and identify age-appropriate needs.

On the Nature of Conditioned Stimuli

While our brains evolved to find certain stimuli naturally rewarding, threatening, or disgusting, there are many more stimuli in our environment for which such feelings did not evolve. Nevertheless, they may be important for survival and require an appropriate behavioral response. Learning enables humans and other animals to produce such a response. It allows us to form associations between an unconditioned stimulus and a temporarily paired neutral stimulus so that the neutral stimulus acquires the emotional significance of the unconditioned stimulus and can motivate behavior accordingly.

Ivan Pavlov (1927), a Russian physiologist, was the first to describe the mechanism by which neutral stimuli in the environment form associations with naturally emotional or unconditioned stimuli. As part of his efforts to understand the mammalian digestive system, he explored salivation in dogs. During his explorations, Pavlov noticed that food triggered the release of saliva from the salivary gland and thus inferred that food must be an unconditioned stimulus that naturally provokes salivation. After a while, Pavlov also observed an increase in

FIGURE 5.3 Imprinting in Geese: A Temporary Attachment Mechanism

Konrad Lorenz demonstrated that geese form a parental attachment with the first individual they encounter within a few hours after hatching. The geese in this photo became attached to Lorenz and accepted him as a parent. As they matured, however, their need to be with their adoptive parent changed, and separation was no longer stressful to them.

Source: Courtesy of the Konrad Lorenz Archive, Altenberg, Austria.

salivation when his dogs saw the experimenter who typically fed them. Thus, he speculated, the dogs learned the association between experimenter and food, and after a while would respond to them in similar ways.

After this chance discovery, Pavlov went on to specifically explore associative learning (Figure 5.4). Among other things, he presented his dogs with a tone prior to food delivery. After a few pairings, the dogs started to salivate when hearing the tone, indicating that they had learned the relationship between the tone and the food. Researchers now refer to this form of learning as classical conditioning. The stimulus that naturally elicits salivation is called the unconditioned stimulus and salivation the unconditioned response. During conditioning, tones or other arbitrary stimuli that are paired with an unconditioned stimulus change from a neutral stimulus into a stimulus that has the same effect as the unconditioned stimulus for the individual. This neutral stimulus thus becomes a **conditioned stimulus** able to evoke a conditioned response.

Note that a conditioned response does not remain stable but depends on future encounters with the conditioned stimulus. If these encounters consistently fail to produce the unconditioned stimulus, then the conditioned response becomes gradually weaker and eventually disappears. Thus, Pavlov's dogs would eventually stop salivating to the tone if food no longer followed. Within the conditioning framework, this process is termed **extinction**.

Pavlov's results created a lot of interest among psychologists who applied them to the study of emotions. While psychologists extended Pavlov's work by showing that positive unconditioned stimuli such as food can be used to produce positive affect to seemingly neutral stimuli (Chapter 7), they first and foremost focused on the role of conditioning in fear (Chapter 9). The results of this work clearly indicate that unconditioned threats (e.g., a loud noise or electric shock) are powerful stimuli that readily extend their emotional significance to other, temporarily associated stimuli. Moreover, unconditioned threats produce conditioning not only in dogs but in humans as well as in numerous nonmammalian species including birds (Gallup, Rosen, & Brown, 1972), fish (Lee et al., 2010), amphibians (von Frisch, 1965), and insects (Roman & Davis, 2001).

Another fact that was uncovered about conditioning is that it occurs not only directly, as in the examples given above, but also indirectly, in the form of **vicarious learning**. In the latter case, the research animal or human participant does not learn the association between the unconditioned and conditioned stimulus through personal experience but through someone else's experience. For example, mice that observe other mice being bitten by a particular fly will subsequently avoid this fly without having been bitten themselves (Kavaliers, Choleris, & Colwell, 2001). In humans, such observational learning is complemented by verbal learning. Being told that a particular stimulus is dangerous leads to conditioned responses similar to those from observing the effect of the stimulus on someone else or experiencing its effect oneself. Notably, however, verbally conditioned responses require a conscious perception of the conditioned stimulus and thus are not as automatic as observationally or directly conditioned responses (Olsson & Phelps, 2004).

The use of conditioned stimuli in emotion research has a number of advantages over the use of unconditioned stimuli. One advantage is that conditioned stimuli allow better control of differences between emotional and neutral experimental conditions. As mentioned earlier, such differences ideally should involve emotions only—a criterion that is impossible to observe when unconditioned stimuli are used. Conditioned stimuli, however, can easily be equated so that differences arise solely from their association to an unconditioned stimulus. For example, some subjects could be exposed to a high and a low tone, with only the high tone being paired with threat. Other subjects could undergo the same procedure, with only the low tone being paired with threat. Thus, on subsequent tests, the conditioned tone would produce an emotion, whereas the tone that was not conditioned, and that was essentially identical to the conditioned tone for the other subject group, would not.

A second advantage of using conditioned stimuli in emotion research is that they are often more suitable for repeated presentations. Imagine researchers wanting to explore the

FIGURE 5.4 Classical Conditioning

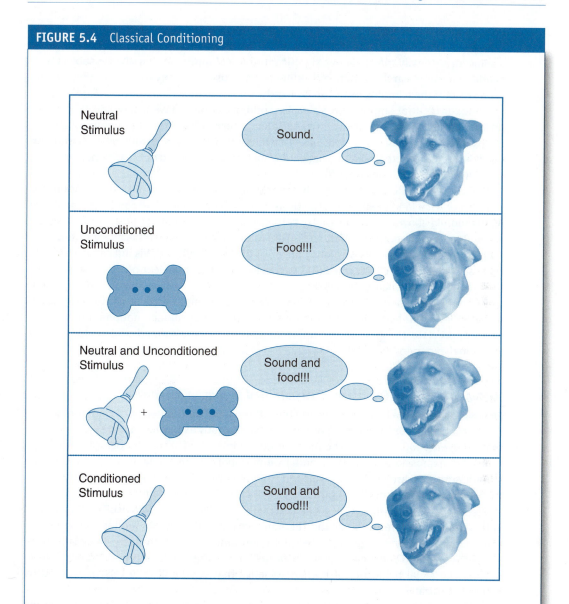

During the course of classical conditioning, an animal learns the association between a previously neutral stimulus and an unconditioned stimulus such as food. Following a few pairings of both stimuli, the neutral stimulus becomes a conditioned stimulus that now elicits similar physiological (e.g., salivation) and emotional (e.g., joy) reactions as the unconditioned stimulus. Thought bubbles in the picture are merely meant to illustrate associative learning by the dog. They are not meant to imply that dogs think in words or that the process of conditioning is a reflective, conscious process.

brain mechanisms involved in the joy of receiving a food reward. After using actual food, satiety would soon set in and interfere with the researchers' objective. Likewise, punishing a subject repeatedly may produce significant physical injury and terrify the subject to an extent that the research cannot be continued. Thus, using a proxy for an emotional stimulus instead of the stimulus itself can be handy.

Although neutral stimuli can be easily conditioned and have a few advantages over unconditioned stimuli, their use in experimental research is not entirely unproblematic. For example, they evoke emotions based on a memory that was formed during conditioning. It is unclear whether and to what extent such memory-based or conditioned emotions differ from unconditioned emotions.

Furthermore, although it is relatively easy to condition neutral stimuli, we still lack understanding of what kind of emotions can be associated with them in the conditioning process. As mentioned above, we can be pretty certain of the conditioning of positive and negative states. But how emotionally differentiated are these states? Do they reflect specific emotions such as joy, surprise, sadness, jealousy, anger, or disgust? While there is indication that some of these states can be conditioned (Klucken et al., 2012), it is unclear how emotion-specific their mental representations really are.

Given the prominent role that conditioned stimuli like money, grades, brand names, and so forth play in our lives, closing these gaps will reveal much about emotions and will allow us to appreciate the potentially different effects of conditioned and unconditioned emotional experiences.

Typical Unconditioned and Conditioned Stimuli Used in Human Research

Pictures. Now that we better understand the nature of unconditioned and conditioned emotion stimuli, let us examine some of the popular stimulus examples that are typically used in human emotion research. The most popular stimuli by far are photographs of human nonverbal expressions or other potentially emotional content. To facilitate the use of such stimuli, some researchers have developed and publicized photograph sets such as the "Pictures of Facial Affect" or the "International Affective Picture System."

Pictures of Facial Affect was developed by the American psychologist Paul Ekman and is therefore often referred to as the "Ekman faces." As already mentioned, Ekman spent much of his career investigating the way we communicate emotions through facial expressions. He observed the facial behaviors of his fellow Americans and traveled overseas to explore the facial behaviors of human societies that were still relatively untouched by Western civilization.

Through this work, he identified a set of facial action units and linked these to the expression of different kinds of emotions such as sadness, surprise, and fear (Ekman & Friesen, 1976). For example, one action unit consists of raising the inner brows, which is an action shared among the three mentioned emotions. Another action unit consists of depressing the lip corners or pulling them downward. This action unit would be specific to sadness only.

To enable research on facial expression perception, Ekman developed a controlled facial expression set in which actors were instructed in the deployment of facial action units and posed a range of what Ekman considered to be basic emotions. This set has been used widely in emotion research and formed the basis for many discoveries to be discussed later in this book. The stimulus set, as well as other facial expression materials, are available for purchase from the Paul Ekman Group, LLC (http://www.paulekman.com).

The International Affective Picture System (IAPS) was developed by Peter Lang, Margaret Bradley, and Bruce Cuthbert at the Center for the Study of Emotion and Attention at the University of Florida (Lang, Bradley, & Cuthbert, 2008). The goal of this system was to provide emotionally evocative stimuli from a wide range of semantic categories. These categories include nature scenes, everyday objects, people, animals, and food. Moreover, the images are of neutral, pleasant, or unpleasant valence. For example, they may show a peaceful landscape, a cute young animal, or a mutilated person.

All images of the IAPS have been validated in a rating study with undergraduate students from the University of Florida. In this study, the authors used a rating instrument called the Self-Assessment Manikin (Bradley & Lang, 1994), which assesses emotional responses along the dimensions of valence, arousal, and dominance, and thus conceptualizes emotions in a multidimensional space rather than as distinct categories.

Like the Ekman faces, the IAPS pictures have made significant contributions to our understanding of emotions. Researchers around the world used them in behavioral studies, psychophysiological research, and neuroimaging work. The IAPS, as well as other stimulus sets, are freely available from the center's website (http://csea.phhp.ufl.edu/Media.html).

Photographs and other pictorial stimuli (e.g., drawings, symbols, words) have several advantages over alternative means to elicit emotions. For one thing, they are cheaply and easily used. More important, however, they enable good control over important experimental parameters. Their emotional impact can be normalized in studies using self-reports or other modes of emotion assessment, to be discussed in Chapter 6. Additionally, their presentation can be timed precisely, and they need not be visible for long for an emotion to be elicited. This allows estimating or predicting the time point of an experienced emotion with relative accuracy. Last, pictorial stimuli allow researchers to explore both unconscious and conscious emotion aspects. Unconscious emotion aspects reveal themselves when pictures are presented too quickly to be consciously identified or when they are preceded and/or followed by another, longer visible, or more salient image that functions as a mask.

An example of the use of very short stimulus presentations is the study by Kunst-Wilson and Zajonc (1980) mentioned in Chapter 2 (Figure 2.9). In this study, the experimenters flashed geometrical shapes for only a single millisecond and could show that participants later, when shapes were presented long enough for conscious recognition, preferred these shapes over new shapes.

An example of the use of masked stimulus presentations is work by Öhman and Soares (1994), who presented spider and snake pictures to phobic individuals and healthy controls. In a first experiment, these researchers showed pictures followed by a mask (i.e., a distorted, unrecognizable image) at various intervals and established that conscious picture recognition was unsuccessful when masks followed the onset of target pictures by 30 milliseconds. The researchers then conducted a second experiment, where they measured skin conductance to pictures that were masked after 30 milliseconds' exposure or that were unmasked pictures. Skin conductance was greater in phobics relative to controls, irrespective of whether snakes and spiders were viewed unconsciously or consciously. Thus, phobics may experience aspects of fear without consciously perceiving their phobic objects.

A CLOSER LOOK 5.1

Using Published Stimulus Systems of Conditioned and Unconditioned Stimuli in Emotion Research

Several stimulus sets have been developed and made available for emotion research. Using these sets confers a number of advantages. First, the establishment of such corpora requires time and can be quite costly. Researchers can avoid these costs and progress at a faster rate when relying on existing material than when generating stimuli for each experiment anew. Second, the establishment of such corpora requires a certain expertise—for example, with human facial expressions and/or access to special populations such as actors or tribespeople. Thanks to established corpora, researchers can use stimuli that they would be unable to create themselves. Finally, established corpora enable researchers to compare findings across a wide range of studies and to easily replicate and extend them.

Yet an exclusive reliance on a few published stimulus sets also creates problems. It greatly limits the type of stimuli and emotions that are subjected to emotion research and thus curtails the generalizability of findings. Condition differences may be due to idiosyncrasies in the material.

For example, the instructions given to actors in Ekman's "Pictures of Facial Affect" and the fact that actors posed rather than felt an emotion may have produced stimulus-specific effects. Moreover, several decades have passed since these stimuli were created, and their somewhat antique appearance may influence subject responses.

Likewise, there are some idiosyncrasies in the IAPS pictures. For example, emotional pictures more frequently involve living or human content relative to neutral pictures so that putative emotion effects may result from social processing. Moreover, careful investigations also identified valence-specific differences in low-level perceptual image properties such as spatial frequency content (Delplanque, N'Diaye, Scherer, & Grandjean, 2007). Thus, a careful selection of stimuli from this and other published sets is required in order to avoid emotion effects being confounded (Delplanque et al., 2007; Knebel, Toepel, Hudry, le Coutre, & Murray, 2008).

Another potential concern with the use of published stimulus sets is that they were created against the backdrop of a particular theoretical perspective. For example, the Ekman faces were created with the assumption of a certain number of basic emotion categories. Thus, only stimuli that fall neatly within these categories are available in the set. In contrast, the IAPS was created with the assumption that emotions are organized along a few key dimensions and cannot be neatly sorted into categories. Thus, the IAPS pictures fall along these dimensions without clear category boundaries. Therefore, using one or the other stimulus set has implications for the kind of research questions that can be asked and answered.

Finally, the preceding stimulus sets were developed within a specific cultural context. The facial set contains Caucasian faces that may be less appropriate for emotion research in non-Caucasian individuals. Specifically, although emotion expressions seem to have a universal basis, there is enough cross-cultural variation to impair the accuracy with which expressions can be universally recognized (Jack, Blais, Scheepers, Schyns, & Caldara, 2009). Likewise, the IAPS has cultural elements. For example, cultures differ in their relation to animals. While Western societies typically view dogs as a favorite pet, others perceive dogs as unclean, or an ordinary food item. Thus, an image of puppies may elicit very different emotions in these different societies.

Due to these caveats, researchers typically carefully select stimuli from published sets and normalize their stimulus selection for their study population. Moreover, they also develop their own stimuli, as these can be better tailored to a particular study question. Thus, a range of stimulus sets has become available over the years and include, among other things, traditional facial displays and affective images as well as less traditional means for emotion elicitation, including video clips, body gestures, vocalizations, environmental sounds, or music. Some have been reviewed for their respective properties and suitability in emotion research (Cowie, Douglas-Cowie, & Cox, 2005; Gunes & Piccardi, 2006).

Sounds. Most emotional events not only impact our visual sense, they also produce olfactory, tactile, or auditory impressions. For example, a raging fire cannot only be seen, it can also be smelled, felt, and heard. Of these latter impressions, olfaction (Ferdenzi et al., 2011) and somatosensation (Löken, Wessberg, Morrison, McGlone, & Olausson, 2009; Schirmer et al., 2011) have been relatively rarely used to elicit emotions and are only now gaining significance. The elicitation of emotions via sounds, however, is already well documented. As for pictures, different variants have been used that range from vocal expressions and music to environmental sounds.

Like facial expressions, vocal expressions can communicate another person's emotional state and behavioral intent and therefore modify emotions in receivers (Banse & Scherer, 1996; Darwin, 1872). Additionally, vocalizations vary with respect to their intrinsic pleasantness (Bachorowski & Owren, 2003). Some of the sounds that humans and other animals produce are pleasing to the ear (e.g., a song), whereas other sounds are irritating or obnoxious (e.g., screams). Thus, perceiving such sounds is thought to produce affective or emotional states that bias approach and avoidance behaviors, respectively (Bachorowski & Owren, 2003). For example, an individual pursued by another may scream not only to rally support but also to fend off the attacker, who can avoid the obnoxious sound by leaving the victim alone.

The effect of music on listener emotion is closely related to that of vocalizations. Melodies sung by individuals, being most likely the first form of human music, necessarily leveraged on basic vocal properties and vocal expression (Escoffier, Zhong, Schirmer, & Qiu, 2013; Juslin & Laukka, 2003; Scherer, 1986). Moreover, the eventual development of instruments to accompany or replace the voice in music (e.g., flute; Higham et al., 2012) did little to abate structural and functional similarities. Thus, music, whether sung or not, can elicit emotions in listeners because it conveys emotion signals and because it may be inherently pleasant (e.g., consonant) or unpleasant (e.g., dissonant).

The kinds of vocalizations that found repeated application in emotion research include nonverbal exclamations like screams, sighs, laughter, or crying. However, they also include words or sentences spoken in an emotional voice. Although these latter stimuli are typically less emotionally salient, they are still capable of producing an emotional response, and they can do so in fairly implicit experimental designs in which emotions are not highlighted as the topic of interest to research participants (Brosch, Grandjean, Sander, & Scherer, 2008; Schirmer et al., 2008).

When eliciting emotions via music, experimenters typically select excerpts or segments from classical compositions like Tchaikovsky's *Nutcracker Suite* or *Swan Lake* (Eich, Ng, Macaulay, Percy, & Grebneva, 2007). Additionally, they may compose melodies or chord sequences for which they vary simple parameters such as key (i.e., minor, major) or harmony.

Apart from voices and music, our auditory environment is filled with other sounds that may be emotionally provoking. As already mentioned, the sound of a fire may be alarming, the sound of a car race may be thrilling, and the sound of ocean waves gently breaking on a shore may be calming. Thus, sounds, irrespective of whether they come from a conspecific, can and are used to elicit emotions in the laboratory. Moreover, their advantages and disadvantages vis-à-vis the use of pictorial material are relatively comparable.

One of the key advantages is that sounds cannot be "overlooked." Unlike pictures, for which experimenters need to ensure that participants attend a particular spatial location, sounds simply need to be audible. This advantage comes in handy when researchers want to reduce the probability that participants disengage with the stimulus material (e.g., looking away from disgusting images) or when they work with populations that have difficulties directing and maintaining attention (e.g., infants and small children).

However, the use of sounds also brings a number of disadvantages. For example, it is more difficult to create auditory stimulus sets in which different emotion conditions differ with respect to emotional content only. Sounds that carry different emotions typically contrast with one another. Someone speaking with a happy voice is typically much louder than someone speaking with a sad or dejected voice. Thus, researchers need to employ controls to determine whether condition differences result from simple acoustic differences or whether they are due to emotion (Grandjean et al., 2005; Schirmer & Escoffier, 2010). Furthermore, sounds, unlike images, emerge in time, so that the time-locking between stimulus presentation and emotion elicitation is not as tight. Related to this, sounds cannot be presented subconsciously simply by reducing presentation time. Instead, researchers must reduce sound intensity to be just below hearing threshold (Knight, Nguyen, & Bandettini, 2003).

Films. Given the multimodality of most natural emotions, there is much merit in using stimuli that combine one modality with one or more other modalities. Films are an example of this. They combine visual with auditory input and thus excite emotions in a fairly realistic manner. Efforts to leverage on films in emotion research have focused largely on popular films available on television or in movie theaters. Excerpts from such films have been selected and shown to participants who then evaluated the film and their emotions on postfilm questionnaires. Using this technique, researchers could demonstrate that films effectively evoke both changes in general affect but also more specific emotional responses including amusement, anger, disgust, fear, sadness, and surprise (Gross & Levenson, 1995; Rottenberg, Ray, & Gross, 2007).

An example of this is work by Gross and Levenson (1995), who tested a number of film clips in a large student sample. Students viewed the clips in groups of 3 to 30 students. After each clip, they completed an emotion questionnaire on which they indicated for 16 separate emotions how much they felt each emotion after watching the clip. Based on the students' responses, the authors selected two clips with the best ratings for each of the 16 emotions. Among the clips, they selected one from *When Harry Met Sally* that elicited amusement, one from *The Silence of the Lambs* that elicited fear, and one from *Bambi* that elicited sadness. For their neutral condition they selected films with abstract shapes or color bars.

Films have a number of advantages over unimodal stimuli such as pictures and sounds. As already mentioned, in most cases films have probably a greater ecological validity than their unimodal counterparts. Perceiving a fire from film is certainly more "real" than simply seeing or hearing a fire. Additionally, films are well suited to capture the participants' attention. Due to the combined visual and auditory sensory input, attention is less likely to wander. Last, films often enable researchers to evoke stronger emotions than would be possible via other means. Most participants are exposed to films on an almost daily basis, and as such may perceive them as less harmful and ethically problematic than other experimental manipulations such as mild electric shocks (Rottenberg et al., 2007).

Associated with these benefits, however, are a number of costs. First, it is unclear to what extent the emotions from films are "real." Because most of the films used in emotion research require participants to suspend disbelief and to engage with an illusion, it has been argued that the resulting feelings are aesthetic responses rather than true emotions (Frijda, 1989). Second, film clips typically require longer presentations than do pictures and sounds. Because a story or scenario needs time to develop, experiments become overly long or entail relatively few trials or data points. Associated with this, films make it difficult to tell when exactly an emotion occurs. They also often suffer from significant variation in content and complexity, which limits how well researchers can match experimental conditions (e.g., an emotional with a neutral film condition) and how films can be employed in the context of the time-sensitive emotion assessment techniques introduced in Chapter 6.

Social psychological methods. When social psychologists study emotions, they often prefer "real-life" scenarios to ensure the ecological validity of their results. One approach to bringing such scenarios into the lab relies on so-called **deception techniques**, whereby participants are given a "cover story" aimed at concealing the true experimental purpose (e.g., emotion; Harmon-Jones, Amodio, & Zinner, 2007). As deception requires that certain aspects of an experiment are wrongly or not explained to participants, it falls under much ethical scrutiny. Moreover, researchers can only use deception if other approaches are inappropriate and participants are not unduly harmed in the process.

A famous example of the use of deception is the study by Schachter and Singer (1962) mentioned in Chapter 2 (Figure 2.6). In this study, the researchers gave participants adrenaline or a placebo under the guise of testing the effects of a new vitamin. Some participants received correct information about potential side effects, whereas other participants received incorrect or no information. The researchers then explored the effect of both the drug and the side-effects information on how participants responded to a confederate who either annoyed or amused them. Schachter and Singer found that it was the cognitive interpretation of physiological state and emotional stimulus that mattered for the participants' subjective experience of an emotion. This finding was unlikely to have emerged had participants been aware of the nature of the drug and that the confederate had instructions to provoke them emotionally. Had they known, participants probably would have responded very differently. Hence, deception, although ethically sensitive, is a useful tool in emotion research.

Another popular social psychology approach is to bring two participants into the lab and to induce them to interact. The premise for this is that we often experience our strongest emotions with or because of the people around us. In everyday life, feelings like joy, disappointment, and anger often result from encounters with acquaintances, friends, and family. Thus, interactions with them provide a rich fountain of emotions that is valuable to emotion researchers.

One example of the interaction approach is to bring two romantic partners into the lab for a discussion of shared interests or points of disagreement in the relationship (Roberts, Tsai, & Coan, 2007). This is typically done via a facilitator who first solicits potential discussion topics from the couple, inquires about associated emotions with each individual, and helps dispel any negative feelings at the end of the experiment. Among other things, this approach was applied to questions regarding the role of positive affect during marital conflict (Gottman, Coan, Carrere, & Swanson, 1998) and the role of emotions in domestic violence (Coan, Gottman, Babcock, & Jacobson, 1997).

As already mentioned, a significant advantage of social psychological methods is that they elicit emotions in a fairly realistic way and therefore have better ecological validity than the presentation of isolated pictures, sounds, or films. Moreover, they take into account the dynamics of emotional processes in that they allow emotions to emerge and dissipate relatively naturally. Unlike the presentation of isolated stimuli, social psychological methods do not constrain participant emotions by massed and mixed emotion elicitation, or by temporal parameters such as short interstimulus intervals. Last, social psychology methods are well suited to study emotions such as sadness or anger that are otherwise difficult to elicit in the lab.

Again, however, there are problems arising from the use of these social psychological methods. For example, they tend to be more involved and costly than other methods. Instead of computer-based mass testing, participants have to be treated individually or in small groups. Instead of multicondition sessions, single-condition sessions typically must be conducted. In other words, one emotion would be elicited in one sitting, so another emotion or control condition would have to be elicited in another sitting or from another participant. A second problem with social psychological methods is that they are more difficult to control than other methods. Felt emotions may vary more among participants, and experimental comparisons may potentially be more confounded by extraneous variables (e.g., experimenter behavior, cognitive demands). Last, there is danger that participants rightly or wrongly guess the intention of the experiment and that such guessing systematically influences their response.

Autobiographical Memories

An alternative strategy to presenting participants with emotional events is to ask them to recall such events from their own past. For example, a researcher interested in studying fear might ask participants to recall a frightening memory, as well as another memory with similar characteristics that is emotionally neutral. The experimenter would assess these memories before the study and then provide participants with reminders or retrieval cues that would prompt the recall of one or the other memory during the experiment.

This technique has facilitated the investigation of emotional reactions to scenarios that are difficult or impossible to create in the lab. For example, it played an important role in research on events that cause traumatic or flashbulb memories—memories that individuals experience as more vivid and powerful than memories of mundane events (Sharot, Martorella, Delgado, & Phelps, 2007; Figure 5.5). It has also been important for studying social emotions such as love, jealousy, or sadness (Harris, 2002; Zubieta et al., 2003) that result from existing relationships to other individuals—relationships that are person-specific and that take time to develop.

One interesting phenomenon in the context of autobiographical research is that individuals remember self-relevant information differently and better than information that is not self-relevant. This was first shown in a study by Rogers and colleagues (Rogers, Kuiper, & Kirker, 1977) in which participants rated adjectives with respect to structural, phonemic, and semantic properties or with respect to how well an adjective described themselves. After this encoding task, participants were given a surprise recall test in which they had to recall as many words as possible. Their recall was better for words in the self-relevance rating as compared with all other ratings, suggesting a memory advantage for material that undergoes a self-attribution or comparison process.

There are two reasons why this so-called self-reference effect is important in the context of autobiographical emotion research. First, there is evidence that individuals derive pleasure from relating self-relevant information to others (Tamir & Mitchell, 2012). Second, autobiographical memories differ in self-relevance. Of the things we experience in our lives, some involve us more directly than others. For example, a car accident that we cause has greater self-relevance than a car accident that we merely witness. As a consequence, the storage processes underpinning the former will differ from the storage processes underpinning the latter, irrespective of potential emotional differences (Herbert, Pauli, & Herbert, 2011). Together, these points imply that self-relevance needs to be carefully considered when using autobiographical memories to study emotions.

Apart from self-relevance, other issues arise from the use of autobiographical memories that are not as easily addressed. For example, one cannot exclude the possibility that emotions triggered by memories differ from emotions triggered by the first experience of the event. Mnemonic processes may attenuate some and enhance other aspects of the event. Additionally, it is uncertain whether and how these events are recalled when prompted. Participants may not want to fully retrieve a former emotionally intense experience or engage in concurrent emotion regulation strategies.

Despite these issues, the autobiographical approach is a valuable tool in the emotion researcher's toolkit. It opens avenues to pursue otherwise inaccessible research questions and offers good ecological validity. By using this technique, researchers can study emotional events that are truly important to their participants.

FIGURE 5.5   Outstanding Events—Outstanding Memories

Flashbulb memories are associated with outstanding events that have an unusually high emotional significance. The 9/11 terrorist attacks on the World Trade Center in 2001 had such significance for many individuals around the world.

Source: Flickr/TheMachineStops (CC BY-SA 2.0).

Behavioral Responses as Emotion Stimuli

As postulated by William James (Chapter 1) and later scientifically proven, our behavior has a pivotal role in how we feel. If we adopt a happy face, chances are good that we will feel happier than if we adopt a neutral or angry face.

In their pursuit of emotions, researchers are leveraging on this phenomenon. An example of this is the Directed Facial Action Task developed by Ekman and colleagues (Ekman, Levenson, & Friesen, 1983). These researchers found that different emotions are linked to different facial expressions, each characterized by a particular combination of muscular contractions or facial actions. While the researchers' initial work served merely to classify facial expressions, they subsequently used these actions as instructions in the context of emotion elicitation. Without naming an emotion, they asked their participants to perform and hold a specific combination of facial actions. For example, they might have asked participants to do the following:

1. pull eyebrows down and together,
2. raise the upper eyelids,
3. tighten the lower eyelids, and
4. narrow, tighten, and press both lips together while pushing the lower lip a bit upward.

After holding these or other expressions for 15 seconds, participants could relax and the researchers assessed a potentially felt emotion by examining physiological recordings (e.g., heart rate) or by asking participants to reflect on their feelings. In the preceding example, such feelings would likely tilt away from neutral and toward anger.

Apart from facial expressions, other behaviors are linked to emotions and can be used for emotion elicitation. For example, vocalizations, touch, and body posture can be used to this effect. Individuals are more likely to feel angry when speaking with a loud and harsh voice than when speaking with a low and soft voice (Hatfield, Hsee, Costello, Weisman, & Denney, 1995). Stroking a dog can reduce physiological signs of stress and induce positive affect (Handlin et al., 2011; Odendaal & Meintjes, 2003). Moreover, leaning forward can produce approach motivation, while leaning backward can produce avoidance motivation and thus make an approach (e.g., happy) and avoidance (e.g., fear) emotion more likely, respectively (Price & Harmon-Jones, 2011).

In terms of advantages, the behavioral approach boasts a low cognitive load and the potential to elicit a wide range of feeling states. Unlike many of the aforementioned techniques, it does not require stimulus analysis or event appraisal. Moreover, using seemingly similar demands (i.e., lean forward versus lean backward), different affect but also varied discrete emotions can be elicited.

In terms of disadvantages, the behavioral approach requires participants to follow behavioral instructions that may be too complex and difficult. Perhaps you have tried producing the facial actions described above? If you found this challenging, you are not alone. In fact, quite a number of people have difficulties with the Directed Facial Action Task, and this difficulty varies depending on what emotion is being examined (Boiten, 1996). Additionally, the exact role of behavioral responses for emotions is still unclear. As already noted by the opponents of William James, individuals incapable of movement can still feel emotions. Moreover, movements do not always elicit an emotion. Some individuals when asked to adjust their facial expression, voice, or posture remain emotionally unaffected (Laird & Strout, 2007).

Electrical Brain Stimulation

A last method of emotion elicitation that shall be mentioned here is the stimulation of brain tissue, a method that grew out of the discovery that muscles contract when electrically stimulated. This discovery raised the question of how the brain would respond if electrically stimulated and led inquisitive scientists to search for an answer in living nonhuman animals. To this end, they inserted electrodes into brain tissue and, after the animal recovered from the operation, observed stimulation effects on the animal's behavior.

The first to successfully apply this technique in the context of emotions was the psychologist James Olds (1956, 1958). After inserting electrodes into the brain of a rat, he moved his subject into a test chamber and electrically stimulated the implanted electrode only if the rat entered a particular corner of that chamber. After several attempts, he found a brain region that, when electrically stimulated, influenced the rat's space preference. Specifically, the rat would prefer staying in the corner in which it received an electrical stimulation. Based on this and subsequent work, Olds and others described a **pleasure center** in the brain that ultimately facilitated the discovery of the dopamine system and our understanding of positive states such as sexual pleasure or joy (Figure 5.6).

FIGURE 5.6   Emotion Induction Through Electrical Brain Stimulation

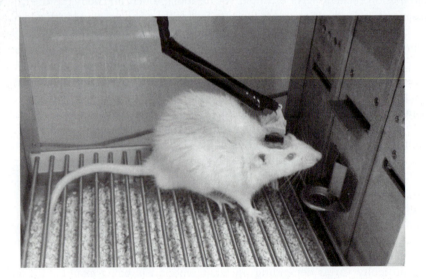

Whether or not electrical brain stimulation elicits positive emotions can be explored by placing a rat in an operant chamber and stimulating an implanted electrode when the rat presses the lever. If the stimulation was pleasant, the rat will soon learn to press the lever deliberately to gain the reward.

More recently, the idea of brain stimulation has been combined with insights from optics, genetics, and bioengineering (Deisseroth et al., 2006). The result of this is a new method called optogenetics, which uses light to modulate activity in brain tissue (Figure 5.7). In short, target neurons in a model organism such as a mouse are genetically modified to include light-sensitive components such as ion channels. By shining light on these neurons, its new light-sensitive components can be activated and, depending on their role within the neuron, may enhance or reduce the probability of an action potential. Thus, like electrical brain stimulation, a light shining on optogenetically modified brain structures can trigger or inhibit an emotion. Compared with electrical brain stimulation, however, the precision of optogenetics is much greater, as is its utility for stimulating specific neuronal populations or networks (Ciocchi et al., 2010; Liu et al., 2012).

Although optogenetics holds a lot of promise for the future of emotion research, it is largely limited to use in nonhu-

FIGURE 5.7   Fiber-optic Cable Sending Light Into a Mouse's Brain

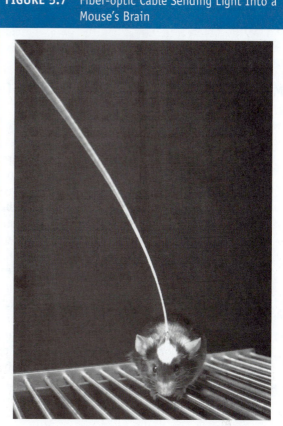

Light projected via a fiber-optic cable may cause a transient disruption or activation of brain function in localized areas and signaling pathways.

Source: Courtesy of Karl Deisseroth, professor of bioengineering and of psychiatry and behavioral sciences at Stanford University, and a key figure in the development of optogenetics. Deisseroth lab.

man animals. Moreover, optogenetics and electrical brain stimulation are highly invasive techniques that, in the context of humans, require a clear medical indication. Such indication may be given when patients undergo brain surgery and surgeons have to probe the function of tissue targeted for an operation. Alternatively, it may be given when patients suffer from psychiatric or neurological symptoms that are otherwise nontreatable, and for which the targeted stimulation/suppression of brain sites could offer relief (Ressler &

Mayberg, 2007; Vaca, Lüders, Basha, & Miller, 2011). If a medical indication is given, patients may be asked to volunteer in research, and if they agree to do so their reports are of great value.

EMOTION ELICITATION IN THE CONTEXT OF CURRENT EMOTION THEORIES

Current emotion theories discriminate between affects and emotions (Chapter 3). Affects are seen as fairly general or undifferentiated feelings of something being good or bad, whereas emotions are considered to be more specific feelings linked to a particular subset of events that are good (e.g., love, success) or bad (e.g., threat, disappointment). The elicitation methods introduced here have different specificity with respect to affects and emotions and thus are differently suited to study one or the other. This specificity, as well as other factors, need to be considered when planning an experiment or interpreting its results (Quigley, Lindquist, & Barrett, 2014).

Take the examples of negative affect and fear. If you were interested in negative affect, you would need to ensure that your elicitation method does not provoke a specific feeling state. To this end, you may choose a fairly general approach, such as leaning backward, over other approaches, such as forming a particular facial expression. Alternatively, you may present participants with mixed events that sample across a range of discrete negative emotions (e.g., fear, sadness, anger, disgust). Response measurements collected to these emotions could then be averaged with the hope that commonalities (e.g., negative affect) are retained and differences (e.g., conceptual knowledge) discarded. Both approaches have found application in existing work (Bradley & Lang, 1994; Price & Harmon-Jones, 2011).

If you were interested in studying fear, you would need to create a condition in which the events used for emotion elicitation are clearly linked to fear. Additionally, however, you would need to create a control condition in which you elicit one or more other negative emotions. This is necessary for you to dissociate commonalities and differences between fear and other negative states. Again, commonalities would point to shared negative affect, whereas differences would tell you what aspects of your experimental condition are unique to fear.

SUMMARY

The study of mental processes is very challenging. This is particularly true for the study of emotions, which are varied and complex phenomena that so far have eluded a universally accepted definition. Emotion research is further complicated by ethical and practical constraints concerning what can be done to research animals and human participants in a laboratory setting.

Nevertheless, to advance our understanding of emotions, ways have been devised to work within these constraints. They include the presentation of unconditioned stimuli such as food or mild pain, and conditioned stimuli that have been formerly associated with an unconditioned stimulus. For humans, examples of emotionally significant conditioned stimuli include money, grades, and weapons.

When researchers study emotions, they may do so by presenting unconditioned and conditioned stimuli in the form of images, sounds, or multisensory events such as films. They may also create them "online" through the use of deception and interpersonal inter-actions. These different approaches balance experimental control and ecological validity to varying degrees.

In addition to the presentation of isolated stimuli or the creation of actual emotional events, researchers may elicit emotions through other techniques. For example, they may ask participants to engage in the recall of emotional and neutral personal memories. The assumption is that emotional and neutral states are relived during recall and can thus be characterized and compared. Another technique involves tasks in which participants produce the motor actions that typically accompany an emotion. For example, participants may be asked to lean backward or pull their eyebrows up. Last, emotion elicitation may be achieved through manipulating the brain structures underlying a particular emotion. For example, electrical brain stimulation of areas supporting the representation of rewards may be used to elicit a positive state.

Which emotion elicitation technique is appropriate for a given study depends on a range of factors. One of these factors concerns whether affects or emotions are being investigated. Affects would require more general elicitation techniques, whereas emotions would require more specific elicitation techniques. Other factors include the study population (e.g., What can infants easily perceive?), the question that is being asked (e.g., Can an emotion be unconscious?), the way emotions are measured (e.g., Is my assessment technique time sensitive?), and economic considerations (e.g., How much time and money does this require?). Thus, careful planning and consideration are needed for a research project to become successful.

THINKING CRITICALLY ABOUT "ELICITING EMOTIONS"

1. What needs and emotions stay the same throughout an animal's lifetime, and what needs and emotions change? Why would these changes be important for emotion research?

2. One mode to elicit emotions is to ask participants to recall a previously experienced emotional event and a neutral control event. What memory characteristics would need to be controlled for or kept constant across the emotional and neutral memory condition? Try to come up with two appropriately controlled examples from your personal history.

3. Emotions can be induced through electrical brain stimulation. Is such stimulation a conditioned or an unconditioned emotion stimulus?

MEDIA LIBRARY

Basics of optogenetics: http://video.mit.edu/watch/optogenetics-controlling-the-brain-with-light-7659/

Emotion Stimuli from the Center for the Study of Emotion and Attention at the University of Florida: http://csea.phhp.ufl.edu/Media.html

Ethics Guidelines from the American Psychological Association: http://www.apa.org/science/leadership/care/guidelines.aspx

Ethics Guidelines from the World Medical Association: http://www.wma.net/en/30publications/10policies/b3

Ivan Pavlov's *Conditioned Reflexes:* http://books.google.com.sg/books?id = cknrYDqAClkC& printsec = frontcover&dq = ivan + pavlov&hl = en&sa = X&ei = BP4xT5ewJMrKrAfukP C6BA&redir_esc = y#v = onepage&q = ivan % 20pavlov&f = false

CHAPTER 6

Methodological Foundations II

Exploring Emotions

After successfully evoking an emotion in a human or nonhuman research subject, experimenters want to explore and characterize that emotion. In this chapter we will deal with the methods from which experimenters can choose to pursue their scientific goals. Moreover, we will detail the pros and cons of each method, provide insights into the kind of data that experimenters obtain, and critically examine the inferences that can be made.

The chapter is organized based on whether methods explore emotions by tapping on associated behaviors, peripheral nervous system activity, or brain function. Moreover, with respect to brain function, we will consider approaches that record brain processes as they unfold in time as well as approaches that explore how distortions of normal brain mechanisms (e.g., lesions, drug use) affect normal emotional responding.

BEHAVIORAL CORRELATES OF EMOTIONS

Because emotions evolved as a means to bias individuals to avoid danger and to seek stimuli and situations that increase chances of reproduction and survival, behavior can serve as a reliable and sensitive indicator for emotions. Thus, many paradigms and measurement techniques have been devised to assess behavior in the context of emotions.

The large majority of these techniques examine emotions implicitly in the sense that emotions are task-irrelevant. Nonhuman or human subjects are unaware that their behavioral responses inform the experimenter about what they feel. Unbeknownst to them, the experimenter may measure emotions in their gross behavioral responses (e.g., speed of running through an open maze), subtle changes in emotional expression (e.g., smiling while viewing neutral and emotional images), and response tendencies as expressed in traditional reaction time measures (e.g., recognition of emotional and neutral words).

In humans, these implicit techniques can be complemented by explicit techniques that presuppose some sort of emotional awareness in participants. In explicit techniques, emotions are, therefore, task-relevant. Emotional stimuli are the focus of attention and have to be evaluated based on a given emotion criterion. For example, participants may be shown facial expressions and asked to categorize them into basic emotion categories. Alternatively, they may be shown affective images and asked to rate each image on a valence or arousal dimension.

Implicit Explorations of Behavior

Implicit explorations of behavior form a substantial part of emotion research in both humans and nonhuman animals. In the following section, we will review a subset of techniques that received particular attention in the literature, including the assessment of gross behavioral responses to emotional events, more subtle nonverbal expressions, and psychological tasks in which response parameters (e.g., reaction times) are indicative of emotional processing.

Gross Behaviors

Gross behaviors are an obvious starting point from which to explore emotions. After all, emotions make us seek out the things that we like and avoid the things that we dislike. However, because emotions need to be sufficiently strong in order to affect gross behavior, studying gross behavior in the lab is a nontrivial matter. Moreover, it entails a number of ethical restrictions that make it more viable for research in nonhuman animals than for research in humans.

One exemplary class of gross behavior is that which reflects the tendency to approach. This behavior can be provoked by rewards (e.g., food, the presence of a bonded partner, electrical brain stimulation) and includes working for the reward by, for example, pressing a lever or crossing a maze. The effort directed at obtaining the reward can be quantified as lever-pressing frequency or maze-crossing speed and may serve as an indicator of the anticipated pleasure of consuming the reward (Chapter 7).

Gross behavioral responses may also be elicited in the context of negative or punishing events that threaten an individual's physical integrity or access to valuable resources (e.g., territory). Apart from running away, there exist other protective responses, such as the startle reflex and hiding, that better lend themselves to the laboratory, where subjects are spatially confined.

The **startle reflex** occurs in response to physical threats that announce themselves through sudden sensory changes such as an unexpected noise, a visual change, or a tactile stimulus (Landis & Hunt, 1939; Yeomans & Frankland, 1995). High-speed camera and targeted muscle recordings of this reflex in nonhuman and human animals revealed a wave of muscle actions that begins in the face and moves down through the body. During this wave, the eyes close, the mouth opens, and the body tenses in a forward-bent position (Figure 6.1).

In human research, the full startle reflex is rarely elicited. Instead, it is typically only approximated by stimuli that are just strong enough (e.g., a sudden loud noise) to trigger a facial component, the eyeblink. The eyeblink can be easily measured through eye-tracking or facial muscle recordings. Presumably, the function of this and the other startle components is to activate the body for action. Additionally, some speculate that the startle serves to reduce chances of injury (Yeomans & Frankland, 1995).

Hiding, another threat-related behavior, can be a passive or an active response. Often, hiding starts as a passive response, whereby individuals arrest in their movements for a short amount of time. Such arrests, called freezing, reduce the likelihood of attracting the attention of a potential predator and enable individuals to explore the threat. An initially passive response may be followed by an active response, whereby individuals move toward shelter. This occurs after they appraise, rightly or wrongly, that a threat is directed at them. For example, individuals may realize that a nearby predator is not simply passing by but is in pursuit of them, making escape necessary.

Both passive and active hiding can be studied in the lab. For example, researchers may study the duration of freezing after the presentation of a tone that was previously paired with an electric shock. Additionally, they may measure running speed toward a covered area after animals are released into an open field.

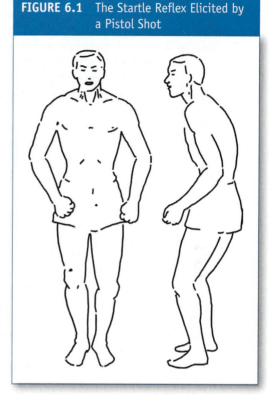

FIGURE 6.1 The Startle Reflex Elicited by a Pistol Shot

Source: Adapted from C. Landis and W. A. Hunt, *The Startle Pattern* (New York: Farrar & Rinehart, Inc., 1939).

Nonverbal Expression

Nonverbal expressions are closely linked to the gross behavioral responses discussed earlier. In fact, many nonverbal expressions prepare and accompany gross behavioral responses, making it difficult or impossible to clearly dissociate between the two. For example, in many animals physical fights are prepared for and accompanied by exposed teeth, an enlarged body frame, and tensed muscles—which are nonverbal expressions that help one individual intimidate or fend off another. However, because these nonverbal expressions are relatively subtle and may show in the absence of gross behaviors such as biting or scratching, they are often considered separately. For this reason, we consider them separately here as well.

A popular nonverbal expression in the context of human research results from the movements of facial muscles (Ekman & Rosenberg, 2005). Research has demonstrated that emotions can automatically trigger such movements, which then converge to a particular facial expression. For example, positive emotions may trigger a smile that involves the contraction of the orbicularis oculi (i.e., the muscle that surrounds the eyes) and the zygomaticus major (i.e., the muscle that retracts the mouth corners).

Using facial expressions to explore emotions requires researchers to somehow quantify the expressions. This is often done from videos recorded during emotion elicitation.

Using coding systems such as the Facial Action Coding System (Ekman & Friesen, 1978; Chapter 5), trained observers then identify individual muscle movements. Because these movements are sometimes very subtle, they are not always visible to the naked eye. In these instances researchers can use electrical recordings from the face or high-speed videos to assist with expression analysis.

Other nonverbal expressions include bodily gestures such as clenching one's fists in anger or moving forcefully and erratically (Pollick, Paterson, Bruderlin, & Sanford, 2001). In analogy to the Facial Action Coding System, some researchers developed a Body Action and Posture Coding System that can be used to classify individual bodily gestures and to make inferences about underlying emotions (Dael, Mortillaro, & Scherer, 2012).

Vocalizations can also be used to explore emotions. They depend on a range of facial muscular movements as well as breathing patterns that change as a function of emotion. In anger, for example, individuals tend to talk with a loud and relatively rough voice (Banse & Scherer, 1996). These characteristics can be quantified in speech recordings by measuring sound intensity or frequency parameters such as the energy distribution across the speech frequency bands.

Finally, humans and other animals express emotions chemically through pheromones contained in body fluids such as sweat or urine (Albrecht et al., 2011; Mathuru et al., 2012). Although the release of pheromones can, as yet, not be directly measured, pheromones can be collected and their potency to elicit emotions in conspecifics can be used as an exploratory tool.

An individual's ability to control nonverbal expressions depends on whether these expressions arise from autonomic or somatic nervous system activity (Chapter 4). Some expressions, such as the widening of the pupils, are triggered by the autonomic nervous system and are thus strictly involuntarily. Other expressions, however, arise from activity of the somatic nervous system that issues automatic as well as controlled responses. Thus, most facial, gestural, and vocal signals occur involuntarily; but they may also be produced, suppressed, or modulated by voluntary motor commands. Because of this, they are subject to large situational and individual variation. For example, in humans, they differ as a function of gender and culture (Chapters 13 and 14).

Unlike gross behaviors, which are studied mostly in the context of nonhuman emotions, nonverbal expressions are mostly studied in the context of human emotions. This, however, is beginning to change, as researchers recognize that many of the nonverbal expressions thought to be uniquely human are also present in nonhuman animals. For example, there are studies revealing facial expression in mice and dogs. In mice, such expressions were shown in response to pain (Langford et al., 2010); in dogs, they were shown in response to rewards and social isolation (Schirmer, Seow, & Penney, 2013). Moreover, the dogs' expressions actually resembled those of humans obtained under similar conditions (Figure 6.2).

Apart from facial expressions, there is evidence that humans share aspects of their vocal expressions with other species. Among other things, this evidence includes the fact that rats, when tickled, exhibit a vocal pattern resembling that of human laughter (Panksepp & Burgdorf, 2003). These and similar findings are important because they open new avenues for researchers to explore and compare emotions across species.

FIGURE 6.2 Facial Expressions Reveal Emotions in a Range of Species

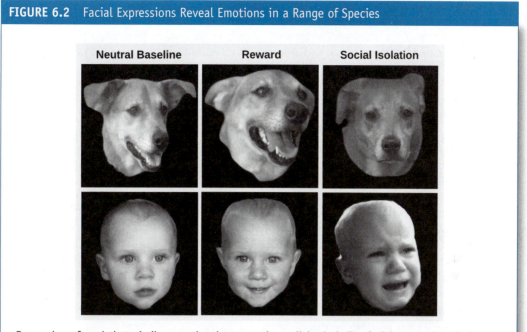

Researchers found that similar emotional provocations elicited similar facial expressions in human infants and dogs. Naive human adults could infer the emotions from the images irrespective of species.

Source: "Humans Process Dog and Human Facial Expressions in Similar Ways," by A. Schirmer, T. B. Penney, and C. S. Seow, 2013, *PLOS ONE, 8,* p. e74591.

Psychological Tasks

Finally, psychologists devised a range of behavioral tasks in which performance sheds light on emotions. Popular among these tasks are those that use the affective priming paradigm borrowed from cognitive psychology. In this paradigm, participants are presented with a leading stimulus called the prime, which is followed by an imperative stimulus called the target. Primes are typically task-irrelevant and may be presented both above and below the participants' threshold for awareness by modulating prime duration or intensity (Chapter 5). Targets are typically task-relevant in that they require participants to make some sort of judgment. Researchers then explore whether the speed and accuracy of these judgments depend on the affective relationship between target and prime.

A classic example of affective priming uses emotion words as primes and as targets (Fazio, Sanbonmatsu, Powell, & Kardes, 1986; Figure 6.3). Primes represent concepts one may evaluate as good or bad (e.g., flower, sunshine), and targets are positive or negative adjectives (e.g., appealing, repulsive). A positive prime may be followed by a positive or negative target. Likewise, a negative prime may be followed by a positive or negative target.

FIGURE 6.3 Affective Priming

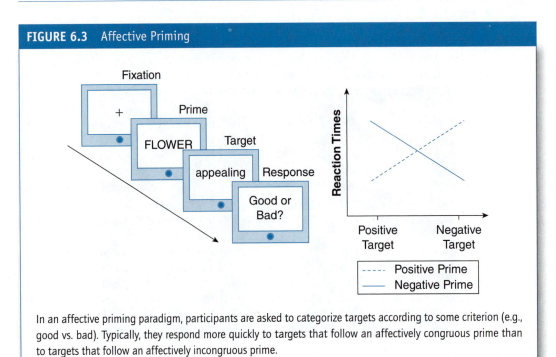

In an affective priming paradigm, participants are asked to categorize targets according to some criterion (e.g., good vs. bad). Typically, they respond more quickly to targets that follow an affectively congruous prime than to targets that follow an affectively incongruous prime.

Participants are required to categorize targets as "good" or "bad" as quickly and accurately as possible.

Response accuracy tends to be high and comparable across conditions. However, reaction times are significantly faster to targets that had an affectively congruous as compared to an affectively incongruous prime. Thus, reaction times implicitly inform about affective evaluations of the prime and suggest that our emotional responses are context-dependent. We seem to more readily admit those emotions that are congruous with preceding affective evaluations or emotional states.

Another popular emotion paradigm is the IAT, which stands for Implicit Association Test (Greenwald, McGhee, & Schwartz, 1998). This paradigm comprises elements of affective priming but is overall more complex. The IAT has different phases in which participants have to assign a given word to one of two target categories (Figure 6.4). In the first phase, words represent objects that one may evaluate as good or bad, pleasant or unpleasant. However, instead of evaluating them in this way, participants have to assign these words to one of two supraordinate categories. For example, words like *rose, bee, tulip, wasp,* and *horsefly* would have to be categorized as flowers or insects, respectively. Accordingly, participants may press the left button of a response box for words that name flowers and the right button for words that name insects.

In a second phase, words represent evaluative adjectives such as *lucky, hateful, despicable,* or *friendly* that now have to be classified as unpleasant or pleasant by pressing the left and right response button, respectively. In a third test phase, participants see words from both phases intermixed and have to categorize them according to the previously used categories. That means objects have to be categorized as flowers or insects, while adjectives have to be categorized as unpleasant or pleasant. The mapping of object and evaluation categories is arranged in accordance with the preceding two phases. So, in our example, flowers would be responded to with the same hand as unpleasant words and insects with the same hand as pleasant words. The third phase is followed by a fourth phase, in which the initial object categorization is reversed. Now, insects will be responded to with the left hand and flowers with the right hand. Last, participants will enter a final experimental phase in which they again receive objects intermixed with adjectives. This time the mapping of objects and adjectives is reversed from that in the third phase. Now, insects will be mapped with unpleasant and flowers with pleasant responses.

If you, like most people, were to implicitly evaluate flowers as pleasant and insects as unpleasant, you would find phases 3 and 5 of the IAT easier if the response hand mapping for objects and adjectives were affectively congruous as compared with incongruous. In our example, then, you would perform better in phase 5 than you would in phase 3. Thus, although insects are considered ecologically useful and this may bias explicit evaluations, such considerations play a subordinate role for implicit evaluations as tested with the IAT. Hence, the natural dislike we have for insects despite better knowledge comes to light (Curtis, Aunger, & Rabie, 2004; Greenwald et al., 1998).

Explicit Explorations of Behavior

While many of the implicit measures mentioned above can be used to assess emotions in both humans and nonhuman animals, explicit measures can be used in humans only. They refer to techniques that require participants to reflect about their past, current, or future emotions and to communicate their reflections to the experimenter.

A typical explicit measure involves affective or emotion judgments of target stimuli or events. In an affective judgment, participants may see pictures, as those used in the International Affective Picture System, and rate these pictures on a scale ranging from 1 (maximally negative) to 9 (maximally positive; Bradley & Lang, 1994). In an emotion judgment, they may categorize these pictures into different emotion categories such as joy, sadness, fear, or disgust and rate emotion intensity.

Affective and emotion judgments may also be applied to other stimuli such as sounds, tactile impressions, or smells. They can be very useful because they allow experimenters to relate self-reported emotions to other concurrent measures or independent variables. For example, affective judgments may be used as a continuous variable in the analysis of psychophysiological or brain measures, which will be introduced later. This would allow experimenters to identify the psychophysiological patterns or brain areas that are activated during specific affective or emotional states (Posner et al., 2009). Self-reported emotions may also be used to assess intra- and inter-individual differences. For example, differences in self-reported emotions between brain lesion patients and healthy controls can inform experimenters about the potential neural substrate of an emotion (Calder, Keane, Manes, Antoun, & Young, 2000).

FIGURE 6.4 Paradigm and Results of the Implicit Association Test

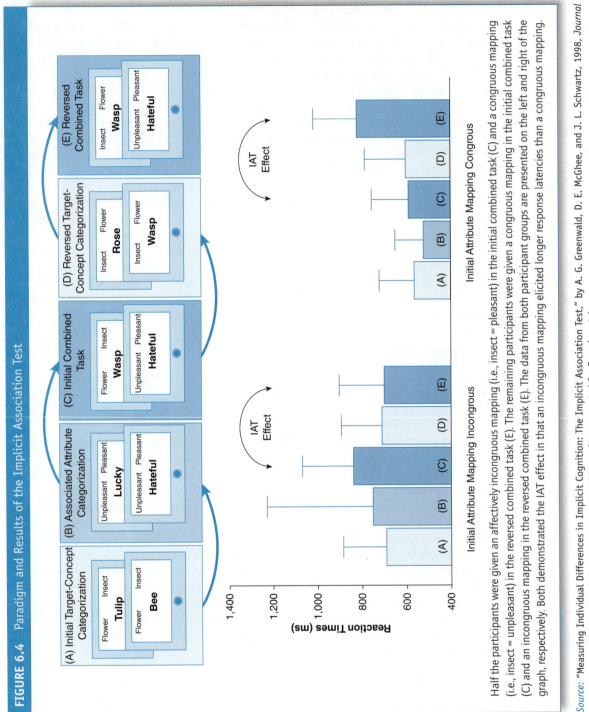

Source: "Measuring Individual Differences in Implicit Cognition: The Implicit Association Test," by A. G. Greenwald, D. E. McGhee, and J. L. Schwartz, 1998, *Journal of Personality and Social Psychology, 74,* pp. 1464–1480; results as reported for Experiment 1.

Half the participants were given an affectively incongruous mapping (i.e., insect = pleasant) in the initial combined task (C) and a congruous mapping (i.e., insect = unpleasant) in the reversed combined task (E). The remaining participants were given a congruous mapping in the initial combined task (C) and an incongruous mapping in the reversed combined task (E). The data from both participant groups are presented on the left and right of the graph, respectively. Both demonstrated the IAT effect in that an incongruous mapping elicited longer response latencies than a congruous mapping.

In addition to these simple judgments, researchers developed more elaborate instruments or emotion questionnaires. These instruments are typically employed to assess stimulus-unspecific states or to assess emotional experiences more holistically. Popular among these instruments is the Positive and Negative Affect Schedule (PANAS; Watson, Clark, & Tellegen, 1988). In its original form, this instrument comprises 10 positive affect words (*attentive, interested, alert, excited, enthusiastic, inspired, proud, determined, strong, active*) and 10 negative affect words (*hostile, irritable, scared, afraid, ashamed, guilty, nervous, jittery, upset, distressed*) for which participants have to rate on a 5-point scale how strongly each word applies to their own feelings in a specified time frame (e.g., right now). Their ratings are then summed up to derive separate scores for negative and positive affect. The original PANAS and its subsequently extended version PANAS-X (Watson & Clark, 1999), which includes emotion-specific scales, have found wide application. Also important have been instruments that measure one emotional state in detail. Examples here are the instruments developed by Charles Spielberger and colleagues that measure anxiety, depression, and anger (Spielberger & Reheiser, 2003).

Pros and Cons of Implicit and Explicit Exploration Techniques

Although there are many measures available to study emotions, not all measures are equally suited. Moreover, each measure has advantages and disadvantages that make it a better fit for one research project and a worse fit for another.

Implicit measures are advantageous because they enable the study of emotions in non-human research animals. There, they can serve as useful indicators for the effect of brain lesions, genetic mutations, or pharmacological treatments on emotion. Implicit measures are also useful for the study of human emotions. First, they enable research in preverbal infants and other populations for which verbal communication would be inappropriate. Second, they enable the investigation of emotion aspects that may be inaccessible to consciousness. For example, some feeling states may be too fleeting or subtle to evoke a conscious change in feeling. Yet these states might affect implicit measures such as facial expressions or reaction times. Implicit measures also reduce the potential of participants intentionally or unintentionally regulating their emotional response. Specifically in the context of negative emotions, human participants may downplay their feelings if these feelings are brought to their attention or made task-relevant. Finally, implicit measures do not presuppose that an emotional experience has a corresponding verbal label, and thus they enable researchers to explore such experiences without the categorical biases imposed by language.

One key disadvantage pitted against these many advantages arises from the fact that behaviors are the result of many processes—emotions being only one of them. Thus, behavioral changes between two conditions may or may not be due to emotion. For example, an animal's lever pressing for a food reward depends on a number of factors. One factor is a positive or appetitive state; other factors are learning, memory, motor abilities, or satiety. Thus, if an animal fails to work for food, it may be because of a change in affect. However, it may also be because of a change in learning, memory, or motor abilities, or simply because the animal feels full.

Explicit measures are advantageous because they can tap into an individual's subjective emotional experience. These experiences are believed to form an important part of human emotions and are, as of now, inaccessible to other measurement approaches. Additionally, explicit measures are easy and cheap to apply.

Disadvantages of explicit measures include the fact that many aspects or qualities of an emotion may not be accessible to consciousness or find no expression in verbal language (Roberson, Damjanovic, & Kikutani, 2010). Specifically, individuals may experience feelings that they are unaware of or that they cannot put into words. A second disadvantage is that explicit measures are often used to assess emotions retrospectively and thus depend on possibly inaccurate or patchy memory representations. Third, explicit measures are easily manipulated by the participants. Their beliefs about "normal" responses and concerns about social acceptability undoubtedly affect their reported emotions. Last, individuals differ in self-awareness, verbal aptitude, memory, and desires to conform, and these differences necessarily shape their self-reports. Thus, they introduce much variance and potentially create spurious inter-individual differences in emotion, which arise from inter-individual differences in nonemotional traits.

PERIPHERAL CORRELATES OF EMOTIONS

Emotion effects on behavior are intimately connected with emotion effects on body physiology. In fact, many of the behaviors described earlier depend on emotion-induced changes in the activity of major organs and the supply of bodily tissue with nutrients. These changes are regulated by the autonomic nervous system and the endocrine system. The autonomic nervous system can largely be divided into a parasympathetic and a sympathetic component (Chapter 4). Both components originate in the central nervous system, from where they project nerves to other parts in the body. Parasympathetic and sympathetic projections have complementary effects directed at the storage and expenditure of bodily energy, respectively. They involve effects on muscle tone, heart rate, blood pressure, and insulin production, among other things. The endocrine system represents a second mode of bodily regulation. It comprises glands such as the pituitary situated at the base of the brain, releasing hormones into the bloodstream. The binding of these hormones to target receptors can then influence tissue function. In the following section, we review some approaches to measure autonomic and endocrine peripheral activity.

Heart Rate

The heart is responsible for blood circulation and the body's provision with oxygen and other nutrients. Its rhythmic contractions vary as a function of emotional, motor, cognitive, and other bodily processes such as breathing. They result from action potentials that spread from the sinoatrial node to other parts of the heart and that generate voltage changes measurable on the skin with surface electrodes. Measuring the heart's electrical activity is also called doing an electrocardiogram (ECG). It reveals several types of voltage changes, the most prominent of which is the QRS complex representing the depolarization of the heart's ventricles (Figure 6.5). This complex is commonly used as an indicator of the speed or rate at which the heart contracts. Moreover, it forms the basis for two popular

FIGURE 6.5 Electrocardiogram

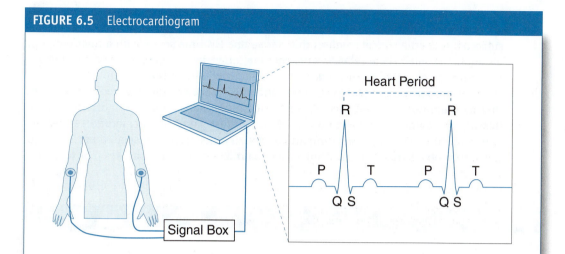

The electrocardiogram can be recorded by electrodes placed on a participant's left and right forearm (for clinical recordings, additional electrodes may be placed on the chest). The recordings are subjected to amplification, digitization, and filter mechanisms signified by the "signal box." The resulting data are illustrated on the right. They contain typical voltage changes that William Einthoven, a Dutch physiologist, labeled with the letters P, Q, R, S, and T.

heart-rate measures: heart-rate variability and event-related heart rate (Berntson et al., 2007).

Heart-rate variability (HRV) can be quantified as the range or variance of heart periods—that is, the periods between successive QRS complexes (Figure 6.5). Given the many factors that influence the heart, variability in the duration of heart periods is healthy and indicates flexibility in the heart's response to environmental challenges (Appelhans & Luecken, 2006; Thayer & Lane, 2009).

Experiments that use HRV as a dependent measure typically have a blocked design. Neutral and emotional conditions are presented for extended periods, respectively, allowing the accumulation of a sufficient number of heart periods. Subsequently, the range or variance in the duration of heart periods is compared across conditions. Research using this approach found that stress or threat reduces HRV (Elliot, Payen, Brisswalter, Cury, & Thayer, 2011) and that emotion regulation (e.g., reappraisal) helps the heart to maintain its flexibility by increasing HRV (Denson, Grisham, & Moulds, 2011).

Event-related heart rate (HR) measures examine the decrease or increase in heart periods in response to a target event relative to a pretarget baseline. Emotion research that examines event-related HR typically presents brief emotional and neutral stimuli in random order. The stimuli are spaced a few seconds apart to allow HR changes elicited by one stimulus to return to baseline before the onset of the next stimulus. Because the heart beats relatively slowly, an event or target stimulus would overlap with only one or maximally two heart periods. Thus, for analysis purposes, the HR data recorded to multiple targets are subjected to mathematical routines that derive one HR time series with a finer temporal resolution (Berntson et al., 2007). A typical time series derived in this way is illustrated in Figure 6.6. It comprises an initial deceleration followed by an acceleration.

Event properties modulate the amplitude of HR deceleration and acceleration, and this modulation provides insights into the functional significance of HR change. Research studying such change revealed that event-related HR deceleration arises primarily through increased parasympathetic activity (Berntson, Boysen, Bauer, & Torello, 1989; Palomba, Sarlo, Angrilli, Mini, & Stegagno, 2000). Brain processes that represent

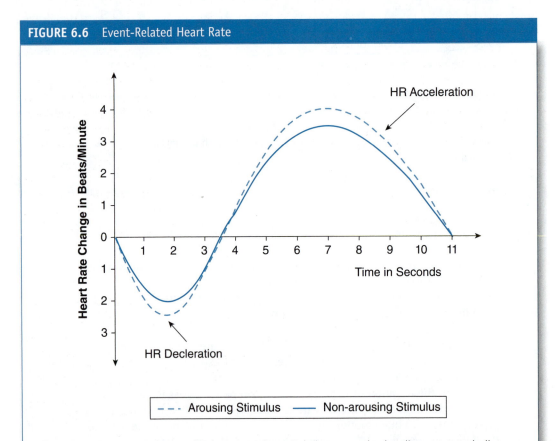

FIGURE 6.6   Event-Related Heart Rate

Event-related heart rate is expressed in beats per minute. Relative to a resting baseline, events typically cause an initial prolongation in heart period—and thus, a decelerating heart rate. This is often followed by a shortening of heart period and heart-rate acceleration. Research suggests that these event-related heart-rate changes are more pronounced for important stimuli such as emotionally arousing pictures or sounds than for more mundane, neutral stimuli.

the event activate the vagus nerve, a key parasympathetic nerve that carries axons from the brain to the heart as well as other organs. Outputs from this nerve then slow the heart down. Event-related HR acceleration has been linked to both parasympathetic and sympathetic mechanisms, which may reduce inhibitory and increase excitatory influences on the heart, respectively (Bradley, Codispoti, Cuthbert, & Lang, 2001; Thayer & Lane, 2009).

Early work on the mental processes underlying event-related HR changes suggested that stimulus registration and attentional orienting drive initial HR deceleration (Bradley et al., 2001; Lacey & Lacey, 1980). Moreover, it revealed that emotional stimuli, particularly if they are threatening, exaggerate deceleration as part of a more general freezing response (Berntson et al., 1989; Bradley et al., 2001; Harrison & Turpin, 2003). HR acceleration has been viewed as sign of resource mobilization directed at facilitating overt behaviors such as fight or flight (Bradley et al., 2001). Like the deceleration response, it is increased in the context of emotionally arousing as compared to neutral, unarousing events (Adenauer, Catani, Keil, Aichinger, & Neuner, 2010; Dellacherie, Roy, Hugueville, Peretz, & Samson, 2011; Harrison & Turpin, 2003; Lang, Greenwald, Bradley, & Hamm, 1993).

While subsequent work corroborated emotion effects on event-related HR changes, it raised some issues concerning existing functional interpretations. Specifically, evidence was found that challenged the role of HR deceleration in stimulus registration and attentional orienting. Such a role would imply that HR deceleration positively relates to stimulus memory. However, the relationship appears to be negative instead (Harrison & Turpin, 2003). Moreover, traditional functional interpretations of HR deceleration and acceleration imply a conscious awareness of the eliciting stimulus. However, research revealed that such conscious awareness is unnecessary. HR deceleration and acceleration have been found for stimuli that were masked or ignored (Lewis-Evans, de Waard, Jolij, & Brookhuis, 2012; Schirmer & Escoffier, 2010; but see Peira, Golkar, Ohman, Anders, & Wiens, 2012). Hence, the exact mental processes that trigger HR changes are still unclear and await further investigation.

Electrodermal Activity

The skin constitutes another popular psychophysiological target in emotion research (Dawson, Schell, & Filion, 2007). Among its many purposes, the skin is responsible for maintaining an appropriate body temperature and facilitating interactions with the environment. Eccrine sweat glands, seated in the skin, help with that. They are distributed across most of the body's surface, including the hands and the feet, and expel sweat via a duct to the skin's surface. While the primary function of eccrine glands is to promote cooling on hands and feet, they also assist in gripping by making the skin's surface a bit sticky. As such, their activity is tightly coupled to motor action and dependent on sympathetic innervation (Wallin, 1981).

Measurements of eccrine activity are typically accomplished via two electrodes placed on a participant's palm (Dawson et al., 2007). Such measurements can take the shape of a skin potential response, in which case researchers record changes in the electrical potential between the two electrodes. Alternatively, measurements of eccrine activity can take the shape of a skin resistance or skin conductance response, in which case the researchers run a small current across the two electrodes. If they keep the current constant the resultant measure will be skin resistance, whereas if they keep the voltage constant the resultant measure will be skin conductance. Across these measurements, electrical recordings are sensitive to sweat secretion. Increased sweating due to sympathetic arousal facilitates current flow across the skin.

After their initial discovery, electrodermal measures were soon brought into connection with changes in emotion (Neumann & Blanton, 1970). The psychoanalyst Carl Jung, for example, integrated them into his work on word association as an additional means to assess the emotional significance of words for his patients (Jung, 1907). In his hands and the hands of others, electrodermal measures revealed an increase in skin conductance following the encounter of emotional relative to neutral words (Jones & Wechsler, 1928; Osgood, 1952). Subsequent research, however, indicated that such increases are not emotion-specific. They were also observed in wakefulness relative to sleep, for intense relative to weak stimuli, or for novel relative to familiar events (Woodworth & Schlosberg, 1955). Thus, they seem to reflect a general increase in sympathetic arousal that may have emotional, circadian, or cognitive causation.

Apart from the peripheral measures mentioned above, many other measures have been developed and applied to emotion research. These include measures of pupil size, respiratory activity, muscle tension, blood pressure, and body temperature, among other things.

Initial attempts to link these measures to specific emotions such as anger or fear have failed. It quickly became apparent that individual measures provide only a very general estimate of an individual's alertness or arousal state. Thus, efforts were directed at examining multiple peripheral measures in conjunction and to relate the resulting peripheral profiles to particular emotions.

Some of these efforts seemed successful. For example, Ekman and colleagues showed that different emotions have different peripheral profiles. Among other things, they found that anger and fear have similar effects on heart rate and skin conductance but different effects on finger temperature (Ekman, Levenson, & Friesen, 1983; Levenson, Ekman, & Friesen, 1990). However, subsequent attempts to replicate these findings failed (Cacioppo et al., 1993). Therefore, researchers still debate whether peripheral activity serves as a specific or unspecific indicator of emotions.

BRAIN CORRELATES OF EMOTIONS

Over the past few decades, behavioral and peripheral research paradigms were increasingly complemented with methods that explore the brain basis for emotions. This development reflects an increasing appreciation that knowledge about the brain enables insights into the mind. Additionally, it arose from a number of technical developments that facilitated brain research and enabled the study of brain processes as they unfold in time. Some of the techniques that were of primary importance for advancing our understanding of emotions are detailed next.

Lesion Studies

Before the advent of modern neuroimaging, researchers largely relied on lesion studies to make inferences about brain function. To date, the lesion approach is still useful and as relevant as other brain-based approaches for our understanding of emotions. In humans,

A CLOSER LOOK 6.1

Lie Detection

Many a time in history, the conviction of a suspect depended on a verbal witness. Because such a witness is easily manipulated, different means were developed to tell truth from lie. Not that long ago, a prevalent approach in Western Europe was to burn or drown individuals to determine whether they were truthful when asked whether they were a witch. Suspects who died were believed innocent, whereas suspects who survived were believed guilty because they must have employed witchcraft to save themselves.

A somewhat more sensible approach in Asia was to ask suspects to chew rice for a while and then to spit the rice on a sacred leaf. Because it was observed that fear reduces salivation, the wetness of the chewed rice was taken as an indicator of the suspect's fear of discovery (Cannon, 1915).

Modern justice has further developed attempts to use physiological markers in lie detection. An example is the Control Question Test (CQT). This test takes peripheral measures such as electrodermal activity while a suspect is asked three types of yes/no questions—relevant questions, control questions, and neutral questions.

When used to identify a car thief, the question "Did you steal a car from the dealership?" would be an example of a relevant question, which directly addresses the crime. "Did you ever take something that did not belong to you?" would be an example of a control question. Like the relevant question, it focuses on misconduct but is presumably irrelevant to the crime. "Are you a wife and mother?" is an example of a neutral question, with no relationship to misconduct. Neutral questions are presented at the beginning of the investigation and as fillers in between relevant and control questions. Suspects are believed to be guilty if they show a greater increase in electrodermal activity to relevant as compared to control and neutral questions.

Rigorous tests of the CQT have challenged its validity (Patrick & Iacono, 1991). The expected peripheral patterns are theoretically unfounded and cannot be sufficiently replicated across guilty and innocent individuals.

To address these issues, psychologists developed an alternative test called the Guilty Knowledge Test (GKT) or the Concealed Information Test (CIT). In this test, the suspect is given multiple-choice questions that are followed by several alternatives, only one of which applies to the crime. For example, the suspect may be asked "Which color was the stolen car?" and presented with the options "Yellow," "Green," Red," "Blue," and "Black." An individual truly unfamiliar with the crime could be expected to show similar skin responses to the different color options. In contrast, an individual familiar with the crime might be expected to show increased skin conductance in response to the color of the stolen car, but not to any other color. Thus, if individuals are found to respond more strongly to crime-compatible as compared to incompatible information for a range of multiple-choice questions, they are believed to be guilty or knowledgeable of the crime.

Laboratory tests of the GKT/CIT indicate that it is better suited than the CQT to identify deception. Although GKT/CIT discrimination of deception from innocence comes to only ~80%, it boasts a rate of only ~4% false positives and thus has a relatively low probability of falsely implicating an individual in a crime (Ben-Shakhar & Elaad, 2003). Nevertheless, the GKT/CIT finds relatively little application in applied settings, where the simpler and less accurate CQT is still preferred.

FIGURE 6.7 Cabinet Portrait of Phineas Gage Holding the Tamping Iron That Injured Him

Source: Wikimedia Commons.

the lesion approach involves the investigation of behavioral, peripheral, and/or mental processes in individuals with brain damage. Some causes for such damage include cardiovascular incidents, tumors, or head trauma. In the past, the exact location of the damage could only be determined postmortem, thus often requiring a wait of several years before mental changes could be linked to specific brain regions. To date, neurological patients routinely undergo brain-imaging procedures that reveal the site of the damage.

The human lesion approach has enabled original insights into the brain basis for emotions. One famous example is the case of Phineas Gage, a railroad construction worker who injured himself with a tamping iron in 1848 (Harlow, 1868, 1993; Macmillan, 2000). An explosion propelled the iron through the front of his head, injuring a substantial part of his medial frontal lobe (Figure 6.7). While the injury left Gage's general health and cognitive abilities seemingly unaffected, his contemporaries noted a change in his personality. Responsible and orderly before the accident, Gage turned unpredictable and guided by spontaneous impulses rather than reflection. Thus, clinicians and scientists of the time concluded that the frontal regions, which were damaged in Gage's accident, control the "animalistic" aspects of the mind, including emotions (Harlow, 1868, 1993). More recently, alternative proposals emerged, claiming that these regions receive information about emotion-induced bodily states and use this information for decision making (Damasio, 1996).

Over the last century, individual case reports like Gage's were increasingly supplemented by group studies. In these studies, a number of patients with similar lesions were examined and compared to healthy controls or patients with lesions located elsewhere in the brain. This was advantageous because it reduced the impact of idiosyncrasies associated with an individual case and made observations more generalizable.

However, the group approach is not without problems. As it is relatively rare to meet neurological patients with exactly the same kind of damage, group studies almost always introduce noise that complicates inferences about the brain's role in behavioral, peripheral, and mental processes. Furthermore, like the case approach, the group approach is limited by the brain's plastic nature. In case of injury, functions originally subserved by damaged tissue may be taken over by intact tissue. Another limitation, particularly pertinent for emotion research, is that brain damage often produces a range of changes in a person's life that undoubtedly influence emotions. For example, many patients are forced out of their employment and become dependent on others for care. Thus, they lose part of their social network, financial security, and individual freedom—all of which may trigger emotional disorders such as anxiety or depression.

These and other issues can be better addressed by applying the lesion approach to nonhuman animals. Here, experimenters can produce circumscribed lesions in a group of animals while keeping everything else in the animals' environment constant. Moreover, lesions can be induced surgically, with minimal collateral damage, allowing for short recovery periods in which neuronal reorganization is unlikely. Additionally, researchers are now able to produce highly targeted lesions transiently and remotely, simply by exposing an animal's brain to light (Deisseroth et al., 2006). This is achieved through optogenetic manipulations (Chapter 5) that make targeted brain regions photosensitive so that they can be turned off and on in freely behaving animals. The drawback of this work, however, is that these animals have brains and possibly emotions that differ from those of humans. Therefore, it is uncertain what their results tell us about human emotions.

Techniques to Influence Brain Function

Another approach to study emotions is to dynamically influence brain function through pharmacological agents. Rather than producing a structurally targeted lesion, these agents alter the workings of specific types of neurons that may be widely distributed in the brain. For example, the application of morphine produces its analgesic effects by acting on neurons with µ-opiod receptors located in the spinal cord, brainstem, diencephalon, and cerebrum.

Drugs like morphine, which facilitate the action of a particular neurotransmitter system, are called agonists, whereas drugs that reduce the activity of a particular neurotransmitter system are called antagonists. Agonists and antagonists may act directly by binding to the receptor of a naturally occurring neurotransmitter and by mimicking or blocking its action, respectively. They may also act indirectly by affecting secondary mechanisms such as the breakdown of neurotransmitters in the synaptic cleft or the reuptake of neurotransmitters into the presynaptic neuron (Chapter 4).

Due to its invasive nature, and the fact that many drugs act for several hours to days, the pharmacological approach finds only limited application in human research. It is important in the context of clinical studies and the development of pharmacological treatments of emotional disorders. However, it plays a lesser role in the context of nonclinical studies. Here, researchers rely primarily on relatively benign pharmacological agents that have only minor effects on the central nervous system. Such agents include the hormone and neuropeptide oxytocin, which plays a role in regulating human social behavior, and over-the-counter pain killers that have been used in the study of sadness (Chapter 8).

While limited in the context of human research, the pharmacological approach plays a major role in nonhuman animal research. Clinical nonhuman animal research involves the development of so-called animal models for human disorders such as anxiety or depression. Animal models are established by exposing an animal to a certain environmental stressor (e.g., social isolation) or by manipulating its genes to produce behavioral or physiological symptoms that mirror the symptoms of a particular human disorder. If successful, the animal can then be used to test the healing and side effects of various pharmacological tools.

Pharmacological manipulations also represent an important mode of nonclinical animal research. They have advanced our understanding of the different neurotransmitter systems and chemical processes that underlie emotions. They are typically used in the context of specific behavioral paradigms that have formerly been linked to a target emotion. For example, paradigms that provoke startle or freezing in an animal can be used to test the effect of pharmacological agents on fear. Paradigms that provoke motivated behaviors toward a food or social reward (e.g., a mate) can be used to test the effect of pharmacological agents on joy or love. Moreover, through the application of agonists and antagonists, researchers can delineate the effect of individual neurotransmitters on facilitating and inhibiting these emotions.

Because the pharmacological approach finds only restricted application in humans and the results from nonhuman animals may not be fully generalizable, researchers have looked for other means to influence brain function. A method born of these efforts is called transcranial magnetic stimulation (TMS). It involves the generation of an electric current via a magnetic coil placed over the participant's head (Luber, Peterchev, Nguyen, Sporn, & Lisanby, 2007). The generated current affects the electrical properties of cortical tissue directly below the coil and thus its excitability. Moreover, by propagating depolarization or hyperpolarization of cortical neurons, TMS can temporarily increase the activity of a target region or induce a temporary functional lesion, respectively (Fitzgerald, Fountain, & Daskalakis, 2006).

Initially, TMS was applied primarily to the study of the motor system. However, recently researchers have begun to explore its usefulness in the study of other phenomena, including emotions. For example, they have measured muscle activity induced by stimulation of the primary motor cortex and found that this activity was greater when participants concurrently viewed emotional as compared to neutral pictures (van Loon, van den Wildenberg, van Stegeren, Hajcak, & Ridderinkhof, 2010). This provides evidence that emotional stimuli increase an individual's readiness for action.

Techniques to Assess Electrical Brain Activity

Neuronal activity depends on a range of electrical changes, including action potentials and postsynaptic potentials. While action potentials reflect neuronal firing that can be measured through intracranial recordings, postsynaptic potentials reflect changes in the probability of neuronal firing that can be measured through both intra- and extracranial recordings.

Intracranial recordings are done in nonhuman research animals and humans with clinical indication. For example, humans undergoing neurosurgery for pharmacologically intractable epilepsy are routinely subjected to intracranial recordings in an effort to better delineate the surgical target tissue. Because recordings are done over an extended period of time in which epileptogenic activity is measured, they are sometimes combined with short psychological experiments. Thus, albeit very limited, emotion research includes intracranial recordings from humans.

To obtain intracranial recordings, the skull is opened and individual electrodes or electrode grids are placed along the cortical surface or into subcortical structures such as the amygdala. Depending on the nature and placement of electrodes, researchers and clinicians can measure the firing of individual neurons or the summed postsynaptic electrical activity of neuronal populations. These two measurement modes are referred to as single-cell recordings and local field potential recordings, respectively. They help determine whether and how specific neurons or brain regions respond to emotional and neutral events and how these responses relate to ensuing behavior.

Extracranial recordings of neuronal activity are typically achieved by placing electrodes on an individual's head using a technique called electroencephalography (EEG; Figure 6.8A). While currents generated through the activity of individual neurons are too small to be measurable at the scalp, the summed postsynaptic activity of several thousands of neurons is not. However, to be measurable, the active neurons need to be aligned in parallel to one another, and they need to have a perpendicular orientation in relation to the recording electrode. Because these conditions are met by some (e.g., pyramidal neurons in certain layers of the cortex) but not other neuronal assemblies (e.g., subcortical structures such as the amygdala), the EEG records only a subset of neural processes. Specifically, it is sensitive primarily to cortical activity.

EEG research comprises a range of approaches and measurements. Some of them involve blocked designs in which experimenters explore oscillations in neuronal activity in different frequency bands. Such oscillations result from neurons synchronizing their activity along different temporal rhythms, some of which are very slow and others of which are very fast. Which it is depends on how "busy" these neurons are, and what demands they must tackle. For example, most neuronal oscillations have a relatively slow tempo/low frequency when physiological arousal is low and a relatively fast tempo/high frequency when physiological arousal is high. States such as deep sleep, relaxed wakefulness, or focused attention are associated with progressively faster oscillations expressed as greater oscillatory activity in higher-frequency bands (Figure 6.8B).

EEG research can also be done in the context of event-related designs, where stimuli of interest are presented in random order. These designs are often combined with the investigation of event-related potentials (ERPs). ERPs can be derived by averaging stimulus-locked EEG epochs. Such averaging reduces or eliminates random signal components while amplifying those that occur regularly for a particular stimulus class. The amplified components can be classified into those driven by primarily physical stimulus features such as intensity or brightness and those that depend largely on psychological stimulus features including goal relevance, contextual significance, or previous encounters with a stimulus. These components are referred to as exogenous and endogenous

FIGURE 6.8   Electroencephalography (EEG)

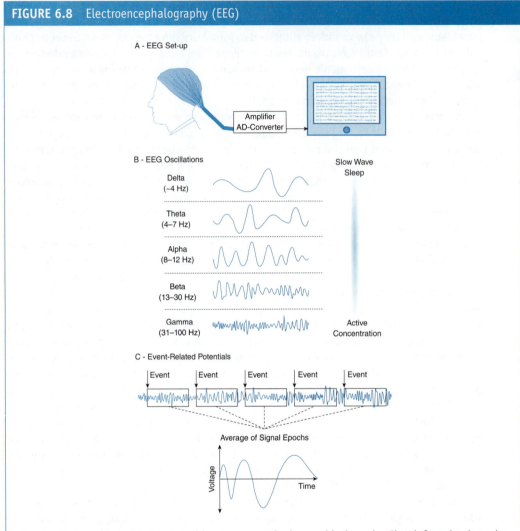

Panel A illustrates the EEG setup. A participant wears an elastic cap with electrodes. Signals from the electrodes are amplified, converted from analog to digital format, and sent to a computer for recording and analysis. Panel B illustrates typical voltage recordings from one scalp electrode within time windows of one second. The recordings differ with respect to prominent frequencies depending on the participant's mental state. Faster oscillations are more prominent during increased arousal and cognitive engagement. Panel C illustrates the averaging procedure underlying the event-related potential technique. EEG signal epochs associated with the presentation of a particular stimulus class are averaged. Through this averaging, signal content that is not time-locked to the event is removed. Signal content that is time-locked to the event is amplified. The resulting event-related potential is characterized by a series of positive and negative deflections. Early deflections occurring immediately after event onset are typically considered exogenous and linked to the processing of physical stimulus features (e.g., brightness). Later deflections occurring after 200 milliseconds following event onset are typically considered endogenous and linked to the processing of psychological stimulus features (e.g., goal relevance).

components, respectively, and contribute equally to our understanding of emotions (see Figure 6.8C).

Intra- and extracranial electrical recordings have different advantages and disadvantages. Intracranial recordings are useful because they allow the precise localization of neuronal activity and because they are less susceptible to movement artifacts. Hence, they can be used in small brains, such as those of rodents, and in freely behaving animals. However, researchers are relatively limited in the number of sites from which they can record and need to have a clear idea about the brain regions for which they expect experimental effects to occur.

Extracranial recordings have a comparatively lower spatial resolution than intracranial recordings. Due to volume conduction, scalp-recorded electrical potentials cannot be unequivocally localized. However, many channels can be recorded in parallel covering most of the brain's surface. Moreover, because electrodes are simply attached to the head, recordings can be done easily and without significant discomfort to the research animal or human participant. The development of wireless EEG systems further adds to the advantages of extracranial recordings by enabling research animals and participants to move freely and by reducing potential artifacts that hitherto arose from such movement.

Techniques to Assess Brain Metabolism

The brain processes underlying human thought and feeling are not only characterized by electrical changes, they are also characterized by metabolic changes that can be largely defined as chemical processes that sustain life. Metabolic changes include the provision of nutrients (e.g., oxygen, glucose) to active brain tissue via the bloodstream. They also include changes associated with brain activity itself (e.g., neurotransmitter binding to postsynaptic receptors) and the by-products of brain activity (e.g., neurotransmitter disposal through enzymes). Techniques that measure the availability of the chemicals affected by these changes thus provide insights into brain function. Specifically, by identifying regions with high brain metabolism as a function of emotion, they imply that these regions are "active" or involved in emotion.

One technique to study brain metabolism is called **positron emission tomography** (PET; Bailey, Townsend, Valk, & Maisey, 2005; Figure 6.9). It relies on radionuclides, which are atoms with an unstable nucleus. For the purpose of PET brain imaging, radionuclides are combined with chemicals that are functionally important in the brain. The combined substance, called a radiotracer, is injected into a person's bloodstream, from where it diffuses throughout the body and into the brain.

Given their unstable nature, the radionuclides of the injected tracer soon decay and emit positrons in the process (Figure 6.9B). Their time of decay varies across different radionuclides and ranges from several minutes to several hours. When positrons are emitted, they are attracted by oppositely charged, local electrons. Once a positron and electron collide, they annihilate and create two gamma ray photons that move away from each other in opposite directions and with the same speed. These photons are absorbed by a specially devised ring of detectors placed around the participant's head. The origin of photon generation and thus positron emission is inferred from photons that arrive more or less coincidentally at 180 degrees on the detector ring. Photons arriving with a larger delay or nondiagonally are ignored.

FIGURE 6.9   Positron Emission Tomography (PET)

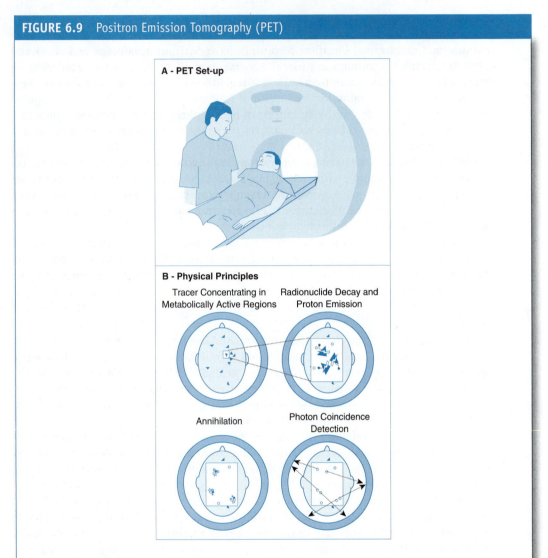

Panel A shows a PET scanner. The experimenter has injected a radiotracer into the participant's bloodstream and is positioning the participant's head inside the donut-shaped detector ring of the PET scanner. Panel B illustrates the physical principles underlying PET. The injected tracer, indicated by filled blue triangles, moves to metabolically active regions. Eventually, the radionuclides that are part of the tracer break down and emit positrons indicated by filled blue circles. Positrons are attracted by local electrons, indicated by open circles. Once a positron and an electron collide, they annihilate and produce two photons, indicated by open circles. The photons move away from each other at the same speed and in opposite directions. They are absorbed by the PET scanner. Photons that arrive more or less coincidentally and with 180 degrees at the detector ring are marked by arrows. They are used for data processing and image construction.

The nature or type of brain activity that can be inferred from PET imaging depends on the radiotracer that was used. For example, the metabolically relevant tracer fludeoxyglucose containing the radionuclide fluorine-18 will concentrate in regions with an increased demand for glucose. Thus, PET would reveal a greater rate of positron annihilation and photon generation in these regions than in metabolically less active regions.

Radiotracers that act like a neurotransmitter will attach or bind to relevant receptor types and thus provide a measure of how busy these receptors are. For example, radiotracers that bind to dopamine receptors will do so readily if there is a lack of endogenous dopamine such that dopamine receptors sit idle. Moreover, the radiotracer and the resultant photon generation would be well concentrated in dopaminergic structures if these structures are currently inactive. If, however, dopamine structures are active, photon generation would be less concentrated and more distributed across the brain. As such, it would fail to highlight dopaminergic structures.

Another technique used to measure brain metabolism is called **magnetic resonance imaging** (MRI; Huettel, Song, & McCarthy, 2009; Figure 6.10). It takes advantage of the magnetic properties of hydrogen protons—which are present, albeit to different degrees, in all bodily tissue. When left alone, the body axis of hydrogen protons has a random spatial orientation and serves as the center for the protons' rotational movement or spinning (Figure 6.10B, "Outside the Scanner"). Placing protons into the strong magnetic field of an MRI scanner causes them to orient like little compass needles (Figure 6.10B, "In the Scanner"). Most protons align their axis in parallel with the scanner's magnetic field, while a minority of protons assume a more energy costly, antiparallel orientation. In addition to changing their alignment, the protons begin a type of rotational movement called **precession**. Apart from rotating around their body axis, they now move so that their axis describes a cone oriented vertically to the scanner's magnetic field.

Once in this state, the protons can be excited into a more energy costly state whereby more of them align antiparallelly to the scanner's magnetic field and whereby they precess in phase synchrony rather than randomly. This excitement is achieved through the application of a short radio frequency pulse tuned to the protons' movement frequency (Figure 6.10B, "After RF-Pulse"). When the radio frequency pulse is turned off, the protons start to relax and will fall into their former, less energy costly state. In other words, most will revert to a parallel field orientation, and precession phases will desynchronize (Figure 6.10B, "After Relaxation").

Images of the brain and its metabolic activity can be derived after the protons were excited by the radio frequency pulse. When the frequency pulse is turned off, the energy supplied to the protons will be emitted and this process, called relaxation, is measured by the MRI scanner. Relaxation varies as a function of the protons' molecular environment. For example, relaxation is delayed when there is more oxygenated relative to de-oxygenated blood, yielding a stronger MRI signal. Thus, by comparing MRI signal strength, researchers can dissociate between brain regions with high as compared to low metabolic activity. This dissociation forms the basis for functional MRI (fMRI).

Although fMRI reflects blood oxygenation, it is typically used as an indirect measure of neuronal activity. This use is founded on correlations between intracranially recorded local field potentials or the EEG on one hand, and the fMRI's blood oxygen level dependent (BOLD)

FIGURE 6.10 Magnetic Resonance Imaging (MRI)

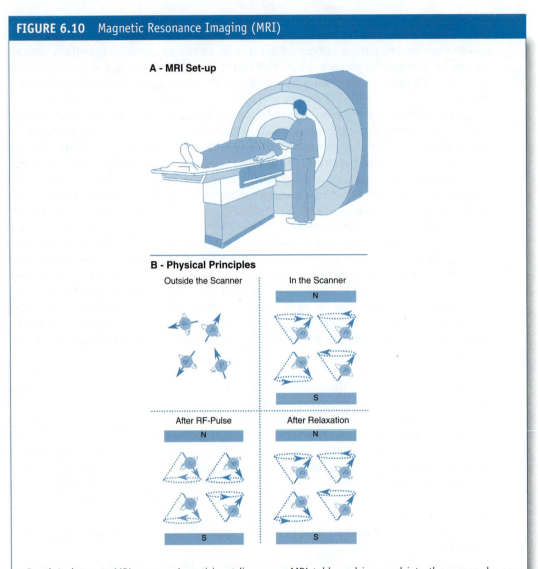

Panel A shows an MRI scanner. A participant lies on an MRI table and is moved into the scanner by an experimenter. Panel B illustrates the physical principles underlying MRI/fMRI. Magnetic resonance imaging depends on the activity of hydrogen protons in the body. Outside the MRI scanner, these protons are randomly oriented and spin around their axis. In the scanner, their body axis aligns parallelly or, in some cases, antiparallelly with the magnetic field and shows a movement called precession. The application of a radiofrequency (RF) pulse supplies the protons with energy. Now more will orient antiparallelly with the magnetic field. Moreover, the protons' precession temporarily synchronizes. When the frequency pulse is turned off, the protons relax into their former state. In the course of relaxation, the protons emit energy that is detected by the MRI scanner. Because energy emission differs as a function of tissue properties, it can be used to make inferences about brain structure and function.

response on the other hand (Conner, Ellmore, Pieters, DiSano, & Tandon, 2011; Logothetis, Pauls, Augath, Trinath, & Oeltermann, 2001; Scheeringa et al., 2011). However, as such correlations depend on tissue properties (Conner et al., 2011) and the nature of neural activity (Scheeringa et al., 2011), they are not consistently found. Therefore, fMRI research is blind to some mental processes that are visible with the electrical recording techniques mentioned earlier, and vice versa. Yet its noninvasive nature, high spatial resolution, and flexibility in the application of blocked and event-related designs have made fMRI a great favorite among today's emotion researchers.

Apart from the techniques mentioned here, there exist other techniques to image chemical substances and processes in the brain (e.g., optical imaging, mass spectrometry). Each technique has its advantages and disadvantages and thus is more or less appropriate for a given research question. PET enables the analysis of a wide range of brain chemicals and is thus particularly useful in the study of research questions related to neurotransmitters, neuropeptides, or enzymes. However, radiotracer decay rate greatly limits the temporal resolution of PET and necessitates the use of blocked designs. fMRI is more flexible in this regard. Yet it measures neuronal processes even more indirectly and creates a more constrained experimental environment. For example, the noise produced by the MRI scanner greatly restricts the utility of fMRI for auditory paradigms. Moreover, the strong magnetic field of the MRI scanner necessitates security measures that prevent the investigation of certain populations (e.g., individuals with metal implants) and the use of additional ferromagnetic equipment (e.g., non–fMRI compatible heart-rate monitor).

SUMMARY

Current means to measure emotions tap into behavioral, peripheral, and brain changes. Behavioral changes are assessed through gross behavioral responses (e.g., flight), nonverbal expressions, as well as response characteristics in psychological tasks. These assessments are considered implicit if the research participant is unaware that his or her emotions are monitored and does not intentionally express felt emotions. Behavioral measures also include verbal self-reports of emotions, which are necessarily explicit in nature.

Peripheral changes prepare and support behavioral changes. A range of measures have been devised for their assessment. These include measures of cardiac activity such as heart rate and heart-rate variability and electrodermal measures such as skin resistance, among other things. Together, peripheral measures inform about endocrine and autonomic engagement. Beyond this engagement, however, they provide as yet little insight into specific emotions or emotion categories.

Emotion-related changes in the body's periphery arise from brain processes. Traditionally, these processes were studied by examining individuals who suffered from brain damage. Now, this approach is complemented by a host of techniques that influence and monitor brain function. Methods that influence brain function include the application of pharmacological agents that excite (i.e., agonist) or inhibit (i.e., antagonist) the activity of a particular neurotransmitter system. The excitation or inhibition of particular brain regions can also be achieved through the application of a strong, focused, and rapidly changing magnetic field, as is done during transcranial magnetic stimulation (TMS). Methods that monitor brain function include electrical recording techniques such as single-cell recordings, local field potentials, and the scalp-recorded electroencephalogram (EEG). They also include techniques that measure brain metabolism such as positron emission tomography (PET) and functional magnetic resonance imaging (fMRI).

Of the many techniques available to study emotions, only a few could be covered here. Moreover, their coverage was necessarily superficial and did not include recent advances and developments to further improve and expand on existing techniques. Yet what was presented should provide a basic understanding of the ways in which emotions are typically studied. Moreover, it should highlight the importance of seeking and considering evidence from multiple methodological approaches when trying to understand emotion phenomena.

THINKING CRITICALLY ABOUT "EXPLORING EMOTIONS"

1. Emotions can be explored through implicit and explicit measures. Identify one research question that is more appropriately studied with implicit measures and one research question that is more appropriately studied with explicit measures.

2. What do brain measures add to emotion research that is not available from behavioral or peripheral measures?

3. After an experimental treatment, a research animal no longer shows overt fear behaviors such as freezing or running away. What could the researchers do to determine whether a loss of fear accounts for this change in behavior?

MEDIA LIBRARY

Facial muscles and their role in facial expressions can be explored using an interactive tool: http://www.artnatomia.net/uk/artnatomiaIng.html

Illustrations for the Facial Action Coding System: http://www.cs.cmu.edu/afs/cs/project/face/www/facs.htm

Jaak Panksepp demonstrating rat laughter: http://www.freesciencelectures.com/video/rats-laugh-when-you-tickle-them

Virtual physiology lab with demonstrations (e.g., see cardiovascular lab): http://www.medicine.mcgill.ca/physio/vlab/default.htm

PART 3

Emotions

[D]ifferent emotions should be studied as separate functional units.

—Joseph LeDoux (1998, p. 127)

The human mind is multifaceted. Different senses enable the exploration of different aspects of our environment and give rise to auditory, visual, somatosensory, olfactory, and gustatory impressions. Different cognitive faculties exist that enable a wide range of functions and that are mediated by dedicated brain systems. For example, aspects of spatial attention have been linked to the right parietal lobe, our ability to form long-term memories has been linked to the hippocampus, and our capacity for language and speech has been linked to areas in the left frontal and temporal cortex.

Like sensation and traditional cognitive functions, emotions are highly differentiated. Humans possess not one but multiple emotions, each of which fulfills a specific purpose and arises from a dedicated representation in body and mind. Thus, in order to understand their nature, emotions cannot be explored as a unitary phenomenon but have to be tackled individually.

The three chapters in this part of the book serve this purpose. They introduce the emotions of joy, sadness, and fear, which researchers relatively thoroughly investigated and often consider "basic" emotions. For each of them, there is a review of eliciting conditions or emotion triggers, followed by an account of the different feeling components including behavioral, mental, and bodily expressions. With respect to bodily expressions, both the peripheral and the central nervous system are explored. Additionally, the links between individual emotions and relevant mental disorders are examined, and regulatory strategies for extreme or dysfunctional emotional experiences are outlined.

CHAPTER 7

Joy and Positive Emotions

Unlike the study of negative emotions, the study of positive emotions was long marginalized by psychology. Initially, clinical psychologists were the only ones concerned with emotions, and their primary focus was on understanding and treating psychological disorders. As these disorders seemed linked almost exclusively to negative emotions such as fear, sadness, or anger, negative emotions took center stage.

This changed with the emergence of humanistic psychology, which sought to identify the means that enable individuals to achieve fulfillment, or self-actualization. Abraham Maslow (1943), one of the main theoretical drivers of humanistic psychology, proposed a hierarchy of needs. Within this hierarchy, Maslow considered the fulfillment of lower needs, such as satisfying one's hunger, to be a necessary precondition for the fulfillment of higher needs, such as making friends or achieving status. Moreover, he stressed the importance of understanding the positive forces that move individuals up the hierarchy of needs toward self-actualization (Figure 7.1).

Maslow's ideas fell on fertile ground both among his clinical colleagues and among psychologists from other domains. Two individuals who took his work further were Mihaly Csikszentmihalyi and Martin Seligman. Csikszentmihalyi (1988) developed the concept of flow, which he defined as a positive state of complete immersion in a rewarding activity or task. Seligman (1992) achieved fame through his work on learned helplessness (Chapter 8). Together, these two scientists initiated a broad movement called positive psychology that turned positive emotions into a key area of research (Seligman & Csikszentmihalyi, 2000).

Outside psychology, within the area of neuroscience, positive emotions were also initially neglected. The dominant view, which saw all emotions as mediated by a single neural system, limited emotion-specific inquiry and insights. Only after the psychologist Edward Thorndike introduced the notion of operant conditioning did positive emotions receive attention from neuroscience. Thorndike (1927) demonstrated that nonhuman animals repeat behaviors for which they have been rewarded, and he developed paradigms to study the underlying learning processes. These paradigms were readily adopted by neuroscientists who sought to understand the effect of brain stimulation and lesions on animals. In their hands, operant conditioning research generated valuable knowledge about reward mechanisms in the brain.

FIGURE 7.1 Hierarchy of Needs

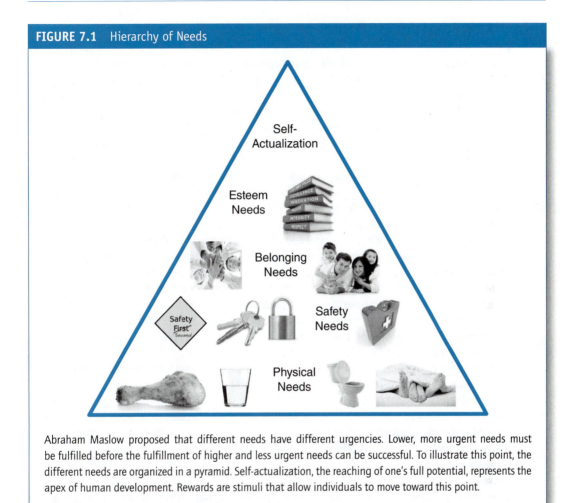

Abraham Maslow proposed that different needs have different urgencies. Lower, more urgent needs must be fulfilled before the fulfillment of higher and less urgent needs can be successful. To illustrate this point, the different needs are organized in a pyramid. Self-actualization, the reaching of one's full potential, represents the apex of human development. Rewards are stimuli that allow individuals to move toward this point.

Sources: © iStockphoto.com/Warchi (books); © iStockphoto.com/mediaphotos (group holding hands); © Andres Rodriguez—Fotolia.com (family); Composite of © Neyro—Fotolia.com and © marslander—Fotolia.com (keys and padlock); © iStockphoto.com/klenger (first-aid box); © Givaga—Fotolia.com (chicken leg); © iStockphoto.com/Pgiam (water glass); © iStockphoto.com/Rouzes (toilet); © iStockphoto.com/jaroon (couple in bed).

More recently, positive emotions have attracted interest from fields outside psychology and neuroscience. For example, economics, which for a long time followed the dogma that human decisions are rational, began to appreciate the impact of emotions on decision processes (Kahneman, Slovic, & Tversky, 1982). Economists became particularly interested in positive emotions as driving forces of choice behavior. Thus, over the past couple of decades, the study of positive emotions has evolved from a largely ignored topic into a popular, multidisciplinary endeavor.

HOW MANY POSITIVE EMOTIONS ARE THERE?

Most languages comprise a wide range of terms denoting positive emotions. A few English terms are *joy, excitement, amusement, bliss, contentment, pride, love, pleasure,* and *lust.* Do these terms describe different emotions, or do they refer to a fundamentally similar, "happy" state? Existing emotion theories offer different answers to this question (Chapter 3).

Categorical or basic emotions theories, which conceptualize emotions as a set of qualitatively different physical and mental states, often recognize only a few as distinct positive emotions. For example, a primary positive emotion in the theory put forth by Jaak Panksepp is "seeking." According to Panksepp, seeking motivates exploration and play by promoting the anticipation of rewards (Alcaro & Panksepp, 2011; Siviy & Panksepp, 2011). Others, like Paul Ekman (1999), have postulated a few more positive states including excitement, amusement, contentment, pride in achievement, sensory pleasure, and satisfaction.

There is some evidence that positive states such as these could reflect qualitatively different emotions. For example, Shiota and colleagues identified different groups of facial action units for portrayals of awe, amusement, and pride (Shiota, Campos, & Keltner, 2003). Sauter and Scott (2007) found that speakers use different vocal patterns to express achievement, amusement, contentment, sensual pleasure, and relief. Nevertheless, whether these patterns are culturally universal is questionable (Sauter, Eisner, Ekman, & Scott, 2010). Moreover, whether they concur with other defining criteria for basic emotions still needs to be ascertained.

Dimensional accounts view emotions as instances in a multidimensional space. One of the dimensions in this space typically specifies valence and ranges from good to bad, pleasure to displeasure, or positive to negative. Various positive emotions emerge from a combination of this valence dimension, with other dimensions such as arousal and a possible contribution of cognitive mechanisms (Russell, 1980, 2003). For example, excitement may be conceptualized as intermediate in pleasure but high in arousal, whereas contentment may be conceptualized as high in pleasure and intermediate in arousal. Further differentiation of states that compare in valence and arousal (e.g., contentment and satisfaction) presumably involves higher-order mental operations that represent the cause, temporal trajectory, probability, and so forth of an emotional event. Thus, on one hand, dimensional accounts assume that all positive emotions are fundamentally similar with respect to the underlying affect. On the other hand, these accounts afford the possibility that multiple positive emotions can be differentiated based on their exact position in a multidimensional space and based on associated cognitions.

Appraisal theory also accepts the idea of multiple positive emotions. It considers emotions the result of multiple appraisal processes that, depending on appraisal outcomes, can produce a multitude of feelings. Because of its flexibility, appraisal theory poses few constraints on the upper limit of possible positive emotions and thus easily accommodates the various feeling states that were listed earlier. With the exception of being appraised as good, pleasurable, or positive, these feeling states may be quite different as regards other appraisal outcomes (e.g., novelty, normative significance). Moreover, some appraisal theories (e.g., Scherer, 2001) even imply a differentiation as regards an intrinsic pleasantness appraisal by proposing that not all positive emotions require intrinsic pleasantness. Instead, some positive emotions may arise from other appraisal values such as goal relevance. For example, flying on a plane may not be intrinsically pleasant, but it could still produce a positive emotion if the plane ride is necessary for reaching a holiday destination.

While most theoretical approaches converge on the notion that we feel more than one positive emotion, actual empirical work has largely been restricted to the study of what might be conceptualized as joy. In contrast, research on negative emotions has been less restrained and elucidated a number of states including fear, anger, sadness, and disgust. What accounts for this imbalance?

A likely explanation is that although we can differentiate a number of positive emotions, these emotions may be more similar and their number may not be as large as the number of negative emotions. In line with this, the English language (Averill, 1980) as well as existing emotion taxonomies (Ellsworth & Smith, 1988) identify fewer positive than negative emotions. Additionally, positive and negative emotional events differ in their significance for an individual's survival (Fredrickson, 1998). Overlooking the occasional positive event is undoubtedly unfortunate, but it is certainly less detrimental than ignoring a threat to one's life. Thus, some suggest that there was great evolutionary pressure on the development of different negative emotions that propagated threat-specific coping behaviors. In contrast, there was less pressure on the development of a comparable range of positive emotions.

WHAT TRIGGERS JOY?

Although several positive emotions may exist, in this chapter, we focus on only one of them—joy. There are several reasons for this focus.

First, much research explored joy-related states. In contrast, little effort has been made to investigate other positive emotions and to determine how these emotions compare or differ from one another. Second, aspects of what here is defined as joy are shared among other positive emotions. Thus, the following information is relevant not only to joy but extends to affectively related states. Last, the goal for this part of the book is to explore a few emotions in depth and to develop a feeling for the complexity of these emotions. Other positive emotions such as love, gratitude, or pride will be dealt with more superficially in later sections of the book, when we consider emotions in their wider context. For example, there is a discussion of love in the context of developmental issues such as maternal attachment and mate selection (Chapter 12).

For the present purpose, joy shall be defined as a state elicited by the unexpected prospect of a reward. What is meant by "unexpected prospect," and what is meant by "reward"? The phrase "unexpected prospect" expresses the idea that joy is maximal to rewards that are unanticipated and that it is their sudden anticipation rather than their consumption that is critical (Scherer, 2001). To appreciate this latter distinction, consider a dreary Saturday evening when you are alone at home with nothing interesting to while away your time. Suddenly, you receive a text message from a friend inviting you to a party. Undoubtedly, this invitation lifts your spirits, even though the party is still a couple of hours away. Moreover, the effect of this invitation is likely greater if the party is an unexpected event as opposed to a gathering that you join routinely every Saturday night.

The term "reward" used in the above definition refers to events or stimuli that satisfy an existing need. Accordingly, food is perceived as rewarding when you are hungry but not when you are satiated. Likewise, an excellent grade brings joy when such a grade is the exception rather than when it is the norm. Note that some theorists consider only the latter kind of reward to be relevant for joy. Specifically, sensory rewards associated with maintaining bodily homeostasis are sometimes thought to evoke an emotion called sensual pleasure rather than joy (Fredrickson, 1998; Seligman & Csikszentmihalyi, 2000). Moreover, many reserve the term *joy* for rewards that address needs further up in Maslow's pyramid—for example, needs associated with companionship, play (e.g., Fredrickson, 1998; Panksepp & Burgdorf, 2003), and achievement (e.g., Seligman & Csikszentmihalyi, 2000). For the purpose of this book, however, we ignore this discrimination and consider the prospect of sensual and nonsensual rewards as equally relevant for joy (A Closer Look 7.1). This is because they are often treated interchangeably in empirical work, and the results appear to justify this treatment.

A CLOSER LOOK 7.1

Humor: A Funny Reward?

Humor takes a prominent place among the things that bring us joy. Like other basic rewards such as food or companionship, it is an everyday necessity that we readily provide for others and that we readily receive in return. Humor finds expression in physical play and tickling, silly acts meant to entertain, or witty repartee and jokes.

Existing theoretical proposals as to what exactly makes something humorous agree in that it is an incongruity of ideas (Bekinschtein, Davis, Rodd, & Owen, 2011; Gervais & Wilson, 2005; Wyer & Collins, 1992). In the case of physical play, such incongruity may arise from the play's pretended and actual intent. The former is often intimidating, whereas the latter is always benign. In the case of silly acts, the incongruity lies between an individual's expressed and actual capabilities, whereas in the case of jokes, the incongruity lies at the semantic level. To appreciate the latter consider the following joke:

"Why did Cleopatra bathe in milk?

Because she could not find a cow tall enough to take a shower."

Clearly, the joke stretches what is semantically acceptable, because who would shower under a cow? Although the act is in principle possible, it is incongruous with our concept of what it means to take a shower. Yet such incongruity by itself is unlikely to account for why the joke is funny. Other incongruities, such as "She could not find a kangaroo tall enough to take a shower," would not be equally amusing. Thus, additional elements such as the possibility to solve or understand incongruity as well as its social and personal relevance are likely to play a role.

Despite giving the appearance of folly, humor serves a number of important functions. Its resultant positive affect enhances social ties, promotes skill development and learning, and confers a range of health benefits. Like other rewards, it has analgesic effects (Dunbar et al., 2012), reduces inflammation, and enhances cardiovascular functioning (Miller & Fry, 2009). Thus, it is often employed deliberately toward individuals suffering from pain or illness or in social settings that are tense, stressful, or potentially boring.

When considering the origins of human humor, many theorists suspect a long evolutionary history (Fredrickson, 1998; Gervais & Wilson, 2005; Panksepp & Burgdorf, 2003). The young of many species engage in rough-and-tumble play and thus show something akin to humor. Its further development in humans has been accounted for by the emergence of group living and a rising pressure for more than a couple of individuals to share in the fun. Because of this pressure, our primate ancestors likely became more sensitive toward the play overtures of others. Eventually, they were able to derive pleasure from such overtures alone as well as from the mere observation of physical play. This vicarious enjoyment may have been a stepping-stone toward the development of other forms of humor, including its abstract, linguistic variants.

Humor elicits amusement, which many consider to be an emotion distinct from joy or happiness (Ekman, 1999; Sauter & Scott, 2007). This distinction is partially justified by the fact that humor differs from other rewards in that it is decidedly social and in that it elicits laughter. Humans and other animals don't typically laugh about food, warmth, or shelter. But they do laugh about a silly playmate.

Nevertheless, there are ways in which humor compares to other rewards. For example, humor is only effective if it takes you by surprise. If you know the ending of a joke already, you won't laugh about it. Thus, the behavioral, mental, and bodily effects of amusement resemble those of other positive emotions; this suggests that, albeit nonidentical, these states are certainly very similar.

FEELING JOY—BEHAVIORAL TENDENCIES, MENTAL PROCESSES, AND BODILY CORRELATES

What we call feelings are complex sensations that result from a multitude of changes that, for convenience, are here categorized into behavioral tendencies, mental processes, and bodily correlates. Behavioral tendencies are emerging biases to behave in a particular way and are hence measurable through behavior. Mental processes are subjective feeling changes or changes in thinking patterns. They may occur consciously or unconsciously. Finally, bodily correlates are changes in the workings of the body and are commonly quantified by peripheral and central nervous system measures.

Although treated as separate categories here, behavioral, mental, and bodily changes overlap and depend on one another. Behavioral tendencies emerge from mental processes, which arise from bodily correlates. Moreover, there are also feedback connections in that behaviors affect mental processes, and together they affect body physiology. Thus, their separation should not be understood as implying a functional independence. It is a mere effort to present joyful feeling aspects in an accessible way.

Behavioral Tendencies

Like other emotions, joy promotes characteristic behavioral, mental, and bodily effects. Joy's behavioral effects can best be described as a bias to approach the eliciting stimulus. Thus, at a very basic level, joy promotes the pursuit and consumption of unconditioned positive stimuli such as food or mating opportunities, also known as primary rewards. Moreover, via association with conditioned stimuli (e.g., money), also known as secondary rewards, joy enables more complex behaviors such as working for a salary or gambling in a casino.

In the lab, the tendency to approach can be measured in numerous ways. In nonhuman animal studies, it is often operationalized as the speed with which a subject approaches or how hard it will work for a reward. For example, in a typical Skinner box used for operant conditioning, researchers may record the frequency with which a subject operates a lever that produces a food reward (Figure 7.2). In a maze, the researchers may measure how speedily an animal runs toward a previously rewarded location.

In human studies, measures of speed are also relevant. For example, human participants may be presented with joy-relevant and irrelevant stimuli and asked to respond to each stimulus by operating a lever. In different conditions, they would be instructed either to pull the lever toward them or to push it away. Stimuli that are joy relevant typically speed up the former and slow down the latter action relative to joy-irrelevant stimuli (Cacioppo, Priester, & Berntson, 1993; Chen & Bargh, 1999; Zhou et al., 2011).

Other behavioral effects of joy include changes in the individual's nonverbal expressions. Here, two signals stand out. The first signal, the smile, is a prominent facial expression (Figure 7.3). It can be produced involuntarily or voluntarily. Joyful smiles are typically produced involuntarily and, in humans, comprise two critical components—an activation of the zygomaticus major, which extends the mouth horizontally, and an activation of the

---

FIGURE 7.2   Paradigms to Study Reward-Directed Behaviors in Nonhuman Animals

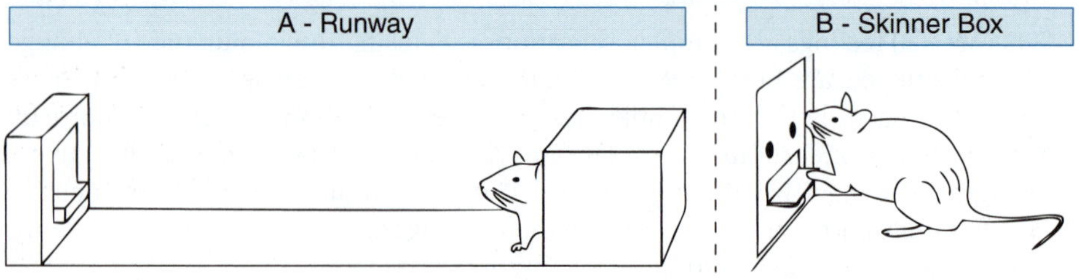

| A - Runway | B - Skinner Box |

Two typical reward-directed behaviors measured in nonhuman animal research are (A) running across an alley and (B) lever pressing in a Skinner box. Nonhuman animals run faster and show a higher frequency of lever pressing when these behaviors are followed by a reward than when they are not rewarded.

orbicularis occuli, which contracts the eye. Together, these components form what is called a Duchenne smile—named after Duchenne de Boulogne (1862), who first identified the facial muscles of joy. Voluntary smiles may involve the same components as involuntary smiles. However, more often than not, they are contained within the mouth region and fail to reach the eyes (Ekman, Davidson, & Friesen, 1990; but see Krumhuber & Manstead, 2009). As such, they serve as a social gesture rather than as a reflection of the sender's emotional state.

The human smile has parallels in other species, including nonhuman primates and canines. Nonhuman primates, such as chimpanzees, show a silent bared-teeth display, which is focused on the mouth region with only occasional involvement of the eyes (Parr, Waller, Vick, & Bard, 2007). It is displayed by individuals who initiate contact with others or who are subject to aggression from others. In these contexts, the silent bared-teeth display has been found to increase the likelihood of affiliation and to reduce the likelihood of aggression between interaction partners. Because of its instrumental character, the silent bared-teeth display is thought to be a signal of "benign intent" (Waller & Dunbar, 2005) rather than joy and to compare more closely to the human voluntary smile than to the Duchenne smile. Another primate expression, called the "play face," is seen primarily during playful encounters and seems a more likely candidate for the expression of joy (Waller & Dunbar, 2005). Morphologically, it is quite similar to the silent bared-teeth display, with the addition of a relaxed, open jaw.

Primates are not the only taxon that communicates emotions facially. Interestingly, canines, which are evolutionarily more distantly related to us than are nonhuman primates or even rodents, have facial expressions that parallel those described earlier (Bloom & Friedman, 2013; Fox, 1970; Schirmer, Seow, & Penney, 2013). They may show something called the submissive grin during interactions with an intimidating or seemingly threatening individual. As the name suggests, canines such as wolves, foxes, or dogs then give the appearance of grinning by retracting their mouth corners and exposing their teeth. Canines also show something called the play face. Like the homologous primate expression, it is enacted during playful encounters and involves both a retraction of the mouth corners and a relaxed, open jaw. Again, the latter expression is clearly more joy-relevant than the former (Figure 7.3).

The second nonverbal signal closely linked to experiences of joy is laughter. In humans, laughter involves the respiratory and vocal systems (Meyer, Baumann, Wildgruber, & Alter, 2007; Ross, Owren, & Zimmermann, 2009). It begins with a vocalized inhalation that is followed by a series of isochronous laugh bouts consisting of an aspiration (i.e., the release of air) and a vowel. Together, this typically sounds like *hahaha*. Humans can laugh voluntarily, for example, in an effort to follow social convention or involuntarily during playful physical encounters or when perceiving something as funny (Box 7.1).

Like the smile, human laughter has parallels in other species. It has been found in our closest relative, the chimpanzee. The observation of natural chimpanzee behavior allowed scientists such as Charles Darwin and Jane Goodall to discern a heavy guttural grunting and panting during joyful social interactions of a relatively physical nature including chasing, wrestling, and tickling. Subsequent acoustic investigation of these sounds revealed a range of not only similarities but also differences to human laughter (Ross et al., 2009).

FIGURE 7.3 Related Positive Facial Expressions in Three Mammalian Species

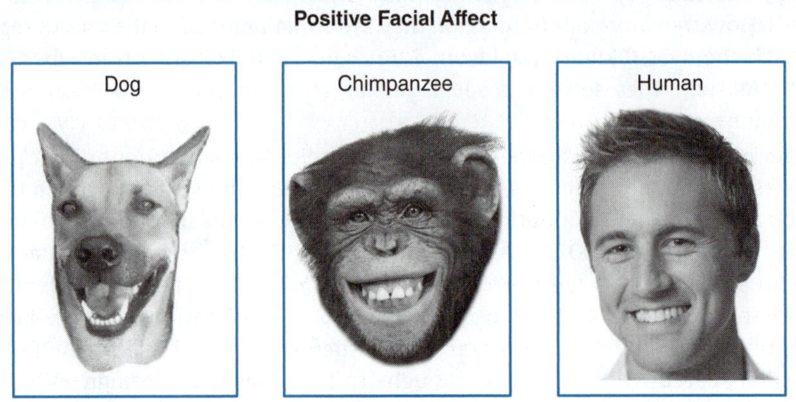

Positive Facial Affect

| Dog | Chimpanzee | Human |

From left to right, dog play face; chimpanzee silent bared-teeth display; and human smile.

Source: © iStockphoto.com/GlobalP (chimpanzee); © Photodisc/Thinkstock (human).

There also exist laughter-like expressions in canines. The ethologist Konrad Lorenz published a book called *Man Meets Dog* in which he described joyful interactions among dogs and between dogs and their human owners (Lorenz & Wilson, 2002). He observed that these interactions are typically accompanied by smile-like facial expressions and panting that is too heavy to be explained solely by physical exertion. Lorenz thus suggested that the facial expressions and panting have a laughter-like quality.

A last laughing species to be mentioned here is rats. Panksepp and his collaborators noted that rats produce a series of ultrasonic vocal bursts during rough-and-tumble play that are akin to human laughter (Burgdorf, Panksepp, & Moskal, 2011; Panksepp, 2007; Panksepp & Burgdorf, 2003). The vocal bursts are too high in frequency to be heard by the human ear, but can be made audible with special audio equipment. Following their initial discovery, Panksepp and colleagues further explored rat laughter and found that it could also be elicited by a human experimenter tickling a rat's belly. Rats that had been tickled this way would follow the experimenter's hand in the hope for more tickles while chirping happily.

Mental Processes

Joy is an altogether pleasant state that most of us wish to maximize during our lifetime. That is, we purposefully seek out activities from which we believe to derive joy. Apart from this positive feeling aspect, joy facilitates certain aspects of thought. Indeed, multiple lines of evidence point to the fact that joy enhances mental capacity and supports learning (Ashby, Isen, & Turken, 1999). Its effect on mental capacity seems to derive from a relaxation of mental focus and an increased readiness to explore and connect distantly related concepts or ideas.

Language research supporting this supposition shows that individuals generate unusual word associations (Isen, Johnson, Mertz, & Robinson, 1985) and process unusual language constructions more effortlessly when they are in an affectively positive as compared to a neutral state.

Exemplary for this is an event-related potential (ERP) study conducted by Federmeier and colleagues (Federmeier, Kirson, Moreno, & Kutas, 2001). These researchers gave their participants sentences like, "They wanted to make the hotel look more like a tropical resort. So, in the driveway they planted . . . ." In different conditions, the sentences were completed with an unexpected word such as *tulips* or an expected word such as *palms*. Typically, unexpected words elicit a more negative ERP than expected words around 400 milliseconds following word onset, indicating that processing effort is greater. Federmeier and colleagues found that this effect was reduced after participants viewed positive images, suggesting that the feelings induced by these images made it easier for participants to process unexpected words (Federmeier et al., 2001; Figure 7.4).

Further evidence for a mind-broadening effect of joy comes from research on creativity and problem solving. When asked to indicate whether certain items (e.g., bananas, apples) belong to a target category (e.g., fruits), individuals in an affectively positive state are more

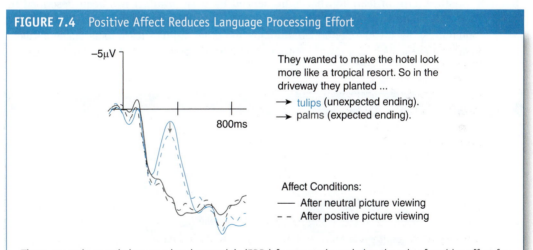

FIGURE 7.4 Positive Affect Reduces Language Processing Effort

They wanted to make the hotel look more like a tropical resort. So in the driveway they planted ...

→ tulips (unexpected ending).
→ palms (expected ending).

Affect Conditions:
—— After neutral picture viewing
– – After positive picture viewing

These are scalp-recorded event-related potentials (ERPs) from a study exploring the role of positive affect for language processing. The ERPs are time-locked to the onset of the target word at the end of the sentence. Compared to expected target words, unexpected target words elicited a greater negativity around 400 milliseconds following word onset. This effect was smaller after participants viewed positive images compared to a condition where they viewed neutral images.

Source: "Effects of Transient, Mild Mood States on Semantic Memory Organization and Use: An Event-Related Potential Investigation in Humans," by K. Federmeier & M. Kutas, in *Neuroscience Letters, 305,* pp. 149–152. Copyright 2001, with permission from Elsevier.

likely to extend category membership to include atypical items such as avocados (Isen & Daubman, 1984). They are also more likely to solve problems such as Duncker's (1945) candle task. In this task, participants are given a candle, matches, and a box of pins and are asked to attach the candle on a pin board in a way that prevents wax from dripping onto the floor. To solve this task, participants must overcome what is called "functional fixedness" and use the box that originally functioned as a pin container to hold the candle (Figure 7.5). Participants can do this more easily when they are in an affectively positive as compared to neutral state (Isen, Daubman, & Nowicki, 1987).

Last, and perhaps most important, joy has been shown to promote learning. During classical conditioning, humans and other animals learn to associate an unconditioned stimulus or primary reward (e.g., food) with a conditioned stimulus or secondary reward (e.g., tone; Pavlov & Anrep, 2003; Chapter 5). Developing such associations enables individuals to use secondary rewards as predictors or guides in their pursuit of primary rewards. On one hand, such guides enable spatial prediction about where primary rewards are located. For example, a certain vegetation may inform an animal where it makes sense to search for a particular type of fruit. On the other hand, secondary rewards enable temporal predictions concerning when in time it makes sense to expect a primary reward. For example, an individual may learn that a particular behavior in another individual indicates readiness for sexual intercourse and that sexual advances after this behavioral cue are likely to succeed.

Another form of learning that is influenced by positive affect has been described by Thorndike as the law of effect (Thorndike, 1927) and is now commonly known as operant conditioning. As already mentioned, humans and other animals learn to associate a salient emotional event such as a reward with an immediately preceding behavior. In a laboratory

---

FIGURE 7.5   Duncker's Candle Task

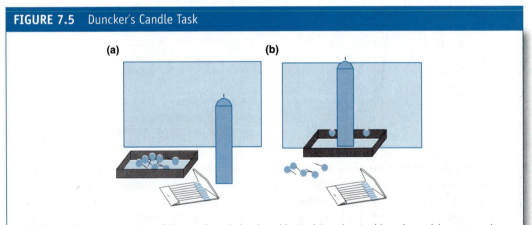

This figure illustrates a variant of the candle task developed by Karl Duncker. In this task, participants are given a container with pins, a candle, and matches and are asked to attach the candle to a nearby board so that wax won't drop on the floor. In order to solve this task, participants have to use the pin container as a candle holder. Participants do this more readily when they are in a positive as compared to a neutral or negative state.

setting this may go something like this. A hungry lab animal may explore its cage and in doing so accidentally push a lever. If a food pellet is delivered every time this happens, the animal will soon learn that lever pushing produces food and start to operate the lever intentionally.

Thus, actions with apparent positive consequences are more likely to be retained in memory and to be repeated subsequently than are actions without consequences. Through this, positive affect or joy facilitates the learning and execution of behaviors necessary for an animal to obtain the rewards that secure survival and reproduction.

Bodily Correlates

The following sections elucidate the bodily processes that underpin joyful emotions by exploring associated changes in the peripheral and central nervous system including effects on neurochemical messenger systems and brain structures.

Peripheral Correlates

Current opinions regarding the usefulness of peripheral responses as emotion indicators are divided. Some consider them to be relatively unspecific physiological activations and thus unsuited to provide much insight into emotions (Feldman-Barrett, 2006), whereas others believe them to be highly specific and informative (Ekman, Levenson, & Friesen, 1983). Although much research has been dedicated to settling this controversy, definite answers have remained elusive. Variation in emotion terminology and modes of emotion induction complicate comparisons between studies and obscure potential insights. On one hand, many studies use the term *happiness* to describe responses to positive pictures, films, or music even though the actual responses may be more differentiated and better described as *awe, amusement,* or *contentment.* On the other hand, the same or very similar states are often termed differently, such as *seeking, joy, happiness,* and *anticipatory enthusiasm* (Shiota, Neufeld, Yeung, Moser, & Perea, 2011). This makes it difficult to derive a holistic picture.

Despite these obstacles, however, some peripheral patterns appear to recur for a given emotion or emotion class across multiple studies (Kreibig, 2010). Here, we review these patterns for the class of emotions related to joy, considering both nonhuman and human evidence.

Nonhuman animal research inspired a dual systems model of behavioral activation and behavioral inhibition in response to rewards and threats, respectively (Gray, 1975). Linked to the behavioral activation system, rewards as well as opportunities of escape or relief from threat are believed to trigger behaviors that enable active pursuit. Experimental attempts to establish associated psychophysiological markers revealed some fairly specific changes (Fowles, 1980). Notable among them is an acceleration in heart rate, which occurs most consistently.

Research in humans corroborates this impression. Here, studies exploring responses to stimuli of joy or happiness revealed an increase in heart rate relative to neutral stimuli and relative to a resting baseline period (Kreibig, 2010). Moreover, this increase seemed linked to a decrease in vagal or parasympathetic innervation as it was accompanied by vasodilation, increased heart-rate variability and blood pressure, faster breathing, and elevated skin conductance. Thus, in line with the notion that rewards are generally activating (Fowles, 1980; Gray, 1975), these findings imply increased bodily arousal and action readiness.

Central Nervous System Correlates

Research on the brain's role in joy has elucidated relevant structures, neurochemicals, and mechanisms. These are described separately below.

Structures

The psychologist James Olds pioneered research into the structural basis of joy (Olds, 1956, 1958). He used Thorndike's operant conditioning approach as a means to assess the effect of electrical brain stimulation (EBS) on the development of place preferences. Specifically, Olds inserted an electrode into a rat's brain and, after the rat recovered from the operation, moved the rat into a testing chamber. In this chamber, Olds allowed the rat to move around freely and applied EBS any time the rat reached a particular corner. Otherwise, he withheld EBS.

After several such experiments, the placement and stimulation of one electrode successfully influenced the rat's behavior. Now, the rat stayed or returned to the corner that had previously produced EBS, suggesting that the rat found EBS rewarding. To probe this further, Olds placed the rat into a Skinner box and applied EBS any time the rat pressed a lever. The rat would press the lever up to 5,000 times per hour until too weak from exhaustion.

At the outset of his work, Olds roughly aimed his electrodes at parts of the Papez circuit (Chapter 2). After successfully conditioning rat behavior, he began to place his electrodes more carefully and to map out the areas for which stimulation was rewarding. Thus, Olds found brain structures for which EBS elicited operant responses depending on the animal's bodily states (e.g., hunger, testosterone; Olds, Allan, & Briese, 1971). Additionally, he identified a brain structure for which EBS elicited operant responses regardless of such states (except physical exhaustion; Olds, 1956, 1958). This latter structure is called the medial forebrain bundle, and connects the ventral tegmental area in the midbrain with the hypothalamus and the nucleus accumbens. The latter two structures are part of the forebrain, which is composed of diencephalon and cerebrum (Figure 7.6). Olds referred to the medial forebrain bundle as the "pleasure center" (A Closer Look 7.2).

Modern neuroimaging research in humans confirmed a role for the medial forebrain bundle in reward and joy. Moreover, it revealed reward-related activations in structures connected by this bundle (e.g., ventral tegmental area and nucleus accumbens) as well as neighboring structures such as the medial prefrontal cortex and the amygdala. The rewards that have been tested and found to excite one or more of these structures include, among other things, food (Grabenhorst, Rolls, & Bilderbeck, 2008; Rolls & McCabe, 2007), monetary gains (Breiter, Aharon, Kahneman, Dale, & Shizgal, 2001; Peters & Büchel, 2010), cartoons (Mobbs, Greicius, Abdel-Azim, Menon, & Reiss, 2003), pleasant images, music, and the recall of joyful memories (Phan, Wager, Taylor, & Liberzon, 2002).

The ventral striatum, which comprises the nucleus accumbens and forms the inferofrontal aspect of the basal ganglia, is the structure most consistently activated across this body of work. Interestingly, the ventral striatum is also involved in feelings of *Schadenfreude* (English translation, "malicious joy") elicited when we discover that an envied person or competitor has met misfortune (Takahashi et al., 2009). Thus, it seems that this part of the basal ganglia represents an important component of a brain system dedicated to the processing of a wide range of reward-related stimuli and resultant feelings of joy.

A CLOSER LOOK 7.2

Electrical Brain Stimulation in Humans

After Olds's discovery of a "pleasure center" in the brain of nonhuman animals, researchers and clinicians were naturally eager to explore the effect of EBS on humans. EBS promised to revolutionize the treatment of mental disorders, which, at the time, were subjected to lobotomy (Freeman & Watts, 1950) or left in the hands of psychotherapists.

One individual who attempted EBS in the context of human health care was Robert Heath (Bishop, Elder, & Heath, 1963). Heath inserted electrodes into the "pleasure center" of patients with depression and other mental disorders and allowed these patients to self-administer EBS. In line with Olds's reports, the patients found EBS rewarding and showed EBS-contingent mood improvements (Heath, John, & Fontana, 1976). Encouraged by these results, Heath also attempted to "cure" homosexuality by using EBS to reward heterosexual intercourse between a patient and a prostitute (Moan & Heath, 1972). Needless to say, Heath's proceedings met a lot of criticism. Apart from many ethical concerns, the highly addictive nature of EBS in the medial forebrain bundle made it inadequate for self-administration and long-term application. This and the emergent development of pharmaceutical treatment approaches led to a temporary suspension of clinical EBS.

Renewed interest in the use of EBS for human health care came with a better understanding of brain structures and their function. Today, EBS is successfully employed in the treatment of movement disorders such as Parkinson's disease (Fasano, Daniele, & Albanese, 2012). Here, an electrode regularly stimulates the subthalamic nucleus to facilitate movement initiation. The electrode is powered by a small battery implanted under the patient's collar bone. Through trial and error, researchers also identified long-term EBS treatment sites for other conditions, including epilepsy and depression. While initial results are promising, research is still ongoing to advance current treatments and to identify potential limitations and side effects (Massano & Garrett, 2012).

Neurochemicals

One prominent feature of the ventral striatum as well as other structures implicated in reward and joy is that they synthesize and/or use the neurotransmitter dopamine. Dopamine belongs to the monoamine and the catecholamine families (Chapter 4). Its precursor amino acids, phenylalanine and tyrosine, are available in various foods such as milk products, certain meats (e.g., chicken), or fruits (e.g., banana), and readily pass the blood-brain barrier for conversion to dopamine.

Initial evidence for a role of dopamine in the processing of rewards came from pharmacological studies. Some of these studies used drugs that block dopaminergic effects by attaching themselves to dopamine receptors. Thus, any dopamine released into the synapse was prevented from influencing the postsynaptic neuron. Comparisons between the effect of such dopamine blockage and a placebo treatment revealed a reduction in reward-directed behaviors. For example, rats previously trained to press a lever in return for an EBS

FIGURE 7.6 Brain Dopamine Pathways

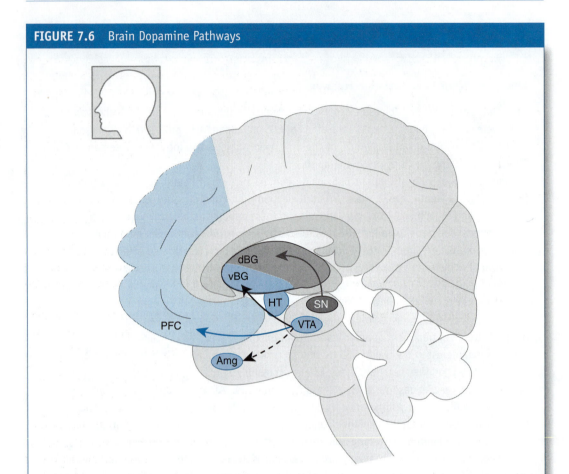

Neurons that produce the neurotransmitter dopamine are located in the substantia nigra and ventral tegmental area. The medial forebrain bundle, indicated by the solid black arrow, contains fiber connections between the ventral tegmental area, hypothalamus, and ventral striatum. It forms the "pleasure center," as discovered by James Olds, and overlaps with what has subsequently been defined as the mesolimbic dopaminergic pathway. In its present conceptualization, this pathway also includes the amygdala, marked by a dashed black arrow. The mesocortical pathway is indicated by a blue arrow leaving the ventral tegmental area and extending to the prefrontal cortex. The mesostriatal pathway is indicated by a gray arrow connecting substantia nigra with the dorsal basal ganglia. Amg = amygdala, dBG/vBG = dorsal/ventral basal ganglia, HT = hypothalamus, PFC = prefrontal cortex, SN = substantia nigra, VTA = ventral tegmental area.

reward eventually stopped working (Gallistel, Boytim, Gomita, & Klebanoff, 1982). Moreover, the decline in their conditioned behavior was comparable to that seen during (drug-free) extinction training, when lever pressing no longer produced EBS.

Importantly, there are studies showing that these effects of dopamine blockage are context- or behavior-specific and reflect an emotional rather than a motor retardation. For example, Gallistel and colleagues trained rats to perform two conditioned behaviors in two separate contexts (Gallistel et al., 1982). In one context, the rats received an EBS reward for lever pressing, whereas in the other context they received an EBS reward for crossing a runway. Rats then treated with a dopaminergic blocker and repeatedly tested for lever pressing showed the expected decline in reward-directed behavior. Eventually, they would stop pressing the lever. Notably, however, they initially recovered their reward-directed behavior when placed in the runway. Again, a few trials with the dopamine blocker were necessary to abolish the rats' conditioned efforts (Figure 7.7). This indicates that, during dopamine blockage, the rats learned that lever pressing was no longer rewarding. Moreover, they maintained the notion that crossing the runway leads to good things until they had the opportunity to realize the futility of their efforts. Studies that employed other rewards (e.g., sucrose solution) and paradigms confirmed these results (Wise, 2008).

In addition to laboratory work in research animals, clinical work in humans implied a role of dopamine in reward and joy. First, the dopamine blockers introduced earlier proved useful in the treatment of schizophrenia and bipolar disorder. Initially conceived as tranquilizers, they effectively reduce a patient's emotional excitability.

Second, there are converging insights from drug treatments that promote rather than hinder dopaminergic activity. In his famous book called *Awakenings,* the physician Oliver Sacks (2011) describes a first attempt to treat patients with Postencephalitic Parkinsonism with the dopamine precursor L-Dopa. Prior to the treatment, the patients had low mood and a number of motor problems typical for Parkinson's disease. During the treatment, both mood and motor problems improved dramatically. Moreover, the patients became more active, showed greater sexual interest, and found the world to be a better place.

Recent neuroimaging work complements these clinical reports. Using PET, researchers found increased dopamine release in the basal ganglia during a monetary incentive task as compared to a pre-task resting baseline (Peciña et al., 2013; Urban et al., 2012). Using EEG/ERPs and fMRI, researchers found a relationship between reward processing and genes that influence dopaminergic function.

For example, such a relationship was identified for the COMT gene, which enables the creation of an enzyme (i.e., catechol-O-methyltransferase protein) that inactivates dopamine in the synapse. Humans vary in a part of this gene that codes for the integration of two essential amino acids into the construction of the enzyme. Some individuals have two alleles for methionine (i.e., they are "Met-Met"), whereas others have one or two alleles for valine (i.e., they are "Met-Val" or "Val-Val").

Individuals who are homozygous for the methionine allele (i.e., "Met-Met") have reduced COMT enzyme synthesis as compared to individuals who are nonhomozygous for the methionine allele (i.e., "Met-Val") or who are homozygous for the valine allele (i.e., "Val-Val"). As a consequence, their dopamine remains in the synapse longer and is thus more likely to affect the postsynaptic neuron (Figure 7.8).

If, as previously suggested, dopamine is critical for reward processing, one would expect the "Met-Met" individuals to show enhanced reward sensitivity relative to the other groups. This is indeed the case (Dreher, Kohn, Kolachana, Weinberger, & Berman, 2009; Foti &

FIGURE 7.7 Dopamine Action Enables Feelings of Pleasure

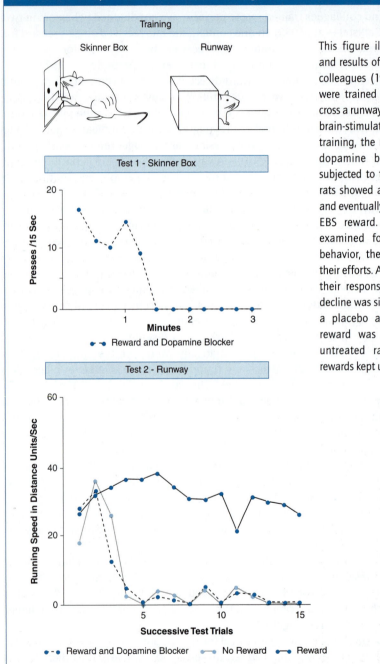

This figure illustrates the procedure and results of a study by Gallistel and colleagues (1982). In this study, rats were trained to press a lever and to cross a runway in return for an electrical brain-stimulation (EBS) reward. After training, the rats were treated with a dopamine blocker (pimozide) and subjected to two tests. During Test 1, rats showed a decline in performance and eventually stopped working for the EBS reward. During Test 2, when examined for a different operant behavior, the rats initially recovered their efforts. After a few trials, however, their responses again declined. This decline was similar to rats treated with a placebo and for which the EBS reward was withheld. A group of untreated rats still receiving EBS rewards kept up their operant behavior.

Source: "Does Pimozide Block the Reinforcing Effect of Brain Stimulation?" by C. R. Gallistel, M. Boytim, Y. Gomita, & L. Klebanoff, *Pharmacology, Biochemistry, & Behavior, 17,* pp. 769–781. Copyright 1982, adapted with permission from Elsevier.

Hajcak, 2012; Yacubian et al., 2007). Moreover, the brain areas with enhanced reward sensitivity in these individuals are the prefrontal cortex and ventral striatum and thus overlap with the brain's dopamine system and the structures previously identified for reward (Dreher et al., 2009; Yacubian et al., 2007).

Mechanisms

While the previously mentioned studies leave little doubt that dopamine and dopaminergic structures play a role in reward and joy, they do not specify what exactly that role might be. Their methodology typically implicates a range of processes, each of which may or may not be subject to the influence of dopamine. Specifically, for humans and nonhuman animals to enjoy a reward, three conditions have to be met. First, they have to positively appraise or *like* the reward. Second, they must desire or *want* the reward. Third, they need to know the conditions that produce the reward and thus must have previously *learned* its predicting stimuli and necessary actions (Berridge & Kringelbach, 2008).

Reward-directed behavior or brain responses to reward signals are reduced if any of these three conditions are unmet. For example, a rat may stop working a lever because it no longer likes the reward, because its motivation is too low to want the reward, or because its memory for the relationship between lever pushing and the reward was erased. Likewise, a human participant's joy over a monetary gain would be reduced if riches are no longer liked, if riches are not wanted, or if the stimulus used to signal monetary gain is no longer associated with an increase in wealth.

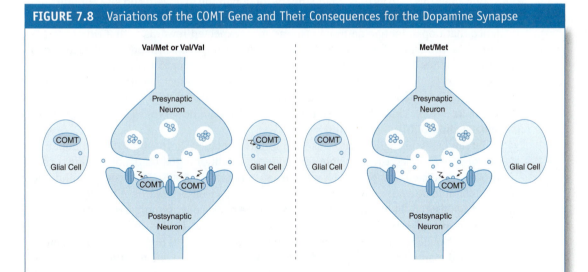

FIGURE 7.8 Variations of the COMT Gene and Their Consequences for the Dopamine Synapse

The gene coding for the enzyme catechol-O-methyltransferase (COMT) varies among individuals. Some individuals have two alleles for methionine (Met/Met), whereas others have one or two alleles for valine (Val/Met, Val/Val). The former individuals differ from the latter in that they produce less COMT and, as a consequence, have more synaptic dopamine (open circles) that can bind to post-synaptic receptors (blue ovals).

One approach to dissociate between these three components or processes has been to employ paradigms that temporarily separate reward predictors from actual rewards and to measure the temporal course of ongoing brain operations. This has been done in nonhuman primates that, prior to testing, had learned that an arbitrary stimulus (e.g., light) predicted a food reward (Mirenowicz & Schultz, 1996). During testing, these primates were presented with unannounced food rewards or the reward predictor (i.e., appetitively conditioned stimulus) while activity of midbrain dopaminergic neurons was recorded. Neuronal firing to the unannounced rewards and the reward predictor showed a phasic increase around 200 milliseconds following stimulus onset.

Further investigations into the emergence of this response during the course of conditioning revealed a response shift from the reward to the reward predictor (Schultz, 2010; Schultz, Dayan, & Montague, 1997). Thus, after conditioning established an expectation for a reward predictor to be followed by a reward, the predictor rather than the reward itself triggered dopamine release (Figure 7.9). Moreover, if the reward was unexpectedly withheld, dopaminergic activity was temporarily depressed (Romo & Schultz, 1990).

Together, these findings have been interpreted in the context of mathematical learning models that specify a reward prediction error (Glimcher, 2011; Waelti, Dickinson, & Schultz, 2001). According to these models and to the obtained electrophysiological data, dopamine neurons phasically increase their firing rate in the case of a positive reward prediction error—that is, when the individual encounters an unpredicted reward. In contrast, dopamine neurons phasically decrease their activity in the case of a negative reward prediction error—that is, when the individual finds that an expected reward did not materialize.

How does this help us understand the role of dopamine in reward and joy? For one thing, it lends support to a role of dopamine in "liking." Specifically, the abovementioned evidence that dopaminergic neurons respond to unexpected rewards with a firing increase and to the omission of an expected reward with a firing decrease suggests that they code affective value (Romo & Schultz, 1990). This is corroborated by evidence that many researchers find the dopamine prediction error effect to reflect reward magnitude and to be absent from or considerably weaker for aversive stimuli and their predictors (Mirenowicz & Schultz, 1996). Thus, it has been proposed that dopamine serves as the brain's pleasure signal (Schultz, 2010; Wise, 2008).

Yet not everyone agrees with this "liking" interpretation. Some argue that, if dopamine neurons were indeed responsible for "liking," conditioning should not diminish firing bursts to predicted rewards (Redgrave, Gurney, & Reynolds, 2008). After conditioning, such bursts should be evident for both reward predictors as well as rewards. A further argument raised against the "liking" interpretation is that the phasic dopaminergic response observed for unpredicted rewards and reward predictors was also identified for nonrewards. Specifically, unexpected neutral but perceptually salient events (e.g., door opening) elicit a burst in dopaminergic firing that fades away after a few event repetitions (Ljungberg, Apicella, & Schultz, 1992). This burst is maintained during classical conditioning, if the event reliably predicts an upcoming aversive stimulus such as an air-puff blown into the individual's face (Matsumoto & Hikosaka, 2009). It is also occasionally seen to unpredicted aversive stimuli (Matsumoto & Hikosaka, 2009). Thus, some argue that rather than signaling

FIGURE 7.9 Reward Prediction Error

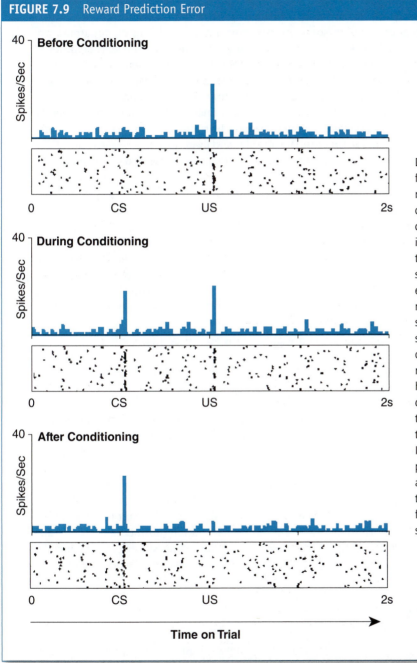

During reward conditioning, the firing pattern of dopaminergic neurons in the midbrain changes. At the beginning of conditioning, these neurons increase their firing rate weakly to the conditioned stimulus and strongly to the reward. At the end of conditioning, these neurons increase their firing rate strongly to the conditioned stimulus (CS) and no longer change their firing rate to the reward. This can be seen in the histograms at the top of each data graph. The histograms sum the action potentials for a given time bin across a number of trials. Individual action potentials are presented below the histogram as dots. Each line marks the time course of a trial ranging from 0 to 2 seconds following stimulus onset.

Source: "Dopamine Signaled Reward Predictions Generated by Competitive Excitation and Inhibition in a Spiking Neural Network Model," by P. Chorley and A. K. Seth, *Frontiers in Computational Neuroscience, 5,* 21; doi: 10.3389/fncom.2011.00021. Copyright 2011 by Chorley and Seth.

"liking" in particular, dopamine codes the presence of stimuli with behavioral relevance. In other words, its release reflects "wanting" (Berridge, Ho, Richard, & DiFeliceantonio, 2010).

To complicate matters further, some investigators found an effect of dopamine on "learning" (Redgrave et al., 2008). Animals undergoing avoidance training learned faster if their dopaminergic system was stimulated (Messier & White, 1984; Mondadori, Ornstein, Waser, & Huston, 1976). For example, animals trained to avoid a metal grid that shocked their feet would do so faster if they had received EBS immediately after having crossed the grid (Mondadori et al., 1976). In line with this, it is now known that dopamine modulates some of the molecular mechanisms thought to support learning. Dopamine promotes both long-term potentiation (Lisman, Grace, & Duzel, 2011) and long-term depression (Law-Tho, Desce, & Crepel, 1995)—two mechanisms that, respectively, increase and decrease neural signaling.

Taken together, existing work has implicated dopamine in "liking," "wanting," and "learning," and thus divided opinions as to dopamine's role in reward and joy. However, does dopamine have to serve only one of these functions, or could it possibly be more versatile? Several points speak for the latter possibility. First, apart from the phasic dopaminergic effects reported previously, there are tonic changes in dopaminergic firing that build up across a few seconds following a reward predictor. There is now evidence that these tonic changes reflect reward anticipation (Bromberg-Martin, Matsumoto, & Hikosaka, 2010a; Howe, Tierney, Sandberg, Phillips, & Graybiel, 2013) and thus could serve to differentiate between "liking," "wanting," and "learning."

Second, not all dopamine neurons are alike. As reported earlier, some neurons are excited by rewards only, whereas other neurons are excited by any stimulus that is behaviorally imperative. Thus, different neuronal populations may be dedicated to coding value or "liking" and behavioral urgency or "wanting" (Bromberg-Martin, Matsumoto, & Hikosaka, 2010b).

Third, the different dopamine neurons have different subcortical and cortical targets. Activation of these targets may further contribute to representations of "liking" and "wanting" as well as to learning processes. For example, much speaks for a role of the orbitofronal cortex in representing value (Berridge & Kringelbach, 2008).

Finally, the function of midbrain dopamine neurons is influenced by other, currently less explored structures such as the habenula. The habenula is a small nucleus situated below the thalamus. It projects to the midbrain and sends signals relevant for motivating behavior and could thus form part of a "wanting" representation (Bromberg-Martin et al., 2010b; Lee et al., 2010). Together, these facets of the dopamine system clearly enable multiple functions and support the possibility that dopamine serves all aspects of joy.

WHY DO WE FEEL JOY?

In Chapter 3, we defined emotions as the mental states elicited by events that are relevant for an individual's needs and that motivate behaviors to fulfill these needs. When applying this definition to joy, it is easy to see how rewards qualify as joy-eliciting events. After all, rewards are desired objects or sensations. Yet what behaviors do they motivate?

For one thing, individuals who behold a reward will be driven to secure and consume it. For example, a hungry rat will follow its nose to find and eat scraps of food in the garbage. Likewise, after separation, a pet dog will run toward its owner and solicit petting and play. Although both behaviors are quite different, they are each directed toward reward consumption and the satisfaction of an imminent need.

Exploratory behaviors are a second response to rewards (Alcaro & Panksepp, 2011; Fredrickson, 1998). Specifically, the joy experienced from rewards broadens the individual's mind and enhances playfulness and interest in novel places, objects, and actions. Far from being merely entertaining, these interests secure the individual's future survival. Because of them, a young bird may probe the surface of a water puddle and find it suitable for drinking and bathing. A cat may playfully chase up a tree and thus discover a nest with chicks. In these and similar instances, the urge to explore reveals life-sustaining resources as well as actions that bring these resources about.

Last, rewards and joy promote the storage of reward-related information in memory. As formally described by Pavlov in the last century, stimuli that are followed by a reward become associated with the reward. Animals learn to use such stimuli as guides to survey their environment and to plan reward-directed behaviors. Furthermore, Thorndike's work on operant conditioning revealed that animals repeat behaviors that were previously rewarded. Thus, a young bird retains the information that reflecting surfaces can be a source of water and will seek them out in the future. Likewise, a cat, after having harvested its first bird nest in a tree, will climb other trees when hungry thereafter. By enabling such learning, joy expands an animal's mental and behavioral repertoire and increases its probability of success in the pursuit of future rewards (Figure 7.10).

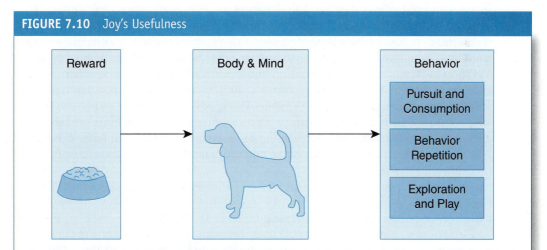

FIGURE 7.10 Joy's Usefulness

Emotions have a range of effects on the individual's body and mind. Together, these effects increase the likelihood of certain behaviors over others. In the case of joy, the behaviors that increase in likelihood are the pursuit and consumption of an identified reward, the repetition of successful behaviors, and exploration and play.

In sum, joy triggers a wide range of behaviors that secure immediate rewards and that maximize the chances of prospective rewards. Because there are many types of rewards, each requiring a different mode of pursuit and consumption, reward-related behaviors are necessarily diverse. The exploratory drive following joyful experiences as well as the reinforcement learning further contribute to this diversity. While some lament this and suggest that joy's behavioral impact is rather unspecific and perhaps too flexible (Lazarus, 1994), the work described here highlights behavioral diversity as an important feature of joy—a feature without which we would be ill-equipped to find and cherish the things we need (Fredrickson, 1998).

CAN FEELING GOOD BE BAD?

Joyful states are pleasurable and promote a range of positive cognitions and behaviors. Additionally, they confer a number of health benefits. Among other things, joy counteracts pain through activation of the dopaminergic and the endogenous opioid systems (Becker, Gandhi, & Schweinhardt, 2012). It has also been linked to improved cardiovascular function and resilience to infection (Steptoe, Dockray, & Wardle, 2009). Thus, it seems only reasonable that joy should be a forceful motivator that is frequently conceived as life's main purpose (Freud & Gay, 1989). Yet would continual joy be advantageous?

The answer to this question is a certain "no." For one thing, joy signals that our needs are met. If we were continually joyful, we would become insensitive to the needs that must necessarily arise from changes in our body or dangers in the environment. We would be like an EBS lab rat that in the face of pleasure forgoes all life-sustaining impulses to eventually break down and die. Furthermore, a number of clinical reports suggest that increased dopaminergic transmission compromises rather than enhances an individual's mental and physical state and could potentially cause disorder. Foremost among the disorders discussed in this context is addiction—a chronically relapsing condition that is characterized by compulsive reward consumption and a negative affective tone when rewards are unavailable (Koob, 2009).

Different factors related to the reward and the individual influence whether and how easily an addiction develops. Critical reward-related factors include the potency to promote dopaminergic action in the synapse (Volkow, Wang, Fowler, Tomasi, & Telang, 2011). Most addictive drugs such as cocaine directly or indirectly increase dopamine availability by exciting dopamine release or by preventing its re-uptake or breakdown (Wise & Kiyatkin, 2011). The greater the potency of a drug or other stimulus to increase dopaminergic action, the more addictive is its effect.

Another reward-specific factor is the speed of affected neurochemical changes (Wise & Kiyatkin, 2011). Humans and other animals prefer immediate over delayed rewards, even if the former are smaller than the latter (Figure 7.11). This form of temporal discounting is also seen during conditioning where the delay between a stimulus or action and its associated reward determines conditioning success (Kobayashi & Schultz, 2008). Fast rewards like EBS or cocaine produce faster and stronger conditioning and are hence more addictive than slow rewards such as a good grade or a friend's visit. However, as all rewards ultimately excite the dopamine system, they are all potentially addictive. This is evident from

FIGURE 7.11 Temporal Discounting

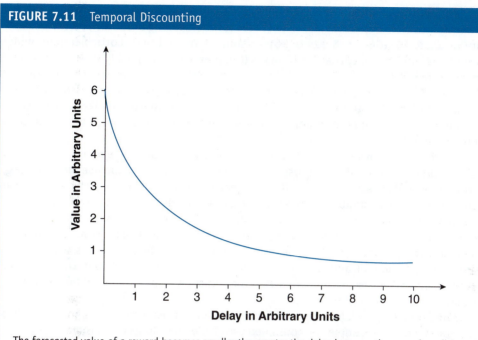

The forecasted value of a reward becomes smaller the greater the delay between the reward predictor and the reward itself. Individuals experience greater joy upon learning that they will receive $50 today as compared to $100 in a year. Moreover, if asked to choose between both possibilities, they will pick the former. This phenomenon has been termed *temporal discounting.*

the range of reported addictions, which include behaviors like eating, Internet surfing, gaming, masturbating, or shopping.

Apart from reward-related factors, factors related to the individual's biological makeup and environment influence the development of dependency. Biological predispositions include a greater exploratory drive, also referred to as "sensation seeking," and increased dopaminergic activity to novel stimuli and rewards. The latter is currently explored in relation to the Met/Val variation of the COMT gene (Tunbridge et al., 2012).

Another individual factor concerns learning and the readiness to develop conditioned responses. During conditioning, addiction-prone individuals show an exaggerated shift of dopaminergic firing from a rewarding to a conditioning stimulus so that, eventually, the latter more effectively excites dopaminergic neurons in situations where both stimuli are equally expected (Alcaro & Panksepp, 2011; Volkow et al., 2011).

Other biological differences between addiction-prone and control individuals include the metabolism in the prefrontal cortex and the density of dopamine receptors in the ventral striatum. Both markers are reportedly lower in the former as compared to the latter group. However, whether they are cause or consequence of addiction is still unclear (Volkow et al., 2011).

Within the individual's environment, stress stands out as a contributor to addiction. Research demonstrates that stress increases reward-seeking behavior and the possibility of addiction (George & Koob, 2010). Animals treated with corticosterone, which functions similarly to cortisol in humans (Chapter 4), more quickly develop a cocaine dependency than do control animals (Mantsch, Saphier, & Goeders, 1998). This has been attributed to interactions between the stress hormone and the release of dopamine in the ventral striatum (George & Koob, 2010). Furthermore, like reward, stress promotes learning and thus readily increases the salience of reward predictors and the urgency of conditioned behaviors.

Together and individually, the factors mentioned above contribute to the development of an addiction. During the course of this development, the addictive stimulus (e.g., cocaine) as well as associated stimuli (e.g., injection needle) become more rewarding than addiction-irrelevant stimuli. At the same time, however, their absolute power to elicit joy declines. Over time, more of the addictive stimulus is necessary to evoke the same sense of pleasure experienced upon first exposure. Moreover, individuals become dysphoric or anxious during prolonged periods of abstinence. Their stress level increases, which in turn motivates them to seek and consume the longed-for reward (Koob, 2009). Thus, a vicious cycle emerges that sustains and intensifies the addiction at the expense of the individual's health.

While addiction itself is a mental disorder, it often causes secondary mental and physical conditions. For example, the continued use of addictive drugs may produce symptoms of hypersexuality, aggression, and delusions (Sacks, 2011), which may mature into full-fledged schizophrenia or bipolar disorder. Additionally, during the emergence of an addiction, individuals become disregarding of other rewards that formerly were able to excite their dopamine system. Thus, they neglect things like eating, socializing, or exercising and often present with substantial organic damage when admitted for treatment. The costs to treat addiction as well as costs arising from addiction-related accidents and crimes are tremendous. In the United States, one of the most developed nations to date, they are estimated at $559 billion a year (National Institute of Drug Abuse, http://www.drug abuse.gov).

SUMMARY

We have many words that express the positive feelings in our life. The word *joy* is one of them, and it was used here to describe the emotion elicited by the unexpected prospect of a reward. Like other emotions, joy is characterized by a set of behavioral, mental, and bodily responses that increase an individual's evolutionary fitness.

Behaviorally, joy motivates reward pursuit and consumption and stimulates an individual's exploratory drive. In social species, joy additionally triggers a set of nonverbal behaviors that facilitate inter-individual interactions. For example, joyful social encounters make rodents, canines, and primates laugh.

Mentally, joy broadens ongoing thought processes, making people more creative and improving their ability to solve problems. Moreover, by enhancing learning, joy ensures that individuals remember the stimuli and the actions that that led up to the emotion.

Together, these behavioral and mental effects are supported by a range of bodily changes. At the peripheral level, these changes are linked to activational processes in the cardiovasular system as well as other organs such as the lungs and the skin. At the central level, they are linked to an activation of dopamine neurons in the ventral tegmental area and the nucleus accumbens as well as relevant neuronal targets (e.g., amygdala, orbitofrontal cortex).

Dopamine, an ancient neurochemical, seems to contribute to all aspects of joy, including that of liking a reward, wanting to work for it, and knowing what to do. Its activity follows what has been termed the *reward prediction error*. Unexpected prospects of a reward, signified by a conditioned stimulus or the reward itself, excite dopaminergic neurons, whereas the omission of an expected reward silences the same. The role of dopamine in reward prediction and learning makes it a key player in joy but also in the development of addiction, a debilitating mental disorder. Thus, while joy is something to be enjoyed—it can and should not last forever.

THINKING CRITICALLY ABOUT "JOY"

1. This chapter introduced the notion of primary rewards such as food, love, or warmth. Are these rewards truly primary, or should they be considered secondary to the bodily states or pleasurable feelings they produce?

2. What is the relative importance of liking and wanting for joy?

3. When considering the functions of joy, the author of this textbook stresses the importance of behavioral over bodily and mental consequences. Why this emphasis on behavior? Is it justified?

4. What are health risks associated with continuous reward consumption?

MEDIA LIBRARY

Mihaly Csikszentmihalyi talks about his idea of "flow" on TED: http://www.ted.com/talks/mihaly_csikszentmihalyi_on_flow.html

Martin Seligman talks about the inception of positive psychology on TED: http://www.ted.com/talks/martin_seligman_on_the_state_of_psychology.html

Nora Volkow talks about addiction and dopamine on "Big Think": http://bigthink.com/users/noravolkow

CHAPTER 8

Sadness

O f the negative emotions, sadness is most closely associated with joy. Laypeople typically view sadness and joy as opposing ends of the same emotion continuum. Whether this view is justified, however, is still a matter of debate. Some scientists advocate for the layperson view and propose a neural system that operates like a seesaw. If one end of the seesaw moves up, individuals feel joy, and if the other end moves up, individuals feel sadness. Thus, joy depends on the absence of sadness, and vice versa (for a review, see Lang & Davis, 2006).

Other scientists, however, challenge this conceptualization. They hold that sadness serves a purpose separate from that of joy and that, therefore, sadness has a separate representation in body and mind (Ekman, 1992; Panksepp, 1992). In principle, this view accommodates simultaneous feelings of joy and sadness. In reviewing the causes and effects of sadness, this chapter speaks to this debate and highlights relevant evidence.

WHAT TRIGGERS SADNESS?

At first glance, the stimuli or events that trigger sadness appear quite varied. They include social partners (e.g., a scolding parent) as well as nonsocial objects (e.g., a broken gadget) and abstract ideas (e.g., a poor grade). They can be expected or unexpected, such as when prolonged illness or a car accident take away a loved one. They can be intrinsically or extrinsically generated, such as when failure is due to a lack of aptitude or a lack of instruction. And they can violate or adhere to moral standards, such as when sadness results from a perceived injustice or some form of moral sacrifice.

Despite this disparity, however, there are certain characteristics shared among sadness-provoking events (Ellsworth & Smith, 1988; MacDonald & Leary, 2005; Panksepp, 2005b; Scherer, 1997). First, these events are typically considered negative in the sense that they exacerbate an individual's needs. Second, they afford little chances for problem-based coping because they concern established facts that are not easily undone. Last, they have significant primary or secondary social consequences. Primary social consequences result from social events that directly sever an individual's social connectedness such as a relationship breakup or an unkind word or action from a social partner. Secondary social consequences result from nonsocial events that impact an individual's ability to maintain current

FIGURE 8.1 Feeling Sad

Sadness is elicited in situations in which individuals experience some sort of social loss or exclusion.

Source: © iStockPhoto/DianaHirsch.

relationships, such as the loss of a gadget or poor grades—both of which are modern currencies for social recognition and status.

While the role of negative events and the apparent futility of problem-based coping are widely recognized as being important for sadness (Ellsworth & Smith, 1988; Scherer, 1997), the role of social consequences has received comparatively weaker emphasis. Specifically, it has been raised by only a few theorists who linked sadness to social and physical pain and/or who explored sadness in nonhuman animals (MacDonald & Leary, 2005; Panksepp, 2005b).

FEELING SAD—BEHAVIORAL TENDENCIES, MENTAL PROCESSES, AND BODILY CORRELATES

Sadness is a complex emotion. From your own experience, you may know that it can take the form of powerful sobbing or silent suffering. This was also evident to Charles Darwin (1872), who dissociated the two by referring to the former as a "paroxysm of grief" and to the latter as "low spirits." A paroxysm of grief, he suggested, is triggered initially, when an extremely sad event has just occurred. Low spirits are experienced subsequently, when one thinks that "there is no hope of relief." Similar distinctions were made by other researchers (Ekman, 2009; Levine, Wiener, Coe, Bayart, & Hayashi, 1987). These researchers used terms like *protest* or *distress* for the initial stage and *sadness* or *despair* for the following, more passive stage (Figure 8.2). Given that both stages arise from the same event, we will here subsume them under the term *sadness*. In the following section, we will refer to them separately as distress and despair only when existing research allows this.

Behavioral Tendencies

Sadness behaviors elicited during the initial distress stage differ from those expressed subsequently, when individuals despair. Initially, the confrontation with the sadness-provoking event elicits nonverbal outbursts that are clearly intended to restore the physical or affective proximity to a receding social partner (Farrell & Alberts, 2002; Levine et al., 1987).

In humans and other animals, this outburst entails vocal exclamations or wailing. Offspring of species that engage in parental care will wail for their parents if they have been separated. Moreover, this wailing typically induces the parents to maintain or decrease their distance to the offspring (Farrell & Alberts, 2002; Levine et al., 1987). As adults, many social species continue to show vocal signs of distress when separated from important others. For example, dogs may bark and whine when separated from their owners (Pongrácz, Molnár, & Miklósi, 2006; Pongrácz, Molnár, Miklósi, & Csányi, 2005). Likewise, parrots produce characteristic vocalizations that facilitate reunion (Colbert-White, Covington, & Fragaszy, 2011).

FIGURE 8.2 Stages of Sadness

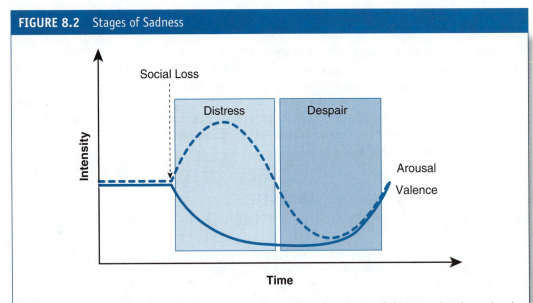

Sadness is a multistage process. During an initial stage, sadness is arousing. If this arousal and associated behavioral expositions remain unanswered, arousal declines and distress behaviors are suppressed. The individual now becomes withdrawn.

While on the surface these vocalizations appear quite varied across species, certain acoustic elements are evolutionarily preserved. Evidence for this comes from studies that examined call patterns in different species (Owren & Rendall, 2001). Additionally, it comes from studies that presented human listeners with the vocalizations of another species and found that they rate separation calls as more negative than calls produced during reunion (Tallet, Špinka, Maruščáková, & Šimeček, 2010). Moreover, when asked to determine whether a given vocalization was produced in a social separation context, human listeners could do this more accurately than would be expected by chance (Pongrácz et al., 2006, 2005; Tallet et al., 2010).

In humans, the vocalizations emitted during the initial stage of sadness are often accompanied by the shedding of tears. While it is known that tears serve to nourish and lubricate the eye, their shedding in the context of sadness has puzzled researchers for a while. Clues to this puzzle came from a recent investigation demonstrating that, apart from being salty, tears contain an airborne pheromone that reduces arousal (Gelstein et al., 2011). Thus, the shedding of tears may dampen the crier's own emotional reaction and reduce the likelihood of aggression from others (A Closer Look 8.1).

Apart from vocalizations and tears, specific facial expressions accompany initial responses to sad events. Humans typically look down and avoid extended periods of eye contact (Adams & Kleck, 2003). Additionally, they raise their inner eyebrows and pull them together. One may also note squinting eyes caused by an activation of the orbicularis oculi muscle, a protruding lower lip, turned-down mouth corners, and a raised and wrinkled chin (Darwin, 1872; Ekman & Friesen, 1978; Figure 8.4). Whether these facial responses are evident in other species has received little attention to date. However, given the shared vocal expressions, it is likely that some aspects of the human sad facial display are shared as well (Bloom & Friedman, 2013; Parr, Waller, Vick, & Bard, 2007; Schirmer, Seow, & Penney, 2013).

After the initial stage of emotional agitation, sadness takes on a less violent form and the individual's behavior becomes largely withdrawn. Now, humans and nonhuman animals vocalize less, and if they do vocalize, their expressions are less salient (Levine et al., 1987). Additionally, human facial expressions are downcast rather than pleading. They may "drop" their head and shoulders and move more slowly or even refrain from movement

A CLOSER LOOK 8.1

Manipulative Tears

The eye is a very delicate organ that needs constant lubrication. Tears help with that task, and in addition, they facilitate the expulsion of foreign particles and harmful substances that may have entered the eye (Montagu, 1959). Apart from these protective functions, tears also serve as a communicative signal. Moreover, they contain a pheromone—an odorless chemical substance that activates chemical receptors in the nose and thereby alters brain function.

(Continued)

(Continued)

Researchers have begun to investigate the effects of tears on others (Gelstein et al., 2011; Oh, Kim, Park, & Cho, 2012). They collected tears from women watching a sad movie and presented the tears together with a saline solution to male participants. The participants could not discriminate between tears and the saline solution; they rated both as smelling equally intense, pleasant, and familiar. However, the participant's hormonal, psychophysiological, and neural responses differentiated both substances. Sniffing tears, but not the saline solution, triggered a reduction in

FIGURE 8.3 Tear Pheromones Alter Physiological Arousal

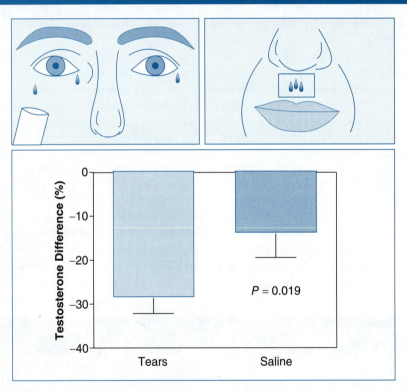

Tears were collected from women who cried while watching a sad video. The collected tears or a saline solution were dropped onto cotton pads, which were then placed under the noses of male participants. Participants exposed to tears showed a greater reduction in testosterone levels relative to a pre-exposure baseline, as compared to participants exposed to the saline solution.

Source: Data from "Effects of Chemosignals From Sad Tears and Postprandial Plasma on Appetite and Food Intake in Humans," by T. J. Oh et al., 2012, *PLoS ONE, 7,* p. e42352. © Oh et al.

testosterone levels, skin conductance, and abdominal respiration, indicating a reduction in physiological arousal. In line with this, the researchers also observed a reduction in self-reported sexual arousal. Thus, they argued that tears are functional because they reduce the likelihood of male sexual advances when a woman feels unwell (Gelstein et al., 2011).

Apart from reducing sexual desire, however, the effect of tears on testosterone and physiological arousal suggests a general reduction in aggressive tendencies. Testosterone, the main male sex hormone, has been linked to aggression, with higher levels being associated with a reduced threshold for violence (Archer, Birring, & Wu, 1998; Bronson & Desjardins, 1968). Thus, a reduction of this hormone would increase the threshold for violence and protect the crying individual from assault.

Related to this, the findings by Gelstein and colleagues also raise the possibility that tears protect the crying individual from him or herself. Desperate situations may trigger auto-aggression such as self-mutilation and suicide. These might be inhibited, and individuals may experience a reduction in arousal and perhaps a sense of calm after perceiving the pheromones of their own tears. Future research will have to test these possibilities.

(Darwin, 1872; Michalak et al., 2009). Together, these changes give the impression of the individual wanting to shrink and might serve to avoid harassment.

Mental Processes

Sadness affects both the subjective feeling and thinking aspects of the mind. Its feeling aspects have been explored with self-report measures such as the Positive and Negative Affect Scale (PANAS; Watson, Clark, & Tellegen, 1988; Chapter 6). This scale comprises a range of adjectives for which participants indicate to what extent these adjectives describe their current state. Individuals who are reportedly sad associate this state with feeling blue, downhearted, alone, and lonely. Moreover, they often express a sense of being "hurt."

As with other emotions, subjective feelings of sadness overshadow many aspects of an individual's life.

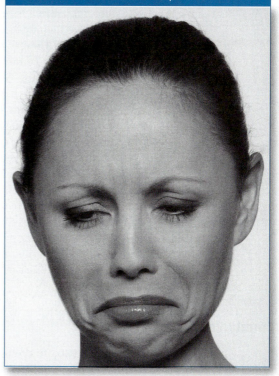

FIGURE 8.4 Human Facial Expression of Sadness

Source: © iStockphoto.com/OSTILL.

For example, they taint one's general life satisfaction and promote the assimilation of sadness-relevant concepts and ideas. Thus, individuals process sadness-relevant information more easily than they do sadness-irrelevant information (Albarracin & Hart, 2011; Schirmer, Kotz, & Friederici, 2005). Furthermore, they are more likely to apply sad appraisal patterns to incidental events. For example, sad individuals, when confronted with a mishap or a problem, are likely to engage in fatalistic attributions (Yang & Tong, 2010) and to find the situation difficult to overcome (Lasauskaite, Gendolla, & Silvestrini, 2013).

Despite such tainted thought patterns, however, sadness does not necessarily impair the efficiency of ongoing mental processes or the individual's ability to succeed in a task. On the contrary, there is evidence that sad individuals increase their mental efforts so that their performance exceeds that of individuals in neutral or joyful states (Lasauskaite et al., 2013). Sad individuals also demonstrate a heightened attentional focus that enables them to block out information that is irrelevant for a task.

This has been shown in studies using interference tasks like the one developed by John Ridley Stroop (1935). Participants doing the Stroop task have to name the print color of a word as quickly and accurately as possible. This sounds easier to do than it is. Print color and word content vary from trial to trial so that they are sometimes congruous (e.g., the word *red* printed in red) and sometimes incongruous (e.g., the word *red* printed in blue). Not surprisingly, participants perform better on congruous than on incongruous trials. Important for us is that incongruous trials are more challenging when participants are in a neutral as compared to a sad state (Melcher, Obst, Mann, Paulus, & Gruber, 2012), suggesting that sadness helps to filter out irrelevant word content.

Further evidence for sadness helping to suppress the influence of irrelevant information comes from research on attitudes. Here, it was found that sad participants remained unbiased by stereotype information (e.g., ethnic minority) when asked to give a verdict on an alleged crime (Bodenhausen, Sheppard, & Kramer, 1994). Another study found that sad individuals were unlikely to be persuaded by weak arguments but remained susceptible to strong arguments (Bless, Bohner, Schwarz, & Strack, 1990).

Taken together, the extant literature suggests that sadness propagates negative feelings and thoughts. At the same time, however, certain aspects of cognition become enhanced. Specifically, sad individuals appear exceedingly motivated in their tasks and show little susceptibility to distraction. Nevertheless, there are reasons to consider these findings with caution. Specifically, most published work on sadness relies on a comparison with happiness and lacks a proper neutral control condition. Furthermore, many emotion manipulations simply involved the presentation of nonverbal expressions to induce sadness, with the implicit assumption that participants empathize with the expressed emotions. However, this may not necessarily be the case. Instead, such expressions may evoke compassion and the urge to help. Future research needs to tackle these issues and confirm whether the reported effects hold.

Bodily Correlates

In the following section, we explore the bodily mechanisms that support the behavioral and mental processes mentioned earlier. Again, emphasis is placed on peripheral and central nervous system correlates.

Peripheral Correlates

Little research systematically explored endocrine and peripheral nervous system responses for the two stages of sadness. Nevertheless, there is some indication that the initial stage of distress is characterized by energy mobilization, whereas the later stage of despair is characterized by energy conservation.

Evidence for this comes from studies in nonhuman animals that revealed an activation of the HPA axis during social separation. For example, rat pups (Litvin et al., 2010) and primate infants (Levine et al., 1987) were found to experience a surge in stress hormones when separated from their mothers. Notably, such hormonal responses were not always correlated with overt sadness behaviors. For example, infant squirrel monkeys that were reared by their mothers in a group with other female relatives failed to cry when their mothers were taken away. Nevertheless, their cortisol levels compared with infants that were separated both from their mothers and other relatives and that showed clear vocal distress (Coe, Mendoza, Smotherman, & Levine, 1978). Mothers, when separated from their young, showed a similar increase in cortisol that returned to baseline levels during reunion (Coe et al., 1978; Stanton & Levine, 1985).

Complementing these results in nonhuman animals, work in humans suggests sympathetic activation during the initial stage of sadness (for a review, see Kreibig, 2010). Specifically, studies in which sadness manipulations evoked crying found autonomic responses similar to those excited by fear. Individuals watching sad movies or imagining situations of social rejection and failure displayed increased heart rate, skin conductance, and respiratory rate. In contrast, sadness unaccompanied by tears appears to be characterized by sympathetic withdrawal (Kreibig, 2010). Among other things, this is evident from studies of music listening, which revealed reduced heart rate and skin conductance, together with mixed breathing patterns. Common across both forms of sadness is a reduction in finger temperature or feeling cold (IJzerman et al., 2012; Kreibig, 2010).

Although it is possible that the crying and noncrying forms of human sadness map onto the two stages of sadness defined earlier in this chapter, evidence for this is still weak. Moreover, other proposals have been made that link human crying to an anticipation of loss and noncrying sadness to a realization of loss (Kreibig, 2010). To clarify this issue, the temporal course of sadness needs to be better scrutinized in future studies.

Central Nervous System Correlates

Structures

The brain structures implicated in sadness were pursued primarily by presenting human participants with neutral or sad stimuli such as facial expressions, stories, or music, and by recording brain metabolism using fMRI or PET. For example, Wang and colleagues (Wang, McCarthy, Song, & LaBar, 2005) showed intact sad and neutral faces as well as images with scrambled face parts to participants. The authors assumed that brain structures implicated in the processing of sadness-relevant information would be more active when participants watched sad as compared to neutral or scrambled faces. They found evidence for this in the fusiform gyrus, a region implicated in face processing; the inferior frontal gyrus, a region implicated in a number of cognitive tasks such as language processing and decision making; and the amygdala, one of the dopaminergic targets discussed in the preceding chapter. Do these regions then form the neural network underlying sadness?

Likely, the answer is no. Other neuroimaging studies rarely replicated these results. Moreover, across published studies activation patterns are highly variable. Exemplary for this are findings by Eugčne and colleagues (2003), who conducted the same experiment on two groups of participants. Participants were randomly assigned to these groups and matched on basic characteristics such as age, sex, and education. Both groups viewed the same sadness-inducing film excerpts with very different brain activation patterns. While one group activated anterior temporal pole and insula, the other group activated medial prefrontal and orbitofrontal cortex.

Several factors may account for this variability. First, individuals differ in their life experiences and thus respond differently to the stimulus material that experimenters use to elicit sadness. For example, a situation portrayed in a sad film clip may be differently familiar to different individuals, and hence the memories triggered and the empathy for characters in the clip will vary. Second, sadness may not be as easily empathized with as other emotions, such as happiness or fear. For example, sad music may produce pleasant feelings, and sad faces may evoke concern. Last, different materials or conditions may activate different stages of sadness. For example, sad film clips may effectively provoke distress by allowing observers to take part in the unfolding of sadness-eliciting events. In contrast, such distress may not easily arise from listening to music. Instead, the latter may more readily trigger despair.

When reviewing existing work with these issues in mind, some consistency seems to emerge. Specifically, there appears to be replicable evidence from studies exploring the initial stage of sadness by creating experiences of social loss in the lab. One successful approach to this has been to invite participants to a game of "cyberball" (Eisenberger, Lieberman, & Williams, 2003). In this game, participants interact with two other players over a computer by throwing and catching a virtual ball. Unbeknown to the participants, the two other players are also virtual, and the experimenter determines the participants' involvement in the game. Thus, the experimenter can easily create situations of social in- and exclusion.

One of the studies that used this paradigm consisted of three experimental phases (Eisenberger et al., 2003). In the first phase, the participant lay in the scanner and watched the other two players exchange balls. The participant was informed that there were some technical difficulties that needed to be resolved before the participant could join in the game. Subsequently, the participant engaged in the game throwing balls back and forth with the other players. Eventually, the other players stopped throwing the ball to the participant and thus effectively excluded the participant from the game. After the experiment was finished, the participant completed a self-report measure on social distress, likely tapping into the initial stage of sadness.

The results of this study isolated three structures as more active in the final phase of the experiment than in the initial or middle phases (Figure 8.5). The first structure was the anterior cingulate cortex (ACC), a region that is typically activated when we experience physical pain. The other two structures were the insula, a region that also receives pain information as well as other information from the body, and the right ventral prefrontal cortex (vPFC). Notably, activity in the ACC correlated positively with self-reported social distress, while activity in the right vPFC correlated negatively with self-reported social

FIGURE 8.5   Brain Regions Activated During the Distress Stage of Sadness

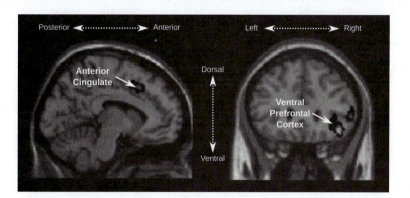

Social distress elicited by exclusion from a cyberball game is accompanied by increased cerebral blood flow in the anterior cingulate, the anterior insula, and the right ventral prefrontal cortex.

Source: "Does Rejection Hurt? An fMRI Study of Social Exclusion," by N. I. Eisenberger et al., 2003, *Science, 302,* pp. 290–292. Adapted with permission from AAAS.

distress. In other words, individuals who reported high levels of social distress showed increased activity in the ACC and decreased activity in the vPFC relative to individuals who reported low levels of social distress. Thus, it is possible that the right vPFC plays a regulatory role in dampening the "hurt" from social exclusion (Chapter 11).

Subsequent work that employed a similar approach could replicate these findings (Bolling et al., 2011; DeWall et al., 2010; Masten et al., 2009; Sebastian et al., 2011).

Neurochemicals

Inquiries into the neurochemical underpinnings of sadness have revealed a role for monamines and beta-endorphins.

Monoamines. The term *monoamine* refers to neurotransmitters such as serotonin, dopamine, or norepinephrine, which have one amino group (Chapter 4). The possibility that these neurotransmitters could play a role in sadness was first discovered in the late 1950s. Back then, clinicians noted that drugs prescribed to patients with tuberculosis induced positive changes in mood and improved symptoms of depression (López-Muñoz & Alamo, 2009; Ruhé, Mason, & Schene, 2007). Once noted, these drugs quickly became the focus of neurological research showing that they increase the availability of monoamines in the synapse. Specifically, it was found that monoamineoxidase (MAO) inhibitors, which reduce the breakdown of monoamines, and tricyclic antidepressants, which reduce the reuptake of serotonin and norepinephrine into the presynaptic neuron, both increase the potential for monoamines to activate postsynaptic receptors (Figure 8.6).

FIGURE 8.6 Monoamine (MA) Disposal

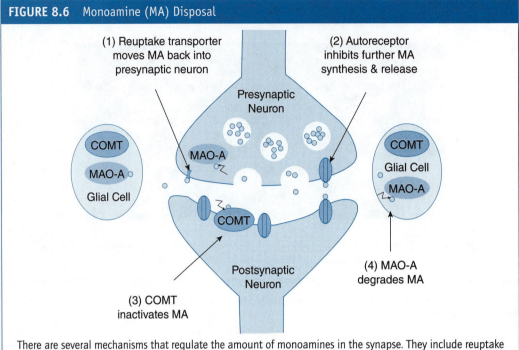

(1) Reuptake transporter moves MA back into presynaptic neuron

(2) Autoreceptor inhibits further MA synthesis & release

Presynaptic Neuron

COMT

MAO-A

Glial Cell

COMT

MAO-A

Glial Cell

MAO-A

COMT

Postsynaptic Neuron

(4) MAO-A degrades MA

(3) COMT inactivates MA

There are several mechanisms that regulate the amount of monoamines in the synapse. They include reuptake transporters, autoreceptors, monoamineoxidase A (MAO-A), and catechol-O-methyltransferase (COMT). The more active these mechanisms are, the fewer monoamines can bind to receptors of the postsynaptic neuron. MAO-A inhibitors, tricyclic antidepressants, and selective serotonin reuptake inhibitors downregulate these mechanisms and thus increase the availability of monoamines in the synapse.

Although useful in the treatment of depression, MAO-inhibitors and tricyclic antidepressants have very general effects on the central nervous system and produce a number of side effects. Thus, efforts were directed at isolating the most effective monoamine. In the 1970s, these efforts culminated in the introduction of selective serotonin-reuptake inhibitors (SSRIs). These had fewer and less dramatic side effects than did earlier generic drugs, while being equally potent. To date, SSRIs are still the most widely prescribed medicine in the treatment of depression (for reviews, see Krishnan & Nestler, 2008; López-Muñoz & Alamo, 2009).

Serotonin, also called 5-hydroxytryptamine (5-HT), is synthesized in the raphe nuclei in the brainstem and from there distributed to the rest of the brain. Its wide distribution, in conjunction with a relatively large receptor family, makes 5-HT a highly complex neurotransmitter. Moreover, a simple change in its concentration likely has a range of effects, very few of which are currently understood.

A role for 5-HT in sadness may be inferred from the effect of SSRIs in depression. Additionally, it is evident from studies that looked at the effect of depleting individuals of the 5-HT precursor tryptophan. Like other essential amino acids, tryptophan is obtained from certain foods, and abstaining from foods that contain tryptophan reduces

5-HT availability in the brain. Studies that used tryptophan depletion in previously depressed patients and relatives of depressed individuals found that it lowers mood fairly consistently (Ruhé et al., 2007). Similar but less consistent effects have been reported in healthy individuals without a family history of depression (Ruhé et al., 2007). Thus, one may speculate that 5-HT plays a role in sadness and that a certain vulnerability of the 5-HT system exacerbates the effect of short-term 5-HT depletion on mood (Silber & Schmitt, 2010).

However, because mood was typically assessed as a combination of decreased happy and increased sad feelings, this work could not decide whether 5-HT is more critical for the former or the latter. Evidence in favor of 5-HT increasing sad feelings is now starting to emerge. Specifically, researchers have begun to include dependent variables besides self-reports in tryptophan depletion studies. For example, researchers have measured behavioral responses in experimental tasks and looked at brain activity. Thus, it was observed that tryptophan depletion slows reaction times and reduces sensitivity to social information from faces (Beacher et al., 2011). Additionally, there is evidence that, in healthy individuals, tryptophan depletion increases activity in the ACC and that this increase correlates with self-reported negative mood (Talbot & Cooper, 2006). Thus, the effects of tryptophan depletion can be linked to social processing and one of the key brain structures implicated in sadness.

Another line of evidence for a role of 5-HT in sadness and depression comes from studies exploring the phenotype of genetic variations of the 5-HT transporter gene (Figure 8.7). Like other genes, the 5-HT transporter gene represents a snippet on a chromosome of which one exemplar came from the maternal and the other from the paternal side. In humans, the 5-HT transporter gene is located on chromosome 17 and exists in many variants, the most common of which are referred to as short and long. A human may have two short variants, one short and one long variant, or two long variants. Compared to the long variant, the short variant has been associated with a decreased number of 5-HT transporters and thus a reduced reuptake of 5-HT into the presynaptic neuron (for a review, see Homberg & Lesch, 2011).

Based on what we know about the effect of 5-HT reuptake (Chapter 4), one would guess that individuals with two short variants of the gene are less likely to suffer from depression than are individuals with two long variants. For them, more 5-HT should remain in the synapse. Curiously, however, the opposite is the case (Caspi et al., 2003; but see Risch et al., 2009). Moreover, individuals with the short variant also respond more strongly to negative emotional stimuli as compared to individuals with the long variant (Hariri, 2002; Murphy et al., 2013). Such differences have been observed in both adults and children. For example, Fortier and colleagues (2010) found that children showed increased activation of the ACC when watching sad as compared to neutral movies, and this increase was greater in children with one or two short gene variants relative to children who were homozygous for the long variant.

Different proposals were made to explain these findings. One proposal holds that genetically determined 5-HT transporter availability influences brain development, resulting in a range of structural and neurochemical changes (Ansorge, 2004). It is likely that these changes predispose carriers of the short variant to react to extreme social stress with depression (Caspi et al., 2003). Support for this idea comes from studies that found parts

FIGURE 8.7   Serotonin Transporter Gene

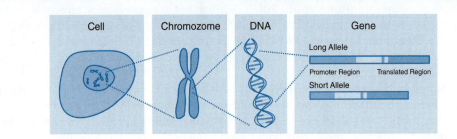

The serotonin transporter gene is located on chromosome 17. This gene comes in two variants. One has a longer promoter region than the other. This means that transcription of the former gene will be greater than that of the latter gene, theoretically resulting in more serotonin transporters. However, gene transcription depends on factors besides the length of the promoter region (e.g., DNA methylation). Therefore, one cannot infer differences in the availability of serotonin transporters from the length of the promoter region alone.

of the ACC and the amygdala to be smaller (Pezawas et al., 2005) and parts of the thalamus to be larger (Young et al., 2007) in individuals with the short as compared to the long variant of the 5-HT transporter gene.

A second proposal is based on evidence that exaggerated responses of short variant carriers are not restricted to negative stimuli but include positive ones. For example, Beevers and colleagues found that short variant carriers spend more time exploring positive scenes relative to long variant carriers (Beevers, Ellis, Wells, & McGeary, 2010). Furthermore, social support seems a more critical buffer for depression in short as compared to long variant carriers (Kaufman et al., 2004). Thus, it has been argued that 5-HT transporter gene variability creates variability in how individuals attend to both negative and positive events (Homberg & Lesch, 2011). Individuals with the short variant are presumably overtly vigilant to the emotional nature of these events. This may be advantageous in many instances where emotions usefully inform decisions and behavior. However, it also poses a risk under adverse conditions. Here, a generally heightened emotional sensitivity may lead to psychological maladjustment.

In sum, monoamines appear relevant for some aspects of sadness. Their availability in the synapse influences various things such as liking, wanting, and learning (see Chapter 7). Monoamines also appear to play a role in depression, which has prolonged feelings of sadness as one of its possible symptoms (see the later discussion). Nevertheless, research failed to consistently support the idea that a reduction in monoamine binding directly causes sadness and/or depression. Instead, a complex picture emerged in which monoamines, and in particular serotonin, moderate sensitivity to emotional events. Both acute and sustained changes in the serotonin system affect the workings of one of the key structures implicated in sadness—the ACC. Additionally, such changes seem instrumental for a generally heightened emotional sensitivity. Through one or both of these mechanisms, social losses may have a greater impact on individuals, leading to enhanced feelings of sadness and vulnerability to depression.

Beta-endorphin. Beta-endorphin is another type of neurotransmitter implicated in sadness (Chapter 4). It is produced in subcortical structures such as the pituitary gland and the hypothalamus. Severe physical injury, orgasm, or strenuous physical activity may trigger the release of beta-endorphin, which then binds to μ-opioid receptors to reduce pain and to promote positive feelings. μ-opioid receptors are located in a number of structures including periaqueductal gray, nucleus accumbens, amygdala, ACC, and insula. As some of these structures were found to support the processing of sad events, one may speculate that they also promote a link between beta-endorphin and sadness.

To investigate this, Zubieta and colleagues (2003) conducted a positron emission tomography (PET) study. As detailed in Chapter 6, the PET technique involves the injection of a radioactive tracer derived by combining a functionally important chemical with a radionuclide. In their study, Zubieta and colleagues selected a chemical that preferentially attached to μ-opioid receptors and hence would travel to these receptors for binding. Once at the receptors, the radionuclide that was piggybacked onto the chemical would break down and trigger the creation of gamma ray photons. Reading these photons with the PET scanner allowed the researchers to reconstruct the chemical's location (Figure 8.8). In their study, this should reveal brain regions that had free μ-opioid receptors to which the chemical could bind.

To determine whether the μ-opioid system is implicated in sadness, Zubieta and colleagues asked their participants to recall sad autobiographical memories. They compared the PET scans obtained during this condition with a condition in which participants simply focused on current physical sensations. To understand the predictions of Zubieta and colleagues, let us first reconsider the effect of beta-endorphin release in the brain. In response to physical injury, such a release dampens pain as beta-endorphin binds to μ-opioid receptors. Moreover, pain ensues if only some or no beta-endorphin is released and μ-opioid receptors sit idle. Thus, if being sad is similar to feeling pain, then beta-endorphin release should be reduced and more beta-endorphin receptors should sit idle during the sad recall condition as compared to the neutral baseline condition. This is what Zubieta and colleagues observed. Moreover, regions that showed significant differences in μ-opioid receptor availability were the ACC, the amygdala, and the ventral pallidum (Figure 8.9). Thus, we can infer that sadness is linked to a lack of beta-endorphin in brain sites associated with the perception of pain.

Following these and similar findings, researchers explored whether the opioid system could be an effective target in the treatment of depression (for a review, see Berrocoso, Sánchez-Blázquez, Garzón, & Mico, 2009). Nonhuman animal studies that used learned helplessness as a model for depression found positive results. Agonists for the μ-opioid system produced antidepressive effects, whereas antagonists produced depressive effects (Besson, Privat, Eschalier, & Fialip, 1996). Although this could be extended to humans (Stoll & Rueter, 1999), the effects of beta-endorphin in alleviating depression were found to be less potent than the effects of SSRIs. Thus, beta-endorphin may be only a minor player in human depression. Moreover, sadness and depression may have somewhat different representations in the brain.

FIGURE 8.8   PET Research Can Estimate the Availability of Free μ-opioid Receptors

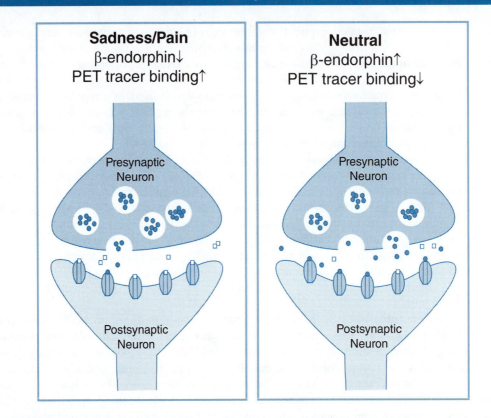

As beta-endorphin (small circles) is released into extracellular space, it binds to available μ-opioid receptors. When individuals are sad or in pain, most μ-opioid receptors sit idle. In contrast, when individuals feel comfortable, most μ-opioid receptors are activated by beta-endorphin. PET imaging can assess the availability of μ-opioid receptors by measuring how much of an injected chemical (small squares) can bind to them.

Mechanisms

Throughout this chapter, we encountered several indicators for a potential relationship between sadness and pain. For example, we noted that sadness is associated with feeling "hurt" and relies on brain structures and neurochemicals that are active during physical injury. Additionally, the behaviors elicited by sadness such as crying and withdrawal are clearly reminiscent of the behaviors displayed during body ache. Thus, one may reasonably venture that the brain mechanisms of sadness and pain overlap. Moreover, sadness may be an emotion that developed on top of an evolutionarily older pain system (A Closer Look 8.2).

FIGURE 8.9   PET Study Reveals Reduced Beta-endorphin Activity During Sadness

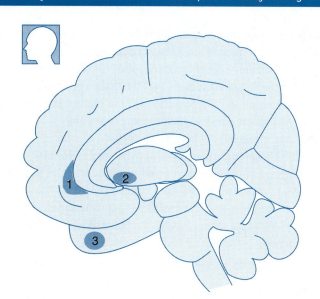

Zubieta and colleagues (2003) found greater availability of μ-opioid receptors linked to reduced beta-endorphin activity when participants recalled sad memories as compared to when the participants focused on current sensations. This difference was observed in (1) the anterior cingulate, (2) the ventral pallidum, and (3) the amygdala.

A CLOSER LOOK 8.2

How We Feel Pain

A complex somatosensory system supports our ability to sense bodily position and bodily contact with the environment. This system comprises cells that register mechanical and thermal impressions and cells dedicated to the perception of pain. The latter cells, called nociceptors, are located externally on the skin or internally in the muscles and organs.

Nociceptors come in different variants. Some respond to high mechanical pressure, others respond to extremely hot or cold temperature, and yet others are multimodal in that they respond to any stimulus that causes cellular damage.

Information from the nociceptors is sent to the brain via the spinal cord. Interestingly, pain fibers take a different route than do most other somatosensory fibers. The latter travel within the dorsal

(Continued)

(Continued)

root of the spinal cord (i.e., back side) to the medulla in the brainstem, where they cross over to the other hemisphere and reach the primary somatosensory cortex via the thalamus.

Pain fibers cross sides immediately after entering the spinal cord dorsal root and travel within the contralateral ventral root to the medulla and then onto the thalamus. From there, some fibers take a similar route as the other somatosensory projections to the primary somatosensory cortex. The remaining fibers, however, bypass the primary somatosensory cortex and travel to more specific "pain regions" such as the ACC and insula directly from the thalamus.

For some time, researchers believed the pain pathway to be unique. However, more recent research demonstrated the participation of projections involved in pleasant social touch (Olausson et al., 2002). These projections are activated by the slow, gentle stroking of hairy skin—a stimulation typically obtained from grooming, human affectionate touch, and massages. The anatomical overlap between this socially important tactile sense and pain perception is telling in that it provides further clues to a functional relationship between pain and social processing.

Evidence for this assertion comes from research that explicitly investigated the relationship between sadness and pain. In some of this work, researchers applied hot or cold stimuli to the participants' skin and asked them to rate pain intensity. When combined with the recall of sad memories or the perception of sadness-related stimuli (e.g., music), pain intensity ratings were higher than when combined with the recall or perception of neutral and positive events (Berna et al., 2010; Boettger, Schwier, & Bär, 2011; Wagner, Koschke, Leuf, Schlösser, & Bär, 2009; Yoshino et al., 2010; but see Zelman, Howland, Nichols, & Cleeland, 1991).

Further corroborating these findings are clinical reports indicating that depressed individuals are more likely than nondepressed individuals to suffer from chronic pain (Bär et al., 2005). Counterintuitively, however, their sensitivity to short-term noxious stimulation is reduced (Bär et al., 2005), suggesting qualitative changes in the pain system when low mood is sustained over a longer period. Perhaps the sustained recruitment of pain-related areas by sad mood makes these areas less sensitive to acute pain but more sensitive to chronic pain.

Another line of evidence for a relationship between sadness and pain comes from research that alleviated pain experiences and looked at an accompanying effect on social interest and sadness. For example, in nonhuman primates, researchers applied lesions to the ACC and found that this not only reduced pain sensitivity but also the primate's prosociality or interest in social stimuli (MacLean & Newman, 1988; Rudebeck, Buckley, Walton, & Rushworth, 2006; Rudebeck et al., 2007).

In humans, researchers applied painkillers and observed resulting effects on emotion. For example, DeWall and colleagues (2010) asked their participants to take a placebo or acetaminophen, a centrally active painkiller also known as paracetamol, once daily for three weeks. During this time, participants recorded for each day the frequency with which they experienced feelings of hurt from social interactions. Over the course of the study, the researchers observed a significant reduction in the number of instances that caused social pain in participants who took the painkiller. No such reduction was seen in participants who took the placebo.

A link between sadness and pain also emerged from neuroimaging studies. For example, acetaminophen was found to reduce activity in the ACC and anterior insula of participants who experienced social exclusion in the cyberball game (DeWall et al., 2010). Furthermore, fMRI studies found ACC activation to physical pain stimuli to be increased in a sad context as compared to a neutral or happy context (Berna et al., 2010; Yoshino et al., 2010).

Apart from changes in the ACC, researchers also observed changes in thalamic activity. The thalamus is a subcortical structure relaying sensory information, such as pain, from the brainstem to the cerebral hemispheres. Additionally, it has been implicated in vocal crying during social separation in nonhuman animals (Herman & Panksepp, 1981). As for the ACC, neuroimaging research in humans found greater thalamic activation to pain when participants were in a sad as compared to a neutral or happy state (Berna et al., 2010; Wagner et al., 2009).

Together, this evidence led researchers to suggest that sadness alters how individuals attend to or regulate pain—allowing noxious stimuli to receive more processing resources (Berna et al., 2010; Wagner et al., 2009). Equally possible, however, is a cognition-independent modulation of pain sensitivity that is caused simply because pain and sadness have a common neuronal substrate. Future research will have to determine whether the proposed cognitive regulation mechanism, neuronal overlap, or both in combination explain the interaction between sadness and pain.

WHY DO WE FEEL SAD?

Sadness has multiple functions. In its initial form, sadness is directed at regaining physical or affective proximity to a receding social partner. The offspring of many species, including humans, cry violently when left by their parents. Offspring crying is a special signal to most parents that elicits greater activity relative to control sounds in brain structures such as the amygdala (Sander, Brechmann, & Scheich, 2003; Seifritz et al., 2003). Moreover, mammalian mothers in particular are sensitive to offspring crying, and this seems mediated by oxytocin surges experienced during breast-feeding (Kim et al., 2011; Riem et al., 2011; Chapter 12). Thus, infant crying is very effective in restoring the comfort of the mother's breast. Observations in a number of species suggest that crying and other behaviors characteristic of separation distress also serve to restore social proximity in adulthood.

When the initial stage of agitation fails to produce the longed-for social response, individuals fall into a second stage called despair. Many researchers agree that this stage reduces behaviors with risky social consequences and promotes behaviors that signal submission or defeat. For example, Price (1967) proposed that individuals within a group compete for resources and status, and that feelings of sadness or depression evolved to signal when such competitions are no longer worthwhile because an individual is clearly losing and should avoid further damage or costs (Figure 8.10). Recognizing this would not only minimize harm to the competing individuals, it would also allow group relationships to stabilize.

The view of despair as a submission response resonated with other researchers. Nevertheless, it was developed further by shifting the focus from harm avoidance and group benefits to the individual's need for belonging. According to this revised view, individuals keep track of how many resources they are able and willing to invest in social relationships and how much recognition and support they receive in return. When an individual's investments are high and his or her perceived returns are low, social relationships and possibly group belonging are threatened (Allen & Badcock, 2003; Knowles & Gardner, 2008; Molden, Lucas, Gardner, Dean, & Knowles, 2009).

To illustrate this, let us imagine that you organized a party to which you invited all your friends, but only a few came. You would have made a substantial financial and social investment with little return, and you might realize that you are not as socially connected as you thought you were. In this case, feelings of despair would make you adopt strategies to avoid further damage to your social position. Central to these strategies would be to steer away from confrontation and to minimize being a nuisance to others (Allen & Badcock, 2003; Knowles & Gardner, 2008; Molden et al., 2009). Thus, you might avoid further rejection and elicit caring or supporting behaviors from individuals with whom you still engage in norm-based reciprocity—that is, the few friends who came to your party (Allen & Badcock, 2003; Watson & Andrews, 2002).

Apart from its immediate effects on behavior, sadness also has prospective effects on behavior that operate even when individuals are no longer sad. To appreciate what these effects might be, let us return to the party scenario. It is likely you would ask yourself why only a few friends came, and you would think of ways to increase your popularity. In other words, you would revisit your investment in existing relationships and change investment strategies, if that appears both possible and profitable. For example, if you affronted many of your friends by being selfish or unfair, you might venture an apology. You may become more sensitive and responsive to their needs, and you may make greater contributions to shared tasks (e.g., a class project). Together, these efforts would make you more valuable to your peers and therefore increase your sense of belonging (Allen & Badcock, 2003; Knowles & Gardner, 2008; Molden et al., 2009).

By promoting both immediate and prospective responses, the function of sadness seems comparable to that of pain. Like social hurt, physical hurt serves as a signal to disengage from potentially damaging activities and to take measures to prevent such hurt in the future. If you play soccer and painfully twist your foot in the game, it is likely that you will stop playing and attend to your injury instead. Moreover, depending on the severity of your injury, you may want to retreat from other activities and remain passive for a while. Additionally, however, you might consider why you twisted your foot and whether there is something you can do to prevent this from happening in the future. Perhaps you were wearing the wrong type of shoes and will now invest in a proper pair.

FIGURE 8.10   Primate Aggression

When conflicts become too costly, submitting to the opponent is a useful strategy. Nonverbal signs of submission show similarities to those used to express sadness. For example, individuals lower their posture and avert their gaze.

Source: © bra_nec—Fotolia.com.

Taken together, sadness and pain have similar adaptive value in that they both reduce behaviors that harm and increase behaviors that benefit an individual in the longer term. While pain concerns an individual's basic bodily well-being, sadness concerns his or her social well-being—a condition equally important for the survival of human as well as other species that care for offspring and lead social lives.

WHEN SADNESS BECOMES A PROBLEM

Depression

Laypeople as well as scientists often associate the emotion sadness with the mood disorder depression. The term *depression* comes from the Latin verb *deprimere,* which means "to press down." As such, it is a relatively generic term. Apart from its use in psychology, it finds application in the context of economics, where it refers to the downturn of an economic market, or in the context of medicine, where it refers to the downregulation of an organ or physiological function.

The commonly perceived association between sadness and psychological depression springs from the fact that major life events that elicit sadness potentially trigger psychological depression. For example, many depressed individuals have experienced a death in the family or another social incision, such as unemployment. Additionally, many of the symptoms of psychological depression compare to those experienced during sadness. Like sad individuals, depressed patients are withdrawn and express complaints related to physical pain (for a review, see Robinson et al., 2009).

Despite these similarities, however, there are several factors that dissociate the emotion from the mood disorder. First, by virtue of being an emotion, sadness is adaptive and short-lived, whereas depression is maladaptive and prolonged. Second, the role of external events in eliciting sadness and depression is not entirely comparable. Although stressful life events may trigger sadness, not everyone who experiences such events becomes depressed. Moreover, depressive symptoms may develop in the absence of such events. Thus, whereas sadness appears to be event-based, depression seems more dependent on an individual's biological predisposition.

Last, clinical diagnostic criteria as well as empirical work dissociate sadness from depression. Clinicians refer to a major depressive episode when a patient shows five or more of the following symptoms for a period of two or more weeks (American Psychiatric Association & DSM-5 Task Force, 2013):

1. Depressed mood
2. Diminished interest or pleasure in daily activities
3. Changes in body weight
4. Sleeping problems
5. Changes in motor activity
6. Fatigue
7. Feelings of worthlessness or guilt
8. Problems concentrating
9. Thoughts of death

Of the symptoms shown by a patient with depression, one has to be depressed mood or diminished pleasure. Thus, clinicians allow for the possibility that these patients, instead of being exceedingly sad, are simply unable to feel happy. This possibility is supported by empirical work showing that some depressed individuals cry no more than do healthy individuals, but lack the motivation to go on with life (Chentsova-Dutton et al., 2007). Thus, the relationship between sadness and depression may vary across patients, making the diagnostic category heterogeneous and pointing to different etiological mechanisms (Krishnan & Nestler, 2008).

Treatment Approaches for Depression

Pharmacological Approaches. Like for any other disorder, the importance of specifying etiological mechanisms lies with the development of treatment methods. Naturally, such treatments are more effective if they address the causes underlying a disorder as opposed to its symptoms. In the case of depression, disturbances in the monoamine systems are one suspected culprit. This is because drugs that increase monoamine levels (e.g., tricyclic antidepressants, SSRIs) in the synapse were found to alleviate depression.

Curiously, however, the effects that these drugs have on raising monoamine levels are immediate, whereas their effects on the patients' mood are relatively delayed.

Patients have to take monoamine-enhancing drugs for a couple of weeks before they experience subjective improvements. Therefore, a simple relationship between monoamine levels and feelings of depression does not exist. Instead, monoamines seem to trigger other long-term mechanisms that eventually moderate mood.

One of the mechanisms that is currently being explored concerns the interaction between monoamines and the endogenous opioid system (Berrocoso et al., 2009). Another mechanism concerns the brain's general housekeeping. Monoamine levels appear to have epigenetic effects on the expression of genes that support the development and maintenance of neurons (Krishnan & Nestler, 2008). As current pharmacological treatments of depression have low remission rates, the exploration of these and other potential mechanisms holds a lot of promise.

FIGURE 8.11 "Old Man in Sorrow," by Vincent Van Gogh (1890)

Source: Wikimedia Commons.

Brain Stimulation Approaches. In 1938, Italian psychiatrist Ugo Cerletti and his student Lucio Bini introduced a device that produced electrical seizures in patients (Aruta, 2011). The device induced an electric current via two electrodes that were attached to the patients' temples. Without much evidence, Cerletti claimed to cure mental illness and advertised his technique to fellow practitioners—who, for lack of alternatives, eagerly followed his lead.

Despite a questionable start, Cerletti's technique developed into an accepted treatment approach that is still used today under the name of electroconvulsive therapy (ECT). However, unlike in Cerletti's days, it is now applied only if patients consent and if other treatment approaches are either ineffective or not indicated. Additionally, the technique is done under general anesthesia, with muscle relaxants to prevent painful experiences.

Although the application of ECT proved useful for depression, it can cause a range of adverse effects, including delirium and amnesia (Tokutsu et al., 2013). Looking for ways to achieve safer treatment success, clinicians and scientists turned to other stimulation approaches, including vagus nerve stimulation and transcranial magnetic stimulation of the brain (TMS; Chapter 6). As of now, however, these approaches have lower remission rates than does ECT (Wani, Trevino, Marnell, & Husain, 2013).

Cognitive Techniques. In the absence of a clear etiological understanding, the current treatment of depression is based on trial and error and involves, in addition to the aforementioned medical therapies, a range of cognitive and behavioral techniques. One of the cognitive techniques relies on the assumption that depression results from learned helplessness (Peterson & Seligman, 1984). According to this assumption, individuals who experience negative life events as uncontrollable are prone to attribute these events to internal, stable, and global causes. In other words, they are likely to assume that some negative outcome resulted from their own shortcomings, is not a singular incident, and is diagnostic of large aspects of their life. Thus, an approach has been to alter these assumptions by making people realize the errors in their thinking. For example, therapists may help patients appreciate external contributors to their misfortune and the specificity of the event, as well as available resources in the patient's life (e.g., skills and possessions).

Mindfulness. A further approach to the treatment of depression and sadness is mindfulness training (MT). MT has a long tradition in Buddhist meditation and has recently been adopted in Western medicine. The basic principle of this training is to engage in meta-cognition—that is, the monitoring of bodily and mental states as they are experienced—and to accept these states as part of one's self. Bringing bodily and mental sensations into awareness presumably enables individuals to reduce the overall impact of negative appraisals.

Researchers noted that MT changes the way individuals respond to sadness-provoking events (Farb et al., 2010). After regular training, individuals reported lower depression scores and differed from waitlist controls in their response to sadness-provoking movies. Although their self-reported sadness from these movies was comparable, the MT group was more likely to activate the ACC, the insula, and the thalamus. Moreover, insula activation was negatively correlated with depression scores. The authors concluded that MT shifts emotional responses from cognitive-affective processes to more bodily-affective processes, thereby making emotional experiences more adaptive.

Physical Exercise. Physical exercise also combats depression and sadness. Studies in humans and nonhuman animals have revealed a positive relationship between physical activity and mood. Extended running, for example, produces temporary positive feelings described as "runner's high"; this suggests an immediate impact of exercise on mood.

However, there also appear to be more sustained effects. Valtonen and colleagues (2009) found that individuals are less likely to report feelings of hopelessness if they are physically active in their leisure time. Furthermore, individuals with depression appear to benefit from prescribed physical training (Archer, Fredriksson, Schütz, & Kostrzewa, 2011; Cotman, Berchtold, & Christie, 2007).

The mechanisms underlying these effects are still poorly understood. One possibility is that exercise alleviates depression through a modulation of the endogenous opioid system. Research suggests that physical exercise triggers the release of endogenous opioids such as beta-endorphin and thus acts similarly to some recreational drugs (Kanarek, D'Anci, Jurdak, & Mathes, 2009).

Another potential mechanism involves the body's inflammatory system. Typically, people who are sick also feel emotionally unwell, suggesting a link between the immune system and mood. The idea is that sickness triggers feelings that promote protective behaviors, or inactivity, to support recuperation. In line with this, individuals who suffer from prolonged illnesses often also develop depression, and patients with depression that did not arise from illness frequently show elevated inflammatory activity (Dantzer, O'Connor, Freund, Johnson, & Kelley, 2008). Exercise has been shown to decrease inflammation (Archer et al., 2011; Cotman et al., 2007).

Sleep. Another factor contributing to mood and mood disorders is the circadian rhythm. This rhythm is tightly coupled to daily changes in light. These changes are registered by the brain, which then adjusts the release of neurotransmitters and hormones that wake us to activity or allow us to fall asleep. Irregular or too little sleep has negative health consequences and is another weak spot in individuals with depression. Moreover, some suggest that seasonal depression, observed during the winter months when days are short, results from disruptions of normal sleeping (Lewy et al., 2009).

To address this problem, clinicians introduced light therapy to supplement natural light, to improve sleep, and to alleviate mood disturbances. This entails exposing the patient to bright light for about an hour daily, with greatest effects seen for morning exposure. The success of this technique spurred researchers to explore the underlying mechanisms. These likely engage the suprachiasmatic nucleus in the brainstem, which plays a central role in our sleep-wake patterns and regulates the production of hormones such as cortisol and melatonin.

Diet. Finally, sadness and depression may be regulated through food intake. As already mentioned, we obtain the 5-HT precursor tryptophan from some of the things we eat (e.g., meat, cheese; Chapter 4). Although mood improvements with the ingestion of tryptophan have been shown only inconsistently in healthy and severely depressed individuals, such improvements appear relatively consistently in mild to moderately depressed individuals, suggesting that here diet can make a difference (Silber & Schmitt, 2010).

SUMMARY

Humans and other animals may feel sad after losing something dear or costly, such as a valued social partner or a resource that supported ongoing social relationships. Initially, such feelings are arousing and activate behaviors directed at minimizing the perceived loss (e.g., crying). Subsequently, however, when these behaviors prove unsuccessful, sad feelings take on a more passive note and promote decreased physiological arousal and behavioral withdrawal.

The biological processes that support these effects overlap with those involved in pain. The neurotransmitter beta-endorphin and brain structures such as the anterior cingulate and insula are involved both during sadness/distress and physical injury. Thus, it has been proposed that the evolutionarily older pain system formed the basis for social animals like humans to experience sadness.

Interestingly, the biological processes of sadness also appear to be linked to joy. Insufficiency of the monoamines dopamine and serotonin creates sadness symptoms (e.g., withdrawal) that are used in the diagnosis of depression. Additionally, beta-endorphin activity intertwines pain and sadness with joy, as receptors for this neurotransmitter are located not only in primary pain and sadness structures (i.e., the ACC and the insula) but also in structures whose activation we find rewarding (e.g., the ventral pallidum). Thus, it is easy to see why certain pains may be pleasurable and why certain pleasures may provoke tears.

Given its behavioral, mental, and biological effects, sadness likely serves multiple purposes. In the short term, sadness prompts withdrawal, making the individual inoffensive and raising the possibility that others extend support and care. In the long term, sadness reduces the probability of being antisocial and promotes the probability of prosocial behaviors. Moreover, it ensures that individuals maintain the social relationships that are critical for their survival and reproductive success.

The mental disorder most closely linked to sadness is depression. Some, but not all, forms of this disorder are triggered by severe social distress such as the loss of a loved one. These forms can be characterized by intense sadness and tearfulness or by a lack of pleasure. Current insights into the etiology of depression imply a role for both life experiences and biological predisposition. The treatment of depression comprises a range of approaches including pharmaceuticals (e.g., SSRIs), brain stimulation (e.g., ECT), cognitive therapy (e.g., attributional style), and behavioral change (e.g., exercise). Some of these approaches are also useful in helping alleviate nonclinical forms of sadness.

THINKING CRITICALLY ABOUT "SADNESS"

1. Why do we observe so many similarities in the feelings of sadness and pain? Are the two different enough to be considered as separate constructs?

2. Are sadness and joy two ends of the same emotion continuum, or should they be understood as separate emotions with specifically dedicated neuronal systems?

3. The study by Farb and colleagues (2010) was used to support the idea that mindfulness training improves mood. What might be an alternative interpretation of their data?

MEDIA LIBRARY

BBC documentary, *The Truth About Depression*: http://www.bbc.co.uk/programmes/b01sgpd6
BBC website listing a number of videos about social species illustrating what it means to be social: http://www.bbc.co.uk/nature/adaptations/Presociality

Experts in Emotion Research Series by Jane Gruber at Yale University: http://www.yalepeplab .com/teaching/psych131_summer2013/materials.php. Relevant for this chapter is an interview with Naomi Eisenberger on social pain.

Kathryn Schulz talks about regret on TED: http://www.ted.com/talks/kathryn_schulz_ don_t_regret_regret.html

CHAPTER 9

Fear

Sigmund Freud (1930) considered fear a primary motivator for behavior. This was not without reason. A range of species, including nonvertebrates such as snails and flies as well as vertebrates such as fish or primates, experience fear or something like it. Additionally, many species are endowed with both a sophisticated sensory system that detects fear-relevant threat and a broad repertoire of behavioral and mental responses to effectively deal with threat. Traditionally, threat responses have been classified into fight or flight. More recent studies, however, revealed further differentiation into inhibitory and activational responses, the expression of which depends on critical situational factors such as the proximity to threat. Beginning with the work of Walter Cannon in the early 20th century, fear has been an intensive focus of research and is to date the best-studied emotion.

As with the preceding emotion chapters, we will take a look at the work done since the early 20th century and elucidate key aspects of fear such as its triggers; its feeling components, including behavioral tendencies, mental representations, and bodily substrates; and its functions and potential dysfunctions.

WHAT TRIGGERS FEAR?

Fear is an emotion elicited by threat. Threats may be defined as events or stimuli that signal a potential loss of resources and that forecast a need. For example, the open encounter with a predator endangers an individual's physical integrity and the fulfillment of his or her need for safety. A failure at work may result in unemployment and thus jeopardizes an individual's financial situation and his or her ability to secure basic necessities like food and shelter. A public performance bears the risk of public criticism and thus endangers an individual's self-esteem and sense of social belonging.

Although threats such as these may cause fear, whether they do so depends on an individual's appraisal. Threats that seem difficult to avert because they make the individual feel powerless are likely to make individuals fearful. However, threats that seem easy to avert may provoke no emotion or provoke other emotions instead. For example, a child may intimidate another child by using verbal threats. However, the same child may seem hilarious or annoying to an adult. Thus, a threat's relevance to fear lies in the eye of the beholder.

Many researchers dissociate fear from anxiety. Some hold that fear denotes an emotion and thus a short-lived response elicited by a stimulus, whereas anxiety denotes a stimulus-unspecific individual disposition (Averill, 1988). Others hold that fear and anxiety spring from different kinds of threats. From this standpoint, fear is often viewed as arising from the threat of physical injury, whereas anxiety is viewed as arising from threats related to one's self-perception or ego-identity (Lazarus, 1994). Yet other researchers suggest that fear and anxiety differ with respect to the underlying threat appraisal. According to this position, threats that provoke fear are appraised as novel and unexpected, whereas threats that provoke anxiety are appraised as familiar and expected (Scherer, 2001). Finally, the most popular differentiation between fear and anxiety uses a temporal criterion. It holds that immediate threats provoke fear, whereas prospective threats or the possibility of future threats provoke anxiety (Cisler, Olatunji, & Lohr, 2009). In this vein, researchers presume that a rat experiences fear when confronted by a cat and that it experiences anxiety in open spaces that expose it to the possibility of meeting a cat (Korte & De Boer, 2003).

Irrespective of the fact that researchers disagree on how they define fear and anxiety, a case can be made that their definitions refer to very similar processes (Lazarus, 1994). First, that emotions depend on an individual's disposition to experience them makes it difficult to use dispositional markers to dissociate fear from anxiety. Second, nonphysical threats such as the loss of employment often have secondary physical consequences that blur the boundary between physical and nonphysical threat. Third, fear-conditioning research suggests that fear may be sustained even while a threat signal becomes familiar and expected (Olsson & Phelps, 2007; Shurick et al., 2012). Thus, it is hard to dissociate fear and anxiety based on familiarity and expectation. Finally, individuals perceive threat from a range of cues, most of which would be present during immediate threat (e.g., cat and open space), and only some of which would be present during prospective threat (e.g., open space only). Taken together, these points favor the argument that fear and anxiety are largely similar and reflect differences in degree rather than kind. Therefore, we treat them interchangeably in the present discussion.

FEELING FEARFUL—BEHAVIORAL TENDENCIES, MENTAL PROCESSES, AND BODILY CORRELATES

Fear is a very basic emotion. We find evidence of it in a wide range of species, including relatively simple organisms such as worms or flies. Yet the feeling aspects of fear can be very complex. They may involve seemingly opposing behavioral tendencies and a range of mental processes, all of which are supported by sophisticated biological mechanisms. In the following section, we examine these aspects and learn how they make fear a highly useful emotion.

Behavioral Tendencies

Individuals faced with threat may display a range of behaviors that appear unpredictable. A dog, for example, may cower, run away, or attack when frightened. Thus, its fear seems to promote submission, evasion, or opposition toward an aggressor. Researchers suggest that these behaviors, although quite varied, are all directed at avoiding personal harm, and that they are organized along a temporal dimension reflecting the immediacy of threat (Figure 9.1). At low immediacy, when threat is still relatively distant, fear triggers behavioral inhibition, allowing the animal to assess the threat and to minimize the likelihood of detection. In contrast, at high immediacy, when threat is imminent, fear triggers behavioral activation and thus promotes active escape and defense. Because threat is typically distant before it becomes immediate, inhibitory responses are believed commonly to precede activational responses; this has been termed a **defense cascade** (Lang, Davis, & Öhman, 2000).

The startle reflex and freezing are two behaviors that fall into the initial stage of threat detection, during which ongoing activities are inhibited and individuals orient toward threat (Chapter 6). The startle reflex is provoked by a sudden and salient sensory change, such as a loud noise following silence or darkness following light. It is important for individuals to respond to such changes because they often announce actual threat, such as a sudden attack from a predator.

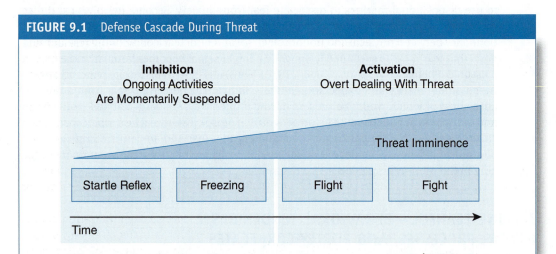

FIGURE 9.1   Defense Cascade During Threat

Researchers proposed that threat responses can be organized in a "defense cascade." Initial responses may be primarily inhibitory. Ongoing activities are interrupted, the body muscles are tensed and prepared for action (startle reflex), and the individual refrains from overt movement (freezing). Subsequently, the individual may flee, if flight is an option, or fight. Initial, inhibitory responses may be most pronounced when threat is relatively distant. They may serve to explore and prepare for threat as well as to prevent detection. The more imminent threat becomes, the more likely the individual engages in active threat responses.

The startle reflex is characterized by a wave of muscular contractions that lower the individual's body frame and produce temporary rigidity (Figure 6.1). Presumably, this protects against physical injury and, like a spring-loaded jack-in-the box, prepares the body for movement. While the startle reflex itself may be an automatic, nonemotional response that is executed at the level of the brainstem (Lang et al., 2000), its neuronal activation feeds into higher brain centers such as the amygdala, and there may generate accompanying feelings of fear. Thus, like other more specific signals of threat, startling stimuli are unpleasant, and apart from eliciting a startle reflex, provoke higher-level behavioral, mental, and bodily aspects of fear (Knight, Nguyen, & Bandettini, 2003; Lanuza, Nader, & LeDoux, 2004).

Freezing may follow the startle response or initial threat perception. During freezing, the body arrests in its movements and body physiology temporarily slows down. In extreme situations, when threat is inescapable, individuals may lose consciousness and give the impression of being dead (Natterson-Horowitz & Bowers, 2013). If consciousness is retained, the individual may deliberately explore the perceived threat. For example, a squirrel in a public park noticing a distant dog will typically freeze in its position and monitor the trajectory of the dog's movement. If the dog moves away from the squirrel, the squirrel will remain fixed for a while longer and thus avoid detection. However, if the dog moves toward the squirrel, the squirrel will break its freezing and run up the nearest tree.

Like the startle reflex, freezing occurs in a range of vertebrates, including small zebrafish (Lee et al., 2010) and nonhuman primates (Kalin, Shelton, Rickman, & Davidson, 1998; Sagaspe, Schwartz, & Vuilleumier, 2011). Moreover, behavioral precursors akin to freezing appear to exist in invertebrates such as snails (Walters, Carew, & Kandel, 1981) and flies (Cho, Heberlein, & Wolf, 2004). Researchers speculate that these responses serve to avoid detection, and in their extreme unconscious form are aimed at making aggressors lose interest (Natterson-Horowitz & Bowers, 2013). Notably, however, the latter response may in itself be deadly, as occasionally body physiology slows down too much, inducing cardiac arrest.

The initial period of behavioral inhibition may be followed by a dramatic increase in behavioral output if an identified threat becomes imminent and behavioral responses seem viable. Depending on the situation, these responses can take two forms. If the situation allows the individual to flee with a reasonable chance for escape, the individual will choose this route and avoid confrontation. However, if the situation makes escape improbable, the individual will defend itself or its social group by attempting to appease, intimidate, or harm an aggressor.

Appeasement and intimidation are pursued through nonverbal communication including facial displays and vocalizations. Darwin noted that such communication shows striking similarities across a range of species, suggesting that "fear was [nonverbally] expressed from an extremely remote period" (Darwin, 1872/2009, p. 356). As part of a facial display of fear, many mammals including humans will expose their teeth. For example, canines confronted by an aggressor often show something called a submissive grin, whereby they raise their upper lip and withdraw their mouth corners. Likewise, nonhuman primates will expose their teeth in an expression called the silent bared-teeth display (Chapter 7). Although seen in antagonistic encounters, these expressions are not strictly defensive displays (de Waal, 2006; Parr, Waller, Vick, & Bard, 2007). They may also occur during affiliative encounters, when one individual tries peacefully to approach another. Thus, many researchers proposed that the silent bared-teeth display and its evolutionary predecessor, the submissive grin, were precursors of the human smile (de Waal, 2006; Parr et al., 2007).

In humans, smiling is not uncommon during fear. Moreover, the typical human fear display contains a smile-like oral component characterized by an open mouth and, possibly, stretched lips. However, oral muscles are involved differently in this as compared to the genuine smile. Additionally, the eyes are affected in a different way. Rather than squinting, the eyes in fear are wide open to facilitate a visual exploration of threat (Ekman & Rosenberg, 2005; Susskind et al., 2008; Figure 9.2).

Vocal expressions form a second line of defense during threat. They typically comprise screams that are characterized by a steep onset, high-piercing sound, and a certain noisiness that presumably reflects deterministic or nonrandom chaos in vocal fold vibration (Owren & Rendall, 2001). Screams broadcast the sender's fear and thus summon allies to come to aid. But perhaps more important, screams help to ward off aggressors because they are an unpleasant stimulus or "auditory pinprick," particularly at close distances (Owren & Rendall, 2001).

While fear behaviors such as intense gazing and screaming might help a frightened individual to defend itself against threat, they may also be useful to other members in its social group. More often than not, a threat to one individual in the group will become a threat to other individuals. For example, a group member that aggresses against one may be likely to aggress against another one of its peers. Likewise, a predator may change pursuit if one individual seems an easier catch than another. Thus, it pays off for group members to be sensitive to their respective levels of fear so as to minimize threat to themselves.

In addition to the nonverbal signals that can be seen or heard, many species evolved a chemical mechanism to communicate fear to peers. For example, fish can detect a

---

FIGURE 9.2   Facial Display of Fear

During fear humans raise their eyebrows, widen their eyes, and open their mouths. Similar facial changes can be seen in other primates, such as the long-tailed macaque.

Source: © palangsi—Fotolia.com (macaque).

pheromone that is released by injury. This pheromone, in the absence of a visible predator, is enough to elicit a fear response from an entire school (Mathuru et al., 2012; von Frisch, 1965). Humans also produce a fear pheromone. It is released with sweat and has been shown to facilitate the perception of fear in others (Zhou & Chen, 2009), to promote actual feelings of fear (Mujica-Parodi et al., 2009; Prehn, Ohrt, Sojka, Ferstl, & Pause, 2006), and to enhance risk taking (Haegler et al., 2010) as well as cognitive functioning (Chen, Katdare, & Lucas, 2006).

If the nonverbal attempts to solicit help or ward off an aggressor fail, the frightened individual becomes more physical and may kick, scratch, bite, or sting. Moreover, nonverbal signs of fear may give way to displays of anger and aggression. Thus, with increasing threat imminence, an individual progresses from a stage of behavioral inhibition and wariness to full-body physical defense.

Mental Processes

In its extreme form, fear is clearly an unpleasant emotion that most individuals try to avoid. Yet, under certain circumstances, lower levels of fear may be pleasant and exhilarating. We know this because some humans devote substantial time and money to dangerous sports such as big-wave surfing, base jumping, high-altitude climbing, or cave diving. Moreover, even more people spend their time and money getting scared at the movies or in theme parks. Thus, it seems that certain thrills are a welcome experience and that a propensity to seek them out may be evolutionarily adaptive. Undoubtedly, willfully facing certain fearful situations enables humans and other animals to defend and expand resources such as territory or food supply. Additionally, it helps to impress others and to secure mating opportunities and status within a group.

In addition to its subjective feeling component, fear influences mental processes associated with attention and memory. Research on attention revealed that threats, more than any other stimuli, automatically grab and hold an individual's attention. Evidence of this comes from visual search studies conducted by Öhman and colleagues (Juth et al., 2005; Lundqvist and Öhman, 2005). In these studies, participants were presented with an array of stimuli that were fully identical or that contained a single odd stimulus. For example, such an array may have comprised neutral faces only or neutral faces with a single happy or angry face. The participants' task was to indicate via button pressing whether the visual array was coherent or contained an odd one out. Participants performed this task better when the odd stimulus was an angry and hence threatening face as compared to when it was a happy face (Figure 9.3).

Further evidence of a precedence of threat in attention and awareness comes from the attentional blink paradigm (Anderson, 2005). In this paradigm, participants are exposed to a rapid stimulus stream that contains one or possibly two targets. For example, the participants may see a series of words in which nontargets are printed in black and targets are printed in green, and they have to push a button as soon as they detect a target. Participants are likely to miss a second target that closely follows a first target, and this likelihood decreases with increasing temporal separation between the first and the second target. The finding that the second of two closely succeeding targets is difficult to detect has been called the "attentional

FIGURE 9.3 The Priority of Threat

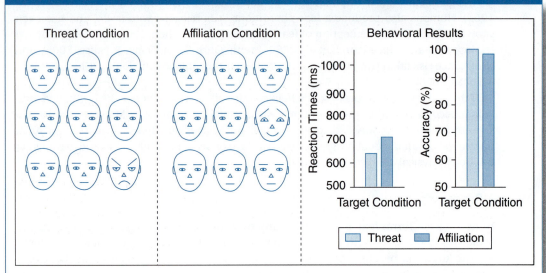

Threat-relevant information captures attention. This has been demonstrated by Lundqvist and Öhman (2005), who presented face arrays to participants. The arrays contained either all neutral faces (nontarget arrays, not shown here) or neutral faces together with a single angry (threat) or happy (affiliation) face (target arrays). Participants discriminated target from nontarget arrays faster and more accurately when the target arrays contained threat as compared to affiliation signals. The data figure is based on performance means provided by Lundqvist and Öhman (2005, Experiment 4). These means were collapsed across multiple conditions in which the above faces as well as faces with limited combinations of expressive features (e.g., only eyebrows and mouth signaled threat or affiliation) were presented.

Source: "Emotion Regulates Attention: The Relation Between Facial Configurations, Facial Emotion, and Visual Attention," by D. Lundqvist and A. Öhman, 2005, *Visual Cognition, 12,* 51–84.

blink," and has been interpreted as a momentary lapse in awareness. Notably, this lapse can be overcome when the second target signals threat (Anderson, 2005).

Apart from attention and awareness, fear plays an important role in learning. Because threat signals a possible loss of resources, it pays off to remember the circumstances that produced threat and the behaviors that prevented or terminated it. Memory of the circumstances of threat is established through classical conditioning (Chapter 5). In humans this was first empirically demonstrated by John Watson and Rosalie Rayner (1920) in a study that is now considered unethical.

These two scientists conducted repeated learning sessions with a 9-month-old-infant named Albert. Prior to the conditioning, Watson and Rayner presented Albert with a live rat and established that the child's reaction was nonfearful. Subsequent presentations of the rat were paired with a loud noise that startled Albert and made him cry. It took only a few such pairings for Albert to begin to fear the rat. Now, when presented with it, he would cry even without noise. Moreover, he would show a similar reaction to a white rabbit or a Santa Claus mask, suggesting that he generalized his fear to all things white and furry.

These findings have been replicated with other, more ethical paradigms in humans. One such paradigm involves the presentation of two colored squares, one of which is followed by a mild electric shock and thus serves as the conditioned stimulus (CS+), whereas the other is not followed by shock and serves as a stimulus control or CS–. It has been shown that human participants learn to associate the electric shock with the colored square that precedes it. Additionally, they develop autonomic and central nervous system responses indicative of fear for the CS+ but not for the CS– (LaBar, Gatenby, Gore, LeDoux, & Phelps, 1998; LaBar, LeDoux, Spencer, & Phelps, 1995; Schiller et al., 2009).

Apart from this work in humans, there is overwhelming evidence of fear conditioning in nonhuman animals, including invertebrates such as snails (Kita et al., 2011) or flies (Galili, Lüdke, Galizia, Szyszka, & Tanimoto, 2011), and vertebrates such as fish (Lee et al., 2010) and rodents (Iwata & LeDoux, 1988). Thus, classical or fear conditioning seems to represent one general mechanism by which fear affects an individual's mind.

Operant conditioning represents another such mechanism. During operant conditioning, behavioral consequences shape future behavioral probabilities. Behaviors that produced positive consequences are more likely to be repeated than behaviors without consequences. In contrast, behaviors that produced negative consequences are less likely to be repeated than behaviors without consequences. Both forms of operant learning are critical in the context of fear and have been empirically examined.

For example, Seligman and Maier (1967) explored how the termination of threat and thus a positive behavioral consequence shapes behavioral probabilities. The researchers placed dogs inside a shuttle-box comprising of two compartments that were separated by a barrier low enough for the dog to jump over (Figure 9.4). They then administered an electric foot shock that the dog could avoid by moving into the adjoining compartment. Dogs that, in an attempt to escape the shock, jumped the shuttle-box barrier were rewarded for this behavior because it terminated the threat. Thus, they would continue to jump the barrier on subsequent trials. Notably, however, not all dogs showed successful operant learning. Specifically, those dogs that prior to the shuttle-box training were subjected to inescapable shocks were considerably less likely to later attempt and master escape. They had developed a condition called "learned helplessness" (Chapter 8).

Another example of the role of fear in operant learning comes from a study in which the consequences of a behavior reduced its probability. In this study, goldfish were trained to press a lever to obtain a food reward (Geller, 1963). After this behavior was well established, the researchers introduced a light and, for the duration of the light, coupled lever pressing both with food delivery and electric shock. Only a few trials were necessary for the goldfish to inhibit lever pressing whenever the light was on. A review of this and similar work in other nonhuman animals and humans suggests that the effect of fear on operant conditioning transcends species (Higgins & Morris, 1984).

Although fear promotes classical and operant learning, certain stimulus-stimulus or stimulus-response associations are learned more easily than others. This variation in

FIGURE 9.4   Fear Promotes Operant Learning

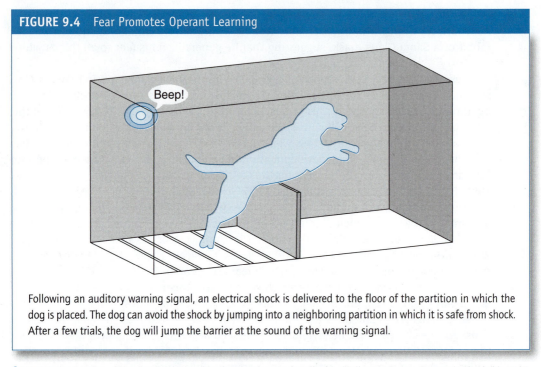

Following an auditory warning signal, an electrical shock is delivered to the floor of the partition in which the dog is placed. The dog can avoid the shock by jumping into a neighboring partition in which it is safe from shock. After a few trials, the dog will jump the barrier at the sound of the warning signal.

Source: Approximation of the shuttle-box used in the experiments described in "Failure to Escape Traumatic Shock," by M. E. Seligman & S. F. Maier, 1967, *Journal of Experimental Psychology, 74*, pp. 1–9.

learning has been linked to the idea of preparedness, which holds that any animal, by virtue of its physical and mental characteristics, is "prepared to associate certain events, unprepared for some, and contraprepared for others" (Seligman 1970, p. 406; A Closer Look 9.1).

For example, in the context of classical conditioning, it has been demonstrated that rats easily associate a particular taste with subsequent illness but are unlikely to associate taste with shock. In other words, they learn to avoid tastes that previously made them ill but fail to avoid tastes that triggered a painful stimulus (Garcia & Koelling, 1966; Figure 9.5). Somehow, a taste is unlikely to be perceived as a precursor to threat. Thus, rats are contraprepared to develop conditioned fear to a taste stimulus.

Research also suggests a role of preparedness for operant conditioning. Most animals are prepared to associate species-typical escape behaviors and contraprepared to associate appetitive or approach behaviors with the termination of threat. Thus, it is relatively easy to teach an animal that jumping away from an area where it receives an electric shock will terminate that shock. In contrast, it is much more difficult to teach the animal that grooming itself will do the same (Seligman, 1970; Thorndike, 1998). Again, similar principles apply to humans (Öhman & Dimberg, 1978; Öhman & Soares, 1998).

FIGURE 9.5 Preparedness and the Classical Conditioning of Fear

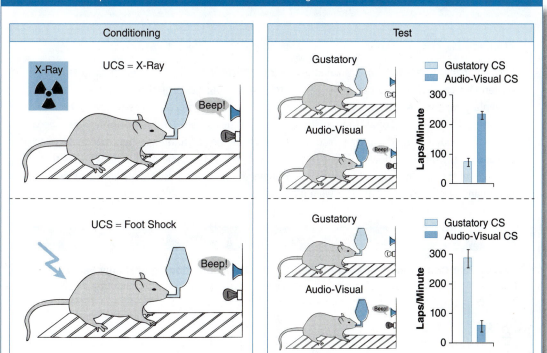

In this study, rats were exposed to a drinking solution with a particular taste, noise, and light. The drinking solution served as the gustatory conditioned stimulus (CS); the noise and light served as the audiovisual CS. One group of rats was exposed to X-rays, a sickness-producing unconditioned stimulus (UCS). Another group was exposed to foot shock, a pain-producing UCS. Both groups then underwent testing for the gustatory CS (i.e., the flavor of the gustatory CS was presented without noise and light) and the audiovisual CS (i.e., noise and light were presented; the flavor of the drinking solution differed from that of the gustatory CS). The group that was X-rayed during conditioning had learned to associate sickness with the gustatory CS. It showed reduced drinking during the gustatory test, but not during the audiovisual test. The group that was foot shocked during conditioning had learned to associate pain with the light and noise. It showed reduced drinking during the audiovisual test, but not during the gustatory test. This demonstrates that sickness and pain produce different conditioning responses, suggesting that both are differently "prepared" for learning.

Source: "Relation of Cue to Consequence in Avoidance Learning," by J. Garcia & R. A. Koelling, 1966, *Psychonomic Science, 4,* pp. 123–124.

Bodily Correlates

Peripheral Correlates

The first researcher to directly explore the effect of fear on the autonomic nervous system was Walter Cannon (1915). While exposing a subject cat to a barking dog, Cannon

A CLOSER LOOK 9.1

Prepared for Fear

Because many threats remained unchanged in the course of evolution, a readiness to fear them conferred a consistent advantage that is now reflected in our genes and those of other animals. Exemplary for this are findings in nonhuman primates on the preparedness to fear snakes and crocodiles. In an observational learning study (Cook & Mineka, 1989), rhesus monkeys were shown one of four video clips. These clips pictured a conspecific being frightened by a toy snake, a toy crocodile, a toy rabbit, or flowers. The clips were edited so that the same fearful monkey was shown with one of the aforementioned objects. Subject monkeys watched these videos across 12 sessions. Before and after these sessions, they were presented with the video objects and their fear response

---

FIGURE 9.6   Fear Conditioning to Facial Threat Displays

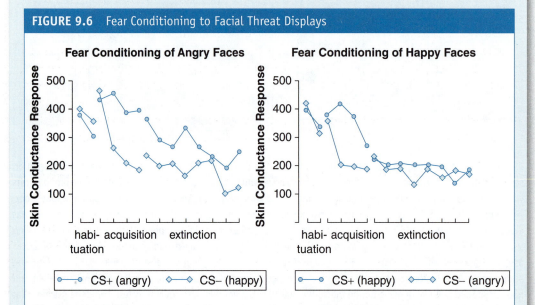

Results of a study by Öhman and Dimberg exploring the preparedness of humans to fear condition to angry versus happy faces. In two separate conditioning groups, either an angry or a happy face was paired with a shock (i.e., acquisition). The fear response measured via skin conductance extinguished more readily when the happy face than when the angry face served as conditioned stimulus (CS+).

Source: Copyright © 2011 by the American Psychological Association. Adapted with permission. "Facial Expressions as Conditioned Stimuli for Extrodermal Responses: A case of Preparedness?" by A. Öhman and U. Dimberg, 1978, *Journal of Personality and Social Psychology, 36*(11), pp. 1251–1258. The use of APA information does not imply endorsement by APA.

was assessed. To this end, the researchers placed the object together with a food item into a see-through box and measured how long the monkeys hesitated before they retrieved the food.

The results showed comparable latencies for the toy rabbit and flower conditions. However, the monkeys took significantly longer to reach for the food in the snake and crocodile conditions. Thus, the authors argue that the monkeys were prepared to fear reptiles but not rabbits and flowers. Possibly, such preparedness is retained in the human gene pool and accounts for the prevalence of reptile phobia.

Apart from being threatened by venomous animals or other predators, humans experience much threat from their own kind. Moreover, the recognition of such threat from an angry face or an angry voice is paramount for children to obey their parents and for adults to place themselves in the hierarchy of their social group. Thus, one may speculate that humans are prepared to fear anger expressions from other humans.

That this is indeed the case has been demonstrated in a study that used happy and angry expressions in a fear-conditioning experiment (Öhman & Dimberg, 1978). Participants were presented with these expressions. While half the participants received an electric shock following the happy expression, the other half received an electric shock following the angry expression. Following this fear acquisition phase, both groups underwent extinction (Chapter 5), where the expressions were presented without shock. During fear acquisition, participants showed a comparable increase in skin conductance to the happy and angry CS+. During extinction, however, skin conductance quickly returned to normal levels for the happy CS+ group, whereas levels remained high for the angry CS+ group. Thus, fear conditioning to angry faces was relatively resistant to extinction, suggesting that we are prepared to fear them.

observed an activation of the cat's "sympathetic" nerves that triggered the release of adrenaline from the adrenal gland. Moreover, he found that this adrenergic release had a number of knock-on effects. Among other things, it reduced the digestion of food by impacting processes like salivation or peristaltic motion. He also observed an increase in blood sugar, blood coagulation, and muscle function. Thus, Cannon famously postulated that "strong" emotions like fear or anger overcome momentary fatigue and prepare the organism for flight or fight.

Researchers after Cannon confirmed and extended his work with nonhuman animals (for a review, see Dantzer, 2001). They termed the system that mediates bodily preparation for flight or fight the sympathetic adrenal medullary system (SAM) and showed that its activation triggers the release of both adrenaline and noradrenaline. Furthermore, they identified a second system that is activated by fear, now known as the hypothalamic-pituitary-adrenal (HPA) axis and part of the body's endocrine system. Unlike SAM, which targets the adrenal medulla, the HPA axis targets the adrenal cortex and promotes its release of glucocorticoids such as cortisol and corticosterone. The release of these stress hormones helps break down the body's energy stores (i.e., protein, carbohydrates, and fat) so that they can be turned into sugar. While SAM immediately mobilizes the organism for action, the HPA axis ensures that this mobilization is sustained (Figure 9.7).

In line with these findings, psychophysiological studies in humans suggest physiological arousal during fear that results from sympathetic and endocrine processes. Among other things, this is evident from increased levels of stress hormones in the blood (Hermans et al., 2011; Merz, Stark, Vaitl, Tabbert, & Wolf, 2013) and the fact that breathing becomes faster and more shallow, the pupils dilate, heart rate increases while heart-rate variability declines, the skin becomes moist and better conducting, and finger temperature decreases (Kreibig, 2010).

Central Nervous System Correlates

Structures

Initial insights into the neuroanatomical substrates of fear came from lesion work in non-human animals. At the beginning of the 20th century, individuals like Cannon, Papez, and MacLean had highlighted structures in the diencephalon such as the hypothalamus as well as cerebral structures such as the cingulate gyrus and hippocampus as being important for emotions. In the second half of the 20th century, their successors began to explore which structures were critical for what emotion.

Valuable insights into this issue came from neuroscientist Joseph LeDoux. To determine which parts of the brain support auditory fear conditioning, LeDoux and colleagues subjected rats to various kinds of lesions (LeDoux, Sakaguchi, & Reis, 1984; LeDoux, Sakaguchi, Iwata, & Reis, 1985). After the animals recovered from the surgery, they underwent a fear-conditioning procedure in which a tone was paired with an electric foot shock.

Among the lesion sites that disrupted fear conditioning was the amygdala. Damage to this region and/or to its sensory input region in the thalamus impaired learning. Such damage prevented animals from acquiring fear responses to tones that were paired with shock (e.g., increased blood pressure and freezing). Thus, LeDoux and colleagues concluded that fear conditioning depends on the amygdala.

Because lesions to the amygdala left responses to the unconditioned stimulus, the foot shock, intact, the researchers went further to discover the neuroanatomical targets of the amygdala (LeDoux, Iwata, Cicchetti, & Reis, 1988). Some of these targets were located in the lateral hypothalamus and the central gray, and lesions to these structures disrupted different aspects of fear. Hypothalamic lesions disrupted changes in blood pressure, whereas central gray lesions disrupted freezing. Work by others revealed additional targets by showing that threat-induced amygdala activation upregulates processing in sensory areas and facilitates the elicitation of a startle reflex in the brainstem (Hitchcock & Davis, 1986; Rosen, Hitchcock, Sananes, & Davis, 1991).

Inspired by these discoveries in nonhuman animals, researchers began to test human patients with amygdala damage. Not surprisingly, these patients failed to properly fear condition. Although they understood and remembered the contingency between a conditioned and an unconditioned stimulus, they failed to develop peripheral signs of fear to the conditioned stimulus (LaBar et al., 1995). In other words, they could tell the experimenter that high tones were followed by an electric shock. However, their skin conductance remained flat whenever they heard these tones.

FIGURE 9.7   Functional Mechanisms of the Sympathetic Adrenal Medullary (SAM) System and the Hypothalamic-Pituitary-Adrenal (HPA) Axis

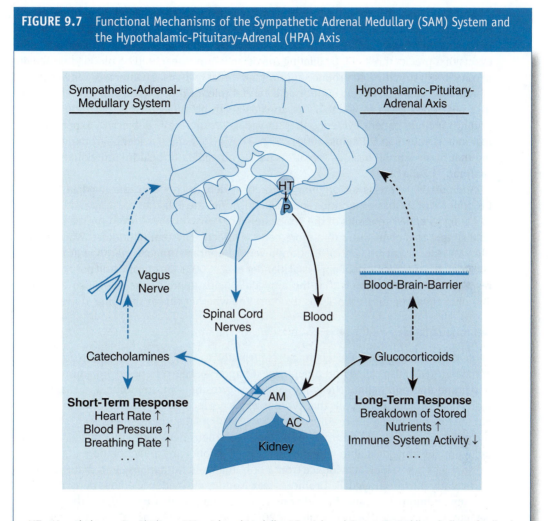

HT = Hypothalamus; P = Pituitary; AM = Adrenal Medulla; AC = Adrenal Cortex. Dotted lines indicate feedback mechanisms to the brain.

Converging evidence also came from neuroimaging studies in healthy individuals, showing that fear conditioning involved an activation of the amygdala (LaBar et al., 1998). Notably, such activation was not only found during standard fear conditioning but also for instructed fear. Specifically, participants who were told that one of two stimuli might be followed by a shock showed differences in amygdala activation and skin conductance between both stimuli. Despite the fact that a shock was never presented, the stimulus they were instructed to fear elicited heightened activation compared to the supposed safe stimulus (Phelps et al., 2001).

Based on this and other work implicating the amygdala in the perception of both conditioned and unconditioned fear stimuli (Phan, Wager, Taylor, & Liberzon, 2002), it was proposed that the amygdala plays a central role in fear by allowing individuals to learn about the events that predict threat, by facilitating the detection of threat, and by modulating activity in other brain structures to produce appropriate threat responses (Öhman & Mineka, 2001).

Although research largely supported a central role for the amygdala in fear, some findings raised doubts as to whether the amygdala can be considered a fear module. Such findings include patient evidence that amygdala lesions leave subjective experiences of fear intact (Anderson & Phelps, 2000, 2002). They also include evidence from neuroimaging that many stimuli besides threat excite the amygdala in healthy individuals (Sander, Grafman, & Zalla, 2003).

Additionally, there is an ongoing theoretical debate concerning amygdala function. Proponents of the basic emotions approach hold onto the idea that the amygdala is central to a fear system. Proponents of the dimensional or constructionist account see the amygdala simply as a contributor to a more general affective system (Lindquist, Wager, Kober, Bliss-Moreau, & Barrett, 2012). Last, followers of appraisal theory view the amygdala as subserving a specific form of appraisal (Sander et al., 2003). One promising possibility with respect to the latter view is that the amygdala helps appraise the relevance of a given stimulus. However, future work has to determine whether this or the other views prevail.

Neurochemicals

Noradrenaline. One potential chemical contributor to fear is the neurotransmitter noradrenaline (NA), also called norepinephrine (Chapter 4). Like other catecholamines such as dopamine and adrenaline, NA is derived from tyrosine—an amino acid available from many high-protein foods. Cells that synthesize NA are located outside the brain in the adrenal medulla and inside the brain in the locus coeruleus (Latin for "blue spot"), situated in the pons (Figure 9.8). NA neurons in the locus coeruleus have multiple projection targets, including the amygdala, into which they release NA following an action potential.

Now, let's take a look at evidence from nonhuman and human research that NA release, particularly into the amygdala, promotes fear. Nonhuman evidence entails demonstrations that unconditioned threats or conditioned stimuli that predict threat trigger the release of NA into the amygdala (Young & Williams, 2010). Nonhuman evidence also includes research showing that the blockage of central NA release reduces fearful responses to threat (Davis et al., 1979; Dębiec et al., 2011; Onaka et al., 1996). For example, pharmacologically induced lesions of NA neurons were found to reduce both endocrine and behavioral measures of agitation to foot shock (Onaka et al., 1996). Additionally, the application of clonidine, a substance that inhibits the firing of NA neurons by binding to α-adrenergic receptors in the locus coeruleus, was shown to suppress the startle response elicited by a conditioned stimulus previously paired with foot shock (Davis et al., 1979).

In line with this, human research revealed a role for NA in fear. An initial study by Cahill and colleagues tested the effect of propranolol, a drug that readily crosses the blood-brain barrier and that blocks β-adrenergic receptors. Thus, propranolol prevents NA from binding in places that express such receptors—for example, the amygdala. In their study, Cahill and colleagues presented participants with a slide story that contained

FIGURE 9.8 The Amygdala and Some Input and Output Regions

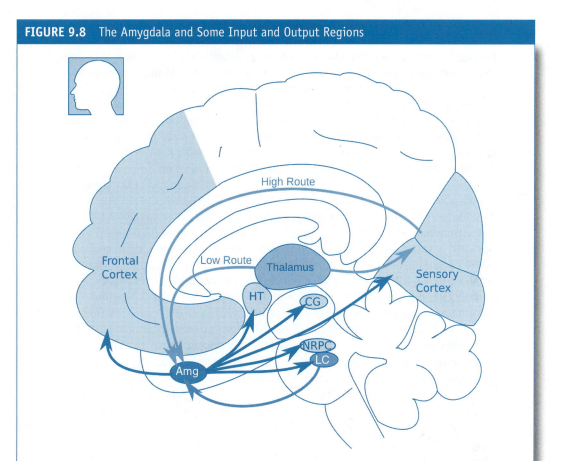

The amygdala is located in the temporal lobe and receives sensory information via the low and high route, indicated in light blue. The representation of threat-relevant sensory information by the amygdala excites the locus coeruleus in the pons, which sends noradrenergic fibers back to the amygdala that facilitate the function of this multinuclei structure. Among other things, amygdala activation affects the frontal cortex, sensory cortex, and a number of subcortical structures. Amg = amygdala; HT = hypothalamus; CG = central gray; NRPC = nucleus reticulopontis caudalis; LC =locus coeruleus.

neutral and threat-relevant information (Cahill, Prins, Weber, & McGaugh, 1994). They found that memory was better for threat-relevant as compared to neutral information in individuals treated with a placebo. In contrast, there was no such memory advantage for threat in individuals treated with propranolol. Thus, as in nonhuman animals, NA transmission seems critical to the processing of threat in humans.

Subsequent research corroborated this point. Using similar pharmacological manipulations, it demonstrated that NA binding underpins fear conditioning (Soeter & Kindt, 2011) and is critical for amygdala activation to threat (Hurlemann et al., 2010; Onur et al., 2009).

Cortisol/corticosterone (CORT). A second substance that may play a role in fear is the human hormone cortisol and its nonhuman analog corticosterone, henceforth referred to as CORT. Despite being produced outside the brain in the adrenal gland, this hormone can pass the blood-brain barrier and affect brain functioning (Figure 9.7). In fact, there are several brain structures with CORT receptors, including the amygdala and the hippocampus (Oitzl, Champagne, van der Veen, & de Kloet, 2010).

Although the influence of CORT on brain function must necessarily be slow, it seems relevant for certain aspects of fear. First, it seems to promote fear conditioning. Several studies in rodents revealed that a CORT injection facilitates (Corodimas, LeDoux, Gold, & Schulkin, 1994; Hui et al., 2004) whereas a depletion of CORT impairs conditioned fear responses (Pugh, Tremblay, Fleshner, & Rudy, 1997). Additionally, CORT seems to increase wariness and avoidance behavior (Korte & De Boer, 2003).

Whereas the above evidence from nonhuman animals is relatively conclusive, the evidence from humans is, at present, quite mixed. Some human studies suggest a contribution of CORT to fear (Jovanovic et al., 2011), while others suggest the opposite—namely, that CORT protects against fear (Putman & Roelofs, 2011). Together, this work highlights the complexity of CORT function and raises the possibility that its effects may vary depending on the CORT dose or level, the duration an individual is exposed to heightened CORT, and the different receptors to which CORT binds (Oitzl et al., 2010; Putman & Roelofs, 2011).

Last, there is evidence that the neurotransmitter γ-aminobutyric acid (GABA) modulates fear. GABA, which is synthesized from glutamate, serves as the main inhibitory neurotransmitter, with neurons and receptor sites widely distributed throughout the brain. Interesting for us is that there are large numbers of GABAergic neurons in the amygdala, and that these neurons seem to play a critical role in fear conditioning. Specifically, their selective inactivation or disruption has been shown to impair both fear acquisition (Ciocchi et al., 2010) and extinction (Amano, Unal, & Paré, 2010). Moreover, GABAergic agonists or the injection of GABA have been shown to reduce fear (Lopes et al., 2012; Korte & De Boer, 2003). Thus, medication that facilitates GABAergic activity is often prescribed to individuals with anxiety disorders. Unfortunately, however, these drugs are not fear-specific and produce a range of side effects. Thus, pharmacological research is still ongoing to provide better help for clinically relevant fear conditions.

Mechanisms

Having reviewed the different feeling aspects of fear, we can now attempt their synthesis and approach the mechanism by which threat stimuli come to influence an individual's behavior. This mechanism begins when the individual experiences threats such as a sudden drop in altitude, a predator, or a conditioned stimulus that was previously associated with threat. Sensory information from these stimuli is conveyed from the primary sense organs to the amygdala.

Rodent work by LeDoux and others suggests that this information can take two routes, referred to as the low and high route, respectively. The low route extends from subcortical sensory centers in the thalamus directly to the amygdala. The high route extends from these same centers to the primary and secondary sensory cortex, and from there to the amygdala. Although definite evidence of the existence of these two routes comes from nonhuman animals only, some studies imply similar projections in the human brain (Morris, DeGelder, Weiskrantz, & Dolan, 2001; Morris, Öhman, & Dolan, 1999; Vuilleumier et al., 2003; Figure 9.8).

Being somewhat shorter, information traveling the low route reaches the amygdala a few milliseconds faster than it does traveling the high route. Yet its sensory acuity is relatively low. In the auditory domain, the low route supports only simple representations of pitch and fails at more complex representations, such as pitch trajectory (e.g., up-down versus down-up; Ohl, Wetzel, Wagner, Rech, & Scheich, 1999). In the visual domain, it supports the representation of low but not high spatial frequencies, which are projected via magno- and parvocellular pathways, respectively. Thus, visual impressions from the low route confer rough changes in brightness that inform about the spatial whereabouts of an object but not its fine perceptual details. Moreover, in the absence of high route input, low route sensation is intuitive rather than definite. Individuals may have a feeling of something being there without actual sensory certainty or conscious awareness.

This phenomenon is illustrated by patients with lesions in primary visual cortex who retain some visual capacity despite lacking a cortical analysis. When presented with objects in their "blind" visual field, these patients typically report not seeing anything. Yet, when forced to make perceptual judgments such as whether a presented object is dark or bright, round or squared, they often perform better than would be expected by chance. Moreover, they also retain a certain emotional sensitivity. For example, they are able to discriminate between different facial expressions (de Gelder, Vroomen, Pourtois, & Weiskrantz, 1999) and respond to visual fear-conditioned stimuli with heightened physiological arousal (Hamm et al., 2003).

Thus, although low route sensory processing is coarse, it often provides enough clues about possible dangers to influence amygdala function without input from the more fine-grained sensory representations of the high route. Moreover, it can direct the focus of fine-grained sensory analysis to dangers that are perceived outside an individual's awareness and initiate a defense cascade before the slower and more resource-dependent cognitive operations can intervene. As such, the low route serves as a kind of emotional safety system, ensuring that critical events are not missed.

Once the amygdala becomes excited through low and/or high route processes, it issues commands to a number of subcortical and cortical targets. Projections to the locus coeruleus in the brainstem presumably excite back projections that release NA into the amygdala and that facilitate the functioning of this multinuclei structure (Liddell et al., 2005; Figure 9.8). Projections from the amygdala to the hypothalamus excite the SAM system and the HPA axis and thus trigger the release of stress hormones into the bloodstream (Figure 9.7). Amygdala projections to other subcortical structures such as the central gray or pons facilitate fear behaviors like freezing and the startle reflex, respectively. Last, amygdala projections to cortical structures such as the primary sensory areas as well as frontal regions facilitate threat awareness, the minute encoding of threatening events, and the selection of appropriate response strategies.

Together, the physiological, behavioral, and mental processes initiated by the amygdala and its projection targets are experienced as fear, and their consequences are closely monitored. Part of this monitoring is achieved via a feedback loop from the body to the brain (McGaugh, 2004). Some of the stress hormones released by the adrenal gland (e.g., adrenaline) can bind to the ascending vagus nerve and through their binding send a return signal to the locus coeruleus and the amygdala. Other stress hormones, such as CORT, can pass the blood-brain barrier and directly bind to dedicated receptors located in the amygdala and elsewhere (Figure 9.7).

Research suggests that this feedback has several important functions. One of these functions is to facilitate the long-term storage of information related to the threatening experience (McGaugh, 2004). Feedback modulation of the amygdala enhances the long-term storage of freshly acquired fear memories, a process that operates across minutes, hours, and days following the threat (Chapter 10).

Another function is to keep ongoing threat responses in check (Tasker & Herman, 2011). This is achieved through the activation of fear inhibitory processes that can be triggered by the binding of CORT to receptors in the amygdala, hippocampus, and pituitary. Specifically, CORT feedback to these structures helps downregulate the HPA axis and reduce the amount of circulating stress hormones.

Together, feedback from the body promotes long-term memories of threat predictors and escape behaviors and thus helps the animal to deal with threat more effectively in the future. Additionally, it contributes to fear recovery and reduces the potentially damaging effect that fear or extended stress can have on the body.

WHY DO WE FEEL FEAR?

Like other emotions, fear has complex consequences on an individual's body, mind, and behavior. Depending on threat proximity, its consequences for the body are inhibitory or activational. Its consequences for the mind include attentional focus on the threat and the memorization of threat-relevant information. Last, its consequences on behavior include responses that reduce discovery, enable threat exploration, and, if threat becomes imminent, allow the individual to defend itself against injury or death. Thus, together, fear promotes processes that minimize both current harm and harm that lies ahead.

WHEN FEAR BECOMES A PROBLEM

Anxiety Disorders

Anxiety disorders overview. Although we often hail fearlessness as a desirable personal characteristic, a person without fear would be doomed. As with other negative emotions, feelings of fear are useful in guiding our behavior and are critical to our survival and the survival of those who depend on us. Thus, it pays off to listen to one's fear instead of wishing it away. Nevertheless, the result of such listening should be a healthy balance between giving in to fear and conquering it. Many events are potentially dangerous. Driving a car, cooking a meal, or approaching an unfamiliar person could all end badly. Yet we need to engage in these activities on a daily basis in order to live normally.

Individuals who are overcome by their fears and who show fearful avoidance of vital everyday activities are said to suffer from anxiety disorder. A large-scale survey conducted in the United States revealed a lifetime prevalence of 28.8 % (Kessler et al., 2005). This suggests that one in three or four individuals suffers from an anxiety disorder at least once in his or her life.

Clinicians recognize a number of anxiety disorders, including **generalized anxiety disorder**, which is characterized by excessive worry about a wide range of commonplace events; **panic disorder**, which is characterized by the fearful anticipation and frequent experience of panic attacks; and **phobias**, which, with a lifetime prevalence of 12.5%, represent the most common anxiety disorder (Kessler et al., 2005). In the following section, we will examine the conditions of phobias and their treatment approaches in more detail.

The term *phobia* derives from the word *phóbos,* which is Greek for "fear." In a clinical context, the term refers to the persistent and excessive fear of a particular object, event, or situation. Typical phobias include arachnophobia, the fear of spiders; acrophobia, the fear of heights; or claustrophobia, the fear of confined spaces. Individuals with such phobias experience intense fear when confronted with their phobic object, spend much time thinking about it, and will avoid their phobic object at great cost.

How phobias develop. Different theories have been proposed to explain how individuals become phobic (Coelho & Purkis, 2009). One such theory refers to learning principles such as classical conditioning. It holds that individuals can form pathological associations between a natural threat and a previously neutral object if both are encountered in close temporal proximity. Thus, subsequent encounters with the previously neutral object become threatening. The classical example of this is little Albert, who developed a fear of anything white and furry after being repeatedly startled in the presence of a white rat (Watson & Rayner, 1920).

Another theory of how phobias develop combines classical conditioning with the notion of biological preparedness (Seligman, 1970). It highlights the fact that typical phobic objects bear actual dangers and suggests that their avoidance conferred an evolutionary advantage that was passed on in our genes. According to this theory, the preparedness to avoid poisonous spiders, heights, and confinement, for example, would have reduced the risk of physical injury or death and increased reproductive success. Thus, a readiness to fear condition to these items came to permeate the human gene pool and is now a typical characteristic of most humans. Due to natural genetic variation, however, some humans are more prepared than others, so their fear develops into an actual phobia.

Interestingly, there is evidence from rodent research that some forms of biological preparedness result from a parent's threat-related experiences and involve epigenetic rather than genetic mechanisms (Dias & Ressler, 2013). Rodents undergoing a fear-conditioning procedure in which a particular odor was paired with a shock produced offspring with a naturally heightened sensitivity to the fear-conditioned odor but not to control odors. An examination of the father's semen showed that fear conditioning had changed the methylation patterns of the gene that codes for the olfactory receptor responsible for perceiving the fear-conditioned odor. Through this, the offspring could more actively transcribe the receptor, giving them an odor-specific perceptual and conditioning advantage.

Treatment Approaches for Phobias

Treatments of phobia often include a medical and a psychological component. To date, the medical component focuses on the application of drugs that have a calming and thus fear-reducing effect. Popular in this respect are benzodiazepines, discovered in the 1950s, which facilitate GABAergic activity and thus are sedative. There are different types of benzodiazepines, some of which are short-acting, with a half-life of 1 hour, and others that are longer acting, with a half-life of up to 10 days. While short-term treatments with benzodiazepines are considered safe, long-term treatments over months or years are problematic because the drug has a range of side effects, including memory impairments; furthermore, it eventually produces tolerance and addiction (Stewart, 2005).

While more appropriate alternative drugs are currently unavailable, research in nonhuman animals points the way to potential future treatments. Specifically, research into the formation of fear memories has revealed that their long-term storage depends on the synthesis of proteins in the amygdala. If a protein synthesis blocker is injected directly into the amygdala, fear memories cannot be formed. Notably, such protein synthesis is also critical after the retrieval of a previously stored fear memory. Such retrieval makes the memory labile and is followed by a renewed process in which the memory must be stabilized. If this process is disturbed, the fear memory can seemingly be erased (Nader, Schafe, & LeDoux, 2000). Although promising, this latter approach cannot yet be used for the treatment of human phobia because it is too invasive (A Closer Look 9.2).

A CLOSER LOOK 9.2

Erasing Fear

Because anxiety disorders represent the most common psychological impediment, much research is dedicated to understanding their representation in the brain. Moreover, because the basic principles of fear acquisition are evolutionarily preserved, this research is frequently pursued in nonhuman animals like rodents. The application of invasive techniques in these animals has shed light on how fear memories are formed and maintained. Specifically, it revealed the amygdala as a site for memory formation and storage. Additionally, it showed that amygdala-dependent memories are not stable but fall into a labile state every time they are recalled. Whether they are maintained after recall depends on a process called reconsolidation.

The mechanisms underlying this process have been uncovered by LeDoux and colleagues (Nader et al., 2000). These researchers presented rats with a tone followed by a foot shock. On the following day, they presented the tone alone and subsequently injected anisomycin, a protein synthesis blocker, or a placebo into the lateral and basal nuclei of the amygdala. A day later, the researchers again presented the tone and measured the animals' propensity to freeze.

They found very little freezing in rats treated with the protein synthesis blocker and substantial freezing in animals treated with the placebo. Further tests showed that these results depended on the fear reminder being presented to the animals prior to the application of anisomycin within a time window of less than 6 hours. Notably, the delay between initial fear conditioning and the reminder

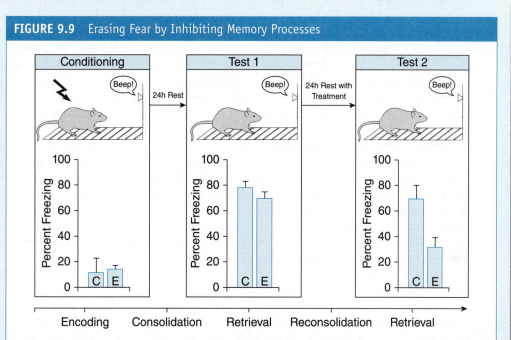

FIGURE 9.9 Erasing Fear by Inhibiting Memory Processes

In this study, control (C) and experimental (E) animals underwent fear conditioning. An electric shock served as the unconditioned stimulus and a tone served as the conditioned stimulus. Following Test 1, the control animals were injected with a placebo, whereas the experimental animals were injected with a protein synthesis blocker. When encountering the conditioned stimulus during Test 2, control animals showed significantly more freezing than did experimental animals (illustrated is the second of three test trials).

Source: "Fear Memories Require Protein Synthesis in the Amygdala for Reconsolidation After Retrieval," by K. Nader, G. E. Schafe, & J. E. LeDoux, 2000, *Nature, 406*, pp. 722–726.

seemed less important. The researchers still found significant differences between treatment groups if they presented the reminder and the pharmacological treatment 14 days after initial fear conditioning.

This demonstrates that protein synthesis initiated within a few hours following a fear reminder reconsolidates an associated fear memory. If this synthesis is blocked, memory reconsolidation is prevented and the fear memory is effectively erased. Notably, however, only the implicit association between a conditioned and an unconditioned stimulus can be modified in this way. Explicit associations or the conscious knowledge that the unconditioned stimulus had once produced the conditioned stimulus are not stored in the amygdala but distributed throughout the brain. Thus, if a similar study were done in humans, they—like the rats—may no longer show peripheral arousal to the tone after treatment with anisomycin. However, they would still be able to report that, on the first day of the experiment, the tone was followed by a shock.

Because current medical treatments of human phobia are relatively unspecific, they typically are combined with psychotherapy. Among the different psychological traditions, behavior therapy seems most effective (Wolitzky-Taylor, Horowitz, Powers, & Telch, 2008). As the name suggests, behavior therapy utilizes the principles of learning theory such as classical and operant conditioning. In the context of phobia, it aims to extinguish an existing fear through the repeated and inconsequential exposure to the phobic object. This may be done in vivo by confronting an arachnophobic with a living spider, through virtual reality by allowing the patient to interact with a spider via a computer, or through suggestion by a therapist.

Although these exposure techniques are relatively effective, patients often relapse into their old fears. This is because phobias easily generalize to a range of similar objects (e.g., anything white and furry in the case of Albert), not all of which can reasonably be produced during behavior therapy. Furthermore, therapeutic exposure necessarily differs from encounters with the phobic object in real life. For example, it is administered in a relatively safe environment in which the phobic object is expected, the patient is informed about the object being benign, and a trusted person—the therapist—is present. Last, although repeated exposure can extinguish fear responses, it does not erase the fear memory. Moreover, encountering a previously feared object sometime after successful extinction can easily activate the fear memory and thus reinstate the fear response.

This latter phenomenon, called spontaneous recovery, has been the target of recent research unearthing a potential psychological remedy (Schiller et al., 2009; Figure 9.10). In a relevant study, healthy human participants underwent a fear-conditioning routine where they saw a succession of blue and yellow squares on a computer screen. One color served as the CS+ that, in 38% of the trials, was paired with a mild electric shock. The other color served as the CS–. On the following day, the participants were divided into three groups. The first group was given a fear reminder in the form of the CS+ without the electric shock. Ten minutes later, this group underwent extinction training during which participants were presented with a series of CS+ and CS– trials, neither of which were paired with a shock. The second group received a comparable treatment with the exception that the delay between the reminder and extinction training was 6 hours. The third group underwent extinction training without a reminder. On the next day, all groups were presented with another stimulus sequence consisting of CS+ and CS–.

Fear responses were quantified as skin conductance differences between the CS+ and the CS–. They were found to be comparable between groups following fear conditioning at Day 1, when they were high, and following extinction at Day 2, when they were close to 0. However, fear responses differed between groups at Day 3. While the first group, which received a fear reminder 10 minutes prior to extinction training, showed no fear response, the other two groups showed spontaneous recovery. Their skin conductance differential (i.e., CS+ minus CS–) was significantly higher for the first couple of trials on Day 3 than it was on the last couple of trials on Day 2. Thus, it seems that a fear reminder encountered a few minutes before extinction training effectively prevented spontaneous recovery. Presumably, the fear reminder opened a reconsolidation window during which extinction training could erase a previously formed fear memory (Schiller et al., 2009).

FIGURE 9.10 Temporal Aspects of Extinction Training Determine Spontaneous Recovery

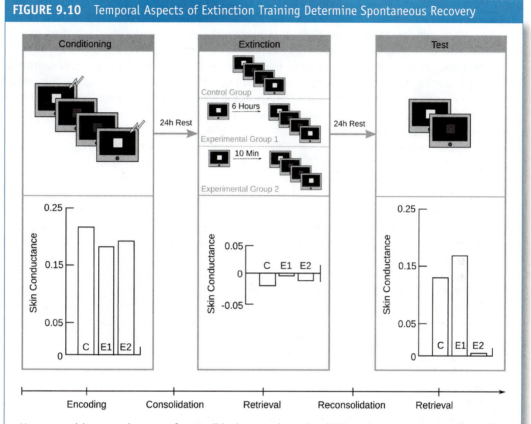

Human participants underwent a fear-conditioning experiment in which a colored square was paired with a shock and thus served as the CS+ and a differently colored square was not paired with a shock and served as the CS−. A reminder presented 10 minutes prior to an extinction phase effectively eliminated an increase in skin conductance to the CS+ not only immediately after extinction, but also after a 24-hour resting period. C = Control Group, E1 = Experimental Group 1, E2 = Experimental Group 2.

Source: "Preventing the Return of Fear in Humans Using Reconsolidation Update Mechanisms," by D. Schiller, M.-H. Monfils, C. M. Raio, D. C. Johnson, J. E. LeDoux, & E. A. Phelps, 2009, *Nature, 463,* pp. 49–53.

SUMMARY

Fear, in its intense form, is clearly a negative emotion. It is evoked by objects or situations that are appraised as harmful and toward which individuals feel powerless. The fear response seems to be a biphasic "defense cascade" comprising an initial inhibitory stage that is followed by an activational stage when threat becomes imminent. During the initial stage, frightened individuals may startle and then freeze. Freezing helps to avoid detection and enables individuals to explore threat. If they perceive that threat is approaching, they will break their freezing and, depending on what seems more feasible, flee or fight.

Many species have a rich nonverbal repertoire, which they deploy as a first line of defense in frightening situations. For example, they may scream, expose their teeth in preparation for biting, or raise their body hair to appear more formidable. Sometimes, these displays are enough to intimidate or appease an aggressor. Additionally, they warn conspecifics or group members about impending danger. Because threat to one individual can potentially implicate an entire group, many species evolved a special sensitivity to the fear of others. For example, both fish and humans developed sensory mechanisms for the perception of a chemical compound called a fear pheromone that is released by frightened conspecifics.

Energy-costly fear responses are supported by changes in the autonomic nervous system and the endocrine system. Activation of the sympathetic adrenal medullary (SAM) system and the hypothalamic-pituitary-adrenal (HPA) axis causes the release of stress hormones such as adrenaline and cortisol/corticosterone. In turn, these hormones activate the organs needed for action (e.g., the heart, the brain) and facilitate their energy supply.

Apart from behavioral and bodily changes, experiences of fear are marked by mental changes. Fear focuses the attention of an individual on threat and facilitates the encoding and consolidation of threat-relevant information in memory. This is enabled by neuronal processes at the heart of which sits the amygdala. This centrally located structure receives sensory information via a low route from the thalamus and via a high route from the cortical sensory areas. If incoming information is threat-relevant, the amygdala sends signals to a range of structures that directly mediate fear behaviors, that control peripheral organs, and that subserve consciousness and cognition. Pharmacological studies suggest that these effects depend on an interplay between noradrenergic and GABAergic neurotransmission within and outside the amygdala.

Given the importance of fear for survival, humans and other animals are naturally fearful and potentially develop pathological fear. In humans, such fears are called anxiety disorders, the most prevalent of which are phobias. Phobias are excessive and disabling fears of specific objects or situations such as spiders, heights, or confinement. They likely spring from a heightened preparedness to fear these objects and thus are challenging to treat. Current treatments comprise pharmacological agents that facilitate GABAergic activity as well as psychological treatments that are based on stimulus exposure and extinction.

THINKING CRITICALLY ABOUT "FEAR"

1. Fear can trigger a wide range of possible responses. What determines how an animal behaves when frightened? Can we predict its behavior?

2. After recalling a memory, its brain representation becomes labile and requires reconsolidation in order to be retained. Is this a flaw or a beneficial feature of memory?

3. Why are anxiety disorders so common? Should we consider them disorders?

MEDIA LIBRARY

Joseph LeDoux talks about fear memories on "Big Think": http://bigthink.com/josephledoux

Research documentary on biological preparedness: http://archive.sciencentral.com/2008/03/27/snakes-on-the-brain

Article with video about blindsight by Beatrice de Gelder: http://blogs.scientificamerican.com/observations/2010/04/22/blindsight-seeing-without-knowing-it

PART 4

Emotions and Other Mental Processes

I used my courage, intelligence and tactics, to get us out of there. . . .

—Odysseus (Homer, *The Odyssey,* Book 12)

Traditionally, Western philosophy and popular wisdom embraced the notion that cognition and emotion represent different aspects of the mind and that we need thought to conquer feeling. Greek mythology illustrates this. It is filled with strong and cunning heroes who rarely give in to the supposed weaker aspects of their nature. One such hero, Odysseus, is said to have resisted the Sirens, a group of attractive females whose singing lured many sailors into dangerous waters and certain death. Foreseeing these dangers, Odysseus filled the ears of his comrades with beeswax so that the Sirens' singing could not turn their hearts. He himself asked to be tied to a mast so that he could enjoy the Sirens' performance without becoming its victim.

While Greek myths such as these remain popular to the present day, dominant thoughts about the relationship between cognition and emotion changed (Niedenthal, Augustinova, & Rychlowska, 2010; Ochsner

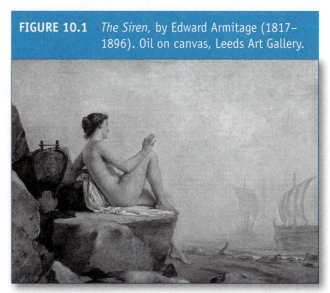

FIGURE 10.1 *The Siren,* by Edward Armitage (1817–1896). Oil on canvas, Leeds Art Gallery.

Source: Wikimedia Commons.

& Phelps, 2007; Pessoa, 2008: Schaefer & Gray, 2007). Both contemporary literature and science admit that emotions are useful and that they don't run isolated from cognition. Moreover, some thinkers even go so far as to challenge that emotion and cognition can be meaningfully separated (Lazarus, 1982; Sander, Grandjean, & Scherer, 2005; Scherer, 2001; Chapter 3).

The chapters in this part of the book tackle this issue and review research that explored how emotions intertwine with mental processes such as attention, memory, or language—which have long been considered purely cognitive. Additionally, the following chapters examine how these processes may be employed to produce, maintain, and subdue emotions.

CHAPTER 10

Emotion Effects on Cognition

The polarization of emotion and cognition has a long tradition in philosophy, medicine, and psychology (Pessoa, 2008). These disciplines typically considered emotions as involuntary and possibly unconscious processes that are mediated by an evolutionarily ancient and primarily subcortical brain system. In contrast, cognitions were seen as voluntary and conscious processes that are mediated by evolutionarily younger and primarily cortical structures. Over the course of the last century, the boundaries between these two types of processes began to blur.

For one thing, psychological research negated many assumptions underlying the traditional conceptual divide. It demonstrated that emotions can be evoked by a willfully produced thought or memory and that cognitions can be involuntarily triggered by events that are both external (e.g., an image) and internal (e.g., pain). Furthermore, psychological research showed that both emotional and cognitive processes can be conscious and unconscious in the sense that individuals can be aware and unaware of a particular feeling, perception, or thought. Last, psychologists have revised their abstract and computer-like notion of thought because they discovered that thought can be embodied in that it involves concrete lower-level representations of the motor and the sensory system—the same representations that appear to be critical for emotions (Niedenthal, Augustinova, & Rychlowska 2010).

Brain research has supported these psychological findings. Work directed at identifying the neural correlates of specific emotions such as joy, sadness, or fear did not only overturn the limbic system theory; it also moved emotional processes into traditional "cognitive territory." Specifically, lesion patient and neuroimaging studies implicated the frontal lobe (Bechara, Damasio, & Damasio, 2000; Hornak, 2003; Schirmer & Kotz, 2006)—a presumed stronghold for mental feats like language, working memory, and decision making—in the feeling aspects of emotions. Additionally, they revealed a role for subcortical structures, such as the hippocampus, in cognition and identified important interconnections between presumed emotional and cognitive structures, suggesting that they work in tandem (Pessoa, 2008; Ray & Zald, 2012; Schaefer & Gray, 2007).

Together, these insights from psychology and neuroscience call the polarization of emotion and cognition into question. Modern scientists answer this in two ways. Some still maintain a conceptual distinction between feeling and thinking and argue that the two interact (Niedenthal et al., 2010; Pessoa, 2008; Ray & Zald, 2012; Schaefer & Gray, 2007). Feeling can alter thinking, and vice versa. Pragmatic reasons to hold onto this position are as strong and possibly stronger than theoretical reasons. After all, the distinction between emotion and cognition is so ingrained in our language and thoughts that it is challenging to communicate about this topic without dividing the two. Yet some more radical minds take up this challenge. On the forefront here are appraisal theorists, who insist that cognitive processes, or appraisals, are the basis for emotions (Lazarus, 1982; Sander, Grandjean, & Scherer, 2005; Scherer, 2001).

Although it is possible that these radical minds are correct, common sense may persuade us otherwise. Don't we know many situations in which feeling and thinking conflict and our hearts speak differently from our minds? After all, it is because of these situations that both appear separate to us.

In order to appreciate that this appearance may be deceiving, let us consider how we make decisions—a mental process that presumably pitches emotions against thought. Decision making requires us to select one alternative from among several, each of which may have positive and negative outcomes. If we give into what we call feelings, often we select alternatives with immediate positive and delayed negative consequences. In contrast, if we are ruled by what we call thinking, often we select alternatives with delayed positive and immediate negative consequences. As an example take Odysseus, the Greek hero of the Trojan War. He needed to pass the Sirens' island and knew that they would tempt him and his comrades to change course. One could consider giving into this temptation as giving into an emotion and that Odysseus, by avoiding the Sirens, was instead governed by his intellect. However, another way to consider this is that Odysseus decided against the immediate pleasures of following the Sirens because of the prospective emotional outcome of injury and death. Thus, rather than being an issue of feeling against thinking, this may be an issue of feeling now against feeling later.

For the present purpose, however, we will not be too radical. We maintain that there are emotions and that these emotions may affect traditional cognitive functions such as attention, memory, or language. Moreover, we explore how these functions are altered to optimize behavior and how their alteration aids in a species' reproductive success.

HOW EMOTIONAL EVENTS MODULATE ATTENTION

Attentional Mechanisms

The natural environment of most species is highly complex. Take, for example, the typical environment of an urban outdoor cat. Among other things, this environment consists of streets with cars and people; market areas with shops and stalls; and public parks with shrubbery, trees, birds, and rodents. The objects in this environment change, as do the cat's needs. Depending on the cat's last meal, she may be hungry or satiated; depending on her estrous cycle, male suitors may interest or annoy her; and, depending on the time of day, she may look for entertainment or a place to rest. Thus, there is continuous change in the environmental objects that are relevant for the cat in that they further or fulfill an existing need.

Attentional mechanisms enable the cat to filter out relevant from irrelevant objects so that the former can become targets for action. One prominent model for how this is accomplished relies on the idea that objects in perception proper compete for perceptual resources (Corbetta & Shulman, 2002; Desimone & Duncan, 1995). Evidence for such competition comes from behavioral studies that revealed a perceptual bottleneck. This bottleneck is characterized by the fact that individuals discern objects more poorly the larger the number of objects that they behold. For example, when chancing upon a bird's nest with only one chick, our urban cat would discern the chick quite clearly. However, if there were several chicks in the nest, perceptual details of individual chicks would be lost.

Research demonstrated that difficulties in the perception of two or more simultaneously presented objects can be ameliorated if one object is singled out for attention or if the objects are viewed in succession rather than simultaneously. Relevant here is a study by Duncan, who presented a 2-by-2 stimulus array with number targets mixed in among letter distractors. Targets could appear singly or doubly. In the latter case, one target showed in the upper and the other target in the lower half of the array. Participants were asked to report targets at the end of each trial. Their reports were more accurate if there was only one target or if upper and lower array halves were presented in succession rather than simultaneously (Duncan 1980). Thus, the perceptual bottleneck appears to arise not from maintaining multiple objects in memory, but from generating perceptual object representations in the first place.

Insights into the mechanisms underpinning the perceptual bottleneck come from nonhuman animals in which single cell recordings uncovered the firing properties of visual neurons. Individual visual neurons don't represent the entire visual field but a circumscribed region referred to as a receptive field. Whereas one unattended object falling into a neuron's receptive field increases neuronal firing, adding one or more unattended objects has the opposite effect (Figure 10.2); it reduces neuronal firing. Interestingly, if one object is task-relevant and therefore singled out for attention, adding other task-irrelevant objects has no effect (Reynolds, Chelazzi, & Desimone, 1999). Moreover, if two or more objects are task-relevant, only one object can effectively be represented (Wiederman & O'Carroll, 2013). Thus, attention facilitates the mental and neural representation of an attended object. However, it can do so properly for only one object at a time, and at the expense of unattended objects.

Please note that many researchers discriminate between attention directed at an object, the features of an object, or a particular point in space. However, as feature and spatial locations are ultimately tied to objects (i.e., each object is composed of features and marked by a spatial location and configuration), and attention eventually serves the representation of objects rather than isolated features or spatial properties, we focus our discussion on objects.

Whether an object wins or loses in the competition for neural representation depends on exogenous factors linked to the object and its environment as well as on endogenous factors linked to the bodily or mental state of the individual. Exogenous factors are thought to influence competition in a bottom-up manner. For example, when resting quietly, our urban cat would perceptually represent and attend to the sudden chirping of a bird irrespective of her desire for food. Against a silent backdrop, the chirp would readily pass the perceptual bottleneck.

Endogenous factors are thought to influence competition in a top-down manner. They arise from the individual's effective needs and goals. These needs and goals dictate what objects in the environment are relevant and should guide behavioral responses. Accordingly, our urban cat will look for food objects such as birds when she is hungry but not when she is satiated. If she then encounters a bird, the cat intentionally selects the bird for neural representation.

FIGURE 10.2   Visual Neuron Activity as a Function of Crowding and Attention

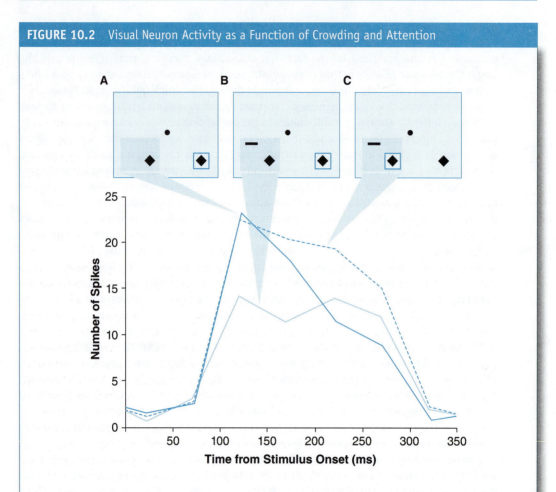

In this experiment, monkeys were trained to look at a central fixation point and to focus their attention on a particular region of the screen (highlighted by the small open square) and to respond any time a target stimulus (black diamond) appeared in that region. Prior to the experiment, the researchers identified a visual neuron for recording and specified its receptive field (highlighted by the large shaded square). On some trials during the experiment (A and B), the attended region was outside the neuron's receptive field. On other trials (C), the attended region was within the neuron's receptive field. Neuronal firing for stimuli presented in the neuron's receptive field differed as a function of crowding and attention. An unattended target presented alone in the neuron's receptive field (A, solid dark blue line) elicited a larger number of spikes than an unattended target that was accompanied by another stimulus (B, solid light blue line). The drop in firing caused by crowding could be recovered when subjects attended to the target (C, dotted dark blue line).

Source: "Competitive Mechanisms Subserve Attention in Macaque Areas V2 and V4," by J. Reynolds, L. Chelazzi, and R. Desimone, 1999, *Journal of Neuroscience, 5,* pp. 1736–1753.

Different proposals exist as to how exogenously driven bottom-up and endogenously driven top-down attentional mechanisms are represented in the brain. One prominent proposal specifies two segregated pathways (Corbetta & Shulman, 2002). Top-down mechanisms are thought to rely primarily on a dorsal attentional system that spans from the dorsal posterior parietal cortex to the dorsal frontal cortex and is fairly bilaterally distributed. Bottom-up mechanisms are thought to rely primarily on a ventral attentional system that spans from the temporo-parietal cortex to the inferior and ventral frontal cortex, and which is lateralized to the right hemisphere. It presumably serves as a circuit breaker for ongoing top-down mechanisms. However, because both systems have been implicated in bottom-up and top-down attentional effects, their exact functional roles still need to be ascertained.

Emotions and Attention

Behavioral Insights

Several paradigms have been developed to explore the effect of emotion on attention (Figure 10.3). The visual search and the attentional blink paradigm, two of the more popular ones, were already mentioned in the discussion of fear in Chapter 9. During a visual search experiment, the participant sees an array of objects and has to decide whether this array is composed of identical objects or contains a single "oddball." Participants are typically slower in detecting an oddball if that oddball is neutral while the remaining images in the array are emotional. In contrast, participants are faster if the oddball is emotional while the remaining images are neutral (Leclerc & Kensinger, 2008; Öhman, Flykt, & Esteves, 2001). This has been demonstrated for both negative and positive stimuli such as faces or manmade objects and for various array sizes (e.g., 3 by 3, 6 by 6, 9 by 9). However, because responses to emotional oddballs become somewhat slower as array sizes increase, their attention capture is unlikely to reflect an automatic "pop-out" effect, whereby the target can be effortlessly discerned. Instead, emotional oddball responses seem to depend on attentional resources and to engage an at least partially serial search, whereby participants scan individual array items (Yiend, 2010).

In the attentional blink paradigm, participants see a rapid picture stream, which contains primarily nontarget pictures interspersed with an occasional target picture. For example, there may be a stream of words printed in upper-case letters that is occasionally interrupted by words printed in lower case letters (Figure 10.3). At the end of a given stream, participants have to report how many words with lower case letters they saw. Typically, participants would miss targets that shortly follow a previous target, suggesting that attention "blinked" or was still engaged with processing the previous target.

A target's emotional significance modulates this effect. If the first of two succeeding targets is emotional, the attentional blink is enhanced (de Jong, Koster, van Wees, & Martens, 2010). In contrast, if the second of two succeeding targets is emotional, the attentional blink is attenuated (Anderson, 2005). In line with the findings from visual search studies, this suggests that, compared to neutral stimuli, emotional stimuli more effectively attract and hold attention.

A third paradigm that is relatively popular in research on the relationship between emotion and attention employs spatial cueing. One variant of this paradigm is called the

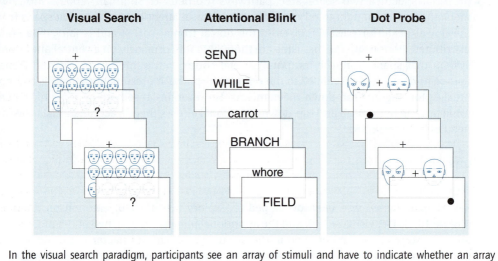

FIGURE 10.3   Popular Paradigms for Research on the Relationship Between Emotion and Attention

In the visual search paradigm, participants see an array of stimuli and have to indicate whether an array contained an "oddball." In the attentional blink paradigm, participants see a string of stimuli at the end of which they have to report how many targets (e.g., words in lower-case letters) they could identify. In the dot probe task, participants see two stimuli presented on the left and right of fixation. These are followed by a dot and participants have to indicate whether the dot is on the left or right side of the screen.

dot-probe task (MacLeod, Mathews, & Tata, 1986). In this task, participants are presented with two images (e.g., faces) positioned to the left and right of a fixation cross (Figure 10.3). Subsequently, a dot appears at the location of one of the former images, and participants have to report that location by pressing a button. They press the left button of a response box if the dot was on the left and the right button if the dot was on the right.

Unsurprisingly, response times are influenced by the emotional nature of the images preceding the dot. They are longer if one of the images was emotional and the location of that image and that of the dot are incongruous rather than congruous (Koster, Crombez Verschuere, & De Houwer 2004). This effect is exaggerated in emotion disorders when pathologically relevant stimuli are presented. For example, individuals with anxiety disorder show increased response times when an anxiety-relevant threat (e.g., a spider) precedes a dot at a spatially incongruous as compared to a congruous location. Moreover, this difference in response times is greater than in healthy controls (Koster, Crombez Verschuere, & De Houwer, 2006; MacLeod et al., 1986). Again, this has been interpreted to mean that, compared with neutral stimuli, emotional stimuli more effectively attract and hold attention (Yiend, 2010).

Insights From Brain Research

Insights into the biological substrates underpinning the relationship between emotion and attention come from studies in patients with neurological damage. Specifically, insights have been gained from two major clinical groups—individuals with hemispatial neglect and individuals with amygdala damage.

Hemispatial Neglect. Damage to the parietal cortex, especially in the right hemisphere, typically causes a neurological syndrome termed hemispatial neglect (Domínguez-Borràs, Saj, Armony, & Vuilleumier, 2012). This syndrome is characterized by a failure to detect and respond to objects in contralesional space, defined as the half of the visual field located opposite to the lesioned hemisphere (Figure 10.4). Problems arising from hemispatial neglect permeate patients' everyday lives, including activities like dressing for the day or eating a meal. In these instances, the patients typically concern themselves with only one half of their body or one half of their plate.

Hemispatial neglect is considered primarily an attentional disorder. This is because early brain responses in primary sensory areas of neglect patients compare to the brain responses in healthy individuals (Rees et al., 2000). It is only for later brain responses that the two groups start to diverge. Thus, neglect patients appear to have lost a regulatory mechanism situated in the parietal cortex that enables representations in sensory areas to reach awareness (Domínguez-Borràs et al., 2012).

FIGURE 10.4 Visual Processing and Hemispatial Neglect

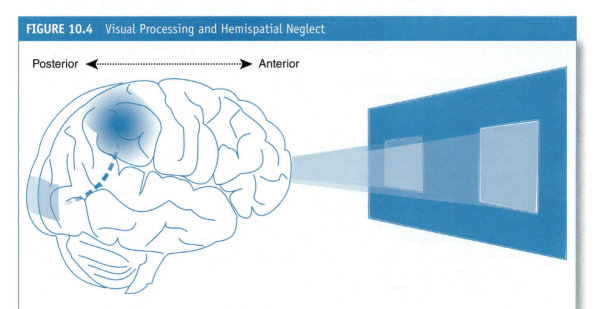

Posterior ◄┈┈┈┈┈┈┈┈┈┈┈┈┈┈┈► Anterior

Hemispatial neglect typically results from lesions to the right parietal cortex. It impairs awareness for information presented in contralesional space. Thus, if two objects are shown simultaneously, the contralesional one is typically ignored.

Extinction is a phenomenon closely associated with hemispatial neglect. It refers to the fact that neglect patients often are able to identify a stimulus presented in contralesional space (i.e., neglected half) if that stimulus is presented individually. However, they fail when the stimulus co-occurs with another stimulus in ipsilesional space (i.e., normal half). This latter, competing stimulus extinguishes awareness for the former stimulus in contralesional space.

Notably, such extinction depends on the emotional significance of the stimuli presented. It can be overcome if the stimulus presented in contralesional space is threatening or rewarding and the stimulus in ipsilesional space is mundane (Vuilleumier & Schwartz 2001). This has been interpreted as an effect of perceptual representations on awareness. An emotional boosting of these representations presumably makes them stronger so that they more effectively compete against other representations and succeed for recognition (Domínguez-Borràs et al., 2012).

Amygdala Lesion. Another clinical group to shed light on the relationship between attention and emotion comprises patients with amygdala lesions. Given the central role of the amygdala in emotion, researchers were interested to determine whether amygdala damage impairs the attentional advantage that emotional material has in healthy brains. Evidence to this effect has been found in two seminal studies.

The first study used the attentional blink paradigm and compared the performance of a patient with bilateral amygdala damage to that of healthy controls (Anderson & Phelps 2001). While the patient and controls showed a similar attentional blink to neutral targets, the patient differed from controls in her response to emotional targets. Here, she failed to show the typical attenuation of the attentional blink for emotional targets that followed neutral targets.

The second study compared healthy controls with a group of patients with sclerosis of the amygdala (Vuilleumier et al., 2004). The stimuli comprised arrays of two faces and two houses in which either the faces or the houses were task-relevant and should be attended. Both patients and controls showed increased activation in the fusiform gyrus when faces as compared to houses were task-relevant. This is in line with prior evidence indicating that the fusiform gyrus, an area in the inferior temporal lobe, is specifically excited by face stimuli (Kanwisher, McDermott, & Chun, 1997). Notably, however, only controls showed a face emotion effect that was independent of whether faces were task-relevant. Specifically, controls, irrespective of whether faces were attended or unattended, showed greater activity in the fusiform gyrus when facial expressions were emotional as compared to neutral. Because this emotion effect was absent in patients, the amygdala was inferred to be critical for the perceptual advantage of emotional over neutral material.

Note, however, that some researchers have challenged this position and called for further research (Bach, Talmi, Hurlemann, Patin, & Dolan, 2011; Piech et al., 2011).

Mechanisms

The preceding evidence clearly shows that whether and to what extent a stimulus engages attention depends on its emotional significance. Specifically, emotional stimuli seem to capture and hold attention more effectively than do neutral stimuli. Different mechanisms may explain this effect.

A first potential mechanism relies on bottom-up processes (Kennedy & Adolphs, 2011; Öhman et al., 2001; Vuilleumier, Armony, Driver, & Dolan, 2001). It rests on the possibility that emotional stimulus properties can be as salient as physical stimulus properties (e.g., intensity or brightness) in the competition for attention and awareness. Such salience may be explained in the following ways. First, it is often the physical properties of a stimulus that make it emotional. For example, a gunshot startles us because of its loud and sudden acoustic onset. Second, emotional stimuli have played an important role in the evolutionary history of our species. Thus, our brains may be especially adapted to perceive these stimuli even if our attention or mental resources are engaged elsewhere (compare with the idea of preparedness discussed in Chapter 9). Last, the repeated association of certain stimuli with emotional outcomes during an individual's lifetime may produce perceptual templates that guide attention in a bottom-up fashion.

A second potential mechanism relies on top-down processes involving memory and current goals (Pessoa & Ungerleider, 2004). According to this view, stimulus information needs to reach sensory areas and from there travel to brain structures implicated in memory and goal representation. Through this, the significance of an object in perception proper could be derived and could govern attention.

A role of top-down processes in attention has been examined by engaging participants in a task with distractors. Typically, distractors impair task performance, and this impairment is greater when distractors are emotional than when they are neutral. Importantly, high task difficulty can eliminate this distractor effect. Because of this, some researchers have argued that emotional influences on attention require processing resources that are allocated in a controlled, top-down fashion (Pessoa, McKenna, Gutierrez, & Ungerleider, 2002).

Last, it is possible that emotions affect attention via a combination of bottom-up and top-down processes. This possibility makes sense from a theoretical and an empirical point of view. Theoretically, it makes sense because the emotional significance of an object or event depends on both object and event properties and the individual's changing needs and mental state. Empirically, a contribution of bottom-up and top-down effects is implied by the findings that support both. Additionally, it is implied by work that directly pitched bottom-up against top-down processing showing their coexistant contribution (Hsu & Pessoa, 2007; Lang, Bradley, & Cuthbert, 1990).

One study in point required participants to identify a target letter from among an array of nontarget letters (Hsu & Pessoa, 2007). Bottom-up processing of emotional and neutral face distractors that flanked the letter array was manipulated by changing the size of the letters. A smaller letter size was associated with a greater salience of the face distractors and enhanced bottom-up processing. Top-down processing of face distractors was manipulated by making the target letter easy to find (i.e., only one type in the array) or hard to find (i.e., many different letter types in the array). The bottom-up manipulation revealed increased amygdala activity for fearful faces when face salience was high as compared to low. The top-down manipulation revealed decreased amygdala activation for fearful faces when target detection was difficult as compared to easy. No such effects were observed for neutral faces.

Due to these and other findings, a combination of bottom-up and top-down mechanisms feature in many contemporary models on the relationship between emotion and attention (Bishop, 2008; Pourtois, Schettino, & Vuilleumier, 2013; Shafer et al., 2012).

HOW EMOTIONAL EVENTS MODULATE MEMORY

Memory Processes and Types

Whereas attention enables an individual to focus mental processes on behaviorally relevant information, memory enables the storage of that information for future purposes. Thus, our urban cat need not worry every day anew about what places in her environment provide food or are dangerous. Instead, she can rely on previously stored representations to guide her actions.

In order for her to do that, these representations have to undergo three processing stages termed encoding, consolidation, and retrieval. The term encoding refers to an initial stage during which external or self-generated information is represented by sensory and association areas in the brain and maintained in short-term or working memory. Although attention may not be necessary for encoding, it greatly facilitates this processing stage and thus benefits overall memory.

The term consolidation refers to the processes that follow encoding and that make the established representation durable. In other words, these processes turn a short-term memory into a long-term memory. Their duration ranges from a few minutes to hours and days.

Last, for stored representations to guide behavior, these representations need to be reactivated. This process, called retrieval, engages brain regions that overlap with those engaged during initial encoding.

Scientific inquiries into the organization of memory revealed different memory systems. Initial evidence for this came from the Swiss neurologist Eduard Claparède (1911/1995). He treated a patient with Korsakoff amnesia, a condition caused by vitamin insufficiency. The patient was seemingly unable to form new memories. Every time Claparède met her, the patient failed to recognize him and treated him like a stranger. One day he tested whether her memory was indeed completely eliminated. To do so, he hid a pin in his hand while extending his hand for a handshake. Naturally, the patient found the handshake painful and quickly withdrew her hand. On subsequent encounters, the patient could still not remember Claparède. However, she was now reluctant to shake hands with him. Claparède thus reasoned that the patient retained some aspect of the painful experience. Moreover, he argued that there are different types of memories, each differently represented in the brain.

This early demonstration of dissociable memory systems was followed by evidence from other patients. Famous among these patients was H. M., a man who underwent medial temporal lobectomy as a treatment for pharmacologically intractable epilepsy (Scoville & Milner, 1957). After the surgery, which created bilateral hippocampal lesions (Figure 10.5; Corkin, Amaral, González, Johnson, & Hyman, 1997), H. M. showed severe anterograde amnesia. Although he could still remember events from before his surgery,

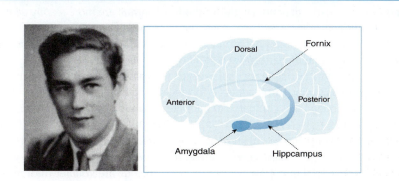

FIGURE 10.5   Lesion Patient Sheds Light on the Brain Basis for Memory

Patient H. M. had parts of his medial temporal lobe—including parts of the amygdala and the hippocampus—removed during epileptic surgery.

Source: Photograph of Henry Gustave (H.M.) by Suzanne Corkin. Copyright © by Suzanne Corkin, used by permission of The Wylie Agency LLC.

events after his surgery appeared to create no lasting impression. Yet, like Claparède's patient, H. M. retained the ability to form certain kinds of memories. For example, he could still acquire new manual skills and develop conditioned responses (Corkin, 2002).

Psychological insights from amnesic patients as well as healthy individuals led to the current conceptualization of multiple memory stores. Specifically, they established the distinction of implicit or procedural memories on one hand and explicit or declarative memories on the other hand (Cohen & Squire, 1980; Schacter & Graf, 1986). Implicit or procedural memories comprise things like habituation, conditioning, skill learning, and semantic priming. These memories are difficult to express in words and may be acquired and retrieved automatically, without awareness. Explicit or declarative memories can largely be divided into autobiographical memories (e.g., one's own wedding day) and factual memories about the world (e.g., the knowledge of what happens at a typical wedding). They can be readily verbalized and typically require effortful processing and awareness both during memory acquisition and retrieval.

Emotions and Memory

Behavioral Insights

Given what was said about the relationship between emotion and attention, it should come as no surprise that emotions also affect the formation of implicit and explicit memories. Both types of memories are formed more readily the greater the incentive for learning. Emotions provide this incentive and have been shown to exert their influence on the three memory stages defined earlier.

Encoding. Insights into emotion effects on encoding came from studies on attention. As mentioned earlier, emotional stimuli possess an innate or acquired salience that is attention-capturing. Compared to neutral stimuli, emotional stimuli are more readily detected and seem to hold attention more effectively. Thus, they are more effectively committed to short-term memory. Exemplary for this phenomenon are studies testing short-term memory for emotional and neutral information (Lindström & Bohlin, 2011; Sutherland & Mather, 2012). In one such study, participants saw a series of images and had to press a button if a current image had been shown two trials earlier. Participants performed this so-called 2-back task more accurately for images with emotional as compared to neutral content (Lindström & Bohlin, 2011).

Consolidation. There is also substantial evidence for a role of emotion in memory consolidation. For example, it has been demonstrated that recall differences between emotional and neutral material immediately after a study episode are smaller than recall differences following a consolidation window of 1 hour (LaBar & Phelps 1998). During this time, memory for emotional but not neutral material was found to increase, indicating that consolidation processes acted more strongly on the former as compared to the latter.

Additional evidence for consolidation effects comes from studies that manipulated emotional or physiological arousal after stimulus encoding. In one such study, participants committed neutral verbal information to memory and then completed the cold-pressor stress task. In this task, participants immersed one hand into ice-cold water and kept it there for a couple of minutes—an act that induces pain and is perceived as stressful. Doing the cold-pressor stress task immediately after verbal encoding was shown to improve verbal memory (Andreano & Cahill, 2006).

Retrieval. Research also supports the notion that emotions influence memory retrieval (Buchanan, 2007). For one thing, individuals are more likely to recall emotional information that matches their current emotional state. For example, a negative autobiographical memory is more readily recounted when an individual is in a negative as compared to a positive mood (Teasdale & Fogarty, 1979). Thus, it seems that emotional information can serve as a retrieval cue.

Additionally, emotional information seems to enhance specific aspects of retrieval. When we meet a person whom we have met once before, we may simply find that the person looks familiar without remembering the details of the initial encounter. Alternatively, we may fully recollect this encounter and the person's identity. The former kind of retrieval is called familiarity, or "feeling of knowing," whereas the latter kind of retrieval is called recollection. Some studies suggest that it is specifically this latter kind of retrieval that is facilitated for emotional relative to neutral memory content (Dolcos, LaBar, & Cabeza, 2005; Kensinger & Corkin, 2003; Ochsner, 2000).

Emotion memory properties. An extreme emotional memory is often referred to with the term flashbulb memory. This term, coined about 40 years ago, concerns memories of autobiographical events of a particularly shocking or arousing nature, as in when an individual becomes the victim or witness of a crime (Brown & Kulik, 1977). The word *flashbulb* captures the idea that memory for such events is particularly salient and vivid—like a picture taken with a camera. Notably, however, the supposed special status of flashbulb memories received incomplete support. Moreover, recent empirical work suggests that the storage of exceedingly emotional events recruits similar processes as the storage of lesser emotional events. The main difference seems to be the degree to which these processes are recruited (Sharot, Martorella, Delgado, & Phelps, 2007; A Closer Look 10.1).

Last, research has highlighted that only some aspects of an emotional event incur mnemonic benefits and that these benefits often come at a cost. Specifically, it seems that only the elements that are central to an emotional episode produce improved retention, and that memory for peripheral elements may suffer as a consequence (Kensinger, 2009). For example, individuals threatened with a gun may well remember the instrument pointed at them but not the perpetrator of the crime. This has been explained by an emotion-induced increase in attentional focusing (Easterbrook, 1959; Kensinger, 2009). In other words, emotional excitation, like a spotlight, highlights some aspects of an event while diminishing others.

Insights From Brain Research

Having reviewed emotions' influence on memory, we may now turn to the brain structures that mediate this influence.

Encoding. That a relevant structure must be the amygdala is evident from the fact that the amygdala supports emotional modulations of attention and thus plays a role in stimulus encoding. Another structure commonly implicated in the enhanced encoding of emotional as compared to neutral information is the hippocampal region including the hippocampus and the parahippocampal gyrus. Imaging studies that contrasted emotional and neutral encoding conditions revealed relatively consistently an activation in this region (Murty, Ritchey, Adcock, & LaBar, 2011).

Consolidation. That the amygdala and the hippocampal region also play a role in emotions' influence on later memory stages has been demonstrated in patient and neuroimaging studies. One such study examined emotional memory in patients with unilateral medial temporal lobe lesions that included the amygdala and the hippocampus (LaBar & Phelps 1998). These patients and a group of healthy controls were asked to remember a series of neutral and emotionally arousing words. Memory for these words was tested immediately after participants had studied them and then again 1 hour later. Healthy controls showed better memory for emotional words during the delayed as compared to the immediate memory test. In contrast, this effect was absent in the patients suggesting a dependence on bilaterally intact amygdalae and/or hippocampi.

Retrieval. Insights into a role of the amygdala and the hippocampal region for emotional retrieval comes from neuroimaging studies (Dolcos et al., 2005; Sharot et al., 2007). In one such study, participants were presented with emotional and neutral pictures, and memory for these pictures was tested one year later (Dolcos et al., 2005). During test, the participants saw the pictures they had studied a year before as well as new pictures and had to indicate which of the pictures were "old" and which were "new." In line with other work, participants were better at discriminating old from new emotional pictures

A CLOSER LOOK 10.1

Flashbulb Memories

It seems intuitive that we should remember particularly significant events better than we remember mundane ones. This intuition accords with empirical attempts to characterize and distinguish the former from the latter. One such attempt is a survey conducted in 1896 inquiring into the memories of American citizens about President Lincoln's assassination in 1865. The survey revealed that about 71% of respondents remembered a lot of information that is typically forgotten for mundane events (Colegrove, 1899). Specifically, they could report where they were when they heard the news, who was with them, and what they were doing. Similar investigations by other researchers revealed comparable results and led to the notion that outstanding events produce memories of a picture-like quality that are stored in more or less the same form as they were experienced (Brown & Kulik, 1977).

However, there are issues with these investigations. For one thing, the results are difficult to verify. Researchers have to rely on their participants' reported memories, which may or may not be accurate. Moreover, the apparent vividness of these memories may have developed after the fact through recounting and embellishment with subsequent information. Research on so-called "false memories"

FIGURE 10.6   9/11 Memories—Flashbulb or Not?

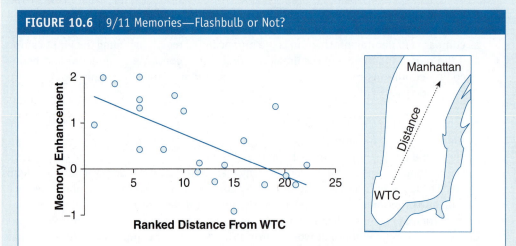

The subjective quality of a memory relates negatively to physical distance or personal involvement with an event. The memory enhancement score is an average difference score derived from recollections of 9/11 events and a summer vacation from that same year. Recollections were assessed with regards to arousal, vividness, reliving, remember/knowing, confidence, and valence. The ranked distance from the World Trade Center (WTC) was derived by rank-ordering participants according to their reported physical distance from the WTC at the time of the attack.

Source: "How Personal Experience Modulates the Neural Circuitry of Memories of September 11," by T. Sharot, E. A. Martorella, M. R. Delgado, and E. A. Phelps, 2006, Proceedings of the National Academy of Sciences, 104, 389–394.

makes this as a viable possibility. It demonstrated that a later interrogation can lastingly alter one's memory of an event. For example, false assumptions implicit in questions asked during an interrogation eventually become accepted truths (Loftus, 1975). Likewise, as-if thinking about an event can lead to the integration of imaginary and true facts so that eventually the two are no longer distinguishable (Wade, Garry, Read, & Lindsay, 2002).

Does this mean that "flashbulb" memories are little more than imagination? Current evidence suggests that outstanding emotional events elicit stronger memories than neutral ones. However, these memories do not seem dramatically different. A study that assessed memories of the 9/11 terrorist attack on the World Trade Center in New York City found that the memories differed quantitatively, not qualitatively, between individuals who were close to the World Trade Center and thus immediately endangered by the falling towers as compared to individuals who were further away (Sharot et al., 2007). Specifically, the researchers observed a negative linear correlation between the individuals' recollective experience and their physical distance to the World Trade Center (Figure 10.6). Moreover, distance likewise accounted for the participants' amygdala responses to memories of the 9/11 attack. These were greater in individuals closer to the World Trade Center as compared to individuals further away. Based on these results, it is likely that outstanding emotional events simply augment the processes that support the formation of more ordinary memories.

than they were at discriminating old from new neutral pictures. Notably, this retrieval effect was accompanied by enhanced activity in the amygdala and hippocampal region. Thus, it seems that these structures more readily support the retrieval of emotional as compared to neutral memories, and that they underpin emotions' mnemonic benefit. Moreover, because their contribution was greater for items that were recollected as compared to familiar items for which participants simply had a feeling of knowing, it seems that the amygdala and the hippocampus underpin emotions' facilitation of recollection (Figure 10.7).

Mechanisms

Structures. The previous section identified the amygdala and the hippocampal region as key structures in the relationship between emotion and memory. But what are their respective roles? An answer to this question comes from lesion studies suggesting that the amygdala and the hippocampal region subserve different memory systems.

Patients with amygdala lesions readily acquire declarative or explicit memories about emotional events. For example, in a fear-conditioning paradigm where a colored square precedes a shock, these patients are able to learn and later report on the association between both stimuli. Thus, their explicit memory is seemingly intact. Yet they fail to develop a conditioned physiological response (e.g., increased skin conductance) to the colored square, suggesting an impaired implicit memory (Bechara et al., 1995; LaBar, LeDoux, Spencer, & Phelps, 1995).

Notably, patients with hippocampal damage show the opposite pattern. They fail to form an explicit memory of the relationship between the colored square and the shock. This means they do not consciously remember that the latter followed the former. Yet they readily acquire a physiological response to the colored square, indicating a preserved implicit memory (Bechara et al., 1995).

Findings such as these nicely illustrate the coexistence of both implicit and explicit memory systems; furthermore, they show that, in healthy individuals, these systems operate in parallel. Implicit and explicit processes are jointly engaged in the storage of significant life events and together enable memories that retain both an event's feeling and thinking aspects.

Molecules. Now that we have identified the key structures supporting emotional memory effects, we can take a look at the molecular mechanisms that underpin their functioning. Because these mechanisms appear largely similar for the two memory systems, implicit and explicit memories will only be differentiated as this becomes necessary.

FIGURE 10.7   The Medial Temporal Lobe Memory System

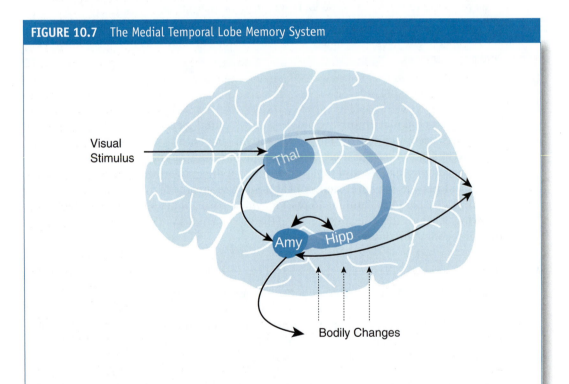

Amygdala and hippocampus situated in the medial temporal lobe support the formation of implicit and explicit memories, respectively. They also mediate the influence of emotions on stimulus encoding (e.g., by upregulating sensory cortex activity), consolidation, and retrieval.

Most learning requires the formation of associations between different stimuli or pieces of information. For example, if our urban cat narrowly escapes the wheels of a car, she will form both implicit and explicit associations between roads, cars, and being scared. A popular model for how these associations are formed involves the notion of Hebbian learning. Donald Hebb (2002), an acclaimed psychologist, once postulated that learning results from the contiguous firing of neighboring neurons, which he believed produces changes in one or both neurons and an increased likelihood of their firing contiguously in the future. This notion has often been paraphrased as "neurons that fire together, wire together."

Modern neuroscience has found support for Hebb's model (Johansen, Cain, Ostroff, & LeDoux, 2011). It identified mechanisms, such as those involving glutamate receptors, that detect contiguous neuronal firing. The activation of these receptors in postsynaptic neurons triggers a signaling cascade that enables the short-term maintenance of contiguous firing patterns with presynaptic neurons through the modification of existing proteins in these neurons.

Naturally, the detection of contiguous firing depends on the strength and duration of neuronal excitation. Because emotional stimuli excite the brain more effectively than neutral stimuli, their contiguous firing may be more readily detected. Additionally, the detection of contiguous firing is subject to neuromodulatory influences from neurotransmitters such as dopamine, noradrenaline, or GABA (Johansen et al., 2011). Therefore, the release of these neurotransmitters into structures that promote learning (e.g., amygdala) represents a further route, whereby emotions can influence memory encoding.

The short-term synaptic remodeling initiated during encoding may trigger a secondary signaling cascade that produces long-term synaptic changes and memory consolidation. Consolidation processes depend on the synthesis of new synaptic proteins through gene transcription and possibly the degradation of existing proteins (Johansen et al., 2011). A phosphate group joining the cellular transcription factor called cAMP response element binding protein (CREB), a process partially influenced by Hebbian learning, plays an important role in this. It is one of several steps in a chain of events that reaches the neuron's nucleus and there initiates DNA transcription and messenger RNA synthesis. Together, these processes result in the creation of new proteins and the strengthening of the synapse (Figure 10.8).

Emotions influence consolidation and long-term synaptic remodeling indirectly, via their influence on encoding and short-term synaptic remodeling. After all, consolidation is triggered during encoding and thus affected by the strength of short-term mnemonic processes. Additionally, emotions influence consolidation directly, through the feedback of emotion-induced bodily changes (McIntyre, McGaugh, & Williams, 2012). Activation of the sympathetic adrenal medullary system and the HPA axis trigger the release of catecholamines and glucocorticoids (Chapters 4 and 9). Apart from modulating things like muscle tone, heart rate, or glucose metabolism, these hormones signal back to the brain.

Catecholamines cannot pass the blood-brain barrier and thus exert their influence through an indirect signaling pathway. Specifically, they attach to receptors on the vagus nerve, which projects from the periphery to the nucleus of the solitary tract (NST) in the brainstem. From there, projections reach the amygdala directly and indirectly via the locus coeruleus. Their outputs increase noradrenergic tone and enhance the formation of

FIGURE 10.8   Molecular Mechanisms Underlying Short- and Long-Term Synaptic Remodeling

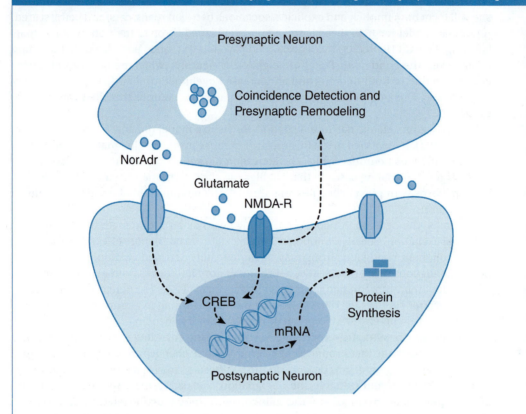

Short- and long-term synaptic remodeling form the basis for memory encoding and consolidation. Short-term remodeling involves the detection of coincident firing of pre- and postsynaptic neurons. Long-term remodeling involves the synthesis of new proteins. NorAdr = noradrenaline; NMDA-R = N-methyl-d-aspartate receptor (a type of glutamate receptor); CREB = cAMP response element binding protein; mRNA = messenger ribonucleic acid.

implicit memories. Additionally, further projections from the amygdala to the hippocampal region facilitate the formation of explicit memories.

Glucosteroids readily pass the blood-brain barrier and have abundant receptors both in the amygdala and the hippocampus. As such, their release by the adrenal gland into the bloodstream forms a direct signaling pathway to the sites that consolidate implicit and explicit memories.

Compared to memory encoding, memory consolidation is a relatively drawn-out process. Why this delay? Why are encoded memories not immediately consolidated? One possible answer to these questions is that a delayed long-term storage accommodates the influence of peripheral emotional responses on memory (Phelps, 2004). Like consolidation, these responses are relatively sluggish and perhaps reflect the actual significance of a stimulus across time more effectively than do instant neural changes associated with stimulus encoding. In other words, they offer a cumulative or temporally integrated estimate of emotional significance. A prolonged consolidation process could profit from this and might ensure that only "worthwhile" memories are stored.

HOW EMOTIONAL EVENTS MODULATE HIGHER-ORDER COGNITIVE PROCESSES

Attentional and mnemonic processes help us sieve through the enormous amount of information that reaches our senses. Because emotions guide this sieving, one can expect them also to play a role in the many cognitive processes that build on attention and memory. These processes, often referred to as "higher-order" cognition, include symbolic communication, the formation of meaningful concepts and categories, time perception, decision making, and problem solving. The following section presents a snapshot of some of these processes and their relation to emotion.

Language and Categorization

Behavioral Observations

The term *language* refers to communication systems that comprise a set of symbols and a set of rules, the latter of which govern the combination of symbols. In natural languages, such as spoken English, words and grammar represent symbols and rules, respectively. Words and their reference to conceptual knowledge are considered to be part of explicit or declarative memory. Grammar, on the other hand, is considered to be part of implicit or procedural memory (Chomsky, 1965; Pinker, 2000; Ullman et al., 2005).

At present, research on the role of emotions for language has focused primarily on word processing and the activation of associated concepts or categories. A popular paradigm has been the affective priming paradigm, which social psychologists and emotion researchers adapted from priming techniques developed within cognitive psychology. In affective priming, two stimuli are presented in succession. The first stimulus is called the prime and the second stimulus is called the target. Typically, participants perceive the prime passively and perform an active task on the target. By measuring responses to the target, researchers can shed light on how affective states activated by the prime influence target processing (Chapter 6, Figure 6.3).

In a seminal application of affective priming, Fazio and colleagues used attitude objects such as *gift* or *crime* as primes and adjectives such as *appealing* or *awful* as targets (Fazio, Sanbonmatsu, Powell, & Kardes, 1986). The participants' task was to classify targets as good or bad. The researchers observed that target classifications depended on the affective congruency between primes and targets. Participants responded more quickly if both had the same affective valence (e.g., *gift → appealing, crime → awful*) as compared to if both had an opposing affective valence (e.g., *gift → awful, crime → appealing*). Moreover, comparisons with a control condition in which targets were preceded by a letter string (e.g., *BBB*) suggested that affective congruency facilitated, whereas affective incongruency impeded the participants' responses. Thus, the researchers proposed that a word's affective value—that is, whether something is considered good or bad—can be automatically activated and may influence subsequent valuations.

The results of Fazio and colleagues were soon replicated and extended. Other labs moved in to demonstrate that affective priming works for primes other than words. Among other things, these labs used emotional images (Zhang, Li, Gold, & Jiang, 2010), nonverbal expressions (Schirmer, Kotz, & Friederici, 2005), or music (Steinbeis & Koelsch, 2011). Furthermore, they showed that, like prime words, these stimuli can facilitate responses to affectively congruent as compared to incongruent target words.

Researchers also began to explore whether an influence of prime affect on target processing could be demonstrated when decisions to the target were nonaffective. An exemplary approach, again borrowed from cognitive psychology, is the lexical decision task. In this task, primes are followed by an ordinary word (e.g., *table*) or "pseudoword" (e.g., *tebal*), a phonologically plausible letter string without an "entry" in the participants' mental lexicon. The participants' task is to decide whether a target is a word or a pseudoword. Research using this paradigm found that target words are judged faster when the preceding prime is affectively congruous as compared to incongruous (Schirmer et al., 2005; Wentura, 2000).

Last, some attempts were made to explore whether, in addition to affect, one could prime proper emotions. The results of these attempts are somewhat contradictory. On one hand, there is evidence for emotion-specific priming. For example, sad voices were shown to prime behavioral responses to sad targets more than to angry targets (Pell, 2005), disgusting facial expressions were shown to prime behavioral responses to disgusting targets more than to fear targets (Neumann & Lozo, 2012), and angry faces were shown to prime behavioral responses to angry targets more than to sad or fearful targets. On the other hand, not all attempts to demonstrate a facilitation for emotionally congruent prime-target pairs were successful. For example, attempts to demonstrate a facilitation of fear-fear pairs relative to fear-sadness pairs failed (Rohr, Degner, & Wentura, 2012; Rossell & Nobre, 2004).

What may account for this seeming contradiction is that some emotions share processing or appraisal aspects with other emotions. As a consequence of such sharing, these emotions are more similar than emotions without overlapping appraisals. As an example, take fear and sadness. Both result from events that are appraised as uncontrollable. Thus, the processing of target words that express a lack of control would be equally facilitated by fear and sadness primes. If true, affective or emotional priming offers a way to test the relationship between different emotions and to probe current emotion theories (Chapter 3).

Mechanisms

The affective priming results mentioned previously raise several questions about the mechanisms through which affective primes influence behavioral responses to a subsequent target.

One such question concerns the processing stage at which priming takes place. Several such stages must run their course before a participant can accurately press an assigned response button. Specifically, a stimulus must be perceived, its meaning must be retrieved from memory, and a response must be prepared and issued. An affective prime could facilitate any of these processing stages. Which stage it is has been tackled using neuroimaging techniques that reveal mental processes as they unfold in time.

Some of this work found evidence for a facilitation of meaning retrieval or semantic processing. For example, using event-related potentials (ERPs; Chapter 6), researchers showed that affective priming modulates an ERP component termed the N400 (Bostanov & Kotchoubey, 2004; Schirmer, Kotz, & Friederici, 2002; Steinbeis & Koelsch, 2011). This component is a negative ERP deflection that peaks around 400 milliseconds following word onset. It was first identified in a sentence processing study (Kutas & Hillyard, 1980). In this study, participants were presented with written sentences in a word-by-word fashion. Sentence final words that were semantically expected given the preceding words elicited a smaller N400 than sentence final words that were semantically unexpected (Figure 10.9).

Studies that recorded ERPs in the context of affective priming revealed similar results. Target words that were affectively congruous to a preceding prime were found to elicit a smaller N400 than did target words that were affectively incongruous (Bostanov & Kotchoubey, 2004; Schirmer et al., 2002; Steinbeis & Koelsch, 2011). Furthermore, studies using functional magnetic resonance imaging (fMRI; Chapter 6) implicated similar brain structures underlying semantic and affective priming. Like semantic priming, affective priming involves the activation of language structures in the left hemisphere (Liu, Hu, Peng, Yang, & Li, 2010; Schirmer, Zysset, Kotz, & von Cramon, 2004). Because these structures were less activated for affectively congruous as compared to incongruous targets, it has been proposed that affective or emotional primes activate semantic representations that, if shared with the target, facilitate target processing.

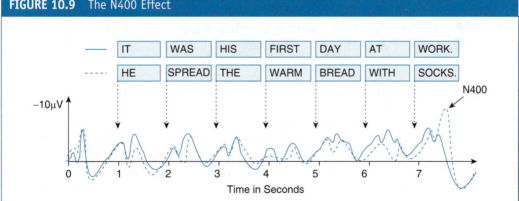

FIGURE 10.9 The N400 Effect

Sentences with semantically incongruous words elicit an increased negativity around 400 milliseconds following word onset.

Source: "Reading Senseless Sentences: Brain Potentials Reflect Semantic Incongruity," by M. Kutas and S. A. Hillyard, 1980, *Science, 207*, pp. 203–205.

However, not everyone holds this view. This is because not every study revealed evidence for semantic processing (e.g., Kissler & Koessler, 2011). Moreover, some studies point to a later stage of response preparation instead. For example, ERP research found an effect of affective priming on the readiness potential (Bartholow, Riordan, Saults, & Lust, 2009; Eder, Leuthold, Rothermund, & Schweinberger, 2012). The readiness potential reflects motor preparation. It emerges as a negative deflection prior to an overt motor response over motor areas contralateral to the intended movement. A right-hand button press, for example, is preceded by a readiness potential over left central electrode sites. Notably, despite the fact that affective primes require no overt response, they elicit a readiness potential suggesting that they are not merely passively perceived, but instead trigger response preparation. If the prepared response matches that required by the target, responses are facilitated. In contrast, if the prepared response conflicts with that required by the target, responses are delayed.

How do we reconcile the evidence for response preparation effects with the evidence that affective priming modulates semantic processing? As so often, it is likely that both sets of findings represent different parts of the truth. Experimental parameters such as stimulus durations, interstimulus intervals, and/or the participants' task have varied between studies and may thus account for the discrepant reports. These parameters undoubtedly determine what processing stage is implicated in affective priming and whether affective priming ensues from a modulation of semantic and/or response processes. Because of this, it has been suggested that affective priming may operate at both processing stages (Eder et al., 2012; Klauer, Musch, & Eder, 2005).

Time Perception

Behavioral Observations

Our ability to track time is fundamental for many activities that we necessarily engage in on a daily basis. Examples of these activities include cooking a meal or crossing a road. They would end badly if we were unable to produce and use temporal estimates. Timing is also critical for the production and the perception of speech, where it helps to differentiate between voiced and unvoiced consonants (e.g., *b* versus *p*) or between stressed and unstressed syllables (e.g., *CONtent* versus *conTENT*). Additionally, temporal processing is necessary for activities we do in synchrony with others, such as playing in an orchestra, dancing, or going for a walk. Thus, there is some truth to the statement that "timing is everything."

From your own experience, you may recall that your perception of time alters as a function of your emotions. This phenomenon is reflected in verbal descriptions of emotional events as "never ending" or "gone in a flash." It is also evident from empirical work. Some of this work supports the notion that emotional events can be experienced as "never ending" in that they increase our perception of passing time. In other words, we find them to be much longer than they really are. This was shown in studies that required participants to categorize emotional and neutral stimuli as "long" or "short," or to reproduce their duration. Emotional stimuli led to more frequent "long" categorizations and longer temporal reproductions than equally long neutral stimuli (Angrilli, Cherubini, Pavese, & Mantredini, 1997; Mella, Conty, & Pouthas, 2011; Noulhiane, Mella, Samson, Ragot, & Pouthas, 2007).

Empirical work also identified conditions under which emotions make events seem to be "gone in a flash" by leading to temporal underestimations. Specifically, it was shown that participants tend to underestimate the presentation time of disgusting relative to neutral images (Gil, Rousset, & Droit-Volet, 2009). Possibly, this reflects a distancing or disengagement from processing disgust. Additionally, underestimations were observed for neutral stimuli that participants timed in the context of an emotional as compared to a neutral distractor (Lui, Penney, & Schirmer, 2011). Here, participants watched two circles that appeared in succession on a screen. The circles were separated by a distractor image of emotional or neutral valence. Participants were more likely to judge the second circle as "shorter" than the first circle, when the intervening distractor image was emotional as compared to neutral.

Mechanisms

Different models have been proposed to account for our ability to perceive time, and these models have different implications for how emotions could come into play. The most influential model is scalar timing theory (Gibbon, Church, & Meck, 1984). It comprises different processing stages including a pacemaker that emits temporal pulses and an accumulator that stores these pulses. Pacemaker and accumulator are connected by a switch so that temporal pulses can only be transmitted if the switch is in a closed state. Temporal pulses that reach the accumulator are made available to working memory and decision processes, where they can be used to issue a behavioral response (e.g., button press) or from where they can enter long-term memory for future reference (Figure 10.10).

A more recent proposal to provide a physiologically realistic model of time perception is the striatal beat-frequency model (Buhusi & Meck, 2005). According to this model, connections between the cortex and the striatum are critical for timing (Buhusi & Meck, 2005; Meck, Penney, & Pouthas, 2008). Specifically, neurons in the striatum detect patterns of oscillatory input from cortical neurons that uniquely identify stimulus durations (Figure 10.10). For example, imagine you hear a loud tone. The tone onset will cause neurons in the substantia nigra and ventral tegmental area to release dopamine onto their target neurons in the striatum and cortex. This dopamine release serves to reset the striatal neurons and synchronizes the oscillations of the cortical neurons. If something important happens during the tone such as the presentation of food, the specific pattern of cortical neuron oscillations at that moment will be encoded by some of the striatal neurons. The next time the tone sounds, those striatal neurons will respond when the previously encoded neural oscillation pattern occurs, thereby enabling an expectation of when food will be presented. Although there are parallels between the striatal beat-frequency model and scalar timing theory, the two don't agree perfectly. Moreover, emotional influences on timing are still largely interpreted within the psychological rather than the physiological framework.

The different processing stages implicated in the psychological framework accommodate the observation that emotional events may feel both longer and shorter than equally long neutral events. Relative overestimations for emotional events could be caused by an increase in pacemaker rate (Droit-Volet & Meck, 2007). This would lead to more temporal pulses being accumulated and to a subjective stretching of passing time. Additionally,

FIGURE 10.10   Models of Time Perception

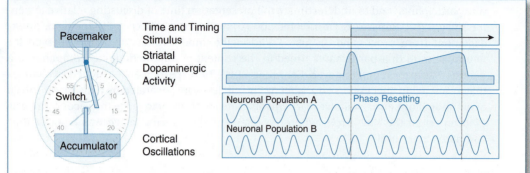

Illustrated on the left is the clock stage of the dominant psychological information processing model of time perception. According to this model, a switch connecting a pacemaker and an accumulator needs to be in a closed state for passing time to be registered. Illustrated on the right is a neurofunctional model, called the striatal beat-frequency model, which integrates psychological evidence with insights from the neurosciences. The oscillations in the firing of many neuronal populations in the frontal cortex are believed to support temporal representations. Their oscillatory phase is aligned when individuals begin to time an event so that the timed duration results in a unique and identifiable oscillatory pattern. Striatal dopaminergic neurons coordinate cortical oscillations and help register passing time.

relative overestimations of emotional as compared to neutral events could be caused by the state of the switch (Lui et al., 2011). Possibly, attention is required to keep the switch in a closed state. If the to-be-timed stimulus is emotional and therefore readily captures and holds attention, the switch may close faster and may be less likely to flicker into an open state than if the to-be-timed stimulus is neutral. Thus, fewer pulses would be lost and time estimates would be longer. Last, processing resources may be needed to retain pulses in the accumulator or short-term memory (Buhusi & Meck, 2009). Again, these resources may be more readily engaged if the to-be-timed event is emotional as compared to neutral.

Similar to emotion-induced overestimations, emotion-induced underestimations may emerge from a modulation of pacemaker, switch, or accumulator processes. For example, some emotional states may reduce rather than increase pacemaker rate. Despair or "low spirits," which form aspects of sadness, could represent such states. However, supporting evidence for this is, at present, lacking. Moreover, because most emotions are behaviorally activating (Droit-Volet & Meck, 2007), emotion-induced underestimations are typically associated with the switch or accumulator stage instead. Underestimations at these stages may result when individuals time neutral events in the context of an emotional event (Buhusi & Meck, 2009; Lui et al., 2011). In such a situation, the emotional event would attract processing resources that would deter individuals from keeping the switch in a closed state or from maintaining representations of the accumulated pulses. As a consequence, the duration of the neutral stimulus would seem shorter than if that same stimulus were timed in the context of a neutral event.

Taken together, emotional states may lengthen or shorten our perception of time relative to a neutral state. Whether we experience a lengthening or a shortening likely depends on whether we intend to time the emotion-evoking stimulus or a concurrent neutral stimulus. An example of the lengthening of time would be an evening that we spend at a party as compared to a relatively quiet evening at home. Even if we are sorry when the party comes to an end, we should perceive it to be longer than the time spent at home. An example of the shortening of time would be a relatively neutral conversation held at the party as compared to one held at the evening at home. Now, the conversation should appear shorter in the former relative to the latter scenario. In each of these situations, a modulation of corticostriatal activity would speed up or slow down temporal processing, respectively.

Decision Making

Behavioral Observations

Our lives are filled with choices. A simple act like going out to dinner requires us to make multiple decisions, including what restaurant to go to, whom to invite, when to go, how to get there, and what to order. We make these choices by selecting one from among many alternatives. But how exactly do we do that? Traditionally, the answer to this question has been "through logical reasoning." Moreover, ancient Western philosophy conceived human behavior as rational, resulting from the weighing of available choices with respect to their benefits and costs. This was contrasted with the behavior of nonhuman animals, which was supposedly governed by inborn reflex-like programs making these animals choiceless.

Contrary to these ancient beliefs, however, modern research revealed that human decisions are not necessarily rational or the result of logical reasoning. Instead, they are influenced by seemingly irrelevant contextual information. One example of this comes from the affective priming literature showing that a currently activated affect influences whether we find something good or bad and thus whether we approach or avoid it. That this extends to real-world decisions outside the laboratory has been shown in a study that examined the relationship between the weather and the stock market. Compared to cloudy days, sunny days—on which individuals are presumably happier—were found to yield greater stock returns (Hirshleifer & Shumway, 2003). On these days, brokers were more likely to buy and/ or less likely to sell, thereby moving the price for individual shares upward.

Apart from current affect, the framing of choices influences decisions. Examples of this come from the work of Daniel Kahneman and Amos Tversky (1979). These researchers presented participants with two choices, one of which was a sure thing and one of which was a gamble. Whether participants opted for the sure thing or the gamble depended on whether the choices were framed as gains or losses. If they were framed as gains, then participants were more likely to choose the sure thing (e.g., receive $100 as compared to having a 50/50 chance of receiving $0 or $200). However, if they were framed as losses, then participants were more likely to choose the gamble (e.g., a sure loss of $100 as compared to a 50/50 chance of losing $0 or $200). Thus, Kahnemann and Tversky concluded that humans are risk-averse in the context of potential gains and risk-seeking in the context of potential losses.

Decisions concerning objects also depend on whether or not we own them. Once we've established ownership over an object, it becomes more valuable to us and we become unwilling to part from it. This phenomenon, called "loss aversion," has been demonstrated in a number of studies. In one of them, half the participants were endowed with a mug that they could trade on a mock market (Kahneman, Knetsch, & Thaler, 1990). They were told that, if they opted to trade, they would receive the market-clearing price computed by the experimenter at the end of the study. Given that very few individuals can be expected to be in need of a mug, for most participants this should have been an easy opportunity to earn a few dollars simply by selling the mug. However, only 10% of the participants endowed with a mug pursued the trading option, and those who did had an asking price more than double of what potential buyers (i.e., participants without a mug) were willing to pay. Thus, simply owning the mug made participants want to keep it.

Mechanisms

Although many human decisions seem rational and thus imply a critical role for intellect and reasoning, psychologists have uncovered a number of instances in which decisions diverge from rationality. **Prospect theory**, developed by Kahneman and Tversky (Kahneman, 2003; Kahneman & Tversky, 1979), represents one attempt to deal with these instances. It posits the existence of two cognitive systems underlying decision making. The first system is based on intuition. It operates quickly and involuntarily, needs limited processing resources, and may draw on emotional mechanisms. The second system is based on reasoning. It operates slowly and in a controlled manner, requires effortful processing, and is unaffected by emotions. Thus, emotions associated with current affective states or responses to prospective gains or losses would impact decisions via the first system only.

Prospect theory was well aligned with research available at the time. However, research generated since then incrementally challenged its validity. Specifically, the assumption of an emotional and a nonemotional system eventually became untenable. Research showed that most mental processes operate differently as a function of emotion. Compared to neutral events, emotional events capture and hold attention more readily, are more readily stored in memory, activate different linguistic processes, and produce different temporal representations. This makes it difficult to dissociate emotions from what are commonly considered the building blocks of intellect and reasoning. Moreover, it suggests that, if a two-system account of decision making is correct, it would have to accommodate emotional influences on both systems, fast and slow. It would need to acknowledge the fact that any decision—as rational as it may seem—is in some way linked to our emotions.

Although a critical role for emotions in decision making is now commonly accepted, disagreement exists concerning the mechanisms through which emotions exert their influence. One possibility is that emotional states or the emotional value of information activated in working memory form a direct and central part of decision making. Another possibility is that they affect decision making indirectly through feedback from emotion-induced bodily changes.

The latter possibility has been explicitly formulated by Antonio Damasio as the somatic marker hypothesis (Damasio, 1994, 1996). Following up on the ideas of William James and Carl Lange (Chapter 2), Damasio linked the experience of an emotion to specific bodily changes such as changes in muscle tone, heart rate, skin temperature, or electrodermal activity. Feedback of these changes reaches the brain through the somatosensory system, the vagus nerve, or hormones that pass the blood-brain barrier. Damasio proposed that this feedback provides somatic markers, which carry emotional information and bias decision-making processes toward beneficial choices (Figure 10.11).

Existing evidence from brain research allows for the possibility that brain-based emotions both directly and indirectly, via somatic markers, influence decision making. In line with the first possibility, many studies implicate structures such as the amygdala, the striatum, and the orbitofrontal cortex in decision making (Seymour & Dolan, 2008; Volz & von Cramon, 2009). These areas are activated while participants weigh their choices (Hsu, Bhatt, Adolphs, Tranel, & Camerer, 2005), and lesions to these areas produces decision-making deficits (Bechara, Damasio, & Damasio, 2000; Gupta, Koscik, Bechara, & Tranel, 2011). Given that these structures seem to contribute directly to the emotional evaluation of incoming information, their implication in decision making suggests that resulting computations immediately bias choices.

In line with the second possibility, concerning an indirect influence via somatic markers, some studies revealed a correlation between bodily changes and ensuing decisions (Bechara & Damasio, 2002; Bechara et al., 2000). These studies typically used the Iowa Gambling Task, in which participants have to select a card from one of four decks. Unbeknownst to the participant, each deck is associated with a certain probability that cards produce financial rewards or costs. Thus, there are "good decks" and there are "bad decks." During the course of the experiment, participants implicitly learn which decks are good and which are bad and eventually are able to explicitly articulate this. In the hands of some researchers, participants showed increased skin conductance prior to selecting from "bad decks." Moreover, participants showed this increase well before they could articulate which decks were good and which were bad. Notably, however, other researchers were unable to replicate this finding, making a role for somatic markers in decision making contentious (Dunn, Dalgleish, & Lawrence, 2006).

Whether directly or indirectly, it is now clear that emotional processes necessarily inform not only the choices of nonhuman animals but also the choices of humans. Moreover, extant work suggests that decision making depends on emotional responses to available options as well as emotional responses to the context in which these options are presented. However, do we consistently choose options associated with positive emotions and shy away from options associated with negative emotions?

Although much of the research on decision making might give this impression, a few studies suggest otherwise. Specifically, work that explored decisions in the context of different emotions that were positive (e.g., happiness, hope) and negative (e.g., anger,

FIGURE 10.11 Structures That Mediate Emotional Influences on Decision Making

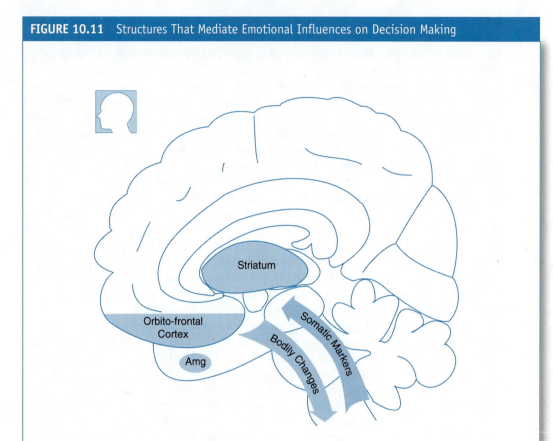

Emotions modulate decision making. Such modulation may occur directly as in when brain computations directly feed into decision processes. However, they may also occur indirectly. Bodily changes triggered via brain computations produce feedback called somatic markers that influences decision processes. Amg = amygdala.

fear) revealed emotion specificity (Lerner & Keltner, 2000; Tiedens & Linton, 2001). For example, emotions that involve uncertainty (e.g., hope, fear) were found to enhance risk assessment relative to emotions that involve certainty (e.g., happiness, anger; Tiedens & Linton, 2001). Undoubtedly, other emotion aspects or appraisal dimensions likewise impact the valuation of choices, making it probable that each emotion affects decision making somewhat differently. However, more research is needed to specify exactly how.

SUMMARY

Many mental processes that help us make sense of our environment have traditionally been considered "cold" cognitive processes. Some of these processes, such as attention and memory, are the building blocks for other, more complex processes such as language, time perception, or decision making. Modern research revealed that both the building blocks and the more complex cognitions are everything else, but cold.

Attention, a set of mental operations that highlight critical information in a bottom-up or top-down fashion, depends on emotion in that emotions determine what is critical. This has been demonstrated in a number of target detection paradigms, which revealed an advantage for emotional as compared to neutral targets. Thus, it has been suggested that emotional stimuli recruit attention more effectively than do neutral stimuli. This effect of emotion on attention may persist after cortical damage that impairs the ability to properly direct attention in a top-down fashion. However, it is abolished by lesions to the amygdala, suggesting that this structure helps emotionally significant sensory representations reach awareness.

Behavioral and neuroimaging studies that pitted bottom-up against top-down processes suggest that both contribute to emotional influences on attention. These influences result from processes that represent stimulus characteristics as well as processes that combine these characteristics with current needs or goals.

In order for perceived stimuli to be stored for future reference, these stimuli have to be encoded into short-term memory and consolidated into long-term memory. Both encoding and consolidation benefit from emotions, and these benefits arise from an engagement of the amygdala and hippocampal region. While the amygdala seems particularly important for implicit emotion memories, the hippocampal region seems particularly important for explicit emotion memories. Both implicit and explicit emotion memories depend on Hebbian learning or synaptic remodeling. The encoding of these memories involves changes in existing proteins that facilitate contiguous firing of neurons activated during the emotional episode. Memory consolidation involves the creation of new proteins through which short-term synaptic "rewiring" becomes durable. While encoding effects largely depend on instantaneous neural activation patterns triggered by an emotional stimulus, consolidation effects additionally involve bodily feedback. Possibly, this ensures that only those memories are kept long-term that had a significant mental and bodily impact.

Because attention and memory form the basis for a range of other cognitive functions, it is not surprising that these functions are likewise influenced by emotions. In the context of language processing, the activation of linguistic and categorical knowledge occurs more readily if that knowledge relates to an individual's current emotional state. This has been shown using the affective priming technique. Priming effects revealed through this technique suggest that affective states facilitate affect congruous semantic and response processes.

Another process that depends on attention and memory is time perception. Emotions influence this process by lengthening or shortening temporal representations, which may be explained through a modulation of pacemaker rate or the attentional and mnemonic processes that accumulate and store temporal pulses.

Last, this chapter introduced a role of emotions for decision making. In contrast to previous belief, human decisions are not strictly rational. Examples for this come again from the affective priming literature as well as from gambling and trading studies. Thus, theories, such as prospect theory, have been developed to account for emotional decision biases. Amygdala, striatum, and orbitofrontal cortex are brain structures that mediate emotional influences on choices. Neuroimaging and lesion evidence suggest that their influence results directly via central pathways and indirectly through feedback from the body. In either case, it seems that decision biases emerge in an emotion-specific rather than a simply affective way.

THINKING CRITICALLY ABOUT "EMOTION EFFECTS ON COGNITION"

1. What are typical paradigms to study memory, and how can these paradigms be used to dissociate emotion effects on different memory stages?

2. Do nonhuman animals have explicit memory? How could you test that?

3. Different studies find evidence for affective priming of semantic and response processes. What aspects of the design might produce these differential effects, and why?

4. Decision making is determined not only by the emotional value of choices, but also by the emotional value of the context in which these choices are presented. Is this problematic? Why did we fail to evolve a mechanism that discounts emotional context in decision making?

MEDIA LIBRARY

Documentary about memory and patient H. M.: http://www.liveleak.com/view?i=fd0_1261475829

Experts in Emotion Research Series by Jane Gruber at Yale University: http://www.yalepeplab.com/teaching/psych131_summer2013/materials.php. Relevant for this chapter would be videos by Derek Isaacowitz and Gerald Clore.

CHAPTER 11

Emotion Regulation

Emotions motivate actions, and because actions have multiple short- and long-term consequences, indulging in an emotion inadvertently impacts the probability of experiencing that same or another emotion in the future. To illustrate this, let's imagine you are working on an assignment and are tempted to browse the Internet instead. Giving in to temptation might mean that in the short term, you escape boredom. In the long term, however, you might fail the assignment. Thus, feeling good now would decrease your probability of feeling good later. Moreover, if this decrease can be expected to be more severe than the good feelings experienced from surfing the Web, you might do well to keep working on your assignment.

Emotion regulation helps with that. It comprises a mental toolkit for increasing, maintaining, or decreasing one or more aspects of an emotion (e.g., physiological response, nonverbal expression, conscious appraisals). Thus, by engaging in emotion regulation, you can change your emotions to both the assignment and the Internet so that the former becomes more interesting and the latter less so. This in turn would increase your motivation for actions associated with the assignment and decrease your need for distraction.

The mechanisms that support emotion regulation have long been of interest within philosophy and psychology. Many centuries ago, the ancient Greeks highlighted one particular aspect of emotion regulation—namely, humans' ability to subdue emotional impulses and to rely on judgment instead. Stoicism, a philosophical school that developed toward the end of the classical period around 300 BC, had this idea as a central tenet of its teachings. This is still reflected in today's use of phrases such as "being Stoic" or showing "Stoic calm."

Although Stoicism and the abomination of emotions eventually fell out of favor, emotion regulation as a topic of interest prevailed. Among other things, it was mentioned as a useful practice in the writings of René Descartes, who, although considering emotions to be generally useful, held that they may occasionally be ill used. To prevent this ill usage, he suggested "a general remedy against the passions" (Descartes, 1643/1989, Article 211). This remedy included the distraction from an emotional situation and the reconsideration or reweighing of associated benefits and costs. Thus, Descartes thought, one can turn a negative state such as boredom into a positive state such as interest.

With the emergence of psychology as a scientific discipline, emotion regulation became relevant for separate lines of inquiry. For example, it gained a central role in budding theories of mental disorders. Famous here is the psychoanalytical school that originated with Sigmund Freud. It postulates the repression of unwanted memories as a defense mechanism through which individuals can take "psychic flight" from a traumatic event (Freud, 1926). Emotion regulation also emerged as an important topic for the psychology of child development (Mischel, Shoda, & Rodriguez, 1989) and the psychology of coping with stress (Lazarus & Alfert, 1964). It is only recently, however, that these lines of inquiry evolved into a holistic study of emotion regulation and its underlying mechanisms (Ochsner & Gross, 2005). The results of this study form the basis for the present chapter.

WHY REGULATE? THE FUNCTIONS OF EMOTION REGULATION

As mentioned earlier, we don't experience emotions in a vacuum. Any time we indulge in a particular emotion, the behaviors associated with that emotion have knock-on effects on our environment and change future emotion probabilities. Our success in life depends on how we negotiate these probabilities and how we regulate a current state so as to maximize overall benefits. Thus, like emotions, emotion regulation helps us satisfy existing and prospective needs, including physical and safety needs, needs to belong and to be esteemed, and needs for self-actualization (Maslow, 1943).

A second important function of emotion regulation is that it helps us prevent needs from developing. In other words, a healthy dose of emotion regulation is a necessary safeguard from being overwhelmed by emotions and from allowing them to interfere with normal mental and bodily functions.

An example of this preventative function comes from research by Vandekerckhove and colleagues (2012), who studied the role of emotion regulation in sleep. Participants in their study performed a difficult cognitive task for which they received discouraging feedback from the experimenter. Following this task, the participants were instructed to regulate their emotions and afterward slept in the lab. Half the participants received an "experiential" emotion regulation instruction, which entailed focusing on their affective state without evaluating this state and its eliciting conditions. The remaining participants received an "analytical" emotion regulation instruction, which entailed dealing with the causes, meanings, and consequences of the emotional episode. Participants in the "experiential" regulation group slept with fewer interruptions and spent less time awake than did participants in the "analytical" regulation group. Thus, the researchers concluded that experiential emotion regulation is more effective than analytical emotion regulation in promoting healthy sleep. Interestingly, the relationship between emotion regulation and sleep is bidirectional. Just like emotion regulation can enhance sleep, healthy sleep can promote an individual's capacity for emotion regulation (Mauss, Troy, & Lebourgeois, 2013).

Extending this line of work, researchers found a reciprocal relationship between other aspects of a person's health and emotion regulation. For example, they linked certain forms of emotion regulation with reduced risk for depression (Berking & Wupperman, 2012), improved cardiovascular function (Dorr, Brosschot, Sollers, & Thayer, 2007), and a better immune system (Appleton, Buka, Loucks, Gilman, & Kubzansky, 2013).

EMOTION REGULATION STRATEGIES

Emotion regulation has been defined as the application of strategies that increase, maintain, or decrease the intensity, duration, and/or quality of an experienced emotion (Gyurak, Gross, & Etkin, 2011). Several attempts have been made to characterize and organize these strategies. A popular one differentiates three major classes referred to as (1) attentional deployment, (2) cognitive change, and (3) response modulation (Webb, Miles, & Sheeran, 2012; Figure 11.1). These classes are examined in more detail in the following.

Attentional Deployment

Strategies that rely on attentional deployment distract attention from or direct attention toward an emotional event and/or experience.

Distraction strategies include behavioral and mental avoidance, such as when individuals steer clear of an emotional stimulus or when they turn away their thoughts. To date, research focusing primarily on the latter, mental avoidance, suggests that it can dampen immediate emotional reactions (Denson, Moulds, & Grisham, 2012; Lieberman, Inagaki, Tabibnia, & Crockett, 2011; Sheppes & Meiran, 2007).

This has been shown by exposing participants to an emotional stimulus with the instruction to think of something else or to perform a secondary, unemotional task. It has also been demonstrated by presenting participants with distracting stimuli. In one such study, negative images were each followed by a positive distractor image (Strick, Holland, van Baaren, & van Knippenberg, 2009). Rated emotions were less negative when the distractor image was humorous as compared to nonhumorous. Moreover, because the effect

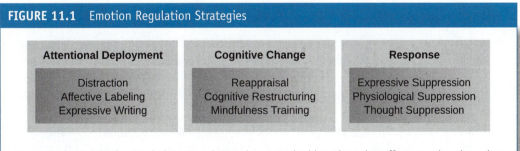

FIGURE 11.1 Emotion Regulation Strategies

Attentional Deployment	Cognitive Change	Response
Distraction	Reappraisal	Expressive Suppression
Affective Labeling	Cognitive Restructuring	Physiological Suppression
Expressive Writing	Mindfulness Training	Thought Suppression

For convenience, emotion regulation strategies can be categorized into those that affect attention, those that affect the nature of thought, and those that affect the response to an emotion. Listed for each category are example strategies discussed in the text.

of humorous distractors correlated with their cognitive complexity, the authors suggested that they helped regulate emotions by disengaging cognitive resources from the negative images.

Similar to distraction, confrontation strategies can involve both behavior and thought. They play an important role in the clinical treatment of emotion disorders. In this context, they have been shown to reduce phobias (Chapter 9) and to help deal with trauma (Goncalves, Pedrozo, Coutinho, Figueira, & Ventura, 2012). Again, in the context of healthy emotions, mental confrontation has received most scientific scrutiny, and this scrutiny has provided mixed results (Webb et al., 2012).

Some studies found that, like mental distraction, mental confrontation dampens felt emotions. For example, the explicit naming of an emotion, also referred to as affect labeling, has been shown to reduce the affective evaluation of both negative and positive stimuli (Lieberman et al., 2011). Furthermore, there is evidence that writing down one's thoughts and feelings produces similar results (A Closer Look 11.1). This evidence includes an investigation on test anxiety, a condition known to reduce performance on tests. Students who were asked to write down their worries prior to taking a challenging exam performed better than did students who were asked to write on an unrelated topic or to write nothing at all (Ramirez & Beilock, 2011).

Nevertheless, there are studies suggesting that concentrating and cognitively elaborating on an emotion fail to reduce and may even increase that emotion (Denson et al., 2012; Kuehner, Huffziger, & Liebsch, 2009). In one such study, anger was induced by asking participants to recall an episode that made them angry (Denson et al., 2012). One group of participants then wrote about the causes and consequences of this episode. Other groups were instructed to write about whatever came to mind or to describe the campus layout. After this writing task, the first group showed significantly greater levels of anger than did the two other groups, suggesting that concentrating on the anger episode prolonged the elicited anger.

A CLOSER LOOK 11.1

Writing Your Worries Away

In many cultures, diaries represent a popular means to unburden the mind from a day's events and worries. The Roman emperor Marcus Aurelius (121–180 CE), for example, committed his thoughts and feelings experienced during military campaigns to a personal journal titled *To Myself* (Aurelius, 1916). Research suggests that, apart from resulting in an external memory, this would have helped Marcus Aurelius grapple with significant events and regulate experienced emotions.

Evidence for this comes from studies linking expressive writing to cognitive and emotional benefits. For example, Klein and Boals required participants to write about current emotional or nonemotional events (Klein & Boals, 2001). Before and after several such writing sessions, the participants underwent a working memory test. The test should determine whether writing about emotional events helped with emotional regulation and freed up mental capacity.

FIGURE 11.2   Writing About Emotions Helps Control Their Negative Impact

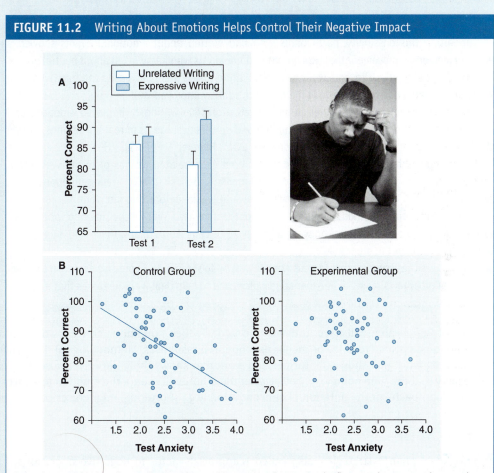

Panel A provides data from college students taking two math tests. On the first test, there was no intervention prior to test taking. On the second test, students in the expressive writing group were instructed to write for 10 minutes about their thoughts and feelings toward the upcoming exam. Students in the unrelated writing group wrote about something else. While both groups performed comparably on test 1, the expressive writing group performed better than the unrelated writing group on test 2. Panel B shows the relationship between test performance and test anxiety in high school students sitting for a biology exam. Students in the experimental group underwent a 10-minute expressive writing session about exam-related thoughts and feelings. Students in the control group were instructed to think about a topic that would not be covered in the exam. Only in the latter group did test anxiety, measured as a trait several weeks prior to this study, predict exam performance.

Sources: "Writing About Testing Worries Boosts Exam Performance in the Classroom," by G. Ramirez and S. L. Beilock, 2011, *Science, 331,* 211–213; "Adult Student With Test Anxiety," © Lisa F. Young–*Fotolia.com.*

(Continued)

(Continued)

Supporting this possibility, participants who had written about emotional events showed a working memory improvement that was absent in participants who had written about neutral events. Moreover, if the emotional events were negative, writing about them decreased the frequency with which participants had to think about them, and thus likely improved well-being.

Extending this line of work, other studies linked expressive writing to improved emotions and better exam performance in both school children and university students in real-life settings outside the laboratory (Frattaroli, Thomas, & Lyubomirsky, 2011; Ramirez & Beilock, 2011).

For example, school kids were asked to write about exam-related worries or to think about an unrelated topic prior to taking a math exam (Ramirez & Beilock, 2011). Their self-reported test anxiety, which the experimenters had obtained several weeks before this intervention, negatively predicted exam scores in the kids who thought about the unrelated topic. In the kids who wrote about exam-related worries, this correlation was no longer significant. Additionally, their exam scores were higher than those of the other kids.

Findings like these suggest that Marcus Aurelius was on to something. Expressive writing in the form of diaries or other texts seems to free mental resources and to help deal with the things that matter.

Future research will have to determine under which conditions concentration on an emotional episode reduces or increases emotional responses. Methodological differences between work that shows the former and work that shows the latter effect raise the possibility that the time point (e.g., before/after the emotional event), the emotion (e.g., avoidance/approach), or the duration of concentration (e.g., short/long) might be critical.

Cognitive Change

Cognitive change strategies, also called reappraisals, refer to cognitive operations that change the way individuals think about an emotional event or experience. They involve the integration of new information—real or imagined. Experimental research today has explored reappraisals by asking participants to imagine a context in which an emotional event or experience would be neutral (Ochsner, Bunge, Gross, & Gabrieli, 2002), in which it recedes into the distance (Davis, Gross, & Ochsner, 2011), or in which the participants themselves act as objective, scientific observers without being emotionally involved (Goldin, McRae, Ramel, & Gross, 2008). Reappraisals have also been explored using more complex instructions that provide new information and additionally tap into the participants' imagination. This has been termed cognitive restructuring.

A fear-conditioning study demonstrated that cognitive restructuring can alleviate negative emotions. In this study, participants saw two types of images, one of which was paired with an electric shock to the wrist (Shurick et al., 2012; Figure 11.3). After the conditioning procedure, participants in the experimental group underwent complex reappraisal treatment. The experimenter explained to them the relationship between thoughts and feelings and that the former can influence the intensity of the latter. Furthermore, the experimenter demonstrated how adding information can alter one's feelings toward a stimulus and asked the participants to come up with thoughts that would make the conditioned image seem less threatening. Participants in the control group were excluded from this treatment.

The researchers reinvited all the participants on the next day and subjected them to a fear-conditioning procedure identical to the one carried out previously. Additionally, they assessed the participants' fear of the conditioned stimulus by asking them to rate the intensity of their fear and by measuring skin conductance. Participants in the experimental condition reported significantly less fear and showed decreased skin conductance relative to participants in the control condition. This suggests that the cognitive representation of

FIGURE 11.3 Methods and Results of a Study Exploring the Effect of Cognitive Restructuring on Fear

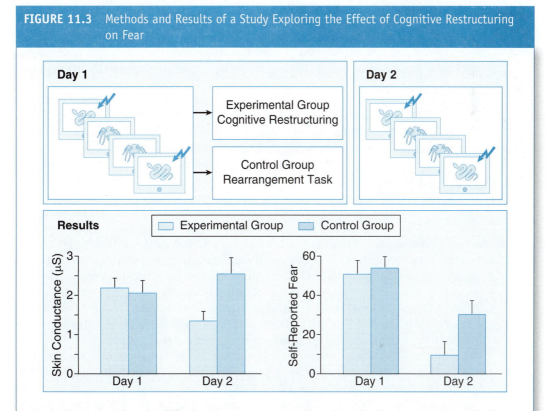

For the illustration of results, difference scores were computed by subtracting the responses to the CS− (image without shock) from the responses to the CS+ (image with shock). There were no differences in physiological and self-reported fear measures between the experimental and the control group on Day 1. However, on Day 2, the experimental group showed significantly less fear on both measures when compared to the control group.

Source: Copyright © 2012 by the American Psychological Association. Adapted with permission from "Durable Effects of Cognitive Restructuring on Conditioned Fear," by A. A. Shurick, J. Hamilton, L. T. Harris, A. K. Roy, J. J. Gross, and E. Phelps, 2012, *Emotion, 12,* pp. 1393–1397. The use of APA information does not imply endorsement by APA.

an emotional episode can be changed to reduce emotional responses and that such changes may be relatively durable.

Research that explored the effect of reappraising one's response to an emotion-eliciting episode overlaps with research on the effects of mindfulness training (Chapter 8). Both share the idea that accepting one's mental and bodily state as something natural and meaningful promotes emotional recovery. The findings that speak to this idea, however, are mixed (Webb et al., 2012). Some attest that acceptance of an emotional response reduces that response (Low, Stanton, & Bower, 2008), whereas others fail to find such an effect (Kuehner et al., 2009). More research is needed to solve this discrepancy.

Response Modulation

Strategies referred to as response modulation involve the enhancement or suppression of one or more aspects of an emotion. These aspects include the nonverbal expressions, physiological responses, subjective feelings, or thoughts that are triggered by an emotional episode.

Much research tackled the suppression of nonverbal expressions. This work demonstrated that individuals can significantly restrict their nonverbal behaviors when told to do so. However, the effect of this restriction on their felt emotions is less clear. While such restriction reduces felt emotions toward positive stimuli fairly reliably, its effect on negative stimuli is often nonsignificant (Webb et al., 2012). Moreover, because there are some reports that expression suppression increases the activity of the sympathetic nervous system (Gross & Levenson, 1993), it is possible that "hiding" one's emotions is more harmful than helpful.

Only a few studies explored the suppression of emotion aspects other than nonverbal expressions. Those that looked at physiological responses suggest possible benefits. Specifically, it was shown that participants can willfully slow down their heart rate or reduce their rate of breathing. Moreover, such reductions affect physiological arousal more generally (Dan-Glauser & Gross, 2011) and ratings of subjective emotion intensity (McCaul, Solomon, & Holmes, 1979). Exemplary for this effect is a study in which participants were subjected to mild electrical shocks. Participants who were asked to reduce their rate of breathing prior to the shock period showed reduced skin conductance and less subjective fear relative to participants who breathed normally (McCaul et al., 1979).

Other emotion suppression research explored the effect of thought both in experimental and clinical settings. Experimental research probed Freud's proposition that we can repress or forget unwanted memories (Anderson & Green, 2001). To demonstrate this, participants were presented with noun pairs (e.g., *steam-train*) and asked to commit them to memory. Subsequently, they saw one member of each pair again. On some trials, they had to retrieve the memory of the other member (i.e., think condition), whereas on other trials they had to suppress the learned association (i.e., no-think condition). After completing this task, participants were again presented with one member of each pair and now had to report the other member for each of them. In line with Freud, the participants' recall was better for think as compared to no-think pairs, suggesting that thoughts had been successfully suppressed.

Follow-up research could replicate these results (Nørby, Lange, & Larsen, 2010; Figure 11.4). At the same time, however, it showed that thought suppression works only for relatively neutral material and is short-lived. As such, it seems a poor strategy for emotion regulation.

FIGURE 11.4 On the Effect of Thought Suppression on Recall

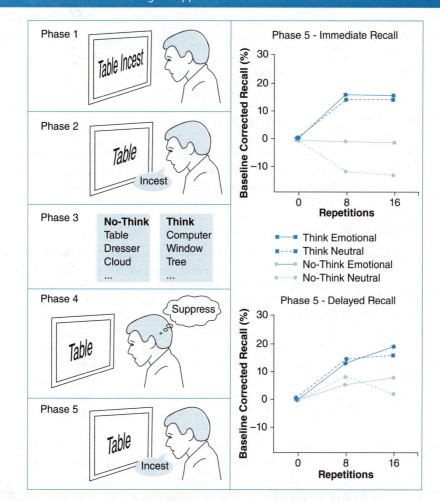

Thought suppression was studied in an experiment with 5 successive phases. In the first phase, participants saw word pairs (cue word on left side, target word on right side) and committed these pairs to memory. In the second phase, they saw only the cue words of the pairs they had studied and had to recall the corresponding target words. In the third phase, the participants received two lists of cue words. One list comprised no-think words and the other list comprised think words. The participants committed to memory which words belonged to which list. In the fourth phase, the participants saw most cue words again (except for a small subset [0 repetition] that served as baseline stimuli). Cues could be repeated 8 or 16 times. For words from the no-think list, participants had to suppress recall of the associated target. For words from the think list, they had to recall the associated target. In the fifth phase, the participants saw all cue words again and had to recall the associated target. They did this immediately, and again one week later. During immediate recall, the percent baseline corrected recall (i.e., the percent of recalled words presented in phase 4 minus the percent of recalled words not presented in phase 4) was greater for the think as compared to the no-think condition. However, a significant memory impairment relative to baseline was seen for only the neutral words in the no-think condition, and this effect disappeared during the delayed recall.

Source: "Forgetting to Forget: On the Duration of Voluntary Suppression of Neutral and Emotional Memories," by S. Nørby, M. Lange, and A. Larsen, 2010, *Acta Psychologica, 133,* pp. 73–80. Copyright © 2010, with permission from Elsevier.

Clinical studies, furthermore, hint that its habitual use may be detrimental. Individuals who habitually engage in thought suppression as compared to other means of emotion regulation report a greater incidence of psychopathological symptoms associated with depression, anxiety, eating disorders, and posttraumatic stress disorder (Aldao & Nolen-Hoeksema, 2010; Amstadter & Vernon, 2008).

PRINCIPLES THAT GOVERN THE USE AND USEFULNESS OF EMOTION REGULATION

Given the many possible ways in which individuals can regulate their emotions, one may ask what determines which strategy they choose, and whether that strategy is effective. The following section reviews some factors of potential relevance for this question.

Factors Associated With the Event

Time of regulation. One possibility is that strategy choice and effectiveness depend on the point in time at which emotion regulation is attempted. Specifically, different strategies may be more or less useful as a function of whether emotion regulation is antecedent- or response-focused (Gross, 1998; Figure 11.5). Antecedent-focused emotion regulation concerns attempts to subdue an emotion before or while that emotion is being elicited. Such regulation addresses incoming information associated with the eliciting event and thus the input to a putative emotion system. For example, a student might attempt to console herself prior to or during a difficult exam with the thought that a bad grade would not be the end of the world. Response-focused emotion regulation concerns attempts to subdue an emotion after that emotion was elicited and is directed at the output processes of a putative emotion system. In this case, the student might attempt consolation after having failed the exam, once she has felt a wave of dejection.

One popular proposal holds that attentional deployment and cognitive change are antecedent-focused strategies, whereas response modulation is a response-focused strategy

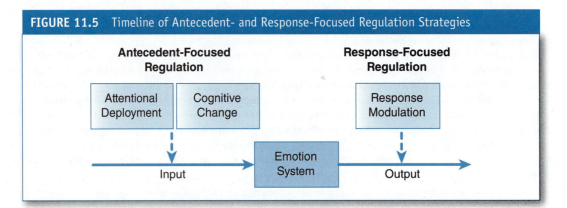

FIGURE 11.5   Timeline of Antecedent- and Response-Focused Regulation Strategies

(Gross, 1998; Webb et al., 2012). Whether this is indeed the case, however, remains to be seen (Sheppes & Gross, 2011). At present, antecedent- and response-focused strategies are difficult to dissociate both at a conceptual and an empirical level.

Conceptually, difficulties rest on the dissociation of input to and output from a putative emotion system. Moreover, whether our brains maintain such a system and at what point in time its input would turn into output are still open questions. We do not know when the mental processes and bodily responses that behold an emotional event represent incoming information and when they represent the emotional response. Problems at the empirical level arise from the fact that there is currently no evidence that clearly dissociates antecedent- from response-focused strategies. Moreover, existing evidence implies a similar time course in the activation of both strategies (Gross, 1998), raising further doubts as to whether they can be meaningfully dissociated.

Although a dissociation between antecedent- and response-focused regulation is still doubtful, it is probable that time matters for regulation success. Specifically, there is evidence that the effectiveness of using a particular strategy depends on when this strategy is recruited relative to the onset of an emotional stimulus. Whereas cognitive change strategies have been associated with substantial regulatory effects when initiated before stimulus onset, these effects decline when strategy initiation occurs during or after the stimulus (Sheppes & Meiran, 2007). Possibly, it is quite difficult to truly change one's view of an event after that view is already established. In contrast, attentional deployment strategies seem equally effective when initiated early or late in an emotional episode (Sheppes & Meiran, 2007). Possibly, new thoughts or impressions effectively dilute an emotional experience regardless of when they occur.

Mental capacity. Another factor that may influence whether an emotion regulation strategy is both used and useful is the strategy's associated mental cost. Most ongoing mental processes tax a limited capacity pool. Thus, how much is left in that pool determines whether and how an additional process can be executed. If little capacity is available, then a costly regulation strategy may not be attempted or attempted suboptimally. Instead, participants may opt for a less costly strategy.

Although there is little insight into how available capacity influences regulation choices and regulation success, there is substantial evidence that different strategies pose different costs (Gross, 2002). Pitting cognitive change against distraction, it has been shown that the former is more taxing than the latter (Sheppes & Meiran, 2008). Specifically, participants were exposed to a sad movie and asked to regulate ensuing emotions either by adopting an objective and analytical point of view or by pursuing thoughts unrelated to the movie. Compared to the cognitive change group, the distraction group performed better on a subsequent cognitive interference task. Its members were less impaired by task-irrelevant information and thus demonstrated greater mental capacity.

Notably, however, distraction disrupted memory for the movie, whereas cognitive change did not. Thus, although potentially less effortful, distraction may be a poorer choice if memory for an emotional event is critical. Moreover, if its eliciting conditions and consequences need to be retained for future reference, then expending the extra effort and freeing capacity for cognitive change may be a better choice.

Other factors. Apart from time and cost, there are many other event-associated factors with potential influence on emotion regulation. These factors include aspects of the emotion-eliciting stimulus and the type of emotion that individuals experience. For example, attentional deployment strategies may be more effective for weak than for strong emotions. For strong emotions, some sort of cognitive engagement and restructuring may be necessary. Furthermore, emotions based on conscious thought or reasoning may be more amenable to cognitive change strategies as opposed to emotions based on relatively automatic evaluations. However, whether this is the case and what other factors are relevant constitute issues for future research.

Factors Associated With the Individual

External factors. Many personal characteristics have been shown to influence whether and how individuals engage in emotion regulation. Some of these characteristics derive from the individual's life or learning experiences. Through such experiences, individuals acquire and ultimately apply regulatory strategies. Applied strategies may then be dismissed if they are ineffective or otherwise problematic. In contrast, effective and otherwise unproblematic strategies may become automatized regulation habits.

An individual's cultural background constitutes one of the life and learning experiences that influence strategy acquisition and utilization. For example, different cultures value nonverbal emotional expressions differently. Such expressions are frowned on in some Asian cultures (e.g., Japan), whereas they are tolerated and even expected in some European cultures (e.g., Italy). As a consequence, individuals from the former cultures are more likely than individuals from the latter cultures to engage in expression suppression (Matsumoto, Yoo, & Nakagawa, 2008).

Internal factors. Other factors influencing whether and how individuals regulate their emotions come from within the individual. They concern the individual's mental resources for engaging regulatory processes in general and certain strategies in particular. These processes and strategies result from a complex interplay of basic mental resources (e.g., for perception and memory) that are subject to genetic variation and developmental conditions (e.g., nutrition). For example, we know that individuals differ in sentience, defined as the ability to apprehend one's own mental and bodily states. Some may detect very subtle state changes, whereas others need changes to be more salient. As a consequence, the former individuals may be better than the latter at learning the conditions that produce state change and are thus better equipped to engage in emotion regulation.

In line with this supposition, recent research identified a link between sentience and an individual's propensity to downregulate negative affect (Füstös, Gramann, Herbert, & Pollatos, 2013). Sentience was quantified as the difference between a participant's perceived and actual heartbeat. Emotion regulation was modulated by presenting participants with negative images and asking them to reappraise or maintain their emotions to the images. The participants' emotions were measured explicitly through self-reports and implicitly through event-related potentials (ERPs). The explicit measure involved scoring on an affective scale. The implicit measure comprised a late positive ERP component (LPC) that is typically larger for more emotionally intense stimuli (Moser, Hajcak, Bukay, & Simons, 2006). Sentience positively predicted regulation success for both the explicit and the implicit measure (Füstös et al., 2013). Individuals who more accurately perceived their own heartbeats showed greater explicit and implicit emotion differences between the "reappraise" and the "maintain" condition, indicating that their reappraisal was more effective (Figure 11.6).

Apart from sentience or self-perception, humans show natural variation in the mental resources that underlie memory. One reason why these resources are relevant for emotion regulation is that they assist in keeping a certain regulatory goal in mind. Thus, individuals do not immediately forget that they intended to regulate their state but can do so over an extended period. That this facilitates emotion regulation was demonstrated in a study that required participants to view a negative or a positive movie while suppressing their

FIGURE 11.6   Exploring the Relationship Between Sentience and Emotion Regulation

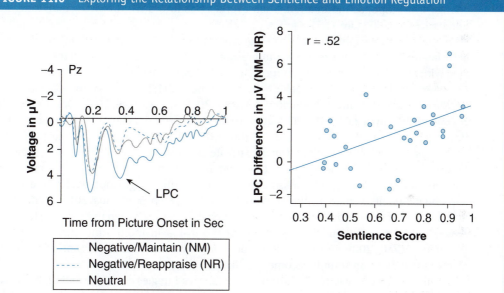

Illustrated on the left is the ERP from one representative scalp electrode (Pz). A late positive component (LPC) is greater for negative images for which participants were instructed to maintain elicited feelings than for negative images for which participants were instructed to reappraise. The latter condition elicited a similar ERP as that obtained for neutral images. Illustrated on the right is the relationship between the sentience score ($1/4\Sigma(1-(|$ recorded heartbeats − counted heartbeats $|)/$ recorded heartbeats)) and emotion regulation success (ERP negative/maintain condition − ERP negative/reappraise). Greater sentience was associated with greater emotion regulation success.

Source: "On the Embodiment of Emotion Regulation: Interoceptive Awareness Facilitates Reappraisal," by J. Füstös, K. Gramann, B. M. Herbert, and O. Pollatos, 2013, *Social, Cognitive, and Affective Neuroscience, 8,* pp. 911–917. Copyright © 2013, Oxford University Press.

expression and keeping a "straight face" (Schmeichel, Volokhov, & Demaree, 2008). The ability to comply with these instructions correlated with the participants' working memory. Those who scored better on a standard working memory test were better able to suppress their emotional expressions. Similar results were obtained when individuals were instructed to quench emotions using a detached viewing strategy; this supported the idea that working memory is a relatively general emotion regulation resource.

BRAIN MECHANISMS THAT SUPPORT EMOTION REGULATION

Research on the brain mechanisms that support emotion regulation has focused primarily on attempts to downregulate negative states. In line with the idea that the different emotion regulation strategies recruit a common set of regulation resources, this research revealed substantial overlap in the neural underpinnings of attentional deployment, cognitive change, and response modulation. Such overlap was found within the frontal, temporal, and parietal lobe (Figure 11.7).

Within the frontal lobe, the different regulation strategies depend on ventrolateral regions associated with language processing and response preparation, dorsolateral regions associated with attention and working memory, as well as dorsomedial regions within or close to the anterior cingulate (Diekhof, Geier, Falkai, & Gruber, 2011; Dolcos, Iordan, & Dolcos, 2011; Kanske, Heissler, Schönfelder, Bongers, & Wessa, 2011; McRae et al., 2009; Ochsner, Silvers, & Buhle, 2012; Ray & Zald, 2012). The latter regions in the anterior cingulate (Chapters 4 and 8) have been implicated in action inhibition (Brass & Haggard, 2007) and the detection of discrepancy between an intended and an actual state (Isomura & Takada, 2004). Thus, they may help to inhibit action tendencies and nonverbal expressions triggered by an emotional stimulus and track how close one is to an intended emotion regulation goal. Some studies additionally point to an involvement of the insula (Firk, Siep, & Markus, 2013; Goldin et al., 2008). However, activation of this structure is typically reduced when individuals effectively downregulate an emotion. Given the role of the insula in monitoring changes in body physiology (Craig, 2009; Chapter 4), its reduced activity in the context of emotion regulation suggests that emotion stimuli become less likely to trigger such changes.

Within the temporal lobe, the different regulation strategies converge in their effects on the amygdala. Like the insula, the amygdala typically becomes less active when participants engage in attentional deployment, cognitive change, or response modulation. Connections between the amygdala and parts of the frontal lobe (e.g., dorsal aspect of anterior cingulate; Ray & Zald, 2012) have been implicated in this effect, and it has been suggested that control processes initiated within the frontal lobe serve to inhibit amygdala function (Ochsner et al., 2012; Ray & Zald, 2012). Thus, emotional stimuli are less likely to excite the amygdala and to trigger emotional changes in mental state and bodily function.

Last, the different emotion regulation strategies overlap in their recruitment of the parietal lobe. Here, most studies identified an area within the inferior parietal cortex that is enhanced when individuals attempt to regulate as compared to when they don't. This enhancement has been interpreted in reference to the concomitant recruitment of dorsolateral prefrontal cortex. Apart from being jointly active during emotion

FIGURE 11.7 Brain Correlates of Emotion Regulation

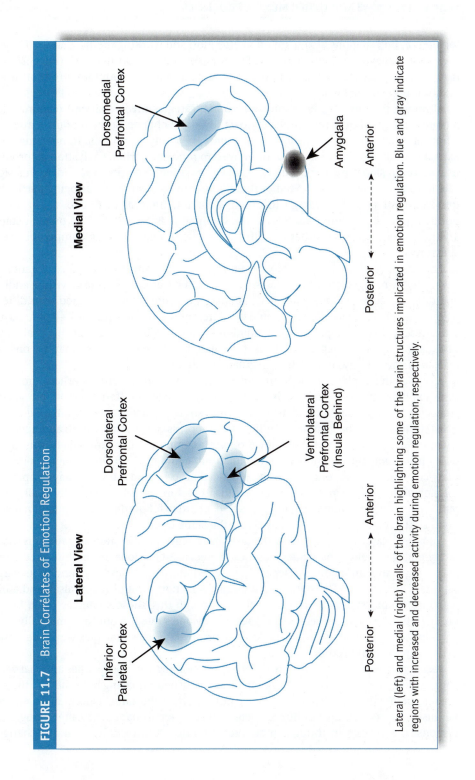

Lateral View

Inferior
Parietal Cortex

Dorsolateral
Prefrontal Cortex

Ventrolateral
Prefrontal Cortex
(Insula Behind)

Posterior ◄┄┄┄┄► Anterior

Medial View

Dorsomedial
Prefrontal Cortex

Amygdala

Posterior ◄┄┄┄┄► Anterior

Lateral (left) and medial (right) walls of the brain highlighting some of the brain structures implicated in emotion regulation. Blue and gray indicate regions with increased and decreased activity during emotion regulation, respectively.

regulation, both regions also team up in attention and working memory tasks. They are, therefore, believed to form part of a frontoparietal attention network (Ptak, 2012). If true, then the parietal activation probably helps direct and maintain attention toward emotion regulation goals.

Although the different emotion regulation strategies involve shared resources (e.g., attention and memory), they differ in how they effect change. Some modulate attention, whereas others modulate associated thoughts or bodily responses. Hence, one would expect that, in addition to the structural overlap reported earlier, each strategy produces its own brain signature. Surprisingly, however, existing attempts to elucidate this signature have been unsuccessful. Studies that highlighted one structure as being particularly important for a given strategy (Giuliani, Drabant, Bhatnagar, & Gross, 2011) could not be replicated by other studies (Kühn, Gallinat, & Brass, 2011). The present state of affairs, therefore, suggests that the different strategies have largely comparable neural substrates.

This state of affairs is worrisome given that, traditionally, functional segregation has been reliably mapped onto structural segregation. If different senses (e.g., vision, audition) and different cognitive processes (e.g., language, attention) are associated with different patterns of brain activity, then so should the different regulation strategies—if, indeed, they are different. Thus, one possible explanation for the lack of strategy-specific brain signatures is that these strategies are in fact comparable. Moreover, there may be only one instead of several ways in which we regulate emotions.

Although this explanation is at present a possibility, there are other, perhaps more plausible, explanations. For example, individuals may engage in different emotion regulation strategies but have very little control over what strategy they use when. Lifelong practice turns strategies into habits that are difficult to suppress or evoke at will. To appreciate this, try to recall the position of the letter *B* on your computer keyboard. Likely, this is quite difficult—despite the fact that you have little trouble finding the *B* while typing. Sometimes practice makes us lose control over the practiced process, and the same may happen to us through a lifetime of emotion regulation. It is, therefore, possible that individuals participating in emotion regulation experiments find it hard to follow different regulation instructions, so that on average they end up doing the same thing.

Another, related explanation for the lack of strategy-specific brain signatures is that we rarely engage in only one strategy at a time. Because emotions are multifaceted experiences, regulating an emotion effectively may require us to change or modify its various aspects. Thus, in real life we may try a bit of distraction, a bit of reappraisal, and a bit of response suppression all at the same time. Through this, these strategies could become linked so that an explicit attempt to engage in only one strategy would automatically trigger participation of the other strategies. As a consequence, these strategies would be difficult to tease apart in an experimental context.

Last, it may well be that there are different emotion regulation strategies and that we can engage them one at a time. Moreover, the reason why neuroimaging links them to the same brain structures may be because they eventually affect the same aspects of an emotion. Because these aspects are tightly connected, an attentional change may alter thoughts and responses, a change in thought may alter attention and responses, and a change in responses may alter attention and thoughts. If true, no matter what strategy you use to regulate, you will ultimately trigger processes that are central to one or more of the other strategies discussed here and thereby recruit comparable brain mechanisms.

EMOTION REGULATION AND MENTAL HEALTH

Since Freud, psychologists and clinicians have embraced the idea that many mental disorders can be traced back to dysfunctional emotion regulation. Such links have been postulated for anxiety, bipolar disorder, depression, eating disorders, and substance abuse, among other disorders (Berking & Wupperman, 2012). Dysfunctional regulation has largely been conceptualized as a shift in the strategies that individuals employ. For example, studies exploring emotion regulation in depression (Chapter 8) found that depressive symptoms are positively associated with the self-reported use of attentional deployment (e.g., distraction, rumination) and response modulation strategies (e.g., suppression of expression and thought), whereas they are negatively associated with the self-reported use of cognitive change strategies (e.g., mindfulness, reappraisal; Aldao, Nolen-Hoeksema, & Schweizer, 2010). In other words, depressed individuals seem to engage attentional deployment and response modulation strategies more and cognitive change strategies less than do healthy individuals.

Although these results implicate emotion regulation in psychopathology, they have little explanatory power. Moreover, they raise several questions concerning the mechanisms and consequences of the observed regulation changes. In the following section, we turn to two of these questions.

Why Do Depressed Individuals Regulate Differently?

A first question concerns the reason why depression biases individuals toward attentional deployment and response modulation strategies. What is wrong so that these strategies become dominant?

A possible answer to this question is that other strategies no longer work. Perhaps the mechanisms underlying cognitive change are broken, and thus are no longer available for regulation. In support of this possibility, a large literature describes cognitive deficits in depression, including reduced working memory (Gotlib & Joormann, 2010; Murrough, Iacoviello, Neumeister, Charney, & Iosifescu, 2011). Contrary to this possibility, however, there is evidence that individuals prone to depression use cognitive change just as effectively as controls if instructed to do so (Ehring, Tuschen-Caffier, Schnülle, Fischer, & Gross, 2010). Therefore, cognitive change, albeit taxing and not a first choice, seems preserved.

Another explanation for the regulation bias in depression may be that depression alters regulation preferences. Specifically, it may change the way in which individuals trade off the costs and benefits associated with the different regulation strategies. As mentioned previously, cognitive change requires more effort than other regulation strategies (Sheppes & Meiran, 2008), and depressed individuals may simply wish to avoid this extraneous effort. Alternatively, the different strategies may differ in how quickly they effect emotion changes. For example, it is possible that attentional deployment and response modulation produce their effects faster than cognitive change—serving as a "quick fix." Thus, individuals with depression may opt for the fast remedy instead of the slow one, even if the slow one is potentially more effective (Gross & Muñoz, 1995).

Are Differences in Emotion Regulation Cause or Consequence of Depression?

Another question associated with the regulation bias in depression is whether this bias is a cause or consequence of depression. Do abnormal patterns in emotion regulation choices contribute to the emergence of depression, or are they the result of it?

Many clinicians and psychologists hold that abnormal patterns of emotion regulation cause psychopathology, despite the fact that this has not been directly proven. Findings, taken as indirect proof, are that a relationship between emotion regulation and depressive symptomatology exists not only in patients currently suffering from depression but also in preclinical populations (Aldao et al., 2010) and in patients who recovered from a previous depressive episode (Ehring, Fischer, Schnülle, Bösterling, & Tuschen-Caffier, 2008; Ehring et al., 2010). Thus, depression-related emotion regulation choices may reflect stable premorbid aspects of an individual's personality that increase the likelihood of developing the disorder.

Additionally, there is evidence that stimulating the dorsolateral prefrontal cortex with repetitive transcranial magnetic stimulation (rTMS; Chapter 6) alleviates symptoms of depression (Downar & Daskalakis, 2013). Given that this brain structure forms part of the emotion regulation network introduced above, this finding suggests that the effectiveness of rTMS in the treatment of depression results from pushing the emotion regulation network (De Raedt et al., 2010; Strafella, Paus, Fraraccio, & Dagher, 2003) and thus potentially altering emotion regulation choices.

Yet, there is also research in favor of the possibility that abnormal patterns of emotion regulation are simply a consequence of depression. As mentioned before, the different regulation strategies are intact and as efficient in individuals prone to depression as they are in healthy controls (Ehring et al., 2010). Moreover, several studies point to the fact that depressed individuals or individuals prone to depression have difficulties accepting negative emotions. When exposed to sadness-relevant information, they show the same increase in self-reported negative affect as do healthy controls. However, they feel less comfortable with this increase and are more likely to attempt regulation (Campbell-Sills, Barlow, Brown, & Hofmann, 2006; Ehring et al., 2010). Therefore, it is possible that negative emotions and associated subjective feelings are the culprit in depression and that changes in the regulation of these emotions emerge as a mere consequence.

Together, the extant literature accommodates both the idea that emotion dysregulation contributes to the development of depression and that it emerges as a secondary feature through depression-related changes in emotion. As both ideas are not mutually exclusive, it is well possible that both are correct. First, depression is a very heterogeneous disorder that may have different causes and symptoms (Chapter 8). Hence, what may be a cause for one individual may be a symptom for another. Second, the pathological course in depression may be circular in that a cause turns into a symptom, and vice versa. Individuals prone to depression may naturally gravitate to strategies that are potentially less optimal in regulating their emotions over the long term (Gross & Muñoz, 1995). They may go for the "quick fix" that addresses their current state and avoid strategies that help minimize such states in the future. This, in turn, may increase the frequency with which individuals experience negative emotions so that these emotions become subjectively more unpleasant and the need to regulate them becomes more pressing. As a consequence, individuals may then go for the "quick fix" more and more frequently.

CHALLENGES AND FUTURE DIRECTIONS OF EMOTION REGULATION RESEARCH

Despite being of interest since antiquity, emotion regulation emerged as a topic for scientific inquiry only in the last few decades. It is therefore a relatively recent addition to the emotion research arena. Moreover, it faces conceptual and methodological challenges that have already been addressed for other, more established topics of inquiry. Addressing them in the context of emotion regulation research will be necessary to move the field forward.

Conceptual Challenges

Strategy Terminology

One of the conceptual challenges concerns the terms that researchers introduced to discuss and study emotion regulation. At present, many of these terms mean different things to different people, and therefore are used inconsistently in research reports. For example, some researchers use the term *suppression* very generally to denote the downregulation of an emotion, whereas others use the term more specifically to denote the suppression of nonverbal expressions. These and other differences in the use of terms make it difficult to compare and integrate research findings.

Furthermore, some of the terms are misleading and inadequately denote associated processes or strategies. For example, the term *reappraisal* implies that something was appraised before and is now appraised a second time, potentially producing a different appraisal outcome. Contrary to this common conception, however, in studies using *reappraisal* participants are instructed how to appraise upcoming events. Strictly speaking, then, these participants appraise rather than reappraise.

Strategy Categorization

Another conceptual challenge that grows out of issues related to terminology concerns the way the different strategies are categorized. We already discussed the popular differentiation between antecedent- and response-focused strategies. This differentiation is perhaps more appealing than useful because, at present, it is impossible to dissociate input from output of a putative emotion system. Moreover, some of the antecedent-focused strategies (e.g., cognitive change of response) seem to more appropriately denote response regulation, and vice versa (e.g., thought suppression).

Related to this are issues of conceptual overlap between regulation strategies from different categories. Specifically, attentional deployment, cognitive change, and response modulation each comprise strategies that share significant features with strategies from another category. Affective labeling is an attentional deployment strategy aimed at putting a label to one's feelings. It is conceptually very similar to an alleged cognitive change strategy in which individuals appraise their emotional response. Likewise similar are distraction, an attentional deployment strategy, and thought suppression, a response modulation strategy. After all, we must think of something, so in thought suppression, one thought must be replaced by another. Hence, it is difficult to see how we can distract ourselves without suppressing mental content or suppress mental content without distracting ourselves.

Last, some researchers have introduced the idea of "good" and "bad" regulation strategies (Aldao et al., 2010; Ehring et al., 2010; Gross & Muñoz, 1995). Cognitive change strategies are typically considered good, whereas attentional deployment and response modulation are considered bad. Some researchers make this distinction based on the supposed effectiveness of the different category strategies. However, the effectiveness of a strategy depends on the conditions (i.e., the regulatory event and individual) under which it is employed. Because of this dependence, there are instances in which cognitive change is more effective (Hofmann, Heering, Sawyer, & Asnaani, 2009; Szasz, Szentagotai, & Hofmann, 2011) and instances in which attentional deployment or response modulation are more effective (Sheppes & Meiran, 2008).

Other researchers discriminate between "good" and "bad" strategies based on their association with psychopathology. Those more typically associated with psychopathology are considered bad, whereas those less typically associated with psychopathology are considered good. Again, such considerations are problematic, as the role of these strategies in the context of psychopathology is unknown. Hence, we don't know whether they are good or bad, and using these labels introduces unwarranted assumptions that hinder rather than further progress.

What Is Emotion Regulation?

We defined emotion regulation as the mental tool set for increasing, maintaining, or decreasing one or more aspects of an emotion. This definition is quite broad. It accommodates all implicit and explicit processes through which individuals change what and how information from outside and inside their body is represented, and thus what is available to produce an emotional response.

The broadness of this definition presents a problem. First, it fails to demarcate differences between emotion regulation and other mental and behavioral processes. Thus, any process that is not an emotion could potentially be a regulatory strategy. Second, it fails to demarcate what distinguishes emotion regulation from the processes that evoke an emotion in the first place. It simply assumes that such a distinction exists. However, this assumption is not fully justified both from a theoretical and an empirical perspective (Gross & Barrett, 2011; Todd, Cunningham, Anderson, & Thompson, 2012).

From a theoretical perspective, the two are hard to separate because they depend on the same mechanisms (e.g., appraisals). From an empirical perspective, emotion regulation and emotion elicitation are hard to separate because one must assume that they co-occur. Given our supposed habitual use of emotion regulation, it is possible that emotional stimuli automatically trigger not only primary emotional responses but also secondary regulatory mechanisms, making it difficult to study one independently of the other.

Methodological Challenges

What Strategy?

Strategy plays a central role in emotion regulation research. Typically, participants are instructed to engage in a certain regulation strategy, which is then compared against another strategy and/or a control condition. Such a comparison can be problematic for a number of reasons.

First, researchers may fail to ensure that a chosen regulatory strategy is sufficiently dissociable from other strategies. In many instances it is possible that the use of one strategy ultimately triggers the use of another strategy, which the researchers did not intend to investigate. For example, the instruction to suppress one's emotional response is unlikely to affect response processes only. Such regulation requires certain mental resources that then become unavailable for the processing of the emotional stimulus. Thus, apart from regulating one's response, response suppression also affects attentional deployment.

Second, researchers have not yet established a standard control condition against which emotion regulation efforts can be measured. Some instruct their participants to engage with their emotional response, whereas others instruct them simply to perceive an eliciting stimulus. Apart from being very different, both control conditions may be construed as instructions to regulate. Participants are told how to respond to an upcoming emotional event. Therefore, a comparison between these control conditions with an experimental regulation condition is potentially problematic.

Third, and perhaps most important, researchers have at present no means to ensure whether participants comply with the regulation instructions. Many researchers rely on the participants' self-report, the validity of which is questionable. Because the regulation instructions give the experimenters' goals away, self-reports may reflect compliance with these goals rather than the instructions. In other words, participants may rate their affect differently in the regulation and the control condition because they know that the experimenter expects them to do so. In recognition of this issue, some researchers have added physiological or brain measures. However, it is currently unclear whether and how these measures reflect regulation success. They need to be further explored and validated.

Emotion Regulation in Other Species

To date, emotion regulation research has focused primarily on humans (but see A Closer Look 11.2). This contrasts with other emotion topics that have been explored in both humans and nonhuman animals and that therefore benefited from invasive techniques that cannot be applied to humans. Why was emotion regulation research not extended this way?

Coming out of social psychology, the dominant approach to studying emotion regulation has been to instruct participants how to regulate and then to assess regulation success through self-reports. Although nonhuman animals share a number of cognitive abilities with humans, their ability to follow verbal instructions is limited, and their ability to

A CLOSER LOOK 11.2

Animals Waiting for More

FIGURE 11.8   Hunting Dog With Game

Source: Flickr/Blaine Hansel (CC BY 2.0).

An important function of emotion regulation is the inhibition of emotional impulses that, if satisfied, may jeopardize future benefits. For example, eating a small portion of ice cream now may jeopardize the possibility of eating a large portion of ice cream later. Thus, a person may decide to temporarily check his appetite for ice cream and to forgo the small portion so as to maximize overall ice cream benefits. This ability to wait for more is called delayed gratification, and it critically determines an individual's success in life (Mischel et al., 1989).

Empirical research provided evidence that species other than humans can wait for more (Dufour, Wascher, Braun, Miller, & Bugnyar, 2012; Leonardi, Vick, & Dufour, 2012). Among other species, such evidence was obtained from dogs (Leonardi et al., 2012). In a clever study, dogs were trained to exchange an object for food, something most dogs do readily and that forms the basis for their ability to play fetch or retrieve. Then, the dogs were trained to exchange a less desired food for a more desired food. To this end, they were presented with the two food items for sniffing and then given the less desired one to hold in their mouths. If they chewed on or ate this item, the more desired food was lost to them, whereas if they dropped the item, they were given the more desired food. All the dogs tested quickly learned this trick, and the experimenters could now proceed to explore the dogs' "delayed gratification" ability. To this end, they systematically increased the duration between giving the less desired food and allowing exchange for the more desired food. As with humans, the dogs' "delayed gratification" ability differed depending on how much better the desired food was and depending on the dogs themselves. Some dogs were able to wait for 10 minutes, whereas other dogs managed only 10 seconds before they fell for the food that was immediately available to them. Overall, however, each of them was able to wait for some amount of time and thus demonstrated emotion regulation.

Food is not the only incentive in a dog's life that is worth waiting for. Being a social animal, dogs value the company of other dogs or humans; thus, they regulate their behavior to maintain or further existing social bonds. Hunting dogs are an example. They retrieve tasty game for their human companions in return for a lesser meal and praise. Clearly, then, the ability to regulate emotions was not specific to the dogs tested in the preceding study. Moreover, because it has also been demonstrated in nonmammalian species (Dufour et al., 2012), it seems to represent a more general phenomenon that, like emotions themselves, has a long evolutionary history predating human primates.

self-report affect is unknown. These obstacles may have discouraged researchers from attempting the study of emotion regulation in other species.

Additionally, researchers may hold the belief that only humans regulate emotions. This belief has a long philosophical tradition and is hence still rooted in our thinking. In the meantime, however, scientific evidence proved this belief to be wrong. Many species other than humans need to negotiate between the short- and long-term consequences that arise from gratifying an acute emotional impulse (Dufour et al., 2012; Goodall, 2010; Leonardi et al., 2012). For example, species living in social groups with a hierarchical structure regulate access to feeding and mating opportunities (Goodall, 2010). Higher-ranked individuals get first pick and lower-ranked individuals have to resist temptation until the higher-ranked individuals have satisfied their needs. Thus, they must suppress acting on an emotion impulse until such acting is no longer punished.

To further our understanding of emotion regulation, it would be valuable to develop techniques through which emotion regulation can be studied without recourse to verbal instruction and self-report. That would enable additional insights from nonhuman animals.

SUMMARY

The questions of how and of why we regulate emotions has enjoyed great interest among thinkers and scientists across the ages. Yet it was only recently that this interest turned into a dedicated study of emotion regulation. This study has identified three classes of regulation strategies referred to as attentional deployment, cognitive change, and response modulation—all of which are aimed at changing one or more aspects of a current emotion so as to maximize future benefits. These strategies modulate how an emotional event is attended to, cognitively represented, or responded to. Thus, they change ensuing emotional feelings by enhancing, maintaining, or subduing them.

Research exploring emotion regulation strategies has focused primarily on the latter—that is, on how emotions can be subdued. This research revealed that regulation success depends on event and personal characteristics. Event characteristics include the time point at which emotion regulation is attempted, the present engagement of mental resources, and the nature of the evoked emotion. Personal characteristics include internalized environmental constraints as well as natural inclinations. A person's cultural background is an example of an internalized environmental constraint because it makes certain strategies (e.g., response modulation) more or less acceptable. Working memory and sentience are examples of natural inclinations that affect emotion regulation. They vary depending on our genes and the environments we meet, and they determine the resources that we devote to emotion regulation.

Several brain structures have been implicated in emotion regulation. They form a fronto-temporo-parietal network that overlaps with networks identified in many standard cognitive tasks. Some structures show increased activation during emotion regulation. They have been linked to language and response preparation, attention and working memory, or the monitoring of goal states. Other structures show a decreased activation during emotion regulation. These structures are commonly known for their involvement in emotions so that their decreased activation may index regulation success.

Clinicians long suspected deficits in emotion regulation to underlie various forms of mental illness including depression. Individuals prone to depression report a more frequent use of attentional deployment and response modulation strategies, and a less frequent use of cognitive change strategies compared to psychologically healthy individuals. However, at present it is unclear whether this difference in emotion regulation is the cause or consequence of depression. Existing evidence makes both possibilities viable.

Due to its relevance for psychopathology, emotion regulation represents an important topic for scientific inquiry and carries significant potential for clinical practice. In order to realize this potential, emotional regulation research needs to overcome existing teething problems and address a number of outstanding conceptual and methodological issues. Conceptual issues include problems associated with terminology and the categorization of emotion regulation strategies. Methodological issues include the experimental isolation of specific regulation strategies, means to ensure whether and how participants regulate, and the restriction of regulation research to humans. Addressing these issues will benefit our understanding of emotion regulation and facilitate its application to other areas of psychology.

THINKING CRITICALLY ABOUT "EMOTION REGULATION"

1. When is an emotion regulation strategy "effective"?
2. What event and personal characteristics, other than the ones described here, could impact the effectiveness of different emotion strategies?
3. How could we measure regulation success implicitly, without the use of self-report?

MEDIA LIBRARY

Experts in Emotion Research Series by Jane Gruber at Yale University: http://www.yalepeplab .com/teaching/psych131_summer2013/materials.php. Relevant for this chapter would be video interviews with James Gross and Kevin Ochsner.

PART 5

Intra- and Inter-individual Differences in Emotion

"Excellent!" I cried. "Elementary," said he.

—Watson and Holmes in "The Adventure of the
Crooked Man" by Sir Arthur Conan Doyle (1893)

We understand emotions as evolutionary adaptations motivating behaviors that are relevant for the successful propagation of a species. Implicit in this understanding is that, when faced with the same circumstances, individuals from the same species should feel similarly. Yet our own life experience tells us that this is not always the case. What makes one person happy can make another person feel neutral, disappointed, afraid, or angry. Do such differences then challenge the evolutionary significance of emotions?

They certainly would if they were the norm rather than the exception. Some amount of consistency in the emotions of a species is necessary for these emotions to be reflected in the species' genome. If every individual of a species felt differently and as a consequence behaved differently, then these feelings would help little in dealing with species-typical challenges (e.g., a particular predator or foraging need). As such, they would be irrelevant for the species' survival and not to be selected in the course of evolution.

However, while some consistency is necessary, differences are necessary as well. One reason for this is that, natural selection, the driving principle of evolution, depends on variance. If all individuals of a species were identical, the species' genome could not adapt to changes in the environment. In the face of such changes, all individuals would be equally fit or doomed. Second, not every individual within a species faces the same life tasks. Individuals with a different age or sex need to behave differently in order to survive, reproduce, and ensure the survival of their offspring. Last, every individual of a species has a unique learning background or life history. Important for the present discussion is that learning and life history shape associations between neutral and emotional stimuli or actions. Thus, no two individuals, even with identical genes, can feel perfectly alike.

This section of the book explores emotion differences between the individuals of a species and elucidates their biological and environmental underpinnings. Three separate chapters detail how emotions change across an individual's life span; how an individual's biological sex shapes emotion systems, and how the functioning of these systems is affected by learning and life history, with a special emphasis on human culture.

Because, age, sex, and culture interweave in their influence on emotions, one should, in principle, examine them in conjunction and consider their potential interaction. That this is not done here and that instead these inter-individual variables are considered relatively independently has the following two reasons. First, practical and theoretical constraints have limited research into the intersection of age, sex, and culture. That is because, like other disciplines, the science of emotions is moving from the study of simple, individual phenomena to the study of how these phenomena behave in a more complex context. The latter efforts are only budding now. Second and related to this is the pedagogical goal of understanding issues related to the different inter-individual variables first before attempting their integration.

CHAPTER 12

Emotions Across the Life Span

During their lifetime, individuals of many species undergo dramatic physical, behavioral, and mental changes (Figure 12.1). For example, newborn humans are on average only 48 centimeters long. They have a hard time moving away from or seeking out objects on their own. Their senses are not acute, and their ability to attend to, remember, or understand events in their environment is extremely limited. This changes as humans mature into adulthood. Over the years, they may reach a size of 180 centimeters or more, acquire complex motor skills, and become apt at adapting their environment to suit their

---

FIGURE 12.1 A Lifetime of Changes

Humans undergo substantial physical changes during their lifetime. These changes are accompanied by different bodily and mental functions as well as different life tasks.

needs. However, these changes are not sustained. As time goes by, gains turn into losses and humans show a slow but progressive physical, behavioral, and mental decline.

In tandem with these physical, behavioral, and mental changes come changes in the individual's needs and in what must be accomplished in order to survive and reproduce successfully. In the case of humans, children need to secure their parents' care and learn about their environment. Young adults must apply what they've learned in order to find a partner and start a family. Middle-aged adults must invest in their family and promote their children's development and life success. Last, elder adults are tasked to continually support their children and their children's children until eventually their bodily resources are exhausted and they pass away.

As prime motivators of behavior, emotions necessarily adapt to these different life periods and tasks. In this chapter, we examine the mechanisms and outcomes of this process for major developmental milestones.

EARLY INFANCY AND CHILDHOOD

The offspring of many species are still immature at birth and require parental care for survival. Among mammals, which are the focus of this chapter, this care comes first and foremost from the mother, who not only nurtures her young but provides body heat, hygienic care, and protection. Thus, a primary life task for a mammalian youngster is to attach itself to its mother and to solicit maximum maternal care. A secondary task is to learn about its environment and to prepare for the days when its mother is no longer available. In the following section, we take a closer look at both tasks and review the emotional mechanisms that enable their fulfillment.

Attachment

During pregnancy, mothers are physically bonded with their offspring; they automatically satisfy the young's needs by taking care of their own needs. If they eat, the offspring receives nutrition, and if they drink, the offspring receives fluids. After birth, however, this is no longer the case. Mother and offspring lose their physical bond and the offspring becomes an independent organism with individual needs. In order for these needs to be met, offspring and mother must form a bidirectional relationship. On one hand, the offspring has to care about the mother in order to stay physically close to her. On the other hand, the mother has to care about the offspring in order to be motivated to extend resources and protection. Dedicated mechanisms evolved that tap into the emotions of both offspring and mother and that help replace the initial physical bond with an emotional one.

Caring About Mother

One of the mechanisms that support the attachment of immature offspring to their mother or other attachment figures is called **imprinting**. Konrad Lorenz studied imprinting in a wide range of birds. He showed that chicks attach themselves to an object they encounter within a few hours after hatching and that has one or more characteristics typical of a mother bird. For the offspring of some species, these characteristics include species-typical calls and movements, whereas for other species, they simply include some form of movement (Lorenz, 1935). Thus, by mimicking these characteristics, Lorenz was able to imprint the offspring of various bird species on himself or on an experimental object (Chapter 5, Figure 5.3).

Although imprinting represents a feasible solution for offspring attachment in birds, it would be unfeasible in most mammals. Unlike avian parents, most mammalian parents don't keep their offspring in isolated nests that only they visit. Moreover, because many live and raise their young in large social groups, an offspring could easily attach itself to a different individual that is unprepared for parenthood. Thus, offspring attachment in mammals is necessarily more complex and flexible than in birds.

Immediately after birth, mammals show orientation preferences for stimuli that remind them of the womb—stimuli such as amniotic fluid or maternal sounds. Human newborns, for example, when placed on their mother's belly are more likely to crawl to a breast treated with the mother's amniotic fluid than to an untreated breast (Varendi, Porter, & Winberg, 1996). Thus, the odor of this fluid must be appetitive. Likewise appetitive is the mother's voice. When given a pacifier that, with different sucking, can turn on their mother's voice or the voice of another woman, newborns quickly learn and prefer to suck in a way that allows them to hear their mother (DeCasper & Fifer, 1980).

Initial preferences at birth, however, are not set in stone. Instead, they are easily modified to accommodate potential changes in the mother. Such changes may be caused by changes in the mother's living conditions—for example, in the food sources that are available to her. Changes in food alter bodily fluids and odors, making them fickle cues for maternal recognition (Sullivan, Wilson, Wong, Correa, & Leon, 1990).

That offspring perceive and track these changes has been demonstrated extensively in rodents. Here, researchers placed a novel odor (e.g., lemon) on the mother's coat and later tested the young's preferences for this odor and a control substance (Hudson, 1985). They found that offspring were more likely to approach the odor that was linked to mom than they were to approach the odor alternative.

Researchers also explored odor learning in rodent pups that were separated from their mothers. Using classical conditioning, they paired novel odors with some of the typical maternal comforts such as milk, warmth, or grooming, and showed that rodent pups quickly acquired a preference for the conditioned as compared to a control odor (Landers & Sullivan, 2012). Nonintuitively, a similar preference emerged for odors that were paired with painful stimuli such as an electric shock.

The finding that pain fosters attachment to a mother has been linked to observations of abusive parenting (Maestripieri & Carroll, 1998; Troisi & D'Amato, 1984). Offspring of abusive mothers receive second-rate care relative to offspring of nonabusive mothers. Nevertheless, second-rate care is better than no care, and avoiding it would mean certain death. Thus, like offspring of nonabusive mothers, offspring of abusive mothers form maternal attachments.

The mechanism through which this occurs depends on a suppression of fear conditioning. In rodents, such a suppression is initially guaranteed by low levels of cortisol that are kept low by intensive maternal care (Landers & Sullivan, 2012). Thus, painful stimulation or other stressors are ineffective in raising the offspring's cortisol level and producing a typical stress response. Later, when cortisol activity acquires a more adult-like pattern, the presence of the mother effectively reduces cortisol and subdues a cortisol surge in response to stress. Through this, the offspring is buffered against negative emotions and will continue to turn to its mother even if she is a source of stress.

Although comparable research in humans is naturally quite limited, available evidence raises the possibility of analogous mechanisms (Gunnar & Donzella, 2002).

Making Mother Care

For the offspring-mother relationship to work, it is not enough that the offspring attaches to the mother; the mother has to return this attachment and to willingly offer her care. Two mechanisms contribute to this. On one hand, hormonal and brain-related changes associated with pregnancy and birth prepare a mother for her responsibilities and produce some amount of natural concern. One example of this is change in the oxytocin system that occur in tandem with mother-infant interactions and that underpin a mother's love (Chapter 4; A Closer Look 12.1). On the other hand, an infant can stimulate the mother's love by engaging in social behaviors. In the following section, we examine this infant-driven mechanism in more detail.

A CLOSER LOOK 12.1

Mothers' Brains Prepared for Love

Research in a range of species has shown how the simple presence of offspring triggers neural processes in the mother that reward her for interacting with her offspring (Broad, Curley, & Keverne, 2006). Specifically, at birth and at times when the mother is grooming (Shahrokh, Zhang, Diorio, Gratton, & Meaney, 2010) or feeding (Ferris et al., 2005; McNeilly, Robinson, Houston, & Howie, 1983) her offspring, she experiences a surge in oxytocin that hijacks her reward system. By facilitating dopaminergic and μ-opioid activity, the oxytocin release experienced during offspring care excites the brain's pleasure center more effectively than do other kinds of rewards, including the consumption of addictive drugs (Broad et al., 2006; Ferris et al., 2005). Through this, a mother literally falls in love with her offspring (Figure 12.2).

In addition to simply being there and sucking on mom's breast, the offspring can solicit maternal care by crying. Already developed at birth, crying serves as a universal signal of distress that arises from bodily discomfort (e.g., hunger, pain) or maternal separation. Apart from being a salient cue that is difficult to ignore, crying has a special effect on the brain of receivers. It activates the anterior cingulate (Laurent, Stevens, & Ablow, 2011; Noriuchi, Kikuchi, & Senoo, 2008; Seifritz et al., 2003), a structure relevant for pain perception and sadness. Moreover, activity in this structure is especially pronounced in mothers listening to their own as compared to other offspring cry (Laurent et al., 2011; Noriuchi et al., 2008). Thus, by crying, the offspring does more than simply communicate distress; it actually induces distress in the mother and motivates her to help.

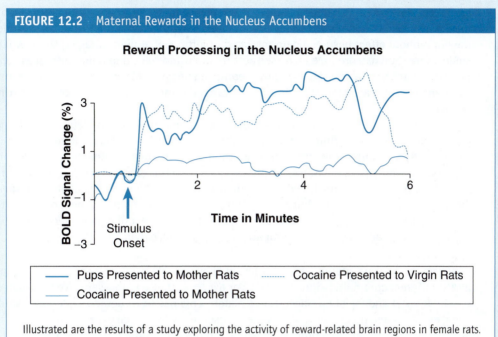

FIGURE 12.2 · Maternal Rewards in the Nucleus Accumbens

Illustrated are the results of a study exploring the activity of reward-related brain regions in female rats. Lactating rats 4 days after delivery were presented with either their pups (thick solid lines) or cocaine (thin sold line). FMRI measurements taken in the nucleus accumbens indicated a larger response to the pups than to cocaine. Virgin rats presented with cocaine (dashed line) showed a response comparable to that of mother rats presented with their own offspring.

Source: "Pup Suckling Is More Rewarding Than Cocaine: Evidence From Functional Magnetic Resonance Imaging and Three-Dimensional Computational Analysis," by C. F. Ferris, P. Kulkarni, J. M. Sullivan, J. A. Harder, T. L. Messenger, and M. Febo, 2005, *The Journal of Neuroscience, 25*, pp. 149–156.

Newborn. Initially, an infant's behaviors and associated mental representations are still quite limited. In human newborns they include things like crying, sucking, and simple forms of acknowledging the mother's presence. The latter is demonstrated by the newborn's ability to engage in mutual gaze (Farroni, Csibra, Simion, & Johnson, 2002; Keller & Zach, 1993) and to mimic some of the mother's facial expressions and gross motor actions (Meltzoff & Moore, 1977). Newborns also show spontaneous expressions that are similar to what we might call a smile. However, in the first weeks of life, these expressions are rarely contingent on a particular event such as the mother's touch or voice (Wolff, 1959). Hence, they do not yet qualify as true smiles.

First 6 months. At about 4 months after birth, the infant acquires additional behaviors that can be employed to make mother care. At this time, the infant begins to smile more reliably in response to her attentions (Mendes, Seidl-de-Moura, & Siqueira, 2009). That these smiles are not without effect has been demonstrated in a functional neuroimaging study. Infant smiles were shown to produce increased activity in the mother's dopamine system as compared to infant neutral expressions (Strathearn, Li, Fonagy, & Montague, 2008). Thus, one can conclude that an infant's smile truly rewards the mother and reinforces her caring behavior.

Another developing skill set comprises the categorization and interpretation of maternal emotional expressions. While infants seem able to discriminate different kinds of expressions shortly after birth, some maturation is required before they can link these expressions to particular emotion states (Walker-Andrews, 1997). That this emerges midway into the first year of life has been demonstrated in a study with 5-month-olds. Happy, neutral, or angry faces were paired with a noise-burst loud enough to elicit the blink component of the startle reflex. Like adults, infant participants startled less in the context of a happy face and more in the context of an angry face as compared to a neutral face (Balaban, 1995).

First year. By the time infants are 7 months old, they are able to integrate emotional signals across different communication channels. For example, they are now sensitive to instances in which vocal and facial emotions don't match. This has been demonstrated in a study using event-related potentials (ERPs). When presented with a facial expression followed by an emotional voice, an ERP component, similar to the adult N400 (Chapter 10), was modulated by emotional incongruity. This ERP component was larger when facial and vocal emotions were incongruous as compared to congruous (Grossmann, Striano, & Friederici, 2006; Figure 12.3). Thus, similar to adults, 7-month-old infants notice emotional incongruity in others and dedicate additional resources to processing this incongruity. As such, they possess the cognitive and emotional basis to understand simple forms of humor and pretend play (Semrud-Clikeman & Glass, 2010).

The fact that, at 7 months, infants appreciate that other individuals can have emotions that differ from what they themselves feel suggests that they may also appreciate that others can perceive the world differently. To explore this possibility, researchers presented 7-month-old infants with short movie clips in which the infants shared their perceptual experience with an agent in the clip or in which infant and agent developed different perceptions (Kovács, Téglás, & Endress, 2010).

In more detail, the infant and the agent saw a ball rolling behind a wooden block or rolling past the block out of the scene. Then the agent left the scene and the ball stayed where it was, or, if it was behind the block, it could roll out of the scene. Finally, the block was lifted to reveal what was behind (Figure 12.4). Crucially, in all conditions—that is, regardless of whether or not the ball should be behind the block—lifting the block revealed an empty space. Thus, if the infant expected the ball to be there, the infant should be surprised and look longer than if the ball were unexpected.

This is what the researchers found when comparing the condition in which the ball rolled behind the block and remained hidden there with the condition in which the ball rolled immediately out of the scene. Moreover, this effect was also present when the

FIGURE 12.3 Emotion Recognition in 7-Month-Old Infants

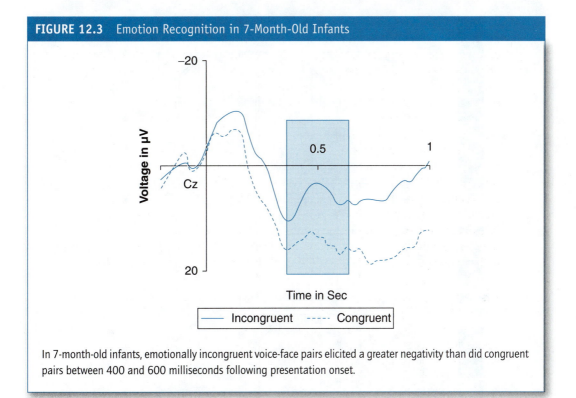

In 7-month-old infants, emotionally incongruent voice-face pairs elicited a greater negativity than did congruent pairs between 400 and 600 milliseconds following presentation onset.

Source: "Crossmodal Integration of Emotional Information From Face and Voice in the Infant Brain," by T. Grossmann, T. Striano, and A. D. Friederici, 2006, *Developmental Science 9,* pp. 309–315. The results are illustrated for one centrally located scalp electrode (Cz). Adapted with permission. Copyright © 2006 John Wiley & Sons, Inc.

ball rolled behind the block and out of the scene after the agent left compared with when the ball rolled out immediately (Figure 12.5). Notably, when the ball left the scene after the agent, the infant should not be surprised about the later absence of the ball—only the agent should be. The fact that the infant is nevertheless surprised suggests that the infant took the agent's perspective into account and integrated it with a personal perspective of the world.

One year onward. Together, the aforementioned evidence suggests that, during their first year, infants develop the basis for representing the emotions and mental states of others. As such, they begin to understand their mother as an individual with feelings and thoughts of her own. Over the course of the following months and years, this understanding evolves into a more sophisticated mind-reading ability that researchers refer to as Theory of Mind (ToM). In line with the old divide between emotion and cognition, many divide ToM into an affective and a cognitive component. Efforts have been made to determine which component develops first (O'Brien et al., 2011) and what brain systems support their respective operation (Abu-Akel & Shamay-Tsoory, 2011).

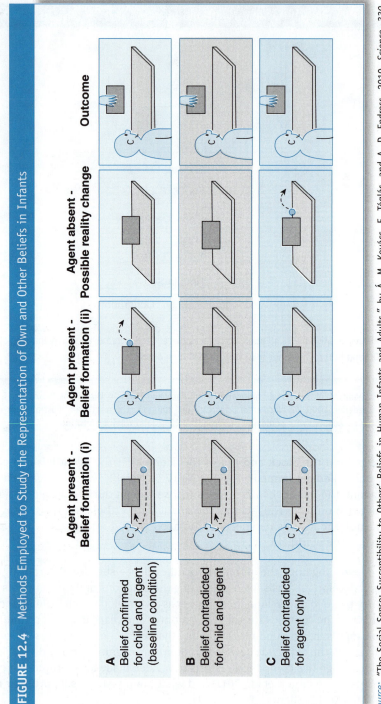

FIGURE 12.4 Methods Employed to Study the Representation of Own and Other Beliefs in Infants

Source: "The Social Sense: Susceptibility to Others' Beliefs in Human Infants and Adults," by Á. M. Kovács, E. Téglás, and A. D. Endress, 2010, *Science, 330,* pp. 1830–1834.

FIGURE 12.5   Infant Looking Results

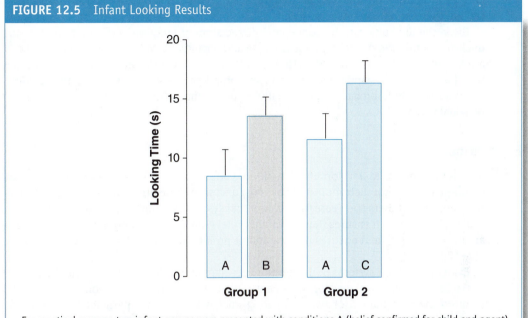

For practical reasons, two infant groups were presented with conditions A (belief confirmed for child and agent) and B (belief contradicted for child and agent), and with conditions A (belief confirmed for child and agent) and C (belief contradicted for agent only), respectively (refer to Figure 12.4). When presented with the outcome of the ball scenario, infants looked longer when their beliefs and/or the agent's beliefs were contradicted than when their beliefs and the agent's beliefs were confirmed.

Source: "The Social Sense: Susceptibility to Others' Beliefs in Human Infants and Adults," by Á. M. Kovács, E. Téglás, and A. D, Endress, 2010, *Science, 330,* pp. 1830–1834.

Affective ToM has been linked to a network comprising the ventromedial and orbitofrontal cortices, the ventral anterior cingulate cortex, the amygdala, and the ventral striatum (Abu-Akel & Shamay-Tsoory, 2011). This network presumably supports emotion recognition and emotional perspective taking. An example of emotional perspective taking is the ability to understand that one may feel good about winning a game, while someone else may feel bad about losing the same game.

Cognitive ToM has been linked to a network comprising the dorsomedial prefrontal cortex, the dorsal anterior cingulate cortex, and the dorsal striatum (Abu-Akel & Shamay-Tsoory, 2011). It presumably serves the ability to infer another individual's beliefs. An example of this is identity beliefs that depend on identity surface features to which individuals are differently privy. Specifically, if a child with cognitive ToM observes twins change their clothes in order to confuse their parents, the child will know that the parents may indeed be confused if they did not witness the clothes change. The child will also know that the parents would not be confused if they spied on the twins during their clothes change. Moreover, the child would then foresee the twins' disappointment once they realize that their prank was unsuccessful.

Given the difficulties in the conceptual dissociation of emotion and cognition, it is still unclear whether the divide between affective and cognitive ToM holds. But the fact is, both are related (Harwood & Farrar, 2006; Hughes & Dunn, 1998; O'Brien et al., 2011), and together they foster an understanding of the motives behind people's actions. This understanding enables the child to predict and eventually influence the mother and other individuals for personal benefit.

Exploration

In order for infants to develop into functioning adults, it is not enough that they forge an emotional bond with their mother. They must also show a healthy curiosity for their environment. Researchers speculate that two mental systems support these fairly antagonistic goals. A social system ensures that the infant prefers the mother over other individuals, and an object-based system ensures that the infant prefers novel over familiar objects (Quinn et al., 2011).

Evidence for both systems in the developing infant comes from studies using the **preferential looking paradigm** developed by Fantz (1964). In its initial conception, this paradigm involved the presentation of two competing images to an infant participant. One image remained the same across trials, whereas the other image changed. By studying the infant's gaze, Fantz could determine whether the infant preferred familiarity or novelty. If the infant's gaze fell more frequently on the constant as compared to the changing image, then the infant preferred familiarity. However, if the infant's gaze fell more frequently on the changing as compared to the constant image, then the infant preferred novelty.

A similar logic applies to more recent variants of this paradigm that expose infants to only one image during a so-called habituation phase (Quinn et al., 2011; Walker-Andrews, 1997). After this phase, infants are presented with a test image representing a concept similar to that of the habituation phase or a novel concept. Again, greater looking at the similar concept indicates a preference for familiarity, whereas greater looking at the novel concept indicates a preference for novelty.

Studies in which infants were exposed to social stimuli such as faces revealed a preference for familiarity. For example, infants were found to spend more time looking at their mother as compared to a stranger. Likewise, they showed greater fondness for looking at faces from their own race than at faces from another race (Anzures, Quinn, Pascalis, Slater, & Lee, 2010; Quinn et al., 2011).

This spontaneous preference for familiar social stimuli is contrasted by a spontaneous preference for unfamiliar nonsocial stimuli. Studies using environmental objects in preferential looking paradigms observe a fairly consistent orientation toward novel rather than familiar or habituated objects (Fantz, 1964; Quinn et al., 2011; Figure 12.6).

Moreover, this novelty preference has been linked to the brain's reward system and dopamine. Variants in DRD4, a gene that regulates the production of dopamine D4 receptors, has been shown to predict novelty preference from infancy into adulthood (Ebstein et al., 1998; Laucht, Becker, & Schmidt, 2006). Several DRD4 variants have been identified in the human

FIGURE 12.6   Infant Looking Preferences for Novel Objects

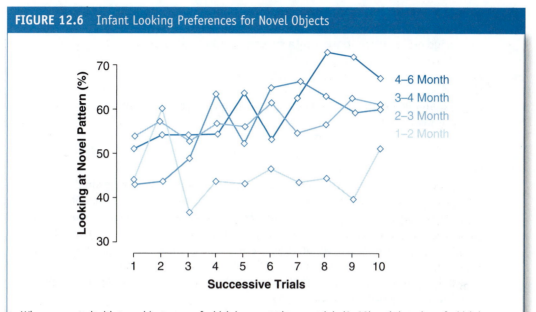

When presented with two objects, one of which is repeated across trials (1–10) and the other of which is new, 4- to 6-month-old infants spend proportionally more time looking at the new as compared to the repeated object. This preference is absent in 1- to 2-month-old infants.

Source: "Visual Experience in Infants: Decreased Attention to Familiar Patterns Relative to Novel Ones," by R. L. Fantz, 1964, *Science, 146,* pp. 668–670.

genome, some of which are characterized by the number of repeats of a part of the gene called exon III. While the exact functional consequences of the different repeat lengths are still unclear, it has been shown that individuals with a greater number of repeats (> 6) are more novelty-seeking than are individuals with fewer repeats (Ebstein et al., 1998; Laucht et al., 2006). This is presumably because their D4 receptors are less efficient (Schoots & Van Tol, 2003; Van Craenenbroeck et al., 2005, 2011).

Interestingly, DRD4 variation affects not only responses to novel objects but also to novel people. Infants with many repeats show less anxiety during the approach of a stranger than do infants with fewer repeats (Lakatos et al., 2003). Thus, although antagonistic, the familiarity preference that typically emerges in the context of people can be overwritten by the novelty preference that typically emerges in the context of objects.

Perhaps not surprisingly, there seems to be a link between novelty preference and cognitive development. In this context, it has been shown that novelty preference predicts intelligence as well as academic achievement in childhood (McCall & Carriger, 1993) and adulthood (Fagan, Holland, & Wheeler, 2007). Infants who more quickly habituate to repeated stimuli and who show a stronger preference for novel stimuli score better on intelligence and academic tests later in life. This highlights the importance of curiosity to drive exploration during early development. Moreover, it suggests that, together with attachment formation, a healthy curiosity enables individuals to acquire the skills and knowledge necessary for becoming a successful adult.

Emotion Regulation

Whether and in what way infants and young children regulate their emotions has been a vivid but challenging area of research. Unlike adults, participants of this age cannot be explicitly asked to employ a particular regulation strategy or to report their regulation success. Instead, implicit techniques need to be applied, and these occlude insights into certain aspects of emotion regulation.

A typical approach to study emotion regulation in infants and young children has been to engage them in a stressful situation involving an unresponsive or unavailable parent, the presence of a stranger, or a delayed reward. For example, reward-related research has used the so-called Marshmallow test (Mischel, Ebbesen, & Zeiss, 1972; Mischel, Shoda, & Rodriguez, 1989), in which children are shown a marshmallow and another sweet and asked which one they like better. Afterward, they are told that they can have one of the two sweets. However, while the nonpreferred sweet is immediately available, the preferred sweet can only be eaten after some delay.

Researchers studied the participants' behavior elicited in this and other paradigms and subsequently identified certain behavioral categories and emotional expressions as indicative of emotion regulation and regulation success. Two major categories, attentional deployment and response modulation, have been identified to date, and these map onto two of the three categories introduced in the context of adult emotion regulation (Chapter 11).

Attentional Deployment

A key regulatory strategy that emerges shortly after birth is distraction. Initially, distraction is achieved through disengagement from an emotionally arousing stimulus. Research exploring disengagement in early infancy has used the still-face procedure (Tronick, Als, Adamson, Wise, & Brazelton, 1978). Here, a mother faces her child and either interacts normally or stays motionless. Naturally, infants find the latter condition irritating. They show less positive and more negative affect than when their mother behaves normally. Additionally, they gaze less at their mothers, suggesting that they avoid confrontation with her strange new ways. Gaze aversion has also been observed in other emotionally arousing situations—for example, when infants meet a stranger (Mangelsdorf, Shapiro, & Marzolf, 1995) or in the Marshmallow test (Mischel et al., 1972, 1989).

As the infant's motor abilities develop, disengagement through gaze aversion is complemented by more active means of distraction that involve moving away from the emotion object, manipulating other objects, thinking about other things, or engaging with other individuals in interaction (Grolnick, Bridges, & Connell, 1996; Mangelsdorf et al., 1995; Mischel et al., 1972). That these means are effective suggests a negative correlation between the frequency with which children engage in distraction and the amount of negative affect they show. Children who are more likely to engage their attention elsewhere show fewer signs of distress (Grolnick et al., 1996) and can hold out longer for a preferred reward (Mischel et al., 1972, 1989).

Response Modulation

A popular mode of emotion regulation in adulthood is the suppression of emotion-associated responses. Such suppression requires the inhibition of a potent behavioral impulse and is thus a relatively basic mechanism that enables meaningful interactions with the environment. Although far from being fully developed, rudimentary forms of response suppression emerge shortly after birth. Observations of gaze behavior in 4-month-old infants revealed that these infants learn to suppress an automatic gaze shift triggered by the onset of a visual cue if that cue occurs opposite of a more interesting target stimulus shown shortly afterward (Johnson, 1995; Figure 12.7). Thus, infants eventually inhibit a basic orienting response to be better prepared for an upcoming positive event.

The suppression of more complex cognitive and motor responses, however, requires additional maturation. For example a go/no-go task, in which targets but not nontargets call for a specific action (e.g., pushing a button), can only be mastered by the time a child reaches 3 years old (Posner & Rothbart, 1998; Wiebe, Sheffield, & Espy, 2012). Then the child has some capacity to keep a relatively abstract goal in memory, to monitor deviation from this goal, and to inhibit goal-incongruous responses. This capacity rests on the maturation of certain brain structures such as the anterior cingulate. Moreover, it predicts reduced negative affect and better inhibitory control of problem behaviors that children may show in their home environment (Posner & Rothbart, 1998).

Apart from suppressing an emotional response, there is evidence that infants and small children attempt to change this response. Specifically, many researchers report self-soothing strategies such as sucking, hair twisting, or seeking out a "security blanket" or favorite toy. Some researchers report that these strategies are relatively more common among younger

---

FIGURE 12.7 Suppression of a Visual Orienting Response in 4-Month-Old Infants

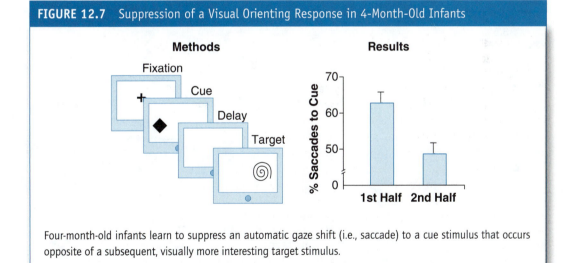

Four-month-old infants learn to suppress an automatic gaze shift (i.e., saccade) to a cue stimulus that occurs opposite of a subsequent, visually more interesting target stimulus.

Source: Eye movement results are plotted for the first and second half of Experiment 1, published in "The Inhibition of Automatic Saccades in Early Infancy," by M. H. Johnson, 1995, *Developmental Psychobiology 28,* pp. 281–291. Adapted with permission. Copyright © 1995 John Wiley & Sons, Inc.

infants, aged 18 months or less (Mangelsdorf et al., 1995). Moreover, their effectiveness in regulating emotions is unclear. One study showed a positive correlation between self-soothing and negative affect, suggesting that attempts at self-soothing may up- rather than downregulate distress (Grolnick et al., 1996).

Getting Help

As in adults, emotion regulation in infants and children can be facilitated by another person. Moreover, in infants and children such facilitation is critical because their own resources for emotion regulation are still quite limited. Thus, they depend on their mother and other attachment figures for help.

Fussing and crying solicit such help. A mother who hears her child cry will attempt to soothe the child through rocking and holding, by distracting the child, and/or by removing the source of distress (Harman, Rothbart, & Posner, 1997; Figure 12.8). Thus, children learn that their mother is a good emotion regulator and will continue to turn to her in the future.

Additionally, children learn about the means through which their mother achieves emotion regulation and how to employ these means in an independent manner. Initially, such employment remains dependent on the mother's presence. Research has shown, for example, that children use active distraction more frequently and more effectively when they are with their mother or an experimenter than when they are alone (Grolnick et al., 1996). As the child matures, emotion regulation becomes less dependent on social support. Nevertheless, social support remains important into adulthood (Coan, Schaefer, & Davidson, 2006).

FIGURE 12.8   Distress Ratings Before, During, and After the Presentation of a Distractor in 3- and 6-Month-Old Infants

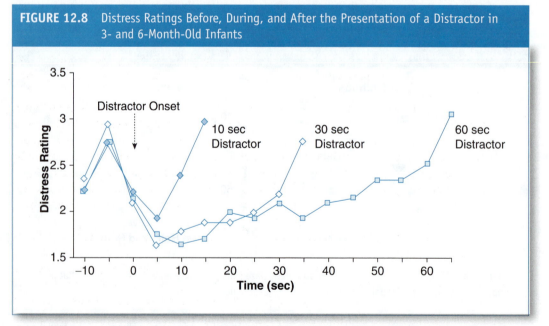

Source: "Distress and Attention Interactions in Early Infancy," by C. Harman, M. K. Rothbart, and M. I. Posner, 1997, *Motivation and Emotion, 21,* pp. 27–43.

ADOLESCENCE AND YOUNG ADULTHOOD

Human development is not a linear process during which infants gradually turn into adults. Instead, it comprises distinct developmental phases, each of which is tailored toward age-specific needs and tasks. Adolescence is such a phase. It differs qualitatively from both childhood and adulthood in that it involves unique bodily and mental processes. These processes prepare the adolescent for the mastery of two new life tasks. The first life task is to gain independence from parental care and to become a self-sufficient individual. The second life task is to find and bond with a sexual partner. Again, emotional mechanisms are what enable individuals to accomplish these tasks.

Gaining Independence

The emotional mechanisms that move adolescents toward independence entail changes in attachments and behavioral preferences. On one hand, adolescents loosen their parental attachment in favor of a greater orientation toward peers. On the other hand, adolescents develop an increased exploratory drive. Novel experiences become even more tempting and rewarding than they were earlier during development. In the following paragraphs, we explore both kinds of changes in more detail.

Bonding—From Parents to Peers

Attachment mechanisms ensure that an infant forms an emotional bond with its mother and other relevant figures in its life. While this bond is functionally important during early development, it would be problematic if maintained into adulthood. If adolescents felt the same kind of closeness to their parents that they felt when they were younger, they'd never leave the comfort of their home and acquire the means to start a family. To ensure that this does not happen, humans as well as many other species evolved the means to change childhood attachments.

Research in humans has shown that, during the course of adolescence, individuals spend less and less time with their family (Arnett, 1999; Larson & Richards, 1991). This is accompanied by a transitory dip in positive affect experienced from interactions with parents and other adult relatives. Additionally, adolescents, particularly girls, spend more time with peers and find interactions with peers more rewarding (Larson & Richards, 1991). Now, peers rather than parents critically shape opinions and behaviors (Aral & Walker, 2012). They become role models against which individuals compare themselves and from which they seek approval and acceptance.

The significance of peer acceptance was demonstrated in an online chatting study during which experimenters manipulated whether participants were invited to chat with or were rejected by virtual peers (Silk et al., 2012). Measurements of pupil size indicated that rejections increased physiological arousal relative to chat invitations. Moreover, this effect grew linearly between the ages of 9 and 17, suggesting that, during this time, peer acceptance and bonding become increasingly important.

Research in nonhuman animals implies interesting parallels. Like human adolescents, rodent adolescents develop a preference for the company of peers. This was revealed by place-conditioning experiments in which rats were placed in one of two separated compartments of a testing chamber (Douglas, Varlinskaya, & Spear, 2004). In one compartment they would meet an unrelated peer, whereas in the other compartment they would be by themselves. After a few repetitions of these conditions, the rats were tested for their place preference (Figure 12.9). To this end, they were positioned in the middle of the chamber and allowed to enter both compartments, which were now empty. Compared to adults, adolescents were more likely to spend time in the compartment in which they had previously met a peer than in the compartment in which they had been alone. In contrast, place preferences matched across adult and adolescent control animals that had undergone similar handling by the researchers but that had not been paired with a peer.

More Exploration—A Risky Business

Curiosity and the drive to explore are already important during childhood. However, they become even more important during adolescence. In order to establish themselves as independent individuals, adolescents must step out of their parents' shadow and meet the

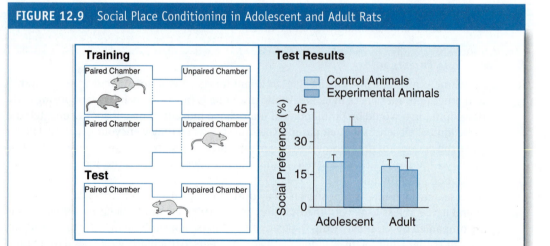

FIGURE 12.9   Social Place Conditioning in Adolescent and Adult Rats

Experimental animals were placed repeatedly in one of two conditioning chambers. In one of these chambers (unpaired) they were always alone. In the other chamber (paired) they were always in the company of a same-age and same-sex conspecific. Control animals were also placed in both chambers but were always alone. Social place conditioning in experimental animals was assessed by computing a social preference score during test (time in paired chamber − time in unpaired chamber/time in both chambers × 100). A behavioral coefficient for control animals was defined somewhat differently (time in preferred chamber − time in nonpreferred chamber/time in both chambers × 100). Experimental adolescents spent more time in the paired chamber than did experimental adults. Adolescent and adult control animals did not differ in their propensity to develop a place preference.

Source: "Rewarding Properties of Social Interactions in Adolescent and Adult Male and Female Rats: Impact of Social Versus Isolate Housing of Subjects and Partners," by L. A. Douglas, E. I. Varlinskaya, and L. P. Spear, 2004, *Developmental Psychobiology, 45,* pp. 153–162. Test results adapted with permission. Copyright © 2004 Wiley Periodicals, Inc.

world on their own. They must test their strengths and find out their weaknesses. They must develop new skills to obtain resources of their own and to position themselves within their social group. Consequently, they have to try new things and they need to willingly take risks.

To facilitate this, human children (Somerville, Hare, & Casey, 2011) and the offspring of nonhuman animals (Stansfield & Kirstein, 2006) moving into adolescence change the ways they evaluate novelty and risk. Specifically, novel stimuli that promise a reward become more salient and are more likely to elicit approach behaviors. At the same time, risks under certain conditions are increasingly discounted.

One study on reward salience used a go/no-go procedure (Somerville et al., 2011). This procedure involved a sequence of face stimuli for most of which participants had to press a button and for some of which button-presses had to be withheld. Children and adults experienced the same difficulty withholding button-presses to happy no-go faces as they did to calm no-go faces. Adolescents, however, pressed the button on no-go trials more frequently when they encountered a happy as compared to a calm face (Figure 12.10). Thus, to them, happy faces were more captivating.

FIGURE 12.10 Positive Novel Faces Elicit Greater Approach Responses in Adolescents as Compared to Children and Adults

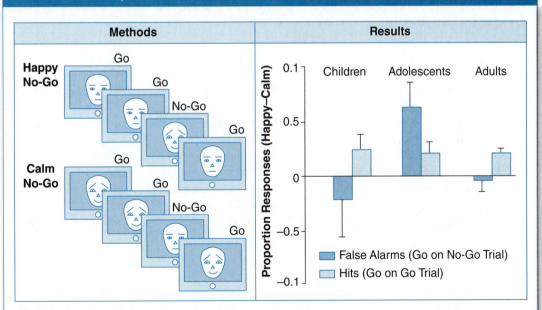

Results are plotted as the proportion of false alarms relative to the total number of no-go trials and the proportion of hits relative to the total number of go trials. The proportion of responses in the condition with calm go trials was subtracted from the proportion of responses in the condition with happy go trials.

Source: "Frontostriatal Maturation Predicts Cognitive Control Failure to Appetitive Cues in Adolescents," by L. H. Somerville, T. Hare, and B. Casey, 2011, *Journal of Cognitive Neuroscience, 23*, pp. 2123–2134.

Developmental changes in risk evaluation are evident from the fact that adolescents are more likely than both younger and older individuals to engage in risky behaviors such as consuming addictive drugs, stealing, breaking traffic rules, or engaging in unsafe sex (Arnett, 1999; Moffitt, 1993). Because most of these behaviors are publicly regulated, adolescence is a time when many individuals come into first conflict with the law—with the number of first-time offenders rising from late childhood and returning to lower levels after the age of 17 (Moffitt, 1993).

Although these real-life facts imply that risks become less threatening during adolescence, laboratory research indicates that the full story is more complicated than that. Specifically, by themselves adolescents behave in a way that implies a linear improvement from childhood to adulthood with respect to risk assessment and decision making (Cassotti, Houdé, & Moutier, 2011; Van Leijenhorst, Westenberg, & Crone, 2008). Only in the company of others do adolescents deviate from this pattern and take excessive risks (Hensley, 1977).

This has been shown in a study that used a computer game called "Chicken" (Gardner & Steinberg, 2005). In this game, players earn points by moving a car on a road. As in real life, traffic lights indicate when cars should be halted and when they can go. Whereas a halting car can earn no points, a car crossing an intersection on red costs points. Thus, players need to trade off potential earnings against the risk of losing the same. When playing this game, both adolescents and adults are more likely to favor risk when they are surrounded by peers than when they are alone. However, the peer effect is significantly greater in adolescents than it is in adults.

Finding Love

Gaining independence from one's parents sets the stage for the formation of adult romantic relationships and for finding Mr. or Ms. Right. On one hand, the weakening of parental bonds makes room for bonds with other individuals. On the other hand, the strengthening of novelty and peer orientation helps meeting those individuals. However, not every meeting turns into a romantic relationship. Who is attracted to who depends on a range of factors. Moreover, initial attraction or sexual engagement may or may not lead to the formation of a lasting emotional attachment. Folk wisdom as well as scientific evidence suggest that these are functionally and temporally separable phenomena. In the following section, we explore these phenomena and learn how they relate to emotions.

Mate Choice

Reproduction is the ultimate goal of any living organism, including that of nonhuman animals and humans. Because reproduction is costly, individuals try to maximize reproductive success by choosing the best available mating partner. Rather than taking the first one that comes along, they assess potential mating candidates for species-typical mate choice markers (Edward & Chapman, 2011; Puts, Jones, & DeBruine, 2012; but see Lykken & Tellegen, 1993).

During adolescence, individuals become increasingly sensitive to these markers. As they discover their own sexuality, they develop an interest in the courtship displays and sexual characteristics of others, particularly those of the opposite sex. Others who promise reproductive success become magnets of attention and objects of infatuation. Thinking about them or being in their presence is experienced as rewarding and becomes a primary motivator for behavior. Exemplary evidence for this comes from anthropologists studying nonhuman primates. Galdikas (1996), for example, gave a vivid description of a male orangutan named Throatpouch being "smitten" by a female named Priscilla. Throatpouch followed the female for days, without much appetite for food and seemingly unable to take his eyes off her (Galdikas, 1996).

Throatpouch's symptoms of infatuation are very similar to those experienced by humans and remind us of what happens when individuals develop an addiction. Indeed, brain research has shown that both falling in love and becoming addicted involve similar neural processes. Individuals with a recent attraction to another person activate the brain's reward system differently when seeing that person as compared to when seeing someone else. Specifically, looking at a desired individual preferentially activates the ventral tegmental area (Fisher, Aron, & Brown, 2005), a site for the production of dopamine, and the caudate nucleus (Bartels & Zeki, 2000; Fisher et al., 2005), a dopaminergic target (Chapter 7).

A CLOSER LOOK 12.2

Things to Look for in a Mate

Mate selection is nonarbitrary. If there is choice, individuals compare potential mates with respect to certain characteristics. For some of these characteristics, it is relatively easy to see how they reflect a mate's quality or fit, whereas for other characteristics the usefulness for mate selection is dubious.

An example of a relatively transparent mate choice characteristic is an individual's major histocompatibility complex (MHC)—a molecular player within the body's immune system. Genes that code for MHC affect body odor, so MHC information becomes accessible to potential mates. Research in both humans and nonhuman animals suggests that this information determines mate choices possibly because it predicts disease resilience in offspring (Chaix, Cao, & Donnelly, 2008; Garver-Apgar, Gangestad, Thornhill, Miller, & Olp, 2006; Wedekind, Seebeck, Bettens, & Paepke, 1995).

An example of a more dubious mate choice characteristic is the courtship display of bowerbirds indigenous to Australia and its wider regions (Kelley & Endler, 2012; Madden, 2008). Male bowerbirds build bowers, which they use to attract females. In some bowerbird species, these bowers are true pieces of art for which their creators gathered and arranged colorful materials such as sticks, shells, stones, and feathers. Notably, the males' bowers have no apparent function other than to impress

(Continued)

(Continued)

female visitors. The females decide on a mate based on the aesthetic quality of his bower, as well as other aspects of his courtship display.

Humans are little different from bowerbirds in that some aspects of their courtship are not obviously related to mate quality. During adolescence and young adulthood, for example, many individuals explore their artistic talents and begin to sing, paint, or write poetry. Individuals mastering these arts stand a better chance of attracting the opposite sex than do individuals with no apparent artistic talent (Griskevicius, Cialdini, & Kenrick, 2006; Miller, 2000).

Because a pretty bower or poetry do not immediately translate into suitability as a mate or parent, the role of art or aesthetics in mate selection is unclear. It is possible that it evolved due to arbitrary preferences in the opposite sex (Prum, 2012). For example, female bowerbirds may have developed a taste for bowers independently of their reproductive desires, and males evolved the means to cater to that taste. Alternatively, artful displays may reveal a mate's social, cognitive, and/or physical aptitudes, which would benefit prospective offspring (Miller, 2000).

FIGURE 12.11 Great Bowerbird With Bower

The entrance to the bower is carefully decorated and constructed in a way that suggests perspective, making it seem longer and the bower taller than in reality (Kelley & Endler, 2012).

Source: Images courtesy of and © Laura Kelley.

Mate Attachment

Many humans dream of finding someone with whom they can spend the rest of their life. They consider a true and faithful sexual partnership as an important precondition for happiness. Interestingly, however, such partnerships are extremely rare within the animal kingdom. Our close relative the chimpanzee, is notoriously promiscuous. Female chimpanzees in heat will offer themselves to virtually all unrelated males within their group (Goodall, 2010). Moreover, only about 3% of animal species scattered across insects, fish, birds, and mammals are monogamous, meaning that they bond with only one sexual partner in a given breeding season. Hardly any animals bond for life, and even those that do have the occasional sexual interlude with another conspecific.

Why, then, do many humans wish to selectively attach themselves to only one individual? One potential reason is that the raising of human offspring is an exceptionally long, costly, and risky process (Fraley & Shaver, 2000). Women typically bear only one child at a time, and while nursing this child are unlikely to be fertile. Moreover, even after they stop nursing, they have to invest substantial time and effort for the child to make it into adulthood, and this becomes more challenging as additional children arrive. Having a committed male partner in this process is useful. It increases the mother's fitness and promotes offspring survival.

Although many dream of finding Mr. or Ms. Right for their journey into parenthood, nature ensures that, in their actual choices, humans are not unreasonably picky. Attachment mechanisms evolved that emotionally bind humans as well as some of the other monogamous species to their sexual partners. Psychology and neuroscience contributed differently to uncovering these mechanisms.

Psychological approach. One mechanism explored by psychologists depends on the infant attachment system. Because this system must work up until individuals reach adolescence, psychologists speculate that its extended duration was hijacked for the formation of mate attachments. This speculation received support from empirical parallels between infant and mate attachment styles.

Although all infants attach to their mother, the quality of this attachment varies. Mary Ainsworth and colleagues explored this variation and identified attachment styles referred to as secure and insecure (Ainsworth, Blehar, Waters, & Wall, 1978). Secure attachments presumably result from warm, supportive, and consistent care, which enables infants to experience their caretaker as a "secure base" from which they can safely explore the environment. Insecure attachments presumably result from unresponsive and/or inconsistent care, which disturbs the development of a "secure base."

The exploration of mate attachment styles suggests that they map onto those identified by Ainsworth and colleagues for infants. Specifically, self-reported mate attachment experiences could be categorized as secure and insecure and their respective proportion matched that observed in infancy and childhood. Additionally, longitudinal research revealed that infant attachment styles positively predict mate attachment styles (Hamilton, 2000; Simard, Moss, & Pascuzzo, 2011). In other words, infants and children who are securely attached to their caretaker are likely to form secure romantic relationships as adults. In contrast, infants and children who are insecurely attached are likely to form insecure mate attachments. A potential discontinuity in attachment style seems linked to experiences of negative life events (Hamilton, 2000).

Neuroscience approach. While psychologists approached mate attachment by exploring infant mechanisms, neuroscientists took a different route. They approached mate attachment by exploring parental mechanisms. Much of this work was done on a small rodent called the prairie vole (Figure 12.12). Like humans, this rodent forms monogamous pair bonds in which both the male and the female care for offspring. Studying this rodent showed that oxytocin- and dopamine-dependent mechanisms, which facilitate parental care, are also critical for the formation of mate attachment (McGraw & Young, 2010).

An important role for oxytocin was identified in female prairie voles. During sexual interactions, female voles, like humans (Caldwell, 2002), release oxytocin into the nucleus accumbens, where it promotes positive feelings as well as the formation of long-term attachments (Ross et al., 2009). Blocking and stimulating oxytocin receptors in the nucleus accumbens impairs (Insel & Hulihan, 1995) and furthers (Williams, Insel, Harbaugh, & Carter, 1994) such attachments, respectively. Although oxytocin is also present in males, its role in pair bonding is less critical. Instead, such bonding depends on the release of arginine vasopressin into the ventral pallidum or the lateral septum (Lim & Young, 2004; Liu, Curtis, & Wang, 2001). Arginine vasopressin is a neuropeptide with a similar structure and function as oxytocin. As for oxytocin, blocking its action impairs, whereas stimulating its action furthers attachment formation (Lim & Young, 2004; Liu et al., 2001).

FIGURE 12.12   Prairie Vole Family

Source: Picture courtesy of and © Larry Young.

Together, the release of oxytocin and vasopressin during sexual intercourse produce partner preferences and initiate the formation of attachments. Additionally, they help these attachments endure. The latter is achieved by kick-starting alterations in the density of dopamine receptors within the nucleus accumbens. After the initial formation of an attachment, the proportion of D1 receptors increases relative to the proportion of D2 receptors (Aragona et al., 2006). Because the development of partner preferences after sexual intercourse is inhibited by the activation of D1 receptors and promoted by the activation of D2 receptors, these changes reduce the probability that such intercourse with a new individual endangers an existing parental commitment.

Based on the findings from psychology and neuroscience, one may conclude that both infant attachment experiences as well as the biological mechanisms underlying parental attachment contribute to the emergence of romantic relationships in adolescence and early adulthood. These relationships seem to involve especially adapted social mechanisms that interact with the brain's reward system and our capacity to experience joy.

LATE ADULTHOOD AND AGING

Although most adults wish for a long life, old age is not equally appealing. This is because aging brings with it a number of life changes that are typically considered negative. One such change concerns the retirement from the workforce. Although retirement may have its superficial appeals, for many it means financial restraints and a loss of significance to one's family and to society. Another change concerns an individual's physical and mental fitness. This fitness abates with age and thus begins to curtail active participation in life and to increase dependence on others. Last, old age is a time when many individuals lose one or more persons dear to them. The longer a life is lived, the greater becomes the probability that family members, friends, and life partners are taken by accident or disease, leaving the bereaved with a shrinking social circle. Thus, many conceive of old age as a sad and lonely time (Gluth, Ebner, & Schmiedek, 2010; Röcke & Lachman, 2008).

Surprisingly, this conception conflicts with the actual feelings of older adults. Investigations suggest that their emotional well-being is comparable to if not better than that of younger adults. Using a **mixed longitudinal design**, Carstensen and colleagues (2011) followed 18- to 94-year-olds for 10 years. At the beginning of their study and then every 5 years, the researchers assessed their participants' well-being using the **experience sampling method**. To this end, the participants were alerted five times a day over the course of a week to complete a set of questionnaires provided by the researchers.

Compared to younger adults, older adults reported more positive emotional experiences (Figure 12.13). Additionally, older adults showed greater stability in their emotions, meaning that they were less likely than younger adults to experience a change in emotion from one measurement point to the next. Their emotions also became more complex in the sense that negative and positive states were more frequently experienced at the same time. Thus, aging seems to improve the ability to see "the silver lining" in a sky of clouds, while

FIGURE 12.13   Emotional Changes in Old Age

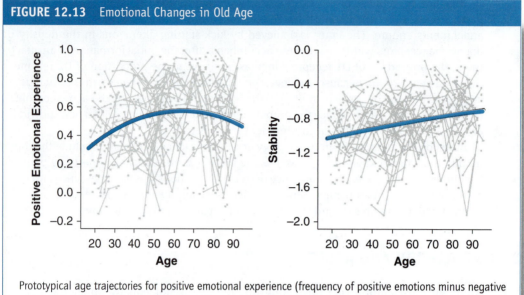

Prototypical age trajectories for positive emotional experience (frequency of positive emotions minus negative emotions) and emotional stability. Data points connected by lines represent one participant.

Source: Copyright © 2011 by the American Psychological Association. Reproduced with permission. "Emotional Experience Improves With Age: Evidence Based on Over 10 Years of Experience Sampling," by L. L. Carstensen, B. Turan, S. Scheibe, N. Ram, H. Ersner-Hershfield G. R. Samanez, K. P. Brooks, and J. R. Nesselroade, 2011, *Psychology and Aging, 26*, pp. 21–33. The use of APA information does not imply endorsement by APA.

also recognizing the "darker side" of things. This presumably promotes mental health by enabling richer and perhaps more balanced emotional experiences (Ong & Bergeman, 2004).

In the following section, we look at some of the mechanisms that produce these age-related changes in emotion.

Socioemotional Selectivity Theory

One consequence of biological aging is that one's lifetime eventually runs out. In industrialized nations, women live on average into their mid-80s and men live into their late 70s. As individuals approach these temporal markers, the expectations and opportunities that seemed unlimited when they were young eventually become finite. Many personal goals that were not achieved by late adulthood are unlikely ever to be achieved. Moreover, new goals become less tenable if they have a long as compared to a short tenure. Thus, the emphasis shifts from future-oriented concerns and behaviors to the "here and now." Socioemotional selectivity theory (SST) holds that it is this shift that produces age-related changes in emotion.

Caring About the "Here and Now"

Evidence that a shortened life perspective changes the relative priority of short- as compared to long-term goals comes from studies investigating younger and older adults' preferences for social partners or merchandise. For example, when given the alternative of meeting a member of their family, a recent acquaintance, or the author of a book they have read, older adults more frequently than younger adults select the family member (Fung, Carstensen, & Lutz, 1999). This suggests that the maintenance of existing relationships becomes of greater importance than the forging of new ones.

Another example of the gaining importance of the "here and now" comes from a study that explored framing effects in the context of advertisements (Figure 12.14). Compared to younger adults, older adults preferred products presented with slogans such as "Capture those special moments" over products with slogans such as "Capture the unexplored world" (Fung & Carstensen, 2003).

Importantly, these preferences change in the face of information that alters subjective life expectancy. Older adults, instructed to imagine that modern medicine allows their life to be extended by 20 more years, adjust their preferences to match those of younger adults (Fung & Carstensen, 2003; Fung et al., 1999). Likewise, younger adults, whose normal life expectancy is jeopardized, adjust their preferences to match those of older adults.

The latter was shown in the context of major security or health threats such as the terrorist attacks on the United States in 2001 or the outbreak of SARS (sever acute respiratory syndrome), a viral respiratory disease, at the end of 2002 in Asia. When dealing with such threats, young like old adults preferred to invest in the "here and now" as compared to a doubtful future (Fung & Carstensen, 2006).

The Positivity Effect

Information processing in young and middle-aged adults shows a negativity bias (Chapter 9). Negative stimuli, especially if threatening, capture and hold attention more effectively than neutral or positive stimuli. Additionally, they are more effectively stored and remembered. This has been explained in reference to the special survival value of negative information. While there are no immediate consequences to ignoring neutral or positive stimuli, ignoring negative stimuli can be dangerous. Moreover, engaging with the latter and learning about their eliciting conditions and effective countermeasures are useful because that reduces the likelihood of both immediate and future harm.

SST holds that aging alters the negativity bias (Carstensen, 2006). Because current states gain in importance relative to future states, individuals change the way they trade off current emotions against future emotions. Current emotions are thought to increase in importance relative to future emotions. Therefore, older adults more than younger adults maximize present over future positive states. Moreover, they shift their engagement from negative to positive information in the here and now. Engaging with negative information on the off-chance of future emotional payoffs loses its worth.

The relative change in the significance of negative and positive information, termed the positivity effect (Carstensen, 2006), has been explored behaviorally and with functional brain imaging. Together, these explorations revealed that attention capture by negative

FIGURE 12.14   Older Adults Value the "Here and Now"

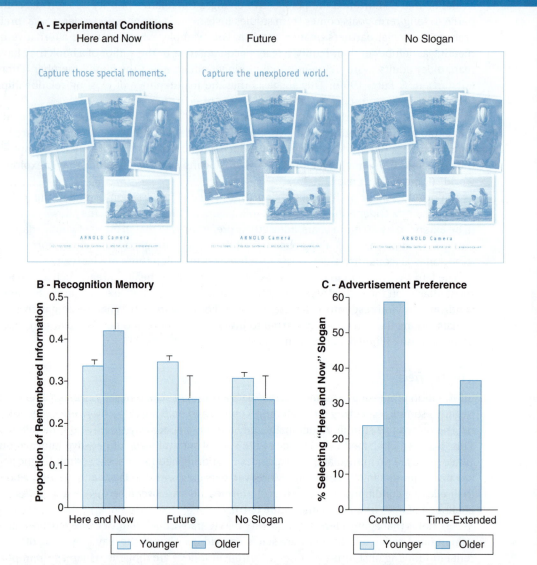

In a study by Fung and Carstensen (2003), younger and older adults saw advertisements (A) with a "here and now" slogan, a future-directed slogan, or no slogan. (B) Older but not younger adults remembered more information presented with a "here and now" slogan than with a future-oriented slogan or no slogan. Error bars represent standard error of the mean. (C) Older adults asked to imagine that their life could be extended by 20 more years showed a reduced preference for the "here and now" advertisement relative to older adults in a control condition. Imagining a life extension had no effect on younger adults.

Source: Adapted with permission from "Sending Memorable Messages to the Old: Age Differences in Preferences and Memory for Advertisements," by H. H. Fung and L. L. Carstensen, 2003, *Journal of Personality and Social Psychology, 85,* pp. 163–178.

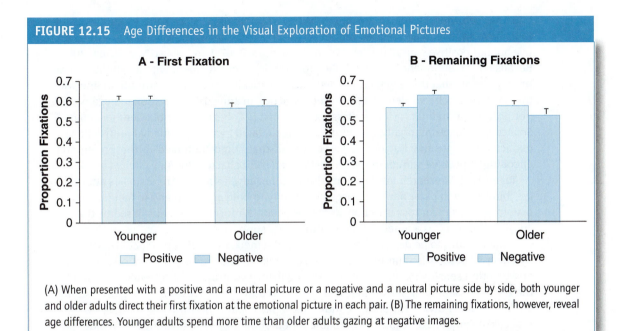

FIGURE 12.15   Age Differences in the Visual Exploration of Emotional Pictures

(A) When presented with a positive and a neutral picture or a negative and a neutral picture side by side, both younger and older adults direct their first fixation at the emotional picture in each pair. (B) The remaining fixations, however, reveal age differences. Younger adults spend more time than older adults gazing at negative images.

Source: Adapted with permission from "Aging and Goal-Directed Emotional Attention: Distraction Reverses Emotional Biases," by M. Knight, T. L. Seymour, J. T. Gaunt, C. Baker, K. Nesmith, & M. Mather, 2007, *Emotion, 7,* pp. 705–714.

information is maintained in older adults, while attention holding and memory facilitation decline. This was demonstrated in an eye-tracking study in which younger and older adults saw a sequence of image pairs composed of a negative and a neutral image or a positive and a neutral image (Knight et al., 2007). Eye-tracking measures indicated that younger and older adults' first fixations on an image pair were comparable (Figure 12.15). Both were more likely to glance at the negative and positive images as compared to the neutral images. However, age differences emerged for the remaining fixations in negative-neutral image pairs. Here, older adults were less likely than younger adults to continue gazing at the negative image. No age differences emerged for gazing at the positive-neutral pairs.

To examine the "positivity effect" on memory, researchers presented participants with negative, positive, and neutral images and subsequently tested recognition performance (Kensinger, Garoff-Eaton, & Schacter, 2007; Kensinger & Schacter, 2008). Under these conditions, younger adults were more likely to remember negative as compared to positive or neutral images. Additionally, they remembered positive and neutral images equally well. Older adults, in contrast, remembered negative and positive images equally well and better than they remembered neutral images. Specifically, while their memory performance dropped for negative and neutral images relative to young adults, it seemed constant for positive images.

These behavioral findings are supported by brain imaging. For example, studies using ERPs have shown an age-related reduction in the late positive component (LPC) for negative but not positive stimuli (Kisley, Wood, & Burrows, 2007; Langeslag & van Strien, 2009). Because this component has been linked to attentional engagement with a stimulus, these findings imply that this engagement declines specifically for negative stimuli. In line with this, fMRI research revealed an age-related reduction in amygdala activation to negative but not positive stimuli (St. Jacques, Bessette-Symons, & Cabeza, 2009; but see Kensinger & Schacter, 2008). Additionally, it identified an age-related increase in medial prefrontal cortex activity to positive but not negative stimuli that could be linked to the preferential encoding of positive stimuli in memory (Kensinger & Schacter, 2008).

Together, this research implies that, although negative information retains its attention-grabbing effect in older adults, it loses its capacity to hold attention and to facilitate memory storage. A similar loss is not observed for positive information. Thus, it seems that the "positivity effect," as a tenet of SST, is empirically supported.

What remains to be determined, however, is the mechanism that produces the "positivity effect." Does it arise automatically from age-related changes in information processing and emotion sensitivity, or does it require regulatory control? Existing evidence points to the latter possibility. It shows that age differences in the processing of negative stimuli disappear under divided attention conditions. If participants perform a secondary task that reduces the amount of resources available for emotion processing, younger and older participants engage similarly with negative information (Knight et al., 2007). Additionally, fMRI research has linked age-related reductions in amygdala activity to negative stimuli and age-persistent amygdala activity to positive stimuli to a concurrent recruitment of the prefrontal cortex—a known substrate for emotion regulation (Mather, 2012; Chapter 11). Thus, these results suggest that age-related emotion changes arise, at least partially, from enhanced emotion regulation. Whether such regulation is made fairly automatically or requires intentionality remains to be determined.

Functional Decline Affects Emotions

Although SST received much empirical support, it is rivaled by an alternative account that links age-related emotional change to a decline in the bodily structures and functions that support emotions. Rather than holding goal changes responsible, this account considers aging itself to be the factor driving enhanced well-being and the "positivity effect."

In support of this idea, researchers identified age-related changes in brain morphology and function. Aging causes widespread atrophy through loss in both gray and white matter. Although this atrophy is most prominent in the frontal and temporal cortex, it is also evident in subcortical structures such as the amygdala (Allen, Bruss, Brown, & Damasio, 2005). Because structural damage to the amygdala in young and middle-aged individuals produces elderly-like emotional responses, some researchers attribute age-related emotional change to brain atrophy (Cacioppo, Berntson, Bechara, Tranel, & Hawkley, 2011).

Apart from decreasing brain matter, aging also affects the peripheral nervous system and its ability to produce somatic markers of emotion. Both negative and positive stimuli seem to lose some of their capacity to provoke peripheral arousal. When recounting emotional events from their lives, when posing emotional expressions, or when viewing emotionally charged movies, older adults show weaker cardiovascular responses than do younger adults (Levenson, Carstensen, Friesen, & Ekman, 1991; Tsai, Levenson, & Carstensen, 2000).

Last, aging affects the feedback signaling from the periphery to the brain. Elderly individuals are less aware than younger individuals of visceral sensations such as intestinal distensions (Lasch, Castell, & Castell, 1997) or heartbeats (Khalsa, Rudrauf, & Tranel, 2009). The aging of both the peripheral and central mechanisms potentially contributes to this. Notably, the insula and somatosensory cortex, two major hubs for representing the body, show age-related structural and functional decline (Good et al., 2001; Kalisch, Ragert, Schwenkreis, Dinse, & Tegenthoff, 2009).

Together, a reduced functionality of emotion structures as well as weaker peripheral changes and feedback dampen emotional experiences in old age. A particular impact on negative emotions may arise from structural changes in the amygdala that specifically alter negative appraisals (Cacioppo et al., 2011) and/or from a stronger association between negative emotions and bodily arousal. Alternatively, they may arise from the processes postulated by SST.

SUMMARY

The bodily and mental changes that occur in the course of a lifetime are accompanied by changes in emotion. Through this, age-specific feelings enable age-appropriate environmental interactions.

In a first life period, here referred to as infancy and early childhood, individuals experience emotions that facilitate two major life tasks: (1) attaching to a caregiver and (2) learning about the environment. It has been proposed that the former is achieved through interaction between emotions and a dedicated social system that makes engaging with socially familiar information rewarding. The latter is presumably achieved through interaction between emotions and a dedicated object system that makes engaging with novel objects rewarding.

Additionally, both systems are complemented by a developing tool set that individuals can use to meaningfully interact with and shape their environment. Notably, social interactions are supported by the emergence of Theory of Mind—the ability to represent another's affective and cognitive state. Moreover, both social and nonsocial interactions are supported by the development of emotion regulation skills such as distraction and response suppression.

In a second major life period, called adolescence, children mature into adults. During this period, early childhood attachments diminish and individuals achieve parental independence. Now, being with peers becomes more rewarding than being with one's family, novel experiences become exceedingly motivating, and proper risk assessments become compromised by the company of others. Through this, adolescents push their boundaries, find out their strengths and weaknesses, and position themselves within their social group.

In the course of these developments, adolescents undergo sexual maturation and develop a sexual interest in their own body and that of others. Individuals who display relevant mate choice markers become objects of infatuation. Being with them is experienced as rewarding and may develop into something akin to an addiction. If infatuations result in sexual interactions, they may develop into more lasting attachments. As the basis for these, psychologists point to infant attachment mechanisms, whereas neuroscientists point to parental attachment mechanisms.

A final life period associated with emotion-related changes comprises late adulthood. During this period individuals undergo physical and mental decline and face major life stressors such as the termination of their employment or the loss of a significant other. It is hence considered to be a relatively sad period. Yet research suggests that the emotional well-being of older adults compares favorably with that of younger adults.

One potential explanation for this is offered by socioemotional selectivity theory. This theory holds that the approaching end of life leads older adults to change their priorities from long-term goals and future emotions to short-term goals and current emotions. Moreover, in the context of current emotions, positive emotions gain in importance relative to negative emotions. Evidence for this comes from behavioral and neuroimaging research showing that aging reduces responses to negative information, while responses to positive information are maintained.

Apart from an approaching end of life, older adults face a number of bodily changes that undoubtedly produce emotion changes and that contribute to well-being. These changes include a decline in the brain structures that support emotion and cognition, a reduced excitability of the peripheral nervous system, and a deficient feedback of peripheral responses to the brain. Together, these changes dampen emotional experiences and help make our sunset years comfortable and contented.

THINKING CRITICALLY ABOUT "EMOTIONS ACROSS THE LIFE SPAN"

1. Researchers have used a habituation paradigm to explore novelty orientation in infancy. What are the cognitive functions that contribute to an infant's performance in this paradigm? How would they impact the assessed novelty orientation?

2. The chapter discusses monogamy as a preferred mating strategy in humans. How can this be reconciled with the fact that many humans engage in extramarital sexual relations?

3. The chapter introduces two theories to account for emotional changes in late adulthood. Are these two theories complementary or mutually exclusive?

MEDIA LIBRARY

Sarah-Jayne Blakemore talks about the adolescent brain on TED: http://www.ted.com/talks/sarah_jayne_blakemore_the_mysterious_workings_of_the_adolescent_brain.html

Laura Carstensen talks about socioemotional selectivity theory on TED: http://www.ted.com/talks/laura_carstensen_older_people_are_happier.html

Laurence Steinberg gives a lecture on the social neuroscience of adolescent risk taking: http://www.cornell.edu/video/a-social-neuroscience-perspective-on-adolescent-risk-taking

Short video clips on monogamous life-forms: http://www.bbc.co.uk/nature/adaptations/Monogamous_pairing_in_animals#intro

CHAPTER 13

Emotions and Sex Differences

It is indisputable that men are physically different from women. But do they also think and feel differently? Popular opinion answers this question in the affirmative. Folk philosophy, literature, and public norms are dominated by stereotypes according to which men and women have different interests, personal strengths, and weaknesses. Most researchers, however, regard these stereotypes skeptically. The primary reason for their skepticism is that stereotypes were and are used to inform alleged scientific theories, and to justify sexual discrimination and the suppression of women.

Popular historical examples for this are the theories of Darwin and Freud. Applying his principles of natural and sexual selection, Darwin concluded that men must be superior to women because they engage in fiercer competition for sexual partners (Darwin, 1871). As such, he argued, men must be endowed with greater "courage, perseverance, and determined energy" as well as greater "reason" (Darwin 1871, pp. 316–354). Half a century later, Freud, although taking a different approach, arrived at the same conclusion (Freud, 1927). He considered men superior to women because women don't have a penis. Women, Freud theorized, are sexually castrated and, hence, overcome with an envy for male genitals. This envy, he argued, clouds their mental state and makes them psychologically ill adapted.

Women in many parts of the world still suffer from these and other testimonials of male dominance. This is also true for many modern societies including the United States or the European Union in which women obtained legal rights equal to those of men many decades ago. For example, in the United States women still hold only about 14% of leading positions in companies and governmental organizations (www.catalyst.org) and earn on average 40% less than men do (www.census.gov).

It is because of these imbalances in power that most researchers today are especially careful in their examination and interpretation of sex differences. Moreover, while sex differences have been found, it is now clear that they are much more complex than initial theories and prevailing stereotypes made us believe. Sexual differentiation does not simply make men smarter and women more emotional. Instead, it weaves itself intricately into the minds of men and women, affecting different aspects of thought and feeling in a multifaceted manner. In this chapter, we explore these aspects and examine how they shape emotional experiences and associated behaviors in a sex-specific way.

WHAT IS SEX? THE ORIGINS OF SEXUAL DIFFERENTIATION

Before considering differences between men and women, we may ask ourselves why we have two sexes in the first place. Why do humans and most other animals divide into male and female individuals? Why is it rare that animals proliferate without sexual differentiation, and why are there hardly any species with three or more sexes? (For such an exception, see Cervantes et al., 2013.) While definite answers to these questions are still outstanding, biologists gained some clues from the physical properties of sex cells called gametes and the importance of these properties for reproduction.

One such property that seems relevant is the size of gametes (Parker, Baker, & Smith, 1972). Compared to large gametes, small gametes are energetically cheaper to produce, and organisms can produce them in greater quantity. Additionally, small gametes need less energy to disperse, allowing them to disperse faster and wider than large gametes. However, small gametes must make do with little cytoplasm, and therefore contribute hardly more than genetic instructions to an emerging organism (Figure 13.1). In this respect, large gametes, which have substantial cytoplasm, are better. They contain life-sustaining substances that help bridge the time until the developing organism is ready to produce these substances itself. Because of their respective benefits, both small and large gametes were presumably more successful than medium-sized gametes. Moreover, their success is held responsible for the development of what we now call sperm and eggs.

Other factors that may have assisted in the development of sperm and eggs relate to the kind of genetic mixing these gametes afford. Too little mixing, as may be the case with only one type of gamete, curtails genetic adaptability in the face of environmental change. Too much mixing, however, as would be the case with infinite gamete types, may also be problematic. One problem that arises here concerns again the cytoplasm (Hurst, 1990, 1996). Cytoplasm albeit nourishing the cell, may contain parasitic elements that potentially harm the offspring. By specializing into sperm and eggs, with only the eggs containing cytoplasm, organisms reduce the likelihood that gamete parasites compromise reproductive success.

The evolution of two specialized gametes led to a corresponding evolution of two sex-typed organisms, males and females, that produce these gametes. Notably, these organisms are typically dimorphic, meaning that females and males are built and function differently. Researchers speculate that this dimorphism arose at least partially from differences in how sperm and eggs are best put to use (Low, 2001). Sperm may best be used by individuals whose physique and mindset enable them to roam and reach a maximum of mating partners. Eggs, in contrast, may best be used by individuals whose physique and mindset keep them safe and promote careful partner selection.

While such speculations are certainly reasonable, we have to be cautious when using sex-specific reproductive strategies to explain sexual dimorphism in body build and function. This is because the latter varies considerably across species. For example, although in most species the male is larger and stronger than the female, this is not always the case. In some species, including certain mammals, the female is larger. Moreover, size differences range from very little, as in the case of humans, to very much, as in the case of triplewart

FIGURE 13.1 Gamete Properties and Reproductive Success

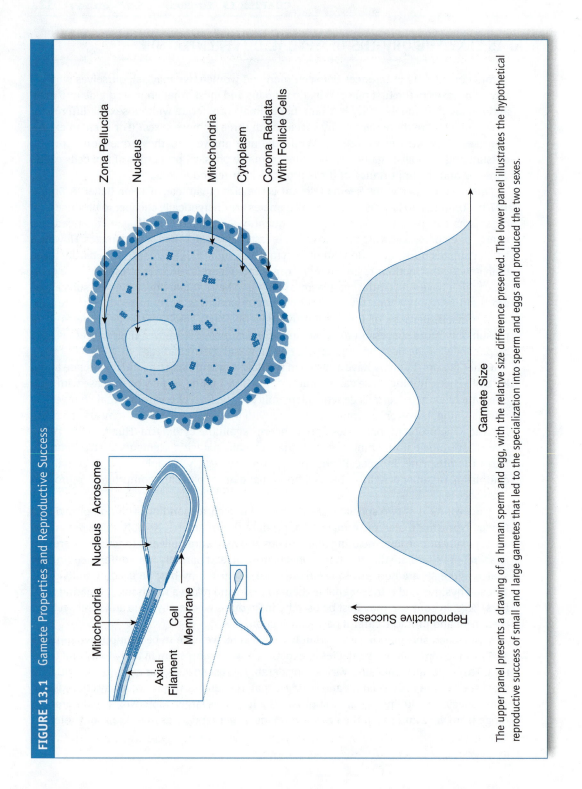

The upper panel presents a drawing of a human sperm and egg, with the relative size difference preserved. The lower panel illustrates the hypothetical reproductive success of small and large gametes that led to the specialization into sperm and eggs and produced the two sexes.

seadevils, where the male is only one fifth the size of the female (www.fishbase.org). Thus, factors other than gamete specialization have affected sexual dimorphism and broken up its evolutionary trajectory into manifold species-specific variations. For this reason, and because the present focus is on understanding sex differences in human emotions, evidence from nonhuman animals will be used sparingly and only if it concerns sex-specific phenomena that are clearly shared between humans and other animals.

DOES SEX MATTER FOR EMOTIONS?

Theoretical Positions

"Give me a child and I'll shape him into anything." This famous quote attributed to the behaviorist B. F. Skinner holds that every thought, feeling, and behavior of an individual is learned. A person's biological sex becomes relevant only insofar as it influences how others interact with the person and in what kinds of environments the person is placed. However, it is irrelevant for how the person responds to these environments.

That things are not as simple as that became clear when medical professionals tried to put Skinner's terms into practice and attempted to solicit gender conforming behaviors and emotions in individuals with sexual abnormalities. Bruce Reimer was such an individual (Colapinto, 2001). He lost his penis in a circumcision accident when he was 6 months old. In an effort to repair the damage, medics constructed a vagina, turning Bruce into a girl. Additionally, they put Bruce on hormone therapy and advised the parents to dress him and treat him like a girl. Despite all this, however, Bruce never fully identified as a female. He felt lost, became an outsider with his peers, and threatened suicide at the age of 13. Moreover, when he finally learned his true sexual identity from his parents, Bruce insisted on a sex change and lived thereafter as a man.

Cases such as these suggest that individuals are not born as "blank slates" or unformed entities that mold to their environments. Inborn characteristics such as biological sex matter. But how much do they matter, and how relevant are they for something so seemingly universal as emotions? Opinions divide drastically on this point.

Gendered Minds Position

Echoing Skinner, some researchers consider biological sex to be fairly irrelevant. Exemplary for this position are Wendy Wood and Alice Eagly, who developed a biosocial model concerning the role of sex (Wood & Eagly, 2002). According to their model, nature, as reflected in the physical differences between men and women, dictates sex-typed roles in the care for offspring and produces different physical aptitudes (e.g., strength). However, what produces different mental aptitudes is the placement within society. Because in many societies the sexes occupy different roles, these societies inadvertently create gendered minds—that is, they masculinize or feminize individuals (http://www.who.int/gender/whatisgender/en).

Men, typically conceived of as "breadwinners" and the makers of society, are placed in more powerful or high-income positions than women, who are expected to support their men and to take care of their home and family. These gender roles, as a cultural institution, then produce male- and female-typical emotions.

In support of their model, Wood and Eagly (2002) cite research demonstrating a relationship between environment or culture on one hand and sex differences on the other. Among other things, they point to lab-based social psychology studies on **stereotype threat**, a phenomenon experienced when individuals face situations that raise the possibility of failure and where such failure might be expected based on existing stereotypes (A Closer Look 13.1). In the context of sex differences, stereotype threat has been shown to explain performance differences between men and women in male- and female-typical tasks.

For example, men were found to score worse than women on a social perception test when informed that this test assesses social perception and that women typically fare better at this. However, when the test was framed as an information processing test and stereotypes were not highlighted, both sexes performed similarly (Koenig & Eagly, 2005). Comparable results were found in a study that explored sex-typed performances on a science test conducted after participants read a science lesson. When the lesson was accompanied by stereotypical male images, women performed worse than men on the test. Notably, this pattern disappeared when the lesson included mixed-sex images and reversed when it was accompanied by only counterstereotypical female images (Good, Woodzicka,

A CLOSER LOOK 13.1

Stereotype Threat and Its Role for Gender Differences

"Self-fulfilling prophecies" are folk wisdom. They hold that beliefs about events affect event outcomes; or, put more simply, that if you expect something to turn out badly, it probably will. Like most folk wisdom, self-fulfilling prophecies have a kernel of truth in them. Moreover, they seem to underpin what psychologists have termed "stereotype threat"—a phenomenon by which individuals feel threatened when they engage in activities for which they know that members of their group typically perform poorly. This knowledge, or the activated stereotype, hampers their performance.

In the context of gender stereotypes, stereotype threat has been used to explain the poorer performance of women in tasks that lie within the traditional male purview. Research has shown that women's ability to solve math or science problems declines when they are explicitly or implicitly reminded that their ability to solve such problems is generally poorer than that of men (Johns, Schmader, & Martens, 2005).

Importantly, it is not only ability or skill that is impacted by prevailing stereotypes. Researchers also found effects on learning and decision making. One learning example is a study that required participants to scan stimulus arrays for a target character. Normally, time on task improves scanning speed, irrespective of sex. However, researchers found this improvement to be absent in female participants who were told that women typically fare worse than men in visual processing tasks (Rydell, Shiffrin, Boucher, Loo, & Rydell, 2010). Similarly, a study that probed the ability of women to acquire mathematical rules showed that rule acquisition was impaired when women were told that the study's goal was to determine why math skills are poorer in women than in men (Rydell, Rydell, & Boucher, 2010).

In the context of decision making, stereotype threat was found to increase women's risk aversion. Stereotype threat was induced by framing a task as relevant for math and asking participants to indicate their sex. In a control condition, participants were simply told that they would solve puzzle exercises. Women in the "math" condition were less likely to accept a gamble and opted for less risky choices than did women in the "puzzle" condition (Carr & Steele, 2010).

Unfortunately for women, their environments are filled with reminders of male superiority that make it hard to break the vicious cycle of stereotypes and gendered performances. Fortunately, however, researchers discovered a way to dampen the impact of stereotype reminders. In a clever study, participants were subjected to a math task with one of the following instructions (Johns et al., 2005). One group was told that the task assessed general problem solving, whereas another group was told

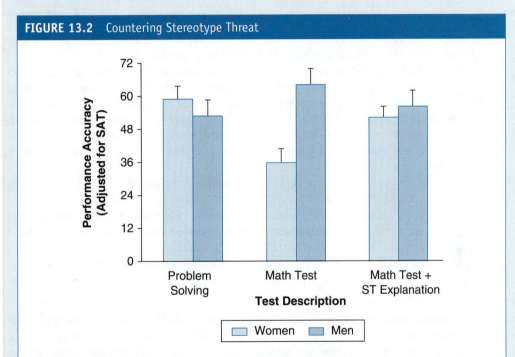

FIGURE 13.2 Countering Stereotype Threat

Women's and men's accuracy scores (adjusted for quantitative Scholastic Assessment Test, or SAT, scores) on the math test as a function of test description (ST = stereotype threat). Error bars represent standard errors.

Source: "Knowing Is Half the Battle: Teaching Stereotype Threat as a Means of Improving Women's Math Performance," by M. Johns, T. Schmader, and A. Martens, 2005, *Psychological Science, 16,* pp. 175–179. Adapted with permission. Copyright © 2005, Association for Psychological Science.

(Continued)

(Continued)

that the task assessed mathematical skills. Thus, in line with previous work, women should experience stereotype threat in the latter but not the former condition. A last group was instructed that the test assessed mathematical skills and was additionally informed about stereotype threat. Specifically, participants were told that "anxiety [experienced during the task] could be the result of . . . negative stereotypes that are widely known in society and have nothing to do with [one's] actual ability to do well on the test" (Johns, Schmader, & Martens, 2005, p. 176). While the first two conditions produced the expected results, showing that sex differences emerge only under stereotype threat, the third condition produced no sex differences, showing that although prophecies may fulfill themselves, they only do if we believe them (Figure 13.2).

& Wingfield, 2010). Thus, gender identity and associated performance expectations seem to play a role in how men and women think, feel, and behave.

Other research highlighted by Wood and Eagly in support of their biosocial model concerns hormonal differences between men and women. Although such differences naturally arise from differences in reproductive physiology, they are malleable by environmental factors. Societies in which men are emotionally close to their women and contribute significantly to childcare seemingly shape male hormonal patterns to become more female-like. Evidence for this was found from expectant parents in Canada, a typical modern society in which fathers are significantly involved in pregnancy and parenting (Figure 13.3). Maternal increases in the concentration of prolactin, a hormone regulating milk production, were partially matched by the fathers (Storey, Walsh, Quinton, & Wynne-Edwards, 2000). Additionally, the fathers showed a sustained reduction in testosterone, the main male sex hormone and an important contributor to male aggression (Muller, Marlowe, Bugumba, & Ellison, 2009; Storey et al., 2000). Thus, the biosocial model argues, gender, as an institutionalized system, is more important than biological sex for the emotions of men and women.

Sex-Typed Minds Position

Opposing the gendered minds position is the sex-typed minds position, according to which differences between men and women arose in the course of human evolution due to selection pressures. Specifically, selection pressures linked to human reproduction presumably created differences in the genetic makeup of men and women so that, today, the sexes differ not only physically but also mentally. Like the gendered minds position, the sex-typed minds position sees male and female reproductive roles at the root of sexual differentiation. Additionally, however, it postulates that these roles brought with them further, genetically fixed mental specializations that are not strictly linked to reproduction and that include aspects of emotions.

Anthropologists and evolutionary psychologists link this further specialization to the division of labor between men and women. According to them, this division emerged in the late Stone Age around 50,000 years ago and gave modern humans an advantage over other human species such as the Neanderthals (Kuhn & Stiner, 2006). Archeological evidence suggests that Neanderthals maintained hunter-gatherer traditions in which men and women

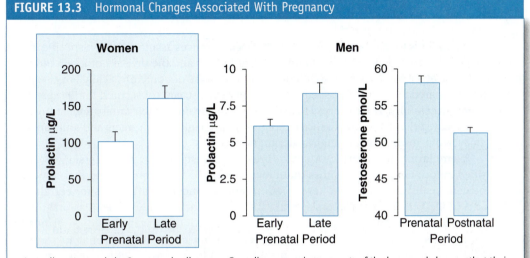

FIGURE 13.3 Hormonal Changes Associated With Pregnancy

According to a study by Storey and colleagues, Canadian men mirror aspects of the hormonal changes that their female partners experience during pregnancy. Additionally, they show a reduction in testosterone. The early prenatal period was defined as 16 to 35 weeks after conception; the late prenatal period was defined as the last 3 weeks before birth; the early postnatal period was defined as the 3 weeks after birth. Testosterone measures are presented from the late prenatal and early postnatal period.

Source: "Hormonal Correlates of Paternal Responsiveness in New and Expectant Fathers," by A. E. Storey, C. J. Walsh, R. L. Quinton, and K. E. Wynne-Edwards, 2000, *Evolution and Human Behavior, 21*, pp. 79–95. Adapted with permission. Copyright © 2000, with permission from Elsevier.

contributed fairly equally to all tasks. In contrast, homo sapiens began to more strategically organize who did what and when. Shifting away from large-game hunting as a primary means of subsistence and developing new food acquisition strategies, our species took on a more diverse set of activities and recognized the benefits of activity-specific manual skills and knowledge. In the wake of this, men and women adopted somewhat complementary subsistence roles that formed the basis for the multifaceted specializations of modern human societies.

How the sexes originally divided labor may be inferred from an analysis of present human cultures living in traditional tribal or nomadic settings as well as in modern rural and urban dwellings (Kuhn & Stiner, 2006; Murdock & Provost, 1973; Wood & Eagly, 2002). Records from these cultures reveal a set of tasks primarily done by men that include large-game hunting, mining, lumbering, and the making of musical instruments, among other things. Tasks primarily performed by women are rarer and include child care; the gathering and preparation of vegetables, fruits, and drinks; and the making and washing of clothes. Researchers speculate that the reason why women did not become more specialized was their primary role in child care. Caring for one or more children that needed to be carried and tended to more or less constantly limited women's labor to tasks that were physically not too demanding, that could be accomplished in the face of distraction, and that could be interrupted on an as-needed basis (Wood & Eagly, 2002).

Proponents for a role of genes in mental sex differences assume that sex-specific minds evolved because these benefited human reproduction and the division of labor and were hence selected for. They hold that individuals who were not only physically but also mentally prepared for their reproductive as well as their societal roles could fulfill these roles more successfully. Their success then would have advanced their family and community and enabled their offspring to thrive. Apart from archeological artifacts and anthropological insights, research experiments support this view.

Exemplary here is work by Melissa Hines and her student Vicky Pasterski, who identified emotional sex differences that emerge early in development and that appear to be genetically determined. These sex differences concern preferences for certain toys (e.g., dolls versus cars; Pasterski et al., 2005), playmates, play styles (Pasterski et al., 2011), and levels of aggression (Pasterski et al., 2007) and were explored in healthy individuals as well as in individuals suffering from congenital adrenal hyperplasia (CAH). CAH exposes girls to male-typical levels of testosterone, which delay or impair their development of typical female sexual characteristics and behaviors. While healthy girls and boys show toy selection, play styles, and aggression levels that conform with existing stereotypes, girls affected with CAH don't. They develop more male-typical preferences and emotional displays despite their parents' best efforts to raise them as girls (Figure 13.4).

Merging Positions

Taken together, researchers are still divided as to the role of environment and genes for mental processes such as emotions. While some consider the environment to be minimally important and ascribe differences between men and women chiefly to genes, others hold the opposite view. The research done in pursuit of both positions accumulated evidence that both environment and genes affect the emergence of sex-typed minds. More recently, it also uncovered mechanisms (Chapter 4) through which upbringing and gender norms can influence the expression of existing biological dispositions. Thus, it becomes increasingly clear that environment and genes matter, perhaps equally, in the preparation of girls and boys for their reproductive and societal roles. In the following section, we explore respective influences in more detail.

Factors Relevant for Sex Differences in Emotion

Environment

Of the environmental factors contributing to sexual differentiation, parenting has received the most attention to date. It has been explored by observing the interactions between parents and their children, by assessing parenting styles through parent self-reports, and by asking individuals to recall how their parents interacted with them. Across these different approaches, some fairly consistent patterns emerged. Most prominent among them are the findings that parents discuss emotions more frequently and that these discussions tend

FIGURE 13.4 Prenatal Testosterone Influences Toy Preferences

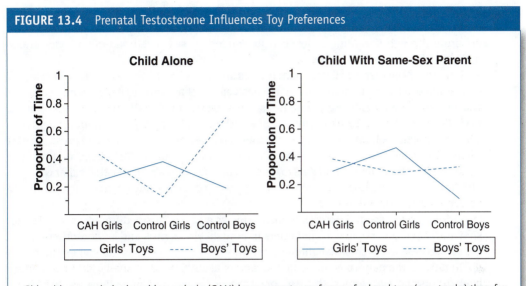

Girls with congenital adrenal hyperplasia (CAH) have a greater preference for boys' toys (e.g., trucks) than for girls' toys (e.g., dolls). This pattern seems largely independent of whether they are by themselves or whether they are with their same-sex parent.

Source: "Prenatal Hormones and Postnatal Socialization by Parents as Determinants of Male-Typical Toy Play in Girls With Congenital Adrenal Hyperplasia," by V. L. Pasterski, M. E. Geffner, C. Brain, P. Hindmarsh, C. Brook, and H. Melissa, 2005, *Child Development, 76,* pp. 264–278.

to be more complex or varied, with girls than with boys (Adams, Kuebli, Boyle, & Fivush, 1995; Dunn, Bretherton, & Munn, 1987; Kuebli, Butler, & Fivush, 1995; Kuebli & Fivush, 1992). Additionally, parents seem to engage differently with girls and boys when they discuss the events and emotions of others—as, for example, in the context of storytelling. With girls, parents tend to be warmer and more involved than with boys (Fabes et al., 1994).

Apart from these general emotion effects, there are also emotion-specific effects. For example, sadness, in particular, is discussed more frequently with girls than with boys (Adams et al., 1995; Kuebli & Fivush, 1992); and, if expressed by girls, it attracts greater parental attention (Chaplin, Cole, & Zahn-Waxler, 2005). Additionally, parents are more likely to tackle the causes of sadness with girls than with boys (Cassano, Perry-Parrish, & Zeman, 2007). Anger, another emotion potentially affected by parenting, is more likely to be a topic of discussion with boys (Fivush, 1989). Moreover, parents punish boys more frequently than they do girls, and the amount of punishment—especially when it is physical— has been shown to positively predict the child's level of physical aggression (Kuppens, Grietens, Onghena, & Michiels, 2009).

Although these effects are interesting and speak for a role of parenting in the development of sex differences, they are inconclusive as to what exactly this role is. It is possible that parents simply cater to the child's perceived needs and aptitudes. If true, parenting would be an expression of sex differences rather than a cause for them. Alternatively, how-ever, cultural norms and the parents' own biological predispositions may be infused into offspring through parenting styles. If true, gender- or sex-typed parenting styles create male- and female-typical minds.

Supporting the first possibility (parenting as an expression of sex differences) is research on cognitive development. Girls begin to speak earlier than boys, and they acquire a larger vocabulary more quickly (Berglund, Eriksson, & Westerlund, 2005; Huttenlocher, Haight, Bryk, Seltzer, & Lyons, 1991; Zhang, Jin, Shen, Zhang, & Hoff, 2008). Additionally, girls are a bit more talkative than boys; and, when they talk, they are more likely to express support for and agreement with an interaction partner (Leaper & Smith, 2004). Boys, on the other hand, are a bit more likely than girls to demand or criticize in their speech (Leaper & Smith, 2004). These and other existing differences between girls and boys may induce parents to treat them somewhat differently.

Supporting the second possibility (parenting as a cause for sex differences) is research showing that mothers differ from fathers in how they treat girls and boys. Mothers report greater distress when their daughters experience negative emotions than when their sons do. In fathers, the pattern is reversed (Cassano et al., 2007). Additionally, fathers are more likely to discuss emotions with their sons than with their daughters (Suveg et al., 2008). Thus, cultural norms or the parent's own biological predispositions may produce stronger parental bonds to same-sex as compared to opposite-sex children, thereby promoting the development of sex-specific emotional styles.

Further support for the second possibility comes from research demonstrating causal links between parenting and offspring development in nonhuman animals. In rodents, the frequency with which dams groom and lick their pups has been shown to affect the expression of genes in the brain and thus to shape emotion mechanisms in the offspring (Chapter 4). Pups of caring dams have better regulated stress responses (Champagne et al., 2008; Liu et al., 1997) and, in the case of females, turn out to be more caring mothers than pups of noncaring dams (Champagne & Meaney, 2001). That this is due to the licking and grooming rather than to genetic similarities between mother and offspring was shown by placing offspring with surrogate mothers providing high and low levels of tactile care (see Chapter 14, Figure 14.4).

Extrapolating these findings to humans suggests that the differential treatment human infants receive as a function of sex could affect infant development. Moreover, sex differ-ences that emerge in childhood and sustain into adulthood could be driven by parents raising girls and boys according to prevailing gender stereotypes or based on their own biological predispositions. However, because experiments confirming these suppositions are ethically problematic, they remain for the present just that—suppositions.

Genes

Genes that are relevant for sex differences in emotion are located on the sex chromosomes X and Y. Normally developing individuals receive one X chromosome from their mother and either one X or one Y chromosome from their father. Fetal sexual differentiation depends on the presence or absence of the Y chromosome. If present, this chromosome initiates the development of testes. If absent, development follows the default building plan, which is that of female sex characteristics.

Testes, once developed, begin to produce testosterone, the main male sex hormone. Prenatally, this production peaks between weeks 8 and 24 of gestation and during this time kick-starts the development of male-typical characteristics throughout the body. As such, it also affects brain development and produces mental differences between male and female offspring (Hines, 2011).

Original insights into these mechanisms came from research in guinea pigs (Figure 13.5). The administration of testosterone to pregnant females was found to affect genital development and sexual preferences in the offspring (Phoenix, Goy, Gerall, & Young, 1959). Offspring that were genetically female and were given testosterone prenatally developed male genitals and showed male-typical sexual behaviors such as mounting. Similar results were obtained in many other species, suggesting that the role of prenatal testosterone for masculinization is fairly universal and extends to our own species. Importantly, however, and as mentioned before in this chapter, the exact form of masculinization differs between species and thus needs to be considered in isolation.

In humans, it is challenging to study the role of prenatal testosterone for the development of a male-typical body and mind. Researchers cannot simply manipulate testosterone levels, as is done in nonhuman animals. Instead, they have to rely on natural variation by exploring healthy infant boys and girls as well as infants with known hormonal abnormalities. Albeit indirect, evidence from this research (Garcia-Falgueras & Swaab, 2008) confirms some of the findings from nonhuman animals that link prenatal testosterone to structural brain differences between males and females (Döhler et al., 1984; Jacobson, Csernus, Shryne, & Gorski, 1981). It also implicates testosterone in some of the psychological sex differences discussed elsewhere in this chapter that concern social preferences, aptitudes, and emotional responses (Hines, 2011).

Although the Y chromosome seems most critical for sexual differentiation, information on the X chromosome is also relevant. This has been shown by examining the social and emotional functioning of girls with Turner syndrome (TS), a genetic defect characterized by only one fully intact X chromosome. Researchers have identified differences between TS girls who inherited their intact X from the father and those who inherited their intact X from the mother (Skuse et al., 1997). Girls with the paternal X scored better than girls with the maternal X on a social cognition test including items such as "lacking an awareness for other people's feelings" or "difficult to reason with when upset." Moreover, compared to the latter group, the former group's performance was more similar to that of healthy girls, who had both paternal and maternal X chromosomes. Additionally, TS girls with the paternal X were more different than those with the maternal X from healthy boys who had only a maternal X chromosome. This suggests that genes on the paternal X chromosome make a special contribution toward feminizing the mind (Marco & Skuse, 2006).

Sex and the Brain

Male and female brains look quite similar. Apart from differences in overall brain volume, which relate to differences in body size, the brains of men and women share the same

FIGURE 13.5   Sexual Behaviors Depend on Prenatal Testosterone

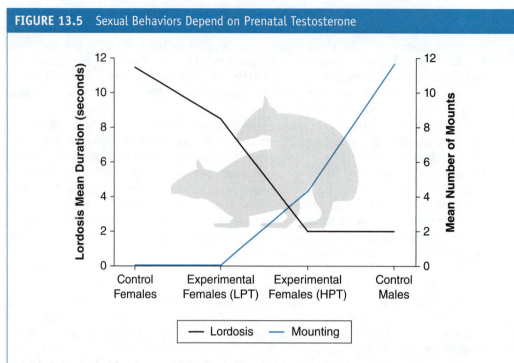

Lordosis is a typical female sexual behavior during which an animal arches its back and makes its genitals accessible from behind. Mounting is a typical male sexual behavior during which the animal climbs on top of another animal. Both behaviors are displayed by both sexes, but to different degrees. Moreover, females whose mothers received testosterone during pregnancy are less likely than female controls to show lordosis and more likely to show mounting. Data in the above figure come from a study using adult guinea pigs. Experimental females were exposed to low prenatal testosterone (LPT) and high prenatal testosterone (HPT). Mothers of the former group received an initial 1 mg of testosterone between Day 10 and 27 after conception and then 1 mg every 3 or 4 days until the end of pregnancy. Mothers of the latter group received an initial 5 mg of testosterone followed by a daily dose of 1 mg. Both experimental and control animals were sex-sterilized shortly after birth. Behavioral observations were made within a 12-hour period once the animals reached adulthood.

Source: "Organizing Action of Prenatally Administered Testosterone Propionate on the Tissues Mediating Mating Behavior in the Female Guinea Pig," by C. H. Phoenix, R. W. Goy, A. A. Gerall, and W. C. Young, 1959, *Endocrinology, 65,* pp. 369–382.

structures and overall organization. Thus, at a first glance, the organ that produces sex differences in feeling, thinking, and behavior seems suspiciously sex-neutral. This first glance, however, is deceiving. Closer inspection reveals structural differences at a finer level that undoubtedly contribute to the emergence of male and female minds.

Some of these differences concern the relative contribution of certain tissues, substances, or structures to overall brain volume. For example, compared to men, women have proportionally more gray matter, the tissue containing primarily cell nuclei (Gur et al., 1999). In contrast, men have proportionally more white matter, the tissue containing myelinated

FIGURE 13.6   Sex Differences in Gross Brain Morphology

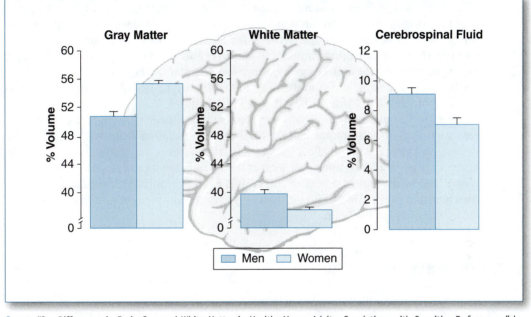

Source: "Sex Differences in Brain Gray and White Matter in Healthy Young Adults: Correlations with Cognitive Performance," by R. C. Gur, B. I. Turetsky, M. Matsui, M. Yan, W. Bilker, P. Hughett, and R. E. Gur, 1999, *The Journal of Neuroscience, 19*, pp. 4065–4072.

neuronal axons, as well as more cerebrospinal fluid (Gur et al., 1999; Figure 13.6). In addition to these gross morphological differences, there are also differences in the relative size of many brain structures, including those relevant for emotions. Among other differences, women have smaller amygdalae, but greater anterior cinguli and orbitofrontal cortices than men do (Goldstein et al., 2001).

While the relative size of certain brain tissues, substances, and structures may influence mental processes, other aspects of the brain may be as or perhaps more important. One of these aspects concerns how the different brain structures are connected and can hence communicate with one another. Researchers assess such connectivity by examining white matter fiber tracts or the extent to which there exist regional correlations in brain metabolism. The former is referred to as structural connectivity, whereas the latter is referred to as functional connectivity.

With respect to structural connectivity, explorations revealed that the corpus callosum, the white matter tract connecting left and right hemisphere, is larger in men than in women (Gong, He, & Evans, 2011). Nevertheless, overall interhemispheric connections appear to be stronger in women than in men (Duarte-Carvajalino et al., 2012; Jahanshad et al., 2011). Additionally, women show greater overall cortical connectivity with the underlying cortical networks having more nodes, shorter path lengths, and, thus, greater efficiency (Duarte-Carvajalino et al., 2012; Gong et al., 2011).

With respect to functional connectivity, examinations of resting state or default network activity revealed interesting differences. The default network comprises several structures including medial prefrontal and medial temporal cortex that are active when participants are at rest. Rest in this case does not mean that participants are sleeping. It simply means that they are not performing a specific task and hence probably engage in self-referential processing or mind wandering (Anticevic et al., 2012; Buckner, Andrews-Hanna, & Schacter, 2008; Gruberger, Ben-Simon, Levkovitz, Zangen, & Hendler, 2011).

When men and women rest in this way, they differ in the laterality of the default network (Kilpatrick, Zald, Pardo, & Cahill, 2006; Tian, Wang, Yan, & He, 2011). Men show greater right lateralization, especially for connectivity between the right amygdala and areas such as the sensorimotor cortex, striatum, and thalamus (Kilpatrick et al., 2006). Women, on the other hand, show greater left lateralization, especially for connectivity between the left amygdala and areas such as the hypothalamus and the subgenual cortex, a region below the frontal aspect of the corpus callosum (Kilpatrick et al., 2006). Thus, when men and women mind-wander, their amygdala activity synchronizes differently with activity elsewhere in the brain.

SEX DIFFERENCES IN EMOTION

In line with the identified differences in brain structure and function, researchers discovered a number of differences in the emotional experiences of men and women. These differences concern early aspects of an emotional episode, such as the way men and women appraise events in their environment or, phrased differently, in what they find important and why. They also concern later aspects, such as the proclivity to feel certain emotions and to express these emotions in certain ways. In the following section, we examine early and late emotion aspects separately.

Emotion Elicitation—How Sex Shapes the Appraisal of Emotion Antecedents

Personal experience probably taught you that men and women have decidedly different tastes. For example, men are often more interested than women in sports, technical gadgets, and motorized vehicles. Women, in contrast, often have greater appreciation for pets, fashion, and cooking. Thus, although men and women may experience the same emotions, they differ in the events and objects that cause these emotions. The same events or objects may be appraised very differently by each sex. Although the number of such instances may be high, only a few concrete examples have been subjected to scientific scrutiny.

Risks are one of them. On average, men are less likely than women to appraise something as risky, and when they do, they take greater joy in facing the risk. This is evident from the traditional division of labor and the tasks typically fulfilled by men (e.g., large-game hunting, mining; Murdock & Provost, 1973). It is also evident in more modern phenomena such as

gun ownership or risky driving. Men are more likely than women to own a gun (http://www
.statisticbrain.com/gun-ownership-statistics-demographics). Additionally, they perceive
risky driving as affectively more positive, less harmful, and less likely to cause accidents
than women do (DeJoy, 1992; Rhodes & Pivik, 2011). Notably, sex differences in the appraisal
of risk appear to be largely independent of social upbringing (Hardies, Breesch, & Branson,
2013) and are greater when men are in the company of other men than when they are in
the company of other women (Fischer & Hills, 2012).

This male peer effect was demonstrated in a computer-based experiment using the Balloon
Analogue Risk Task (BART; Lejuez et al., 2002). The task requires participants to pump-up
virtual balloons and enables them to gain money for each pump as long as their balloon
remains intact while pumping (Fischer & Hills, 2012). In the study, participants were assigned
a BART team member with whom their earnings would be shared. The number of pumps per
unexploded balloon was used as a measure of risk taking. This number was greater in male
as compared to female participants. Additionally, male participants were greater risk takers
when teamed up with another male than when teamed up with a female. Female participants,
in contrast, showed the same level of risk taking irrespective of their partner's sex. Thus, emotion elicitation under risk differs for men and women, and this difference is exaggerated in
men in the company of same-sex peers.

Another antecedent that men appraise more positively than women is sex. Compared
to women, men more readily endorse premarital and casual sex (Oliver & Hyde, 1993), take
greater pleasure engaging with pornographic material (Bradley, Codispoti, Sabatinelli, &
Lang, 2001), and have more positive attitudes toward sex (Fisher, White, Byrne, & Kelley,
1988; Geer & Robertson, 2005). This was shown using explicit self-report surveys as well
as implicit measures such as the Implicit Association Test (IAT; Geer & Robertson, 2005;
Chapter 6).

In an IAT variant used to study sex differences, participants classified words into sexual/
nonsexual and positive/negative categories by pressing one of two response buttons
(Figure 13.7). In a "sex-positive" condition, one button was used for sexual and positive
words and the other for nonsexual and negative words. In a "sex-negative" condition, one
response button was used for sexual and negative words and the other for nonsexual and
positive words. Performing both conditions in separate blocks, men showed comparable
reaction times, suggesting that they had no preexisting verbal biases. However, women
were faster during the second block, when it comprised the sex-negative as compared to
the sex-positive condition. In other words, it was easier for them to switch button assignment when sex words were previously paired with positive responses than when they
were previously paired with negative responses. Thus, women but not men showed an
appraisal bias, indicating that they automatically evaluate sex-related words as negative
(Geer & Robertson, 2005).

Apart from differences in the appraisal of risk and sex, men and women have different
concerns about the infidelity of a romantic partner. Compared to women, men are more
strongly affected if their partner had sexual intercourse outside the relationship. Compared
to men, women are more strongly affected if their partner committed emotional infidelity
and formed a new romantic attachment (Duntley & Buss, 2012; Graham-Kevan & Archer,
2009; Kuhle, 2011; Sagarin, Becker, Guadagno, Wilkinson, & Nicastle, 2012). Because these

FIGURE 13.7 Exploring Implicit Attitudes to Sex

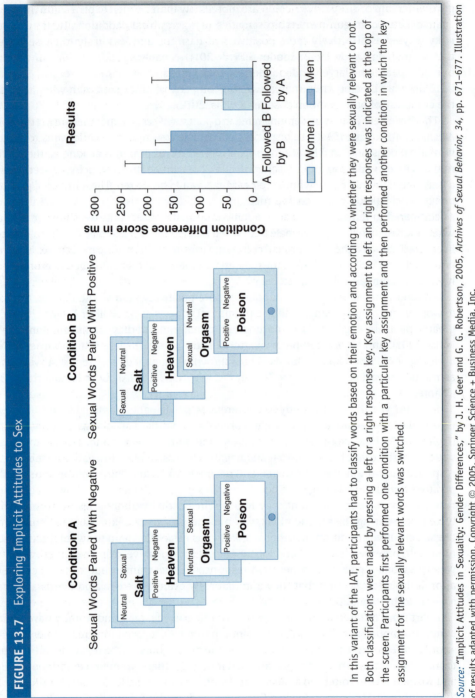

In this variant of the IAT, participants had to classify words based on their emotion and according to whether they were sexually relevant or not. Both classifications were made by pressing a left or a right response key. Key assignment to left and right responses was indicated at the top of the screen. Participants first performed one condition with a particular key assignment and then performed another condition in which the key assignment for the sexually relevant words was switched.

Source: "Implicit Attitudes in Sexuality: Gender Differences," by J. H. Geer and G. G. Robertson, 2005, *Archives of Sexual Behavior, 34*, pp. 671–677. Illustration of results adapted with permission. Copyright © 2005, Springer Science + Business Media, Inc.

differences are more pronounced in hetero- as compared to homosexual individuals and for infidelity with heterosexual as compared to homosexual partners, it seems that reproductive interest is critical here. Men having no easy means to ascertain their parentage of a child, and women being dependent on the men's commitment to childcare, face somewhat different issues when negotiating a relationship.

A last sex difference that shall be mentioned here concerns interest in the physical and the social world (Graziano, Habashi, & Woodcock, 2011; Woodcock et al., 2013). When asked to indicate how much they would enjoy fixing their watch, observing the workings of a machine, or breeding rare tropical fish, men typically indicate greater enjoyment than do women. In contrast, for activities such as eavesdropping on a conversation, chatting with a homeless person, or comforting a stranger, women typically indicate greater enjoyment than do men. Thus, generally speaking, men are more interested in things, whereas women are more interested in people.

The latter, in particular, has been corroborated by empirical studies showing that, compared to men, women express greater concern for others, especially children (Proverbio, Riva, Zani, & Martin, 2011; Proverbio, Zani, & Adorni, 2008; Sander, Frome, & Scheich, 2007; Schirmer, Chen, Ching, Tan, & Hong, 2013; Seifritz et al., 2003); are more likely to attempt mind reading (Skuse et al., 1997), and experience greater emotional benefits from being with loved ones (Guerra, Sánchez-Adam, Anllo-Vento, Ramírez, & Vila, 2012). For example, using a startle paradigm, researchers showed that individuals startle less from a loud noise when looking at the pictures of a loved one as compared to an unfamiliar individual. Importantly, this reduction in startle was significantly greater in women than in men for both romantic and nonromantic love (Guerra et al., 2012; Figure 13.8). Because some of these social effects have been linked to genes on the X chromosome (Skuse et al., 1997) and female sex hormones such as estrogen (Schirmer et al., 2013), it seems they have a biological and thus a possible evolutionary origin.

Although some of the work discussed in this section implies biological or evolutionary explanations for sex differences in the appraisal of certain emotion antecedents, this does not mean that socialization and cultural practices are irrelevant. Their role, albeit rarely investigated, becomes clear if we consider known variations in the above antecedents across different human populations.

For example, there are traditional societies in which women engage in risky and male-typical activities such as hunting. One such society is the Agta people of the Philippines, in which all-female hunting groups are common and boast greater success than all-male hunting groups (Goodman, Griffin, Estioko-Griffin, & Grove, 1985). The appraisal of social partners also varies between cultures. As discussed in the next chapter, some societies are considered interdependent because they promote strong concern for others in both men and women (Markus & Kitayama, 1991). Last, there are cultural differences in how romantic relationships are formed and defined. In some societies such relationships are arranged by the couple's family, whereas in others they are left up to the individuals. In some societies relationships require marriage and may be polygamous, whereas in others they may be extramarital and strictly monogamous. Undoubtedly, this and other variation in how men and women divide labor, define social responsibility, and forge family bonds influence how they appraise their environment.

FIGURE 13.8 Sex Differences in the Relevance of Positive Social Stimuli

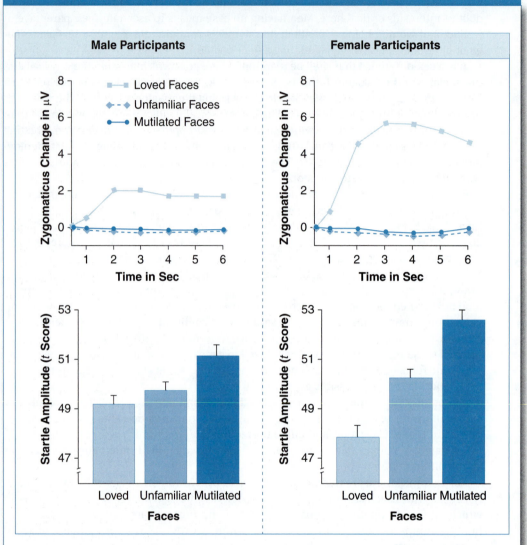

In this study, participants saw images that were combined with startle probes (i.e., a sudden loud noise). Recordings from the zygomaticus major muscle indicated that images of loved ones elicited more smiling in women than in men. Additionally, these images more effectively suppressed the startle response (here measured as eye-blink reflex) in women than in men.

Source: "Viewing Loved Faces Inhibits Defense Reactions: A Health-Promotion Mechanism?" by P. Guerra, A. Sánchez-Adam, L. Anllo-Vento, I. Ramírez, and J. Vila, 2012, *PLoS ONE, 7,* p. e41631.

Emotional Response—How Sex Shapes Emotions in Mind, Body, and Behavior

A popular stereotype is that women feel emotions more frequently and more intensely than do men (Barrett, Robin, Pietromonaco, & Eyssell, 1998; Robinson, Johnson, & Shields, 1998). Again, reality is more complicated than that. As mentioned earlier, emotion elicitation shows multifaceted sex differences in that the sexes are differently predisposed toward certain events, objects, and actions. Some antecedents are more emotionally salient to women, whereas others are more emotionally salient to men. Additionally, sex differences in emotional responding are faceted in that they differ for different emotions and the ways in which these emotions affect mind, body, and behavior. The following paragraphs describe these differences in more detail.

Mental Responses

The mind aspects of an emotional experience have been explored by asking participants to report feelings provoked by emotional stimuli or to recall the frequency and intensity with which such feelings are experienced in daily life. Although some of these studies accord with the popular stereotype of women being more emotional than men (Barrett et al., 1998; Tobin, Graziano, Vanman, & Tassinary, 2000), most studies don't. Instead, they suggest that sex differences in the subjective feeling aspects of emotions are affect or emotion specific.

Negative affect and emotions. Most negative emotions seem subjectively more relevant to women than to men. In an analysis of affective responses to negative images from the International Affective Picture System (IAPS), women reported stronger feelings of displeasure and greater arousal than did men (Bradley et al., 2001). A closer look at the negative emotions that produced these sex differences highlighted fear (Bradley et al., 2001; Fischer et al., 2004), sadness (Bradley et al., 2001; Hess et al., 2000; Simon & Nath, 2004), and disgust (Bradley et al., 2001; Curtis, Aunger, & Rabie, 2004). Notably, anger seems comparable between the sexes (Archer, 2004; Bradley et al., 2001; Fischer et al., 2004; Simon & Nath, 2004).

Researchers warn that sex differences in self-reports have to be interpreted cautiously. Methodological limitations open loopholes for potential alternative explanations. One of these explanations is that men and women differ in their ability to label or verbalize emotions. On average, women appear to be better at this than men (Levant, Hall, Williams, & Hasan, 2009), which may produce differences in verbal self-reports. Additionally, men and women differ in their ability to recall emotional events from episodic memory (Barrett et al., 1998; Seidlitz & Diener, 1998). Hence, such events may seem more prevalent to women than to men and bias their emotion ratings. Last, emotional self-reports may be influenced by internalized gender stereotypes. If true, differences between men and women might reflect these stereotypes rather than true sex differences in emotional experiences (Robinson et al., 1998).

Addressing these concerns is possible by complementing self-reports with other research approaches that evoke emotions in the lab and that assess emotional responses implicitly through their impact on mental functions such as attention, memory, or decision making. Results from these approaches provide some support for the observations concerning self-reported negative emotions.

An example of this is a study in which participants operated a driving simulator while occasional images popped up on their windscreen (Figure 13.9). Compared to neutral images, negative images slowed down the driving of women but not the driving of men (Lewis-Evans, de Waard, Jolij, & Brookhuis, 2012). This suggests that, to women, the negative images were emotionally more salient and captured attention more effectively.

Surprisingly, however, in the typical lab setting, women do not necessarily remember negative images better than men do. It seems that the safety of this setting encourages them to disengage from negative content after the initial alerting effect has worn off (Glaser, Mendrek, Germain, Lakis, & Lavoie, 2012). In line with this, different results are obtained during exposure to stress that cannot be avoided. For example, when asked to immerse one hand into painfully cold water, women but not men show a stress-induced facilitation for memorizing negative visual content studied prior to the cold procedure (Felmingham, Tran, Fong, & Bryant, 2012). Thus, with appropriate tests, negative memories appear to be affected by sex.

Positive affect and emotions. Unlike negative emotions, positive emotions appear more subjectively relevant to men than to women. An analysis of subjective responses to positive IAPS images implied stronger feelings of pleasure and arousal in male as compared to female participants (Bradley et al., 2001). A similar pattern also emerged in studies that assessed the recollection of emotions from the participants' life. Here, men were more likely than women to report pride or happiness (Hess et al., 2000; Kitayama, Markus, & Kurokawa, 2000; Simon & Nath, 2004; but see Steptoe, Wardle, & Marmot, 2005).

Notably, however, a closer look into the specific situations that produce positive states suggests that these patterns are not universal. Risk (Rhodes & Pivik, 2011) and sexual settings (Bradley et al., 2001; Geer & Robertson 2005) provoke more positive emotions in men than in women. In contrast, nonsexual social settings provoke more positive emotions in women than in men, including what some have termed "friendly feelings" (Kitayama et al., 2000), gratitude (Kashdan, Mishra, Breen, & Froh, 2009), or love (Bradley et al., 2001).

To date, relatively few efforts have been made to study sex differences in implicit emotion responding to positive information. Moreover, available results are somewhat mixed. Using the IAPS, memory for pleasant images was found to be comparable in men and women (Glaser et al., 2012). Taking a look at erotic information specifically, however, revealed sex differences. Initially, women seem more easily distracted than men when confronted with erotic stimuli (Geer & Bellard, 1996). Eventually, however, their memory for erotic stimuli is poorer, possibly because they disengage from them. Instead, they better remember love or emotional bonding–related information (McCall, Rellini, Seal, & Meston, 2007).

Also in the context of decision making, a greater relevance of positive affect or reward in men as compared to women received mixed support. Some researchers using the Iowa Gambling Task (Chapter 10) found that men acquire the most advantageous gambling strategy more quickly than women do. This was attributed to men placing greater emphasis than women on the long-term payoffs they receive (van den Bos, Homberg, & de Visser, 2013). However, others have failed to observe this effect and instead found that testosterone levels predict an increased tendency to make disadvantageous choices (Stanton, Liening, &

FIGURE 13.9 Sex Differences in Driving Speed in the Context of Negative and Neutral Images

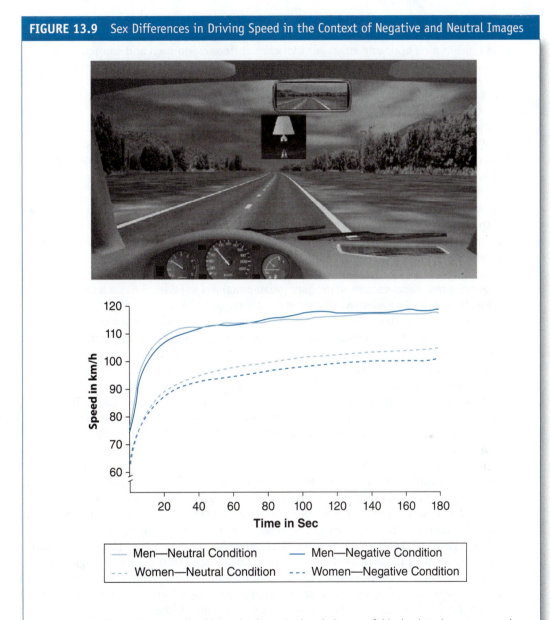

Participants in this study operated a driving simulator. On the windscreen of this simulator images occurred that could be neutral or negative. Women drove at slower speeds than men. Additionally, they were slower in the context of negative relative to neutral images. This difference was absent in men.

Source: "What You May Not See Might Slow You Down Anyway: Masked Images and Driving," by B. Lewis-Evan, D. De Waard, J. Jolij, and K. A. Brookhuis, 2012, *PLoS ONE, 7*, p. e29857.

Schultheiss, 2011). This essentially opposite result was linked to a male preponderance for risk. Possibly, prospective rewards and luring risks exert different pulls in the Iowa Gambling Task, promoting opposing strategies that cater differently to men and women. The exact nature of these differences, however, needs to be further defined.

Bodily Responses

Naturally, any mental changes associated with an emotion have a biological substrate. They emerge from specific processes or signaling patterns within the central and peripheral nervous system. Investigating these patterns has corroborated basic findings from self-reports and cognitive assessments while adding some interesting twists.

Negative affect and emotions. Looking at negative affect in general revealed greater bodily responses in women than in men. Using a wide variety of negative pictures as stimulus material, researchers found sex differences in brain activity. This included women showing greater activity than men in the amygdala, the hypothalamus, and the cerebellum (Domes et al., 2010; Stevens & Hamann, 2012; Figure 13.10). Additionally, sex differences emerged indicating that negative stimuli produce greater changes in heart rate and a greater startle reflex in women than in men (Bradley et al., 2001).

Looking at the different negative emotions separately suggests that sex differences arise again primarily for fear, sadness, and disgust. As was observed for mental processes, bodily processes of fear are enhanced in women relative to men. Relevant research demonstrating this includes electrical stimulation of the medial temporal lobe, a procedure done in patients undergoing surgical therapy for drug-resistant epilepsy. This preparatory procedure was found to elicit more fear responses in women than in men (Meletti et al., 2006), suggesting that, in women, neuronal tissue associated with fear is more widely distributed and/or more efficiently connected and activated. In line with this possibility, women show greater amygdala activity, skin conductance, and heart rate changes in the context of fear than men do (Hubbard et al., 2011; Labouvie-Vief, Lumley, Jain, & Heinze, 2003; Williams et al., 2005). Moreover, they demonstrate further enhancement of bodily responses when threats are encountered against the backdrop of stress that already elevated their cortisol levels (Merz et al., 2010).

Notably, however, not all threat excites women more than men. Threat that arises from human or animal attack reverses sex differences in certain bodily responses. For example, the amygdala activates more in male as compared to female brains (Schienle, Schäfer, Stark, Walter, & Vaitl, 2005). While this may indicate that physical aggression frightens men more than women, another explanation is that men find such aggression more provoking or challenging than women do. Moreover, for them it may be more likely to trigger emotions other than fear, motivating approach rather than avoidance.

Sadness is another negative emotion that reveals fairly consistent sex differences. Research that explored bodily responses in sadness identified both arousing/sympathetic and inhibitory/parasympathetic components that likely reflect distress and despair aspects of sadness, respectively (Chapter 8). Tapping into the distress aspects, researchers observed that increases in skin conductance and heart rate are greater in women than in men (Benenson et al., 2013; Eisenberg et al., 1988; Fernández et al., 2012). Tapping into the despair aspects, researchers observed a reduction in body temperature. Apparently, being

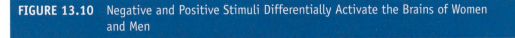

FIGURE 13.10 Negative and Positive Stimuli Differentially Activate the Brains of Women and Men

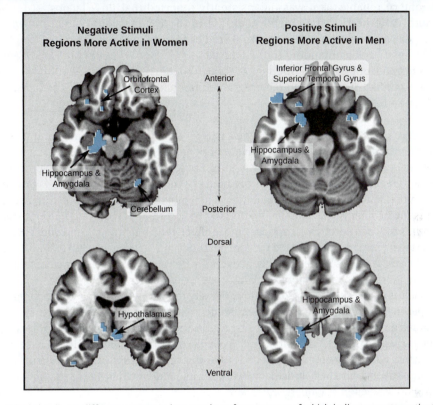

For negative stimuli, sex differences emerge in a number of areas, most of which indicate greater activation in women than in men. The latter effects are illustrated on the left. For positive stimuli, sex differences emerge in a number of areas, most of which indicate greater activation in men than in women. The latter effects are illustrated on the right.

Source: Reprinted from *Neuropsychologia*, 50, J. S. Stevens and S. Hamann, "Sex differences in brain activation to emotional stimuli: A meta-analysis of neuroimaging studies," 1578–1593, Copyright 2012, with permission from Elsevier.

sad and lonely makes people—and women, in particular (Kunzmann & Grühn, 2005)—feel cold (IJzerman et al., 2012). Last, neuroimaging research of sadness revealed sex differences. When sad, brain activations are more widespread in women than in men (Kinoshita et al., 2012).

A last set of negative emotions that received considerable attention in the study of sex differences are disgust and its social variant, contempt. Recall that disgust is subjectively more relevant to women than to men, as indicated by self-reports. In line with this, some researchers showed that disgusting stimuli provoke corresponding sex differences in skin conductance, with women showing greater increases than men do (Rohrmann, Hopp, & Quirin, 2008). Nevertheless, this difference may not be very strong or reliable, as it was inconsistently reported (Balzer & Jacobs, 2011; Meissner, Muth, & Herbert, 2011; Schienle et al., 2005). More consistent so far are sex differences at the level of the brain. Here, several studies found that women more strongly activate a range of areas, including the insula (Aleman & Swart, 2008) and its extension into lateral prefrontal cortex (Aleman & Swart, 2008; Caseras et al., 2007). However, contempt, unlike disgust, again reverses sex differences and leads to greater activity in men (Aleman & Swart, 2008).

Positive affect and emotions. As is the case for negative emotions, men and women differ in their bodily responses for positive emotions in a way that largely confirms the mentioned behavioral findings and self-reports. Erotic stimuli and competitive or risky rewards evoke greater autonomic and brain-related effects in men as compared with women.

In the context of erotic stimuli, this was demonstrated through measures of skin conductance (Bradley et al., 2001). Additionally, the presentation of startle probes showed that erotica reduced defensive responses more effectively in men than in women. Related neuroimaging research highlighted the amygdala (Stevens & Hamann, 2012; Wrase et al., 2003) and visual areas as more strongly active in male than in female participants (Sabatinelli, Flaisch, Bradley, Fitzsimmons, & Lang, 2004; Wrase et al., 2003).

Autonomic responses to competitive or risky rewards were explored in betting or gaming experiments. In a betting experiment, student participants watched a horse race and were offered the opportunity to bet course credits on a suspected champion. Regardless of whether they accepted the bet, the heart rate of male participants was greater than that of female participants while watching the race. A similar effect was also evident at the end of the race, irrespective of whether participants were betting and whether the betting participants had won or lost (Seifert & Wulfert, 2011).

In gaming experiments, participants were exposed to various scenarios ranging from simple slot-machine-type games (Op de Macks et al., 2011), where rewards depend purely on chance, to more sophisticated games, such as those involving the inflation of virtual balloons mentioned earlier in this chapter (Lighthall et al., 2012). Across these scenarios, the brain's reward system was activated, including ventral and dorsal aspects of the striatum (Hermans et al., 2010; Hoeft, Watson, Kesler, Bettinger, & Reiss, 2008; Lighthall et al., 2012; Op de Macks et al., 2011). Moreover, corroborating the results on horse betting, these activations were greater in men than in women, and they positively correlated with testosterone (Hermans et al., 2010; Op de Macks et al., 2011).

However, sex differences in the bodily responses during positive emotions don't always favor men. With the right antecedents, women activate their peripheral and central nervous systems similarly or more strongly than men do. As already suggested by behavioral studies and self-reports, the antecedents that are "right" for women concern emotional bonds with others. Stimuli or events indicative of such bonds accelerate the female heart more than the male heart (Bradley et al., 2001). Additionally, they reduce female as compared to male defensive responses more effectively (Guerra et al., 2012).

At the level of the brain, bond-related stimuli, like other rewards, excite the dopaminergic system, and this excitement differs between women and men (Azim, Mobbs, Jo, Menon, & Reiss, 2005; Spreckelmeyer et al., 2009). This was shown using a delayed incentive task in which participants were presented with a cue indicating the kind of reward participants would receive when hitting a button fast enough (Spreckelmeyer, Kutas, Urbach, Altenmuller, & Munte, 2006). When fast responses were rewarded with verbal praise, female participants showed greater striatal activity than did male participants. However, when fast responses produced monetary gains, this sex difference was reversed (Figure 13.11). Thus, it seems that the striatum and associated dopaminergic activity support positive states of both men and women. The initiation of this support, however, depends on the kind of reward and how it appeals to the sexes.

Behavioral Responses

Sex differences in the behavioral responses to emotions are prominent for emotional expressions as well as more large-scale behaviors such as the fight-or-flight response.

Facial expressions. For emotional expressions, researchers found that, in line with existing stereotypes and somewhat contrary to the mental and bodily measures discussed above, women tend to be more expressive than men, irrespective of emotion. This is evident from facial muscle activity recorded while participants viewed negative and positive IAPS images (Bradley et al., 2001). In the context of negative images, women were more likely than men to activate the corrugator muscle located between the eyes and involved in frowning. In the context of positive images, women were more likely than men to activate the zygomaticus major and the orbicularis occuli muscles indicating a greater readiness to smile. The only exception here was positive images with erotic content, which, in women only, activated the corrugator instead.

That in general women frown more than men accords with existing sex differences in the experience of negative emotions. However, that they smile more is contradicting. Yet it is a finding that was noted by many researchers (LaFrance, Hecht, & Paluck, 2003). Numerous studies identified a sex bias for smiling (LaFrance et al., 2003), and some found this bias to emerge early in development. In one such study, yearbook photos in schoolchildren revealed that girls smile more than boys starting in the sixth grade (Wondergem & Friedlmeier, 2012).

Different explanations were advanced for this phenomenon. One of them links smiling not to happy feelings, but to dominance and status (Hess, Adams, & Kleck, 2005). Cultural norms, so the argument goes, produce an imbalance in status and make women relatively dependent. As a consequence, women, more than men, show signs of affiliation and submission, with smiling being one of these signs (Chapter 7).

Yet other explanations are equally viable. For example, sex differences in smiling may reflect evolutionary pressures arising from sex-typed reproductive roles and the division of labor. Possibly, these pressures shaped facial expressions to be differently threatening and affiliative in the two sexes. Support for this possibility comes from an examination of male and female facial features (Becker, Kenrick, Neuberg, Blackwell, & Smith, 2007). Female inner

FIGURE 13.11 Sex Differences in the Processing of Monetary and Social Rewards

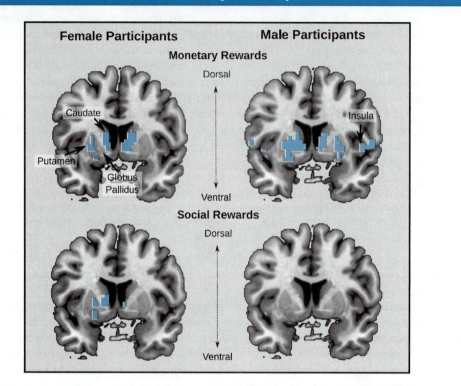

In a study by Spreckelmeyer and colleagues, participants performed a speeded response task during which fast responses could produce either monetary or social rewards. The anticipation of monetary rewards activated dopaminergic structures in the basal ganglia of both men and women. However, the activations in men were larger and encompassed the insula. The anticipation of social rewards (i.e., praise) also activated dopaminergic structures, but in women only.

Source: "Anticipation of Monetary and Social Reward Differently Activates Mesolimbic Brain Structures in Men and Women," by K. N. Spreckelmeyer, S. Krach, G. Kohls, L. Rademacher, A. Irmak , K. Konrad, T. Kircher, and G. Gründer, 2009, *Social Cognitive and Affective Neuroscience, 4,* pp. 158–165.

eyebrows are less bushy and appear less bent down than do male inner eyebrows (Figure 13.12). Also, women's lips are fuller and their jaws rounder, making the mouth region look more relaxed. Thus, even when expressing neutrality, the average woman appears somewhat more happy and approachable than does the average man (Becker et al., 2007).

Related to this, and as we have seen earlier, women tend to care more about others and to derive greater pleasure from affective bonds than men do. Hence, their greater propensity to smile may simply be an expression of this. Moreover, this expression may be shaped equally by past evolutionary mechanisms and today's cultured environments.

FIGURE 13.12 Facial Features of Prototypical Caucasian Male and Female Faces

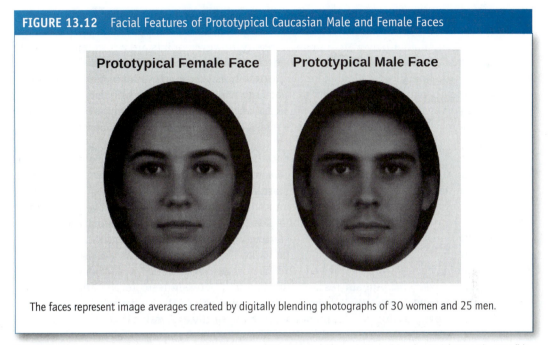

Prototypical Female Face   **Prototypical Male Face**

The faces represent image averages created by digitally blending photographs of 30 women and 25 men.

Source: Reprinted by permission from Macmillan Publishers Ltd: "Effects of Sexual Dimorphism on Facial Attractiveness," by D. I. Perrett, K. J. Lee, I. Penton-Voak , D. Rowland, S. Yoshikawa, D. M. Burt, S. P. Henzi, D. L. Castles, and S. Akamatsu, 1998, *Nature, 394,* pp. 884–887. Copyright © 1998.

Gross behavior. Apart from emotional expression, the sexes differ in how readily they engage in more large-scale emotional behaviors. Of these behaviors, aggressive acts stand out. Compared to women, men are significantly more likely to engage in physical violence. According to the U.S. Bureau of Justice Statistics (http://bjs.ojp.usdoj.gov) there are 3.5 times more male than female offenders committing hate crimes defined as violent acts directed against out-group individuals based, for example, on their religion, ethnicity, or sexual orientation. Moreover, for homicides the number of male offenders soars to 8.5 times the number of female offenders.

Empirical research within noncriminal populations corroborates these sex differences. Studies relying on self- and other-report techniques fairly consistently show that the average man is more ready to aggress than is the average woman (Archer, 2004; Cross & Campbell, 2011; Knight, Guthrie, Page, & Fabes, 2002). Although this difference declines in the context of more minor aggressive acts or verbal assault, it nevertheless remains significant (Knight et al., 2002). Thus, some researchers were able to explore it experimentally in the lab under conditions of minor provocation and relatively mild forms of retaliation.

A paradigm that meets these conditions is the **Point Subtraction Aggression Paradigm** (PSAP; Cherek, Moeller, Schnapp, & Dougherty, 1997). Here, participants gain points by pushing a particular button, and their total number of points at the end of the task determines their overall success. Sometimes, gained points disappear and the participant is told that another player stole them. In reality, however, points are not stolen but simply deducted by the experimenter. When their points are threatened, participants can subtract points from the alleged thief by pressing an additional button. Any subtracted points, however, are not added to the participant's account, which makes them costly as they must be traded off against the opportunity to increase one's own points. As might be expected, men are more likely than women to sacrifice task success and to avenge a perceived affront (Carré, Putnam, & McCormick, 2009).

While the exact causes for sex differences in aggression are still debated, it is certain that they are at least partially biologically mediated. Nonhuman and human research provides substantial evidence for a role of testosterone. In rodents, injections of testosterone increase the frequency and violence with which subjects attack another animal in their cage (Bronson & Desjardins, 1968; Pinna, Costa, & Guidotti, 2005). This effect seems mediated by the GABAergic system. Testosterone reduces GABAergic transmission, thereby dampening inhibitory activity within the brain (Pinna et al., 2005). As a consequence, the threshold decreases for a perceived affront to trigger aggression.

In line with this, human research draws a link between testosterone and aggression (Archer, Birring, & Wu, 1998). For example, women with CAH who have male levels of testosterone early during development are more physically aggressive than are healthy controls (Mathews, Fane, Conway, Brook, & Hines, 2009). Testosterone also correlates with aggressive behavior in the point subtraction aggression paradigm (Carré et al., 2009) as well as with the brain's response to threatening stimuli such as angry faces (Stanton et al., 2011). Additionally, it has been linked to impulsivity. A person's testosterone level positively predicts the number of responses to no-go trials on a go/no-go task (Bjork, Moeller, Dougherty, & Swann, 2001). With increasing testosterone, the likelihood that a to-be-withheld response on no-go trials is wrongly executed increases. This corroborates the notion that testosterone's effect on aggression arises indirectly, through the dampening of the brain's inhibitory mechanisms.

Emotion Regulation—How Sex Shapes an Individual's Attempts to Manage Emotions

Because the behavioral responses triggered by an emotion may conflict with long-term interests, individuals frequently engage in emotion regulation (Chapter 11). Research on the role of sex for emotion regulation has focused primarily on negative emotions or stress. Relevant studies relying on self-reports typically indicated that men regulate less than women do. Moreover, they found that if men regulate, they do so preferentially by seeking instrumental means to solve problems, by blaming others (Zlomke & Hahn, 2010), by disengaging themselves from the emotional episode, or by taking substances of abuse (Nolen-Hoeksema, 2012).

Women share with men a subjective preference for instrumental coping but also favor other emotion regulation strategies, including rumination and social support (Kaiseler, Polman, & Nicholls, 2012; Nolen-Hoeksema, 2012; Tamres, Janicki, & Helgeson, 2002; Zlomke & Hahn, 2010). Compared with men, women are more likely to endorse the discussion of emotions with others and the request for help and comfort as useful actions (Gentzler, Kerns, & Keener, 2010; Kaiseler et al., 2012; Tamres et al., 2002).

Brain research underlines these differences. When asked to regulate emotional responses to an experimental stimulus, men and women engage different neuronal networks, implying that their regulation strategies differ (Mak, Hu, Zhang, Xiao, & Lee, 2009). Brain activations in male participants appear most pronounced for dorsal and lateral prefrontal cortex as well as for anterior cingulate cortex. In contrast, the brain activations of female participants focus more ventrally, in orbitofrontal regions.

These differences change when participants are asked to regulate their emotions specifically using cognitive reappraisal, a technique by which a stimulus is reinterpreted to make it seem less negative (McRae, Ochsner, Mauss, Gabrieli, & Gross, 2008). Under these conditions, women show greater activity than do men in both dorsal and ventral aspects of the prefrontal cortex as well as in the ventral striatum known to be relevant for pleasurable feelings. Men, in contrast, demonstrate a greater reduction of activity in the amygdala (Figure 13.13), possibly reflecting a reduction in perceived threat or emotional significance.

Together, these findings give a tentative picture of sex differences in the brain processes of emotion regulation. Women seem to regulate negative emotions by trying to change them into positive emotions, whereas men seem to subdue their emotions. However, in light of other research raising difficulties in the identification of brain-based regulation networks (Chapter 11), these sex differences need further scientific scrutiny.

Sex differences in emotion regulation have been linked to differences in how women and men respond to stress. In addition to the traditional fight-or-flight response, researchers have identified a **tend-and-befriend response** that promotes social affiliation (Dawans, Fischbacher, Kirschbaum, Fehr, & Heinrichs, 2012; Smeets, Dziobek, & Wolf, 2009; Taylor, 2006). Specifically, tend-and-befriend coping refers to stress-induced affiliative behaviors directed at creating or maintaining social bonds that are reproductively important (e.g., caring for offspring) or that may aid in times of need (e.g., relatives, allies). As such, the tend-and-befriend response overlaps with the emotion regulation mechanisms that involve social support.

Biologically, the tend-and-befriend stress response is mediated by the release of oxytocin, an anxiolytic and stress buffering hormone that promotes affiliative tendencies (Chapters 4 and 12). Because estrogen stimulates the release of oxytocin and the transcription of oxytocin receptor genes (Gabor, Phan, Clipperton-Allen, Kavaliers, & Choleris, 2012; Jezová, Juránková, Mosnárová, Kriska, & Skultétyová, 1996; Lischke et al., 2012), the contribution of oxytocin to stress is greater in women than in men. Moreover, it has been hypothesized that whereas fight-or-flight mechanisms dominate in men, tend-and-befriend mechanisms dominate in women (Taylor, 2006). This hypothesis receives support from the fact that men are more likely than women to aggress and are less likely to emotion regulate with strategies that involve social support.

CHALLENGES FOR RESEARCH ON SEX DIFFERENCES IN EMOTION

The goal of this chapter was to review the literature on sex differences in emotion in a relatively coherent, easy-to-understand way. Because of this goal, findings that conflict with prevailing

FIGURE 13.13 Sex Differences in Emotion Regulation

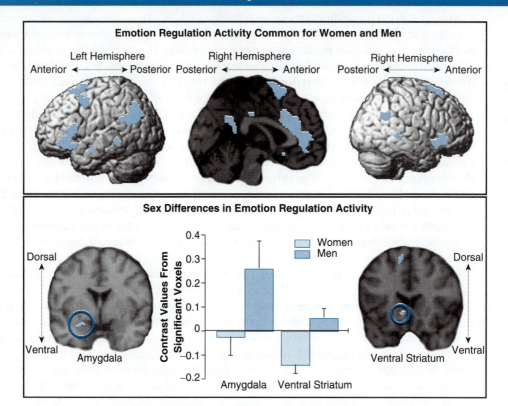

When asked to reinterpret a negative stimulus as to reduce its emotional impact, men and women engage largely overlapping neural networks including parts of the lateral and medial prefrontal cortex, parietal and temporal regions, and the basal ganglia. These areas are illustrated in the upper panel of the figure. The lower panel shows areas for which researchers find sex differences. In the amygdala, emotion regulation effects (perceive normally minus reappraise) are greater in men than in women. Specifically, men show greater activity in this structure when perceiving a negative stimulus normally than when attempting to reappraise it. In the ventral striatum, emotion regulation effects are greater in women than in men. Here, women show greater activity when reappraising a negative stimulus than when perceiving it normally.

Source: "Gender Differences in Emotion Regulation: An fMRI Study of Cognitive Reappraisal," by K. McRae, K. N. Ochsner, I. B. Mauss, J. J. D. Gabrieli, and J. J. Gross, 2008, *Group Processes Intergroup Relations, 11,* pp. 143–162. Copyright © 2008 by Sage. Reprinted by permission of Sage.

theories were occasionally omitted and the complexity and ambiguity of this literature reduced to a simple narrative. Yet the number of conflicting findings is not negligible, and ignoring them would mean losing valuable insights into the minds of men and women. Moreover, there may be particular reasons why some findings deviate from prediction—reasons that are relevant for existing theories. The following paragraphs offer some clues to help explain inconsistent results and to better understand the factors that may produce them.

Hormonal changes. One significant obstacle is that rather than being fully fixed, many sex differences depend on current hormonal levels. Specifically, they vary as a function of male and female sex hormones that show not only inter- but also intra-individual variations. Female sex hormones, in particular, change dramatically on a day-to-day basis in the course of a woman's menstrual cycle. Before considering how these changes may affect sex differences, let's take a look at exactly what happens.

The menstrual cycle can be divided into a follicular and a luteal phase. The follicular phase spans across the first 14 days of the cycle, during which the follicles in the ovaries mature. At the beginning of this phase, the woman menstruates and the sex hormones estrogen and progesterone are at a low. Toward the end of the follicular phase, estrogen rises and with it other hormones that cause a mature follicle to rupture and to release its egg into the Fallopian tubes for fertilization. During the luteal phase, estrogen remains relatively high; progesterone rises and will stay elevated until the end of the cycle and the beginning of menstruation (Figure 13.14).

Cyclic changes in hormonal levels play an important role in female emotions. For example, the normal advantage for the detection of threat is increased during the luteal as compared to the follicular phase (Masataka & Shibasaki, 2012). Additionally, memory for emotionally negative information is better (Ertman, Andreano, & Cahill, 2011), and the rewarding effects of certain drugs are lower (Terner & de Wit, 2006). The latter observation has been attributed to estrogen and progesterone facilitating dopaminergic function (Ossewaarde et al., 2011). The decline of these hormones at the end of the luteal phase and the onset of menstruation has been described as causing a short period of dopaminergic withdrawal. Moreover, this withdrawal has been proposed to be responsible for the decreased mood that many women experience at this point in time (Ossewaarde et al., 2011).

Given these dramatic cycle-dependent changes, research that fails to consider cycle information runs the risk of producing null-results or sex effects that, unbeknownst to the experimenters, are hormone-dependent.

Social versus nonsocial stimuli. Another obstacle in the research on sex differences concerns the stimulus material that experimenters use to elicit an emotion. This material may comprise nonsocial events such as a startling sound, an electric shock, or images of food. But it may also comprise social events such as a crying infant, an injured adult, or a fearful facial expression. At present, researchers treat these two kinds of stimuli interchangeably and sometimes even mix them within a single experimental condition. This, however, is problematic, as the sexes differ in their interest in the physical and the social world (Graziano et al., 2011; Woodcock et al., 2013). As we have discussed earlier, on average, men are more interested in things, and women are more interested in people.

That these differences are critical for the study of emotions is self-evident. Moreover, studies that use things to evoke emotions are bound to produce different results than studies that use people or social information to evoke emotions. For example, a startling sound

FIGURE 13.14   Human Menstrual Cycle

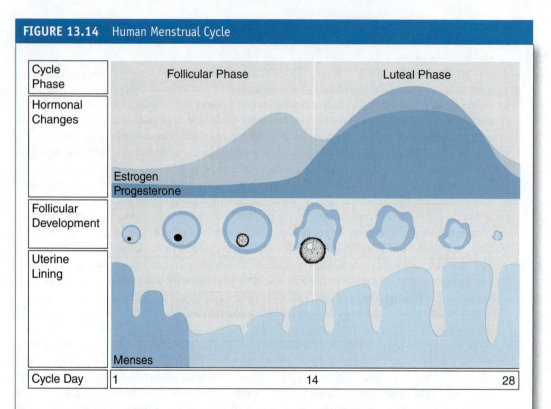

The human menstrual cycle can be divided into a follicular and a luteal phase, each of which is characterized by specific hormonal and structural changes (follicular development, uterine lining). During the follicular phase, the uterine lining is removed, estrogen increases, and the follicles ripen. During the luteal phase, a ripe follicle releases an egg into the Fallopian tubes, where it can be fertilized. Uterine lining increases in preparation for a potential pregnancy.

may be more effective than a fearful face in eliciting fear in men, whereas the opposite may be true in women. Although such a direct comparison between inanimate and animate emotional stimulation has rarely been done (but see Schirmer, Simpson, & Escoffier, 2007), much research has explored sex differences for socioemotional information. This research supports the idea that most emotions communicated by others affect women more than men. Specifically, women tend to recognize these emotions more accurately (Hall, Hutton, & Morgan, 2010) and to integrate them more readily with ongoing mental processes (Schirmer et al., 2013; Schirmer, Striano, & Friederici, 2005).

Thus, to further our understanding of how the sexes differ with respect to emotions, future research will need to consider the previously mentioned obstacles and be more meticulous in controlling participant and stimulus characteristics.

SUMMARY

Sexual differentiation represents nature's solution to the problem of how to maximize reproductive success. Sperm, which are relatively cheaply produced and able to roam far and wide, illustrate the benefits of small gametes. Eggs, which are richly endowed, illustrate the benefits of large gametes. To leverage on these benefits and to compensate for associated costs, individuals that produce sperm or eggs are sexually dimorphic. They differ in how they look, how they represent their environment, and how they behave.

Whether and to what extent sex matters for human thinking and feeling was and is hotly debated. While most researchers admit sex effects on body build, physical strength, and sexual orientation, not all accept the idea that sex impacts seemingly nonsexual aspects of the mind. Thus, some see the different thinking and feeling in men and women as arising from genetic and hormonal factors, whereas others point to gendered environments.

In line with both positions, evidence accumulated for innate and environmental influences on the mental development of men and women. One of the innate factors concerns prenatal testosterone that is dependent on genes on the Y chromosome. One of the environmental influences concerns parenting styles that differ for girls and boys. Research points to a complex interplay between innate and environmental factors showing that biological predispositions can shape an individual's developmental context (e.g., elicit different parenting) and that developmental context regulates the expression of biological predispositions (e.g., by influencing gene expression).

Together, genes and environment shape male and female brains and prepare each sex for their respective reproductive and societal roles. Relevant for the topic of emotions are sex differences in the morphology as well as the structural and functional connectivity of "emotion regions" such as the amygdala. Together, these sex differences underpin sex differences in the evaluation of emotion antecedents as well as sex differences in emotional responding.

Some emotion antecedents that men and women appraise differently include situations that entail risk, opportunities for sexual intercourse, infidelity, and interactions with nonsexual social partners. Differences in emotional responding include the mental changes triggered by emotion antecedents, bodily changes, and behaviors. With a few exceptions (e.g., anger), women appear to feel negative emotions more strongly than men. In contrast, positive emotions, particularly if they arise from sexual stimulation and risk, are felt more keenly by men. An exception here are positive emotions that arise from affectively relevant bonds; these seem more relevant to women than to men.

Sex differences observed in the mental or bodily aspects of emotions don't fully map onto the sex differences in emotional expression and behavior. In particular, women appear to be facially more expressive than men, irrespective of emotion. Men, however, are more likely than women to respond behaviorally in the context of anger or provocation. Across many measures, men were found to be more aggressive than women, and this difference could be linked to the sex hormone testosterone.

Emotion regulation also differs between the sexes. In general, women report regulating emotions more often than men do. Moreover, if they regulate they tend to prefer somewhat different strategies. While both sexes share a tendency to use instrumental coping and to solve the situation that caused negative emotions, women differ from men in that they are more likely to ruminate and to seek social support. The latter strategy has also been referred to as a tend-and-befriend coping response and contrasted with the fight-or-flight response more typical for men.

Although existing research allows us to roughly characterize emotional differences between men and women, many questions remain. To tackle these questions, it will be important to step back and consider methodological issues that have hitherto been ignored. Some of these include hormonal changes that vary within participants as well as the specific antecedents used to elicit emotions.

THINKING CRITICALLY ABOUT "EMOTIONS AND SEX DIFFERENCES"

1. Can you see parallels between how parents interact with boys and girls and how adult men and women differ in their emotions? To what extent do you think are these latter sex differences caused by parenting styles?

2. In many species, males are more aggressive than females. What other emotional aspects (mind, body) may account for these behavioral differences? How may they have been adaptive in the course of evolution?

3. Self-report studies suggest that women regulate their emotions more than men do. What might cause these results?

MEDIA LIBRARY

BBC documentary on Bruce Reimer: http://www.bbc.co.uk/sn/tvradio/programmes/horizon/dr_money_prog_summary.shtml

Research documentary on sex differences in math: http://archive.sciencentral.com/2009/09/10/girls-vs-boys-at-math

Simon Baron-Cohen talks about sex differences in the interest for things versus people: http://tedxtalks.ted.com/video/Autism-Sex-and-Science-Simon-Ba;search%3ABaron-Cohen

Melissa Hines talks about sex and gender: http://www.thebrainandthemind.co.uk/The_Films/Film5

Emotions and Culture

Much of what we know about human emotions stems from a relatively select group of people who have been referred to as the citizens of WEIRD nations—meaning nations that are Western, educated, industrialized, rich, and democratic (Henrich, Heine, & Norenzayan, 2010). Apart from being "weird," research participants from these nations typically also live in urban environments, are young, and are currently undergoing college education. Thus, major findings regarding emotions are limited to a small, highly homogenous group and cannot easily be generalized to humans as a whole.

Cross-cultural research is an attempt to address this issue. With origins in anthropology and, later, adoption by psychology, linguistics, and neuroscience, it explored a wide array of human societies and provided substantial evidence for variation in basic psychological phenomena. Thus, studying this variation seems necessary if we are to understand the human mind.

This chapter reviews cross-cultural research that is relevant for emotions. It asks important questions, such as how we should define culture, what causes variations in culture, and how does this variation shape the mental processes underlying emotions? Because cultural research on emotion has been slowly developing, however, answers to these questions are still preliminary. Moreover, our understanding of the relation between culture and emotions remains, at present, patchy and speculative.

WHAT IS CULTURE?

Before we consider a potential role of culture for emotions, we need to concern ourselves with the meaning of culture. What are cultural building blocks, and on what basis can we distinguish one culture from another?

Answers From Cultural and Evolutionary Anthropology

Answers to these questions are still vague and conflicting. Although "culture" has been intensely investigated, the concept itself proved difficult to define (Martínez Mateo, Cabanis, Loebell, & Krach, 2012). Existing definitions have a cultural or evolutionary anthropological origin and thus differ in important ways.

Cultural anthropology concerns itself first and foremost with humans. Its definition of culture emphasizes civilization and societal artifacts or practices including language, literature, religion, law, and art. Evolutionary anthropology has a somewhat wider focus, which extends beyond our species. One of its driving questions is the evolutionary origin of culture and the potential existence of culture in nonhuman animals. The cultural definition arising from this tradition invokes adaptive advantages and biological mechanisms.

Definitions deriving from cultural anthropology have obvious face value. After all, we know that human societies possess the things we consider cultural. Perhaps less intuitive are definitions deriving from biological anthropology, which imply that culture is not an exclusively human phenomenon. Is such an implication reasonable? Research suggests that it is. Among other findings, it identified instances of cumulative learning in nonhuman animals that are akin to what we call cultural transmission in humans, and which many consider a hallmark of culture. During cumulative learning, a behavior first acquired by an individual is copied by other individuals, who maintain and potentially modify the behavior so that it is preserved and improved across several generations.

One of the first discoveries of nonhuman cumulative learning was made in the Japanese macaque (Matsuzawa & McGrew, 2008). In 1953, an individual macaque was spotted that washed a potato in a small stream prior to eating it. Subsequently, the behavior spread within the colony and was modified to washing potatoes in the ocean, presumably as a means to add salt (Figure 14.1). Other nonhuman animals showing cumulative learning include songbirds or whales that develop vocal dialects (Luther & Baptista, 2010; Rendell & Whitehead, 2001); rats that strip pinecones for consumption (Aisner & Terkel, 1992); and chimpanzees that demonstrate group-specific grooming habits, among other things (Whiten et al., 1999).

Issues With Accepting the Evolutionary Approach

Despite such evidence, however, evolutionary conceptualizations of culture remain contentious (Martínez Mateo et al., 2012; Michaels, 1995). This is because of fears that to accept culture as a biological phenomenon means to accept it as fixed and as something that could be evolved to different degrees. World history suggests that these fears are not unreasonable. In the late 19th and early 20th centuries, theories became popular that discriminated so-called primitive human cultures from more advanced ones and that offered pseudoscientific explanations for putative differences. These theories were then used to legitimate colonialism, as well as racial discrimination and persecution (Fredrickson, 2011).

Although history more than justifies the caution many exert when dealing with issues of culture, science has since advanced and excited a rethinking of the term *evolution*. Evolution is no longer seen as a progression from primitive to advanced or inferior to superior. It is seen as a process through which organisms adapt to the environments they meet. Hence, comparisons of evolutionary progress between different species or subgroups within a species are meaningless. It makes no sense to describe one group as less or more evolved, worse or better than another. Each species evolved for its own environmental niche and developed physical and/or mental adaptations best suited for that niche. Cockroaches, for example, don't have the elaborate mental life of a human. Yet they are as, if not more, successful than humans when it comes to survival and propagation—the currency of evolution.

FIGURE 14.1 Koshima Monkeys Eating Washed Potatoes

Source: Image taken by Tetsuro Matsuzawa. Reprinted with permission from "Kinji Imanishi and 60 Years of Japanese Primatology," by T. Matsuzawa and W. C. McGrew, 2008, *Current Biology, 18*(14), pp. R587–R591. Copyright © 2008, with permission from Elsevier.

Apart from changing the way we think about evolution, scientific progress changed how we conceptualize the mind. It is now accepted that all mental processes have a biological basis; that they rely on the brain and its physical and chemical mechanisms. Moreover, mental processes are no longer considered to be fixed. On the contrary, they like any other bodily processes are accepted as highly dynamic and dependent on an individual's environment. Understanding this brought us one step closer toward shaping mental functions similarly to the way we've shaped bodily functions in the context of physical exercise, diet, environmental design, or medicine over the past decades and centuries.

Taken together, scientific progress led to a rethinking of evolution and the relationship between body and mind. This rethinking should dispel some of the fears harbored against the evolutionary anthropology tradition and should lead us to consider issues of culture more rationally and responsibly than was done in the past. Moreover, it should encourage us to keep our minds open and to conceive of culture relatively broadly by integrating ideas from existing schools of thought—cultural and evolutionary alike.

A Holistic Definition of Culture

Tapping on cultural and evolutionary anthropology, this chapter defines culture as a group-specific practice that emerged from the interaction between a group and its environment. The terms *group* and *practice* are conceptualized as follows.

What is meant by "group"? The term *group* is used broadly to include subgroups within a species as well as species and higher-order biological units. The reason for this is that boundaries between these units are to some extent arbitrary. Species, for example, are not the neat categories we make them out to be, but show gradual transitions across both time and geographical regions. Hence, it is sometimes impossible to decide whether two sets of organisms are from the same or different species.

What is meant by "practice"? The term *practice* is defined with the following two considerations in mind. First, it is used to refer to all behaviors that characterize a group. In the context of human cultures, this includes things like language, cuisine, and art, as well as forms of emotion expression or upright gait. Thus, no distinction is made between practices that are learned and those that are strictly genetically determined. The reason for this is that, again, both are difficult to dissociate, and in most cases learning about one's environment and appropriate genes are necessary for a "practice" to emerge.

To appreciate this, consider the first Japanese macaque washing its potato. Probably, the primate did so by toying around with a type of food that was appealing. Moreover, it repeated the effort most likely because the result of it significantly improved meal quality and was thus naturally rewarding. In other words, without a natural predisposition to forage for food, to play, and to prefer tasty over nontasty food, the practice of washing potatoes prior to consumption would not have come about.

Second, the term *practice* is defined to include behaviors that are transmitted based on ordinary learning and imitation processes as well as behaviors whereby transmission involves genetic mechanisms. The reason for this is that in many instances genetic mechanisms like natural selection or epigenetic programming (Chapter 4) likely help in the establishment of group-specific practices and the maintenance of these practices across generations. For example, whether a particular group of rodents practices intensive grooming and licking of offspring depends on how much grooming and licking these rodents received from their own parents. However, rather than being transmitted via ordinary learning, this behavior is transmitted via grooming-induced changes in DNA expression that affect brain structure and function. At the surface, these genetic processes are impossible to dissociate from ordinary learning and imitation.

Definition considerations. By integrating cultural and evolutionary anthropological positions, the present definition of culture considers both social and biological factors as relevant and is thus fairly holistic. Being holistic is advantageous because there is little danger of missing important perspectives. At the same time, however, it may have unappealing consequences. In the present case, one may argue that including cultural and evolutionary positions makes any behavior shared among the individuals in a group a cultural phenomenon and, hence, fails to discriminate noncultural phenomena. However, as our definition focuses on *group-specific* practices, this is not a serious concern. Moreover, it is countered by the restrictions that emerge naturally from selecting groups for cultural research. These groups are typically closely related (e.g., Americans and Asians) as opposed to distantly related (e.g., humans and snails), thus helping us isolate the cultural phenomena of interest.

Another consequence of the present approach is that it defines culture as behavioral expressions and seemingly ignores mental processes. Given the title of this chapter and the

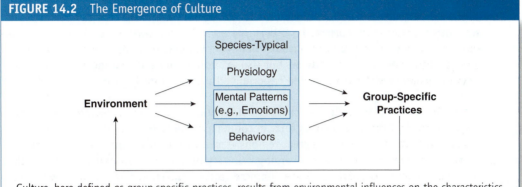

FIGURE 14.2 The Emergence of Culture

Culture, here defined as group-specific practices, results from environmental influences on the characteristics shared among the individuals of a species or group. Group-specific practices imprint on the environment so that they themselves become contributors to further cultural adaptations.

considerable research being done on the relationship between culture and emotions, one would expect that mental processes also play a role. Notably, the present definition does not rule out this possibility. Emotions and other mental processes may be relevant in leading to cultural practices and may be influenced by them (Figure 14.2). However, this does not require that we subsume them under the same conceptual umbrella. In fact, treating them separately should make it easier for us to study their reciprocal relationship.

With these considerations in mind, we may now embark on a scientific journey through landmark research and theoretical work regarding culture and emotions.

DOES CULTURE MATTER FOR EMOTIONS?

Theoretical Positions

The relationship between culture and emotions is a long-standing topic of debate. Proponents for the existence of basic emotions defend the position that emotions are universal and therefore relatively resistant to culture (Ekman, 1992; Panksepp, 1992). They acknowledge that regionally separated human populations faced different environmental challenges that produced behavioral and thus cultural differences. At the same time, however, they posit that differences in environmental challenges were too small to affect traditional life tasks or that potential changes in life tasks are too recent to have altered the biological substrate underpinning human emotions. In other words, not much has changed since humans left Africa about 120,000 years ago and distributed across the globe (Callaway, 2011).

Opposing the basic emotions position are positions that conceive of emotions as social constructions or products of culture that necessarily vary between human societies (Fisher & Chon, 1989; Harré & Gillett, 1994; Sabini & Silver, 1998). This position developed from observations of cultural disparity in emotional descriptions and the language used to characterize emotions. For example, historical studies revealed significant changes in the use of the English term *emotions* (Harré & Gillett, 1994). At the beginning of the 18th century, this term was used primarily to describe an agitated crowd. By mid-century, it was used to describe an agitated or unusually behaving individual. By the end of the 18th century, it referred not only to behaviors but also to bodily states and was increasingly romanticized and feminized as something experienced primarily during the turmoils of youth and, regardless of age, by women.

Our modern understanding of culture and emotions makes extreme interpretations of basic emotion and social constructionist accounts untenable. Humans came to inhabit very diverse environments including polar regions, deserts, or tropical rain forests. To survive in these places, humans developed diverging living styles that range from urban city dwelling to nomadic wandering and that are characterized by different relationships with living and nonliving things. As such, emotional responses to these things must necessarily be different. Yet to consider emotions a human invention would be going too far. Substantial overlap across human societies and similarities between human and nonhuman animals imply a role for evolution and a shared biological basis (Russell, 1991).

Current theories recognize this and allow emotions to have both universal and culturally varied components. However, they still differ in the degree to which they admit a role for biology and social construction. Proponents for basic emotions still weigh biology more heavily. They admit a role of social construction through an "add-on" concept called display rules (Matsumoto, 2007; Matsumoto & Hwang, 2012). Specifically, they hold that individuals acquire cultural norms about whether and how emotions should be expressed in social situations. During development, interactions with family and peers indicate what emotions are acceptable and reinforce individuals for regulating their expressions accordingly. Notably, the emphasis here is on regulating expression rather than feeling. Any changes to the latter are believed to be secondary and to result from peripheral changes only (Chapter 5). Moreover, display rules supposedly operate primarily in social settings, leaving emotions and their expression in nonsocial settings intact and ultimately universal.

A current social constructionist attempt to integrate biological determination has been to propose the existence of a neural valuation system that is shared among mammals and that produces core affect (Barrett, 2006). This core affect is understood as "a neurophysiological barometer of the individual's relation to an environment at a given point in time" (Barrett, 2006, p. 31). It returns simple values such as pleasure, pain, reward, or threat that, in humans, are interpreted by higher-order cognitive systems involved in language and the representation of conceptual knowledge. These systems, which depend on learning and are hence socially constructed, are thought to turn core affect into an emotion. According to this position, then, humans may share core affect cross-culturally. Emotions, however, are bound to be different.

Some Environmental Conditions Relevant to Culture and Cultured Emotions

Mate selection. All aspects of an environment can, in principle, shape an individual's behavior and thus contribute to the emergence of culture and cultured emotions. This begins with the individual's biological conception, which is anything but random. Apart from being determined by a potential sexual attraction between parents, social norms as to what constitutes a proper partner influence partner choice and thus the genes endowed to offspring. In many societies, partner choices are constrained by social class, economic status, religious orientation, ethnic background, and/or age, among other characteristics. Thus, genetic mixing, within these constraints, contributes to the culture of new generations (Parkinson, 2012).

Parental stress. Apart from the parents' DNA, the parents' environment shapes the developing offspring. Parental stress arising from traumatic events but also daily hassles and worries (e.g., being stuck in traffic) have proven critical here (Huizink, Robles de Medina, Mulder, Visser, & Buitelaar, 2003; Laplante et al., 2004).

Some of the mechanisms underlying this may occur before pregnancy and involve the epigenetic modification of DNA that parents pass to their children (Dias & Ressler, 2014). Other mechanisms may occur during pregnancy and relate to the mother's physiological condition. Although these latter mechanisms are still poorly understood, there is evidence that maternal stress harms the developing organism and affects emerging emotion systems. For example, it impacts mental development (Huizink et al., 2003; Laplante et al., 2004), thereby jeopardizing perceptual, analytical, and mnemonic systems that enable emotional evaluations. Maternal stress also shapes the fetal HPA axis and thus alters bodily aspects of emotions (Schuurmans & Kurrasch, 2013; Sierksma et al., 2013).

The reason why stress is relevant for the relationship between emotions and culture is because it differs between different human populations. This is evident from a comparison of the different ethnic groups living in the United States. Hispanics and African Americans have on average a lower socioeconomic status than do White Americans and, as a consequence, face greater stress (A Closer Look 14.1). Not surprisingly, this stress has been linked to developmental adversities and delays in children of Hispanic and African American mothers (Gaffney et al., 1997; Rosenthal & Lobel, 2011).

Maternal diet. Diet is another factor that differs among human populations and that is relevant for fetal development. It contains many substances that can be harmful, beneficial, or simply necessary. One of the necessary substances is choline, an essential nutrient available in most animal products such as eggs and meat. Choline plays an important role for a range of bodily functions; and, as a component of the neurotransmitter acetylcholine, it supports neural signaling (Zeisel, 2012).

Recent evidence from rodents suggests a role for choline in emotions. Compared to subjects whose mothers received a choline-sufficient diet, subjects whose mothers received a choline-enhanced diet were less impulsive and better able to deal with frustration (Cheng, Scott, Penney, Williams, & Meck, 2008). If maternal choline intake has a similar effect during human development, known population differences in choline intake (Chu, Wahlqvist, Chang, Yeh, & Lee, 2012) are relevant for existing emotional differences.

Parental care. After birth, parental care and the home environment become primary determinants for an individual's emotional development. Again, different social groups or human

A CLOSER LOOK 14.1

Wealth Matters for Health

From a global perspective, there is a positive relation between a country's wealth and the health of its citizens. Individuals living in wealthy, industrialized nations have, on average, a longer life expectancy than do individuals living in developing nations. However, as is evident in Figure 14.3, the relationship between a country's wealth and health is not exactly linear. Moreover, at the upper end on the wealth scale, the relationship ceases to exist. Does this mean that here wealth is no longer relevant?

No, it does not. Wealth remains relevant, but not so much in absolute terms and at the level of the country but in relative terms, at the level of the citizens within a country. Wealth distribution among these citizens predicts health outcomes. Citizens with greater earnings live longer than citizens with lesser earnings even when everyone has a decent living standard and access to health

FIGURE 14.3   The Relationship of Wealth and Health at the Country Level

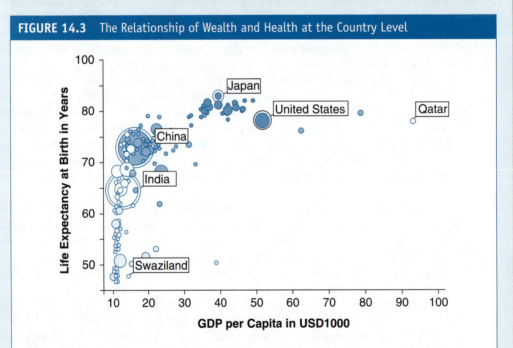

Illustrated on the X axis is gross domestic product (GDP), an index of a country's market value or economic standing. Illustrated on the Y axis is the average life expectancy for the different countries, a marker for citizen health. Circle size corresponds to country population size.

Source: Adapted from the United Nations Development Programme website (http://hdr.undp.org/en/data/explorer).

care (Wilkinson, 1992). Notably, countries with greater wealth discrepancy between the rich and the poor end up with a correspondingly greater health discrepancy and fare worse on international health measures than countries with a smaller wealth discrepancy and better social equality (Lynch et al., 2001; Pickett & Wilkinson, 2010; Wilkinson & Pickett, 2006).

Taken together, this means that both one's absolute and relative wealth matter for health. Absolute wealth enables individuals to gain access to valuable resources ranging from food and shelter to education and medical support. Relative wealth, on the other hand, enables individuals to achieve social recognition. In most cases, being wealthier than others means having a higher status and greater negotiation power in social interactions.

The reason these latter relationships are relevant is because they are central to the level of stress that individuals face in their lives. Evidence for this comes from research in both humans and nonhuman animals. In humans, researchers showed that being looked down on or being devalued by others is one of the greatest sources of stress (Dickerson & Kemeny, 2004). Moreover, there appears to be a link between such stress and poor health outcomes. Some of these outcomes are caused directly through the impact of stress on the individual's body; others result from a greater incidence of health-damaging behaviors such as smoking or drinking (Dohrenwend, 1967; Finkelstein, Kubzansky, & Goodman, 2006; Mortensen, Jensen, Sanders, & Reinisch, 2006).

In nonhuman animals, similar relationships exist. A direct link between social status and health was established in nonhuman primates. Individuals of higher rank reproduce more successfully and are healthier than individuals of lower rank in the group (Altmann, Sapolsky, & Licht, 1995; Cohen et al., 1997; Sapolsky & Mott, 1987; but see Petticrew & Davey Smith, 2012). Evidence for an indirect relationship involving health behaviors comes from work in rodents. As in humans, subordinate rodents are more likely to consume alcohol made available to them than are dominant rodents. This difference emerged after these rodents interacted and established their relative status (Hilakivi-Clarke & Lister, 1992).

Thus, both poor and rich countries need to worry about the health of their citizens. However, covering safety, nutritional, and medical needs goes only halfway toward this goal. Equally relevant is to avoid social disparity.

populations care quite differently for their offspring. In today's hunter-gatherer societies, which continue the lifestyle of humans before the introduction of agriculture 10,000 years ago, mothers spend about 90% of their time in physical contact with their newborn (Lozoff & Brittenham, 1979). In these societies, a woman typically breast-feeds for a year or more and holds or carries her child during daytime activities until the child is 3 or 4 years old.

In modern, developed societies, industrialization and the integration of women into the workforce have altered this pattern of childcare dramatically. Breast-feeding is often supplemented with or replaced by bottle-feeding, and children, instead of being carried by their mom, are sent to day-care or kindergarten, where tactile contact with the caretaker is limited by practical constraints and concerns about physical abuse.

Research in rodents and humans revealed how such differences in childcare may affect offspring development. In rodents, maternal licking and grooming were shown to influence the expression of genes in the brain and thus impact the development of brain structure and function. More specifically, such effects were demonstrated for the genetic transcription of hippocampal glucocorticoid receptors, a class of proteins involved in monitoring the activity of the HPA axis. As mentioned in Chapters 4 and 8, activation of this axis triggers the release of glucocorticoids from the adrenal gland into the bloodstream. Some of these glucocorticoids pass the blood-brain barrier and, by attaching to receptors in the hippocampus, provide feed-back about the body's arousal. This feedback induces the hippocampus to inhibit the HPA axis. Maternal licking and grooming were shown to facilitate the genetic transcription of glucocor-ticoid receptors in the hippocampus and thus to reduce stress responsiveness in offspring (Cameron et al., 2005; Champagne et al., 2008; Liu et al., 1997; see Figure 14.4).

Ethical considerations make identical investigations in humans impossible. Nevertheless, research on mother–child interactions suggests similar mechanisms. For example, interven-tions that increase bodily contact between mother and child were found to improve the child's maternal attachment as well as his or her physical health, cognitive development, and emotion regulation ability (Anisfeld, Casper, Nozyce, & Cunningham, 1990; Field, 2000; Weller & Feldman, 2003). Additionally, the analysis of postmortem human brains revealed indices for effects of childcare on gene expression that mimic the effects in rodents. Specifically, individuals who committed suicide and had a history of childhood abuse were found to have fewer glucocorticoid receptors in the hippocampus than did individuals who committed suicide without a history of child abuse and individuals whose death was not self-determined (McGowan et al., 2009).

Family size. Another aspect of the home environment that is relevant for culture and emo-tions is the number of siblings present while an individual grows up (Cameron, Erkal, Gangadharan, & Meng, 2013). It has long been known that this number is relevant for the individual's cognitive development by benefiting those with fewer siblings and a greater share of their parents' attention. More recently, evidence emerged that sibling number is also relevant for emotions. This evidence was obtained in a natural experiment based on the one-child policy instituted in China in 1979. This policy was aimed at regulating overpopulation and meant that, with a few exceptions, families could have only one child. Although still in effect, the policy has been repeatedly reviewed and declared as problematic because of behavioral changes in the one-child generation. Compared to former generations, these indi-viduals have been described as "little emperors" who lack an ability to socialize with peers.

To empirically probe these impressions, researchers subjected individuals from the one-child generation and controls born before the one-child policy to a series of economic games. In these games, participants received a monetary endowment that they could spend or invest in some way. For example, in a "trust" game (Berg, Dickhaut, & McCabe, 1995), one player was given an endowment and asked to decide whether and how much of it to pass along to an anonymous second player. The money passed on to that second player was then topped up by the experimenter, and the second player could decide whether and how much of it to return to the first player. Trust was quantified as the amount passed on by Player 1, whereas trustworthiness was quantified as the amount returned by Player 2.

FIGURE 14.4 Maternal Licking and Grooming Shape Brain Structure and Function

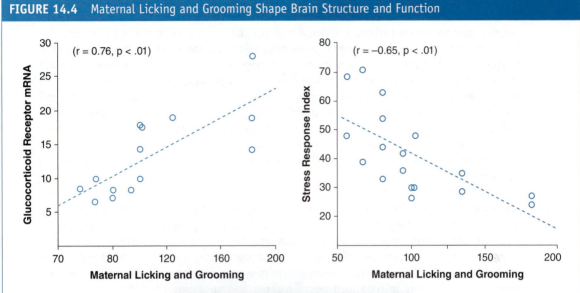

Illustrated in the upper left graph is the relationship between the frequency of maternal licking and grooming during the first 10 days of life and the expression of glucocorticoid receptor (GR) mRNA in the hippocampus as measured in adulthood. Offspring that received more licking and grooming when young have more GR mRNA and consequentially more GRs. Illustrated in the upper right graph is the relationship between the frequency of maternal licking and grooming during the first 10 days of life and an index of the animal's stress sensitivity in adulthood. The index is based on the animal's plasma corticosterone response during restraint stress.

Sources: **Both panels reflect data presented in "Maternal Care, Hippocampal Glucocorticoid Receptors, and Hypothalamic-Pituitary-Adrenal Responses to Stress," by Liu et al., 1997, *Science, 277*(5332), pp. 1659–1662. The rodent image is reprinted with permission from "Maternal Programming of Steroid Receptor Expression and Phenotype Through DNA Methylation in the Rat," by Szyf et al., 2005, *Frontiers in Neuroendocrinology, 26*, pp. 139–162. Copyright © 2005, with permission from Elsevier**

Comparing the behavior of individuals from the one-child generation with older controls revealed that those without siblings tended to be less trusting and less trustworthy than those with siblings (Cameron et al., 2013). Additionally, results from a risk game in which participants could choose to invest their endowment in a risky gamble revealed a significantly lower readiness to take risk in one-child as compared to control individuals. Together, the results from these games suggest that being an only child affects an individual's emotional evaluations by increasing the dread of threats and reducing the lure of rewards. This is reflected in the individual's personality, which becomes on average less optimistic and more neurotic (Cameron et al., 2013). Thus, societal norms and regulations regarding the upbringing of children can have substantial effects on child development and on how new generations interact with and shape the environment they find.

Disease prevalence. A last class of environmental factors that shall be mentioned here concerns pathogens. Pathogens are parasitic microorganisms such as bacteria and viruses that enter other life-forms and that may cause disease. The prevalence of pathogens and their propensity to sicken hosts differ across time and geographical region. Like other organisms, pathogens face an ever-changing environment to which they have to adapt or perish. The resulting fluctuations in pathogen pervasiveness and virulence produce corresponding fluctuations in host health and health behaviors. For example, at times or in regions with many potent flu viruses, large proportions of human populations fall ill and/or engage in behaviors that mitigate or prevent illness.

One class of these behaviors concerns the way individuals treat others. When pathogen threat is high, affective bonds to kin and one's immediate social group become stronger and individuals become more concerned about them. As a consequence, more of their behaviors are directed at maintaining these bonds. At the same time, strangers or out-group others are evaluated as affectively more negative and attempts to avoid them increase. This has been shown in studies that compared other-oriented behaviors during times of high pathogen threat, such as the SARS (Severe Acute Respiratory Syndrome) episode in 2002, with times of low pathogen threat (Fung & Carstensen, 2006). Additionally, it is evident from research mapping the prevalence of infectious diseases against a country's index of "other-orientation." The residents of countries with high prevalence of infectious disease are more concerned about their immediate social groups and less tolerant toward out-group individuals than are the residents of countries with low disease prevalence (Fincher & Thornhill, 2012; Thornhill, Fincher, Murray, & Schaller, 2010; see Figure 14.5).

Two reasons may account for this. First, in times of distress, help is more likely to come from kin or bonded individuals than from strangers. Moreover, in the evolutionary history of humankind as well as in many contemporary societies, kin and bonded individuals are the only available health insurance. Caring for them and ensuring that one is valuable to them was and is critical to ensuring one's own health (Navarrete & Fessler, 2006).

Second, out-group contact increases risk of disease. This increase results from a lesser resilience against novel pathogens carried by strangers as compared to common pathogens found within one's own social group (de Barra & Curtis, 2012; Fincher & Thornhill, 2012). An example of this is the European conquest of America, which brought many European-evolved

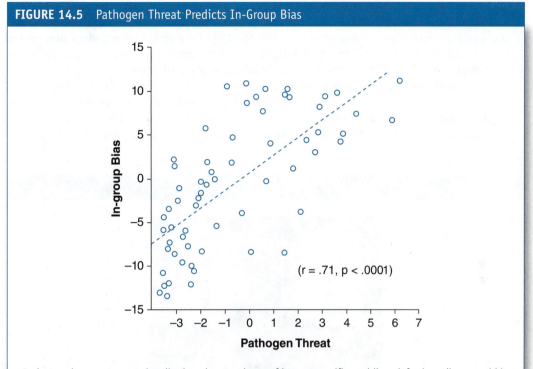

FIGURE 14.5 Pathogen Threat Predicts In-Group Bias

Pathogen threat was operationalized as the prevalence of human-specific, multihost infectious diseases within 65 nations. In-group bias was derived from measures of religiosity and strength of family ties within these nations.

Source: "Parasite-Stress Promotes In-Group Assortative Sociality: The Cases of Strong Family Ties and Heightened Religiosity," by C. L. Fincher and R. Thornhill, 2012, *Behavioral and Brain Sciences, 35*(2), pp. 61–79.

pathogens to the New World. These pathogens were relatively harmless to the European invaders but killed many of the native people who had not yet developed immunity.

The Cultured Brain

Given that an individual's ability to feel, think and behave depends on the functioning of the brain, we may consider the brain as an intermediary between the abovementioned environmental conditions and culture. In interaction with other bodily systems (e.g., cardiovascular, digestive), the brain registers environmental influences and adjusts its function accordingly. Adjustments occur at multiple levels, ranging from molecular processes that determine gene transcription and the construction of proteins to the deployment of large-scale neural networks. Together, these adjustments form the basis for the mental processes and behaviors that differentiate existing human cultures.

Insights into the relationship between brain and culture come from neuroimaging studies using structural MRI. Although still limited in number, these studies uncovered several interesting facts. First, brain shape differs as a function of ethnicity. This fact accords with the more apparent head-shape differences and failed attempts to create "cross-cultural" headware such as goggles or helmets. Chinese, for example, have rounder heads with a flatter front and back as compared to Caucasians (Ball et al., 2010). Similarly, their brains are rounder. Compared to Caucasians, the average Chinese brain is shorter on the anterior-posterior axis and longer on both the dorsal-ventral and the left-right axes (Tang et al., 2010; see Figure 14.6).

Second, there are differences in brain volume that remain even after researchers control for ethnic differences in body size. Hispanics, for example have larger brains than Caucasians and African Americans (DeCarli et al., 2008). Related to this there are size differences in individual brain structures after controlling for differences in overall brain

FIGURE 14.6   Cultural Differences in Gross Brain Morphology

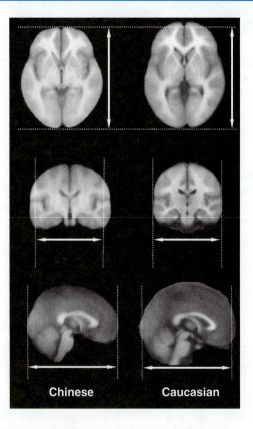

The average Chinese brain is rounder than the average Caucasian brain.

Source: Reprinted from "The Construction of a Chinese MRI Brain Atlas: A Morphometric Comparison Study Between Chinese and Caucasian Cohorts," by Tang et al., 2010, *NeuroImage, 51*(1), pp. 33–41. Copyright © 2010, with permission from Elsevier.

volume. Of primary interest for the present purpose, are structures with an acknowledged role in emotions. These include the orbitofrontal cortex, the insula, cingulate, the striatum, hippocampus, and the amygdala—all of which were identified to vary between cultures (DeCarli et al., 2008; Tang et al., 2010).

In addition to structure, function varies. Moreover, functional variation has been reported with respect to the brain structures that are recruited and the way these brain structures are connected or communicate with each other. Evidence for this has been obtained in a number of paradigms indicating ethnic differences in aspects of perception, attention, language, memory, and emotions, among other mental processes (Han & Northoff, 2008). In the context of emotional paradigms, it has been shown that compared to Koreans, Caucasian Americans activate the ventral striatum more strongly when choosing a smaller immediate reward over a larger delayed reward (Kim, Sung, & McClure, 2012). This and similar studies are further detailed later as we turn to cultural differences in emotional responding.

Taken together, research contrasting different ethnic groups on brain measures revealed evidence for the idea that different living environments alter structural and functional aspects of the brain. These alterations may emerge through genetic adaptations across multiple generations (e.g., head shape), through epigenetic modifications that are passed on from parents to offspring, or through lifetime experiences (e.g., stress). In either case, they are fundamental for the emergence of cultural differences not only between different ethnic groups but also between groups of comparable ethnicity facing disparate living conditions (e.g., economic status, technological access).

PSYCHOLOGICAL DIMENSIONS OF CULTURE

The preceding comparison of different ethnic groups seems an obvious starting point for research on culture. Yet it provides a relatively limited perspective. For one thing, changing political boundaries and migration make it difficult to define ethnicity. Additionally, ethnicity inadequately reflects culture. Two different ethnic groups may vary in some but may be quite similar in other aspects of their culture. For example, Chinese and Indonesians vary in their physiognomy, language, art, and political systems, yet both practice Buddhism as a major religion and have rice as a major component of their diet. Moreover, one ethnic group may comprise subgroups that are culturally more different from each other than they are from a third "foreign" group. For example, urban and rural populations in China may be more different from each other than they are from urban and rural populations of Indonesia, respectively. Thus, studying culture based on ethnic boundaries is relatively crude.

Independence and Interdependence as Cultural Characteristics

One approach to overcome this issue has been to identify psychological dimensions that appear culturally relevant and that differentiate human subgroups (Cohen, 2009). A dimension that proved successful in this regard polarizes an individual's self-construal as independent and individualistic versus interdependent and collectivistic (Hofstede, 1980; Markus & Kitayama, 1991). An independent self-construal is one in which the individual perceives him- or herself as unique and clearly separated from others. His or her personal value derives from own thoughts, feelings, and abilities and how these help establish the individual as a self-sufficient and autonomous agent within society. An interdependent self-construal is one in which the individual perceives him- or herself as part of a group and in relation to members of that group. His or her personal value derives from the ways in which own thoughts, feelings, and abilities enhance group connectedness and help establish the group as a functional unit (see Figure 14.7).

All human societies require individuals to be both independent and interdependent. Although these forms of self-construal seem antagonistic, both are relevant for societal functioning. Independence is relevant because it enables individuals to explore and develop their own aptitudes. Naturally, not every individual is equally suited for all tasks. Identifying and leveraging on individual aptitudes thus promotes an effective division of labor, a hallmark of civilization (Kuhn & Stiner, 2006). Additionally, independence enables individuals to break new grounds. The discovery of new territories, the development of new tools, scientific advances, and artistic creations often hinge on individual efforts to overcome group norms and traditions.

Interdependence, however, is equally relevant. It is a prerequisite for the human ability to live in groups and cooperate in daily activities (Kuhn & Stiner, 2006). Traditional activities such as large-game hunting as well as modern activities such as working in a company all require that humans understand themselves as part of a larger whole and that they coordinate their behaviors for joint success. Additionally, division of labor within this larger whole establishes dependence between individuals and necessitates some amount of bonding, trust, and responsibility.

FIGURE 14.7   Independent and Interdependent Self-Construal

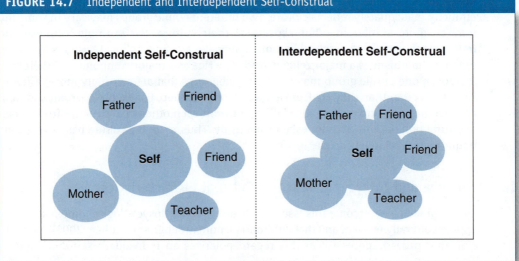

Given the importance of both independence and interdependence, existing societies must negotiate the emphasis they place on one or the other. As a result of this, some societies lean more toward independence, whereas others lean more toward interdependence. Examples of the former include many of the ethnic groups that can be found in northern Europe and that emigrated from Europe to North America. Examples of the latter include Asian nations such as China, Japan, and Thailand, as well as certain populations in Africa and South America (Markus & Kitayama, 1991).

Caveats of the Independence–Interdependence Dimension

Much research explored the independence–interdependence dimension and its impact on how people think and behave. Although proving this dimension is useful, this research also highlighted a couple of issues (Fiske, 2002; Oyserman, Coon, & Kemmelmeier, 2002).

First, it revealed that initial categorizations into independent and interdependent cultures were imprecise. Often, Westerners, defined as individuals of European descent, were considered independent and contrasted against Easterners, defined as individuals of Asian descent, who were considered interdependent. However, within these loose categories substantial variation exists on the independence-interdependence dimension.

Second, there are other psychological dimensions on which social groups vary and that may explain differences between these groups more accurately. Some of these dimensions were proposed several decades ago and include power distance defined as a group's tolerance for hierarchy; uncertainty avoidance defined as a group's effort to make its environment predictable and safe (e.g., through laws); and masculinity defined as the differentiation of gender roles (Hofstede, 1980). Other dimensions that were recognized somewhat more recently include religion, socioeconomic status, or positivity (Cohen, 2009; Lamoreaux & Morling, 2012).

Despite these alternatives, the independence–interdependence dimension has and is being used most frequently. It, therefore, plays a more prominent role than other dimensions in the following discussion of how emotions differ between cultures.

CULTURAL DIFFERENCES IN EMOTION

In line with basic emotions theory, certain events are associated with certain emotions in a similar fashion across the human population. All humans feel sad if they lose a loved one and feel joy when fate reunites them with a loved one thought lost (Ekman, Sorenson, & Friesen, 1969). Yet, in line with social constructionist accounts, this similarity is qualified by cultural differences. Initial efforts to characterize these differences have focused primarily on variation in the presence and frequency of acknowledged "Western" emotions across human societies.

Research predictions were derived from existing findings concerning the independence-interdependence dimension and associated notions about cultural differences in self-construal (Markus & Kitayama, 1991). Independent and interdependent self-construals were proposed to bias individuals toward the feeling of ego-focused and other-focused emotions, respectively. Ego-focused emotions, so the theory goes, are emotions that primarily concern the self and that are triggered by antecedents that are immediately relevant to the self. Other-focused emotions, in contrast, supposedly arise from antecedents with primary relevance for others or for the relationship that the individual has with them. Anger and pride are alleged examples of ego-focused emotions, whereas shame and guilt are alleged examples of other-focused emotions.

Research testing these predictions confirmed a role of self-construal in emotion. At the same time, however, it proved that the initial division into ego- and other-focused emotions was too simplistic. Although there is some evidence that individuals with a more independent self-construal feel anger more frequently and shame less frequently than do individuals with a more interdependent self-construal (Bender, Spada, Rothe-Wulf, & Rauss, 2012), these differences have not been consistently reported (Kitayama, Markus, & Kurokawa, 2000; Matsumoto, Kudoh, Scherer, & Wallbott, 1988; Matsumoto & Willingham, 2006).

Additionally, pride, a supposed ego-focused emotion, can be felt equally by individuals with a primarily independent self-construal and those with a primarily interdependent self-construal. What matters is the source for pride and the attribution of achievement. Individuals with a more independent self-construal feel pride more readily for own achievements, whereas individuals with a more interdependent self-construal feel pride more readily for another's achievements or the achievements of their group (Neumann, Steinhäuser, & Roeder, 2009).

Together, this and other evidence indicates that cultural differences cannot be reduced to differences in the propensity to feel certain emotions. Instead, culture is more pervasive in that it affects the very essence of how emotions are generated; how emotions affect body, mind, and behavior; and how individuals attempt to regulate them (Mesquita & Frijda, 1992). In the following section, we take a look at these emotion aspects and explore their variation as a function of culture.

Emotion Elicitation—How Culture Shapes the Appraisal of Emotion Antecedents

Emotions are triggered by objects or events that are relevant to an existing or prospective need. These objects and events are called emotion antecedents and, with a few exceptions, must be learned. Through experience, individuals come to know that certain foods are edible and tasty, that certain parts of their environment are dangerous, and that certain others are essential for their well-being. Thus, experience turns largely neutral stimuli into elicitors of an emotion. Moreover, because experience differs for individuals in different social groups, it generates cultured or group-specific modes of emotion elicitation.

Appraisal theory (Chapters 2 and 3) offers a suitable framework from which to explore and characterize these cultural effects (Mesquita & Ellsworth, 2001). Unlike other emotion theories, it provides useful psychological dimensions presumed to govern the assessment and mental representation of an emotion antecedent. The psychological dimensions refer to antecedent aspects that are appraised by individuals and whose appraisals ultimately determine whether and how strongly an emotion is elicited. Novelty, goal conduciveness, and causality are a few examples of such dimensions and are further detailed here.

Novelty

During novelty appraisal, individuals compare an emotion antecedent against existing memory content to determine whether and how frequently they have encountered the antecedent before. This appraisal is relevant in the context of culture because emotion antecedents may be absent or rare in some environments, while being plentiful in others. As such, their novelty would be appraised differently, leading to a different emotion. Although the effect of novelty appraisal on felt emotion depends on other appraisals (e.g., intrinsic pleasantness), there is some indication that novelty contributes fairly generally to emotion strength. Compared to rare or relatively novel antecedents, common antecedents are less potent in eliciting emotions because associated needs have been satisfied or because individuals have habituated to the antecedent.

Common antecedents of positive valence are likely to satisfy relevant needs and to prevent these needs from becoming urgent. A dog that has free access to food will be able to still its hunger and avoid a growling stomach. At the same time, it will experience less pleasure from seeing, smelling, or tasting the food, so the food will no longer work as a behavioral incentive. Its owner may use food with little success during dog training.

Common antecedents of negative valence may lose their effectiveness because individuals habituate to them. For example, humans habituate to the presence of certain dangers despite the fact that their need for safety remains the same (Bleich, 2003; Li et al., 2009; Rozin, 2008). Among other things, this was demonstrated in studies exploring the psychological impact of natural disasters or wars. Immediately affected individuals show a surprising emotional resilience (Bleich, 2003) and a lower risk perception than do individuals who are more distantly affected (Li et al., 2009).

Of the many emotion antecedents that show cultural effects related to novelty, one stands out. This antecedent concerns the group membership of an interaction partner and derives its importance from the fact that group membership defines social groups and discriminates in- from out-group individuals. Moreover, it specifies targets for interaction such that interactions are more likely to occur within than across groups.

Research suggests that the relative novelty of out-group interactions triggers negative emotions. Compared to in-group interactions, out-group interactions are perceived as less pleasant, the interacting individuals as less friendly, and the interaction outcomes as less satisfying (Toosi, Babbitt, Ambady, & Sommers, 2012). Additionally, out-group individuals instill more fear and less empathy than do in-group individuals (Olsson, Ebert, Banaji, & Phelps, 2005; Stanley, Sokol-Hessner, Banaji, & Phelps, 2011).

In a fear-conditioning study, out-group individuals, as defined by the individuals' ethnic background, were more readily associated with an aversive stimulus than were in-group individuals (Olsson et al., 2005). When paired with a mild electric shock, photographs of out-group individuals produced a greater elevation in bodily arousal than did photographs of in-group individuals. Moreover, while the response to in-group individuals was readily extinguished, the response to out-group individuals was relatively resistant to extinction (Figure 14.8).

Effects of social group membership on empathy were explored by presenting research participants with images that depicted others in emotional distress (e.g., during a natural disaster) or pain. Across several such explorations, neural markers of empathy were found

FIGURE 14.8 Fear Conditioning to In- and Out-Group Faces

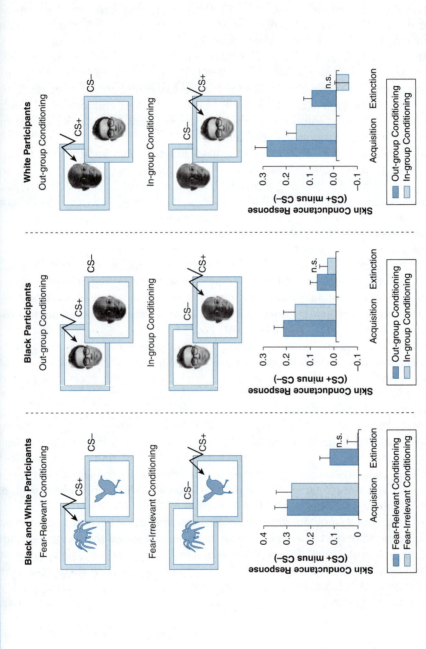

Olsson and colleagues studied fear conditioning in white and black Americans. In a baseline session, they presented naturally fear-relevant images (e.g., spider) and fear-irrelevant images to both groups of participants. In one condition, the fear-relevant images were paired with a mild shock to the participants' wrist, whereas in the other condition, the fear-irrelevant images were paired with shock. After this fear acquisition phase, the participants underwent an extinction phase in which they saw all the images again, but without the shock. In an experimental session using a similar procedure, the researchers presented faces of black and white individuals. Skin conductance responses indicated that participants fear conditioned to all stimuli. However, only fear to non-fear-relevant images and in-group faces readily extinguished. "n.s." indicates skin conductance responses that failed to differ from 0.

Sources: "The Role of Social Groups in the Persistence of Learned Fear," by Olsson et al., 2005, *Science, 309*(5737), pp. 785–787. Human images © Minerva Studio—Fotolia.com.

to emerge faster and to be stronger when participants observed others who shared their ethnic identity as compared to others who did not (Avenanti, Sirigu, & Aglioti, 2010; Cheon et al., 2011; Sessa, Meconi, Castelli, & Dell'Acqua, in press; Xu, Zuo, Wang, & Han, 2009). In line with this, there is also evidence that emotional displays are more readily recognized from in- as compared to out-group individuals (Elfenbein & Ambady, 2002).

Together, these findings have been linked to biologically prepared learning and an evolutionary advantage for shunning strangers (Olsson et al., 2005). Notably, this shunning does not depend on differences between one's own and a stranger's skin color or physiognomy. Instead, it depends on how often strangers, like this one, have been encountered before, and whether these encounters were benign or positive (Toosi et al., 2012). Individuals with numerous such encounters will be more comfortable with the stranger than will individuals without such encounters. What matters is the strangers' relative novelty.

A CLOSER LOOK 14.2

Emotion Outliers

FIGURE 14.9 New Guinea Man of the Dani Tribe

Source: Flickr/710928003 (CC BY 2.0).

Much of the research exploring cultural differences in emotion has been conducted in industrialized nations, in urban environments, and on college students. Although participants representing different cultural groups were geographically separated, they nevertheless shared many aspects of their day-to-day experiences. Hence, resultant findings provide only limited insights. More interesting and revealing in this regard are explorations of individuals living in drastically different environments, such as those of traditional societies with tribal or village lifestyles that are still found on the African continent, in the Arctic, or in the tropical rain forest.

Albeit challenging and rare, such explorations have been made by researchers traveling to and living with indigenous people. Through close personal contact, these researchers were able to document a number of interesting emotional phenomena that are at odds with the cultural norms of most developed countries. As would be expected, some of these phenomena concern emotion antecedents or the things that indigenous people find emotionally significant. For example, the Utku Eskimo experience joy from chasing lemmings, a small rodent;

(Continued)

(Continued)

they also enjoy stoning ptarmigans, a kind of bird (Briggs, 1970). Naturally, these pastimes are unheard of in warmer climates that are unsuitable for these species and that have other attractions to while away time.

Also unusual is what tickles the funny bone of the Kubo tribe in New Guinea. Kubos seem to derive pleasure from the misfortunes of their friends and family (Dwyer & Minnegal, 2008). Dwyer and Minnegal report the case of a boy who damaged one of his eyes with an exploding firestone and lost the other eye in a hunting accident. The boy became the joke of his village, and people enjoyed teasing him to no end. Dwyer and Minnegal explain this teasing as a form of self-irony arising from Kubos' interdependent self-construal. Apparently, the Kubo feel themselves intricately related to others in their group, and their teasing acknowledges that misfortunes are shared experiences that can and do affect everyone.

Apart from differing in emotion antecedents, indigenous people differ in several aspects of their emotional responses. One particularly striking example is that of "fear sleep" found in Indonesian tribes. In frightening or stressful situations such as being caught stealing, individuals from these tribes fall asleep more or less instantaneously (Warren, 2007). Possibly, this relates to an enhanced freezing response during which autonomic functions are reduced to the bare minimum (Natterson-Horowitz & Bowers, 2013).

Another interesting difference concerns how people deal with or regulate their emotions. The Fore people of New Guinea practice cannibalism as a means to deal with the death of a significant person. In other words, they eat the person for whom they are grieving (Ekman, 2012). There are also drastic cultural differences associated with the expression of frustration or anger. Some indigenous people, like the Kaluli in New Guinea, express their anger very dramatically and openly to others in their group, who both fear and admire the expression (Schieffelin, 1983). In contrast, the Utku Eskimo appear entirely void of anger. Moreover, they tend to socially exclude those who express frustration openly (Briggs, 1970).

Together, these remarkable differences nicely demonstrate the importance of environmental conditions for culture and emotion and highlight the limitations of cultural research that is focused exclusively on the industrialized world.

Goal Conduciveness

Although novelty is important in shaping emotions during in- and out-group encounters, other forms of appraisal contribute. One of them, called goal conduciveness, deals with whether and to what extent an emotion antecedent furthers personal goals. Compared to out-group encounters, in-group encounters are particularly relevant for relational goals such as the attempt to secure a romantic partner, to establish one's self among peers, or to provide for one's family. In these respects, then, in-group encounters would likely be appraised as more goal conducive than out-group encounters. As a consequence, they would have a greater propensity to elicit positive emotions and a readiness to share in the emotion of interaction partners.

Support for this was already mentioned earlier in this chapter from studies that made ethnic comparisons (Cheon et al., 2011; Toosi et al., 2012). However, because ethnic comparisons typically conflate goal conduciveness with novelty, other approaches controlling for novelty are needed.

A study that took such an approach used a minimal group paradigm in which partici- pants performed a phony personality test and were then randomly assigned to one of two "personality groups" that were color coded as red and green (Young & Hugenberg, 2010). This served to instill group identity by suggesting to the participants that their personality was more similar to individuals in their own group than to individuals in the other group. Group assignment was followed by an emotion recognition task in which participants saw facial expressions superimposed on red or green backgrounds, indicating that the faces belonged to individuals with their own or the other group's personality type. Participants were better at identifying the emotion of supposed in-group as compared to out-group individuals (Figure 14.10). Moreover, because this effect disappeared when image presenta- tions were shortened or when faces were presented upside-down, the researchers reasoned that the in-group advantage did not result from a more automatic access to the emotions of in-group individuals. Instead, they attributed it to a greater motivation to engage with in- as compared to out-group faces and the employment of different processing strategies.

Causality and Other Appraisals

Studies that investigated other types of appraisals in their relation to culture and emotions are few and far in between. This is not because these appraisals are less relevant; it is because inter- est in this matter is still young (Mesquita & Ellsworth, 2001). Moreover, the few existing studies suggest that further pursuit is promising. A study comparing individuals from Germany and Tonga, for example, revealed a role for causality appraisal defined as the attribution of responsi- bility for an event or emotion antecedent (Bender et al., 2012). Compared to Germans, Tongans have a more interdependent self-construal and are less likely to blame others for negative events. Instead, Tongans blame themselves or circumstantial factors that put others in a more favorable light. These differences in the attribution of responsibility are linked to differences in emotion. Compared to Germans, Tongans feel less anger, an emotion that results from externally caused frustrations, but more guilt, an emotion that results from personal responsibility.

Future research has to replicate and extend these results. Moreover, it will need to con- sider other appraisals concerning, for example, one's perceived ability to cope with an emo- tion antecedent, societal norms regarding responses to this antecedent, and moral values.

Emotional Response—How Culture Shapes Emotions in Mind, Body, and Behavior

Cultural differences in the appraisal of emotion antecedents necessarily translate into cul- tural differences in emotional responding. If one culture promotes appraisals of positive events as being due to the action of others, it will also promote feelings of gratitude. If, on the contrary, a culture promotes self-attribution for positive events, it will promote feelings of pride or self-satisfaction instead. Because of this relationship between appraisals and subsequent emotions, it is challenging to study the two separately. Any differences between cultures in their emotional responses may be due to appraisal differences or to differences in the responses themselves. For this reason, the following discussion should be considered a reflection of known cultural differences in emotional responses that may or may not arise from cultural differences in the processes that lead up to these responses.

FIGURE 14.10   Group Belonging Improves In-Group Emotion Recognition

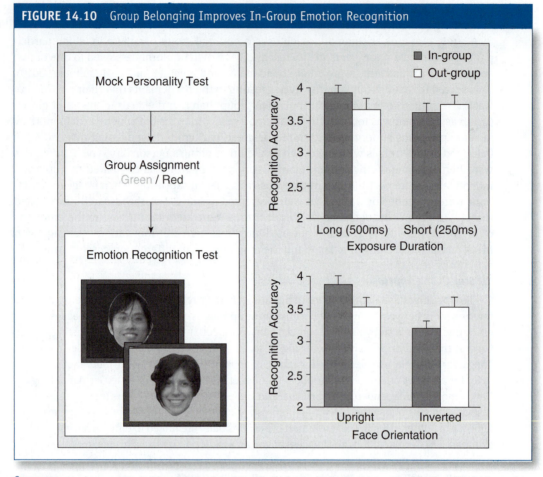

Source: Data graphs are adapted with permission from "Mere Social Categorization Modulates Identification of Facial Expressions of Emotion," by S. G. Young and K. Hugenberg, 2010, *Journal of Personality and Social Psychology, 99*(6), pp. 964–977. Copyright © 2010 by the American Psychological Association. The use of APA information does not imply endorsement by APA.

Mental Responses

One of the best studied aspects of cultured emotional responses concerns the subjective feelings emerging from emotional events. These feelings are typically assessed through questionnaires and other forms of self-report that query individuals from different social groups about the frequency and strength with which they feel certain emotions. Some results from this work were already mentioned above in an effort to illustrate the role of culture in the processing and mental representation of emotion antecedents (Bender et al., 2012; Bleich, 2003; Cheon et al., 2011; Li et al., 2009; Rozin, 2008; Toosi et al., 2012). They will not be repeated here. Instead, we look at how subjective feelings may be influenced by language and by the folk wisdom that differentiates human cultures.

When we are taught a new language, we are typically informed about the correspondence between words in our native language and words in the new language. For example, we might learn that *table* means *Tisch* in German. However, not every word in our native language has a perfect translation in the other. For some words, there may be several possibilities that fit more or less, and for other words there may be no fit at all.

Many emotion words have poor cross-linguistic correspondence. For example, the English words *happiness, surprise, anger, fear, sadness,* and *disgust* don't necessarily exist in other languages (Russell, 1991). One such instance is Tahitian, in which the word *sadness* is missing and which uses words related to feelings of bodily fatigue or illness instead (Levy, 1973). Additionally, there are many emotion words in other languages for which there exist no proper English translations. The German word *Schadenfreude* is an example. A literal translation would be "damage-joy," which means nothing to an English speaker. In German, the word is used to refer to joyful feelings that result from someone else's misfortune.

Such language disparity may have different explanations. One explanation is that only those emotions felt by individuals are linguistically expressed. Hence, emotions that are not felt, don't have a word in the individuals' language. If true, this would mean that Germans feel *Schadenfreude,* whereas English speakers do not. A second possibility is that all humans share the same emotions but differ in how they reflect on them. Emotions that confer a particular meaning within one's group may be verbally labeled to help think and talk about them. Moreover, depending on how a group conceptualizes the relationship of body, mind, and behavior, verbal labels may take different shapes. If true, all humans may feel what Germans call *Schadenfreude*; they simply differ in how they attend to and describe these feelings. Although we cannot decide between these possibilities at present, linguistic differences are informative in that they bear witness to differences in the subjective feeling of emotions.

Another aspect of culture that is relevant to the subjective feeling aspect of emotions relates to folk wisdom. Human societies differ in how they make sense of their experiences and how they deal with frustration and contradiction (Peng & Nisbett, 1999). In societies of European descent, reasoning about the world and the self is rooted in Greek philosophy and is based on simple logical deductions that enable inferences about truth or untruth. In this tradition, contradictions are not tolerated. In societies of Chinese descent, reasoning is governed by somewhat different principles. It is based on the ideas that all things are changing constantly; that they entail opposites such as strength and weakness, good and bad; and that they are connected or part of a greater whole. As such, contradictions are not only tolerated, but expected.

In line with such folk wisdom, individuals of European and Chinese descent differ in the extent to which they report feeling contradictory emotions. Individuals of European descent typically report an absence of negative emotions when they feel good and an absence of positive emotions when they feel bad. When asked, they are rarely aware of feeling both good and bad at the same time, although such awareness increases as people age (Chapter 12). In comparison, Chinese individuals don't pin the presence of a positive emotion on the absence of a negative one, and vice versa. Thus, the negative correlation between positive and negative emotions that is typically found in European individuals is nonsignificant or even positive in Chinese individuals (Kitayama et al., 2000; Miyamoto, Uchida, & Ellsworth, 2010; Shiota, Campos, Gonzaga, Keltner, & Peng, 2010). Whether this means that Europeans feel mixed emotions less frequently than do Chinese, or whether they are simply less aware of them, has to be determined by future studies. What we know for sure is that their subjective experience of mixed emotions differs.

Bodily Responses

While substantial efforts have been directed at obtaining insights into the role of culture in subjective feelings of emotions, relatively fewer attempts have been made to explore other emotion aspects such as central and peripheral nervous system changes. Moreover, the results from these attempts are still inconclusive.

A study on the central nervous system compared the responses of Americans and Koreans to reward. Specifically, participants of both nationalities were placed in an MRI scanner and presented with a series of choices (Kim et al., 2012). In these choices, two varying monetary amounts were contrasted—one amount would, hypothetically, be available today, whereas the other amount would, hypothetically, be available in a few weeks. Because the future is more uncertain than the present, most individuals prefer immediate over delayed rewards—unless, of course, the delayed rewards are significantly greater than immediate ones and outweigh the waiting costs. In line with this, the researchers found that, across participants, brain activity was greater in reward processing areas when opting for immediate as compared to delayed choices. Effect areas included the ventral striatum, amygdala, and ventromedial prefrontal cortex (Chapter 7). Importantly, looking at nationalities separately revealed that the ventral striatum effect was present in American participants only. This suggests that compared to Koreans, Americans experience a greater pull from immediate rewards (Figure 14.11).

Inquiries into the peripheral nervous system have been made using self-reports and psychophysiological assessments. Both point to the notion that response differences between individuals within a social group are greater than response differences between individuals across groups (Scherer, Wallbott, & Summerfield, 1986; Soto, Levenson, & Ebling, 2005; Tsai, Chentsova-Dutton, Freire-Bebeau, & Przymus, 2002; Tsai, Levenson, & McCoy, 2006). In other words, culture does not matter. An example of this is a study comparing Chinese and Mexican participants in a startle paradigm. Although self-reported negative emotions in response to the startle probe were weaker in Chinese as compared to Mexican participants, their peripheral nervous system responses as reflected by heart rate, blood pressure, skin temperature, and skin conductance were comparable. Thus, one may conclude that, unlike bodily responses at the level of the brain, bodily responses at the peripheral level are culturally independent.

This conclusion, however, is at odds with what we know about the relationship of the central and peripheral nervous systems. Central nervous system changes in subcortical areas such as the ventral striatum are linked to peripheral changes in arousal (Blood & Zatorre, 2001), in that the former play a major role in regulating the latter. Thus, central changes should translate into peripheral changes. That the present literature fails to reflect this may be due to the fact that brain and autonomic measures were explored in isolation and for different emotional scenarios and cultural groups. Future research must resolve this issue.

Behavioral Responses

Emotions produce varied behavioral responses that potentially differ by culture (e.g., freezing, flight, fight, choosing a reward). Most thoroughly explored today are the nonverbal signals by which humans express emotions. These signals were initially considered universal (Ekman et al., 1969; Scherer, Banse, & Wallbott, 2001). Subsequent work, however, challenged this position in the following ways.

First, a closer scrutiny of the methods of cross-cultural research revealed a bias toward cultural similarity (Russell, 1994). For example, the fact that posed rather than natural

FIGURE 14.11   Cultural Differences in the Brain Responses to Reward

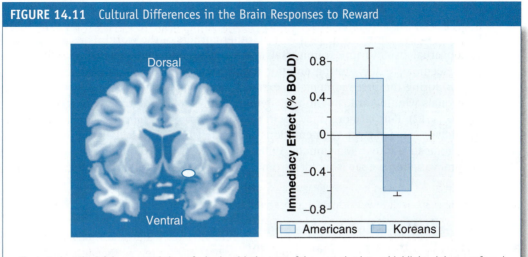

Illustrated on the left is a coronal view of a brain with the part of the ventral striatum highlighted that was found to function differently in Americans and Koreans. Only in Americans was this area more strongly activated when choosing immediate rewards as compared to when choosing delayed rewards.

Source: "The Neural Basis of Cultural Differences in Delay Discounting," by S. Kim, Y. S. Sung, and S. M. McClure, 2012, *Philosophical Transactions of the Royal Society B, 367*(1589), pp. 650–656.

expressions were used and that responses were collected in a forced-choice format were raised as problematic. Posed expressions are typically exaggerated expression prototypes that make recognition easier. They are not as variable as natural expressions. Moreover, the same expression (e.g., frustrated) may be judged differently depending on the available response choices (e.g., sad, angry).

Another issue with the initial idea of universality in emotion expression was that researchers began to find evidence for cultural differences. For example, Jack and colleagues examined the eye gaze patterns of Caucasian and Asian observers during the identification of facial emotions (Jack, Blais, Scheepers, Schyns, & Caldara, 2009). They found that Caucasians distribute their gaze evenly across the face, whereas Asians tend to focus on the eye region. Thus, it is likely that these cultures also differ in how they naturally display emotions on the face.

Evidence supporting this possibility comes from research showing better recognition of expressions from culturally familiar as compared to unfamiliar individuals (Elfenbein & Ambady, 2002). It also comes from work that identified actual expression differences. The Duchenne smile, a facial expression long thought to be culturally universal, was recently shown to vary across cultures, suggesting that aspects of this expression are learned. Specifically, the engagement of the eyes, the defining feature of a Duchenne smile, is largely absent in African Gabonese (Elfenbein, Beaupré, Lévesque, & Hess, 2007), who consider Duchenne and non-Duchenne smiles to be equally genuine or authentic (Thibault, Lévesque, Gosselin, & Hess, 2012).

Although this and similar evidence implies cultural differences in emotion expression, it does not negate the existence of substantial commonalities (Elfenbein & Ambady, 2002;

Matsumoto & Willingham, 2009; Sauter, Eisner, Ekman, & Scott, 2010). After all, the African Gabonese express happiness by retracting their mouth, relaxing their jaw, and laughing in the same way as people from other corners of the world. Thus, key aspects of nonverbal displays appear universal. Moreover, cultural elements that alter these displays seem secondary during emotional communication. They appear to be largely absent during the first moments of extreme emotions, such as those experienced by individuals winning or losing in the Olympic Games (Matsumoto & Willingham, 2009; Figure 14.12). Furthermore, they seem to emerge primarily during later moments, as individuals come to grasp their emotions and as they begin to use their expressions with communicative intent (Matsumoto, Willingham, & Olide, 2009). As such, much of the cultural variation we see is molded from more original displays through the application of display rules.

Emotion Regulation—How Culture Shapes an Individual's Attempts to Manage Emotions

A last emotion aspect to be discussed here concerns emotion regulation. Emotion regulation, defined as the processes that sustain, enhance, or subdue an emotion (Chapter 11), is considered to require some amount of control or effort and to be shaped by societal norms about the appropriateness of feeling or expressing an emotion. It should hence come as no surprise that emotion regulation shows considerable variation across human societies.

For example, there is evidence for cultural differences in the regulation of subjective feeling aspects. Many cultures of European descent value positive emotions more strongly and make greater efforts at sustaining these emotions than do many Asian cultures (Miyamoto & Ma, 2011). At the same time, however, they are less likely to attempt suppressing negative emotions such as anger (Cheung & Park, 2010).

Additionally, cultural differences were reported for regulating behavioral aspects of the emotional response. Again, some European cultures are less likely to suppress or mask their emotions than are some Asian cultures. Moreover, while this form of emotion regulation—also termed expressive suppression—has been linked with negative health outcomes in the former group, such a link appears absent in the latter group. In ethnically European individuals, expressive suppression was found to correlate positively with cardiovascular stress and symptoms of depression, whereas an opposite or nonsignificant correlation was found in ethnically Asian individuals (Soto, Perez, Kim, Lee, & Minnick, 2011; Zhou & Bishop, 2012).

Like other cultural differences in emotion, these differences appear linked to independent and interdependent self-construals. Feeling and expressing an emotion are more consequential in societies with a primarily interdependent self-construal because here these emotions are seen as more relevant and potentially damaging to existing relationships. Feeling and expressing an emotion could unduly shift one's own focus and that of others in the group to the self, thereby disrupting group harmony (Markus & Kitayama, 1991). Many Asians, having a more interdependent self-construal, would therefore be more likely than individuals of European descent to quench their emotional response.

FIGURE 14.12 Universal Emotion Expressions Surface in Extreme Situations

Source: © Jupiterimages/liquidlibrary/Thinkstock.

SUMMARY

Despite the fact that we all seem to know what we mean when we talk about culture, the concept itself is difficult to define. Perhaps counterintuitively, both biological and social factors contribute to the emergence of cultural hallmarks such as language and art. Therefore, both need to be considered and integrated in discussions of culture. Additionally, their dependence on environmental constraints and affordances needs to be recognized.

There are opposing theoretical positions regarding the role of culture for emotions. Some researchers believe that emotions are fundamentally similar across human societies. They admit for cultural differences only in the display of emotion. Other researchers believe emotions to be largely constructed by individuals within a society based on existing norms and beliefs. They admit cultural similarities only for very basic aspects of emotions such as the generation of core affect.

Despite such conflict, however, it is now understood that emotions are universal in some respects and culturally specific in other respects. In fact, many environmental factors have been identified that produce cultured emotions. These include aspects of the natural environment such as available foods and pathogen threat as well as aspects of the manmade environment, including reproductive and childcare practices or the distribution of wealth. Together, these aspects shape the development of individuals within a society and impact the brain as the biological substrate for emotions. These brain changes then determine how individuals process or appraise emotion antecedents, how they respond to them, and how they regulate responses.

One important finding in the context of antecedent appraisal concerns encounters with in- and out-group individuals. Compared to in-group encounters, out-group encounters have greater novelty and are more risky. Additionally, they offer fewer means to realize relevant goals such as social belonging. Therefore, individuals tend to prefer in- over out-group encounters, and this preference is stronger among those who define themselves interdependently, in relation to others, as compared to independently, based on their own achievements and aptitudes.

Cultural differences are also evident for emotional responding. In the context of subjective feelings, these differences were linked to the different languages enabling the expression of some but not other emotional states. Additionally, they were linked to differences in folk wisdom allowing or denying the concurrent experience of positive and negative feelings. Unlike subjective feelings, bodily and behavioral responses have been little explored, and findings are still inconclusive.

Last, culture is relevant for emotion regulation. In line with theoretical suppositions of diversity in the social value of emotions, different cultures deal with emotions in their own ways. Those placing greater emphasis on the individual are less likely to regulate emotions than are those placing greater emphasis on the group. As a consequence, emotion regulation cultivates emotional responding and, due to its long-term mental and bodily consequences, allows the significance of group practices to turn full circle. Not only do these practices shape emotions; they also shape individuals and their social groups—and therefore the very basis of culture.

THINKING CRITICALLY ABOUT "EMOTIONS AND CULTURE"

1. Identify subgroups that coexist within wealthy industrialized nations. Do they differ in their emotions, and if so, how?

2. One approach to increase the sensitivity of cultural research has been to identify psychological dimensions that appear culturally relevant and that differentiate human subgroups. What other approaches might one take?

3. Some cultures suppress the expression of certain emotions. Could this possibly affect other aspects of the emotion, and if so, how?

MEDIA LIBRARY

Information on the definition of a species: http://evolution.berkeley.edu/evosite/evo101/VADefiningSpecies.shtml

Jean Briggs's report on Eskimo life and emotions "*Never in anger: Portrait of an Eskimo family*":   http://books.google.com.sg/books?id=A9QuJjQbh7MC&printsec=frontcover&dq=Never+in+anger+Briggs&hl=en&sa=X&ei=jWgUUePUNoTorQeoh4HIDw&redir_esc=y

Richard Wilkinson talks about wealth and health on TED: http://www.ted.com/talks/richard_wilkinson.html

Data explorer of the United Nations Development Programme: http://hdr.undp.org/en/data/explorer

References

Aalto, S., Näätänen, P., Wallius, E., Metsähonkala, L., Stenman, H., Niem, P. M., & Karlsson, H. (2002). Neuroanatomical substrata of amusement and sadness: A PET activation study using film stimuli. *Neuroreport, 13,* 67–73.

Abu-Akel, A., & Shamay-Tsoory, S. (2011). Neuroanatomical and neurochemical bases of theory of mind. *Neuropsychologia, 49,* 2971–2984.

Adams, R. B., Jr., & Kleck, R. E. (2003). Perceived gaze direction and the processing of facial displays of emotion. *Psychological Science, 14,* 644–647.

Adams, S., Kuebli, J., Boyle, P. A., & Fivush, R. (1995). Gender differences in parent-child conversations about past emotions: A longitudinal investigation. *Sex Roles, 33,* 309–323.

Adenauer, H., Catani, C., Keil, J., Aichinger, H., & Neuner, F. (2010). Is freezing an adaptive reaction to threat? Evidence from heart rate reactivity to emotional pictures in victims of war and torture. *Psychophysiology, 47,* 315–322.

Ainsworth, M. D. S., Blehar, M. C., Waters, E., & Wall, S. (1978). *Patterns of attachment: A psychological study of the strange solution.* Hillsdale, NJ: Lawrence Erlbaum Associates.

Aisner, R., & Terkel, J. (1992). Ontogeny of pine cone opening behaviour in the black rat, Rattus rattus. *Animal Behaviour, 44, Part 2,* 327–336.

Albarracin, D., & Hart, W. (2011). Positive mood + action = negative mood + inaction: Effects of general action and inaction concepts on decisions and performance as a function of affect. *Emotion, 11,* 951–957.

Albrecht, J., Demmel, M., Schöpf, V., Kleemann, A. M., Kopietz, R., May, J., Schreder, T., Zernecke, R., Brückmann, H., & Wiesmann, M. (2011). Smelling chemosensory signals of males in anxious versus nonanxious condition increases state anxiety of female subjects. *Chemical Senses, 36,* 19–27.

Alcaro, A., & Panksepp, J. (2011). The SEEKING mind: Primal neuro-affective substrates for appetitive incentive states and their pathological dynamics in addictions and depression. *Neuroscience & Biobehavioral Reviews, 35,* 1805–1820.

Aldao, A., & Nolen-Hoeksema, S. (2010). Specificity of cognitive emotion regulation strategies: A transdiagnostic examination. *Behaviour Research and Therapy, 48,* 974–983.

Aldao, A., Nolen-Hoeksema, S., & Schweizer, S. (2010). Emotion-regulation strategies across psychopathology: A meta-analytic review. *Clinical Psychology Review, 30,* 217–237.

Aleman, A., & Swart, M. (2008). Sex differences in neural activation to facial expressions denoting contempt and disgust. *PLoS ONE, 3,* e3622.

Allen, J. S., Bruss, J., Brown, C. K., & Damasio, H. (2005). Normal neuroanatomical variation due to age: The major lobes and a parcellation of the temporal region. *Neurobiology of Aging, 26,* 1245–1260.

Allen, N. B., & Badcock, P. B. T. (2003). The social risk hypothesis of depressed mood: Evolutionary, psychosocial, and neurobiological perspectives. *Psychological Bulletin, 129,* 887–913.

Allman, J. M., Tetreault, N. A., Hakeem, A. Y., Manaye, K. F., Semendeferi, K., Erwin, J. M., Park, S., Goubert, V., & Hof, P. R. (2011). The von Economo neurons in the frontoinsular and anterior cingulate cortex. *Annals of the New York Academy of Sciences, 1225,* 59–71.

Altmann, J., Sapolsky, R., & Licht, P. (1995). Baboon fertility and social status. *Nature, 377,* 688–689.

Amano, T., Unal, C. T., & Paré, D. (2010). Synaptic correlates of fear extinction in the amygdala. *Nature Neuroscience, 13,* 489–494.

American Psychiatric Association, & DSM-5 Task Force. (2013). *Diagnostic and statistical manual of mental disorders: DSM-5.* Arlington, VA: American Psychiatric Association.

Amstadter, A. B., & Vernon, L. L. (2008). A preliminary examination of thought suppression, emotion regulation, and coping in a trauma-exposed sample. *Journal of Aggression, Maltreatment & Trauma, 17,* 279–295.

Anderson, A. K. (2005). Affective influences on the attentional dynamics supporting awareness. *Journal of Experimental Psychology: General, 134,* 258–281.

Anderson, A. K., & Phelps, E. A. (2000). Expression without recognition: Contributions of the human amygdala to emotional communication. *Psychological Science, 11,* 106–111.

Anderson, A. K., & Phelps, E. A. (2001). Lesions of the human amygdala impair enhanced perception of emotionally salient events. *Nature, 411,* 305–309.

Anderson, A. K., & Phelps, E. A. (2002). Is the human amygdala critical for the subjective experience of emotion? Evidence of intact dispositional affect in patients with amygdala lesions. *Journal of Cognitive Neuroscience, 14,* 709–720.

Anderson, M. C., & Green, C. (2001). Suppressing unwanted memories by executive control. *Nature, 410,* 366–369.

Andreano, J. M., & Cahill, L. (2006). Glucocorticoid release and memory consolidation in men and women. *Psychological Science, 17,* 466–470.

Angrilli, A., Cherubini, P., Pavese, A., & Mantredini, S. (1997). The influence of affective factors on time perception. *Perception & Psychophysics, 59,* 972–982.

Anisfeld, E., Casper, V., Nozyce, M., & Cunningham, N. (1990). Does infant carrying promote attachment? An experimental study of the effects of increased physical contact on the development of attachment. *Child Development, 61,* 1617–1627.

Ansorge, M. S. (2004). Early-life blockade of the 5-HT transporter alters emotional behavior in adult mice. *Science, 306,* 879–881.

Anticevic, A., Cole, M. W., Murray, J. D., Corlett, P. R., Wang, X.-J., & Krystal, J. H. (2012). The role of default network deactivation in cognition and disease. *Trends in Cognitive Sciences, 16,* 584–592.

Anzures, G., Quinn, P. C., Pascalis, O., Slater, A. M., & Lee, K. (2010). Categorization, categorical perception, and asymmetry in infants' representation of face race. *Developmental Science, 13,* 553–564.

Appelhans, B. M., & Luecken, L. J. (2006). Heart rate variability as an index of regulated emotional responding. *Review of General Psychology, 10,* 229–240.

Appleton, A. A., Buka, S. L., Loucks, E. B., Gilman, S. E., & Kubzansky, L. D. (2013). Divergent associations of adaptive and maladaptive emotion regulation strategies with inflammation. *Health Psychology, 32,* 748–756.

Aragona, B. J., Liu, Y., Yu, Y. J., Curtis, J. T., Detwiler, J. M., Insel, T. R., & Wang, Z. (2006). Nucleus accumbens dopamine differentially mediates the formation and maintenance of monogamous pair bonds. *Nature Neuroscience, 9,* 133–139.

Aral, S., & Walker, D. (2012). Identifying influential and susceptible members of social networks. *Science, 337,* 337–341.

Archer, J. (2004). Sex differences in aggression in real-world settings: A meta-analytic review. *Review of General Psychology, 8,* 291–322.

Archer, J., Birring, S. S., & Wu, F. C. W. (1998). The association between testosterone and aggression among young men: Empirical findings and a meta-analysis. *Aggressive Behavior, 24,* 411–420.

Archer, J., Birring, S. S., & Wu, F. C. W. (1998). The association between testosterone and aggression among young men: Empirical findings and a meta-analysis. *Aggressive Behavior, 24,* 411–420.

Archer, T., Fredriksson, A., Schütz, E., & Kostrzewa, R. M. (2011). Influence of physical exercise on neuroimmunological functioning and health: Aging and stress. *Neurotoxicity Research, 20,* 69–83.

Arias-Carrión, O., Stamelou, M., Murillo-Rodríguez, E., Menéndez-González, M., & Pöppel, E. (2010). Dopaminergic reward system: A short integrative review. *International Archives of Medicine, 3,* 24.

Arnett, J. J. (1999). Adolescent storm and stress, reconsidered. *The American Psychologist, 54,* 317–326.

Arnold, M. B. (1961). *Emotion and personality.* New York: Columbia University Press.

Aruta, A. (2011). Shocking waves at the museum: The Bini-Cerletti electro-shock apparatus. *Medical History, 55,* 407–412.

Ashby, F. G., Isen, A. M., & Turken, A. U. (1999). A neuropsychological theory of positive affect and its influence on cognition. *Psychological Review, 106,* 529–550.

Avenanti, A., Sirigu, A., & Aglioti, S. M. (2010). Racial bias reduces empathic sensorimotor resonance with other-race pain. *Current Biology, 20,* 1018–1022.

Averill, J. R. (1980). On the paucity of positive emotions. *Advances in the Study of Communication and Affect, 6,* 7–45.

Averill, J. R. (1988). Disorders of emotion. *Journal of Social and Clinical Psychology, 6,* 247–268.

Azim, E., Mobbs, D., Jo, B., Menon, V., & Reiss, A. L. (2005). Sex differences in brain activation elicited by humor. *Proceedings of the National Academy of Sciences of the United States of America, 102,* 16496–16501.

Azmitia, E. C. (2001). Modern views on an ancient chemical: Serotonin effects on cell proliferation, maturation, and apoptosis. *Brain Research Bulletin, 56,* 413–424.

Azmitia, E. C., & Segal, M. (1978). An autoradiographic analysis of the differential ascending projections of the dorsal and median raphe nuclei in the rat. *The Journal of Comparative Neurology, 179,* 641–667.

Bach, D. R., Talmi, D., Hurlemann, R., Patin, A., & Dolan, R. J. (2011). Automatic relevance detection in the absence of a functional amygdala. *Neuropsychologia, 49,* 1302–1305.

Bachorowski, J.-A., & Owren, M. J. (2003). Sounds of emotion: Production and perception of affect-related vocal acoustics. *Annals of the New York Academy of Sciences, 1000,* 244–265.

Bailey, D. L., Townsend, D. W., Valk, P. E., & Maisey, M. N. (Eds.). (2005). *Positron emission tomography: Basic sciences.* London: Springer.

Balaban, M. T. (1995). Affective influences on startle in five-month-old infants: Reactions to facial expressions of emotions. *Child Development, 66,* 28–36.

Ball, R., Shu, C., Xi, P., Rioux, M., Luximon, Y., & Molenbroek, J. (2010). A comparison between Chinese and Caucasian head shapes. *Applied Ergonomics, 41,* 832–839.

Balzer, A., & Jacobs, C. M. (2011). Gender and physiological effects in connecting disgust to political preferences. *Social Science Quarterly, 92,* 1297–1313.

Banse, R., & Scherer, K. R. (1996). Acoustic profiles in vocal emotion expression. *Journal of Personality and Social Psychology, 70,* 614–636.

Bär, K.-J., Brehm, S., Boettger, M. K., Boettger, S., Wagner, G., & Sauer, H. (2005). Pain perception in major depression depends on pain modality. *Pain, 117,* 97–103.

Bard, P. (1928). A diencephalic mechanism for the expression of rage with special reference to the sympathetic nervous system. *American Journal of Physiology—Legacy Content, 84,* 490.

Bard, P. (1934). On emotional expression after decortication with some remarks on certain theoretical views: Part I. *Psychological Review, 41,* 309.

Barrett, L. F. (2006). Solving the emotion paradox: Categorization and the experience of emotion. *Personality and Social Psychology Review, 10,* 20–46.

Barrett, L. F., Robin, L., Pietromonaco, P. R., & Eyssell, K. M. (1998). Are women the "more emotional" sex? Evidence from emotional experiences in social context. *Cognition & Emotion, 12,* 555–578.

Barron, A. B., Søvik, E., & Cornish, J. L. (2010). The roles of dopamine and related compounds in reward-seeking behavior across animal phyla. *Frontiers in Behavioral Neuroscience, 4.* doi:10.3389/fnbeh.2010.00163

Bartels, A., & Zeki, S. (2000). The neural basis of romantic love. *Neuroreport, 11,* 3829–3834.

Bartholow, B. D., Riordan, M. A., Saults, J. S., & Lust, S. A. (2009). Psychophysiological evidence of response conflict and strategic control of responses in affective priming. *Journal of Experimental Social Psychology, 45,* 655–666.

Bartolo, A., Benuzzi, F., Nocetti, L., Baraldi, P., & Nichelli, P. (2006). Humor comprehension and appreciation: An FMRI study. *Journal of Cognitive Neuroscience, 18,* 1789–1798.

Beacher, F. D. C. C., Gray, M. A., Minati, L., Whale, R., Harrison, N. A., & Critchley, H. D. (2011). Acute tryptophan depletion attenuates conscious appraisal of social emotional signals in healthy female volunteers. *Psychopharmacology, 213,* 603–613.

Bechara, A., & Damasio, H. (2002). Decision-making and addiction (Part I): Impaired activation of somatic states in substance dependent individuals when pondering decisions with negative future consequences. *Neuropsychologia, 40,* 1675–1689.

Bechara, A., Damasio, H., & Damasio, A. R. (2000). Emotion, decision making and the orbitofrontal cortex. *Cerebral Cortex, 10,* 295–307.

Bechara, A, Tranel, D., Damasio, H., Adolphs, R., Rockland, C., & Damasio, A. R. (1995). Double dissociation of conditioning and declarative knowledge relative to the amygdala and hippocampus in humans. *Science, 269,* 1115–1118.

Becker, D. V., Kenrick, D. T., Neuberg, S. L., Blackwell, K. C., & Smith, D. M. (2007). The confounded nature of angry men and happy women. *Journal of Personality and Social Psychology, 92,* 179–190.

Becker, M. W., & Leinenger, M. (2011). Attentional selection is biased toward mood-congruent stimuli. *Emotion, 11,* 1248–1254.

Becker, S., Gandhi, W., & Schweinhardt, P. (2012). Cerebral interactions of pain and reward and their relevance for chronic pain. *Neuroscience Letters, 520,* 182–187.

Beevers, C. G., Ellis, A. J., Wells, T. T., & McGeary, J. E. (2010). Serotonin transporter gene promoter region polymorphism and selective processing of emotional images. *Biological Psychology, 83,* 260–265.

Bekinschtein, T. A., Davis, M. H., Rodd, J. M., & Owen, A. M. (2011). Why clowns taste funny: The relationship between humor and semantic ambiguity. *The Journal of Neuroscience, 31,* 9665–9671.

Bender, A., Spada, H., Rothe-Wulf, A., & Rauss, K. (2012). Anger elicitation in Tonga and Germany: The impact of culture on cognitive determinants of emotions. *Frontiers in Cultural Psychology, 3,* 435.

Benenson, J. F., Markovits, H., Hultgren, B., Nguyen, T., Bullock, G., & Wrangham, R. (2013). Social exclusion: More important to human females than males. *PLoS ONE, 8,* e55851.

Bennett, M. R. (2007). Development of the concept of mind. *Australian and New Zealand Journal of Psychiatry, 41,* 943–956.

Ben-Shakhar, G., & Elaad, E. (2003). The validity of psychophysiological detection of information with the Guilty Knowledge Test: A meta-analytic review. *Journal of Applied Psychology, 88,* 131–151.

Berg, J., Dickhaut, J., & McCabe, K. (1995). Trust, reciprocity, and social history. *Games and Economic Behavior, 10,* 122–142.

Berglund, E., Eriksson, M., & Westerlund, M. (2005). Communicative skills in relation to gender, birth order, childcare and socioeconomic status in 18-month-old children. *Scandinavian Journal of Psychology, 46,* 485–491.

Berking, M., & Wupperman, P. (2012). Emotion regulation and mental health. *Current Opinion in Psychiatry, 25,* 128–134.

Berna, C., Leknes, S., Holmes, E. A., Edwards, R. R., Goodwin, G. M., & Tracey, I. (2010). Induction of depressed mood disrupts emotion regulation neurocircuitry and enhances pain unpleasantness. *Biological Psychiatry, 67,* 1083–1090.

Berntson, G. G., Boysen, S. T., Bauer, H. R., & Torello, M. S. (1989). Conspecific screams and laughter: Cardiac and behavioral reactions of infant chimpanzees. *Developmental Psychobiology, 22,* 771–787.

Berntson, G. G., Thomas Bigger, J., Eckberg, D. L., Grossman, P., Kaufmann, P. G., Malik, M., Nagaraja, H. N., Porges, S. W., Saul, J. P., Stone, P. H., & Van der Molen W, M. (2007). Heart rate variability: Origins, methods, and interpretive caveats. *Psychophysiology, 34,* 623–648.

Berridge, K. C., Ho, C.-Y., Richard, J. M., & DiFeliceantonio, A. G. (2010). The tempted brain eats: Pleasure and desire circuits in obesity and eating disorders. *Brain Research, 1350,* 43–64.

Berridge, K. C., & Kringelbach, M. L. (2008). Affective neuroscience of pleasure: Reward in humans and animals. *Psychopharmacology, 199,* 457–480.

Berrocoso, E., Sánchez-Blázquez, P., Garzón, J., & Mico, J. A. (2009). Opiates as antidepressants. *Current Pharmaceutical Design, 15,* 1612–1622.

Besson, A., Privat, A. M., Eschalier, A., & Fialip, J. (1996). Effects of morphine, naloxone and their interaction in the learned-helplessness paradigm in rats. *Psychopharmacology, 123,* 71–78.

Bishop, M. P., Elder, S. T., & Heath, R. G. (1963). Intracranial self-stimulation in man. *Science, 140,* 394–396.

Bishop, S. J. (2008). Neural mechanisms underlying selective attention to threat. *Annals of the New York Academy of Sciences, 1129,* 141–152.

Bjork, J. M., Moeller, F. G., Dougherty, D. M., & Swann, A. C. (2001). Endogenous plasma testosterone levels and commission errors in women: A preliminary report. *Physiology & Behavior, 73,* 217–221.

Björklund, A., & Dunnett, S. B. (2007). Dopamine neuron systems in the brain:

An update. *Trends in Neurosciences, 30,* 194–202.

Bleich A, G. M. (2003). Exposure to terrorism, stress-related mental health symptoms, and coping behaviors among a nationally representative sample in Israel. *JAMA: The Journal of the American Medical Association, 290,* 612–620.

Bless, H., Bohner, G., Schwarz, N., & Strack, F. (1990). Mood and persuasion: A cognitive response analysis. *Personality and Social Psychology Bulletin, 16,* 331–345.

Blood, A. J., & Zatorre, R. J. (2001). Intensely pleasurable responses to music correlate with activity in brain regions implicated in reward and emotion. *Proceedings of the National Academy of Sciences of the United States of America, 98,* 11818.

Bloom, T., & Friedman, H. (2013). Classifying dogs' (Canis familiaris) facial expressions from photographs. *Behavioural Processes, 96,* 1–10.

Bodenhausen, G. V., Sheppard, L. A., & Kramer, G. P. (1994). Negative affect and social judgment: The differential impact of anger and sadness. *European Journal of Social Psychology, 24,* 45–62.

Bodnar, R. J. (2011). Endogenous opiates and behavior: 2010. *Peptides, 32,* 2522–2552.

Boettger, M. K., Schwier, C., & Bär, K.-J. (2011). Sad mood increases pain sensitivity upon thermal grill illusion stimulation: Implications for central pain processing. *Pain, 152,* 123–130.

Boiten, F. (1996). Autonomic response patterns during voluntary facial action. *Psychophysiology, 33,* 123–131.

Bolling, D. Z., Pitskel, N. B., Deen, B., Crowley, M. J., McPartland, J. C., Mayes, L. C., & Pelphrey, K. A. (2011). Dissociable brain mechanisms for processing social xclusion and rule violation. *NeuroImage, 54,* 2462–2471.

Bostanov, V., & Kotchoubey, B. (2004). Recognition of affective prosody: Continuous wavelet measures of event-related brain potentials to emotional exclamations. *Psychophysiology, 41,* 259–268.

Bouret, S., & Sara, S. J. (2002). Locus coeruleus activation modulates firing rate and temporal organization of odour-induced single-cell responses in rat piriform cortex. *The European Journal of Neuroscience, 16,* 2371–2382.

Bradley, M. M., Codispoti, M., Cuthbert, B. N., & Lang, P. J. (2001). Emotion and motivation I: Defensive and appetitive reactions in picture processing. *Emotion, 1,* 276–298.

Bradley, M. M., Codispoti, M., Sabatinelli, D., & Lang, P. J. (2001). Emotion and motivation II: Sex differences in picture processing. *Emotion, 1,* 300–319.

Bradley, M. M., & Lang, P. J. (1994). Measuring emotion: The self-assessment manikin and the semantic differential. *Journal of Behavior Therapy and Experimental Psychiatry, 25,* 49–59.

Brass, M., & Haggard, P. (2007). To do or not to do: The neural signature of self-control. *The Journal of Neuroscience, 27,* 9141–9145.

Breiter, H. C., Aharon, I., Kahneman, D., Dale, A., & Shizgal, P. (2001). Functional imaging of neural responses to expectancy and experience of monetary gains and losses. *Neuron, 30,* 619–639.

Brennan, T. (2007). *The Stoic life: Emotions, duties and fate.* Oxford, UK: Clarendon Press.

Briggs, J. L. (1970). *Never in anger: Portrait of an Eskimo family.* Cambridge, MA: Harvard University Press.

Broad, K. D., Curley, J. P., & Keverne, E. B. (2006). Mother–infant bonding and the evolution of mammalian social relationships. *Philosophical Transactions of the Royal Society B: Biological Sciences, 361,* 2199–2214.

Brodmann, K. (2006). *Brodmann's: Localisation in the cerebral cortex.* New York: Springer.

Bromberg-Martin, E. S., Matsumoto, M., & Hikosaka, O. (2010a). Distinct tonic and phasic anticipatory activity in lateral habenula and dopamine neurons. *Neuron, 67,* 144–155.

Bromberg-Martin, E. S., Matsumoto, M., & Hikosaka, O. (2010b). Dopamine in motivational control: Rewarding, aversive, and alerting. *Neuron, 68,* 815–834.

Bronson, F. H., & Desjardins, C. (1968). Aggression in adult mice: Modification by neonatal injections of gonadal hormones. *Science, 161,* 705–706.

Brosch, T., Grandjean, D., Sander, D., & Scherer, K. R. (2008). Behold the voice of wrath: Cross-modal modulation of visual attention by anger prosody. *Cognition, 106,* 1497–1503.

Brown, R., & Kulik, J. (1977). Flashbulb memories. *Cognition, 5,* 73–99.

Buchanan, T. W. (2007). Retrieval of emotional memories. *Psychological Bulletin, 133,* 761–779.

Buchanan, T. W., Tranel, D., & Adolphs, R. (2004). Anteromedial temporal lobe damage blocks startle modulation by fear and disgust. *Behavioral Neuroscience, 118,* 429–437.

Buckner, R. L., Andrews-Hanna, J. R., & Schacter, D. L. (2008). The brain's default network: Anatomy, function, and relevance to disease. *Annals of the New York Academy of Sciences, 1124,* 1–38.

Buhusi, C. V., & Meck, W. H. (2005). What makes us tick? Functional and neural mechanisms of interval timing. *Nature Reviews Neuroscience, 6,* 755–765.

Buhusi, C. V., & Meck, W. H. (2009). Relative time sharing: New findings and an extension of the resource allocation model of temporal processing. *Philosophical Transactions of the Royal Society B: Biological Sciences, 364,* 1875–1885.

Burgdorf, J., & Panksepp, J. (2006). The neurobiology of positive emotions. *Neuroscience and Biobehavioral Reviews, 30,* 173–187.

Burgdorf, J., Panksepp, J., & Moskal, J. R. (2011). Frequency-modulated 50 kHz ultrasonic vocalizations: A tool for uncovering the molecular substrates of positive affect. *Neuroscience & Biobehavioral Reviews, 35,* 1831–1836.

Cacioppo, J. T., Berntson, G. G., Bechara, A., Tranel, D., & Hawkley, L. C. (2011). Could an aging brain contribute to subjective well-being? The value added by a social neuroscience perspective. In A. Todorov, S. Fiske, and D. Prentice (Eds.), *Social neuroscience: Toward understanding the underpinnings of the social mind* (pp. 249–277). New York: Oxford University Press.

Cacioppo, J. T., Berntson, G. G., Larsen, J. T., Poehlmann, K. M., & Ito, T. A. (1993). The psychophysiology of emotion. In M. Lewis & J. M. Haviland (Eds.), *Handbook of emotions* (pp. 119–142). New York: Guilford Press.

Cacioppo, J. T., Priester, J. R., & Berntson, G. G. (1993). Rudimentary determinants of attitudes. II: Arm flexion and extension have differential effects on attitudes. *Journal of Personality and Social Psychology, 65,* 5–17.

Cahill, L., Prins, B., Weber, M., & McGaugh, J. L. (1994). Beta-adrenergic activation and memory for emotional events. *Nature, 371,* 702–704.

Calder, A. J., Keane, J., Manes, F., Antoun, N., & Young, A. W. (2000). Impaired recognition and experience of disgust following brain injury. *Nature Neuroscience, 3,* 1077–1078.

Caldwell, J. D. (2002). A sexual arousability model involving steroid effects at the plasma membrane. *Neuroscience & Biobehavioral Reviews, 26,* 13–30.

Callaway, E. (2011). Early human migration written in stone tools. *Nature News.* doi:10.1038/news.2011.55

Cameron, L., Erkal, N., Gangadharan, L., & Meng, X. (2013). Little emperors: Behavioral impacts of China's one-child policy. *Science.* doi:10.1126/science.1230221

Cameron, N. M., Champagne, F. A., Parent, C., Fish, E. W., Ozaki-Kuroda, K., & Meaney, M. J. (2005). The programming of individual differences in defensive responses and reproductive strategies in the rat through variations in maternal care. *Neuroscience and Biobehavioral Reviews, 29,* 843–865.

Campbell-Sills, L., Barlow, D. H., Brown, T. A., & Hofmann, S. G. (2006). Acceptability and suppression of negative emotion in anxiety and mood disorders. *Emotion, 6,* 587–595.

Cannon, W. B. (1915). *Bodily changes in pain, hunger, fear and rage, an account of recent researches into the function of emotional excitement.* New York and London: D. Appleton and Co. Retrieved from http://archive.org/details/cu31924022542470

Cannon, W. B. (1927). The James-Lange theory of emotions: A critical examination and an alternative theory. *The American Journal of Psychology, 39,* 106–124.

Cannon, W. B. (1931). Again the James-Lange and the thalamic theories of emotion. *Psychological Review, 38,* 281.

Carr, P. B., & Steele, C. M. (2010). Stereotype threat affects financial decision making. *Psychological Science, 21,* 1411–1416.

Carré, J. M., Putnam, S. K., & McCormick, C. M. (2009). Testosterone responses to competition predict future aggressive behaviour at a cost to reward in men. *Psychoneuroendocrinology, 34,* 561–570.

Carstensen, L. L. (2006). The influence of a sense of time on human development. *Science, 312,* 1913–1915.

Carstensen, L. L., Turan, B., Scheibe, S., Ram, N., Ersner-Hershfield, H., Samanez-Larkin, G. R., . . . Nesselroade, J. R. (2011). Emotional experience improves with age: Evidence based on over 10 years of experience sampling. *Psychology and Aging, 26,* 21–33.

Caseras, X., Mataix-Cols, D., An, S. K., Lawrence, N. S., Speckens, A., Giampietro, V., . . . Phillips, M. L. (2007). Sex differences in neural responses to disgusting visual stimuli: Implications for disgust-related psychiatric disorders. *Biological Psychiatry, 62,* 464–471.

Caspi, A., Sugden, K., Moffitt, T. E., Taylor, A., Craig, I. W., Harrington, H., . . . Poulton, R. (2003). Influence of life stress on depression: Moderation by a polymorphism in the 5-HTT gene. *Science, 301,* 386–389.

Cassano, M., Perry-Parrish, C., & Zeman, J. (2007). Influence of gender on parental socialization of children's sadness regulation. *Social Development, 16,* 210–231.

Cassotti, M., Houdé, O., & Moutier, S. (2011). Developmental changes of win-stay and loss-shift strategies in decision making. *Child Neuropsychology, 17,* 400–411.

Cauda, F., Cavanna, A. E., D'Agata, F., Sacco, K., Duca, S., & Geminiani, G. C. (2011). Functional connectivity and coactivation of the nucleus accumbens: A combined functional connectivity and structure-based meta-analysis. *Journal of Cognitive Neuroscience, 23,* 2864–2877.

Cervantes, M. D., Hamilton, E. P., Xiong, J., Lawson, M. J., Yuan, D., Hadjithomas, M., . . . Orias, E. (2013). Selecting one of several mating types through gene segment joining and deletion in Tetrahymena thermophila. *PLoS Biology, 11,* e1001518.

Chaix, R., Cao, C., & Donnelly, P. (2008). Is mate choice in humans MHC-dependent? *PLoS Genetics, 4,* e1000184.

Champagne, D. L., Bagot, R. C., Hasselt, F. van, Ramakers, G., Meaney, M. J., Kloet, E. R. de, . . . Krugers, H. (2008). Maternal care and hippocampal plasticity: Evidence for experience-dependent structural plasticity, altered synaptic functioning, and differential responsiveness to glucocorticoids and stress. *The Journal of Neuroscience, 28,* 6037–6045.

Champagne, F., & Meaney, M. J. (2001). Like mother, like daughter: Evidence for non-genomic transmission of parental behavior and stress responsivity. *Progress in Brain Research, 133,* 287–302.

Chaplin, T. M., Cole, P. M., & Zahn-Waxler, C. (2005). Parental socialization of emotion expression: Gender differences and relations to child adjustment. *Emotion, 5,* 80–88.

Chen, D., Katdare, A., & Lucas, N. (2006). Chemosignals of fear enhance cognitive performance in humans. *Chemical Senses, 31,* 415–423.

Chen, M., & Bargh, J. A. (1999). Consequences of automatic evaluation: Immediate behavioral predispositions to approach or avoid the stimulus. *Personality and Social Psychology Bulletin, 25,* 215–224.

Cheng, R.-K., Scott, A. C., Penney, T. B., Williams, C. L., & Meck, W. H. (2008). Prenatal-choline supplementation differentially modulates timing of auditory and visual stimuli in aged rats. *Brain Research, 1237,* 167–175.

Chentsova-Dutton, Y. E., Chu, J. P., Tsai, J. L., Rottenberg, J., Gross, J. J., & Gotlib, I. H. (2007). Depression and emotional reactivity: Variation among Asian Americans of East Asian descent and European Americans. *Journal of Abnormal Psychology, 116,* 776–785.

Cheon, B. K., Im, D., Harada, T., Kim, J.-S., Mathur, V. A., Scimeca, J. M., . . . Chiao, J. Y. (2011). Cultural influences on neural basis of intergroup empathy. *NeuroImage, 57,* 642–650.

Cherek, D. R., Moeller, F. G., Schnapp, W., & Dougherty, D. M. (1997). Studies of violent and nonviolent male parolees: I. Laboratory and psychometric measurements of aggression. *Biological Psychiatry, 41,* 514–522.

Cheung, R. Y. M., & Park, I. J. K. (2010). Anger suppression, interdependent self-construal, and depression among Asian American and European American college students. *Cultural Diversity & Ethnic Minority Psychology, 16,* 517–525.

Chikama, M., McFarland, N. R., Amaral, D. G., & Haber, S. N. (1997). Insular cortical projections to functional regions of the striatum correlate with cortical cytoarchitectonic organization in the primate. *The Journal of Neuroscience, 17,* 9686–9705.

Cho, W., Heberlein, U., & Wolf, F. W. (2004). Habituation of an odorant-induced startle response in Drosophila. *Genes, Brain, and Behavior, 3,* 127–137.

Chomsky, N. (1965). *Aspects of the theory of syntax.* Cambridge, MA: MIT Press.

Chu, D.-M., Wahlqvist, M. L., Chang, H.-Y., Yeh, N.-H., & Lee, M.-S. (2012). Choline and betaine food sources and intakes in Taiwanese. *Asia Pacific Journal of Clinical Nutrition, 21,* 547–557.

Ciocchi, S., Herry, C., Grenier, F., Wolff, S. B. E., Letzkus, J. J., Vlachos, I., . . . Lüthi, A. (2010). Encoding of conditioned fear in central amygdala inhibitory circuits. *Nature, 468,* 277–282.

Cisler, J. M., Olatunji, B. O., & Lohr, J. M. (2009). Disgust, fear, and the anxiety disorders: A critical review. *Clinical Psychology Review, 29,* 34–46.

Claparède, E. (1911). Recognition et moïté. *Archives de Psychologie, 11,* 79–90.

Claparède, E. (1995). Recognition and selfhood. *Consciousness and Cognition, 4,* 371–378.

Claverie, J.-M. (2001). What if there are only 30,000 human genes? *Science, 291,* 1255–1257.

Coan, J., Gottman, J. M., Babcock, J., & Jacobson, N. (1997). Battering and the male rejection of influence from women. *Aggressive Behavior, 23,* 375–388.

Coan, J. A., Schaefer, H. S., & Davidson, R. J. (2006). Lending a hand: Social regulation of the neural response to threat. *Psychological Science, 17,* 1032–1039.

Coe, C. L., Mendoza, S. P., Smotherman, W. P., & Levine, S. (1978). Mother-infant attachment in the squirrel monkey: Adrenal response to separation. *Behavioral Biology, 22,* 256–263.

Coelho, C. M., & Purkis, H. (2009). The origins of specific phobias: Influential theories and current perspectives. *Review of General Psychology, 13,* 335–348.

Cohen, A. B. (2009). Many forms of culture. *The American Psychologist, 64,* 194–204.

Cohen, N. J., & Squire, L. R. (1980). Preserved learning and retention of pattern-analyzing skill in amnesia: Dissociation of knowing how and knowing that. *Science, 210,* 207–210.

Cohen, S., Line, S., Manuck, S. B., Rabin, B. S., Heise, E. R., & Kaplan, J. R. (1997). Chronic social stress, social status, and susceptibility to upper respiratory infections in non-human primates. *Psychosomatic Medicine, 59,* 213–221.

Colapinto, J. (2001). *As nature made him: The boy who was raised as a girl.* New York: HarperCollins.

Colbert-White, E. N., Covington, M. A., & Fragaszy, D. M. (2011). Social context influences the vocalizations of a home-raised African Grey parrot (Psittacus erithacus erithacus). *Journal of Comparative Psychology, 125,* 175–184.

Colegrove, F. W. (1899). Individual memories. *The American Journal of Psychology, 10,* 228–255.

Colibazzi, T., Posner, J., Wang, Z., Gorman, D., Gerber, A., Yu, S., Zhu, H., Kangarlu, A., Duan, Y., Russell, J.A., & Peterson, B. S. (2010). Neural systems subserving valence and arousal during the experience of induced emotions. *Emotion, 10,* 377–389.

Conner, C. R., Ellmore, T. M., Pieters, T. A., DiSano, M. A., & Tandon, N. (2011). Variability of the relationship between electrophysiology and BOLD-fMRI across cortical regions in humans. *The Journal of Neuroscience, 31,* 12855–12865.

Cook, M., & Mineka, S. (1989). Observational conditioning of fear to fear-relevant versus fear-irrelevant stimuli in rhesus monkeys. *Journal of Abnormal Psychology, 98,* 448–459.

Corbetta, M., & Shulman, G. L. (2002). Control of goal-directed and stimulus-driven attention in the brain. *Nature Reviews Neuroscience, 3,* 201–215.

Corkin, S. (2002). What's new with the amnesic patient H. M.? *Nature Reviews. Neuroscience, 3,* 153–160.

Corkin, S., Amaral, D. G., González, R. G., Johnson, K. A., & Hyman, B. T. (1997). H. M.'s medial temporal lobe lesion: Findings from magnetic resonance imaging. *The Journal of Neuroscience, 17,* 3964–3979.

Corodimas, K. P., LeDoux, J. E., Gold, P. W., & Schulkin, J. (1994). Corticosterone potentiation of conditioned fear in rats. *Annals of the New York Academy of Sciences, 746,* 392–393.

Cotman, C. W., Berchtold, N. C., & Christie, L.-A. (2007). Exercise builds brain health: Key roles of growth factor cascades and inflammation. *Trends in Neurosciences, 30,* 464–472.

Cowie, R., Douglas-Cowie, E., & Cox, C. (2005). Beyond emotion archetypes: Databases for emotion modelling using neural networks. *Neural Networks, 18,* 371–388.

Craig, A. D. B. (2009). How do you feel—now? The anterior insula and human awareness. *Nature Reviews Neuroscience, 10,* 59–70.

Craik, F. I. M., & Lockhart, R. S. (1972). Levels of processing: A framework for memory research. *Journal of Verbal Learning and Verbal Behavior, 11,* 671–684.

Crivellato, E., & Ribatti, D. (2007). Soul, mind, brain: Greek philosophy and the birth of neuroscience. *Brain Research Bulletin, 71,* 327–336.

Cross, C. P., & Campbell, A. (2011). Women's aggression. *Aggression and Violent Behavior, 16,* 390–398.

Cryan, J. F. & Slattery, D. A. (2010). GABAB receptors and depression: Current status. *Advances in Pharmacology, 58,* 427–451.

Csikszentmihalyi, M. (1988). The flow experience and its significance for human psychology. In M. Csikszentmihalyi & I. S. Csikszentmihalyi (Eds.), *Optimal Experience: Psychological Studies of Flow in Consciousness.* Cambridge, UK: Cambridge University Press, pp. 15–35.

Cunningham, W. A., Raye, C. L., & Johnson, M. K. (2004). Implicit and explicit evaluation: FMRI correlates of valence, emotional intensity, and control in the processing of attitudes. *Journal of Cognitive Neuroscience, 16,* 1717–1729.

Curtis, V., Aunger, R., & Rabie, T. (2004). Evidence that disgust evolved to protect from risk of disease. *Proceedings of the Royal Society B: Biological Sciences, 271,* S131–S133.

Dael, N., Mortillaro, M., & Scherer, K. R. (2012). Emotion expression in body action and posture. *Emotion, 12,* 1085–1101.

Dahlstroem, A., & Fuxe, K. (1964). Evidence for the existance of monoamine-containing neurons in the central nervous system. I. Demonstration of monoamines in the cellbodies of brain stem neurons. *Acta Physiologica Scandinavica, Suppl. 232,* 1–55.

Damasio, A. R. (1994). *Descartes' Error.* New York: HarperCollins Publishers.

Damasio, A. R. (1996). The somatic marker hypothesis and the possible functions of the prefrontal cortex. *Philosophical Transactions of the Royal Society of London. Series B, Biological Sciences, 351,* 1413–1420.

Dan-Glauser, E. S., & Gross, J. J. (2011). The temporal dynamics of two response-focused forms of emotion regulation: Experiential, expressive, and autonomic consequences. *Psychophysiology, 48,* 1309–1322.

Dantzer, R. (2001). Stress, emotions and health: Where do we stand? *Social Science Information, 40,* 61–78.

Dantzer, R., O'Connor, J. C., Freund, G. G., Johnson, R. W., & Kelley, K. W. (2008). From inflammation to sickness and depression: When the immune system subjugates the brain. *Nature Reviews Neuroscience, 9,* 46–56.

Darwin, C. (1864). *On the origin of species by means of natural selection: Or, The preservation of favored races in the struggle for life.* New York: D. Appleton and Company.

Darwin, C. (1871). *The descent of man.* New York: D. Appleton and Co.

Darwin, C. (1872). *The expression of the emotions in man and animals.* London: John Murray.

Darwin, C. (2009). *The expression of the emotions in man and animals.* London: Penguin Classics. (Originally published in 1872)

Davis, J. I., Gross, J. J., & Ochsner, K. N. (2011). Psychological distance and emotional experience: What you see is what you get. *Emotion, 11,* 438–444.

Davis, M., Redmond, D. E., & Baraban, J. M. (1979). Noradrenergic agonists and antagonists: Effects on conditioned fear as measured by the potentiated startle paradigm. *Psychopharmacology, 65,* 111–118.

Dawans, B. von, Fischbacher, U., Kirschbaum, C., Fehr, E., & Heinrichs, M. (2012). The social dimension of stress reactivity acute stress increases prosocial behavior in humans. *Psychological Science, 23,* 651–660.

Dawson, M. E., Schell, A. M., & Filion, D. L. (2007). The electrodermal system. In J. T. Cacioppo, L. G. Tassinary, & G. G. Berntson

(Eds.), *Handbook of psychophysiology* (pp. 159–181). New York: Cambridge University Press.

de Barra, M., & Curtis, V. (2012). Are the pathogens of out-groups really more dangerous? *The Behavioral and Brain Sciences, 35,* 85–86.

De Gelder, B., Vroomen, J., Pourtois, G., & Weiskrantz, L. (1999). Non-conscious recognition of affect in the absence of striate cortex. *Neuroreport, 10,* 3759–3763.

de Jong, P. J., Koster, E. H. W., van Wees, R., & Martens, S. (2010). Angry facial expressions hamper subsequent target identification. *Emotion, 10,* 727–732.

De Raedt, R., Leyman, L., Baeken, C., Van Schuerbeek, P., Luypaert, R., Vanderhasselt, M.-A., & Dannlowski, U. (2010). Neurocognitive effects of HF-rTMS over the dorsolateral prefrontal cortex on the attentional processing of emotional information in healthy women: An event-related fMRI study. *Biological Psychology, 85,* 487–495.

de Waal, F. de. (1990). *Peacemaking among primates.* Cambridge, MA: Harvard University Press.

de Waal, F. B. M. (2006). Darwin's legacy and the study of primate visual communication. *Annals of the New York Academy of Sciences, 1000,* 7–31.

Dębiec, J., Bush, D. E. A., & LeDoux, J. E. (2011). Noradrenergic enhancement of reconsolidation in the amygdala impairs extinction of conditioned fear in rats—a possible mechanism for the persistence of traumatic memories in PTSD. *Depression and Anxiety, 28,* 186–193.

DeCarli, C., Reed, B. R., Jagust, W. J., Martinez, O., Ortega, M., & Mungas, D. (2008). Brain behavior relationships amongst African Americans, Caucasians, and Hispanics. *Alzheimer Disease and Associated Disorders, 22,* 382–391.

DeCasper, A. J., & Fifer, W. P. (1980). Of human bonding: Newborns prefer their mothers' voices. *Science, 208,* 1174–1176.

Deisseroth, K., Feng, G., Majewska, A. K., Miesenböck, G., Ting, A., & Schnitzer, M. J. (2006). Next-generation optical technologies for illuminating genetically targeted brain circuits. *The Journal of Neuroscience, 26,* 10380–10386.

DeJoy, D. M. (1992). An examination of gender differences in traffic accident risk perception. *Accident Analysis & Prevention, 24,* 237–246.

Dellacherie, D., Roy, M., Hugueville, L., Peretz, I., & Samson, S. (2011). The effect of musical experience on emotional self-reports and psychophysiological responses to dissonance. *Psychophysiology, 48,* 337–349.

Delplanque, S., N'Diaye, K., Scherer, K., & Grandjean, D. (2007). Spatial frequencies or emotional effects? A systematic measure of spatial frequencies for IAPS pictures by a discrete wavelet analysis. *Journal of Neuroscience Methods, 165,* 144–150.

Denny, B. T., Kober, H., Wager, T. D., & Ochsner, K. N. (2012). A meta-analysis of functional neuroimaging studies of self- and other judgments reveals a spatial gradient for mentalizing in medial prefrontal cortex. *Journal of Cognitive Neuroscience, 24,* 1742–1752.

Denson, T. F., Grisham, J. R., & Moulds, M. L. (2011). Cognitive reappraisal increases heart rate variability in response to an anger provocation. *Motivation and Emotion, 35,* 14–22.

Denson, T. F., Moulds, M. L., & Grisham, J. R. (2012). The effects of analytical rumination, reappraisal, and distraction on anger experience. *Behavior Therapy, 43,* 355–364.

Descartes, R. (1989). *The passions of the soul* (S. Voss, Trans.). Indianapolis, IN: Hackett

Publishing. (Original work published in 1649)

Desimone, R., & Duncan, J. (1995). Neural mechanisms of selective visual attention. *Annual Review of Neuroscience, 18,* 193–222.

DeWall, C. N., MacDonald, G., Webster, G. D., Masten, C. L., Baumeister, R. F., Powell, C., Combs, D., Schurtz, D. E., Stillman, T. F., Tice, D. M., & Eisenberger, N. I. (2010). Acetaminophen reduces social pain: Behavioral and neural evidence. *Psychological Science, 21,* 931–937.

Di, X., & Biswal, B. B. (2014). Identifying the default mode network structure using dynamic causal modeling on resting-state functional magnetic resonance imaging. *NeuroImage, 86,* 59.

Dias, B. G., & Ressler, K. J. (2013). Parental olfactory experience influences behavior and neural structure in subsequent generations. *Nature Neuroscience.* doi:10.1038/nn.3594

Dias, B. G., & Ressler, K. J. (2014). Parental olfactory experience influences behavior and neural structure in subsequent generations. *Nature Neuroscience, 17,* 89–96.

Dickerson, S. S., & Kemeny, M. E. (2004). Acute stressors and cortisol responses: A theoretical integration and synthesis of laboratory research. *Psychological Bulletin, 130,* 355–391.

Dickinson, D., & Elvevåg, B. (2009). Genes, cognition and brain through a COMT lens. *Neuroscience, 164,* 72–87.

Diekhof, E. K., Geier, K., Falkai, P., & Gruber, O. (2011). Fear is only as deep as the mind allows: A coordinate-based meta-analysis of neuroimaging studies on the regulation of negative affect. *NeuroImage, 58,* 275–285.

Döhler, K. D., Coquelin, A., Davis, F., Hines, M., Shryne, J. E., & Gorski, R. A. (1984). Pre- and postnatal influence of testosterone propionate and diethylstilbestrol on differentiation of the sexually dimorphic nucleus of the preoptic area in male and female rats. *Brain Research, 302,* 291–295.

Dohrenwend, B. P. (1967). Social status, stress, and psychological symptoms. *American Journal of Public Health and the Nation's Health, 57,* 625–632.

Dolcos, F., Iordan, A. D., & Dolcos, S. (2011). Neural correlates of emotion–cognition interactions: A review of evidence from brain imaging investigations. *Journal of Cognitive Psychology, 23,* 669–694.

Dolcos, F., LaBar, K. S., & Cabeza, R. (2005). Remembering one year later: Role of the amygdala and the medial temporal lobe memory system in retrieving emotional memories. *Proceedings of the National Academy of Sciences of the United States of America, 102,* 2626–2631.

Domes, G., Schulze, L., Böttger, M., Grossmann, A., Hauenstein, K., Wirtz, P. H., Heinrichs, M., & Herpertz, S. C. (2010). The neural correlates of sex differences in emotional reactivity and emotion regulation. *Human Brain Mapping, 31,* 758–769.

Domínguez-Borràs, J., Saj, A., Armony, J. L., & Vuilleumier, P. (2012). Emotional processing and its impact on unilateral neglect and extinction. *Neuropsychologia, 50,* 1054–1071.

Dorr, N., Brosschot, J. F., Sollers, J. J., 3rd, & Thayer, J. F. (2007). Damned if you do, damned if you don't: The differential effect of expression and inhibition of anger on cardiovascular recovery in black and white males. *International Journal of Psychophysiology, 66,* 125–134.

Douglas, L. A., Varlinskaya, E. I., & Spear, L. P. (2004). Rewarding properties of social interactions in adolescent and adult male and female rats: Impact of social versus isolate housing of subjects and partners. *Developmental Psychobiology, 45,* 153–162.

Downar, J., & Daskalakis, Z. J. (2013). New targets for rTMS in depression: A review of convergent evidence. *Brain Stimulation, 6,* 231–40.

Downing, L. (2013). George Berkeley. In E. N. Zalta (Ed.), *The Stanford encyclopedia of philosophy* (Spring 2013.). Retrieved from http://plato.stanford.edu/archives/spr2013/entries/berkeley/

Dreher, J.-C., Kohn, P., Kolachana, B., Weinberger, D. R., & Berman, K. F. (2009). Variation in dopamine genes influences responsivity of the human reward system. *Proceedings of the National Academy of Sciences of the United States of America, 106,* 617–622.

Dremencov, E., Mansari, M., & Blier, P. (2009). Brain norepinephrine system as a target for antidepressant and mood stabilizing medications. *Current Drug Targets, 10,* 1061–1068.

Driscoll, C. A., Macdonald, D. W., & O'Brien, S. J. (2009). From wild animals to domestic pets, an evolutionary view of domestication. *Proceedings of the National Academy of Sciences, 106,* 9971.

Droit-Volet, S., & Meck, W. H. (2007). How emotions colour our perception of time. *Trends in Cognitive Sciences, 11,* 504–513.

Duarte-Carvajalino, J. M., Jahanshad, N., Lenglet, C., McMahon, K. L., de Zubicaray, G. I., Martin, N. G., Wright, M. J., Thompson, P. M., & Sapiro, G. (2012). Hierarchical topological network analysis of anatomical human brain connectivity and differences related to sex and kinship. *NeuroImage, 59,* 3784–3804.

Duchenne, G.B. (1862). *Mécanisme de la physionomie humaine: Ou analyse électrophysilogique de l'expression des passion.* Paris: Jules Renouard.

Dufour, V., Wascher, C. A. F., Braun, A., Miller, R., & Bugnyar, T. (2012). Corvids can decide if a future exchange is worth waiting for. *Biology Letters, 8,* 201–204.

Dunbar, R. I. M., Baron, R., Frangou, A., Pearce, E., Leeuwen, E. J. C. van, Stow, J., Partridge, G., MacDonald, I., Barra, V., & Vugt, M. van. (2012). Social laughter is correlated with an elevated pain threshold. *Proceedings of the Royal Society B: Biological Sciences, 279,* 1161–1167.

Duncan, J. (1980). The locus of interference in the perception of simultaneous stimuli. *Psychological Review, 87,* 272–300.

Duncan, S. (2013). Thomas Hobbes. In E. N. Zalta (Ed.), *The Stanford encyclopedia of philosophy* (Spring 2013.). Retrieved from http://plato.stanford.edu/archives/spr2013/entries/hobbes/

Duncker, K. (1945). On problem-solving. *Psychological Monographs, 58,* 1–113.

Dunn, B. D., Dalgleish, T., & Lawrence, A. D. (2006). The somatic marker hypothesis: A critical evaluation. *Neuroscience & Biobehavioral Reviews, 30,* 239–271.

Dunn, J., Bretherton, I., & Munn, P. (1987). Conversations about feeling states between mothers and their young children. *Developmental Psychology, 23,* 132–139.

Duntley, J. D., & Buss, D. M. (2012). The evolution of stalking. *Sex Roles, 66,* 311–327.

Dwyer, P. D., & Minnegal, M. (2008). Fun for them, Fun for us and fun for all: The "far side" of field work in the tropical lowlands. *Anthropological Forum, 18,* 303–308.

Easterbrook, J. A. (1959). The effect of emotion on cue utilization and the organization of behavior. *Psychological Review, 66,* 183–201.

Ebstein, R. P., Israel, S., Chew, S. H., Zhong, S., & Knafo, A. (2010). Genetics of human social behavior. *Neuron, 65,* 831–844.

Ebstein, R. P., Levine, J., Geller, V., Auerbach, J., Gritsenko, I., & Belmaker, R. H. (1998). Dopamine D4 receptor and serotonin transporter promoter in the determination of neonatal temperament. *Molecular Psychiatry, 3,* 238–246.

Eder, A. B., Leuthold, H., Rothermund, K., & Schweinberger, S. R. (2012). Automatic response activation in sequential affective priming: An ERP study. *Social Cognitive and Affective Neuroscience, 7,* 436–445.

Edward, D. A., & Chapman, T. (2011). The evolution and significance of male mate choice. *Trends in Ecology & Evolution, 26,* 647–654.

Ehring, T., Fischer, S., Schnülle, J., Bösterling, A., & Tuschen-Caffier, B. (2008). Characteristics of emotion regulation in recovered depressed versus never depressed individuals. *Personality and Individual Differences, 44,* 1574–1584.

Ehring, T., Tuschen-Caffier, B., Schnülle, J., Fischer, S., & Gross, J. J. (2010). Emotion regulation and vulnerability to depression: Spontaneous versus instructed use of emotion suppression and reappraisal. *Emotion, 10,* 563–572.

Eich, E., Ng, J. T. W., Macaulay, D., Percy, A. D., & Grebneva, I. (2007). Combining music with thought to change mood. In J. Coan & J. J. B. Allan (Eds.), *Handbook of emotion elicitation and assessment* (pp. 124–136). New York: Oxford University Press.

Eisenberg, N., Schaller, M., Fabes, R. A., Bustamante, D., Mathy, R. M., Shell, R., & Rhodes, K. (1988). Differentiation of personal distress and sympathy in children and adults. *Developmental Psychology, 24,* 766–775.

Eisenberger, N.I., Lieberman, M.D., & Williams, K.D. (2003). Does rejection hurt? An fMRI study of social exclusion. *Science, 302,* 290–292.

Ekman, P. (1992). Are there basic emotions? *Psychological Review, 99,* 550–553.

Ekman, P. (1999). Basic emotions. In T. Dalgleish & M. Power (Eds.), *Handbook of cognition and emotion* (pp. 45–60). Sussex, UK: John Wiley & Sons.

Ekman, P. (2005). Basic emotions. In T. Dalgleish & M. J. Power (Eds.), *Handbook of cognition and emotion* (pp. 45–60). New York: John Wiley & Sons, Ltd.

Ekman, P. (2009). Darwin's contributions to our understanding of emotional expressions. *Philosophical Transactions of the Royal Society of London. Series B, Biological Sciences, 364,* 3449–3451.

Ekman, P. (2012). Respect in a pinch. *Science, 337,* 1173.

Ekman, P., & Davidson, R. J. (1994). *The nature of emotion: Fundamental questions.* New York: Oxford University Press.

Ekman, P., Davidson, R. J., & Friesen, W. V. (1990). The Duchenne smile: Emotional expression and brain physiology. II. *Journal of Personality and Social Psychology, 58,* 342–353.

Ekman, P., & Friesen, W. V. (1976). Measuring facial movement. *Environmental Psychology and Nonverbal Behavior, 1,* 56–75.

Ekman, P., & Friesen, W. (1978). *Facial action coding system: A technique for the measurement of facial movement.* Palo Alto, CA: Consulting Psychologists Press.

Ekman, P., & Friesen, W. V. (2003). *Unmasking the face: A guide to recognizing emotions from facial clues.* Los Altos, CA: Malor Books.

Ekman, P., Levenson, R. W., & Friesen, W. V. (1983). Autonomic nervous system activity distinguishes among emotions. *Science, 221,* 1208–1210.

Ekman, P., & Rosenberg, E. L. (2005). *What the face reveals: Basic and applied studies of spontaneous expression using the facial action coding system (FACS).* Oxford, UK: Oxford University Press.

Ekman, P., Sorenson, E. R., & Friesen, W. V. (1969). Pan-cultural elements in facial displays of emotion. *Science, 164,* 86–88.

Elfenbein, H. A., & Ambady, N. (2002). On the universality and cultural specificity of emotion recognition: A meta-analysis. *Psychological Bulletin, 128,* 203–235.

Elfenbein, H. A., Beaupré, M., Lévesque, M., & Hess, U. (2007). Toward a dialect theory: Cultural differences in the expression and recognition of posed facial expressions. *Emotion, 7,* 131–146.

Elliot, A. J., Payen, V., Brisswalter, J., Cury, F., & Thayer, J. F. (2011). A subtle threat cue, heart rate variability, and cognitive performance. *Psychophysiology, 48,* 1340–1345.

Ellsworth, P. C., & Smith, C. A. (1988). From appraisal to emotion: Differences among unpleasant feelings. *Motivation and Emotion, 12,* 271–302.

Ellsworth, P. C., & Smith, C. A. (1988). Shades of joy: Patterns of appraisal differentiating pleasant emotions. *Cognition & Emotion, 2,* 301–331.

Eroglu, C., & Barres, B. A. (2010). Regulation of synaptic connectivity by glia. *Nature, 468,* 223–231.

Ertman, N., Andreano, J. M., & Cahill, L. (2011). Progesterone at encoding predicts subsequent emotional memory. *Learning & Memory, 18,* 759–763.

Escoffier, N., Zhong, J., Schirmer, A., & Qiu, A. (2013). Emotional expressions in voice and music: Same code, same effect? *Human Brain Mapping, 34,* 1796–1810.

Escoffier, N., Zhong, J., Schirmer, A., & Qiu, A. (2013). Emotional expressions in voice and music: Same code, same effect? *Human Brain Mapping, 34,* 1796–1810.

Etkin, A., Egner, T., & Kalisch, R. (2011). Emotional processing in anterior cingulate and medial prefrontal cortex. *Trends in Cognitive Sciences, 15,* 85–93.

Eugčne, F., Lévesque, J., Mensour, B., Leroux, J. M., Beaudoin, G., Bourgouin, P., & Beauregard, M. (2003). The impact of individual differences on the neural circuitry underlying sadness. *NeuroImage, 19,* 354–364.

Fabes, R. A., Eisenberg, N., Karbon, M., Bernzweig, J., Lee Speer, A., & Carlo, G. (1994). Socialization of children's vicarious emotional responding and prosocial behavior: Relations with mothers' perceptions of children's emotional reactivity. *Developmental Psychology, 30,* 44–55.

Fabri, M., Polonara, G., Mascioli, G., Salvolini, U., & Manzoni, T. (2011). Topographical organization of human corpus callosum: An fMRI mapping study. *Brain Research, 1370,* 99–111.

Fagan, J. F., Holland, C. R., & Wheeler, K. (2007). The prediction, from infancy, of adult IQ and achievement. *Intelligence, 35,* 225–231.

Fantz, R. L. (1964). Visual experience in infants: Decreased attention to familiar patterns relative to novel ones. *Science, 146,* 668–670.

Farb, N. A. S., Anderson, A. K., Mayberg, H., Bean, J., McKeon, D., & Segal, Z. V. (2010). Minding one's emotions: Mindfulness training alters the neural expression of sadness. *Emotion, 10,* 25–33.

Farrant, M., & Nusser, Z. (2005). Variations on an inhibitory theme: Phasic and tonic activation of GABAA receptors. *Nature Reviews Neuroscience, 6,* 215–229.

Farrell, W. J., & Alberts, J. R. (2002). Stimulus control of maternal responsiveness to Norway rat (Rattus norvegicus) pup ultrasonic vocalizations. *Journal of Comparative Psychology, 116,* 297–307.

Farroni, T., Csibra, G., Simion, F., & Johnson, M. H. (2002). Eye contact detection in humans from birth. *Proceedings of the National Academy of Sciences of the United States of America, 99,* 9602–9605.

Fasano, A., Daniele, A., & Albanese, A. (2012). Treatment of motor and non-motor features of Parkinson's disease with deep brain stimulation. *Lancet Neurology, 11,* 429–442.

Fazio, R. H., Sanbonmatsu, D. M., Powell, M. C., & Kardes, F. R. (1986). On the automatic activation of attitudes. *Journal of Personality and Social Psychology, 50,* 229–238.

Fazio, R. H., Sanbonmatsu, D. M., Powell, M. C., & Kardes, F. R. (1986). On the automatic activation of attitudes. *Journal of Personality and Social Psychology, 50,* 229–238.

Federmeier, K. D., Kirson, D. A., Moreno, E. M., & Kutas, M. (2001). Effects of transient, mild mood states on semantic memory organization and use: An event-related potential investigation in humans. *Neuroscience Letters, 305,* 149–152.

Fehr, B., & Russell, J. A. (1984). Concept of emotion viewed from a prototype perspective. *Journal of Experimental Psychology: General, 113,* 464–486.

Feldman-Barrett, L. (2006a). Are emotions natural kinds? *Perspectives on Psychological Science, 1,* 28–58.

Feldman-Barrett, L. (2006b). Solving the emotion paradox: Categorization and the experience of emotion. *Personality and Social Psychology Review, 10,* 20–46.

Feldman-Barrett, L., Lindquist, K. A., Bliss-Moreau, E., Duncan, S., Gendron, M., Mize, J., & Brennan, L. (2007). Of mice and men: Natural kinds of emotions in the mammalian brain? A response to Panksepp and Izard. *Perspectives on Psychological Science, 2,* 297–311.

Felmingham, K. L., Tran, T. P., Fong, W. C., & Bryant, R. A. (2012). Sex differences in emotional memory consolidation: The effect of stress-induced salivary alpha-amylase and cortisol. *Biological Psychology, 89,* 539–544.

Ferdenzi, C., Schirmer, A., Roberts, S. C., Delplanque, S., Porcherot, C., Cayeux, I., Valezco, M.-I., Sander, D., Scherer, K. R., & Grandjean, D. (2011). Affective dimensions of odor perception: A comparison between Swiss, British, and Singaporean populations. *Emotion,* doi:10.1037/a0022853

Fernández, C., Pascual, J. C., Soler, J., Elices, M., Portella, M. J., & Fernández-Abascal, E. (2012). Physiological responses induced by emotion-eliciting films. *Applied Psychophysiology and Biofeedback, 37,* 73–79.

Fernstrom, J. D. (1977). Effects of the diet on brain neurotransmitters. *Metabolism, 26,* 207–223.

Ferris, C. F., Kulkarni, P., Sullivan, J. M., Harder, J. A., Messenger, T. L., & Febo, M. (2005). Pup suckling is more rewarding than cocaine: Evidence from functional magnetic resonance imaging and three-dimensional computational analysis. *The Journal of Neuroscience, 25,* 149–156.

Field, T. (2000). Infant massage therapy. In *Handbook of infant mental health* (2nd ed.). New York: Guilford Press.

Fincher, C. L., & Thornhill, R. (2012). Parasite-stress promotes in-group assortative sociality: The cases of strong family ties and heightened religiosity. *Behavioral and Brain Sciences, 35,* 61–79.

Finkelstein, D. M., Kubzansky, L. D., & Goodman, E. (2006). Social status, stress, and adolescent smoking. *Journal of Adolescent Health, 39,* 678–685.

Firk, C., Siep, N., & Markus, C. R. (2013). Serotonin transporter genotype modulates cognitive reappraisal of negative emotions: A functional magnetic resonance imaging study. *Social Cognitive and Affective Neuroscience, 8,* 247–258.

Fischer, A. H., Rodriguez Mosquera, P. M., van Vianen, A. E. M., & Manstead, A. S. R. (2004). Gender and culture differences in emotion. *Emotion, 4,* 87–94.

Fischer, D., & Hills, T. T. (2012). The baby effect and young male syndrome: Social influences on cooperative risk-taking in women and men. *Evolution and Human Behavior, 33,* 530–536.

Fischer, R. B., & Brown, P. S. (1993). Vaginal secretions increase the likelihood of intermale aggression in Syrian hamsters. *Physiology & Behavior, 54,* 213–214.

Fisher, G. A., & Chon, K. K. (1989). Durkheim and the social construction of emotions. *Social Psychology Quarterly, 52,* 1–9.

Fisher, H., Aron, A., & Brown, L. L. (2005). Romantic love: An fMRI study of a neural mechanism for mate choice. *The Journal of Comparative Neurology, 493,* 58–62.

Fisher, W. A., White, L. A., Byrne, D., & Kelley, K. (1988). Erotophobia-erotophilia as a dimension of personality. *The Journal of Sex Research, 25,* 123–151.

Fiske, A. P. (2002). Using individualism and collectivism to compare cultures—a critique of the validity and measurement of the constructs: Comment on Oyserman et al. (2002). *Psychological Bulletin, 128,* 78–88.

Fitzgerald, P. B., Fountain, S., & Daskalakis, Z. J. (2006). A comprehensive review of the effects of rTMS on motor cortical excitability and inhibition. *Clinical Neurophysiology, 117,* 2584–2596.

Fivush, R. (1989). Exploring sex differences in the emotional content of mother-child conversations about the past. *Sex Roles, 20,* 675–691.

Foley, P., & Kirschbaum, C. (2010). Human hypothalamus-pituitary-adrenal axis responses to acute psychosocial stress in laboratory settings. *Neuroscience & Biobehavioral Reviews, 35,* 91–96.

Fontaine, J. R. J., Scherer, K. R., Roesch, E. B., & Ellsworth, P. C. (2007). The world of emotions is not two-dimensional. *Psychological Science, 18,* 1050–1057.

Fortier, E., Noreau, A., Lepore, F., Boivin, M., Pérusse, D., Rouleau, G. A., & Beauregard, M. (2010). Early impact of 5-HTTLPR polymorphism on the neural correlates of sadness. *Neuroscience Letters, 485,* 261–265.

Foti, D., & Hajcak, G. (2012). Genetic variation in dopamine moderates neural response during reward anticipation and delivery: Evidence from event-related potentials. *Psychophysiology, 49,* 617–626.

Fowles, D. C. (1980). The three arousal model: Implications of Gray's two-factor learning theory for heart rate, electrodermal activity, and psychopathy. *Psychophysiology, 17,* 87–104.

Fox, M. W. (1970). A comparative study of the development of facial expressions in Canids; wolf, coyote and foxes. *Behaviour, 36,* 49–73.

Fraley, R. C., & Shaver, P. R. (2000). Adult romantic attachment: Theoretical developments, emerging controversies, and unanswered questions. *Review of General Psychology, 4,* 132–154.

Frattaroli, J., Thomas, M., & Lyubomirsky, S. (2011). Opening up in the classroom: Effects of expressive writing on graduate school entrance exam performance. *Emotion, 11,* 691–696.

Fredrickson, B. L. (1998). What good are positive emotions? *Review of General Psychology, 2,* 300–319.

Fredrickson, G. M. (2011). *Racism: A short history.* Princeton, NJ: Princeton University Press.

Freeman, W., & Watts, J. W. (1950). *Psychosurgery in the treatment of mental disorders and intractable pain.* Springfield, IL: Charles C Thomas.

Freud, S. (1926). *Inhibitions, symptoms and anxiety.* London: Hogarth Press.

Freud, S. (1927). Some psychological consequences of the anatomical distinction between the sexes. *International Journal of Psychoanalysis, 8,* 133–142.

Freud, S. (1930). *Das Unbehagen in der Kultur* [Civilization and its discontents]. Wien, Austria: Internationaler Psychoanalytischer Verlag.

Freud, S., & Gay, P. (1989). *Civilization and its discontents.* (J. Strachey, Trans.) (The Standard Edition.) New York: W. W. Norton & Company.

Frijda, N. H. (1989). Aesthetic emotions and reality. *American Psychologist, 44,* 1546–1547.

Frühholz, S., Ceravolo, L., & Grandjean, D. (2012). Specific brain networks during explicit and implicit decoding of emotional prosody. *Cerebral Cortex, 22,* 1107–1117.

Fung, H. H, & Carstensen, L. L. (2003). Sending memorable messages to the old: Age differences in preferences and memory for advertisements. *Journal of Personality and Social Psychology, 85,* 163–178.

Fung, H. H., & Carstensen, L. L. (2006). Goals change when life's fragility is primed: Lessons learned from older adults, the September 11 attacks and SARS. *Social Cognition, 24,* 248–278.

Fung, H. H., Carstensen, L. L., & Lutz, A. M. (1999). Influence of time on social preferences: Implications for life-span development. *Psychology and Aging, 14,* 595–604.

Füstös, J., Gramann, K., Herbert, B. M., & Pollatos, O. (2013). On the embodiment of emotion regulation: Interoceptive awareness facilitates reappraisal. *Social Cognitive and Affective Neuroscience, 8,* 911–917.

Gabor, C. S., Phan, A., Clipperton-Allen, A. E., Kavaliers, M., & Choleris, E. (2012). Interplay of oxytocin, vasopressin, and sex hormones in the regulation of social recognition. *Behavioral Neuroscience, 126,* 97–109.

Gaffney, K. F., Choi, E., Yi, K., Jones, G. B., Bowman, C., & Tavangar, N. N. (1997). Stressful events among pregnant Salvadoran women: A cross-cultural comparison. *Journal of Obstetric, Gynecologic, & Neonatal Nursing, 26,* 303–310.

Galdikas, B. M. F. (1996). *Reflections of Eden: My years with the orangutans of Borneo.* Back Bay Books.

Galili, D. S., Lüdke, A., Galizia, C. G., Szyszka, P., & Tanimoto, H. (2011). Olfactory trace conditioning in Drosophila. *The Journal of Neuroscience, 31,* 7240–7248.

Gallistel, C. R., Boytim, M., Gomita, Y., & Klebanoff, L. (1982). Does pimozide block the reinforcing effect of brain stimulation? *Pharmacology, Biochemistry, and Behavior, 17,* 769–781.

Gallup, G. G., Jr, Rosen, T. S., & Brown, C. W. (1972). Effect of conditioned fear on tonic immobility in domestic chickens. *Journal of Comparative and Physiological Psychology, 78,* 22–25.

Garcia, J., & Koelling, R. A. (1966). Relation of cue to consequence in avoidance learning. *Psychonomic Science, 4,* 123–124.

Garcia-Falgueras, A., & Swaab, D. F. (2008). A sex difference in the hypothalamic uncinate nucleus: Relationship to gender identity. *Brain, 131,* 3132–3146.

Gardner, M., & Steinberg, L. (2005). Peer influence on risk taking, risk preference, and risky decision making in adolescence and adulthood: An experimental study. *Developmental Psychology, 41,* 625–635.

Garver-Apgar, C. E., Gangestad, S. W., Thornhill, R., Miller, R. D., & Olp, J. J. (2006). Major histocompatibility complex alleles, sexual responsivity, and unfaithfulness in romantic couples. *Psychological Science, 17,* 830–835.

Gasquoine, P. G. (2013). Localization of function in anterior cingulate cortex: From psychosurgery to functional neuroimaging. *Neuroscience & Biobehavioral Reviews, 37,* 340–348.

Geer, J. H., & Bellard, H. S. (1996). Sexual content induced delays in unprimed lexical decisions: Gender and context effects. *Archives of Sexual Behavior, 25,* 379–395.

Geer, J. H., & Robertson, G. G. (2005). Implicit attitudes in sexuality: Gender differences. *Archives of Sexual Behavior, 34,* 671–677.

Geller, I. (1963). Conditioned "anxiety" and punishment effects on operant behavior of goldfish (Carassius auratus). *Science, 141,* 351–353.

Gelstein, S., Yeshurun, Y., Rozenkrantz, L., Shushan, S., Frumin, I., Roth, Y., & Sobel, N. (2011). Human tears contain a chemosignal. *Science, 331,* 226–230.

Gentzler, A. L., Kerns, K. A., & Keener, E. (2010). Emotional reactions and regulatory responses to negative and positive events: Associations with attachment and gender. *Motivation and Emotion, 34,* 78–92.

George, O., & Koob, G. F. (2010). Individual differences in prefrontal cortex function and the transition from drug use to drug dependence. *Neuroscience and Biobehavioral Reviews, 35,* 232–247.

Gerdes, A. B. M., Wieser, M. J., Mühlberger, A., Weyers, P., Alpers, G. W., Plichta, M. M., Breuer, F., & Pauli, P. (2010). Brain activations to emotional pictures are differentially associated with valence and arousal ratings. *Frontiers in Human Neuroscience, 4,* 175.

Gervais, M., & Wilson, D. S. (2005). The evolution and functions of laughter and humor: A synthetic approach. *The Quarterly Review of Biology, 80,* 395–430.

Gibbon, J., Church, R. M., & Meck, W. H. (1984). Scalar timing in memory. *Annals of the New York Academy of Sciences, 423,* 52–77.

Gigerenzer, G., & Goldstein, D. G. (1996). Mind as computer: Birth of a metaphor. *Creativity Research Journal, 9,* 131–144.

Gil, S., Rousset, S., & Droit-Volet, S. (2009). How liked and disliked foods affect time perception. *Emotion, 9,* 457–463.

Giuliani, N. R., Drabant, E. M., Bhatnagar, R., & Gross, J. J. (2011). Emotion regulation and brain plasticity: Expressive suppression use predicts anterior insula volume. *NeuroImage, 58,* 10–15.

Glaser, E., Mendrek, A., Germain, M., Lakis, N., & Lavoie, M. E. (2012). Sex differences in memory of emotional images: A behavioral and electrophysiological investigation. *International Journal of Psychophysiology, 85,* 17–26.

Glimcher, P. W. (2011). Understanding dopamine and reinforcement learning: The dopamine reward prediction error hypothesis. *Proceedings of the National Academy of Sciences of the United States of America, 108,* 15647–15654.

Gluth, S., Ebner, N. C., & Schmiedek, F. (2010). Attitudes toward younger and older adults: The German aging semantic differential. *International Journal of Behavioral Development, 34,* 147–158.

Goldin, P. R., McRae, K., Ramel, W., & Gross, J. J. (2008). The neural bases of emotion regulation: Reappraisal and suppression of negative emotion. *Biological Psychiatry, 63,* 577–586.

Goldstein, J. M., Seidman, L. J., Horton, N. J., Makris, N., Kennedy, D. N., Caviness, V. S., Faraone, S. V., & Tsuang, M. T. (2001). Normal sexual dimorphism of the adult human brain assessed by in vivo magnetic resonance imaging. *Cerebral Cortex, 11,* 490–497.

Goncalves, R., Pedrozo, A. L., Coutinho, E. S. F., Figueira, I., & Ventura, P. (2012). Efficacy of virtual reality exposure therapy in the treatment of PTSD: A systematic review. *PLoS ONE, 7,* e48469.

Gong, G., He, Y., & Evans, A. C. (2011). Brain connectivity gender makes a difference. *The Neuroscientist, 17,* 575–591.

Good, C. D., Johnsrude, I. S., Ashburner, J., Henson, R. N., Friston, K. J., & Frackowiak, R. S. (2001). A voxel-based morphometric study of ageing in 465 normal adult human brains. *NeuroImage, 14,* 21–36.

Good, J. J., Woodzicka, J. A., & Wingfield, L. C. (2010). The effects of gender stereotypic and counter-stereotypic textbook images on science performance. *Journal of Social Psychology, 150,* 132–147.

Goodall, J. (2010). *In the shadow of man.* New York: Mariner Books.

Goodman, M. J., Griffin, P. B., Estioko-Griffin, A. A., & Grove, J. S. (1985). The compatibility of hunting and mothering among the Agta hunter-gatherers of the Philippines. *Sex Roles, 12,* 1199–1209.

Gotlib, I. H., & Joormann, J. (2010). Cognition and depression: Current status and future directions. *Annual Review of Clinical Psychology, 6,* 285–312.

Gottman, J. M., Coan, J., Carrere, S., & Swanson, C. (1998). Predicting marital happiness and stability from newly-wed interactions. *Journal of Marriage and Family, 60,* 5–22.

Grabenhorst, F., Rolls, E. T., & Bilderbeck, A. (2008). How cognition modulates affective responses to taste and flavor: Top-down influences on the orbitofrontal and pregenual cingulate cortices. *Cerebral Cortex, 18,* 1549–1559.

Graham-Kevan, N., & Archer, J. (2009). Control tactics and partner violence in heterosexual relationships. *Evolution and Human Behavior, 30,* 445–452.

Grandjean, D., Sander, D., & Scherer, K. R. (2008). Conscious emotional experience emerges as a function of multilevel, appraisal-driven response synchronization. *Consciousness and Cognition, 17,* 484–495.

Grandjean, D., & Scherer, K. R. (2008). Unpacking the cognitive architecture of emotion processes. *Emotion, 8,* 341–351.

Grandjean, D., Sander, D., Pourtois, G., Schwartz, S., Seghier, M. L., Scherer, K. R., & Vuilleumier, P. (2005). The voices of wrath: Brain responses to angry prosody in meaningless speech. *Nature Neuroscience, 8,* 145–146.

Gray, J. A. (1975). *Elements of a two-process theory of learning.* London: Academic Press.

Graziano, W. G., Habashi, M. M., & Woodcock, A. (2011). Exploring and measuring differences in person-thing orientations. *Personality and Individual Differences, 51,* 28–33.

Greenwald, A. G., McGhee, D. E., & Schwartz, J. L. (1998). Measuring individual differences in implicit cognition: The implicit association test. *Journal of Personality and Social Psychology, 74,* 1464–1480.

Griskevicius, V., Cialdini, R. B., & Kenrick, D. T. (2006). Peacocks, Picasso, and parental investment: The effects of romantic motives on creativity. *Journal of Personality and Social Psychology, 91,* 63–76.

Grolnick, W. S., Bridges, L. J., & Connell, J. P. (1996). Emotion regulation in two-year-olds: Strategies and emotional expression in four contexts. *Child Development, 67,* 928–941.

Gross, J. J. (1998). Antecedent- and response-focused emotion regulation: Divergent consequences for experience, expression, and physiology. *Journal of Personality and Social Psychology, 74,* 224–237.

Gross, J. J. (2002). Emotion regulation: Affective, cognitive, and social consequences. *Psychophysiology, 39,* 281–291.

Gross, J. J., & Barrett, L. F. (2011). Emotion generation and emotion regulation: One or two depends on your point of view. *Emotion Review, 3,* 8–16.

Gross, J. J., & Levenson, R. W. (1993). Emotional suppression: Physiology, self-report, and expressive behavior. *Journal of Personality and Social Psychology, 64,* 970–986.

Gross, J. J., & Levenson, R. W. (1995). Emotion elicitation using films. *Cognition & Emotion, 9,* 87–108.

Gross, J. J., & Muñoz, R. F. (1995). Emotion regulation and mental health. *Clinical Psychology: Science and Practice, 2,* 151–164.

Grossman, S. P. (1975). Role of the hypothalamus in the regulation of food and water intake. *Psychological Review, 82,* 200–224.

Grossmann, T., Striano, T., & Friederici, A. D. (2006). Crossmodal integration of emotional information from face and voice in the infant brain. *Developmental Science, 9,* 309–315.

Gruberger, M., Ben-Simon, E., Levkovitz, Y., Zangen, A., & Hendler, T. (2011). Towards a neuroscience of mind-wandering. *Frontiers in Human Neuroscience, 5.*

Guerra, P., Sánchez-Adam, A., Anllo-Vento, L., Ramírez, I., & Vila, J. (2012). Viewing loved faces inhibits defense reactions: A health-promotion mechanism? *PLoS ONE, 7,* e41631.

Gunes, H., & Piccardi, M. (2006). Creating and annotating affect databases from face and body display: A contemporary survey. In *Systems, Man and Cybernetics, 2006. SMC '06. IEEE International Conference* (Vol. 3, pp. 2426–2433).

Gunnar, M. R., & Donzella, B. (2002). Social regulation of the cortisol levels in early human development. *Psychoneuroendocrinology, 27,* 199–220.

Güntürkün, O. (2012). The convergent evolution of neural substrates for cognition. *Psychological Research, 76,* 212–219.

Gupta, R., Koscik, T. R., Bechara, A., & Tranel, D. (2011). The amygdala and decision-making. *Neuropsychologia, 49,* 760–766.

Gur, R. C., Turetsky, B. I., Matsui, M., Yan, M., Bilker, W., Hughett, P., & Gur, R. E. (1999). Sex differences in brain gray and white matter in healthy young adults: Correlations with cognitive performance. *The Journal of Neuroscience, 19,* 4065–4072.

Gyurak, A., Gross, J. J., & Etkin, A. (2011). Explicit and implicit emotion regulation: A dual-process framework. *Cognition & Emotion, 25,* 400–412.

Haegler, K., Zernecke, R., Kleemann, A. M., Albrecht, J., Pollatos, O., Brückmann, H., & Wiesmann, M. (2010). No fear no risk! Human risk behavior is affected by chemosensory anxiety signals. *Neuropsychologia, 48,* 3901–3908.

Halford, J., Harrold, J., Lawton, C., & Blundell, J. (2005). Serotonin (5-HT) drugs: Effects on appetite expression and use for the treatment of obesity. *Current Drug Targets, 6,* 201–213.

Hall, J. K., Hutton, S. B., & Morgan, M. J. (2010). Sex differences in scanning faces: Does attention to the eyes explain female superiority in facial expression recognition? *Cognition & Emotion, 24,* 629–637.

Hamann, S., Herman, R. A., Nolan, C. L., & Wallen, K. (2004). Men and women differ in amygdala response to visual sexual stimuli. *Nature Neuroscience, 7,* 411–416.

Hamilton, C. E. (2000). Continuity and discontinuity of attachment from infancy through adolescence. *Child Development, 71,* 690–694.

Hamm, A. O., Weike, A. I., Schupp, H. T., Treig, T., Dressel, A., & Kessler, C. (2003). Affective blindsight: Intact fear conditioning to a visual cue in a cortically blind patient. *Brain, 126,* 267–275.

Han, S., & Northoff, G. (2008). Culture-sensitive neural substrates of human cognition: A transcultural neuroimaging approach. *Nature Reviews Neuroscience, 9,* 646–654.

Han, X., Chen, M., Wang, F., Windrem, M., Wang, S., Shanz, S., Xu, Q., Oberheim, N., Bekar, L., Betstadt, S., Silva, A. J., Takano, T., Goldman, S. A. & Nedergaard, M. (2013). Forebrain engraftment by human glial progenitor cells enhances synaptic plasticity and learning in adult mice. *Cell Stem Cell, 12,* 342–353.

Handlin, L., Hydbring-Sandberg, E., Nilsson, A., Ejdebäck, M., Jansson, A., & Uvnäs-Moberg, K. (2011). Short-term interaction between dogs and their owners: Effects on oxytocin, cortisol, insulin, and heart rate—an exploratory study. *Anthrozoos: A Multidisciplinary Journal of the Interactions of People & Animals, 24,* 301–315.

Hardies, K., Breesch, D., & Branson, J. (2013). Gender differences in overconfidence and risk taking: Do self-selection and socialization matter? *Economics Letters, 118,* 442–444.

Hariri, A. R. (2002). Serotonin transporter genetic bariation and the response of the human amygdala. *Science, 297,* 400–403.

Harlow, J. M. (1868). Recovery from the passage of an iron bar through the head. *Publications of the Massachusetts Medical Society,* 327–347.

Harlow, J. M. (1993). Recovery from the passage of an iron bar through the head. *History of Psychiatry, 4,* 274–281.

Harman, C., Rothbart, M. K., & Posner, M. I. (1997). Distress and attention interactions in early infancy. *Motivation and Emotion, 21,* 27–43.

Harmon-Jones, E., Amodio, D. M., & Zinner, L. R. (2007). Social psychological methods of emotion elicitation. In J. Coan & J. J. B. Allan (Eds.), *Handbook of emotion elicitation and assessment* (pp. 91–105). New York: Oxford University Press.

Harré, R., & Gillett, G. (1994). *The discursive mind.* Thousand Oaks, CA: Sage.

Harris, C. R. (2002). Sexual and romantic jealousy in heterosexual and homosexual adults. *Psychological Science, 13,* 7–12.

Harrison, B. J., Pujol, J., Ortiz, H., Fornito, A., Pantelis, C., & Yücel, M. (2008). Modulation of brain resting-state networks by sad mood induction. *PloS ONE, 3,* e1794.

Harrison, L. K., & Turpin, G. (2003). Implicit memory bias and trait anxiety: A psychophysiological analysis. *Biological Psychology, 62,* 97–114.

Harwood, M. D., & Farrar, M. J. (2006). Conflicting emotions: The connection between affective perspective taking and theory of mind. *British Journal of Developmental Psychology, 24,* 401–418.

Hatfield, E., Hsee, C. K., Costello, J., Weisman, M. S., & Denney, C. (1995). The impact of vocal feedback on emotional experience and expression. *Journal of Social Behavior and Personality, 10,* 293–312.

Heath, R. G., John, S. B., & Fontana, C. J. (1976). Stereotaxic implantation of electrodes in the human brain: A method for long-term study and treatment. *IEEE Transactions on Biomedical Engineering, BME-23,* 296–304.

Hebb, D. O. (2002). *The organization of behavior: A neuropsychological Theory.* Mahwah, NJ: Lawrence Erlbaum Associates.

Henrich, J., Heine, S. J., & Norenzayan, A. (2010). The weirdest people in the world? *The Behavioral and Brain Sciences, 33,* 61–83; discussion 83–135.

Hensley, W. E. (1977). Probability, personality, age, and risk taking. *The Journal of Psychology, 95,* 139–145.

Herbert, C., Pauli, P., & Herbert, B. M. (2011). Self-reference modulates the processing of emotional stimuli in the absence of explicit self-referential appraisal instructions. *Social Cognitive and Affective Neuroscience, 6,* 653–661.

Herman, B. H., & Panksepp, J. (1978). Effects of morphine and naloxone on separation distress and approach attachment: Evidence for opiate mediation of social affect. *Pharmacology Biochemistry and Behavior, 9,* 213–220.

Herman, B. H., & Panksepp, J. (1981). Ascending endorphin inhibition of distress vocalization. *Science, 211,* 1060–1062.

Hermans, E. J., Bos, P. A., Ossewaarde, L., Ramsey, N. F., Fernández, G., & van Honk, J. (2010). Effects of exogenous testosterone on the ventral striatal BOLD response during reward anticipation in healthy women. *NeuroImage, 52,* 277–283.

Hermans, E. J., Marle, H. J. F. van, Ossewaarde, L., Henckens, M. J. A. G., Qin, S., . . .

Fernández, G. (2011). Stress-related noradrenergic activity prompts large-scale neural network reconfiguration. *Science, 334,* 1151–1153.

Hertenstein, M. J., Keltner, D., App, B., Bulleit, B. A., & Jaskolka, A. R. (2006). Touch communicates distinct emotions. *Emotion, 6,* 528–533.

Hess U., Senécal S., Kirouac G., Herrera P., Philippot P., & Kleck R. E. (2000). Emotional expressivity in men and women: Stereotypes and self-perceptions. *Cognition and Emotion, 14,* 609–642.

Hess, U., Adams, R. B., & Kleck, R. E. (2005). Who may frown and who should smile? Dominance, affiliation, and the display of happiness and anger. *Cognition and Emotion, 19,* 515–536.

Higgins, S. T., & Morris, E. K. (1984). Generality of free-operant avoidance conditioning to human behavior. *Psychological Bulletin, 96,* 247–272.

Higham, T., Basell, L., Jacobi, R., Wood, R., Ramsey, C. B., & Conard, N. J. (2012). Testing models for the beginnings of the Aurignacian and the advent of figurative art and music: The radiocarbon chronology of Geißenklösterle. *Journal of Human Evolution, 62,* 664–676.

Hilakivi-Clarke, L., & Lister, R. G. (1992). Social status and voluntary alcohol consumption in mice: Interaction with stress. *Psychopharmacology, 108,* 276–282.

Hines, M. (2011). Gender development and the human brain. *Annual Review of Neuroscience, 34,* 69–88.

Hirshleifer, D., & Shumway, T. (2003). Good day sunshine: Stock returns and the weather. *The Journal of Finance, 58,* 1009–1032.

Hitchcock, J., & Davis, M. (1986). Lesions of the amygdala, but not of the cerebellum or red nucleus, block conditioned fear as measured with the potentiated startle paradigm. *Behavioral Neuroscience, 100,* 11–22.

Hoeft, F., Watson, C. L., Kesler, S. R., Bettinger, K. E., & Reiss, A. L. (2008). Gender differences in the mesocorticolimbic system during computer game-play. *Journal of Psychiatric Research, 42,* 253–258.

Hofmann, S. G., Heering, S., Sawyer, A. T., & Asnaani, A. (2009). How to handle anxiety: The effects of reappraisal, acceptance, and suppression strategies on anxious arousal. *Behaviour Research and Therapy, 47,* 389–394.

Hofstede, G. (1980). *Culture's consequences: International differences in work-related values.* Thousand Oaks, CA: Sage.

Homberg, J. R., & Lesch, K.-P. (2011). Looking on the bright side of serotonin transporter gene variation. *Biological Psychiatry, 69,* 513–519.

Hornak, J. (2003). Changes in emotion after circumscribed surgical lesions of the orbitofrontal and cingulate cortices. *Brain, 126,* 1691–1712.

Howe, M. W., Tierney, P. L., Sandberg, S. G., Phillips, P. E. M., & Graybiel, A. M. (2013). Prolonged dopamine signaling in striatum signals proximity and value of distant rewards. *Nature, 500,* 575–579.

Hsu, M., Bhatt, M., Adolphs, R., Tranel, D., & Camerer, C. F. (2005). Neural systems responding to degrees of uncertainty in human decision-making. *Science, 310,* 1680–1683.

Hsu, S.-M., & Pessoa, L. (2007). Dissociable effects of bottom-up and top-down factors in the processing of unattended fearful faces. *Neuropsychologia, 45,* 3075–3086.

Hubbard, C. S., Ornitz, E., Gaspar, J. X., Smith, S., Amin, J., Labus, J. S., Kilpatrick, L. A., Rhudy, J. L., Mayer, E. A., & Naliboff, B. D. (2011). Modulation of nociceptive and acoustic startle responses to an unpredictable threat in men and women. *Pain, 152,* 1632–1640.

Hudson, R. (1985). Do newborn rabbits learn the odor stimuli releasing nipple-search behavior? *Developmental Psychobiology, 18,* 575–585.

Huettel, S. A., Song, A. W., & McCarthy, G. (2009). *Functional magnetic resonance imaging.* Sunderland, MA: Sinauer Associates.

Hughes, C., & Dunn, J. (1998). Understanding mind and emotion: Longitudinal associations with mental-state talk between young friends. *Developmental Psychology, 34,* 1026–1037.

Hui, G. K., Figueroa, I. R., Poytress, B. S., Roozendaal, B., McGaugh, J. L., & Weinberger, N. M. (2004). Memory enhancement of classical fear conditioning by post-training injections of corticosterone in rats. *Neurobiology of Learning and Memory, 81,* 67–74.

Huizink, A. C., Robles de Medina, P. G., Mulder, E. J. H., Visser, G. H. A., & Buitelaar, J. K. (2003). Stress during pregnancy is associated with developmental outcome in infancy. *Journal of Child Psychology and Psychiatry, 44,* 810–818.

Hunt, M. (1994). *The story of psychology.* New York: Anchor Books.

Hurlemann, R., Patin, A., Onur, O. A., Cohen, M. X., Baumgartner, T., Metzler, S., . . . Kendrick, K. M. (2010). Oxytocin enhances amygdala-dependent, socially reinforced learning and emotional empathy in humans. *The Journal of Neuroscience, 30,* 4999–5007.

Hurlemann, R., Walter, H., Rehme, A. K., Kukolja, J., Santoro, S. C., Schmidt, C., . . . Onur, O. A. (2010). Human amygdala reactivity is diminished by the b-noradrenergic antagonist propranolol. *Psychological Medicine, 40,* 1839–1848.

Hurst, L. D. (1990). Parasite diversity and the evolution of diploidy, multicellularity and anisogamy. *Journal of Theoretical Biology, 144,* 429–443.

Hurst, L. D. (1996). Why are there only two sexes? *Proceedings of the Royal Society of London. Series B: Biological Sciences, 263,* 415–422.

Huttenlocher, J., Haight, W., Bryk, A., Seltzer, M., & Lyons, T. (1991). Early vocabulary growth: Relation to language input and gender. *Developmental Psychology, 27,* 236–248.

IJzerman, H., Gallucci, M., Pouw, W. T. J. L., Weibgerber, S. C., Van Doesum, N. J., & Williams, K. D. (2012). Cold-blooded loneliness: Social exclusion leads to lower skin temperatures. *Acta Psychologica, 140,* 283–288.

Insel, T. R., & Hulihan, T. J. (1995). A gender-specific mechanism for pair bonding: Oxytocin and partner preference formation in monogamous voles. *Behavioral Neuroscience, 109,* 782–789.

Isen, A. M., & Daubman, K. A. (1984). The influence of affect on categorization. *Journal of Personality and Social Psychology, 47,* 1206–1217.

Isen, A. M., Daubman, K. A., & Nowicki, G. P. (1987). Positive affect facilitates creative problem solving. *Journal of Personality and Social Psychology, 52,* 1122–1131.

Isen, A. M., Johnson, M. M., Mertz, E., & Robinson, G. F. (1985). The influence of positive affect on the unusualness of word associations. *Journal of Personality and Social Psychology, 48,* 1413–1426.

Isomura, Y., & Takada, M. (2004). Neural mechanisms of versatile functions in primate anterior cingulate cortex. *Reviews in the Neurosciences, 15,* 279–291.

Israel, S., Lerer, E., Shalev, I., Uzefovsky, F., Riebold, M., Laiba, E., . . . Ebstein, R. P. (2009). The oxytocin receptor (OXTR) contributes to prosocial fund allocations in the dictator game and the social value orientations task. *PLoS ONE, 4,* e5535.

Ito, M. (2008). Control of mental activities by internal models in the cerebellum. *Nature Reviews Neuroscience, 9,* 304–313.

Iwata, J., & LeDoux, J. E. (1988). Dissociation of associative and nonassociative concomitants of classical fear conditioning in the freely behaving rat. *Behavioral Neuroscience, 102,* 66–76.

Izard, C. E. (1992). Basic emotions, relations among emotions, and emotion-cognition relations. *Psychological Review, 99,* 561–565.

Izard, C. E. (1993). Four systems for emotion activation: Cognitive and noncognitive processes. *Psychological Review, 100,* 68–90.

Jack, R. E., Blais, C., Scheepers, C., Schyns, P. G., & Caldara, R. (2009). Cultural confusions show that facial expressions are not universal. *Current Biology, 19,* 1543–1548.

Jacobson, C. D., Csernus, V. J., Shryne, J. E., & Gorski, R. A. (1981). The influence of gonadectomy, androgen exposure, or a gonadal graft in the neonatal rat on the volume of the sexually dimorphic nucleus of the preoptic area. *The Journal of Neuroscience, 1,* 1142–1147.

Jahanshad, N., Aganj, I., Lenglet, C., Joshi, A., Jin, Y., Barysheva, M., Thompson, P. M. (2011). Sex differences in the human connectome: 4-Tesla high angular resolution diffusion imaging (HARDI) tractography in 234 young adult twins. In *2011 IEEE International Symposium on Biomedical Imaging: From Nano to Macro* (pp. 939–943). New York, NY: IEEE.

James, W. (1884). What is an emotion? *Mind, 9,* 188–205.

James, W. (1890). *The principles of psychology.* New York: Henry Holt.

James, W. (1894). Discussion: The physical basis of emotion. *Psychological Review, 1,* 516–529.

Jezová, D., Juránková, E., Mosnárová, A., Kriska, M., & Skultétyová, I. (1996). Neuroendocrine response during stress with relation to gender differences. *Acta Neurobiologiae Experimentalis, 56,* 779–785.

Johansen, J. P., Cain, C. K., Ostroff, L. E., & LeDoux, J. E. (2011). Molecular mechanisms of fear learning and memory. *Cell, 147,* 509–524.

Johns, M., Schmader, T., & Martens, A. (2005). Knowing is half the battle: Teaching stereotype threat as a means of improving women's math performance. *Psychological Science, 16,* 175–179.

Johnson, M. H. (1995). The inhibition of automatic saccades in early infancy. *Developmental Psychobiology, 28,* 281–291.

Jones, H. E., & Wechsler, D. (1928). Galvanometric technique in studies of association. *The American Journal of Psychology, 40,* 607–612.

Jovanovic, T., Phifer, J. E., Sicking, K., Weiss, T., Norrholm, S. D., Bradley, B., & Ressler, K. J. (2011). Cortisol suppression by dexamethasone reduces exaggerated fear responses in posttraumatic stress disorder. *Psychoneuroendocrinology, 36,* 1540–1552.

Jung, C. G. (1907). On psychophysical relations of the associative experiment. *The Journal of Abnormal Psychology, 1,* 247–255.

Juslin, P. N., & Laukka, P. (2003). Communication of emotions in vocal expression and music performance: Different channels, same code? *Psychological Bulletin, 129,* 770–814.

Juth, P., Lundqvist, D., Karlsson, A., & Öhman, A. (2005). Looking for foes and friends: Perceptual and emotional factors when finding a face in the crowd. *Emotion, 5,* 379–395.

Kaas, J. H. (2011). Neocortex in early mammals and its subsequent variations. *Annals of the New York Academy of Sciences, 1225,* 28–36.

Kahn, C. H. (1985). Democritus and the origins of moral psychology. *American Journal of Philology, 106,* 1–31.

Kahneman, D. (2003). A perspective on judgment and choice: Mapping bounded rationality. *American Psychologist, 58*, 697–720.

Kahneman, D., Knetsch, J. L., & Thaler, R. H. (1990). Experimental tests of the endowment effect and the Coase Theorem. *Journal of Political Economy, 98*, 1325–1348.

Kahneman, D., Slovic, P., & Tversky, A. (1982). *Judgment under uncertainty: Heuristics and biases.* Cambridge, UK: Cambridge University Press.

Kahneman, D., & Tversky, A. (1979). Prospect theory: An analysis of decision under risk. *Econometrica, 47, 263–291.*

Kaiseler, M., Polman, R. C., & Nicholls, A. R. (2012). Gender differences in appraisal and coping: *International Journal of Sport Psychology, 43,* 1–14.

Kalin, N. H., Shelton, S. E., Rickman, M., & Davidson, R. J. (1998). Individual differences in freezing and cortisol in infant and mother rhesus monkeys. *Behavioral Neuroscience, 112,* 251–254.

Kalisch, T., Ragert, P., Schwenkreis, P., Dinse, H. R., & Tegenthoff, M. (2009). Impaired tactile acuity in old age is accompanied by enlarged hand representations in somatosensory cortex. *Cerebral Cortex, 19,* 1530–1538.

Kanarek, R. B., D'Anci, K. E., Jurdak, N., & Mathes, W. F. (2009). Running and addiction: Precipitated withdrawal in a rat model of activity-based anorexia. *Behavioral Neuroscience, 123,* 905–912.

Kanske, P., Heissler, J., Schönfelder, S., Bongers, A., & Wessa, M. (2011). How to regulate emotion? Neural networks for reappraisal and distraction. *Cerebral Cortex, 21,* 1379–1388.

Kanwisher, N., McDermott, J., & Chun, M. M. (1997). The fusiform face area: A module in human extrastriate cortex specialized for face perception. *The Journal of Neuroscience, 17,* 4302–4311.

Kappas, A. (2006). Appraisals are direct, immediate, intuitive, and unwitting . . . and some are reflective. . . . *Cognition & Emotion, 20,* 952–975.

Kashdan, T. B., Mishra, A., Breen, W. E., & Froh, J. J. (2009). Gender differences in gratitude: Examining appraisals, narratives, the willingness to express emotions, and changes in psychological needs. *Journal of Personality, 77,* 691–730.

Kaufman, J., Yang, B.-Z., Douglas-Palumberi, H., Houshyar, S., Lipschitz, D., Krystal, J. H., & Gelernter, J. (2004). Social supports and serotonin transporter gene moderate depression in maltreated children. *Proceedings of the National Academy of Sciences of the United States of America, 101,* 17316–17321.

Kavaliers, M., Choleris, E., & Colwell, D. D. (2001). Learning from others to cope with biting flies: Social learning of fear-induced conditioned analgesia and active avoidance. *Behavioral Neuroscience, 115,* 661–674.

Keller, H., & Zach, U. (1993). Developmental consequences of early eye contact behaviour. *Acta Paedopsychiatrica, 56,* 31–36.

Kelley, L. A., & Endler, J. A. (2012). Male great bowerbirds create forced perspective illusions with consistently different individual quality. *Proceedings of the National Academy of Sciences of the United States of America, 109,* 20980.

Kelly, D. (1973). Psychosurgery and the limbic system. *Postgraduate Medical Journal, 49,* 825.

Kennedy, D. P., & Adolphs, R. (2011). Reprint of: Impaired fixation to eyes following amygdala damage arises from abnormal bottom-up attention. *Neuropsychologia, 49,* 589–595.

Kennedy, P. J., & Shapiro, M. L. (2004). Retrieving memories via internal context requires the hippocampus. *The Journal of Neuroscience, 24,* 6979–6985.

Kensinger, E. A. (2009). Remembering the details: Effects of emotion. *Emotion Review, 1,* 99–113.

Kensinger, E. A., & Corkin, S. (2003). Memory enhancement for emotional words: Are emotional words more vividly remembered than neutral words? *Memory & Cognition, 31,* 1169–1180.

Kensinger, E. A., Garoff-Eaton, R. J., & Schacter, D. L. (2007). Effects of emotion on memory specificity in young and older adults. *The Journals of Gerontology. Series B, Psychological Sciences and Social Sciences, 62,* P208–215.

Kensinger, E. A., & Schacter, D. L. (2008). Neural processes supporting young and older adults' emotional memories. *Journal of Cognitive Neuroscience, 20,* 1161–1173.

Kessler, R. C., Berglund, P., Demler, O., Jin, R., Merikangas, K. R., & Walters, E. E. (2005). Lifetime prevalence and age-of-onset distributions of DSM-IV disorders in the National Comorbidity Survey Replication. *Archives of General Psychiatry, 62,* 593–602.

Kettenmann, H., & Verkhratsky, A. (2008). Neuroglia: The 150 years after. *Trends in Neurosciences, 31,* 653–659.

Khalsa, S., Rudrauf, D., & Tranel, D. (2009). Interoceptive awareness declines with age. *Psychophysiology, 46,* 1130–1136.

Kilpatrick, L. A., Zald, D. H., Pardo, J. V., & Cahill, L. F. (2006). Sex-related differences in amygdala functional connectivity during resting conditions. *NeuroImage, 30,* 452–461.

Kim, B., Sung, Y. S., & McClure, S. M. (2012). The neural basis of cultural differences in delay discounting. *Philosophical Transactions of the Royal Society of London. Series B, Biological Sciences, 367,* 650–656.

Kim, P., Feldman, R., Mayes, L. C., Eicher, V., Thompson, N., Leckman, J. F., & Swain, J. E. (2011). Breastfeeding, brain activation to own infant cry, and maternal sensitivity. *Journal of Child Psychology and Psychiatry, and Allied Disciplines, 52,* 907–915.

Kinoshita, A., Okamoto, Y., Okada, G., Demoto, Y., Kunisato, Y., Yoshimura, S., . . . Yamawaki, S. (2012). Sex differences on neural activation to ambiguous facial expression in happy and sad context. *Perceptual and Motor Skills, 115,* 349–359.

Kisley, M. A., Wood, S., & Burrows, C. L. (2007). Looking at the sunny side of life: Age-related change in an event-related potential measure of the negativity bias. *Psychological Science, 18,* 838–843.

Kissler, J., & Koessler, S. (2011). Emotionally positive stimuli facilitate lexical decisions—an ERP study. *Biological Psychology, 86,* 254–264.

Kita, S., Hashiba, R., Ueki, S., Kimoto, Y., Abe, Y., Gotoda, Y., . . . Ito, E. (2011). Does conditioned taste aversion learning in the pond snail Lymnaea stagnalis produce conditioned fear? *The Biological Bulletin, 220,* 71–81.

Kitayama S., Markus H. R., & Kurokawa M. (2000). Culture, emotion, and well-being: Good feelings in Japan and the United States. *Cognition and Emotion, 14,* 93–124.

Klauer, K. C., Musch, J., & Eder, A. B. (2005). Priming of semantic classifications: Late and response related, or earlier and more central? *Psychonomic Bulletin & Review, 12,* 897–903.

Klein, K., & Boals, A. (2001). Expressive writing can increase working memory capacity. *Journal of Experimental Psychology. General, 130,* 520–533.

Kleinhans, N. M., Johnson, L. C., Mahurin, R., Richards, T., Stegbauer, K. C., Greenson, J., Dawson, G., & Aylward, E. (2007). Increased amygdala activation to neutral faces is associated with better face memory performance. *Neuroreport, 18,* 987–991.

Kleinsmith, A., De Silva, P. R., & Bianchi-Berthouze, N. (2006). Cross-cultural differences in recognizing affect from body posture. *Interacting With Computers, 18,* 1371–1389.

Klucken, T., Schweckendiek, J., Koppe, G., Merz, C. J., Kagerer, S., Walter, B., Sammer, G., Vaitl, D., & Stark, R. (2012). Neural correlates of disgust- and fear-conditioned responses. *Neuroscience, 201,* 209–218.

Klüver, H., & Bucy, P. C. (1939). Preliminary analysis of functions of the temporal lobes in monkeys. *Archives of Neurology & Psychiatry, 42,* 979–1000.

Knebel, J.-F., Toepel, U., Hudry, J., le Coutre, J., & Murray, M. (2008). Generating controlled image sets in cognitive neuroscience research. *Brain Topography, 20,* 284–289.

Knight, D. C., Nguyen, H. T., & Bandettini, P. A. (2003). Expression of conditional fear with and without awareness. *Proceedings of the National Academy of Sciences of the United States of America, 100,* 15280–15283.

Knight, G. P., Guthrie, I. K., Page, M. C., & Fabes, R. A. (2002). Emotional arousal and gender differences in aggression: A meta-analysis. *Aggressive Behavior, 28,* 366–393.

Knight, M., Seymour, T. L., Gaunt, J. T., Baker, C., Nesmith, K., & Mather, M. (2007). Aging and goal-directed emotional attention: Distraction reverses emotional biases. *Emotion, 7,* 705–714.

Knowles, M. L., & Gardner, W. L. (2008). Benefits of membership: The activation and amplification of group identities in response to social rejection. *Personality and Social Psychology Bulletin, 34,* 1200–1213.

Kobayashi, S., & Schultz, W. (2008). Influence of reward delays on responses of dopamine neurons. *The Journal of Neuroscience, 28,* 7837–7846.

Koenig, A. M., & Eagly, A. H. (2005). Stereotype threat in men on a test of social sensitivity. *Sex Roles, 52,* 489–496.

Konstan, D. (2006). *The emotions of the ancient Greeks: Studies in Aristotle and classical literature.* Toronto: University of Toronto Press.

Koob, G. F. (2009). Dynamics of neuronal circuits in addiction: Reward, antireward, and emotional memory. *Pharmacopsychiatry, 42,* S32–S41.

Kopell, B. H., Machado, A. G., & Rezai, A. R. (2005). Not your father's lobotomy: Psychiatric surgery revisited. *Clinical Neurosurgery, 52,* 315–330.

Korte, S. M., & De Boer, S. F. (2003). A robust animal model of state anxiety: Fear-potentiated behaviour in the elevated plus-maze. *European Journal of Pharmacology, 463,* 163–175.

Kosfeld, M., Heinrichs, M., Zak, P. J., Fischbacher, U., & Fehr, E. (2005). Oxytocin increases trust in humans. *Nature, 435,* 673–676.

Koster, E. H. W., Crombez, G., Verschuere, B., & De Houwer, J. (2004). Selective attention to threat in the dot probe paradigm: Differentiating vigilance and difficulty to disengage. *Behaviour Research and Therapy, 42,* 1183–1192.

Koster, E. H. W., Crombez, G., Verschuere, B., & De Houwer, J. (2006). Attention to threat in anxiety-prone individuals: Mechanisms underlying attentional Bias. *Cognitive Therapy and Research, 30,* 635–643.

Kötter, R., & Meyer, N. (1992). The limbic system: A review of its empirical foundation. *Behavioural Brain Research, 52,* 105–127.

Kovács, Á. M., Téglás, E., & Endress, A. D. (2010). The social sense: Susceptibility to others' beliefs in human infants and adults. *Science, 330,* 1830–1834.

Kral, J. G., Paez, W., & Wolfe, B. M. (2009). Vagal nerve function in obesity: Therapeutic implications. *World Journal of Surgery, 33,* 1995–2006.

Kreibig, S. D. (2010). Autonomic nervous system activity in emotion: A review. *Biological Psychology, 84,* 394–421.

Krishnan, V., & Nestler, E. J. (2008). The molecular neurobiology of depression. *Nature, 455,* 894–902.

Krumhuber, E. G., & Manstead, A. S. R. (2009). Can Duchenne smiles be feigned? New evidence on felt and false smiles. *Emotion, 9,* 807–820.

Kuebli, J., Butler, S., & Fivush, R. (1995). Mother-child talk about past emotions: Relations of maternal language and child gender over time. *Cognition & Emotion, 9,* 265–283.

Kuebli, J., & Fivush, R. (1992). Gender differences in parent-child conversations about past emotions. *Sex Roles, 27,* 683–698.

Kuehner, C., Huffziger, S., & Liebsch, K. (2009). Rumination, distraction and mindful self-focus: Effects on mood, dysfunctional attitudes and cortisol stress response. *Psychological Medicine, 39,* 219–228.

Kuhle, B. X. (2011). Did you have sex with him? Do you love her? An in vivo test of sex differences in jealous interrogations. *Personality and Individual Differences, 51,* 1044–1047.

Kühn, S., Gallinat, J., & Brass, M. (2011). "Keep calm and carry on": Structural correlates of expressive suppression of emotions. *PLoS ONE, 6,* e16569.

Kuhn, S. L., & Stiner, M. C. (2006). What's a Mother to Do? The division of labor among Neandertals and modern humans in Eurasia. *Current Anthropology, 47,* 953–981.

Kunst-Wilson, W. R., & Zajonc, R. B. (1980). Affective discrimination of stimuli that cannot be recognized. *Science, 207,* 557–558.

Kunzmann, U., & Grühn, D. (2005). Age differences in emotional reactivity: The sample case of sadness. *Psychology and Aging, 20,* 47–59.

Kuppens, S., Grietens, H., Onghena, P., & Michiels, D. (2009). Associations between parental control and children's overt and relational aggression. *British Journal of Developmental Psychology, 27,* 607–623.

Kutas, M., & Hillyard, S. A. (1980). Reading senseless sentences: Brain potentials reflect semantic incongruity. *Science, 207,* 203–205.

LaBar, K. S., Gatenby, J. C., Gore, J. C., LeDoux, J. E., & Phelps, E. A. (1998). Human amygdala activation during conditioned fear acquisition and extinction: A mixed-trial fMRI study. Neuron, *20,* 937–945.

LaBar, K. S., LeDoux, J. E., Spencer, D. D., & Phelps, E. A. (1995). Impaired fear conditioning following unilateral temporal lobectomy in humans. *The Journal of Neuroscience, 15,* 6846–6855.

LaBar, K. S., & Phelps, E. A. (1998). Arousal-mediated memory consolidation: Role of the medial temporal lobe in humans. *Psychological Science, 9,* 490–493.

Labouvie-Vief, G., Lumley, M. A., Jain, E., & Heinze, H. (2003). Age and gender differences in cardiac reactivity and subjective emotion responses to emotional autobiographical memories. *Emotion, 3,* 115–126.

Lacey, B. C., & Lacey, J. I. (1980). Presidential address, 1979. Cognitive modulation of time-dependent primary bradycardia. *Psychophysiology, 17,* 209–221.

LaFrance, M., Hecht, M. A., & Paluck, E. L. (2003). The contingent smile: A meta-analysis of sex differences in smiling. *Psychological Bulletin, 129,* 305–334.

Laird, J. D., & Strout, S. (2007). Emotional behaviors as emotional stimuli. In J. Coan & J. J. B. Allan (Eds.), *Handbook of emotion elicitation and assessment* (pp. 54–64). New York: Oxford University Press.

Lakatos, K., Nemoda, Z., Birkas, E., Ronai, Z., Kovacs, E., Ney, K., Toth, I., Sasvari-Szekely, M., & Gervai, J. (2003). Association of D4 dopamine receptor gene and serotonin transporter promoter polymorphisms with infants' response to novelty. *Molecular Psychiatry, 8,* 90–97.

Lamoreaux, M., & Morling, B. (2012). Outside the head and outside individualism-collectivism further meta-analyses of cultural products. *Journal of Cross-Cultural Psychology, 43,* 299–327.

Landers, M. S., & Sullivan, R. M. (2012). The development and neurobiology of infant attachment and fear. *Developmental Neuroscience, 34,* 101–114.

Landis, C., & Hunt, W. A. (1939). *The startle pattern.* New York: Farrar & Rinehart, Inc.

Lang, P. J., Bradley, M. M., & Cuthbert, B. N. (1990). Emotion, attention, and the startle reflex. *Psychological Review, 97,* 377.

Lang, P. J., Bradley, M. M., & Cuthbert, B. N. (2008). International affective picture system (IAPS): Affective ratings of pictures and instruction manual. *Technical Report,* A-8.

Lang, P., & Davis, M. (2006). Emotion, motivation, and the brain: Reflex foundations in animal and human research. *Progress in Brain Research, 156,* 3–29.

Lang, P. J., Davis, M., & Öhman, A. (2000). Fear and anxiety: Animal models and human cognitive psychophysiology. *Journal of Affective Disorders, 61,* 137–159.

Lang, P. J., Greenwald, M. K., Bradley, M. M., & Hamm, A. O. (1993). Looking at pictures: Affective, facial, visceral, and behavioral reactions. *Psychophysiology, 30,* 261–273.

Langeslag, S. J. E., & van Strien, J. W. (2009). Aging and emotional memory: The co-occurrence of neurophysiological and behavioral positivity effects. *Emotion, 9,* 369–377.

Langford, D. J., Bailey, A. L., Chanda, M. L., Clarke, S. E., Drummond, T. E., Echols, S., . . . Mogil, J. S. (2010). Coding of facial expressions of pain in the laboratory mouse. *Nature Methods, 7,* 447–449.

Lanuza, E., Nader, K., & Ledoux, J. . (2004). Unconditioned stimulus pathways to the amygdala: Effects of posterior thalamic and cortical lesions on fear conditioning. *Neuroscience, 125,* 305–315.

Laplante, D. P., Barr, R. G., Brunet, A., Fort, G. G. D., Meaney, M. L., Saucier, J.-F., Zelazo, P. R., & King, S. (2004). Stress during pregnancy affects general intellectual and language functioning in human toddlers. *Pediatric Research, 56,* 400–410.

Larson, R., & Richards, M. H. (1991). Daily companionship in late childhood and early adolescence: Changing developmental contexts. *Child Development, 62,* 284–300.

Lasauskaite, R., Gendolla, G. H. E., & Silvestrini, N. (2013). Do sadness-primes make me work harder because they make me sad? *Cognition & Emotion, 27,* 158–165.

Lasch, H., Castell, D. O., & Castell, J. A. (1997). Evidence for diminished visceral pain with aging: stdies using graded intraesophageal balloon distension. *The American Journal of Physiology, 272,* G1–3.

Laucht, M., Becker, K., & Schmidt, M. H. (2006). Visual exploratory behaviour in infancy and novelty seeking in adolescence: Two developmentally specific phenotypes of DRD4? *Journal of Child Psychology and Psychiatry, 47,* 1143–1151.

Laurent, H. K., Stevens, A., & Ablow, J. C. (2011). Neural correlates of hypothalamic-pituitary-adrenal regulation of mothers with their infants. *Biological Psychiatry, 70,* 826–832.

Law-Tho, D., Desce, J. M., & Crepel, F. (1995). Dopamine favours the emergence of long-term depression versus long-term potentiation in slices of rat prefrontal cortex. *Neuroscience Letters, 188,* 125–128.

Lazarus, R. S. (1982). Thoughts on the relations between emotion and cognition. *American Psychologist, 37,* 1019.

Lazarus, R. S. (1984). On the primacy of cognition. *American Psychologist, 39,* 124–129.

Lazarus, R. S. (1994). *Emotion and adaptation.* New York: Oxford University Press.

Lazarus, R. S., & Alfert, E. (1964). Short-circuiting of threat by experimentally altering cognitive appraisal. *Journal of Abnormal Psychology, 69,* 195–205.

Leaper, C., & Smith, T. E. (2004). A meta-analytic review of gender variations in children's language use: Talkativeness, affiliative speech, and assertive speech. *Developmental Psychology, 40,* 993–1027.

Leclerc, C. M., & Kensinger, E. A. (2008). Effects of age on detection of emotional information. *Psychology and Aging, 23,* 209–215.

LeDoux, J. E. (2001). Emotion circuits in the brain. *The Science of Mental Health: Fear and Anxiety, 10,* 259.

LeDoux, J. E., Iwata, J., Cicchetti, P., & Reis, D. J. (1988). Different projections of the central amygdaloid nucleus mediate autonomic and behavioral correlates of conditioned fear. *The Journal of Neuroscience, 8,* 2517–2529.

LeDoux, J. E., Sakaguchi, A., Iwata, J., & Reis, D. J. (1985). Auditory emotional memories: Establishment by projections from the medial geniculate nucleus to the posterior neostriatum and/or dorsal amygdala. *Annals of the New York Academy of Sciences, 444,* 463–464.

LeDoux, J. E., Sakaguchi, A., & Reis, D. J. (1984). Subcortical efferent projections of the medial geniculate nucleus mediate emotional responses conditioned to acoustic stimuli. *The Journal of Neuroscience, 4,* 683–698.

Lee, A., Mathuru, A. S., Teh, C., Kibat, C., Korzh, V., Penney, T. B., & Jesuthasan, S. (2010). The habenula prevents helpless behavior in larval zebrafish. *Current Biology, 20,* 2211–2216.

Lee, K. H., & Siegle, G. J. (2012). Common and distinct brain networks underlying explicit emotional evaluation: A meta-analytic study. *Social Cognitive and Affective Neuroscience, 7,* 521–534.

Leiner, H. C. (2010). Solving the mystery of the human cerebellum. *Neuropsychology Review, 20,* 229–235.

Lejuez, C. W., Read, J. P., Kahler, C. W., Richards, J. B., Ramsey, S. E., Stuart, . . . Brown, R. A. (2002). Evaluation of a behavioral measure of risk taking: The balloon analogue risk task (BART). *Journal of Experimental Psychology. Applied, 8,* 75–84.

Leonardi, R. J., Vick, S.-J., & Dufour, V. (2012). Waiting for more: The performance of domestic dogs (Canis familiaris) on exchange tasks. *Animal Cognition, 15,* 107–120.

Lerner, J. S., & Keltner, D. (2000). Beyond valence: Toward a model of emotion-specific influences on judgment and choice. *Cognition & Emotion, 14,* 473–493.

Levant, R. F., Hall, R. J., Williams, C. M., & Hasan, N. T. (2009). Gender differences in alexithymia. *Psychology of Men & Masculinity, 10,* 190–203.

Levenson, R. W., Carstensen, L. L., Friesen, W. V., & Ekman, P. (1991). Emotion, physiology, and expression in old age. *Psychology and Aging, 6,* 28–35.

Levenson, R. W., Ekman, P., & Friesen, W. V. (1990). Voluntary facial action generates emotion-specific autonomic nervous system activity. *Psychophysiology, 27,* 363–384.

Levine, S., Wiener, S. G., Coe, C. L., Bayart, F. E. S., & Hayashi, K. T. (1987). Primate vocalization: A psychobiological approach. *Child Development, 58,* 1408–1419.

Levy, R. T. (1973). *Tahitians.* Chicago, IL: University of Chicago Press. Retrieved from http://www.press.uchicago.edu/ucp/books/book/chicago/T/bo3627764.html

Lewis-Evans, B., de Waard, D., Jolij, J., & Brookhuis, K. A. (2012). What you may not see might slow you down anyway: Masked images and driving. *PLoS ONE, 7,* e29857.

Lewy, A. J., Emens, J. S., Songer, J. B., Sims, N., Laurie, A. L., Fiala, S. C., & Buti, A. L. (2009). Winter depression: Integrating mood, circadian rhythms, and the sleep/wake and light/dark cycles into a bio-psycho-social-environmental model. *Sleep Medicine Clinics, 4,* 285–299.

Li, S., Rao, L.-L., Ren, X.-P., Bai, X.-W., Zheng, R., Li, J.-Z., Wang, Z.-J., & Liu, H.

(2009). Psychological typhoon eye in the 2008 Wenchuan earthquake. *PLoS ONE, 4,* e4964.

Liddell, B. J., Brown, K. J., Kemp, A. H., Barton, M. J., Das, P., Peduto, A., Gordon, E., & Williams, L. M. (2005). A direct brainstem-amygdala-cortical "alarm" system for subliminal signals of fear. *NeuroImage, 24,* 235–243.

Lieberman, M. D., Inagaki, T. K., Tabibnia, G., & Crockett, M. J. (2011). Subjective responses to emotional stimuli during labeling, reappraisal, and distraction. *Emotion, 11,* 468–480.

Lighthall, N. R., Sakaki, M., Vasunilashorn, S., Nga, L., Somayajula, S., Chen, E. Y., Samii, N., & Mather, M. (2012). Gender differences in reward-related decision processing under stress. *Social Cognitive and Affective Neuroscience, 7,* 476–484.

Lim, M. M., & Young, L. J. (2004). Vasopressin-dependent neural circuits underlying pair bond formation in the monogamous prairie vole. *Neuroscience, 125,* 35–45.

Lindquist, K. A., & Barrett, L. F. (2008). Constructing emotion. *Psychological Science, 19,* 898–903.

Lindquist, K. A., Wager, T. D., Kober, H., Bliss-Moreau, E., & Feldman-Barrett, L. (2012). The brain basis of emotion: A meta-analytic review. *The Behavioral and Brain Sciences, 35,* 121–143.

Lindström, B. R., & Bohlin, G. (2011). Emotion processing facilitates working memory performance. *Cognition & Emotion, 25,* 1196–1204.

Lischke, A., Gamer, M., Berger, C., Grossmann, A., Hauenstein, K., Heinrichs, M., . . . Domes, G. (2012). Oxytocin increases amygdala reactivity to threatening scenes in females. *Psychoneuroendocrinology, 37,* 1431–1438.

Lisman, J., Grace, A. A., & Duzel, E. (2011). A neoHebbian framework for episodic memory; role of dopamine-dependent late LTP. *Trends in Neurosciences, 34,* 536–547.

Litvin, Y., Tovote, P., Pentkowski, N. S., Zeyda, T., King, L. B., Vasconcellos, A. J., . . . Blanchard, R. J. (2010). Maternal separation modulates short-term behavioral and physiological indices of the stress response. *Hormones and Behavior, 58,* 241–249.

Liu, D., Diorio, J., Tannenbaum, B., Caldji, C., Francis, D., Freedman, A., Sharma, S., . . . Meaney, M. J. (1997). Maternal care, hippocampal glucocorticoid receptors, and hypothalamic-pituitary-adrenal responses to stress. *Science, 277,* 1659–1662.

Liu, H., Hu, Z., Peng, D., Yang, Y., & Li, K. (2010). Common and segregated neural substrates for automatic conceptual and affective priming as revealed by event-related functional magnetic resonance imaging. *Brain and Language, 112,* 121–128.

Liu, X., Ramirez, S., Pang, P. T., Puryear, C. B., Govindarajan, A., Deisseroth, K., & Tonegawa, S. (2012). Optogenetic stimulation of a hippocampal engram activates fear memory recall. *Nature, 484,* 381–385.

Liu, X., Ramirez, S., Pang, P. T., Puryear, C. B., Govindarajan, A., Deisseroth, K., & Tonegawa, S. (2012). Optogenetic stimulation of a hippocampal engram activates fear memory recall. *Nature, 484,* 381–385.

Liu, Y., Curtis, J. T., & Wang, Z. (2001). Vasopressin in the lateral septum regulates pair bond formation in male prairie voles (Microtus ochrogaster). *Behavioral Neuroscience, 115,* 910–919.

Ljungberg, T., Apicella, P., & Schultz, W. (1992). Responses of monkey dopamine neurons during learning of behavioral reactions. *Journal of Neurophysiology, 67,* 145–163.

Loftus, E. F. (1975). Leading questions and the eyewitness report. *Cognitive Psychology, 7,* 560–572.

Logothetis, N. K., Pauls, J., Augath, M., Trinath, T., & Oeltermann, A. (2001). Neurophysiological investigation of the basis of the fMRI signal. *Nature, 412,* 150–157.

Löken, L. S., Wessberg, J., Morrison, I., McGlone, F., & Olausson, H. (2009). Coding of pleasant touch by unmyelinated afferents in humans. *Nature Neuroscience, 12,* 547–548.

Lopes, A. P. F., Ganzer, L., Borges, A. C., Kochenborger, L., Januário, A. C., Faria, M. S., . . . Paschoalini, M. A. (2012). Effects of GABA ligands injected into the nucleus accumbens shell on fear/anxiety-like and feeding behaviours in food-deprived rats. *Pharmacology, Biochemistry, and Behavior, 101,* 41–48.

López-Muñoz, F., & Alamo, C. (2009). Monoaminergic neurotransmission: The history of the discovery of antidepressants from 1950s until today. *Current Pharmaceutical Design, 15,* 1563–1586.

Lorenz, K. (1935). Der Kumpan in der Umwelt des Vogels. *Journal für Ornithologie, 83,* 137–213.

Lorenz, K., & Wilson, M. K. (2002). *Man meets dog.* London: Routledge.

Low, B. S. (2001). *Why sex matters: A Darwinian look at human behavior.* Princeton, NJ: Princeton University Press.

Low, C. A., Stanton, A. L., & Bower, J. E. (2008). Effects of acceptance-oriented versus evaluative emotional processing on heart rate recovery and habituation. *Emotion, 8,* 419–424.

Lozoff, B., & Brittenham, G. (1979). Infant care: Cache or carry. *The Journal of Pediatrics, 95,* 478–483.

Luber, B., Peterchev, A. V., Nguyen, T., Sporn, A., & Lisanby, S. H. (2007). Application of transcranial magnetic stimulation (TMS) in psychophysiology. In J. T. Cacioppo, L. G. Tassinary, & G. G. Berntson (Eds.), *Handbook of psychophysiology* (pp. 120–138). New York: Cambridge University Press.

Lui, M. A., Penney, T. B., & Schirmer, A. (2011). Emotion effects on timing: Attention versus pacemaker accounts. *PLoS ONE, 6,* e21829.

Lundqvist, D., & Öhman, A. (2005). Emotion regulates attention: The relation between facial configurations, facial emotion, and visual attention. *Visual Cognition, 12,* 51–84.

Luther, D., & Baptista, L. (2010). Urban noise and the cultural evolution of bird songs. *Proceedings of the Royal Society B: Biological Sciences, 277,* 469–473.

Lutz, P.-E., & Kieffer, B. L. (2013). Opioid receptors: Distinct roles in mood disorders. *Trends in Neurosciences, 36,* 195–206.

Lykken, D. T., & Tellegen, A. (1993). Is human mating adventitious or the result of lawful choice? A twin study of mate selection. *Journal of Personality and Social Psychology, 65,* 56–68.

Lynch, J., Smith, G. D., Hillemeier, M., Shaw, M., Raghunathan, T., & Kaplan, G. (2001). Income inequality, the psychosocial environment, and health: Comparisons of wealthy nations. *Lancet, 358,* 194–200.

MacDonald, G., & Leary, M. R. (2005). Why does social exclusion hurt? The relationship between social and physical pain. *Psychological Bulletin, 131,* 202–223.

Machin, A. J., & Dunbar, R. I. M. (2011). The brain opioid theory of social attachment: A review of the evidence. *Behaviour, 148,* 985–1025.

MacLean, P. D. (1949). Psychosomatic disease and the "visceral brain": Recent developments bearing on the Papez theory of emotion. *Psychosomatic Medicine, 11,* 338–353.

MacLean, P. D. (1952). Some psychiatric implications of physiological studies on frontotemporal portion of limbic system (visceral brain). *Electroencephalography and Clinical Neurophysiology, 4,* 407–418.

MacLean, P. D. (1972). Cerebral evolution and emotional processes: New findings on the striatal complex. *Annals of the New York Academy of Sciences, 193,* 137–149.

MacLean, P. D. (1977). The triune brain in conflict. *Psychotherapy and Psychosomatics, 28,* 207–220.

MacLean, P. D., & Newman, J. D. (1988). Role of midline frontolimbic cortex in production of the isolation call of squirrel monkeys. *Brain Research, 450,* 111–123.

MacLeod, C., Mathews, A., & Tata, P. (1986). Attentional bias in emotional disorders. *Journal of Abnormal Psychology, 95,* 15–20.

Macmillan, M. (2000). Restoring Phineas Gage: A 150th retrospective. *Journal of the History of the Neurosciences, 9,* 46–66.

Madden, J. R. (2008). Do bowerbirds exhibit cultures? *Animal Cognition, 11,* 1–12.

Maestripieri, D., & Carroll, K. A. (1998). Child abuse and neglect: Usefulness of the animal data. *Psychological Bulletin, 123,* 211–223.

Mak, A. K. Y., Hu, Z., Zhang, J. X. X., Xiao, Z., & Lee, T. M. C. (2009). Sex-related differences in neural activity during emotion regulation. *Neuropsychologia, 47,* 2900–2908.

Mangelsdorf, S. C., Shapiro, J. R., & Marzolf, D. (1995). Developmental and temperamental differences in emotion regulation in infancy. *Child Development, 66,* 1817–1828.

Mantsch, J. R., Saphier, D., & Goeders, N. E. (1998). Corticosterone facilitates the acquisition of cocaine self-administration in rats: Opposite effects of the type II glucocorticoid receptor agonist dexamethasone. *The Journal of Pharmacology and Experimental Therapeutics, 287,* 72–80.

Marco, E. J., & Skuse, D. H. (2006). Autism-lessons from the X chromosome. *Social Cognitive and Affective Neuroscience, 1,* 183–193.

Marcus Aurelius (1916). *Marcus Aurelius.* In Loeb Classical Library. C. R. Haines (Ed./Trans.) Cambridge, MA: Harvard University Press.

Markus, H. R., & Kitayama, S. (1991). Culture and the self: Implications for cognition, emotion, and motivation. *Psychological Review, 98,* 224–253.

Martínez Mateo, M., Cabanis, M., Loebell, N. C. de E., & Krach, S. (2012). Concerns about cultural neurosciences: A critical analysis. *Neuroscience & Biobehavioral Reviews, 36,* 152–161.

Masataka, N., & Shibasaki, M. (2012). Premenstrual enhancement of snake detection in visual search in healthy women. *Scientific Reports, 2, 307.*

Mashour, G. A., Walker, E. E., & Martuza, R. L. (2005). Psychosurgery: Past, present, and future. *Brain Research Reviews, 48,* 409–419.

Maslow, A. H. (1943). A theory of human motivation. *Psychological Review, 50,* 370–396.

Massano, J., & Garrett, C. (2012). Deep brain stimulation and cognitive decline in Parkinson's disease: A clinical review. *Frontiers in Neurology, 3,* 66.

Masten, C. L., Eisenberger, N. I., Borofsky, L. A., Pfeifer, J. H., McNealy, K., Mazziotta, J. C., & Dapretto, M. (2009). Neural correlates of social exclusion during adolescence: Understanding the distress of peer rejection. *Social Cognitive and Affective Neuroscience, 4,* 143–157.

Mather, M. (2012). The emotion paradox in the aging brain. *Annals of the New York Academy of Sciences, 1251,* 33–49.

Mathews, G. A., Fane, B. A., Conway, G. S., Brook, C. G. D., & Hines, M. (2009). Personality and congenital adrenal hyperplasia: Possible effects of prenatal androgen exposure. *Hormones and Behavior, 55,* 285–291.

Mathuru, A. S., Kibat, C., Cheong, W. F., Shui, G., Wenk, M. R., Friedrich, R. W., & Jesuthasan, S. (2012). Chondroitin fragments are odorants that trigger fear behavior in fish. *Current Biology: CB, 22,* 538–544.

Matsumoto, D. (2007). Culture, context, and behavior. *Journal of Personality, 75,* 1285–1320.

Matsumoto, D., & Hwang, H. S. (2012). Culture and emotion: The integration of biological and cultural contributions. *Journal of Cross-Cultural Psychology, 43,* 91–118.

Matsumoto, D., Kudoh, T., Scherer, K., & Wallbott, H. (1988). Antecedents of and reactions to emotions in the United States and Japan. *Journal of Cross-Cultural Psychology, 19,* 267–286.

Matsumoto, D., & Willingham, B. (2006). The thrill of victory and the agony of defeat: Spontaneous expressions of medal winners of the 2004 Athens Olympic Games. *Journal of Personality and Social Psychology, 91,* 568–581.

Matsumoto, D., & Willingham, B. (2009). Spontaneous facial expressions of emotion of congenitally and noncongenitally blind individuals. *Journal of Personality and Social Psychology, 96,* 1–10.

Matsumoto, D., Willingham, B., & Olide, A. (2009). Sequential dynamics of culturally moderated facial expressions of emotion. *Psychological Science, 20,* 1269–1275.

Matsumoto, D., Yoo, S. H., & Nakagawa, S. (2008). Culture, emotion regulation, and adjustment. *Journal of Personality and Social Psychology, 94,* 925–937.

Matsumoto, M., & Hikosaka, O. (2009). Two types of dopamine neuron distinctly convey positive and negative motivational signals. *Nature, 459,* 837–841.

Matsunami, H., & Amrein, H. (2003). Taste and pheromone perception in mammals and flies. *Genome Biology, 4,* 220.

Matsuzawa, T., & McGrew, W. C. (2008). Kinji Imanishi and 60 years of Japanese primatology. *Current Biology, 18,* R587–591.

Matthiesen, A.-S., Ransjö-Arvidson, A.-B., Nissen, E., & Uvnäs-Moberg, K. (2001). Postpartum maternal oxytocin release by newborns: Effects of infant hand massage and sucking. *Birth, 28,* 13–19.

Mauss, I. B., Troy, A. S., & Lebourgeois, M. K. (2013). Poorer sleep quality is associated with lower emotion-regulation ability in a laboratory paradigm. *Cognition & Emotion, 27,* 567–576.

McCall, K. M., Rellini, A. H., Seal, B. N., & Meston, C. M. (2007). Sex differences in memory for sexually-relevant information. *Archives of Sexual Behavior, 36,* 508–517.

McCall, R. B., & Carriger, M. S. (1993). A meta-analysis of infant habituation and recognition memory performance as predictors of later IQ. *Child Development, 64,* 57–79.

McCaul, K. D., Solomon, S., & Holmes, D. S. (1979). Effects of paced respiration and expectations on physiological and psychological responses to threat. *Journal of Personality and Social Psychology, 37,* 564–571.

McGaugh, J. L. (2004). The amygdala modulates the consolidation of memories of emotionally arousing experiences. *Annual Review of Neuroscience, 27,* 1–28.

McGowan, P. O., Sasaki, A., D'Alessio, A. C., Dymov, S., Labonté, B., Szyf, M., Turecki, G., & Meaney, M. J. (2009). Epigenetic regulation of the glucocorticoid receptor in human brain associates with childhood abuse. *Nature Neuroscience, 12,* 342–348.

McGraw, L. A., & Young, L. J. (2010). The prairie vole: An emerging model organism for understanding the social brain. *Trends in Neurosciences, 33,* 103.

McIntyre, C. K., McGaugh, J. L., & Williams, C. L. (2012). Interacting brain systems modulate memory consolidation. *Neuroscience & Biobehavioral Reviews, 36,* 1750–1762.

McNeilly, A. S., Robinson, I. C., Houston, M. J., & Howie, P. W. (1983). Release of oxytocin and prolactin in response to suckling.

British Medical Journal (Clinical research ed.), 286, 257–259.

McRae, K., Hughes, B., Chopra, S., Gabrieli, J. D. E., Gross, J. J., & Ochsner, K. N. (2009). The neural bases of distraction and reappraisal. *Journal of Cognitive Neuroscience, 22,* 248–262.

McRae, K., Ochsner, K. N., Mauss, I. B., Gabrieli, J. J. D., & Gross, J. J. (2008). Gender differences in emotion regulation: An fMRI study of cognitive reappraisal. *Group Processes & Intergroup Relations, 11,* 143–162.

Meck, W. H., Penney, T. B., & Pouthas, V. (2008). Cortico-striatal representation of time in animals and humans. *Current Opinion in Neurobiology, 18,* 145–152.

Meissner, K., Muth, E. R., & Herbert, B. M. (2011). Bradygastric activity of the stomach predicts disgust sensitivity and perceived disgust intensity. *Biological Psychology, 86,* 9–16.

Melcher, T., Obst, K., Mann, A., Paulus, C., & Gruber, O. (2012). Antagonistic modulatory influences of negative affect on cognitive control: Reduced and enhanced interference resolution capability after the induction of fear and sadness. *Acta Psychologica, 139,* 507–514.

Meletti, S., Tassi, L., Mai, R., Fini, N., Tassinari, C. A., & Russo, G. L. (2006). Emotions induced by intracerebral electrical stimulation of the temporal lobe. *Epilepsia, 47,* 47–51.

Mella, N., Conty, L., & Pouthas, V. (2011). The role of physiological arousal in time perception: Psychophysiological evidence from an emotion regulation paradigm. *Brain and Cognition, 75,* 182–187.

Meltzoff, A. N., & Moore, M. K. (1977). Imitation of facial and manual gestures by human neonates. *Science, 198,* 75–78.

Mendes, D. M. L. F., Seidl-de-Moura, M. L., & Siqueira, J. de O. (2009). The ontogenesis of smiling and its association with mothers' affective behaviors: A longitudinal study. *Infant Behavior & Development, 32,* 445–453.

Merrer, J. L., Becker, J. A. J., Befort, K., & Kieffer, B. L. (2009). Reward processing by the opioid system in the brain. *Physiological Reviews, 89,* 1379–1412.

Mervis, C. B., & Rosch, E. (1981). Categorization of natural objects. *Annual Review of Psychology, 32,* 89–115.

Merz, C. J., Stark, R., Vaitl, D., Tabbert, K., & Wolf, O. T. (2013). Stress hormones are associated with the neuronal correlates of instructed fear conditioning. *Biological Psychology, 92,* 82–89.

Merz, C. J., Tabbert, K., Schweckendiek, J., Klucken, T., Vaitl, D., Stark, R., & Wolf, O. T. (2010). Investigating the impact of sex and cortisol on implicit fear conditioning with fMRI. *Psychoneuroendocrinology, 35,* 33–46.

Mesquita, B., & Ellsworth, P. C. (2001). The role of culture in appraisal. In K. R. Scherer, A. Schorr, & T. Johnstone (Eds.), *Appraisal processes in emotion: Theory, methods, research* (pp. 233–248). New York: Oxford University Press.

Mesquita, B., & Frijda, N. H. (1992). Cultural variations in emotions: A review. *Psychological Bulletin, 112,* 179–204.

Messier, C., & White, N. M. (1984). Contingent and non-contingent actions of sucrose and saccharin reinforcers: Effects on taste preference and memory. *Physiology & Behavior, 32,* 195–203.

Meyer, M., Baumann, S., Wildgruber, D., & Alter, K. (2007). How the brain laughs. *Behavioural Brain Research, 182,* 245–260.

Meyer-Lindenberg, A., Domes, G., Kirsch, P., & Heinrichs, M. (2011). Oxytocin and vasopressin in the human brain: Social neuropeptides for translational medicine. *Nature Reviews Neuroscience, 12,* 524–538.

Michaels, W. B. (1995). *Our America: Nativism, modernism, and pluralism.* Durham, NC: Duke University Press.

Michalak, J., Troje, N. F., Fischer, J., Vollmar, P., Heidenreich, T., & Schulte, D. (2009). Embodiment of sadness and depression—gait patterns associated with dysphoric mood. *Psychosomatic Medicine, 71*, 580–587.

Miller, G. (2000). Sexual selection for indicators of intelligence. *Novartis Foundation symposium, 233*, 260–270; discussion 270–280.

Miller, M., & Fry, W. F. (2009). The effect of mirthful laughter on the human cardiovascular system. *Medical Hypotheses, 73*, 636–639.

Min, C. S., & Schirmer, A. (2011). Perceiving verbal and vocal emotions in a second language. *Cognition & Emotion*, 1–17.

Mirenowicz, J., & Schultz, W. (1996). Preferential activation of midbrain dopamine neurons by appetitive rather than aversive stimuli. *Nature, 379*, 449–451.

Mischel, W., Ebbesen, E. B., & Zeiss, A. R. (1972). Cognitive and attentional mechanisms in delay of gratification. *Journal of Personality and Social Psychology, 21*, 204–218.

Mischel, W., Shoda, Y., & Rodriguez, M. I. (1989). Delay of gratification in children. *Science, 244*, 933–938.

Miyamoto, Y., & Ma, X. (2011). Dampening or savoring positive emotions: A dialectical cultural script guides emotion regulation. *Emotion, 11*, 1346–1357.

Miyamoto, Y., Uchida, Y., & Ellsworth, P. C. (2010). Culture and mixed emotions: Co-occurrence of positive and negative emotions in Japan and the United States. *Emotion, 10*, 404–415.

Miyashita, T., & Williams, C. L. (2006). Epinephrine administration increases neural impulses propagated along the vagus nerve: Role of peripheral β-adrenergic receptors. *Neurobiology of Learning and Memory, 85*, 116–124.

Moan, C. E., & Heath, R. G. (1972). Septal stimulation for the initiation of heterosexual behavior in a homosexual male. *Journal of Behavior Therapy and Experimental Psychiatry, 3*, 23–30.

Mobbs, D., Greicius, M. D., Abdel-Azim, E., Menon, V., & Reiss, A. L. (2003). Humor modulates the mesolimbic reward centers. *Neuron, 40*, 1041–1048.

Moffitt, T. E. (1993). Adolescence-limited and life-course-persistent antisocial behavior: A developmental taxonomy. *Psychological Review, 100*, 674–701.

Molden, D. C., Lucas, G. M., Gardner, W. L., Dean, K., & Knowles, M. L. (2009). Motivations for prevention or promotion following social exclusion: Being rejected versus being ignored. *Journal of Personality and Social Psychology, 96*, 415–431.

Mondadori, C., Ornstein, K., Waser, P. G., & Huston, J. P. (1976). Post-trial reinforcing hypothalamic stimulation can facilitate avoidance learning. *Neuroscience Letters, 2*, 183–187.

Montagu, A. (1959). Natural selection and the origin and evolution of weeping in man. *Science, 130*, 1572–1573.

Monti, J. M. (2011). Serotonin control of sleep-wake behavior. *Sleep Medicine Reviews, 15*, 269–281.

Moore, R. Y., Halaris, A. E., & Jones, B. E. (1978). Serotonin neurons of the midbrain raphe: Ascending projections. *The Journal of Comparative Neurology, 180*, 417–438.

Morris, J. S., DeGelder, B., Weiskrantz, L., & Dolan, R. J. (2001). Differential extrageniculostriate and amygdala responses to presentation of emotional faces in a cortically blind field. *Brain, 124*, 1241–1252.

Morris, J. S., Öhman, A., & Dolan, R. J. (1999). A subcortical pathway to the right amygdala mediating "unseen" fear. *Proceedings of the National Academy of Sciences of the United States of America, 96*, 1680–1685.

Mortensen, E. L., Jensen, H. H., Sanders, S. A., & Reinisch, J. M. (2006). Associations between volume of alcohol consumption and social status, intelligence, and personality in a sample of young adult Danes. *Scandinavian Journal of Psychology, 47,* 387–398.

Moser, J. S., Hajcak, G., Bukay, E., & Simons, R. F. (2006). Intentional modulation of emotional responding to unpleasant pictures: An ERP study. *Psychophysiology, 43,* 292–296.

Mousa, S. A., Shakibaei, M., Sitte, N., Schäfer, M., & Stein, C. (2004). Subcellular pathways of β-endorphin synthesis, processing, and release from immunocytes in inflammatory pain. *Endocrinology, 145,* 1331–1341.

Mujica-Parodi, L. R., Strey, H. H., Frederick, B., Savoy, R., Cox, D., Botanov, Y., . . . Weber, J. (2009). Chemosensory cues to conspecific emotional stress activate amygdala in humans. *PLoS ONE, 4,* e6415.

Muller, M. N., Marlowe, F. W., Bugumba, R., & Ellison, P. T. (2009). Testosterone and paternal care in East African foragers and pastoralists. *Proceedings of the Royal Society B: Biological Sciences, 276,* 347–354.

Murdock, G. P., & Provost, C. (1973). Factors in the division of labor by sex: A cross-cultural analysis. *Ethnology, 12,* 203–225.

Murphy, S. E., Norbury, R., Godlewska, B. R., Cowen, P. J., Mannie, Z. M., Harmer, C. J., & Munafò, M. R. (2013). The effect of the serotonin transporter polymorphism (5-HTTLPR) on amygdala function: A meta-analysis. *Molecular Psychiatry, 18,* 512–520.

Murrough, J. W., Iacoviello, B., Neumeister, A., Charney, D. S., & Iosifescu, D. V. (2011). Cognitive dysfunction in depression: Neurocircuitry and new therapeutic strategies. *Neurobiology of Learning and Memory, 96,* 553–563.

Murty, V. P., Ritchey, M., Adcock, R. A., & LaBar, K. S. (2011). Reprint of: fMRI studies of successful emotional memory encoding: A quantitative meta-analysis. *Neuropsychologia, 49,* 695–705.

N'Diaye, K., Sander, D., & Vuilleumier, P. (2009). Self-relevance processing in the human amygdala: Gaze direction, facial expression, and emotion intensity. *Emotion, 9,* 798–806.

Nader, K., Schafe, G. E., & LeDoux, J. E. (2000). Fear memories require protein synthesis in the amygdala for reconsolidation after retrieval. *Nature, 406,* 722–726.

Natterson-Horowitz, B., & Bowers, K. (2013). *Zoobiquity: The astonishing connection between human and animal health.* New York: Vintage Books.

Navarrete, C. D., & Fessler, D. M. T. (2006). Disease avoidance and ethnocentrism: The effects of disease vulnerability and disgust sensitivity on intergroup attitudes. *Evolution and Human Behavior, 27,* 270–282.

Neary, D., Snowden, J. S., Gustafson, L., Passant, U., Stuss, D., Black, S., . . . Benson, D. F. (1998). Frontotemporal lobar degeneration: A consensus on clinical diagnostic criteria. *Neurology, 51,* 1546–1554.

Nedergaard, M., Takano, T., & Hansen, A. J. (2002). Beyond the role of glutamate as a neurotransmitter. *Nature Reviews Neuroscience, 3,* 748–755.

Neumann, E., & Blanton, R. (1970). The early history of electrodermal research. *Psychophysiology, 6,* 453–475.

Neumann, I. D., & Landgraf, R. (2012). Balance of brain oxytocin and vasopressin: Implications for anxiety, depression, and social behaviors. *Trends in Neurosciences, 35,* 649–659.

Neumann, R., & Lozo, L. (2012). Priming the activation of fear and disgust: Evidence for semantic processing. *Emotion, 12,* 223–228.

Neumann, R., Steinhäuser, N., & Roeder, U. R. (2009). How self-construal shapes emotion: Cultural differences in the feeling of pride. *Social Cognition, 27,* 327–337.

Niedenthal, P. M., Augustinova, M., & Rychlowska, M. (2010). Body and mind: Zajonc's (re)introduction of the motor system to emotion and cognition. *Emotion Review, 2,* 340–347.

Nisbett, R. E., & Schachter, S. (1966). Cognitive manipulation of pain. *Journal of Experimental Social Psychology, 2,* 227–236.

Nolen-Hoeksema, S. (2012). Emotion regulation and psychopathology: The role of gender. *Annual Review of Clinical Psychology, 8,* 161–187.

Nørby, S., Lange, M., & Larsen, A. (2010). Forgetting to forget: On the duration of voluntary suppression of neutral and emotional memories. *Acta Psychologica, 133,* 73–80.

Noriuchi, M., Kikuchi, Y., & Senoo, A. (2008). The functional neuroanatomy of maternal love: Mother's response to infant's attachment behaviors. *Biological Psychiatry, 63,* 415–423.

Noulhiane, M., Mella, N., Samson, S., Ragot, R., & Pouthas, V. (2007). How emotional auditory stimuli modulate time perception. *Emotion, 7,* 697–704.

Nussbaum, M. C. (2001). *The upheavals of thought: The intelligence of emotions.* Cambridge, UK: Cambridge University Press.

O'Brien, M., Weaver, J. M., Nelson, J. A., Calkins, S., Leerkes, E., & Marcovitch, S. (2011). Longitudinal associations between children's understanding of emotions and theory of mind. *Cognition & Emotion, 25,* 1074–1086.

Ochsner, K. N. (2000). Are affective events richly recollected or simply familiar? The experience and process of recognizing feelings past. *Journal of Experimental Psychology. General, 129,* 242–261.

Ochsner, K. N., Bunge, S. A., Gross, J. J., & Gabrieli, J. D. E. (2002). Rethinking feelings: An fMRI study of the cognitive regulation of emotion. *Journal of Cognitive Neuroscience, 14,* 1215–1229.

Ochsner, K. N., & Gross, J. J. (2005). The cognitive control of emotion. *Trends in Cognitive Sciences, 9,* 242–249.

Ochsner, K. N., & Phelps, E. (2007). Emerging perspectives on emotion-cognition interactions. *Trends in Cognitive Sciences, 11,* 317–318.

Ochsner, K. N., Silvers, J. A., & Buhle, J. T. (2012). Functional imaging studies of emotion regulation: A synthetic review and evolving model of the cognitive control of emotion. *Annals of the New York Academy of Sciences, 1251,* E1–E24.

Odendaal, J. S., & Meintjes, R. (2003). Neurophysiological correlates of affiliative behaviour between humans and dogs. *The Veterinary Journal, 165,* 296–301.

Oh, T. J., Kim, M. Y., Park, K. S., & Cho, Y. M. (2012). Effects of chemosignals from sad tears and postprandial plasma on appetite and food intake in humans. *PLoS ONE, 7,* e42352.

Ohl, F. W., Wetzel, W., Wagner, T., Rech, A., & Scheich, H. (1999). Bilateral ablation of auditory cortex in Mongolian gerbil affects discrimination of frequency modulated tones but not of pure tones. *Learning & Memory, 6,* 347–362.

Öhman, A., & Dimberg, U. (1978). Facial expressions as conditioned stimuli for electrodermal responses: A case of "preparedness"? *Journal of Personality and Social Psychology, 36,* 1251–1258.

Öhman, A., & Mineka, S. (2001). Fears, phobias, and preparedness: Toward an evolved module of fear and fear learning. *Psychological Review, 108,* 483–522.

Öhman, A., & Soares, J. J. (1994). "Unconscious anxiety": Phobic responses to masked stimuli. *Journal of Abnormal Psychology, 103,* 231–240.

Öhman, A., & Soares, J. J. (1998). Emotional conditioning to masked stimuli: Expectancies for aversive outcomes following nonrecognized fear-relevant stimuli. *Journal of Experimental Psychology: General, 127,* 69–82.

Öhman, A., Flykt, A., & Esteves, F. (2001). Emotion drives attention: Detecting the snake in the grass. *Journal of Experimental Psychology: General, 130,* 466–478.

Oitzl, M. S., Champagne, D. L., van der Veen, R., & de Kloet, E. R. (2010). Brain development under stress: Hypotheses of glucocorticoid actions revisited. *Neuroscience & Biobehavioral Reviews, 34,* 853–866.

Olausson, H., Lamarre, Y., Backlund, H., Morin, C., Wallin, B. G., Starck, G., . . . Bushnell, M. C. (2002). Unmyelinated tactile afferents signal touch and project to insular cortex. *Nature Neuroscience, 5,* 900–904.

Olds, J. (1956). Pleasure centers in the brain. *Scientific American, 195,* 105–116.

Olds, J. (1958). Self-stimulation of the brain; its use to study local effects of hunger, sex, and drugs. *Science, 127,* 315–324.

Olds, J., Allan, W. S., & Briese, E. (1971). Differentiation of hypothalamic drive and reward centers. *American Journal of Physiology—Legacy Content, 221,* 368–375.

Oliver, M. B., & Hyde, J. S. (1993). Gender differences in sexuality: A meta-analysis. *Psychological Bulletin, 114,* 29–51.

Olsson, A., & Phelps, E. A. (2004). Learned fear of "unseen" faces after Pavlovian, observational, and instructed fear. *Psychological Science, 15,* 822–828.

Olsson, A., & Phelps, E. A. (2007). Social learning of fear. *Nature Neuroscience, 10,* 1095–1102.

Olsson, A., Ebert, J. P., Banaji, M. R., & Phelps, E. A. (2005). The role of social groups in the persistence of learned fear. *Science, 309,* 785–787.

Onaka, T., Palmer, J. R., & Yagi, K. (1996). Norepinephrine depletion impairs neuroendocrine responses to fear but not novel environmental stimuli in the rat. *Brain Research, 713,* 261–268.

Ong, A. D., & Bergeman, C. S. (2004). The complexity of emotions in later life. *The Journals of Gerontology. Series B, Psychological Sciences and Social Sciences, 59,* P117–122.

Onur, O. A., Walter, H., Schlaepfer, T. E., Rehme, A. K., Schmidt, C., Keysers, C., Maier, W., & Hurlemann, R. (2009). Noradrenergic enhancement of amygdala responses to fear. *Social Cognitive and Affective Neuroscience, 4,* 119–126.

Op de Macks, Z. A., Moor, B. G., Overgaauw, S., Güroğlu, B., Dahl, R. E., & Crone, E. A. (2011). Testosterone levels correspond with increased ventral striatum activation in response to monetary rewards in adolescents. *Developmental Cognitive Neuroscience, 1,* 506–516.

Ortony, A., & Turner, T. J. (1990). What's basic about basic emotions? *Psychological Review, 97,* 315–331.

Osgood, C. E. (1952). The nature and measurement of meaning. *Psychological Bulletin, 49,* 197.

Osgood, C. E. (1969). On the whys and wherefores of E, P, and A. *Journal of Personality and Social Psychology, 12,* 194–199.

Osgood, C. E., May, W. H., & Miron, M. S. (1975). *Cross-cultural universals of affective meaning.* Champaign-Urbana, IL: University of Illinois Press.

Ossewaarde, L., Wingen, G. A. van, Kooijman, S. C., Bäckström, T., Fernández, G., & Hermans, E. J. (2011). Changes in functioning of mesolimbic incentive processing circuits during the premenstrual phase. *Social Cognitive and Affective Neuroscience, 6,* 612–620.

Owren, M. J., & Rendall, D. (2001). Sound on the rebound: Bringing form and function back to the forefront in understanding nonhuman primate vocal signaling. *Evolutionary Anthropology: Issues, News, and Reviews, 10,* 58–71.

Oyserman, D., Coon, H. M., & Kemmelmeier, M. (2002). Rethinking individualism and collectivism: Evaluation of theoretical assumptions and meta-analyses. *Psychological Bulletin, 128,* 3–72.

Pakkenberg, B., & Gundersen, H. J. G. (1997). Neocortical neuron number in humans: Effect of sex and age. *The Journal of Comparative Neurology, 384,* 312–320.

Palomares-Castillo, E., Hernández-Pérez, O. R., Pérez-Carrera, D., Crespo-Ramírez, M., Fuxe, K., & Pérez de la Mora, M. (2012). The intercalated paracapsular islands as a module for integration of signals regulating anxiety in the amygdala. *Brain Research, 1476,* 211–234.

Palomba, D., Sarlo, M., Angrilli, A., Mini, A., & Stegagno, L. (2000). Cardiac responses associated with affective processing of unpleasant film stimuli. *International Journal of Psychophysiology, 36,* 45–57.

Panksepp, J. (1992). A critical role for "affective neuroscience" in resolving what is basic about basic emotions. *Psychological Review, 99,* 554–560.

Panksepp, J. (2004). *Affective neuroscience: The foundations of human and animal emotions.* New York: Oxford University Press.

Panksepp, J. (2005a). Affective consciousness: Core emotional feelings in animals and humans. *Consciousness and Cognition, 14,* 30–80.

Panksepp, J. (2005b). Why does separation distress hurt? Comment on MacDonald and Leary (2005). *Psychological Bulletin, 131,* 224–230.

Panksepp, J. (2007). Neuroevolutionary sources of laughter and social joy: Modeling primal human laughter in laboratory rats. *Behavioural Brain Research, 182,* 231–244.

Panksepp, J., & Burgdorf, J. (2003). "Laughing" rats and the evolutionary antecedents of human joy? *Physiology & Behavior, 79,* 533–547.

Papez, J. W. (1937). A proposed mechanism of emotion. *Archives of Neurology and Psychiatry, 38,* 725–743.

Paré, D., & Duvarci, S. (2012). Amygdala microcircuits mediating fear expression and extinction. *Current Opinion in Neurobiology, 22,* 717–723.

Parker, G. A., Baker, R. R., & Smith, V. G. F. (1972). The origin and evolution of gamete dimorphism and the male-female phenomenon. *Journal of Theoretical Biology, 36,* 529–553.

Parker, K. J., Buckmaster, C. L., Schatzberg, A. F., & Lyons, D. M. (2005). Intranasal oxytocin administration attenuates the ACTH stress response in monkeys. *Psychoneuroendocrinology, 30,* 924–929.

Parkinson, B. (1999). Relations and dissociations between appraisal and emotion ratings of reasonable and unreasonable anger and guilt. *Cognition & Emotion, 13,* 347–385.

Parkinson, B. (2007). Getting from situations to emotions: Appraisal and other routes. *Emotion, 7,* 21–25.

Parkinson, B. (2012). Piecing together emotion: Sites and time-scales for social construction. *Emotion Review, 4,* 291–298.

Parr, L. A., Waller, B. M., Vick, S. J., & Bard, K. A. (2007). Classifying chimpanzee facial expressions using muscle action. *Emotion, 7,* 172–181.

Pasterski, V. L., Geffner, M. E., Brain, C., Hindmarsh, P., Brook, C., & Hines, M. (2005). Prenatal hormones and postnatal socialization by parents as determinants of male-typical toy play in girls with congenital adrenal hyperplasia. *Child Development, 76,* 264–278.

Pasterski, V. L., Geffner, M. E., Brain, C., Hindmarsh, P., Brook, C., & Hines, M. (2011). Prenatal hormones and childhood sex-segregation: Playmate and play style preferences in girls with congenital adrenal hyperplasia. *Hormones and Behavior, 59,* 549–555.

Pasterski, V. L., Hindmarsh, P., Geffner, M., Brook, C., Brain, C., & Hines, M. (2007). Increased aggression and activity level in 3- to 11-year-old girls with congenital adrenal hyperplasia. *Hormones and Behavior, 52,* 368–374.

Patrick, C., & Iacono, W. (1991). Validity of the control question polygraph test: The problem of sampling bias. *Journal of Applied Psychology, 76,* 229–238.

Pavlov, I. P. (1927). *Conditioned reflexes: An investigation of the physiological activity of the cerebral cortex.* London: Oxford University Press.

Pavlov, I. P., & Anrep, G. V. (2003). *Conditioned reflexes.* Mineola, NY: Dover Publications.

Peciña, M., Mickey, B. J., Love, T., Wang, H., Langenecker, S. A., Hodgkinson, C., . . . Zubieta, J.-K. (2013). DRD2 polymorphisms modulate reward and emotion processing, dopamine neurotransmission, and openness to experience. *Cortex, 49,* 877–890.

Peira, N., Golkar, A., Ohman, A., Anders, S., & Wiens, S. (2012). Emotional responses in spider fear are closely related to picture awareness. *Cognition & Emotion, 26,* 252–260.

Pell, M. D. (2005). Nonverbal emotion priming: evidence from the facial affect decision task. *Journal of Nonverbal Behavior, 29,* 45–73.

Pell, M. D., & Skorup, V. (2008). Implicit processing of emotional prosody in a foreign versus native language. *Speech Communication, 50,* 519–530.

Pelvig, D. P., Pakkenberg, H., Stark, A. K., & Pakkenberg, B. (2008). Neocortical glial cell numbers in human brains. *Neurobiology of Aging, 29,* 1754–1762.

Peng, K., & Nisbett, R. E. (1999). Culture, dialectics, and reasoning about contradiction. *American Psychologist, 54,* 741–754.

Perea, G., & Araque, A. (2010). GLIA modulates synaptic transmission. *Brain Research Reviews, 63,* 93–102.

Pessoa, L. (2008). On the relationship between emotion and cognition. *Nature Reviews Neuroscience, 9,* 148–158.

Pessoa, L., McKenna, M., Gutierrez, E., & Ungerleider, L. G. (2002). Neural processing of emotional faces requires attention. *Proceedings of the National Academy of Sciences of the United States of America, 99,* 11458–11463.

Pessoa, L., & Ungerleider, L. G. (2004). Neuroimaging studies of attention and the processing of emotion-laden stimuli. *Progress in Brain Research, 144,* 171–182.

Peters, J., & Büchel, C. (2010). Neural representations of subjective reward value. *Behavioural Brain Research, 213,* 135–141.

Peterson, C., & Seligman, M. E. (1984). Causal explanations as a risk factor for depression: Theory and evidence. *Psychological Review, 91,* 347–374.

Petticrew, M., & Davey Smith, G. (2012). The monkey puzzle: A systematic review of studies of stress, social hierarchies, and heart disease in monkeys. *PLoS ONE, 7,* e27939.

Pezawas, L., Meyer-Lindenberg, A., Drabant, E. M., Verchinski, B. A., Munoz, K. E., Kolachana, B. S., . . . Weinberger, D. R. (2005). 5-HTTLPR polymorphism impacts human cingulate-amygdala interactions: A genetic susceptibility mechanism for depression. *Nature Neuroscience, 8,* 828–834.

Phan, K. L., Wager, T., Taylor, S. F., & Liberzon, I. (2002). Functional neuroanatomy of emotion: A meta-analysis of emotion activation Studies in PET and fMRI. *NeuroImage, 16,* 331–348.

Phan, K. L., Wager, T. D., Taylor, S. F., & Liberzon, I. (2004). Functional neuroimaging studies of human emotions. *CNS Spectrums, 9,* 258–266.

Phelps, E. (2004). Human emotion and memory: Interactions of the amygdala and hippocampal complex. *Current Opinion in Neurobiology, 14,* 198–202.

Phelps, E. A., O'Connor, K. J., Gatenby, J. C., Gore, J. C., Grillon, C., & Davis, M. (2001). Activation of the left amygdala to a cognitive representation of fear. *Nature Neuroscience, 4,* 437–441.

Phillips, K. A., & Hopkins, W. D. (2012). Topography of the Chimpanzee Corpus Callosum. *PLoS ONE, 7,* e31941.

Phoenix, C. H., Goy, R. W., Gerall, A. A., & Young, W. C. (1959). Organizing action of prenatally administered testosterone propionate on the tissues mediating mating behavior in the female guinea pig. *Endocrinology, 65,* 369–382.

Pickett, K. E., & Wilkinson, R. G. (2010). Inequality: An underacknowledged source of mental illness and distress. *The British Journal of Psychiatry, 197,* 426–428.

Piech, R. M., McHugo, M., Smith, S. D., Dukic, M. S., Van Der Meer, J., Abou-Khalil, B., & Zald, D. H. (2011). Reprint of: Fear-enhanced visual search persists after amygdala lesions. *Neuropsychologia, 49,* 596–601.

Pinker, S. (2000). *Words and rules: The ingredients of language.* New York: HarperCollins Publishers.

Pinna, G., Costa, E., & Guidotti, A. (2005). Changes in brain testosterone and allopregnanolone biosynthesis elicit aggressive behavior. *Proceedings of the National Academy of Sciences of the United States of America, 102,* 2135–2140.

Planck, M., & Laue, M. von. (1949). *Scientific autobiography, and other papers.* New York: Philosophical Library.

Pollick, F. E., Paterson, H. M., Bruderlin, A., & Sanford, A. J. (2001). Perceiving affect from arm movement. *Cognition, 82,* B51–61.

Pongrácz, P., Molnár, C., & Miklósi, Á. (2006). Acoustic parameters of dog barks carry emotional information for humans. *Applied Animal Behaviour Science, 100,* 228–240.

Pongrácz, P., Molnár, C., Miklósi, Á., & Csányi, V. (2005). Human listeners are able to classify dog (Canis familiaris) barks recorded in different situations. *Journal of Comparative Psychology, 119,* 136–144.

Posner, J., Russell, J. A., Gerber, A., Gorman, D., Colibazzi, T., Yu, S., Wang, A., . . . Peterson, B. S. (2009). The neurophysiological bases of emotion: An fMRI study of the affective circumplex using emotion-denoting words. *Human Brain Mapping, 30,* 883–895.

Posner, M. I., & Rothbart, M. K. (1998). Attention, self-regulation and consciousness. *Philosophical Transactions of the Royal Society B: Biological Sciences, 353,* 1915–1927.

Pourtois, G., Schettino, A., & Vuilleumier, P. (2013). Brain mechanisms for emotional influences on perception and attention: What is magic and what is not. *Biological Psychology, 92,* 492–512.

Prehn, A., Ohrt, A., Sojka, B., Ferstl, R., & Pause, B. M. (2006). Chemosensory anxiety signals augment the startle reflex in humans. *Neuroscience Letters, 394,* 127–130.

Price, J. (1967). The dominance hierarchy and the evolution of mental illness. *The Lancet, 290,* 243–246.

Price, T. F., & Harmon-Jones, E. (2011). Approach motivational body postures lean toward left frontal brain activity. *Psychophysiology, 48,* 718–722.

Proctor, G. B., & Carpenter, G. H. (2007). Regulation of salivary gland function by autonomic nerves. *Autonomic Neuroscience, 133,* 3–18.

Proverbio, A. M., Riva, F., Zani, A., & Martin, E. (2011). Is it a baby? Perceived age affects brain processing of faces differently in women and men. *Journal of Cognitive Neuroscience, 23,* 3197–3208.

Proverbio, A. M., Zani, A., & Adorni, R. (2008). Neural markers of a greater female responsiveness to social stimuli. *BMC Neuroscience, 9,* 56.

Prum, R. O. (2012). Aesthetic evolution by mate choice: Darwin's really dangerous idea. *Philosophical Transactions of the Royal Society of London. Series B, Biological Sciences, 367,* 2253–2265.

Ptak, R. (2012). The frontoparietal attention network of the human brain: Action, saliency, and a priority map of the environment. *The Neuroscientist, 18,* 502–515.

Pugh, C. R., Tremblay, D., Fleshner, M., & Rudy, J. W. (1997). A selective role for corticosterone in contextual-fear conditioning. *Behavioral Neuroscience, 111,* 503–511.

Putman, P., & Roelofs, K. (2011). Effects of single cortisol administrations on human affect reviewed: Coping with stress through adaptive regulation of automatic cognitive processing. *Psychoneuroendocrinology, 36,* 439–448.

Puts, D. A., Jones, B. C., & DeBruine, L. M. (2012). Sexual selection on human faces and voices. *Journal of Sex Research, 49,* 227–243.

Quigley, K. S., Lindquist, K. A., & Barrett, L. F. (2014). Inducing and measuring emotion and affect: Tips, tricks, and secrets. In H. Reis & C. Judd (Eds.), *Handbook of research methods in personality and social psychology* (pp. 220–252). New York: Oxford University Press.

Quinn, P. C., Anzures, G., Izard, C. E., Lee, K., Pascalis, O., Slater, A. M., & Tanaka, J. W. (2011). Looking across domains to understand infant representation of emotion. *Emotion Review, 3,* 197–206.

Quinn, W. G., Harris, W. A., & Benzer, S. (1974). Conditioned behavior in drosophila melanogaster. *Proceedings of the National Academy of Sciences of the United States of America, 71,* 708–712.

Raichle, M. E., MacLeod, A. M., Snyder, A. Z., Powers, W. J., Gusnard, D. A., & Shulman, G. L. (2001). A default mode of brain function. *Proceedings of the National Academy of Sciences of the United States of America, 98,* 676.

Ramirez, G., & Beilock, S. L. (2011). Writing about testing worries boosts exam performance in the classroom. *Science, 331,* 211–213.

Ramsay, P. T., & Carr, A. (2011). Gastric acid and digestive physiology. *Surgical Clinics of North America, 91,* 977–982.

Rapport, M. M., Green, A. A., & Page, I. H. (1948). Serum vasoconstrictor, serotonin; isolation and characterization. *The Journal of Biological Chemistry, 176,* 1243–1251.

Ray, R. D., & Zald, D. H. (2012). Anatomical insights into the interaction of emotion and cognition in the prefrontal cortex. *Neuroscience & Biobehavioral Reviews, 36,* 479–501.

Redgrave, P., Gurney, K., & Reynolds, J. (2008). What is reinforced by phasic dopamine signals? *Brain Research Reviews, 58,* 322–339.

Rees, G., Wojciulik, E., Clarke, K., Husain, M., Frith, C., & Driver, J. (2000). Unconscious activation of visual cortex in the damaged right hemisphere of a parietal patient with extinction. *Brain, 123,* 1624–1633.

Reisenzein, R. (1983). The Schachter theory of emotion: Two decades later. *Psychological Bulletin, 94,* 239–264.

Reisenzein, R. (2006). Arnold's theory of emotion in historical perspective. *Cognition & Emotion, 20,* 920–951.

Renaud, F. L., Colon, I., Lebron, J., Ortiz, N., Rodriguez, F., & Cadilla, C. (1995). A novel opioid mechanism seems to modulate phagocytosis in Tetrahymena. *The Journal of Eukaryotic Mmicrobiology, 42,* 205–207.

Rendell, L., & Whitehead, H. (2001). Culture in whales and dolphins. *The Behavioral and Brain Sciences, 24,* 309–324; discussion 324–382.

Ressler, K. J., & Mayberg, H. S. (2007). Targeting abnormal neural circuits in mood and anxiety disorders: From the laboratory to the clinic. *Nature Neuroscience, 10,* 1116–1124.

Reynolds, J. H., Chelazzi, L., & Desimone, R. (1999). Competitive mechanisms subserve attention in macaque areas V2 and V4. *The Journal of Neuroscience, 19,* 1736–1753.

Rhodes, N., & Pivik, K. (2011). Age and gender differences in risky driving: The roles of positive affect and risk perception. *Accident; analysis and prevention, 43,* 923–931.

Riem, M. M. E., Bakermans-Kranenburg, M. J., Pieper, S., Tops, M., Boksem, M. A. S., Vermeiren, R. R. J. M., Ijzendoorn, M. H. van, & Rombouts, S. A. R. B. (2011). Oxytocin modulates amygdala, insula, and inferior frontal gyrus responses to infant crying: A randomized controlled trial. *Biological Psychiatry, 70,* 291–297.

Risch, N., Herrell, R., Lehner, T., Liang, K.-Y., Eaves, L., Hoh, J., . . . Merikangas, K. R. (2009). Interaction between the serotonin transporter gene (5-HTTLPR), stressful life events, and risk of depression: A meta-analysis. *JAMA: The Journal of the American Medical Association, 301,* 2462–2471.

Roberson, D., Damjanovic, L., & Kikutani, M. (2010). Show and tell: The role of language in categorizing facial expression of emotion. *Emotion Review, 2,* 255–260.

Roberts, N. A., Tsai, J. L., & Coan, J. A. (2007). Emotion elicitation using dyadic interaction tasks. In J. Coan & J. J. B. Allan (Eds.), *Handbook of emotion elicitation and assessment* (pp. 106–123). New York: Oxford University Press.

Robinson, M. D., Johnson, J. T., & Shields, S. A. (1998). The gender heuristic and the database: Factors affecting the perception of gender-related differences in the experience and display of emotions. *Basic and Applied Social Psychology, 20,* 206–219.

Robinson, M. J., Edwards, S. E., Iyengar, S., Bymaster, F., Clark, M., & Katon, W. (2009). Depression and pain. *Frontiers in Bioscience, 14,* 5031.

Röcke, C., & Lachman, M. E. (2008). Perceived trajectories of life satisfaction across past, present, and future: Profiles and correlates of subjective change in young, middle-aged, and older adults. *Psychology and Aging, 23,* 833–847.

Roeper, J. (2013). Dissecting the diversity of midbrain dopamine neurons. *Trends in Neurosciences, 36,* 336–342.

Rogers, T. B., Kuiper, N. A., & Kirker, W. S. (1977). Self-reference and the encoding of personal information. *Journal of Personality and Social Psychology, 35,* 677–688.

Rohr, M., Degner, J., & Wentura, D. (2012). Masked emotional priming beyond global valence activations. *Cognition & Emotion, 26,* 224–244.

Rohrmann, S., Hopp, H., & Quirin, M. (2008). Gender differences in psychophysiological responses to disgust. *Journal of Psychophysiology, 22,* 65–75.

Rolls, E. T., & McCabe, C. (2007). Enhanced affective brain representations of chocolate in cravers vs. non-cravers. *European Journal of Neuroscience, 26,* 1067–1076.

Roman, G., & Davis, R. L. (2001). Molecular biology and anatomy of Drosophila olfactory associative learning. *BioEssays, 23,* 571–581.

Romo, R., & Schultz, W. (1990). Dopamine neurons of the monkey midbrain:

Contingencies of responses to active touch during self-initiated arm movements. *Journal of Neurophysiology, 63,* 592–606.

Roseman, I. J., & Smith, C. (2001). Appraisal theory: Overview, assumptions, varieties, controversies. In K. R. Scherer, A. Schorr, & T. Johnstone (Eds.), *Appraisal processes in emotion: Theory, methods, research* (pp. 3–34). New York: Oxford University Press.

Roseman, I. J., Wiest, C., & Swartz, T. S. (1994). Phenomenology, behaviors, and goals differentiate discrete emotions. *Journal of Personality and Social Psychology, 67,* 206–221.

Rosen, J. B., Hitchcock, J. M., Sananes, C. B., D, J., & Davis, M. (1991). A direct projection from the central nucleus of the amygdala to the acoustic startle pathway: Anterograde and retrograde tracing studies. *Behavioral Neuroscience, 105,* 817–825.

Rosenthal, L., & Lobel, M. (2011). Explaining racial disparities in adverse birth outcomes: Unique sources of stress for black American women. *Social Science & Medicine (1982), 72,* 977–983.

Ross, H. E., Cole, C. D., Smith, Y., Neumann, I. D., Landgraf, R., Murphy, A. Z., & Young, L. J. (2009). Characterization of the oxytocin system regulating affiliative behavior in female prairie voles. *Neuroscience, 162,* 892–903.

Ross, M. D., Owren, M. J., & Zimmermann, E. (2009). Reconstructing the evolution of laughter in great apes and humans. *Current Biology, 19,* 1106–1111.

Rossell, S. L., & Nobre, A. C. (2004). Semantic priming of different affective categories. *Emotion, 4,* 354–363.

Rottenberg, J., Ray, R. D., & Gross, J. J. (2007). Emotion elicitation using films. In J. Coan & J. J. B. Allan (Eds.), *Handbook of emotion elicitation and assessment* (pp. 9–28). New York: Oxford University Press.

Rozin, P. (2008). Hedonic "adaptation": Specific habituation to disgust/death elicitors as a result of dissecting a cadaver. *Judgment and Decision Making, 3,* 191–194.

Rudebeck, P. H., Buckley, M. J., Walton, M. E., & Rushworth, M. F. S. (2006). A role for the macaque anterior cingulate gyrus in social valuation. *Science, 313,* 1310–1312.

Rudebeck, P. H., Walton, M. E., Millette, B. H. P., Shirley, E., Rushworth, M. F. S., & Bannerman, D. M. (2007). Distinct contributions of frontal areas to emotion and social behaviour in the rat. *The European Journal of Neuroscience, 26,* 2315–2326.

Ruhé, H. G., Mason, N. S., & Schene, A. H. (2007). Mood is indirectly related to serotonin, norepinephrine and dopamine levels in humans: A meta-analysis of monoamine depletion studies. *Molecular Psychiatry, 12,* 331–359.

Russell, J. A. (1980). A circumplex model of affect. *Journal of Personality and Social Psychology, 39,* 1161–1178.

Russell, J. A. (1991). Culture and the categorization of emotions. *Psychological Bulletin, 110,* 426–450.

Russell, J. A. (1994). Is there universal recognition of emotion from facial expression? A review of the cross-cultural studies. *Psychological Bulletin, 115,* 102–141.

Russell, J. A. (2003). Core affect and the psychological construction of emotion. *Psychological Review, 110,* 145–172.

Rydell, R. J., Rydell, M. T., & Boucher, K. L. (2010). The effect of negative performance stereotypes on learning. *Journal of Personality and Social Psychology, 99,* 883–896.

Rydell, R. J., Shiffrin, R. M., Boucher, K. L., Loo, K. V., & Rydell, M. T. (2010). Stereotype threat prevents perceptual learning. *Proceedings of the National Academy of Sciences, 107,* 14042–14047.

Sabatinelli, D., Flaisch, T., Bradley, M. M., Fitzsimmons, J. R., & Lang, P. J. (2004). Affective picture perception: Gender differences in visual cortex? *Neuroreport, 15,* 1109–1112.

Sabatinelli, D., Fortune, E. E., Li, Q., Siddiqui, A., Krafft, C., Oliver, W. T., . . . Jeffries, J. (2011). Emotional perception: Meta-analyses of face and natural scene processing. *NeuroImage, 54,* 2524–2533.

Sabini, J., & Silver, M. (1998). The not altogether social construction of emotions: A Critique of Harré and Gillett. *Journal for the Theory of Social Behaviour, 28,* 223–235.

Sacks, O. (2011). *Awakenings.* Toronto: Random House.

Sagarin, B. J., Becker, D. V., Guadagno, R. E., Wilkinson, W. W., & Nicastle, L. D. (2012). A reproductive threat-based model of evolved sex differences in jealousy. *Evolutionary Psychology: An International Journal of Evolutionary Approaches to Psychology and Behavior, 10,* 487–503.

Sagaspe, P., Schwartz, S., & Vuilleumier, P. (2011). Fear and stop: A role for the amygdala in motor inhibition by emotional signals. *NeuroImage, 55,* 1825–1835.

Sander, D., Grafman, J., & Zalla, T. (2003). The human amygdala: An evolved system for relevance detection. *Reviews in the Neurosciences, 14,* 303–316.

Sander, D., Grandjean, D., & Scherer, K. R. (2005). A systems approach to appraisal mechanisms in emotion. *Neural Networks, 18,* 317–352.

Sander, K., Brechmann, A., & Scheich, H. (2003). Audition of laughing and crying leads to right amygdala activation in a low-noise fMRI setting. *Brain Research Protocols, 11,* 81–91.

Sander, K., Frome, Y., & Scheich, H. (2007). FMRI activations of amygdala, cingulate cortex, and auditory cortex by infant laughing and crying. *Human Brain Mapping, 28,* 1007–1022.

Sapolsky, R. M., & Mott, G. E. (1987). Social subordinance in wild baboons is associated with suppressed high density lipo-protein-cholesterol concentrations: The possible role of chronic social stress. *Endocrinology, 121,* 1605–1610.

Sara, S. J. (2009). The locus coeruleus and noradrenergic modulation of cognition. *Nature Reviews Neuroscience, 10,* 211–223.

Sauter, D., & Scott, S. (2007). More than one kind of happiness: Can we recognize vocal expressions of different positive states? *Motivation and Emotion, 31,* 192–199.

Sauter, D. A., Eisner, F., Ekman, P., & Scott, S. K. (2010). Cross-cultural recognition of basic emotions through nonverbal emotional vocalizations. *Proceedings of the National Academy of Sciences of the United States of America, 107,* 2408–2412.

Schachter, S., & Singer, J. (1962). Cognitive, social, and physiological determinants of emotional state. *Psychological Review, 69,* 379–399.

Schacter, D. L., & Graf, P. (1986). Preserved learning in amnesic patients: Perspectives from research on direct priming. *Journal of Clinical and Experimental Neuropsychology, 8,* 727–743.

Schaefer, A., & Gray, J. R. (2007). A role for the human amygdala in higher cognition. *Reviews in the Neurosciences, 18,* 355–363.

Scheeringa, R., Fries, P., Petersson, K.-M., Oostenveld, R., Grothe, I., Norris, D. G., Hagoor, P., & Bastiaansen, M. C. M. (2011). Neuronal dynamics underlying high- and low-frequency EEG oscillations contribute independently to the human BOLD signal. *Neuron, 69,* 572–583.

Scherer, K. R. (1986). Vocal affect expression: A review and a model for future research. *Psychological Bulletin, 99,* 143–165.

Scherer, K. R. (1988). *Facets of emotion: Recent research.* Hillsdale, NJ: Lawrence Erlbaum Associates, Inc.

Scherer, K. R. (1997). The role of culture in emotion-antecedent appraisal. *Journal of Personality and Social Psychology, 73,* 902–922.

Scherer, K. R. (2001). Appraisal considered as a process of multilevel sequential checking. In K. R. Scherer, A. Schorr, & T. Johnstone (Eds.), *Appraisal processes in emotion: Theory, methods, research* (pp. 92–120). New York: Oxford University Press.

Scherer, K. R., Banse, R., & Wallbott, H. G. (2001). Emotion inferences from vocal expression correlate across languages and cultures. *Journal of Cross-Cultural Psychology, 32,* 76–92.

Scherer, K. R., & Ceschi, G. (1997). Lost luggage: A field study of emotion-antecedent appraisal. *Motivation and Emotion, 21,* 211–235.

Scherer, K. R., & Ellgring, H. (2007). Multimodal expression of emotion: Affect programs or componential appraisal patterns? *Emotion, 7,* 158–171.

Scherer, K. R., Wallbott, H. G., & Summerfield, A. B. (1986). *Experiencing emotion: A cross-cultural study.* Cambridge, UK: Cambridge University Press.

Schieffelin, E. L. (1983). Anger and shame in the tropical forest: On affect as a cultural system in Papua New Guinea. *Ethos, 11,* 181–191.

Schienle, A., Schäfer, A., Stark, R., Walter, B., & Vaitl, D. (2005). Gender differences in the processing of disgust- and fear-inducing pictures: An fMRI study. *Neuroreport, 16,* 277–280.

Schienle, A., Stark, R., Walter, B., Blecker, C., Ott, U., Kirsch, P., Sammer, G., & Vaitl, D. (2002). The insula is not specifically involved in disgust processing: An fMRI study. *Neuroreport, 13,* 2023–2026.

Schiller, D., Monfils, M.-H., Raio, C. M., Johnson, D. C., LeDoux, J. E., & Phelps, E. A. (2009). Preventing the return of fear in humans using reconsolidation update mechanisms. *Nature, 463,* 49–53.

Schirmer, A., Chen, C.-B., Ching, A., Tan, L., & Hong, R. Y. (2013). Vocal emotions influence verbal memory: Neural correlates and interindividual differences. *Cognitive, Affective, & Behavioral Neuroscience, 13,* 80–93.

Schirmer, A., & Escoffier, N. (2010). Emotional MMN: Anxiety and heart rate correlate with the ERP signature for auditory change detection. *Clinical Neurophysiology: Official Journal of the International Federation of Clinical Neurophysiology, 121,* 53–59.

Schirmer, A., Escoffier, N., Zysset, S., Koester, D., Striano, T., & Friederici, A. D. (2008). When vocal processing gets emotional: On the role of social orientation in relevance detection by the human amygdala. *NeuroImage, 40,* 1402–1410.

Schirmer, A., & Kotz, S. A. (2006). Beyond the right hemisphere: Brain mechanisms mediating vocal emotional processing. *Trends in Cognitive Sciences, 10,* 24–30.

Schirmer, A., Kotz, S. A., & Friederici, A. D. (2002). Sex differentiates the role of emotional prosody during word processing. *Brain Research. Cognitive Brain Research, 14,* 228–233.

Schirmer, A., Kotz, S. A., & Friederici, A. D. (2005). On the role of attention for the processing of emotions in speech: Sex differences revisited. *Cognitive Brain Research, 24,* 442–452.

Schirmer, A., Seow, C. S., & Penney, T. B. (2013). Humans process dog and human facial affect in similar ways. *PLoS ONE, 8,* e74591.

Schirmer, A., Simpson, E., & Escoffier, N. (2007). Listen up! Processing of intensity change differs for vocal and nonvocal sounds. *Brain Research, 1176,* 103–112.

Schirmer, A., Striano, T., & Friederici, A. D. (2005). Sex differences in the preattentive processing of vocal emotional expressions. *Neuroreport, 16,* 635–639.

Schirmer, A., Teh, K. S., Wang, S., Vijayakumar, R., Ching, A., Nithianantham, D., Escoffier, N., & Cheok, A. D. (2011). Squeeze me, but don't tease me: Human and mechanical touch enhance visual attention and emotion discrimination. *Social Neuroscience, 6,* 219–230.

Schirmer, A., Zysset, S., Kotz, S. A., & von Cramon, D. Y. (2004). Gender differences in the activation of inferior frontal cortex during emotional speech perception. *NeuroImage, 21,* 1114–1123.

Schlosberg, H. (1941). A scale for the judgment of facial expressions. *Journal of Experimental Psychology, 29,* 497–510.

Schlosberg, H. (1952). The description of facial expressions in terms of two dimensions. *Journal of Experimental Psychology, 44,* 229–237.

Schlosberg, H. (1954). Three dimensions of emotion. *Psychological Review, 61,* 81–88.

Schmeichel, B. J., Volokhov, R. N., & Demaree, H. A. (2008). Working memory capacity and the self-regulation of emotional expression and experience. *Journal of Personality and Social Psychology, 95,* 1526–1540.

Schoots, O., & Van Tol, H. H. M. (2003). The human dopamine D4 receptor repeat sequences modulate expression. *The Pharmacogenomics Journal, 3,* 343–348.

Schultz, W. (2010). Dopamine signals for reward value and risk: Basic and recent data. *Behavioral and Brain Functions: BBF, 6,* 24.

Schultz, W., Dayan, P., & Montague, P. R. (1997). A neural substrate of prediction and reward. *Science, 275,* 1593–1599.

Schulze, L., Lischke, A., Greif, J., Herpertz, S. C., Heinrichs, M., & Domes, G. (2011). Oxytocin increases recognition of masked emotional faces. *Psychoneuroendocrinology, 36,* 1378–1382.

Schuurmans, C., & Kurrasch, D. (2013). Neurodevelopmental consequences of maternal distress: What do we really know? *Clinical Genetics, 83,* 108–117.

Scoville, W. B., & Milner, B. (1957). Loss of recent memory after bilateral hippocampal lesions. *Journal of Neurology, Neurosurgery, and Psychiatry, 20,* 11–21.

Sebastian, C. L., Tan, G. C. Y., Roiser, J. P., Viding, E., Dumontheil, I., & Blakemore, S. J. (2011). Developmental influences on the neural bases of responses to social rejection: Implications of social neuroscience for education. *NeuroImage, 57,* 686–694.

Seeley, W. W., Carlin, D. A., Allman, J. M., Macedo, M. N., Bush, C., Miller, B. L., & Dearmond, S. J. (2006). Early frontotemporal dementia targets neurons unique to apes and humans. *Annals of Neurology, 60,* 660–667.

Seeley, W. W., Merkle, F. T., Gaus, S. E., Craig, A. D. (Bud), Allman, J. M., Hof, P. R., & Economo, C. V. (2012). Distinctive neurons of the anterior cingulate and frontoinsular cortex: A historical perspective. *Cerebral Cortex, 22,* 245–250.

Seidlitz, L., & Diener, E. (1998). Sex differences in the recall of affective experiences. *Journal of Personality and Social Psychology, 74,* 262.

Seifert, C. A., & Wulfert, E. (2011). The effects of realistic reward and risk on simulated gambling behavior. *The American Journal on Addictions, 20,* 120–126.

Seifritz, E., Esposito, F., Neuhoff, J. G., Lüthi, A., Mustovic, H., Dammann, G., . . . Di Salle, F. (2003). Differential sex-independent amygdala response to infant crying and laughing in parents versus nonparents. *Biological Psychiatry, 54,* 1367–1375.

Seligman, M. E. (1970). On the generality of the laws of learning. *Psychological Review, 77,* 406–418.

Seligman, M. E. P. (1992). *Helplessness: On depression, development, and death.* New York: W. H. Freeman & Co Ltd.

Seligman, M. E. P., & Csikszentmihalyi, M. (2000). Positive psychology: An introduction. *American Psychologist, 55,* 5–14.

Seligman, M. E., & Maier, S. F. (1967). Failure to escape traumatic shock. *Journal of Experimental Psychology, 74,* 1–9.

Semrud-Clikeman, M., & Glass, K. (2010). The relation of humor and child development: Social, adaptive, and emotional aspects. *Journal of Child Neurology, 25,* 1248–1260.

Sescousse, G., Redouté, J., & Dreher, J.-C. (2010). The architecture of reward value coding in the human orbitofrontal cortex. *The Journal of Neuroscience, 30,* 13095–13104.

Sessa, P., Meconi, F., Castelli, L., & Dell'Acqua, R. (in press). Taking one's time in feeling other-race pain: An event-related potential investigation on the time-course of cross-racial empathy. *Social Cognitive and Affective Neuroscience.* doi:10.1093/scan/nst003

Seymour, B., & Dolan, R. (2008). Emotion, decision making, and the amygdala. *Neuron, 58,* 662–671.

Shafer, A. T., Matveychuk, D., Penney, T., O'Hare, A. J., Stokes, J., & Dolcos, F. (2012). Processing of emotional distraction is both automatic and modulated by attention: Evidence from an event-related fMRI investigation. *Journal of Cognitive Neuroscience, 24,* 1233–1252.

Shahrokh, D. K., Zhang, T.-Y., Diorio, J., Gratton, A., & Meaney, M. J. (2010). Oxytocin-dopamine interactions mediate variations in maternal behavior in the rat. *Endocrinology, 151,* 2276–2286.

Sharot, T., Martorella, E. A., Delgado, M. R., & Phelps, E. A. (2007). How personal experience modulates the neural circuitry of memories of September 11. *Proceedings of the National Academy of Sciences of the United States of America, 104,* 389–394.

Sheppes, G., & Gross, J. J. (2011). Is timing everything? Temporal considerations in emotion regulation. *Personality and Social Psychology Review, 15,* 319–331.

Sheppes, G., & Meiran, N. (2007). Better late than never? On the dynamics of online regulation of sadness using distraction and cognitive reappraisal. *Personality and Social Psychology Bulletin, 33,* 1518–1532.

Sheppes, G., & Meiran, N. (2008). Divergent cognitive costs for online forms of reappraisal and distraction. *Emotion, 8,* 870–874.

Shields, S. A. (2006). Magda B. Arnold's life and work in context. *Cognition & Emotion, 20,* 902–919.

Shiota, M. N., Campos, B., Gonzaga, G. C., Keltner, D., & Peng, K. (2010). I love you but . . . : Cultural differences in complexity of emotional experience during interaction with a romantic partner. *Cognition & Emotion, 24,* 786–799.

Shiota, M. N., Campos, B., & Keltner, D. (2003). The faces of positive emotion. *Annals of the New York Academy of Sciences, 1000,* 296–299.

Shiota, M. N., Neufeld, S. L., Yeung, W. H., Moser, S. E., & Perea, E. F. (2011). Feeling good: Autonomic nervous system responding in five positive emotions. *Emotion, 11,* 1368–1378.

Shulman, G. L., Fiez, J. A., Corbetta, M., Buckner, R. L., Miezin, F. M., Raichle, M. E., & Petersen, S. E. (1997). Common blood flow changes across visual tasks: II. Decreases in cerebral cortex. *Journal of Cognitive Neuroscience, 9,* 648–663.

Shurick, A. A., Hamilton, J. R., Harris, L. T., Roy, A. K., Gross, J. J., & Phelps, E. A. (2012). Durable effects of cognitive restructuring on conditioned fear. *Emotion, 12,* 1393–1397.

Siemer, M., & Reisenzein, R. (2007). Emotions and appraisals: Can you have one without the other? *Emotion, 7,* 26–29.

Sierksma, A. S. R., Prickaerts, J., Chouliaras, L., Rostamian, S., Delbroek, L., Rutten, B. P. F.,

Steinbusch, H. W. M., & van den Hove, D. L. A. (2013). Behavioral and neurobiological effects of prenatal stress exposure in male and female APPswe/PS1dE9 mice. *Neurobiology of Aging, 34,* 319–337.

Silber, B. Y., & Schmitt, J. A. J. (2010). Effects of tryptophan loading on human cognition, mood, and sleep. *Neuroscience and Biobehavioral Reviews, 34,* 387–407.

Silk, J. S., Stroud, L. R., Siegle, G. J., Dahl, R. E., Lee, K. H., & Nelson, E. E. (2012). Peer acceptance and rejection through the eyes of youth: Pupillary, eyetracking and ecological data from the Chatroom Interact task. *Social Cognitive and Affective Neuroscience, 7,* 93–105.

Simard, V., Moss, E., & Pascuzzo, K. (2011). Early maladaptive schemas and child and adult attachment: A 15-year longitudinal study. *Psychology and Psychotherapy, 84,* 349–366.

Simon, R. W., & Nath, L. E. (2004). Gender and Eeotion in the United States: Do men and women differ in self-reports of feelings and expressive behavior? *American Journal of Sociology, 109,* 1137–1176.

Siviy, S. M., & Panksepp, J. (2011). In search of the neurobiological substrates for social playfulness in mammalian brains. *Neuroscience & Biobehavioral Reviews, 35,* 1821–1830.

Skuse, D. H., James, R. S., Bishop, D. V. M., Coppin, B., Dalton, P., Aamodt-Leeper, G., Bacarese-Hamilton, M., Creswell, C., McGurk, R., & Jacobs, P. A. (1997). Evidence from Turner's syndrome of an imprinted X-linked locus affecting cognitive function. *Nature, 387,* 705–708.

Smeets, T., Dziobek, I., & Wolf, O. T. (2009). Social cognition under stress: Differential effects of stress-induced cortisol elevations in healthy young men and women. *Hormones and Behavior, 55,* 507–513.

Smith, C. A., & Ellsworth, P. C. (1985). Patterns of cognitive appraisal in emotion. *Journal of Personality and Social Psychology, 48,* 813–838.

Smith, C. A., & Lazarus, R. S. (1990). Emotion and adaptation. In L. A. Pervin (Ed.), *Handbook of personality: Theory and research* (pp. 609–637). New York: Guilford Press.

Smith, R. H., & Kim, S. H. (2007). Comprehending envy. *Psychological Bulletin, 133,* 46–64.

Smythies, J. (2005). Section III. The norepinephrine system. In John Smythies (Ed.), *International review of neurobiology* (Vol. 64, pp. 173–211). Academic Press.

Soeter, M., & Kindt, M. (2011). Noradrenergic enhancement of associative fear memory in humans. *Neurobiology of Learning and Memory, 96,* 263–271.

Somerville, L. H., Hare, T., & Casey, B. (2011). Frontostriatal maturation predicts cognitive control failure to appetitive cues in adolescents. *Journal of Cognitive Neuroscience, 23,* 2123–2134.

Sorabji, R. (2002). *Emotion and peace of mind: From Stoic agitation to Christian temptation.* Oxford, UK: Oxford University Press.

Soto, J. A., Levenson, R. W., & Ebling, R. (2005). Cultures of moderation and expression: Emotional experience, behavior, and physiology in Chinese Americans and Mexican Americans. *Emotion, 5,* 154–165.

Soto, J. A., Perez, C. R., Kim, Y.-H., Lee, E. A., & Minnick, M. R. (2011). Is expressive suppression always associated with poorer psychological functioning? A cross-cultural comparison between European Americans and Hong Kong Chinese. *Emotion, 11,* 1450–1455.

Spielberger, C. D., & Reheiser, E. C. (2003). Measuring anxiety, anger, depression and curiosity as emotional states and personality traits with the STAI, STAXI and STPI. In M. J. Hilsenroth, D. Segal, & M. Hersen (Eds.), *Comprehensive handbook of psychological assessment.* Hoboken, NJ: John Wiley & Son.

Spreckelmeyer, K. N., Krach, S., Kohls, G., Rademacher, L., Irmak, A., Konrad, K., Kircher, T., & Gründer, G. (2009). Anticipation of monetary and social reward differently activates mesolimbic brain structures in men and women. *Social Cognitive and Affective Neuroscience, 4,* 158–165.

Spreckelmeyer, K. N., Kutas, M., Urbach, T. P., Altenmuller, E., & Munte, T. F. (2006). Combined perception of emotion in pictures and musical sounds. *Brain Research, 1070,* 160–170.

St. Jacques, P. L., Bessette-Symons, B., & Cabeza, R. (2009). Functional neuroimaging studies of aging and emotion: Fronto-amygdalar differences during emotional perception and episodic memory. *Journal of the International Neuropsychological Society, 15,* 819–825.

Stanley, D. A., Sokol-Hessner, P., Banaji, M. R., & Phelps, E. A. (2011). Implicit race attitudes predict trustworthiness judgments and economic trust decisions. *Proceedings of the National Academy of Sciences.* doi:10.1073/pnas.1014345108

Stansfield, K. H., & Kirstein, C. L. (2006). Effects of novelty on behavior in the adolescent and adult rat. *Developmental Psychobiology, 48,* 10–15.

Stanton, M. E., & Levine, S. (1985). Brief separation elevates cortisol in mother and infant squirrel monkeys. *Physiology & Behavior, 34,* 1007–1008.

Stanton, S. J., Liening, S. H., & Schultheiss, O. C. (2011). Testosterone is positively associated with risk taking in the Iowa Gambling Task. *Hormones and Behavior, 59,* 252–256.

Steinbeis, N., & Koelsch, S. (2011). Affective priming effects of musical sounds on the processing of word meaning. *Journal of Cognitive Neuroscience, 23,* 604–621.

Stemmler, G. (2004). Physiological processes during emotion. In P. Philippot & R. S. Feldman (Eds.), *The regulation of emotion* (pp. 33–70). Mahwah, NJ: Erlbaum.

Stemmler, G., Heldmann, M., Pauls, C. A., & Scherer, T. (2001). Constraints for emotion specificity in fear and anger: The context counts. *Psychophysiology, 38,* 275–291.

Steptoe, A., Dockray, S., & Wardle, J. (2009). Positive affect and psychobiological processes relevant to health. *Journal of Personality, 77,* 1747–1776.

Steptoe, A., Wardle, J., & Marmot, M. (2005). Positive affect and health-related neuroendocrine, cardiovascular, and inflammatory processes. *Proceedings of the National Academy of Sciences of the United States of America, 102,* 6508–6512.

Sterpenich, V., D'Argembeau, A., Desseilles, M., Balteau, E., Albouy, G., Vandewalle, G., . . . Maquet, P. (2006). The locus ceruleus is involved in the successful retrieval of emotional memories in humans. *The Journal of Neuroscience, 26,* 7416–7423.

Stevens, J. S., & Hamann, S. (2012). Sex differences in brain activation to emotional stimuli: A meta-analysis of neuroimaging studies. *Neuropsychologia, 50,* 1578–1593.

Stewart, S. A. (2005). The effects of benzodiazepines on cognition. *The Journal of Clinical Psychiatry, 66,* Supplement 2, 9–13.

Stoll, A. L., & Rueter, S. (1999). Treatment augmentation with opiates in severe and refractory major depression. *American Journal of Psychiatry, 156,* 2017–2017.

Storey, A. E., Walsh, C. J., Quinton, R. L., & Wynne-Edwards, K. E. (2000). Hormonal correlates of paternal responsiveness in new and expectant fathers. *Evolution and Human Behavior, 21,* 79–95.

Stowers, L., & Logan, D. W. (2010). Sexual dimorphism in olfactory signaling. *Current Opinion in Neurobiology, 20,* 770–775.

Strack, F., Martin, L. L., & Stepper, S. (1988). Inhibiting and facilitating conditions of the human smile: A nonobtrusive test of the facial feedback hypothesis. *Journal of Personality and Social Psychology, 54,* 768–777.

Strafella, A. P., Paus, T., Fraraccio, M., & Dagher, A. (2003). Striatal dopamine release induced by repetitive transcranial magnetic stimulation of the human motor cortex. *Brain, 126,* 2609–2615.

Strathearn, L., Li, J., Fonagy, P., & Montague, P. R. (2008). What's in a smile? Maternal brain responses to infant facial cues. *Pediatrics, 122,* 40–51.

Strick, M., Holland, R. W., van Baaren, R. B., & van Knippenberg, A. (2009). Finding comfort in a joke: Consolatory effects of humor through cognitive distraction. *Emotion, 9,* 574–578.

Stroop, J. R. (1935). Studies of interference in serial verbal reactions. *Journal of Experimental Psychology, 18,* 643–662.

Sullivan, R. M., Wilson, D. A., Wong, R., Correa, A., & Leon, M. (1990). Modified behavioral and olfactory bulb responses to maternal odors in preweanling rats. *Brain Research. Developmental Brain Research, 53,* 243–247.

Susskind, J. M., Lee, D. H., Cusi, A., Feiman, R., Grabski, W., & Anderson, A. K. (2008). Expressing fear enhances sensory acquisition. *Nature Neuroscience, 11,* 843–850.

Sutherland, M. R., & Mather, M. (2012). Negative arousal amplifies the effects of saliency in short-term memory. *Emotion.*

Suveg, C., Sood, E., Barmish, A., Tiwari, S., Hudson, J. L., & Kendall, P. C. (2008). "I'd rather not talk about it": Emotion parenting in families of children with an anxiety disorder. *Journal of Family Psychology, 22,* 875–884.

Swaab, D. F., & Hofman, M. A. (1995). Sexual differentiation of the human hypothalamus in relation to gender and sexual orientation. *Trends in Neurosciences, 18,* 264–270.

Szasz, P. L., Szentagotai, A., & Hofmann, S. G. (2011). The effect of emotion regulation strategies on anger. *Behaviour Research and Therapy, 49,* 114–119.

Szeto, A., Rossetti, M. A., Mendez, A. J., Noller, C. M., Herderick, E. E., Gonzales, J. A., Schneiderman, N., & McCabe, P. M. (2013). Oxytocin administration attenuates atherosclerosis and inflammation in Watanabe Heritable Hyperlipidemic rabbits. *Psychoneuroendocrinology, 38,* 685–693.

Takahashi, H., Kato, M., Matsuura, M., Mobbs, D., Suhara, T., & Okubo, Y. (2009). When your gain is my pain and your pain is my gain: Neural correlates of envy and Schadenfreude. *Science, 323,* 937–939.

Takahashi, L. K., Nakashima, B. R., Hong, H., & Watanabe, K. (2005). The smell of danger: A behavioral and neural analysis of predator odor-induced fear. *Neuroscience & Biobehavioral Reviews, 29,* 1157–1167.

Talbot, P. S., & Cooper, S. J. (2006). Anterior cingulate and subgenual prefrontal blood flow changes following tryptophan depletion in healthy males. *Neuropsychopharmacology, 31,* 1757–1767.

Tallet, C., Špinka, M., Maruščáková, I., & Šimecˇek, P. (2010). Human perception of vocalizations of domestic piglets and modulation by experience with domestic pigs (Sus scrofa). *Journal of Comparative Psychology, 124,* 81–91.

Tamir, D. I., & Mitchell, J. P. (2012). Disclosing information about the self is intrinsically rewarding. *Proceedings of the National Academy of Sciences of the United States of America, 109,* 8038–8043.

Tamres, L. K., Janicki, D., & Helgeson, V. S. (2002). Sex differences in coping behavior: A meta-analytic review and an examination of relative coping. *Personality and Social Psychology Review, 6,* 2–30.

Tang, Y., Hojatkashani, C., Dinov, I. D., Sun, B., Fan, L., Lin, X., Qi, H., Hua, X., Liu, S., & Toga,

A. W. (2010). The construction of a Chinese MRI brain atlas: A morphometric comparison study between Chinese and Caucasian cohorts. *NeuroImage, 51,* 33–41.

Tasker, J. G., & Herman, J. P. (2011). Mechanisms of rapid glucocorticoid feedback inhibition of the hypothalamic-pituitary-adrenal axis. *Stress, 14,* 398–406.

Taylor, S. E. (2006). Tend and befriend: Biobehavioral bases of affiliation under stress. *Current Directions in Psychological Science, 15,* 273–277.

Teasdale, J. D., & Fogarty, S. J. (1979). Differential effects of induced mood on retrieval of pleasant and unpleasant events from episodic memory. *Journal of Abnormal Psychology, 88,* 248–257.

Terner, J. M., & de Wit, H. (2006). Menstrual cycle phase and responses to drugs of abuse in humans. *Drug and Alcohol Dependence, 84,* 1–13.

Thayer, J. F., & Lane, R. D. (2009). Claude Bernard and the heart–brain connection: Further elaboration of a model of neurovisceral integration. *Neuroscience & Biobehavioral Reviews, 33,* 81–88.

Thibault, P., Lévesque, M., Gosselin, P., & Hess, U. (2012). The Duchenne marker is *not* a universal signal of smile authenticity—but it can be learned! *Social Psychology, 43,* 215–221.

Thorndike, E. L. (1927). The law of effect. *The American Journal of Psychology, 39,* 212–222.

Thorndike, E. L. (1998). *Animal intelligence.* (1911). (Thoemmes Press—Classics in Psychology.) (R. H. Wozniak, Ed.). London: Thoemmes Continuum.

Thornhill, R., Fincher, C. L., Murray, D. R., & Schaller, M. (2010). Zoonotic and non-zoonotic diseases in relation to human personality and societal values: Support for the parasite-stress model. *Evolutionary Psychology, 8,* 151–169.

Tian, L., Wang, J., Yan, C., & He, Y. (2011). Hemisphere- and gender-related differences in small-world brain networks: A resting-state functional MRI study. *NeuroImage, 54,* 191–202.

Tiedens, L. Z., & Linton, S. (2001). Judgment under emotional certainty and uncertainty: The effects of specific emotions on information processing. *Journal of Personality and Social Psychology, 81,* 973–988.

Tobin, R. M., Graziano, W. G., Vanman, E. J., & Tassinary, L. G. (2000). Personality, emotional experience, and efforts to control emotions. *Journal of Personality and Social Psychology, 79,* 656–669.

Todd, R. M., Cunningham, W. A., Anderson, A. K., & Thompson, E. (2012). Affect-biased attention as emotion regulation. *Trends in Cognitive Sciences, 16,* 365–372.

Tokutsu, Y., Umene-Nakano, W., Shinkai, T., Yoshimura, R., Okamoto, T., Katsuki, A., Hori, H., Ikenouchi-Sugita, A., Hayashi, K., Atake, K., & Nakamura, J. (2013). Follow-up study on electroconvulsive therapy in treatment-resistant depressed patients after remission: A chart review. *Clinical Psychopharmacology and Neuroscience, 11,* 34–38.

Tomkins, S. (1962). *Affect imagery consciousness—Vol. I: The positive affects.* New York: Springer Publishing Company.

Tomkins, S. (2008). *Affect imagery consciousness: The complete edition.* New York: Springer Publishing Company.

Toosi, N. R., Babbitt, L. G., Ambady, N., & Sommers, S. R. (2012). Dyadic interracial interactions: A meta-analysis. *Psychological Bulletin, 138,* 1–27.

Tost, H., Kolachana, B., Hakimi, S., Lemaitre, H., Verchinski, B. A., Mattay, V. S., . . . Meyer-Lindenberg, A. (2010). A common allele in the oxytocin receptor gene (OXTR) impacts prosocial temperament and human hypothalamic-limbic structure and function. *Proceedings of the National Academy of Sciences, 107,* 13936–13941.

Trezza, V., Damsteegt, R., Achterberg, E. J. M., & Vanderschuren, L. J. M. J. (2011). Nucleus accumbens μ-opioid receptors mediate social reward. *The Journal of Neuroscience, 31,* 6362–6370.

Trinder, J. (2007). Cardiac activity and sympathovagal balance during sleep. *Sleep Medicine Clinics, 2,* 199–208.

Troisi, A., & D'Amato, F. R. (1984). Ambivalence in monkey mothering. Infant abuse combined with maternal possessiveness. *The Journal of Nervous and Mental Disease, 172,* 105–108.

Tronick, E., Als, H., Adamson, L., Wise, S., & Brazelton, T. B. (1978). The infant's response to entrapment between contradictory messages in face-to-face interaction. *Journal of the American Academy of Child Psychiatry, 17,* 1–13.

Tsai, J. L., Chentsova-Dutton, Y., Freire-Bebeau, L., & Przymus, D. E. (2002). Emotional expression and physiology in European Americans and Hmong Americans. *Emotion, 2,* 380–397.

Tsai, J. L., Levenson, R. W., & Carstensen, L. L. (2000). Autonomic, subjective, and expressive responses to emotional films in older and younger Chinese Americans and European Americans. *Psychology and Aging, 15,* 684–693.

Tsai, J. L., Levenson, R. W., & McCoy, K. (2006). Cultural and temperamental variation in emotional response. *Emotion, 6,* 484–497.

Tsai, S. H., Shih, C. J., & Lin, M. T. (1985). Effects of brain epinephrine depletion on thermoregulation, reflex bradycardia, and motor activity in rats. *Experimental Neurology, 87,* 428–438.

Tunbridge, E. M., Huber, A., Farrell, S. M., Stumpenhorst, K., Harrison, P. J., & Walton, M. E. (2012). The role of catechol-O-methyltransferase in reward processing and addiction. *CNS & Neurological Disorders—Drug Targets* (formerly *Current Drug Targets—CNS&Neurological Disorders*), 11, 306–323.

Ullman, M. T., Pancheva, R., Love, T., Yee, E., Swinney, D., & Hickok, G. (2005). Neural correlates of lexicon and grammar: Evidence from the production, reading, and judgment of inflection in aphasia. *Brain and Language, 93,* 185–238; discussion, 239–242.

Urban, N. B. L., Slifstein, M., Meda, S., Xu, X., Ayoub, R., Medina, O., . . . Abi-Dargham, A. (2012). Imaging human reward processing with positron emission tomography and functional magnetic resonance imaging. *Psychopharmacology, 221,* 67–77.

Vaca, G. F.-B., Lüders, H. O., Basha, M. M., & Miller, J. P. (2011). Mirth and laughter elicited during brain stimulation. *Epileptic Disorders, 13,* 435–440.

Valins, S. (1966). Cognitive effects of false heart-rate feedback. *Journal of Personality and Social Psychology, 4,* 400–408.

Valtonen, M., Laaksonen, D. E., Laukkanen, J., Tolmunen, T., Rauramaa, R., Viinamäki, H., . . . Niskanen, L. (2009). Leisure-time physical activity, cardiorespiratory fitness and feelings of hopelessness in men. *BMC Public Health, 9,* 204.

Van Craenenbroeck, K., Borroto-Escuela, D. O., Romero-Fernandez, W., Skieterska, K., Rondou, P., Lintermans, B., . . . Haegeman, G. (2011). Dopamine D4 receptor oligomerization—contribution to receptor biogenesis. *The FEBS Journal, 278,* 1333–1344.

Van Craenenbroeck, K., Clark, S. D., Cox, M. J., Oak, J. N., Liu, F., & Van Tol, H. H. M. (2005). Folding efficiency is rate-limiting in dopamine D4 receptor biogenesis. *The Journal of Biological Chemistry, 280,* 19350–19357.

Van den Bos, R., Homberg, J., & de Visser, L. (2013). A critical review of sex differences in decision-making tasks: Focus on the Iowa Gambling Task. *Behavioural Brain Research, 238,* 95–108.

van Donkelaar, E. L., Blokland, A., Ferrington, L., Kelly, P. A. T., Steinbusch, H. W. M., & Prickaerts, J. (2011). Mechanism of acute tryptophan depletion: Is it only serotonin? *Molecular Psychiatry, 16,* 695–713.

van Leijenhorst, L., Westenberg, P. M., & Crone, E. A. (2008). A developmental study of risky decisions on the cake gambling task: Age and gender analyses of probability estimation and reward evaluation. *Developmental Neuropsychology, 33,* 179–196.

van Loon, A. M., van den Wildenberg, W. P. M., van Stegeren, A. H., Hajcak, G., & Ridderinkhof, K. R. (2010). Emotional stimuli modulate readiness for action: A transcranial magnetic stimulation study. *Cognitive, Affective & Behavioral Neuroscience, 10,* 174–181.

Vandekerckhove, M., Kestemont, J., Gross, J. J., Weiss, R., Schotte, C., Exadaktylos, V., . . . Verbraecken, J. (2012). Experiential versus analytical emotion regulation and sleep: Breaking the link between negative events and sleep disturbance. *Emotion, 12,* 1415–1421.

Varendi, H., Porter, R. H., & Winberg, J. (1996). Attractiveness of amniotic fluid odor: Evidence of prenatal olfactory learning? *Acta Paediatrica (Oslo, Norway: 1992), 85,* 1223–1227.

Venter, J. C., Adams, M. D., Myers, E. W., Li, P. W., Mural, R. J., Sutton, G. G., . . . Zhu, X. (2001). The sequence of the human genome. *Science, 291,* 1304–1351.

Vertes, R. P. (1991). A PHA-L analysis of ascending projections of the dorsal raphe nucleus in the rat. *The Journal of Comparative Neurology, 313,* 643–668.

Vogt, B. A., Nimchinsky, E. A., Vogt, L. J., & Hof, P. R. (1995). Human cingulate cortex: Surface features, flat maps, and cytoarchitecture. *The Journal of Comparative Neurology, 359,* 490–506.

Volkow, N. D., Wang, G.-J., Fowler, J. S., Tomasi, D., & Telang, F. (2011). Addiction: Beyond dopamine reward circuitry. *Proceedings of the National Academy of Sciences of the United States of America, 108,* 15037–15042.

Volz, K. G., & von Cramon, D. Y. (2009). How the orbitofrontal cortex contributes to decision making—a view from neuroscience. *Progress in Brain Research, 174,* 61–71.

von Frisch, O. (1965). Versuche über die Änderung der Herzfrequenz von Tieren bei psychischer Erregung. *Zeitschrift für Tierpsychologie, 22,* 104–118.

Vuilleumier, P., Armony, J. L., Driver, J., & Dolan, R. J. (2001). Effects of attention and emotion on face processing in the human brain: An event-related fMRI study. *Neuron, 30,* 829–841.

Vuilleumier, P., Armony, J. L., Driver, J., & Dolan, R. J. (2003). Distinct spatial frequency sensitivities for processing faces and emotional expressions. *Nature Neuroscience, 6,* 624–631.

Vuilleumier, P., Richardson, M. P., Armony, J. L., Driver, J., & Dolan, R. J. (2004). Distant influences of amygdala lesion on visual cortical activation during emotional face processing. *Nature Neuroscience, 7,* 1271–1278.

Vuilleumier, P., & Schwartz, S. (2001). Emotional facial expressions capture attention. *Neurology, 56,* 153–158.

Vytal, K., & Hamann, S. (2010). Neuroimaging support for discrete neural correlates of basic emotions: A voxel-based meta-analysis. *Journal of Cognitive Neuroscience, 22,* 2864–2885.

Wade, K. A., Garry, M., Read, J. D., & Lindsay, D. S. (2002). A picture is worth a thousand lies: Using false photographs to create false childhood memories. *Psychonomic Bulletin & Review, 9,* 597–603.

Waelti, P., Dickinson, A., & Schultz, W. (2001). Dopamine responses comply with basic assumptions of formal learning theory. *Nature, 412,* 43–48.

Wagner, G., Koschke, M., Leuf, T., Schlösser, R., & Bär, K.-J. (2009). Reduced heat pain thresholds after sad-mood induction are associated with changes in thalamic activity. *Neuropsychologia, 47,* 980–987.

Walker-Andrews, A. S. (1997). Infants' perception of expressive behaviors: Differentiation of multimodal information. *Psychological Bulletin, 121,* 437–456.

Waller, B. M., & Dunbar, R. I. M. (2005). Differential behavioural effects of silent bared teeth display and relaxed open mouth display in chimpanzees (Pan troglodytes). *Ethology, 111,* 129–142.

Wallin, B. G. (1981). Sympathetic nerve activity underlying electrodermal and cardiovascular reactions in man. *Psychophysiology, 18,* 470–476.

Walters, E. T., Carew, T. J., & Kandel, E. R. (1981). Associative learning in Aplysia: Evidence for conditioned fear in an invertebrate. *Science, 211,* 504–506.

Wang, L., McCarthy, G., Song, A. W., & LaBar, K. S. (2005). Amygdala activation to sad pictures during high-field (4 Tesla) functional magnetic resonance imaging. *Emotion, 5,* 12.

Wani, A., Trevino, K., Marnell, P., & Husain, M. M. (2013). Advances in brain stimulation for depression. *Annals of Clinical Psychiatry, 25,* 217–224.

Warren, J. (2007). *The head trip: Adventures on the wheel of consciousness.* Toronto: Random House.

Watson, D., & Clark, L. A. (1999). *The PANAS-X: Manual for the positive and negative affect schedule—expanded form.* University of Iowa. Retrieved from ir.uiowa.edu/cgi/view content.cgi?article = 1011&context = psychology_pubs

Watson, D., Clark, L. A., & Tellegen, A. (1988). Development and validation of brief measures of positive and negative affect: The PANAS scales. *Journal of Personality and Social Psychology, 54,* 1063–1070.

Watson, J. B., & Rayner, R. (1920). Conditioned emotional reactions. *Journal of Experimental Psychology, 3,* 1–14.

Watson, P. J., & Andrews, P. W. (2002). Toward a revised evolutionary adaptationist analysis of depression: The social navigation hypothesis. *Journal of Affective Disorders, 72,* 1–14.

Watson, R. I., & Evans, R. B. (1991). *The great psychologists: A history of psychological thought.* New York: HarperCollins Publishers.

Watts, S. W., Morrison, S. F., Davis, R. P., & Barman, S. M. (2012). Serotonin and blood pressure regulation. *Pharmacological Reviews, 64,* 359–388.

Webb, T. L., Miles, E., & Sheeran, P. (2012). Dealing with feeling: A meta-analysis of the effectiveness of strategies derived from the process model of emotion regulation. *Psychological Bulletin, 138,* 775–808.

Wedekind, C., Seebeck, T., Bettens, F., & Paepke, A. J. (1995). MHC-dependent mate preferences in humans. *Proceedings of the Royal Society of London. Series B: Biological Sciences, 260,* 245–249.

Weike, A. I., Hamm, A. O., Schupp, H. T., Runge, U., Schroeder, H. W. S., & Kessler, C. (2005). Fear conditioning following unilateral temporal lobectomy: Dissociation of conditioned startle potentiation and autonomic learning. *The Journal of Neuroscience, 25,* 11117–11124.

Weller, A., & Feldman, R. (2003). Emotion regulation and touch in infants: The role of cholecystokinin and opioids. *Peptides, 24,* 779–788.

Wentura, D. (2000). Dissociative affective and associative priming effects in the lexical decision task: Yes versus no responses to word targets reveal evaluative judgment tendencies. *Journal of Experimental Psychology. Learning, Memory, and Cognition, 26,* 456–469.

White, J. G., Southgate, E., Thomson, J. N., & Brenner, S. (1986). The structure of the nervous system of the Nematode Caenorhabditis elegans. *Philosophical Transactions of the Royal Society of London. B, Biological Sciences, 314,* 1–340.

Whiten, A., Goodall, J., McGrew, W. C., Nishida, T., Reynolds, V., Sugiyama, Y., Tutin, C. E. G., Wrangham, R. W., & Boesch, C. (1999). Cultures in chimpanzees. *Nature, 399,* 682–685.

Wicker, B., Keysers, C., Plailly, J., Royet, J. P., Gallese, V., & Rizzolatti, G. (2003). Both of us disgusted in my insula: The common neural basis of seeing and feeling disgust. *Neuron, 40,* 655–664.

Wiebe, S. A., Sheffield, T. D., & Espy, K. A. (2012). Separating the fish from the sharks: A longitudinal study of preschool response inhibition. *Child Development, 83,* 1245–1261.

Wiedemann, H.-R. (1994). Hans Berger. *European Journal of Pediatrics, 153,* 705–705.

Wiederman, S. D., & O'Carroll, D. C. (2013). Selective attention in an insect visual neuron. *Current Biology: CB, 23,* 156–161.

Wilkinson, R. G. (1992). Income distribution and life expectancy. *BMJ, 304,* 165–168.

Wilkinson, R. G., & Pickett, K. E. (2006). Income inequality and population health: A review and explanation of the evidence. *Social Science & Medicine, 62,* 1768–1784.

Williams, J. R., Insel, T. R., Harbaugh, C. R., & Carter, C. S. (1994). Oxytocin administered centrally facilitates formation of a partner preference in female prairie voles (Microtus ochrogaster). *Journal of Neuroendocrinology, 6,* 247–250.

Williams, L. M., Barton, M. J., Kemp, A. H., Liddell, B. J., Peduto, A., Gordon, E., & Bryant, R. A. (2005). Distinct amygdala-autonomic arousal profiles in response to fear signals in healthy males and females. *NeuroImage, 28,* 618–626.

Wilson-Mendenhall, C. D., Feldman-Barrett, L., & Barsalou, L. W. (2013). Neural evidence that human emotions share core affective properties. *Psychological Science, 24,* 947–956.

Winston, J. S., Strange, B. A., O'Doherty, J., & Dolan, R. J. (2002). Automatic and intentional brain responses during evaluation of trustworthiness of faces. *Nature Neuroscience, 5,* 277–283.

Wise, R. A. (2008). Dopamine and reward: The anhedonia hypothesis 30 years on. *Neurotoxicity Research, 14,* 169–183.

Wise, R. A., & Kiyatkin, E. A. (2011). Differentiating the rapid actions of cocaine. *Nature Reviews Neuroscience, 12,* 479–484.

Wittgenstein, L. (1953). Philosophische Untersuchungen. New York: MacMillan.

Wolff, P. H. (1959). Observations on newborn infants. *Psychosomatic Medicine, 21,* 110–118.

Wolitzky-Taylor, K. B., Horowitz, J. D., Powers, M. B., & Telch, M. J. (2008). Psychological approaches in the treatment of specific phobias: A meta-analysis. *Clinical Psychology Review, 28,* 1021–1037.

Wondergem, T. R., & Friedlmeier, M. (2012). Gender and ethnic differences in smiling: A yearbook photographs analysis from kindergarten through 12th grade. *Sex Roles, 67,* 403–411.

Wood, W., & Eagly, A. H. (2002). A cross-cultural analysis of the behavior of women and men: Implications for the origins of sex differences. *Psychological Bulletin, 128,* 699–727.

Woodcock, A., Graziano, W. G., Branch, S. E., Habashi, M. M., Ngambeki, I., & Evangelou,

D. (2013). Person and thing orientations psychological correlates and predictive utility. *Social Psychological and Personality Science, 4,* 116–123.

Woodworth, R. S., & Schlosberg, H. (1955). *Experimental Psychology.* London: Methuen & Co., Ltd.

Wrase, J., Klein, S., Gruesser, S. M., Hermann, D., Flor, H., Mann, K., Braus, D. F., & Heinz, A. (2003). Gender differences in the processing of standardized emotional visual stimuli in humans: A functional magnetic resonance imaging study. *Neuroscience Letters, 348,* 41–45.

Wu, S., Jia, M., Ruan, Y., Liu, J., Guo, Y., Shuang, M., Gong., Z., Zhang, Y., Yang, X., & Zhang, D. (2005). Positive association of the oxytocin receptor gene (OXTR) with autism in the Chinese Han population. *Biological Psychiatry, 58,* 74–77.

Wyer, R. S., Jr., & Collins, J. E., 2nd. (1992). A theory of humor elicitation. *Psychological Review, 99,* 663–688.

Xu, X., Zuo, X., Wang, X., & Han, S. (2009). Do you feel my pain? Racial group membership modulates empathic neural responses. *The Journal of Neuroscience, 29,* 8525–8529.

Yacubian, J., Sommer, T., Schroeder, K., Gläscher, J., Kalisch, R., Leuenberger, B., Braus, D.F., & Büchel, C. (2007). Gene-gene interaction associated with neural reward sensitivity. *Proceedings of the National Academy of Sciences of the United States of America, 104,* 8125–8130.

Yang, Z., & Tong, E. M. W. (2010). The effects of subliminal anger and sadness primes on agency appraisals. *Emotion, 10,* 915–922.

Yeomans, J. S., & Frankland, P. W. (1995). The acoustic startle reflex: Neurons and connections. *Brain Research Reviews, 21,* 301–314.

Yiend, J. (2010). The effects of emotion on attention: A review of attentional processing of emotional information. *Cognition & Emotion, 24,* 3–47.

Yik, M., Russell, J. A., & Steiger, J. H. (2011). A 12-point circumplex structure of core affect. *Emotion, 11,* 705–731.

Yoshino, A., Okamoto, Y., Onoda, K., Yoshimura, S., Kunisato, Y., Demoto, Y., Okada, G., & Yamawaki, S. (2010). Sadness enhances the experience of pain via neural activation in the anterior cingulate cortex and amygdala: An fMRI study. *NeuroImage, 50,* 1194–1201.

Young, E. J., & Williams, C. L. (2010). Valence dependent asymmetric release of norepinephrine in the basolateral amygdala. *Behavioral Neuroscience, 124,* 633–644.

Young, K. A., Holcomb, L. A., Bonkale, W. L., Hicks, P. B., Yazdani, U., & German, D. C. (2007). 5HTTLPR polymorphism and enlargement of the pulvinar: Unlocking the backdoor to the limbic system. *Biological Psychiatry, 61,* 813–818.

Young, S. G., & Hugenberg, K. (2010). Mere social categorization modulates identification of facial expressions of emotion. *Journal of Personality and Social Psychology, 99,* 964–977.

Zajonc, R. B. (1984). On the primacy of affect. *American Psychologist, 39,* 117–123.

Zeisel, S. H. (2012). A brief history of choline. *Annals of Nutrition and Metabolism, 61,* 254–258.

Zelman, D. C., Howland, E. W., Nichols, S. N., & Cleeland, C. S. (1991). The effects of induced mood on laboratory pain. *Pain, 46,* 105–111.

Zhang, Q., Li, X., Gold, B. T., & Jiang, Y. (2010). Neural correlates of cross-domain affective priming. *Brain Research, 1329,* 142–151.

Zhang, Y., Jin, X., Shen, X., Zhang, J., & Hoff, E. (2008). Correlates of early language development in Chinese children. *International Journal of Behavioral Development, 32,* 145–151.

Zhou, T., & Bishop, G. D. (2012). Culture moderates the cardiovascular consequences of anger regulation strategy. *International Journal of Psychophysiology, 86,* 291–298.

Zhou, W., & Chen, D. (2009). Fear-related chemosignals modulate recognition of fear in ambiguous facial expressions. *Psychological Science, 20,* 177–183.

Zhou, Y., Li, X., Zhang, M., Zhang, F., Zhu, C., & Shen, M. (2011). Behavioural approach tendencies to heroin-related stimuli in abstinent heroin abusers. *Psychopharmacology, 221,* 171–176.

Zillmann, D., & Bryant, J. (1974). Effect of residual excitation on the emotional response to provocation and delayed aggressive behavior. *Journal of Personality and Social Psychology, 30,* 782–791.

Zlomke, K. R., & Hahn, K. S. (2010). Cognitive emotion regulation strategies: Gender differences and associations to worry. *Personality and Individual Differences, 48,* 408–413.

Zubieta, J.-K., Ketter, T. A., Bueller, J. A., Xu, Y., Kilbourn, M. R., Young, E. A., & Koeppe, R. A. (2003). Regulation of human affective responses by anterior cingulate and limbic mu-opioid neurotransmission. *Archives of General Psychiatry, 60,* 1145–1153.

Glossary

Action potential. Neuronal signaling process during which a neuron's membrane potential polarizes rapidly along its axon, eventually triggering the release of neurotransmitters into the synaptic cleft.

Action tendency. As defined by Arnold, a bodily response (e.g., acceleration in heart rate) that results from an emotional appraisal and that prepares the body for action. An action tendency makes appraisal-congruent behaviors more likely than appraisal-incongruent behaviors.

Addiction. Chronically relapsing condition that is characterized by compulsive reward consumption and a negative affective tone when rewards are unavailable.

Adrenaline. Bodily chemical that has an arousing or activating effect. It is released by the adrenal gland into the blood stream where it acts as a hormone. Adrenaline is also released in the brain where it acts as a neurotransmitter.

Affect. Feeling states that are simpler or more basic than emotions. For example, states that can be differentiated based on valence only are typically referred to as affective.

Affect labeling. Explicit naming of an experienced emotion. It has been shown to reduce affective responses.

Affective priming. In an affective priming paradigm, participants are exposed to prime-target sequences, and the affective relationship between primes and targets is either congruous or incongruous. Target classifications are facilitated for congruous relative to incongruous cases.

Agonists. Pharmacological agents that enhance the activity of a particular bodily chemical (e.g., neurotransmitter).

American Psychological Association. A body that organizes researching and practicing psychologists in North America. Among other things, the APA sets ethical standards for their work.

Amygdala. Small, roundish nucleus, reminiscent of an almond, that is situated in the medial temporal lobe. It is located anteriorly to the hippocampus.

Antagonists. Pharmacological agents that inhibit the activity of a particular bodily chemical (e.g., neurotransmitter).

Antecedent-focused emotion regulation. Emotion regulation strategy that tackles the input to a putative emotion system.

Anterior. Front of a structure.

Anxiety. Term that is often used to refer to fearful states. Different researchers use different criteria to define anxiety (e.g., that a threat is prospective rather than imminent). At present it is still unclear whether and how it can be distinguished from fear.

Anxiety disorder. Condition diagnosed when individuals experience excessive fears that prevent them from leading an ordinary life. There are different types of anxiety disorders; the most common are phobias.

Appraisals. Cognitive evaluations of an event. Depending on appraisal outcomes, individuals may feel an emotion.

Arginine vasopressin. Hormone/peptide and neurotransmitter/neuropeptide that is structurally very similar to oxytocin. Whereas oxytocin seems more relevant to female emotions, vasopressin seems more relevant to male emotions. Within the context of attachment formation, these two chemicals have overlapping albeit sex-specific functions.

Attachment styles. According to Ainsworth and colleagues, these are different forms of social bonds children develop toward their mother or other caretakers. They include secure and insecure attachments.

Autism. Neurodevelopmental disorder characterized by marked socioemotional deficits.

Automaton. A machine. Descartes viewed the body as an automaton that only in the case of humans is governed by a soul.

Autonomic nervous system. Part of the peripheral nervous system. It operates involuntarily and is responsible for monitoring and regulating the function of bodily organs.

Balloon Analogue Risk Task. Computer-based task that involves participants pumping up virtual balloons and earning money for each pump as long as the balloon remains intact. BART is used as an implicit measure for risk taking.

Basal ganglia. Collection of nuclei situated in the basal center of the cerebrum. They form important connections with diencephalon and cortex.

Basic emotions. Relates to Tomkins's idea of primary affects. Basic emotions are typically identified based on a set of defining criteria (e.g., functionality, associated behaviors).

Behaviorism. Theoretical approach that became popular in the first half of the 20th century. Its main tenet is that mental processes cannot be observed or measured, and that therefore researchers should focus instead on observing and measuring behavior.

Behavior therapy. Clinical psychological approach for the treatment of mental disorders. It is based on the principles of classical and operant conditioning.

Benzodiazepines. Class of drugs that facilitates the activity of GABA in the brain and therefore has a sedative effect. Benzodiazepines are often prescribed to individuals with anxiety disorders.

Beta-endorphins. Chemical messengers that serve as endogenous opioids or "natural painkillers."

Bottom-up. Term that describes mental processes arising from sensory stimuli that stand out from other stimuli (e.g., brighter, louder). These stimuli are said to capture attention via bottom-up processes.

Brainstem. The most ventral part of the brain that connects with the spinal cord.

CAMP response element binding protein. Protein that helps transcribe the DNA sequence. It is called a transcription factor.

Catecholamines. Chemical messengers of the monoamine family that contain the organic compound catechol. Catecholamines include dopamine, norepinephrine, and epinephrine.

Central nervous system. Part of the nervous system that serves as the main information-processing hub. In vertebrates, it is comprised of the brain and the spinal cord.

Cerebellum. Brain structure located at the posterior base of the cerebrum. It looks like a small replica of the cerebrum.

Cerebrum. The brain's largest and uppermost part. Its three main components are the basal ganglia, the white matter, and the gray matter of the cortex.

Choline. Essential nutrient of the vitamin B family that is available in most animal products such as eggs and meat.

Chronic pain. Clinical condition in which individuals suffer from pain for more than 6 months (*DSM-5*). The condition may be caused by tissue damage and/or psychological stress.

Cingulate gyrus. Structure that sits medially, forming part of the inner walls of the two hemispheres. It stretches like a belt around the corpus callosum from frontal to parietal lobe.

Circumplex model. Model of emotions developed by James Russell. It holds that emotions have a circular relationship that can be characterized by two orthogonal dimensions: valence and arousal.

Cognitive arousal theory. Emotion theory proposed by Schachter and Singer. It holds that emotions depend on the cognitive interpretation of unspecific bodily arousal.

Cognitive restructuring. Emotion regulation technique whereby individuals obtain new information and change the way they think about and evaluate existing information.

Component process model. Emotion model proposed by Klaus Scherer. According to the model, emotions arise from a componential appraisal process that operates in a sequential fashion. Its main components include a relevance check, an implications check, an assessment of coping potentials, and an assessment of an event's normative significance.

COMT gene. Gene that regulates the production of the catechol-O-methyltransferase (COMT) protein, a protein that inactivates dopamine in the synapse. In humans, part of this gene comes in two variants (Met/Val) that make the resulting protein more or less effective.

Conditioned stimulus. Stimulus that elicits the same response as an unconditioned stimulus with which it was previously paired. The elicited response is learned rather than innate.

Congenital adrenal hyperplasia. Genetic disorder that impacts hormonal production in the adrenal gland. Excessive or deficient sex hormones affect the individual's development of primary and secondary sexual characteristics.

Connectivity. In neuroscience, this term denotes the structural or functional relation between two or more regions. Structures that are connected via fiber tracts and/or whose activity seems temporally coupled are said to show structural and/or functional connectivity, respectively.

Consolidation. Mental process during which information previously activated in short-term or working memory becomes durable. Short-term or working memory content is moved into long-term memory.

Constructionist account. Account of emotions that grew out of the dimensional approach. It holds that emotions are constructed from core affect and other processes including the attribution of core affect to an event, appraisals, and bodily responses.

Convergent evolution. Describes instances in which two species evolved the same characteristic independently. This characteristic was absent in the common ancestor from which they evolved.

Core affect. Defined by Russell as a basic affective experience that can be fully described based on valence and arousal.

Cortex. Latin word for "tree bark." As a neuroanatomical term, it describes the folding of neuronal layers around the brain's white matter.

Cranial nerves. Set of 12 nerves that emerge directly from the brain into the body without running through the spinal cord. Their name derives from the word *cranium,* which means "skull."

Cultural anthropology. Study of humankind as focused on culture and society.

Culture. Group-specific practice emerging from the interaction between a group and its environment.

Cumulative learning. Cultural phenomenon whereby individuals acquire a behavior that is then preserved and possibly enhanced within their group across several generations. It is also referred to as cultural transmission.

Cytoarchitecture. Term with two major components: *cyto-* and *architecture*. *Cyto-* is a prefix specifying something as cellular. It derives from the Greek term *kutos,* for "hollow." Together with the term *architecture,* it refers to the cellular composition of tissue.

Deception techniques. Psychological techniques that disguise the true purpose of an experiment by giving participants false information. These techniques are ethically sensitive and have to be used with care.

Declarative memory. The conscious, long-term memory of facts and life events that one can recount verbally.

Default network. Brain system comprising a set of regions (e.g., medial prefrontal cortex, medial temporal cortex) that are more active during wakeful rest than effortful thought and that are possibly engaged in mind wandering.

Defense cascade. Term that describes the behavioral responses to threat and outlines two phases. In an initial inhibitory phase, individuals orient toward and explore threat. In a subsequent activational phase, individuals avoid or, if avoidance is impossible, confront threat.

Delayed gratification. An individual's ability to abstain from a presently available reward in order to obtain a larger reward later. This ability depends on the extent to which an individual engages in temporal discounting.

Deoxyribonucleic acid. Cellular storage system for genetic material. It comprises the body's building instructions that organisms receive from their parent(s).

Depression. In psychology/psychiatry, a mood disorder characterized by several symptoms, including increased sadness or lack of happiness. The symptoms need to be present for a period of two or more weeks.

Despair. Term used to refer to a later stage of sadness, after individuals have lost hope. It is characterized by withdrawal.

Diencephalon. Sits between the brainstem and the cerebrum. Its main components are the thalamus and the hypothalamus. Also called the interbrain.

Display rules. Rules that govern emotional expression during communication. They are acquired during an individual's lifetime and reflect internalized norms about what kinds of expressions are appropriate in what kinds of situations.

Distress. Term used to refer to an initial stage of sadness, during which individuals attempt to restore something lost.

Dopamine. Neurotransmitter that belongs to the monoamine and catecholamine families.

Dorsal. Top or back of a structure.

Duchenne smile. Type of smile named after its discoverer, Duchenne de Boulogne; also called a true smile. It involves both the mouth and the eye region. Posed smiles are often non-Duchenne in that they involve the mouth region only.

Ego-focused emotions. Emotions that primarily concern the self and that are triggered by antecedents that are immediately relevant to the self. Original examples include anger and pride. Note, however, that these emotions may also concern others.

Electrocardiogram. Measurement of the heart's electrical activity.

Electroconvulsive therapy. Treatment approach that uses an electric current to induce an epileptic seizure in patients with mental disorders such as depression and schizophrenia. Presumably, the treatment resets brain function. However, the exact treatment mechanisms are not yet understood.

Electrodermal measures. Measures that record the activity of sweat glands in the skin. They comprise skin potentials, skin resistance, and skin conductance.

Electroencephalography. Technique that uses surface electrodes to measure aspects of the brain's electrical activity.

Embodied. Term that describes the influence of bodily properties and states (e.g., leaning forward, being cold) on cognition.

Emotion prototypes. Defined by Russell as best-exemplar emotions that are constructed from changes in core affect and a range of higher-order processes including appraisals, attributions, and subjective feelings.

Emotion regulation. Mental process aimed to increase, maintain, or decrease the intensity, duration, or quality of an emotional experience. Emotion regulation comprises attentional deployment, cognitive change, and response modulation strategies.

Emotions. Conscious or unconscious mental states elicited by events that are appraised as relevant for one's needs and that motivate behaviors to fulfill these needs.

Encoding. Mental process during which external or self-generated information is represented by sensory and association areas in the brain and maintained in short-term or working memory.

Enzymes. Complex proteins that produce chemical reactions with other substances. In the context of the synapse, enzymes exist that help disintegrate superfluous neurotransmitters.

Epinephrine. Neurotransmitter that belongs to the monoamine and catecholamine families. It is synthesized from norepinephine. See adrenaline.

Epigenetic mechanisms. Mechanisms that regulate the transcription of DNA. They involve the modification of information that is stored together with the DNA in a cell's nucleus. The word *epigenetic* is comprised of two parts: *epi-* and *genetic*. *Epi-* is a prefix of Greek origin, meaning "upon." Together with the word *genetic,* it refers to processes acting upon genes.

Epilepsy. Neurological disorder with recurrent episodes of excessive or hypersynchronous neuronal activity. Patients may experience sensory disturbances, a loss of consciousness, or motor spasms, among other things.

Essential amino acid. Amino acid that is needed for the normal functioning of the body but that is not synthesized within the body itself. Instead, it must be obtained from food.

Event-related heart rate. Measure that indicates the heart rate change caused by a particular event (e.g., an emotional stimulus). Most events first slow down and then speed up the heart. Moreover, these changes are typically enhanced when events are emotionally arousing.

Evolution. Derives from the Latin word *evolvo,* which means to "unfurl" or "extricate." Darwin used the term to describe how species emerge and change as a function of environmental conditions.

Evolutionary anthropology. Study of humankind as focused on evolution and biology.

Experience sampling method. Method in which participants are contacted (e.g., through a digital device) several times a day over the course of several days while pursuing their normal activities. Each time they are contacted, they must describe their current state (e.g., what they are doing, where they are, whom they are with, how they feel).

Explicit emotion processing. Occurs when individuals consciously evaluate the emotional significance of a stimulus.

Explicit or declerative memories. Memories that can be verbalized and that typically require effortful processing both during memory storage and retrieval.

Extinction (learning). Process during which a previously conditioned response is extinguished or unlearned. For extinction to occur, a conditioned stimulus must be presented without its unconditioned stimulus (classical conditioning) or a conditioned behavior must no longer produce a previously associated reward or punishment (operant conditioning). After a number of trials, the individual will stop responding to the conditioned stimulus or stop showing the conditioned behavior.

Extinction (perception). Phenomenon observed in patients with hemispatial neglect. When presented with one object in each side of the visual field, patients typically fail to perceive the object in contralesional space.

Facial Action Coding System. System developed by Ekman and Friesen, who identified several action units (e.g., raising of inner eyebrows) that can be used to analyze facial expressions.

Familiarity. Mental state resulting from incomplete memory retrieval. An individual remembers encountering a particular object/event before but has no or little additional information (e.g., location, time).

Fear. Emotion elicited by stimuli that forecast a need and toward which an individual feels powerless.

Fear module. Structure that plays a specific role for fear. Some researchers consider the amygdala a fear module.

5-HT transporter gene. Gene that codes for the production of a membrane protein that removes 5-HT from the synapse by transporting it back into the presynaptic neuron. In the human genome, the gene comes in a long and a short variant.

5-hydroxytryptamine. Neurotransmitter of the monoamine family. Also called serotonin.

Flashbulb memories. Memories of events with great emotional significance. They are believed to differ from ordinary memories in that they are particularly vivid.

Flow. Term used by Mihaly Csikszentmihalyi to describe a positive state of complete immersion into an activity or task.

Follicular phase. Phase that spans across the first two weeks of the menstrual cycle, during which the woman menstruates and her follicles and their content, the egg, mature.

Forebrain. Term that refers to the part of the central nervous system that sits before the midbrain/mesencephalon. It is composed of diencephalon and cerebrum.

Freezing. Term that refers to an inhibition of movement that is caused by the perception of threat.

Frontotemporal dementia. Form of dementia in which frontal and temporal cortex deteriorate. Patients undergo personality changes and become emotionally blunted.

Gametes. Cells that enable sexual reproduction. They are typically referred to as sperm and eggs in males and females, respectively.

Gender. Term that refers to differences between girls and boys, women and men that arise not from biological but from cultural/environmental factors. Gender and sex of a person do not always match. Some individuals may be biologically male or female but take on an opposite-sex gender identity.

Generalized anxiety disorder. Disorder characterized by excessive worries about a wide range of commonplace events.

Genes. The sections of DNA that form functional units responsible for a particular aspect of the body.

Glial cells. Nervous system cells that support the function of neurons and that communicate with other cells through chemical pathways. Unlike neurons, they cannot communicate via action potentials.

Gliotransmitter. Chemical messenger used by glial cells.

Globus pallidus. Part of the basal ganglia, a subcortical gray-matter site. The globus pallidus sits medially of the striatum (i.e., more centrally within the brain).

Go/no-go task. In such a task, participants see a series of stimuli, some of which are targets and others of which are nontargets. Participants must respond (e.g., by pushing a button) when they see a target and withhold their response when they see a nontarget.

Granule cell. Type of neuron that can be found in the second and fourth layer of cortex as well as in other parts of the brain. Granule cells share a small size but are structurally and functionally diverse.

Gustatory cortex. Primary sensory cortex for taste information. It is located in the dysgranular insula.

Heart-rate variability. Range of heart periods that indicates how consistently or inconsistently the heart beats. Healthy hearts beat somewhat inconsistently.

Hebbian learning. Term that refers to the synaptic changes thought to underpin memory formation. It is commonly paraphrased as "neurons that fire together, wire together."

Hemispatial neglect. Neurological syndrome arising from damage to brain tissue responsible for attention. Tissue damage is typically located in right parietal cortex. Hemispatial neglect patients show difficulties perceiving and attending to objects located in contralesional space.

Hippocampus. Elongated structure situated in the medial temporal lobe. Its name stems from the Greek words *hippos* for "horse" and *kampos* for "sea monster," and reflects the fact that the shape of the hippocampus resembles that of a sea horse.

Hormones. Chemical messengers that are released by glands or other bodily tissue into the bloodstream.

Humor. A bodily fluid in Galen's theory of the body. He assumed that humors determined a person's temperament.

Hypothalamus. Subcortical structure that forms part of the diencephalon and that is situated below the thalamus.

Implicit Association Test. Test that can be used to measure implicit affective or emotional responses to attitude objects such as insects, alcohol, and extramarital sex. The test probes the link between these objects and concepts of interest (e.g., positivity, pride, disgust) in an individual's memory.

Implicit emotion processing. Occurs when individuals perceive a stimulus and make no conscious attempts to evaluate its emotional significance. Any such processing occurs spontaneously and possibly unconsciously.

Implicit or procedural memories. Memories that are difficult or impossible to verbalize. They may be stored and retrieved automatically.

Imprinting. A form of attachment formation observed in the offspring of birds. During a few hours after hatching, chicks of many species will treat the first moving object they see as their mother.

Insula. Small stretch of cortical tissue located below frontal, temporal, and parietal cortex.

International affective picture system. Stimulus system that comprises a range of pictures that vary with respect to valence and arousal. The IAPS is often used as a means to modulate affect in research participants.

Joy. Emotion elicited by the unexpected prospect of a reward.

Lamarckian theory. Evolution theory developed by Jean-Baptiste Lamarck (1744–1829), according to which parents were able to pass on characteristics they had acquired during their lifetime. For example, children might be better at learning to play a particular instrument if their parents had already acquired that skill. As Darwin's theory of evolution gained popularity, Lamarck's theory received much critique. In the end, however, we find truth in both accounts, as nature conveniently combines genetic and experiential mechanisms of inheritance.

Lateral. Outer sides of a structure.

Law of effect. Law formulated by Thorndike that underpins operant conditioning. It refers to the fact that behaviors with positive consequences tend to be repeated, whereas behaviors with negative consequences tend to be avoided.

Learned helplessness. Concept developed by Seligman and colleagues to refer to a condition in which humans and other animals have learned that they cannot avert a negative event. As a consequence of such learning, they will remain impassive when faced with the event.

Level of processing. Concept developed within cognitive psychology to explain memory performance differences caused by different levels of engagement with to-be-remembered material. A deeper level of processing is associated with better memory performance than a shallow level of processing. In analogy, the feeling of an emotion may depend on the level of processing an emotion-eliciting event.

Limbic. Term derived from the Latin word *limbus,* which means "rim" or "edge." It was used by MacLean to refer to a circular set of structures lining the inner walls of the two hemispheres and supposedly governing emotions.

Locus coeruleus. Latin for "blue spot." Denotes nucleus situated in the pons of the brainstem. It is the primary brain site for the synthesis of noradrenaline.

Long-term depression. In neuroscience, this term refers to changes in the synapse that inhibit the communication between the pre- and postsynaptic neuron. The underlying processes may be similar to long-term potentiation but occur for lower firing frequencies. LTD keeps LTP in check and enables memory pruning.

Long-term potentiation. In neuroscience, this term refers to changes in the synapse that optimize the communication between the pre- and postsynaptic neuron. Such optimization is thought to result from the simultaneous activity of both neurons. ("Neurons that fire together, wire together.") LTP is thought to be a primary neuronal mechanism for learning.

Luteal phase. Phase that spans across the second half of the menstrual cycle. At the beginning of the luteal phase, an egg is released for fertilization.

Magnetic resonance imaging. Technique that measures the energy fluctuations of hydrogen protons. Energy differences arising from differences in blood oxygenation form the basis for functional magnetic resonance imaging (fMRI).

Major histocompatibility complex. A class of molecules that present incompatible (i.e., foreign) proteins to immune cells for destruction. Genes that code for MHC molecules differ widely in the human genome.

Marshmallow test. Paradigm developed by Mischel and colleagues to examine preschoolers' capacity for delayed gratification. Kids must decide between an unpreferred sweet that is available now and a preferred sweet that is available later. The experimenter measures whether and how long kids hold out for the preferred sweet.

Mask. Stimulus that serves to prevent conscious processing of a target stimulus. It precedes or follows a target and typically differs from the target in that it is viewed for a longer period of time and is therefore perceptually more salient.

Medial. Middle of a structure.

Medial forebrain bundle. Using electrical brain stimulation, Olds identified this structure as a pleasure center. It contains dopaminergic projections spanning from the ventral tegmental area to the forebrain.

Medial prefrontal cortex. Brain structure located in the medial walls of the hemispheres, anteriorly from the central fissure. It surrounds the anterior cingulate cortex.

Mind-body problem. Philosophical problem concerning the relation between mind and body. It is considered a problem because, intuitively, the mind seems immaterial and thus different from the body. However, the mind depends on the body and this dependence confounds the mind's seemingly immaterial nature.

Mindfulness training. Form of meditation in which individuals engage in metacognition, focusing on current bodily and mental states.

Mixed longitudinal design. Method that combines cross-sectional and longitudinal data gathering by following individuals of different ages (e.g., young, middle-aged, old) across a few years.

Monoamineoxidase (MAO) inhibitors. Drugs that inhibit the activity of MAO. Because MAO serves to breakdown superfluous neurotransmitters in the synapse, MAO-inhibitors reduce such breakdown and allow more neurotransmitters to act on postsynaptic receptors.

Monoamines. Chemical messengers that contain one amino group. They comprise catecholamines and tryptamines.

Monogamous. Term that characterizes species in which most individuals form selective pair bonds after mating to jointly care for offspring. Although these individuals are bonded, they may be sexually active outside their pair bond. Moreover, of the monogamous species, only a few stay within the same pair bond for more than one breeding season.

Mood. Prolonged affective or emotional state for which there is no single eliciting event or the eliciting event is no longer present.

Multidimensional scaling. Statistical procedure that helps illustrate the relationship or distance between items (e.g., emotions) in a multidimensional space.

Neocortex. Refers to cortex that has six well-defined layers and that was originally thought to have evolved in higher mammals (e.g., primates). More recent research suggests that it was present in the earliest mammal.

Nervous system. Comprises of nerve cells and enables organisms to represent the information that is necessary for them to usefully interact with their environment.

Neurons. Cells that are capable of firing an action potential. They are considered the primary constituent of a nervous system.

Neuropeptides. Chemical messengers that contain a protein and that are active within the brain.

Neurotransmitters. Chemical messengers that are released by a presynaptic neuron and that influence the activity of a postsynaptic neuron.

Nociceptors. Cells dedicated to the perception of pain.

Norepinephrine. Neurotransmitter that belongs to the monoamine and catecholamine families. It is synthesized from dopamine. Also called noradrenaline,

Oddball procedure. Procedure that involves the presentation of a rare stimulus intermixed with a frequent stimulus. In an active oddball procedure, participants detect the rare stimulus. In a passive oddball procedure, stimulus processing is monitored through online measures such as EEG or heart rate.

Online measures. Physiological and brain imaging measures are referred to as online measures because they measure bodily and mental processes as they unfold in time.

Operant conditioning. Form of learning whereby the consequences of an action determine how well this action is retained.

Opioids. Chemical messengers that bind to opioid receptors. They are referred to as endogenous opioids if they are naturally produced within the body. Opioids can also be derived from poppy (i.e., opium) or they can be synthesized.

Orbicularis occuli. Facial muscle that surrounds the eye and that makes the eye squint when activated.

Other-focused emotions. Emotions that arise from antecedents with primary relevance for others or for the relationship that the individual has with them. Examples include shame and guilt.

Oxytocin. Chemical messenger that acts as a hormone or peptide and as a neurotransmitter or neuropeptide. It has multiple functions, including the regulation of attachment and social behavior.

Paleomammalian brain. Defined by Paul MacLean as a set of brain structures present in all mammals and supporting the limbic system.

Panic disorder. Disorder characterized by the fearful anticipation and frequent experience of panic attacks. During these attacks individuals feel intense fear (e.g., death, loss of control) and show a range of bodily arousal symptoms.

Parahippocampal gyrus. Gray-matter structure that surrounds the hippocampus.

Parallel evolution. Describes instances in which two species share a characteristic because that characteristic was present in a common ancestor.

Parasympathetic nervous system. One of two efferent strands of the autonomic nervous system. It is largely associated with conserving/restoring the body's energy.

Pathogens. Microorganisms such as bacteria or viruses that befall a host and can cause disease.

Peer review. A system whereby research reports are reviewed for quality by scientists unconnected to the research. The reviewers may recommend alterations in the reports. Moreover, the reviewers' comments may form the basis for editorial decisions regarding whether reports should be published.

Perceptual bottleneck. Term that refers to the limited bandwidth of perceptual processing.

When two or more objects reach an individual's senses they compete for awareness. Objects that win this competition will receive better perceptual representation than will objects that lose this competition.

Peripheral nervous system. Part of the nervous system that is distributed across the body and that serves to connect the central nervous system with peripheral sensors (e.g., skin receptors), effectors (e.g., muscles), and internal organs (e.g., heart).

Phenomenological approach. Has a long tradition within philosophy. It is concerned with consciousness and the first-person experience of an object.

Pheromones. Chemicals released by the body that influence the behavior of conspecifics.

Phobia. Anxiety disorder in which patients experience debilitating fears of specific items such as spiders, heights, or enclosed spaces.

Phylogenetically. Refers to the evolutionary relationship between species. A species that is phylogenetically older than another species evolved at an earlier point in history.

Pictures of facial affect. Set of facial expressions posed by actors who were asked to portray different basic emotions. Also known as the "Ekman faces."

Pineal gland. Small endocrine structure located in the middle of the brain. Descartes considered it the point of contact between body and soul.

Pleasure center. Set of dopaminergic structures identified by James Olds. Individuals perceive the activation of these structures as pleasurable.

Point Subtraction Aggression Paradigm. Task that measures aggression implicitly. Participants have to trade off earning points by pushing a button with avenging points stolen by an alleged thief.

Positive and negative affect schedule. Self-report instrument that measures both affect and emotion. It can be used as a state (how does an individual feel now) or a trait (how does an individual feel typically) measure.

Positive psychology. Movement within psychology that stresses the importance of an individual's positive characteristics and resources as a means to optimize mental functioning.

Positivity effect. Term that refers to older adults' propensity to disengage from negative and to engage with positive information.

Positron emission tomography. Technique in which a radioactive tracer is injected into a person's bloodstream. When used for neuroimaging, the tracer travels to the brain where its radionuclides emit positrons. The site of positron emission gives clues about the local availability of brain chemicals.

Posterior. Back of a structure.

Precession. Type of rotational movement whereby a rotating body moves its rotational axis. For example, the rotational axis may move in such a way that its movements describe a cone.

Preferential looking paradigm. Method developed by Fantz (1964) to explore stimulus preferences in preverbal infants. Infants are presented with two stimuli and the duration of orientation to either stimulus is measured.

Premotor cortex. Forms part of the frontal cortex; sits anterior to motor cortex.

Preparedness. Term that refers to the fact that conditioning depends on species-specific biological predispositions that make some stimulus-stimulus or stimulus-response contingencies more relevant for learning than others.

Primary affects. Fundamental feeling states that differ qualitatively, with each state having their own function. Term used by Tomkins.

Principal component analysis. Statistical technique that helps reduce a large number of variables into a smaller set of principal components. The first component produced with this technique explains most of the data, and the contribution of each following component will be weaker and weaker. Researchers decide which components to consider "principal" based on the components' explanatory power.

Problem-based coping. Behavioral coping strategy aimed at improving one's situation by reducing the problem or stressor. Problem-based coping can be dissociated from appraisal or emotion-focused coping, which tackle thoughts and feelings instead.

Prospect theory. Theory developed by Kahneman and Tversky that provides a framework for the psychological processes underlying decision making.

Prototype. Mental representation of the average member of a category. Prototypes help categorize novel instances based on similarity to the prototype.

Psyche. Word that derives from the Greek word *psukhē,* meaning breath, life, or soul.

QRS complex. Prominent wave pattern in the electrocardiogram that comprises three waves referred to as Q, R, and S waves, respectively, by the Dutch physiologist William Einthoven. The QRS complex represents the depolarization of the heart's ventricles.

Readiness potential. Deflection in the event-related potential that emerges over motor cortex in the hemisphere opposite to that of an ensuing motor response. It reflects the preparation of this response.

Receptive field. Term that refers to the property of a sensory neuron. An external stimulus that influences the likelihood of an action potential is said to fall within the neuron's receptive field.

Recollection. Mental state resulting from complete memory retrieval. An individual has access to critical object/event information such as when the object/event was encountered and what the individual did at the time.

Reconsolidation. Process that helps restabilize a previously recalled memory through protein synthesis in relevant memory structures.

Remission rate. Reflects the number of treated patients who experience a temporary relief from symptoms. It is understood that these symptoms may return at a later point. Remission rate differs from the rate of cured patients in which symptoms do not return.

Response-focused emotion regulation. Emotion regulation strategy that tackles the output of a putative emotion system.

Retrieval. Mental process during which information previously stored in long-term memory is accessed and made available to working memory. Depending on how completely information is retrieved, individuals may have a feeling of familiarity or knowing only, or they may be able to recollect a complete memory.

Reward prediction error. Error that results when a reward comes unexpectedly or an expected reward fails to materialize. The brain represents such errors and uses them for learning.

Sadness. Emotion elicited to negative events that allow little opportunity for problem-based coping and that directly or indirectly produce some sort of social loss. Sadness has an initial stage of distress that may be followed by a stage of despair.

Scalar timing theory. Theory developed by John Gibbon and colleagues that outlines a psychological mechanism for time perception.

Sclerosis. Hardening of bodily tissue that is typically associated with reduced tissue functionality.

Selective serotonin reuptake inhibitors. Class of drugs used to treat clinical depression. They act by preventing serotonin from re-entering the presynaptic neuron and thus effectively increase serotonin availability in the synapse.

Self-actualization. Term that refers to the highest-order need in Maslow's pyramid of needs. Individuals fulfill this need if they are able to realize their full potential and achieve all they can possibly achieve.

Self-construal. Concept in social psychology relating to how individuals define themselves. It is typically applied in the context of cultural comparisons, where self-construal can be independent or interdependent.

Self-reference effect. Phenomenon in which individuals remember self-relevant information better than information that is not self-relevant.

Sentience. Awareness of one's mental and bodily state.

Serotonin. Neurotransmitter that belongs to the monoamine and tryptamine families. It is synthesized from tryptophan.

Sexual dimorphism. Structural difference between the two sexes (e.g., height, genitals).

Sham-rage. Excited state caused by slight provocation in an animal after cortex has been surgically removed.

Single nucleotide polymorphism. A position in a gene for which individuals differ in a single base pair.

Socioemotional selectivity theory. Theory developed by Carstensen and colleagues to explain emotional changes in aging. It holds that a shortening life expectancy alters how individuals engage with emotional events in their environment. With less time left, emphasis shifts from the future to the "here and now," away from negative and toward positive emotions.

Socratic thinking. Method developed by Socrates whereby he used questions and dialogues to achieve knowledge and insight.

Somatic marker hypothesis. Hypothesis formulated by Antonio Damasio. It holds that feedback of emotion-induced bodily processes influences decision making.

Spontaneous recovery. Recovery of a conditioned response after this response was extinguished. For example, a fear-conditioned tone loses its power to provoke fear when it is repeatedly presented alone. If, subsequently, the tone is withheld (e.g., for a day) and then presented again, it can spontaneously trigger the old fear response without the need for additional conditioning.

Startle reflex. Reflex that is triggered by a sudden sensory change. It involves muscle contractions that start at the head and move through the body. It is considered a defensive response.

Stereotype threat. Phenomenon experienced by individuals who engage in activities for which they know that members of their group typically perform poorly. This knowledge, or the activated stereotype, hampers their performance.

Stoic school. Emerged during the Hellenistic period of ancient Greece. Its name derives from the Greek word *stoa,* meaning "collonade." One of its tenets was that emotions should be controlled.

Striatal beat-frequency model. Model proposed by Buhushi and Meck. It pins time perception to the striatum and its connections to the frontal cortex. The striatum is thought to regulate and monitor oscillations in frontal cortex activity.

Striatum. Part of the basal ganglia, a subcortical gray-matter site. The striatum is comprised of the putamen and the caudate nucleus, and it has a striped appearance.

Stroop task. Cognitive interference task developed by John Ridley Stroop in 1935. Participants must name the ink color of color words printed with congruous or incongruous ink (e.g., *blue* printed in blue and green).

Subliminally. In a subliminal stimulus presentation, participants cannot fully perceive the stimulus. Images may be flashed and/or followed by a masking stimulus to prevent proper recognition. Sounds may be played just below hearing threshold. Such presentations are made to explore unconscious aspects of stimulus processing.

Sympathetic nervous system. One of two efferent strands of the autonomic nervous system. This system is largely associated with mobilizing the body for action.

Synapses. Points of communication between two neurons. Synapses are formed between the axon terminal of one neuron and the membrane (typically at the dendrite) of another neuron. It is where neutransmitters are released and bind to receptors of the post-synaptic neuron.

Taxon. In biology, refers to a group of individuals such as a species.

Temporal discounting. Phenomenon whereby individuals discount the value of rewards the longer the time that elapses until they receive the reward.

Tend-and-befriend response. Alternative to the fight-or-flight response to threat. It refers to threat-induced affiliative behaviors directed at creating or maintaining social bonds that are reproductively important (e.g., caring for offspring) or that may aid in times of need (e.g., relatives, allies).

Thalamus. Subcortical structure (i.e., below cortex and white matter) that forms part of the diencephalon. It receives input from all the senses except olfaction. It is a key player in Cannon's emotion theory.

Theories. Frameworks of ideas that help understand or explain a particular phenomenon. They can be based on speculation, logical inferences, and/or empirical data. Researchers can use a theory to make predictions that they then test in an experiment.

Theory of Mind. Mental capacity for recognizing that others have minds of their own and for understanding these minds.

Tonic changes. In the context of neural activity, tonic changes refer to changes in firing patterns that are sustained for several seconds or more. They differ from phasic changes in that they extend over a longer time frame.

Top-down. Term that describes mental processes arising from an intention or goal activated in working memory. The goal relevance of a particular stimulus for the individual is said to influence attentional selection via top-down processes.

Total peripheral resistance. Blood pressure measure that takes into account both arterial and venous pressure. It was shown to differentiate fear and anger.

Transcranial magnetic stimulation (TMS). Stimulation that uses a magnetic coil to produce an electric current that interferes with and modulates normal brain function.

Transporters. In the context of a synapse, transporters are a type of protein located within the membrane of the presynaptic neuron. Transporters move superfluous neurotransmitters back into the cell.

Tricyclic antidepressants. Drugs that have a three-ringed molecular structure and are used to treat clinical depression. They block the reuptake of monoamines into the presynaptic neuron.

Tryptophan. Essential amino acid that forms part of most proteins and serves as a precursor for 5-HT.

Turner syndrome. Genetic defect in which girls have only one fully intact X chromosome. The defect causes a range of dysfunctions that are both physical (e.g., webbed neck, sterility) and mental (e.g., memory).

Unconditioned stimuli. Stimuli that elicit an innate response such as an emotion.

Universal antecedent. Stimulus or event that reliably causes an emotion across individuals and cultures.

Vagus nerve. The tenth cranial nerve. It connects the brain with the body's internal organs.

Valence. Refers to the affective value of a stimulus along a dimension, with good and bad or positive and negative as polar opposites.

Ventral. Bottom or front of a structure.

Vicarious learning. Occurs when an individual acquires a response (e.g., emotion) to a stimulus based on observing another individual's encounter with that stimulus.

Viscera. The body's internal organs.

Vomeronasal organ. Part of the olfactory system that serves primarily the perception of pheromones.

Von Economo neurons. Large neurons with a spindle-shaped soma from which only two dendrites protrude in opposite directions. They are found only in large-brained species. Named after one of their discoverers, Constantin von Economo.

White matter. Nerve tissue comprising myelinated axons. The cerebrum's white matter is situated between the basal ganglia and the cortex.

World Medical Association. An international body concerned with developing and preserving high ethical standards in medicine worldwide.

Zygomaticus major. Facial muscle located around the mouth that, when activated, draws the mouth corners backward.

Author Index

Aalto, S., 88
Aamodt-Leeper, G., 331, 337
Abdel-Azim, E., 164
Abe, Y., 211
Abi-Dargham, A., 167
Ablow, J. C., 292
Abou-Khalil, B., 240
Abu-Akel, A., 295, 297
Achterberg, E. J. M., 99
Adams, M. D., 86
Adams, R. B., 345
Adams, R. B., Jr., 181
Adams, S., 329
Adamson, L., 300
Adcock, R. A., 245
Adolphs, R., 88, 241, 247, 248, 259
Adorni, R., 337
Aganj, I., 333
Aglioti, S. M., 375
Aharon, I., 164
Ainsworth, M. D. S., 309
Aisner, R., 356
Akamatsu, S., 347 (figure)
Alamo, C., 187, 188
Albanese, A., 165
Albarracin, D., 184
Albert, M., 92
Alberts, J. R., 180
Albouy, G., 98
Albrecht, J., 48, 128, 209
Alcaro, A., 154, 173, 175
Aldao, A., 272, 279, 280, 282
Aleman, A., 344
Alfert, E., 264
Allan, W. S., 164
Allen, J. S., 316
Allen, N. B., 196
Allman, J. M., 28, 91–92
Alpers, G. W., 56, 57, 58
Als, H., 300

Altenmuller, E., 345
Alter, K., 159
Altmann, J., 363
Amano, T., 220
Amaral, D. G., 89, 242
Ambady, N., 373, 375, 376, 378, 381
Amin, J., 342
Amodio, D. M., 115
Amrein, H., 48
Amstadter, A. B., 272
An, S. K., 344
Anders, S., 137
Anderson, A. K., 200, 208, 209, 210, 218, 237, 240, 282
Anderson, M. C., 270
Andreano, J. M., 244, 351
Andrews, P. W., 196
Andrews-Hanna, J. R., 334
Angrilli, A., 136
Anisfeld, E., 364
Anllo-Vento, L., 337, 338 (figure), 344
Anrep, G. V., 162
Ansorge, M. S., 189
Anticevic, A., 334
Antoun, N., 131
Anzures, G., 298
Apicella, P., 170
App, B., 48
Appelhans, B. M., 135
Appleton, A. A., 265
Aragona, B. J., 311
Aral, S., 303
Araque, A., 78
Archer, J., 183, 335, 339, 347, 348
Archer, T., 200, 201
Arias-Carrión, O., 48, 66
Armony, J. L., 220, 239, 240, 241
Arnett, J. J., 303, 306
Arnold, M. B., 35, 37, 59
Aron, A., 307

Aruta, A., 199
Ashburner, J., 317
Ashby, F. G., 160
Asnaani, A., 282
Atake, K., 199
Auerbach, J., 298, 299
Augath, M., 149
Augustinova, M., 231, 233
Aunger, R., 339
Avenanti, A., 375
Averill, J. R., 155, 205
Aylward, E., 105
Ayoub, R., 167
Azim, E., 345
Azmitia, E. C., 98

Babbitt, L. G., 373, 375, 376, 378
Babcock, J., 116
Bacarese-Hamilton, M., 331, 337
Bach, D. R., 240
Bachorowski, J.-A., 113
Backlund, H., 80, 194
Bäckström, T., 351
Badcock, P. B. T., 196
Baeken, C., 280
Bagot, R. C., 330, 364
Bai, X.-W., 373, 378
Bailey, A. L., 128
Bailey, D. L., 145
Baker, C., 315, 315 (figure), 316
Baker, R. R., 321
Bakermans-Kranenburg, M. J., 195
Balaban, M. T., 294
Ball, R., 368
Balteau, E., 98
Balzer, A., 344
Banaji, M. R., 373, 374 (figure), 375
Bandettini, P. A., 46, 114, 207
Bannerman, D. M., 194
Banse, R., 47, 113, 128, 380
Baptista, L., 356
Bär, K.-J., 194, 195
Baraban, J. M., 218
Baraldi, P., 88
Bard, K. A., 159, 181, 207–208
Bard, P., 21
Bardeleben, U. von, 195, 292
Bargh, J. A., 158

Barlow, D. H., 280
Barman, S. M., 98
Barmish, A., 330
Baron, R., 157
Barr, R. G., 361
Barra, V., 157
Barres, B. A., 78
Barrett, L. F., 33, 58, 122, 218, 282, 339, 360
Barron, A. B., 96, 97
Barsalou, L. W., 56–57, 58
Bartels, A., 307
Bartholow, B. D., 254
Bartolo, A., 88
Barton, M. J., 45, 221, 342
Barysheva, M., 333
Basell, L., 113
Basha, M. M., 122
Bastiaansen, M. C. M., 149
Bauer, H. R., 136, 137
Baumann, S., 159
Baumeister, R. F., 187, 194, 195
Baumgartner, T., 95, 219
Bayart, F. E. S., 179, 180, 181, 185
Beacher, F. D. C. C., 189
Bean, J., 200
Beaudoin, G., 186
Beaupré, M., 381
Beauregard, M., 186, 189
Bechara, A., 233, 247, 248, 259, 316, 317
Beck, S., 93
Becker, D. V., 335, 345–346
Becker, J. A. J., 99
Becker, K., 298, 299
Becker, M. W., 45
Becker, S., 174
Beevers, C. G., 190
Befort, K., 99
Beilock, S. L., 266, 267 (figure), 268
Bekar, L., 78
Bekinschtein, T. A., 156
Bellard, H. S., 340
Belmaker, R. H., 298, 299
Bender, A., 372, 377, 378
Benenson, J. F., 342
Bennett, M. R., 73
Ben-Simon, E., 334
Benson, D. F., 92
Benuzzi, F., 88

Benzer, S., 47
Berchtold, N. C., 200, 201
Berg, J., 364
Bergeman, C. S., 312
Berger, C., 349
Berglund, E., 330
Berglund, P., 222–223
Berking, M., 265, 279
Berman, K. F., 167, 169
Berna, C., 194, 195
Berntson, G. G., 49, 135, 136, 137, 138, 158, 316, 317
Bernzweig, J., 329
Berridge, K. C., 169, 172
Berrocoso, E., 191, 199
Bessette-Symons, B., 316
Besson, A., 191
Betstadt, S., 78
Bettens, F., 307
Bettinger, K. E., 344
Bhatnagar, R., 278
Bhatt, M., 259
Bianchi- Berthouze, N., 48
Bilderbeck, A., 164
Bilker, W., 332–333, 333 (figure)
Birkas, E., 299
Birring, S. S., 183, 348
Bishop, D. V. M., 331, 337
Bishop, G. D., 382
Bishop, M. P., 165
Bishop, S. J., 242
Biswal, B. B., 93
Bjork, J. M., 348
Björklund, A., 96, 97
Black, S., 92
Blackwell, K. C., 345–346
Blais, C., 113, 381
Blakemore, S. J., 187
Blanchard, D.C., 185
Blanchard, R. J., 185
Blanton, R., 138
Blecker, C., 89
Blehar, M. C., 309
Bleich A, G. M., 373, 378
Bless, H., 184
Blier, P., 98
Bliss- Moreau, E., 43, 58
Blokland, A., 98, 99

Blood, A. J., 380
Bloom, T., 159, 181
Blundell, J., 98
Boals, A., 266
Bodenhausen, G. V., 184
Bodnar, R. J., 99
Boesch, C., 356
Boettger, M. K., 194
Boettger, S., 194
Bohlin, G., 244
Bohner, G., 184
Boiten, F., 119
Boivin, M., 189
Boksem, M. A. S., 195
Bolling, D. Z., 187
Bongers, A., 276
Bonkale, W. L., 190
Boone, K., 92
Borges, A. C., 220
Borofsky, L. A., 187
Borroto-Escuela, D. O., 299
Bos, P. A., 344
Bostanov, V., 253
Bösterling, A., 280
Botanov, Y., 209
Böttger, M., 342
Boucher, K. L., 324
Bouret, S., 98
Bourgouin, P., 186
Bower, J. E., 270
Bowers, K., 207, 376
Bowman, C., 361
Boyle, P. A., 329
Boysen, S. T., 136, 137
Boytim, M., 166, 167, 168 (figure)
Bradley, B., 220
Bradley, M. M., 43, 45, 56, 57, 58, 111, 122, 131, 137, 241, 335, 339, 340, 342, 344, 345
Brain, C., 328, 329 (figure)
Braithwaite, A., 189
Brammer, M. J., 344
Branch, S. E., 337, 351
Branson, J., 335
Brass, M., 276, 278
Braun, A., 284, 285
Braus, D. F., 169, 344
Brazelton, T. B., 300
Breen, W. E., 340

Breesch, D., 335
Brehm, S., 194
Breiter, H. C., 164
Brennan, L., 43
Brennan, T., 6
Brenner, S., 85
Bretherton, I., 329
Breuer, F., 56, 57, 58
Bridges, L. J., 300, 302
Briese, E., 164
Briggs, J. L., 376
Brisswalter, J., 135
Brittenham, G., 363
Broad, K. D., 292
Brodmann, K., 82
Bromberg-Martin, E. S., 172
Bronson, F. H., 183, 348
Brook, C., 328, 329 (figure)
Brook, C. G. D., 348
Brookhuis, K. A., 137, 340, 341 (figure)
Brosch, T., 114
Brosschot, J. F., 265
Brown, C. K., 316
Brown, C. W., 108
Brown, K. J., 45, 221
Brown, L. L., 307
Brown, P. S., 106
Brown, R., 244, 246
Brown, R. A., 335
Brown, T. A., 280
Brückmann, H., 48, 128, 209
Bruderlin, A., 128
Brunet, A., 361
Bruss, J., 316
Bryant, J., 33
Bryant, R. A., 340, 342
Bryk, A., 330
Buchanan, T. W., 88, 244
Büchel, C., 164, 169
Buckley, M. J., 194
Buckmaster, C. L., 95
Buckner, R. L., 93, 334
Bucy, P. C., 87
Bueller, J. A., 90, 117, 191, 193 (figure)
Bugnyar, T., 284, 285
Bugumba, R., 326
Buhle, J. T., 276
Buhusi, C. V., 255, 256

Buitelaar, J. K., 361
Buka, S. L., 265
Bukay, E., 275
Bulleit, B. A., 48
Bullock, G., 342
Bunge, S. A., 268
Burgdorf, J., 31, 128, 156, 157, 160
Burrows, C. L., 316
Burt, D. M., 347 (figure)
Bush, C., 92
Bush, D. E. A., 218
Bushnell, M. C., 80, 194
Buss, D. M., 335
Bustamante, D., 342
Buti, A. L., 201
Butler, S., 329
Bymaster, F., 197
Byrne, D., 335

Cabanis, M., 355, 356
Cabeza, R., 244, 245, 316
Cacioppo, J. T., 49, 138, 158, 316, 317
Cadilla, C., 99
Cahill, L., 219, 244, 351
Cahill, L. F., 334
Cain, C. K., 249
Caldara, R., 113, 381
Calder, A. J., 131
Caldji, C., 87, 330, 364, 365 (figure)
Caldwell, J. D., 310
Calkins, S., 295, 298
Callaway, E., 359
Camerer, C. F., 259
Cameron, L., 364, 366
Cameron, N. M., 364
Campbell, A., 347
Campbell-Sills, L., 280
Campos, B., 154, 163, 379
Cannon, W. B., 21, 81, 139, 213, 215
Cao, C., 307
Carew, T. J., 207
Carlin, D. A., 92
Carlo, G., 329
Carpenter, G. H., 84
Carr, A., 84
Carr, P. B., 325
Carré, J. M., 348
Carrere, S., 116

Carriger, M. S., 299
Carroll, K. A., 291
Carstensen, L. L., 312 (figure), 313, 314, 314 (figure), 317, 366
Carter, C. S., 310
Caseras, X., 344
Casey, B., 305, 305 (figure)
Casper, V., 364
Caspi, A., 189
Cassano, M., 329, 330
Cassotti, M., 306
Castell, D. O., 317
Castell, J. A., 317
Castelli, L., 375
Castles, D. L., 347 (figure)
Cauda, F., 48
Cavanna, A. E., 48
Caviness, V. S., 333
Cayeux, I., 113
Ceravolo, L., 94
Cervantes, M. D., 321
Ceschi, G., 63
Chaix, R., 307
Champagne, D. L., 220, 330, 364
Champagne, F., 330
Champagne, F. A., 364
Chanda, M. L., 128
Chang, H.-Y., 361
Chaplin, T. M., 329
Chapman, T., 307
Charney, D. S., 279
Chelazzi, L., 235, 236 (figure)
Chen, C.-B., 93, 159, 352
Chen, D., 209
Chen, E. Y., 344
Chen, M., 78, 158
Cheng, R.-K., 361
Chentsova-Dutton, Y., 380
Chentsova-Dutton, Y. E., 198
Cheok, A. D., 113
Cheon, B. K., 375, 376, 378
Cheong, W. F., 48, 128, 209
Cherek, D. R., 347
Cheung, R. Y. M., 382
Chew, S. H., 96
Chiao, J. Y., 375, 376, 378
Chikama, M., 89
Ching, A., 93, 113, 159, 352

Cho, W., 207
Cho, Y. M., 182
Choi, E., 361
Choleris, E., 108, 349
Chomsky, N., 251
Chon, K. K., 359
Chopra, S., 276
Chorley, P., 171 (figure)
Chouliaras, L., 361
Christie, L.-A., 200, 201
Chu, D.-M., 361
Chu, J. P., 198
Chun, M. M., 240
Church, R. M., 255
Cialdini, R. B., 308
Cicchetti, P., 216
Ciocchi, S., 121, 220
Cirillo, S., 195, 292
Ciruela, F., 299
Cisler, J. M., 205
Claparède, E., 242
Clark, L. A., 133, 183
Clark, M., 197
Clarke, K., 239
Clarke, S. E., 128
Claverie, J.-M., 86
Cleeland, C. S., 194
Clipperton-Allen, A. E., 349
Coan, J., 116
Coan, J. A., 116, 303
Codispoti, M., 43, 45, 56, 57, 58, 137, 335, 339, 340, 342, 344, 345
Coe, C. L., 179, 180, 181, 185
Coelho, C. M., 223
Cohen, A. B., 371
Cohen, M. X., 95, 219
Cohen, N. J., 243
Cohen, S., 363
Colapinto, J., 323
Colbert-White, E. N., 180
Cole, C. D., 310
Cole, M. W., 334
Cole, P. M., 329
Colegrove, F. W., 246
Colibazzi, T., 56, 57, 58, 131
Collette, F., 98
Collins, J. E., 2nd., 156
Colon, I., 99

Colwell, D. D., 108
Combs, D., 187, 194, 195
Conard, N. J., 113
Connell, J. P., 300, 302
Conner, C. R., 149
Conty, L., 254
Conway, G. S., 348
Cook, M., 214
Coon, H. M., 371
Cooper, S. J., 189
Coppin, B., 331, 337
Coquelin, A., 331
Corbetta, M., 93, 235, 237
Corkin, S., 30, 242, 243, 244
Corlett, P. R., 334
Cornish, J. L., 96, 97
Corodimas, K. P., 220
Correa, A., 291
Costa, E., 348
Costello, J., 119
Cotman, C. W., 200, 201
Cousijn, H., 216
Coutinho, E. S. F., 266
Covington, M. A., 180
Cowen, P. J., 189
Cowie, R., 113
Cox, C., 113
Cox, D., 209
Craig, A. D., 91
Craig, A. D. B., 276
Craig, I. W., 189
Craig, K. D., 128
Craik, F. I. M., 61
Crepel, F., 172
Crespo-Ramírez, M., 88
Creswell, C., 331, 337
Critchley, H. D., 189
Crivellato, E., 3
Crockett, M. J., 266
Crombez, G., 238
Crone, E. A., 306, 344
Cross, C. P., 347
Crowley, M. J., 187
Cryan, J. F., 77
Csányi, V., 180, 181
Csernus, V. J., 331
Csibra, G., 293
Csikszentmihalyi, M., 152, 156

Cummings, J., 92
Cunningham, N., 364
Cunningham, W. A., 94, 282
Curley, J. P., 292
Curtis, J. T., 310, 311
Curtis, V., 339, 366
Cury, F., 135
Cusi, A., 208
Cuthbert, B. N., 43, 45, 56, 57, 58, 111, 137, 241

D, J., 216
Dael, N., 128
D'Agata, F., 48
Dagher, A., 280
Dahl, R. E., 303, 344
Dahlstroem, A., 96
Dale, A., 164
Dalgleish, T., 259
Dalton, P., 331, 337
Damasio, A. R., 140, 233, 247, 248, 259
Damasio, H., 233, 247, 248, 259, 316
D'Amato, F. R., 291
Damjanovic, L., 134
Dammann, G., 195, 292
Damsteegt, R., 99
D'Anci, K. E., 201
Dan-Glauser, E. S., 270
Daniele, A., 165
Dannlowski, U., 280
Dantzer, R., 201, 215
Dapretto, M., 187
D'Argembeau, A., 98
Darwin, C., 12–14, 13 (figure), 113, 179,
    181, 183, 207, 320
Das, P., 45, 221
Daskalakis, Z. J., 142, 280
Daubman, K. A., 162
Davey Smith, G., 363
Davidson, R. J., 47, 159, 207, 303
Davis, F., 331
Davis, J. I., 268
Davis, M., 80, 178, 206, 207, 216, 217, 218
Davis, M. H., 156
Davis, R. L., 108
Davis, R. P., 98
Dawans, B. von, 349
Dawson, G., 105
Dawson, M. E., 137

Dayan, P., 170
de Barra, M., 366
De Boer, S. F., 205, 220
de Gelder, B., 221
De Houwer, J., 238
de Jong, P. J., 237
de Kloet, E. R., 220
De Raedt, R., 280
De Silva, P. R., 48
de Visser, L., 340
de Waal, F. B. M., 207–208
de Waal, F. de., 106
de Waard, D., 137, 340, 341 (figure)
de Wit, H., 351
de Zubicaray, G. I., 333
Dean, K., 196
Dearmond, S. J., 92
Dębiec, J., 218
DeBruine, L. M., 307
DeCarli, C., 368, 369
DeCasper, A. J., 291
Deen, B., 187
Degner, J., 252
Degueldre, C., 98
Deisseroth, K., 121, 141, 220
DeJoy, D. M., 335
Delbroek, L., 361
Delgado, M. R., 117, 245, 246 (figure), 247
Dellacherie, D., 137
Dell'Acqua, R., 375
Delplanque, S., 112, 113
Demaree, H. A., 276
Demler, O., 222–223
Demmel, M., 128
Demoto, Y., 194, 195, 343
Denney, C., 119
Denny, B. T., 93, 94
Denson, T. F., 135, 265, 266
Descartes, R., 8–11, 263
Desce, J. M., 172
Desimone, R., 235, 236 (figure)
Desjardins, C., 183, 348
Desseilles, M., 98
Detwiler, J. M., 311
DeWall, C. N., 187, 194, 195
Di, X., 93
Di Salle, F., 195, 292
Dias, B. G., 223, 361

Dickerson, S. S., 363
Dickhaut, J., 364
Dickinson, A., 170
Dickinson, D., 86
Diekhof, E. K., 276
Diener, E., 339
DiFeliceantonio, A. G., 172
Dimberg, U., 212, 214 (figure), 215
Dinov, I. D., 368, 368 (figure), 369
Dinse, H. R., 317
Diorio, J., 87, 292, 330, 364, 365 (figure)
DiSano, M. A., 149
Dockray, S., 174
Döhler, K. D., 331
Dohrenwend, B. P., 363
Dolan, R., 259
Dolan, R. J., 105, 220, 240, 241
Dolcos, F., 242, 244, 245, 276
Dolcos, S., 276
Domes, G., 95, 342, 349
Domínguez-Borràs, J., 239
Donnelly, P., 307
Donzella, B., 292
Dorr, N., 265
Dougherty, D. M., 347, 348
Douglas, L. A., 304, 304 (figure)
Douglas-Cowie, E., 113
Douglas-Palumberi, H., 190
Downar, J., 280
Downing, L., 73
Drabant, E. M., 190, 278
Dreher, J.-C., 90, 167, 169
Dremencov, E., 98
Dressel, A., 221
Driver, J., 220, 239, 240, 241
Droit-Volet, S., 255, 256
Drummond, T. E., 128
Duan, Y., 56, 57, 58
Duarte-Carvajalino, J. M., 333
Duca, S., 48
Duchenne, G.B., 159
Dufour, V., 284, 285
Dukic, M. S., 240
Dulap, C., 185
Dumontheil, I., 187
Dunbar, R. I. M., 99, 157, 159
Duncan, J., 235
Duncan, S., 43, 73

Dunn, B. D., 259
Dunn, J., 298, 329
Dunnett, S. B., 96, 97
Duntley, J. D., 335
Duvarci, S., 88
Duzel, E., 172
Dwyer, P. D., 376
Dziobek, I., 95, 219, 349

Eagly, A. H., 323, 324, 327, 328
Easterbrook, J. A., 245
Eaves, L., 189
Ebbesen, E. B., 300
Ebert, J. P., 373, 374 (figure), 375
Ebling, R., 380
Ebner, N. C., 311
Ebstein, R. P., 96, 298, 299
Echols, S., 128
Eckberg, D. L., 135, 136
Eder, A. B., 254
Edward, D. A., 307
Edwards, R. R., 194, 195
Edwards, S. E., 197
Egan, M. F., 190
Egner, T., 90, 91, 93
Ehring, T., 279, 280, 282
Ehrlich, I., 121, 220
Eich, E., 114
Eicher, V., 195
Eisenberg, N., 329, 342
Eisenberger, N. I., 44, 90, 186, 187, 187 (figure),
    194, 195
Eisner, F., 154, 382
Ejdebäck, M., 119
Ekholm, S., 80, 194
Ekman, P., 45, 46, 47, 48, 49, 110, 119, 127, 138,
    154, 157, 159, 163, 178, 179, 181, 208, 317,
    359, 371, 376, 380, 382
Elder, S. T., 165
Elfenbein, H. A., 375, 381
Elices, M., 342
Ellgring, H., 63
Elliot, A. J., 135
Ellis, A. J., 190
Ellison, P. T., 326
Ellmore, T. M., 149
Ellsworth, P. C., 62–63, 155, 178, 179,
    372, 377, 379

Elvevåg, B., 86
Emens, J. S., 201
Endler, J. A., 307, 308 (figure)
Endress, A. D., 294, 296 (figure),
    297 (figure)
Eriksson, M., 330
Erkal, N., 364, 366
Eroglu, C., 78
Ertman, N., 351
Erwin, J. M., 28, 91–92
Eschalier, A., 191
Escoffier, N., 93, 113, 114, 137, 352
Esposito, F., 195, 292
Espy, K. A., 301
Esteves, F., 237, 241
Estioko-Griffin, A. A., 337
Etkin, A., 90, 91, 93, 265
Eugčne, F., 186
Evangelou, D., 337, 351
Evans, A. C., 333
Evans, C. A., 86
Evans, R. B., 6
Exadaktylos, V., 264
Eyssell, K. M., 339

Fabes, R. A., 329, 342, 347
Fabri, M., 82
Fagan, J. F., 299
Falkai, P., 276
Fan, L., 368, 368 (figure), 369
Fane, B. A., 348
Fantz, R. L., 298, 299 (figure)
Faraone, S. V., 333
Farb, N. A. S., 200
Faria, M. S., 220
Farrant, M., 77
Farrar, M. J., 298
Farrell, S. M., 175
Farrell, W. J., 180
Farroni, T., 293
Fasano, A., 165
Fazio, R. H., 129, 251
Febo, M., 292, 293 (figure)
Federmeier, K. D., 161
Fehr, B., 1, 53, 69
Fehr, E., 95, 349
Feiman, R., 208
Feldman, R., 195, 364

Feldman-Barrett, L., 43, 49, 54, 56–57, 58, 163
Felmingham, K. L., 340
Feng, G., 121, 141
Ferdenzi, C., 113
Fernández, C., 342
Fernández, G., 216, 344, 351
Fernández-Abascal, E., 342
Fernstrom, J. D., 96
Ferrari, M. D., 128
Ferrington, L., 98, 99
Ferris, C. F., 292, 293 (figure)
Ferstl, R., 209
Fessler, D. M. T., 366
Fiala, S. C., 201
Fialip, J., 191
Field, T., 364
Fiez, J. A., 93
Fifer, W. P., 291
Figueira, I., 266
Figueroa, I. R., 220
Filion, D. L., 137
Fincher, C. L., 366, 367 (figure)
Fini, N., 342
Finkelstein, D. M., 363
Firk, C., 276
Fischbacher, U., 95, 349
Fischer, A. H., 339
Fischer, D., 335
Fischer, J., 183
Fischer, R. B., 106
Fischer, S., 279, 280, 282
Fish, E. W., 364
Fisher, G. A., 359
Fisher, H., 307
Fisher, W. A., 335
Fiske, A. P., 371
Fitzgerald, P. B., 142
Fitzsimmons, J. R., 344
Fivush, R., 329
Flaisch, T., 344
Fleshner, M., 220
Flor, H., 344
Flykt, A., 237, 241
Fogarty, S. J., 244
Foley, P., 81
Fonagy, P., 294
Fong, W. C., 340
Fontaine, J. R. J., 62–63

Fontana, C. J., 165
Fornito, A., 44, 45
Fort, G. G. D., 361
Fortier, E., 189
Fortune, E. E., 93
Foti, D., 167–169
Fountain, S., 142
Fowler, J. S., 174, 175
Fowles, D. C., 163
Fox, M. W., 159
Frackowiak, R. S., 317
Fragaszy, D. M., 180
Fraley, R. C., 309
Francis, D., 87, 330, 364, 365 (figure)
Frangou, A., 157
Frankland, P. W., 126
Fraraccio, M., 280
Frattaroli, J., 268
Frederick, B., 209
Fredrickson, B. L., 155, 156, 157, 173
Fredrickson, G. M., 356
Fredriksson, A., 200, 201
Freedman, A., 87, 330, 364, 365 (figure)
Freedman, M., 92
Freeman, W., 27, 165
Freire-Bebeau, L., 380
Freud, S., 174, 264, 320
Freund, G. G., 201
Friederici, A. D., 114, 184, 252, 253, 294, 295 (figure), 352
Friedlmeier, M., 345
Friedman, H., 159, 181
Friedrich, R. W., 48, 128, 209
Fries, P., 149
Friesen, W., 181
Friesen, W. V., 45, 46, 110, 119, 138, 159, 163, 317, 371, 380
Frijda, N. H., 115, 372
Friston, K. J., 317
Frith, C., 239
Froh, J. J., 340
Frome, Y., 337
Frühholz, S., 94
Frumin, I., 181, 182, 183
Fry, W. F., 157
Fujito, Y., 211
Fulton, J., 27

Fung, H. H., 313, 314, 314 (figure), 366
Füstös, J., 274, 275, 275 (figure)
Fuxe, K., 88, 96, 299

Gabor, C. S., 349
Gabrieli, J. D. E., 268, 276
Gabrieli, J. J. D., 349, 350 (figure)
Gaffney, K. F., 361
Galdikas, B. M. F., 307
Galili, D. S., 211
Galizia, C. G., 211
Gallese, V., 88, 89
Gallinat, J., 95, 219, 278
Gallistel, C. R., 166, 167, 168 (figure)
Gallucci, M., 185, 343
Gallup, G. G., Jr., 108
Gamer, M., 349
Gandhi, W., 174
Gangadharan, L., 364, 366
Gangestad, S. W., 307
Ganzer, L., 220
Garcia, J., 212, 213 (figure)
Garcia-Falgueras, A., 80, 331
Gardner, M., 306
Gardner, W. L., 196
Garoff-Eaton, R. J., 315
Garrett, C., 165
Garry, M., 247
Garver-Apgar, C. E., 307
Garzón, J., 191, 199
Gaspar, J. X., 342
Gasquoine, P. G., 91
Gatenby, J. C., 211, 217
Gaunt, J. T., 315, 315 (figure), 316
Gaus, S. E., 91
Gay, P., 174
Geer, J. H., 335, 336 (figure), 340
Geffner, M. E., 328, 329 (figure)
Geier, K., 276
Gelernter, J., 190
Geller, I., 211
Geller, V., 298, 299
Gelstein, S., 181, 182, 183
Geminiani, G. C., 48
Gendolla, G. H. E., 184
Gendron, M., 43
Gentzler, A. L., 349
George, O., 176

Gerall, A. A., 331, 332 (figure)
Gerber, A., 56, 57, 58, 131
Gerdes, A. B. M., 56, 57, 58
Germain, M., 340
German, D. C., 190
Gervai, J., 299
Gervais, M., 156, 157
Giampietro, V., 344
Gibbon, J., 255
Gigerenzer, G., 32
Gil, S., 255
Gillett, G., 359, 360
Gilman, S. E., 265
Giuliani, N. R., 278
Gläscher, J., 169
Glaser, E., 340
Glass, K., 294
Glick, S., 128
Glimcher, P. W., 170
Gluth, S., 311
Godlewska, B. R., 189
Goeders, N. E., 176
Gold, B. T., 252
Gold, P. W., 220
Goldin, P. R., 268, 276
Goldman, D., 167
Goldman, S. A., 78
Goldstein, D. G., 32
Goldstein, J. M., 333
Golkar, A., 137
Gomita, Y., 166, 167, 168 (figure)
Goncalves, R., 266
Gong, G., 333
Gong, Z., 96
Gonzaga, G. C., 163, 379
Gonzales, J. A., 95
González, R. G., 242
Good, C. D., 317
Good, J. J., 324–326
Goodall, J., 285, 309, 356
Goodman, E., 363
Goodman, M. J., 337
Goodwin, G. M., 194, 195
Gordon, E., 45, 221, 342
Gore, J. C., 211, 217
Gorman, D., 56, 57, 58, 131
Gorski, R. A., 331
Gosselin, P., 381

Gotlib, I. H., 198, 279
Gotoda, Y., 211
Gottman, J. M., 116
Goubert, V., 28, 91–92
Govindarajan, A., 121
Goy, R. W., 331, 332 (figure)
Grabenhorst, F., 164
Grabski, W., 208
Grace, A. A., 172
Grafman, J., 57, 63, 65, 88, 218
Graham-Kevan, N., 335
Gramann, K., 274, 275, 275 (figure)
Grandjean, D., 59, 61–62, 63, 67, 94, 112,
      113, 114, 232, 234
Gratton, A., 292
Gray, J. A., 163
Gray, J. R., 232, 233
Gray, M. A., 189
Graybiel, A. M., 172
Graziano, W. G., 337, 339, 351
Grebneva, I., 114
Green, A. A., 98
Green, C., 270
Greenson, J., 105
Greenwald, A. G., 130, 132 (figure)
Greenwald, M. K., 56, 137
Greicius, M. D., 164
Greif, J., 95
Grenier, F., 121, 220
Griem, A., 189
Grietens, H., 329
Griffin, P. B., 337
Grillon, C., 217
Grisham, J. R., 135, 265, 266
Griskevicius, V., 308
Gritsenko, I., 298, 299
Grogÿlu, B., 344
Grolnick, W. S., 300, 302
Gross, J. J., 115, 198, 205, 264, 265, 268,
      269 (figure), 270, 272, 273, 276, 278,
      279, 280, 281, 282, 349, 350 (figure)
Grossman, P., 135, 136
Grossman, S. P., 80
Grossmann, A., 342, 349
Grossmann, T., 294, 295 (figure)
Grothe, I., 149
Grove, J. S., 337
Gruber, O., 184, 276

Gruberger, M., 334
Gruesser, S. M., 344
Grühn, D., 343
Gründer, G., 345, 346 (figure)
Guadagno, R. E., 335
Guerra, P., 337, 338 (figure), 344
Guidotti, A., 348
Gundersen, H. J. G., 78, 85
Gunes, H., 113
Gunnar, M. R., 292
Güntürkün, O., 30
Guo, Y., 96
Gupta, R., 259
Gur, R. C., 332–333, 333 (figure)
Gur, R. E., 332–333, 333 (figure)
Gurney, K., 170, 172
Gusnard, D. A., 93
Gustafson, L., 92
Guthrie, I. K., 347
Gutierrez, E., 241
Gyurak, A., 265

Habashi, M. M., 337, 351
Haber, S. N., 89
Hadjithomas, M., 321
Haegeman, G., 299
Haegler, K., 48, 209
Haex, B., 264
Haggard, P., 276
Hagoor, P., 149
Hahn, K. S., 348
Haight, W., 330
Hajcak, G., 142, 167–169, 275
Hakeem, A. Y., 28, 91–92
Hakimi, S., 96
Halaris, A. E., 98
Halford, J., 98
Hall, J. K., 352
Hall, R. J., 339
Hamann, S., 48, 88, 342, 343 (figure), 344
Hamilton, C. E., 309, 310
Hamilton, E. P., 321
Hamilton, J. R., 205, 268, 269 (figure)
Hamm, A. O., 56, 88, 137, 221
Han, S., 369, 375
Han, X., 78
Handlin, L., 119
Hansen, A. J., 77

Harada, T., 375, 376, 378
Harbaugh, C. R., 310
Harder, J. A., 292, 293 (figure)
Hardies, K., 335
Hare, T., 305, 305 (figure)
Hariri, A. R., 189, 190
Harlow, J. M., 93, 140
Harman, C., 302, 302 (figure)
Harmer, C. J., 189
Harmon-Jones, E., 115, 119, 122
Harré, R., 359, 360
Harrington, H., 189
Harris, C. R., 117
Harris, L. T., 205, 268, 269 (figure)
Harris, W. A., 47
Harrison, B. J., 44, 45
Harrison, L. K., 137
Harrison, N. A., 189
Harrison, P. J., 175
Harrold, J., 98
Hart, W., 184
Harwood, M. D., 298
Hasan, N. T., 339
Hashiba, R., 211
Hasselt, F. van, Ramakers, G., 330, 364
Hatakeyama, D., 211
Hatfield, E., 119
Hauenstein, K., 342, 349
Hawkley, L. C., 316, 317
Hayashi, K., 199
Hayashi, K. T., 179, 180, 181, 185
He, Y., 333, 334
Heath, R. G., 165
Hebb, D. O., 249
Heberlein, U., 207
Hecht, M. A., 345
Heering, S., 282
Heidenreich, T., 183
Heine, S. J., 355
Heinrichs, M., 95, 342, 349
Heinz, A., 344
Heinze, H., 342
Heise, E. R., 363
Heissler, J., 276
Heldmann, M., 49
Helgeson, V. S., 348, 349
Henckens, M. J. A. G., 216
Hendler, T., 334

Henrich, J., 355
Hensley, W. E., 306
Henson, R. N., 317
Henzi, S. P., 347 (figure)
Herbert, B. M., 117, 274, 275, 275 (figure), 344
Herbert, C., 117
Herderick, E. E., 95
Herman, B. H., 99, 195
Herman, J. P., 222
Herman, R. A., 88
Hermann, D., 344
Hermans, E. J., 216, 344, 351
Hernández-Pérez, O.R., 88
Herpertz, S. C., 95, 342, 349
Herrell, R., 189
Herrera P., 339, 340
Herry, C., 121, 220
Hertenstein, M. J., 48
Hess, U., 339, 340, 345, 381
Hickok, G., 251
Hicks, P. B., 190
Higgins, S. T., 211
Higham, T., 113
Hikosaka, O., 170, 172
Hilakivi-Clarke, L., 363
Hillemeier, M., 363
Hills, T. T., 335
Hillyard, S. A., 253, 253 (figure)
Hindmarsh, P., 328, 329 (figure)
Hines, M., 328, 329 (figure), 331, 348
Hirshleifer, D., 257
Hitchcock, J., 216
Hitchcock, J. M., 216
Ho, C.-Y., 172
Hodgkinson, C., 167
Hoeft, F., 344
Hof, P. R., 28, 90, 91–92
Hoff, E., 330
Hofman, M. A., 80–81
Hofmann, S. G., 280, 282
Hofstede, G., 370, 371
Hoh, J., 189
Hojatkashani, C., 368, 368 (figure), 369
Holcomb, L. A., 190
Holland, C. R., 299
Holland, R. W., 265
Holmes, D. S., 270
Holmes, E. A., 194, 195

Homberg, J., 340
Homberg, J. R., 99, 189, 190
Hong, H., 46
Hong, R. Y., 93, 159, 352
Hopkins, W. D., 82
Hopp, H., 344
Hori, H., 199
Hornak, J., 233
Horowitz, J. D., 226
Horton, N. J., 333
Houdé, O., 306
Houshyar, S., 190
Houston, M. J., 292
Howe, M. W., 172
Howie, P. W., 292
Howland, E. W., 194
Hsee, C. K., 119
Hsu, D., 167
Hsu, M., 259
Hsu, S.-M., 241
Hu, Z., 253, 349
Hua, X., 368, 368 (figure), 369
Hubbard, C. S., 342
Huber, A., 175
Hudry, J., 112
Hudson, J. L., 330
Hudson, R., 291
Huettel, S. A., 147
Huffziger, S., 266, 270
Hugenberg, K., 377, 378 (figure)
Hughes, B., 276
Hughes, C., 298
Hughett, P., 332–333, 333 (figure)
Hugueville, L., 137
Hui, G. K., 220
Huizink, A. C., 361
Hulihan, T. J., 310
Hultgren, B., 342
Hunt, M., 4, 6
Hunt, W. A., 126, 127 (figure)
Hurlemann, R., 95, 219, 240
Hurst, L. D., 321
Husain, M., 239
Husain, M. M., 200
Huston, J. P., 172
Huttenlocher, J., 330
Hutton, S. B., 352
Hwang, H. S., 360

Hydbring-Sandberg, E., 119
Hyde, J. S., 335
Hyman, B. T., 242

Iacono, W., 139
Iacoviello, B., 279
Ijzendoorn, M. H. van, 195
IJzerman, H., 185, 343
Ikenouchi-Sugita, A., 199
Im, D., 375, 376, 378
Inagaki, T. K., 266
Ingrao, J., 128
Insel, T. R., 310, 311
Iordan, A. D., 276
Iosifescu, D. V., 279
Irmak, A., 345, 346 (figure)
Isen, A. M., 160, 161, 162
Isomura, Y., 276
Israel, S., 96
Ito, E., 211
Ito, M., 83
Ito, T. A., 49, 138
Iwata, J., 87, 216
Iyengar, S., 197
Izard, C. E., 49, 65, 298

Jack, R. E., 113, 381
Jacobi, R., 113
Jacobs, C. M., 344
Jacobs, P. A., 331, 337
Jacobsen, C., 27
Jacobson, C. D., 331
Jacobson, N., 116
Jagust, W. J., 368, 369
Jahanshad, N., 333
Jain, E., 342
James, R. S., 331, 337
James, W., 17
Janicki, D., 348, 349
Jansson, A., 119
Janurio, A. C., 220
Jaskolka, A. R., 48
Jeffries, J., 93
Jensen, H. H., 363
Jesuthasan, S., 48, 108, 128, 172, 207, 209, 211
Jezová, D., 349
Jia, M., 96
Jiang, Y., 252

Jin, R., 222–223
Jin, X., 330
Jin, Y., 333
Jo, B., 345
Joëls, M., 330, 364
Johansen, J. P., 249
John, S. B., 165
Johns, M., 324, 325, 325 (figure), 326
Johnson, D. C., 211, 226, 227 (figure)
Johnson, J. T., 339
Johnson, K. A., 242
Johnson, L. C., 105
Johnson, M. H., 293, 301, 301 (figure)
Johnson, M. K., 94
Johnson, M. M., 161
Johnson, R. W., 201
Johnsrude, I. S., 317
Jolij, J., 137, 340, 341 (figure)
Jones, B. C., 307
Jones, B. E., 98
Jones, G. B., 361
Jones, H. E., 138
Joormann, J., 279
Joshi, A., 333
Jovanovic, T., 220
Jung, C. G., 138
Juránková, E., 349
Jurdak, N., 201
Juslin, P. N., 113
Juth, P., 209

Kaas, J. H., 28
Kagerer, S., 110
Kahler, C. W., 335
Kahn, C. H., 3
Kahneman, D., 153, 164, 257, 258
Kaiseler, M., 348, 349
Kalin, N. H., 207
Kalisch, R., 90, 91, 93, 169
Kalisch, T., 317
Kamachi, M., 343
Kanarek, R. B., 201
Kanazawa, A., 211
Kandel, E. R., 207
Kangarlu, A., 56, 57, 58
Kangarly, A., 56, 57, 58, 131
Kanske, P., 276
Kanwisher, N., 240

Kaplan, G., 363
Kaplan, J. R., 363
Kappas, A., 36, 38
Karbon, M., 329
Kardes, F. R., 129, 251
Karlsson, A., 209
Karlsson, H., 88
Kashdan, T. B., 340
Katdare, A., 209
Kato, M., 164
Katon, W., 197
Katsuki, A., 199
Kaufman, J., 190
Kaufmann, P. G., 135, 136
Kauhanen, J., 200
Kavaliers, M., 108, 349
Kawai, R., 211
Keane, J., 131
Keener, E., 349
Keller, H., 293
Kelley, K., 335
Kelley, K. W., 201
Kelley, L. A., 307, 308 (figure)
Kelly, D., 27–28
Kelly, P. A. T., 98, 99
Keltner, D., 48, 154, 163, 260, 379
Kemeny, M. E., 363
Kemmelmeier, M., 371
Kemp, A. H., 45, 221, 342
Kendall, P. C., 330
Kendrick, K. M., 95, 219
Kennedy, D. N., 333
Kennedy, D. P., 241
Kennedy, P. J., 30
Kenrick, D. T., 308, 345–346
Kensinger, E. A., 237, 244, 245, 315, 316
Kerns, K. A., 349
Kertesz, A., 92
Kesler, S. R., 344
Kessler, C., 88, 221
Kessler, R. C., 222–223
Kestemont, J., 264
Kesteren, M. T. R. van, Schoots, V. C., 216
Kettenmann, H., 77, 78
Ketter, T. A., 90, 117, 191, 193 (figure)
Keverne, E. B., 292
Keysers, C., 88, 89, 219
Khalsa, S., 317

Kibat, C., 48, 108, 128, 172, 207, 209, 211
Kieffer, B. L., 99
Kikuchi, Y., 292
Kikutani, M., 134
Kilbourn, M. R., 90, 117, 191, 193 (figure)
Kilpatrick, L. A., 334, 342
Kim, B., 369, 380
Kim, J.-S., 375, 376, 378
Kim, M. Y., 182
Kim, P., 195
Kim, S., 381 (figure)
Kim, S. H., 106
Kim, Y.-H., 382
Kimoto, Y., 211
Kindt, M., 219
King, L. B., 185
King, S., 361
Kinoshita, A., 343
Kircher, T., 345, 346 (figure)
Kirker, W. S., 117
Kirouac G., 339, 340
Kirsch, P., 89, 95
Kirschbaum, C., 81, 349
Kirson, D. A., 161
Kirstein, C. L., 305
Kisley, M. A., 316
Kissler, J., 254
Kita, S., 211
Kitayama, S., 337, 340, 370, 371, 372, 379, 382
Kiyatkin, E. A., 174
Klassen-Ross, T., 128
Klauer, K. C., 254
Klebanoff, L., 166, 167, 168 (figure)
Kleck, R. E., 181, 339, 340, 345
Kleemann, A. M., 48, 128, 209
Klein, K., 266
Klein, S., 344
Kleinhans, N. M., 105
Kleinsmith, A., 48
Kloet, E. R. de, 330, 364
Klucken, T., 110, 342
Klüver, H., 87
Knafo, A., 96
Knebel, J.-F., 112
Knetsch, J. L., 258
Knight, D. C., 46, 114, 207
Knight, G. P., 347
Knight, M., 315, 315 (figure), 316

Knowles, M. L., 196
Kobayashi, S., 174
Kober, H., 58, 93, 94
Kochenborger, L., 220
Koelling, R. A., 212, 213 (figure)
Koelsch, S., 252, 253
Koenig, A. M., 324
Koeppe, R. A., 90, 117, 191, 193 (figure)
Koessler, S., 254
Koester, D., 114
Kohls, G., 345, 346 (figure)
Kohn, P., 167, 169
Kolachana, B., 96, 167, 169
Kolachana, B. S., 190
Konrad, K., 345, 346 (figure)
Konstan, D., 5, 59
Koob, G. F., 174, 176
Kopell, B. H., 27
Kopietz, R., 128
Koppe, G., 110
Korte, S. M., 205, 220
Korzh, V., 108, 172, 207, 211
Koschke, M., 194, 195
Koscik, T. R., 259
Kosfeld, M., 95
Koster, E. H. W., 237, 238
Kostrzewa, R. M., 200, 201
Kotchoubey, B., 253
Kötter, R., 31
Kotz, S. A., 93, 184, 233, 252, 253
Kovács, Á. M., 294, 296 (figure), 297 (figure)
Kovacs, E., 299
Kovacs, M., 189
Krach, S., 345, 346 (figure), 355, 356
Krafft, C., 93
Kral, J. G., 84
Kramer, G. P., 184
Kreibig, S. D., 49, 163, 185, 216
Kringelbach, M. L., 169, 172
Krishnan, V., 188, 198, 199
Kriska, M., 349
Krugers, H., 330, 364
Krumhuber, E. G., 159
Krystal, J. H., 167, 190, 334
Kubzansky, L. D., 265, 363
Kudoh, T., 372
Kuebli, J., 329
Kuehner, C., 266, 270

Kuhle, B. X., 335
Kühn, S., 278
Kuhn, S. L., 326, 327, 370
Kuiper, N. A., 117
Kulik, J., 244, 246
Kulkarni, P., 292, 293 (figure)
Kunisato, Y., 194, 195, 343
Kunst-Wilson, W. R., 39 (figure), 111
Kunzmann, U., 343
Kuppens, S., 329
Kurokawa M., 340, 372, 379
Kurrasch, D., 361
Kutas, M., 161, 253, 253 (figure), 345

Laaksonen, D. E., 200
LaBar, K. S., 88, 185, 211, 216, 217, 244, 245, 247
Labouvie-Vief, G., 342
Labus, J. S., 342
Lacey, B. C., 137
Lacey, J. I., 137
Lachman, M. E., 311
LaCroix-Fralish, M. L., 128
LaFrance, M., 345
Laird, J. D., 119
Lakatos, K., 299
Lakis, N., 340
Lakka, T., 200
Lamarre, Y., 80, 194
Lamoreaux, M., 371
Landers, M. S., 291
Landgraf, R., 95, 310
Landis, C., 126, 127 (figure)
Lane, R. D., 137
Lang, P., 178
Lang, P. J., 43, 45, 56, 57, 58, 80, 111, 122, 131, 137, 206, 207, 241, 335, 339, 340, 342, 344, 345
Lange, M., 270, 271 (figure)
Langenecker, S. A., 167
Langeslag, S. J. E., 316
Langford, D. J., 128
Lanuza, E., 207
Laplante, D. P., 361
Larsen, A., 270, 271 (figure)
Larsen, J. T., 49, 138
Larson, R., 303
Lasauskaite, R., 184

Lasch, H., 317
Laucht, M., 298, 299
Laue, M. von, 71
Laukka, P., 113
Laukkanen, J., 200
Laurent, H. K., 292
Laurie, A. L., 201
Lavoie, M. E., 340
Lawrence, A. D., 259
Lawrence, N. S., 344
Lawson, M. J., 321
Law-Tho, D., 172
Lawton, C., 98
Lazarus, R. S., 38, 67, 174, 205, 232, 234, 264
le Coutre, J., 112
Leaper, C., 330
Leary, M. R., 178, 179
Lebourgeois, M. K., 264
Lebron, J., 99
Leckman, J. F., 195
Leclerc, C. M., 237
Ledoux, J. ., 207
LeDoux, J. E., 31, 80, 87, 88, 211, 216, 217, 218, 220, 224, 225 (figure), 226, 227 (figure), 247, 249
Lee, A., 108, 172, 207, 211
Lee, D. H., 208
Lee, E. A., 382
Lee, K., 298
Lee, K. H., 94, 303
Lee, K. J., 347 (figure)
Lee, M.-S., 361
Lee, T. M. C., 349
Lee Speer, A., 329
Leerkes, E., 295, 298
Leeuwen, E. J. C. van, Stow, J., 157
Lehner, T., 189
Leinenger, M., 45
Leiner, H. C., 83
Lejuez, C. W., 335
Leknes, S., 194, 195
Lemaitre, H., 96
Lenglet, C., 333
Leon, M., 291
Leonardi, R. J., 284, 285
Lepore, F., 189
Lerner, J. S., 260
Leroux, J. M., 186

Lesch, K.-P., 99, 189, 190

Letzkus, J. J., 121, 220

Leuenberger, B., 169

Leuf, T., 194, 195

Leuthold, H., 254

Levant, R. F., 339

Levenson, R. W., 46, 115, 119, 138, 163, 270, 317, 380

Lévesque, J., 186

Lévesque, M., 381

Levine, J., 298, 299

Levine, S., 179, 180, 181, 185

Levkovitz, Y., 334

Levy, R. T., 379

Lewis-Evans, B., 137, 340, 341 (figure)

Lewy, A. J., 201

Leyman, L., 280

Li, J., 294

Li, J.-Z., 373, 378

Li, K., 253

Li, P. W., 86

Li, Q., 93

Li, S., 373, 378

Li, X., 158, 252

Liang, K.-Y., 189

Liberzon, I., 89, 93, 94, 164, 218

Licht, P., 363

Liddell, B. J., 45, 221, 342

Lieberman, M. D., 44, 90, 186, 187 (figure), 266

Liebsch, K., 266, 270

Liening, S. H., 340–342, 348

Lighthall, N. R., 344

Lim, M. M., 310

Lin, M. T., 98

Lin, X., 368, 368 (figure), 369

Lindquist, K. A., 33, 43, 58, 122, 218

Lindsay, D. S., 247

Lindström, B. R., 244

Line, S., 363

Lintermans, B., 299

Linton, S., 260

Lipschitz, D., 190

Lisanby, S. H., 142

Lischke, A., 95, 349

Lisman, J., 172

Lister, R. G., 363

Litvin, Y., 185

Liu, D., 87, 330, 364, 365 (figure)

Liu, H., 253, 373, 378

Liu, J., 96

Liu, S., 368, 368 (figure), 369

Liu, X., 121

Liu, Y., 310, 311

Ljungberg, T., 170

Lobel, M., 361

Lockhart, R. S., 61

Loebell, N. C. de E., 355, 356

Loftus, E. F., 247

Logan, D. W., 106

Logothetis, N. K., 149

Lohr, J. M., 205

Löken, L. S., 113

Loo, K. V., 324

Lopes, A. P. F., 220

López-Muñoz, F., 187, 188

Lorenz, K., 106, 160, 291

Loucks, E. B., 265

Love, T., 167, 251

Low, B. S., 321

Low, C. A., 270

Lozo, L., 252

Lozoff, B., 363

Luber, B., 142

Lucas, G. M., 196

Lucas, N., 209

Lüders, H. O., 122

Lüdke, A., 211

Luecken, L. J., 135

Lui, M. A., 255, 256

Lukowiak, K., 211

Lumley, M. A., 342

Lundqvist, D., 209, 210 (figure)

Lust, S. A., 254

Luther, D., 356

Lüthi, A., 121, 195, 220, 292

Lutz, A. M., 313

Lutz, P.-E., 99

Luxen, A., 98

Luximon, Y., 368

Luypaert, R., 280

Lykken, D. T., 307

Lynch, J., 363

Lyons, D. M., 95

Lyons, T., 330

Lyubomirsky, S., 268

Ma, X., 382
Macaulay, D., 114
Macdonald, D. W., 12
MacDonald, G., 178, 179, 187, 194, 195
MacDonald, I., 157
Macedo, M. N., 92
Machado, A. G., 27
Machin, A. J., 99
MacLean, P. D., 25, 26, 194
MacLeod, A. M., 93
MacLeod, C., 238
Macmillan, M., 140
Madden, J. R., 307
Maestripieri, D., 291
Mahurin, R., 105
Mai, R., 342
Maier, S. F., 211, 212 (figure)
Maier, W., 95, 219
Maisey, M. N., 145
Majewska, A. K., 121, 141
Mak, A. K. Y., 349
Makris, N., 333
Malik, M., 135, 136
Manaye, K. F., 28, 91–92
Manes, F., 131
Mangelsdorf, S. C., 300, 302
Mann, A., 184
Mann, K., 344
Mannie, Z. M., 189
Mansari, M., 98
Manstead, A. S. R., 159, 339
Mantsch, J. R., 176
Manuck, S. B., 363
Manzoni, T., 82
Maquet, P., 98
Marco, E. J., 331
Marcovitch, S., 295, 298
Marcus Aurelius, 266, 268
Marino-Neto, J., 220
Markovits, H., 342
Markus, C. R., 276
Markus, H. R., 337, 340, 370, 371, 372, 379, 382
Marle, H. J. F. van, 216
Marlowe, F. W., 326
Marmot, M., 340
Marnell, P., 200
Martens, A., 324, 325, 325 (figure), 326

Martens, S., 237
Martin, E., 337
Martin, J., 189
Martin, L. L., 66
Martin, N. G., 333
Martinez, O., 368, 369
Martínez Mateo, M., 355, 356
Martorella, E. A., 117, 245, 246 (figure), 247
Martuza, R. L., 27–28
Maruščáková, I., 181
Marzolf, D., 300, 302
Masataka, N., 351
Mascioli, G., 82
Mashour, G. A., 27–28
Maslow, A. H., 69, 152
Mason, N. S., 187, 189
Massano, J., 165
Masten, C. L., 187, 194, 195
Mataix-Cols, D., 344
Mather, M., 244, 315, 315 (figure), 316, 344
Mathes, W. F., 201
Mathews, A., 238
Mathews, G. A., 348
Mathur, V. A., 375, 376, 378
Mathuru, A. S., 48, 108, 128, 172, 207, 209, 211
Mathy, R. M., 342
Matsui, M., 332–333, 333 (figure)
Matsumoto, D., 274, 360, 372, 382
Matsumoto, M., 170, 172
Matsunami, H., 48
Matsuura, M., 164
Matsuzawa, T., 356, 357 (figure)
Mattay, V. S., 96, 190
Matthiesen, A.-S., 95
Matveychuk, D., 242
Mauss, I. B., 264, 349, 350 (figure)
May, J., 128
May, W. H., 55–56, 57
Mayberg, H., 200
Mayberg, H. S., 121–122
Mayer, E. A., 342
Mayes, L. C., 187, 195
Mazziotta, J. C., 187
McCabe, C., 164
McCabe, K., 364
McCabe, P. M., 95
McCall, K. M., 340
McCall, R. B., 299

McCarthy, G., 147, 185
McCaul, K. D., 270
McClay, J., 189
McClure, S. M., 369, 380, 381 (figure)
McCormick, C. M., 348
McCoy, K., 380
McDermott, J., 240
McFarland, N. R., 89
McGaugh, J. L., 219, 220, 221–222, 249
McGeary, J. E., 190
McGhee, D. E., 130, 132 (figure)
McGlone, F., 113
McGraw, L. A., 310
McGrew, W. C., 356, 357 (figure)
McGurk, R., 331, 337
McHugo, M., 240
McIntyre, C. K., 249
McKenna, M., 241
McKeon, D., 200
McMahon, K. L., 333
McNealy, K., 187
McNeilly, A. S., 292
McPartland, J. C., 187
McRae, K., 268, 276, 349, 350 (figure)
Meaney, M. J., 87, 292, 330, 364, 365 (figure)
Meaney, M. L., 361
Meck, W. H., 255, 256, 361
Meconi, F., 375
Meda, S., 167
Medina, O., 167
Meintjes, R., 119
Meiran, N., 273, 279, 282
Meissner, K., 344
Melcher, T., 184
Meletti, S., 342
Mella, N., 254
Meltzoff, A. N., 293
Mendes, D. M. L. F., 294
Mendez, A. J., 95
Mendoza, S. P., 185
Mendrek, A., 340
Menéndez-González, M., 48, 66
Meng, X., 364, 366
Menon, V., 164, 345
Mensour, B., 186
Merikangas, K. R., 189, 222–223
Merkle, F. T., 91
Merrer, J. L., 99

Mertz, E., 161
Mervis, C. B., 52–53
Merz, C. J., 110, 216, 342
Mesquita, B., 372, 377
Messenger, T. L., 292, 293 (figure)
Messier, C., 172
Meston, C. M., 340
Metshonkala, L., 88
Metzler, S., 95, 219
Meyer, M., 159
Meyer, N., 31
Meyer-Lindenberg, A., 95, 96, 190
Miao, W., 321
Michaels, W. B., 356
Michalak, J., 183
Michiels, D., 329
Mickey, B. J., 167
Mico, J. A., 191, 199
Miesenböck, G., 121, 141
Miezin, F. M., 93
Miklósi, Á., 180, 181
Miles, E., 265, 266, 270, 273
Mill, J., 189
Miller, B. L., 92
Miller, G., 308
Miller, J. P., 122
Miller, M., 157
Miller, R., 284, 285
Miller, R. D., 307
Millette, B. H. P., 194
Milner, B., 30, 242
Min, C. S., 47
Minati, L., 189
Mineka, S., 214, 218
Mini, A., 136
Minnegal, M., 376
Minnick, M. R., 382
Mirenowicz, J., 170
Miron, M. S., 55–56, 57
Mischel, W., 264, 284, 300
Mishra, A., 340
Mitchell, J. P., 117
Miyamoto, Y., 379, 382
Miyashita, T., 85
Mize, J., 43
Moan, C. E., 165
Mobbs, D., 164, 345
Moeller, F. G., 347, 348

Moffitt, T. E., 189, 306
Mogil, J. S., 128
Molden, D. C., 196
Molenbroek, J., 368
Molnár, C., 180, 181
Mondadori, C., 172
Monfils, M.-H., 211, 226, 227 (figure)
Montagu, A., 181
Montague, P. R., 170, 294
Monti, J. M., 98
Moor, B. G., 344
Moore, M. K., 293
Moore, R. Y., 98
Moreno, E. M., 161
Morgan, M. J., 352
Morin, C., 80, 194
Morling, B., 371
Morris, E. K., 211
Morris, J. S., 220
Morrison, I., 113
Morrison, S. F., 98
Mortensen, E. L., 363
Mortillaro, M., 128
Moser, J. S., 275
Moskal, J. R., 160
Mosnárová, A., 349
Moss, E., 309
Mott, G. E., 363
Moulds, M. L., 135, 265, 266
Mousa, S. A., 99
Moutier, S., 306
Mühlberger, A., 56, 57, 58
Mujica-Parodi, L. R., 209
Mulder, E. J. H., 361
Müller, C., 121, 220
Muller, M. N., 326
Munaf, M. R., 189
Mungas, D., 368, 369
Munn, P., 329
Munoz, K. E., 190
Muñoz, R. F., 280, 281, 282
Munte, T. F., 345
Mural, R. J., 86
Murdock, G. P., 327, 334
Murillo- Rodrguez, E., 48, 66
Murphy, A. Z., 310
Murphy, S. E., 189
Murray, D. R., 366

Murray, J. D., 334
Murray, M., 112
Murrough, J. W., 279
Murty, V. P., 245
Musch, J., 254
Mustovic, H., 195, 292
Muth, E. R., 344
Myers, E. W., 86

Näätänen, P., 88
Nader, K., 207, 224, 225 (figure)
Nagaraja, H. N., 135, 136
Nakamura, J., 199
Nakashima, B. R., 46
Naliboff, B. D., 342
Nara, N., 211
Nath, L. E., 339, 340
Natterson-Horowitz, B., 207, 376
Navarrete, C. D., 366
N'Diaye, K., 64, 65, 112
Neary, D., 92
Nedergaard, M., 77, 78
Nelson, E. E., 303
Nelson, J. A., 295, 298
Nemoda, Z., 299
Nesmith, K., 315, 315 (figure), 316
Nestler, E. J., 188, 198, 199
Neuberg, S. L., 345–346
Neuhoff, J. G., 195, 292
Neumann, E., 138
Neumann, I. D., 95, 310
Neumann, R., 252, 372
Neumeister, A., 279
Newman, J. D., 194
Ney, K., 299
Ng, J. T. W., 114
Nga, L., 344
Ngambeki, I., 337, 351
Nguyen, H. T., 46, 114, 207
Nguyen, T., 142, 342
Nicastle, L. D., 335
Nichelli, P., 88
Nicholls, A. R., 348, 349
Nichols, S. N., 194
Niedenthal, P. M., 231, 233
Niem, P. M., 88
Nilsson, A., 119
Nimchinsky, E. A., 90

Nisbett, R. E., 33, 379
Nishida, T., 356
Niskanen, L., 200
Nissen, E., 95
Nithianantham, D., 113
Nobre, A. C., 252
Nocetti, L., 88
Nolan, C. L., 88
Nolen-Hoeksema, S., 272, 279, 280, 282, 348
Noller, C. M., 95
Norbury, R., 189
Nørby, S., 270, 271 (figure)
Noreau, A., 189
Norenzayan, A., 355
Noriuchi, M., 292
Norrholm, S. D., 220
Norris, D. G., 149
Northoff, G., 369
Noulhiane, M., 254
Nowicki, G. P., 162
Nozyce, M., 364
Nussbaum, 5
Nusser, Z., 77

Oberheim, N., 78
O'Brien, M., 295, 298
Obst, K., 184
O'Carroll, D. C., 235
Ochsner, K. N., 93, 94, 231, 244, 264, 268, 276, 349, 350 (figure)
O'Connor, J. C., 201
O'Connor, K. J., 217
Odendaal, J. S. ., 119
O'Doherty, J., 105
Oeltermann, A., 149
Oh, T. J., 182
O'Hare, A. J., 242
Ohl, F. W., 221
Öhman, A., 80, 111, 137, 206, 207, 209, 210 (figure), 212, 214 (figure), 215, 218, 220, 237, 241
Ohrt, A., 209
Oitzl, M. S., 220
Okada, G., 194, 195, 343
Okamoto, T., 199
Okamoto, Y., 194, 195, 343
Okubo, Y., 164
Olatunji, B. O., 205

Olausson, H., 80, 113, 194
Olds, J., 120, 164
Olide, A., 382
Oliver, M. B., 335
Oliver, W. T., 93
Olp, J. J., 307
Olsson, A., 108, 205, 373, 374 (figure), 375
Onaka, T., 218
Ong, A. D., 312
Onghena, P., 329
Onoda, K., 194, 195, 343
Onur, O. A., 95, 219
Oostenveld, R., 149, 216
Op de Macks, Z. A., 344
Orias, E., 321
Ornitz, E., 342
Ornstein, K., 172
Ortega, M., 368, 369
Ortiz, H., 44, 45
Ortiz, N., 99
Ortony, A., 49, 50
Osgood, C. E., 55–56, 57
Ossewaarde, L., 216, 344, 351
Ostroff, L. E., 249
Ott, J., 189
Ott, U., 89
Overgaauw, S., 344
Owen, A. M., 156
Owren, M. J., 113, 159, 181, 208
Oyserman, D., 371
Ozaki-Kuroda, K., 364

Paepke, A. J., 307
Paez, W., 84
Page, I. H., 98
Page, M. C., 347
Pakkenberg, B., 77, 78, 85
Pakkenberg, H., 77, 78, 85
Palmer, J. R., 218
Palomares-Castillo, E., 88
Palomba, D., 136
Paluck, E. L., 345
Pancheva, R., 251
Pang, P. T., 121
Panksepp, J., 31, 44, 47, 48, 49, 99, 128, 154, 156, 157, 160, 173, 175, 178, 179, 195, 359

Pantelis, C., 44, 45
Papez, J. W., 21
Pardo, J. V., 334
Paré, D., 88, 220
Parent, C., 364
Park, H. W., 375, 376, 378
Park, I. J. K., 382
Park, K. S., 182
Park, S., 28, 91–92
Parker, G. A., 321
Parker, K. J., 95
Parkinson, B., 65, 67, 361
Parr, L. A., 159, 181, 207–208
Parrish, T. B., 375, 376, 378
Partridge, G., 157
Pascalis, O., 298
Paschoalini, M. A., 220
Pascual, J. C., 342
Pascuzzo, K., 309
Passant, U., 92
Pasterski, V. L., 328, 329 (figure)
Paterson, H. M., 128
Patin, A., 95, 219, 240
Patrick, C., 139
Pauli, P., 56, 57, 58, 117
Pauls, C. A., 49
Pauls, J., 149
Paulus, C., 184
Paus, T., 280
Pause, B. M., 209
Pavlov, I. P., 107, 162
Payen, V., 135
Pearce, E., 157
Pearlson, G. D., 167
Pearson, D., 87, 330, 364, 365 (figure)
Peciña, M., 167
Pedrozo, A. L., 266
Peduto, A., 45, 221, 342
Peira, N., 137
Pell, M. D., 47, 252
Pelphrey, K. A., 187
Pelvig, D. P., 77, 78, 85
Peng, D., 253
Peng, K., 163, 379
Penney, T., 242
Penney, T. B., 108, 128, 129 (figure), 172, 181, 207, 211, 255, 256, 361
Pentkowski, N. S., 185

Penton-Voak, I., 347 (figure)
Percy, A. D., 114
Perea, G., 78
Peretz, I., 137
Perez, C. R., 382
Pérez de la Mora, M., 88
Pérez-Carrera, D., 88
Perrett, D. I., 347 (figure)
Perry-Parrish, C., 329, 330
Pérusse, D., 189
Pessoa, L., 232, 233, 241
Peterchev, A. V., 142
Peters, J., 164
Petersen, S. E., 93
Peterson, B. S., 56, 57, 58, 131
Peterson, C., 200
Petersson, K.-M., 149
Petticrew, M., 363
Pezawas, L., 190
Pfeifer, J. H., 187
Phan, A., 349
Phan, K. L., 89, 93, 94, 164, 218
Phelps, E., 232, 250
Phelps, E. A., 88, 108, 117, 205, 211, 216, 217, 218, 226, 227 (figure), 240, 244, 245, 246 (figure), 247, 268, 269 (figure), 373, 374 (figure), 375
Phifer, J. E., 220
Philippot P., 339, 340
Phillips, K. A., 82
Phillips, M. L., 344
Phillips, P. E. M., 172
Phoenix, C. H., 331, 332 (figure)
Piccardi, M., 113
Pickett, K. E., 363
Piech, R. M., 240
Pieper, S., 195
Pieters, T. A., 149
Pietromonaco, P. R., 339
Pinker, S., 251
Pinna, G., 348
Pitskel, N. B., 187
Pivik, K., 335, 340
Plailly, J., 88, 89
Planck, M., 71
Plichta, M. M., 56, 57, 58
Plotsky, P. M., 87, 330, 364, 365 (figure)
Poehlmann, K. M., 49, 138

Pollatos, O., 48, 209, 274, 275, 275 (figure)
Pollick, F. E., 128
Polman, R. C., 348, 349
Polonara, G., 82
Pongrácz, P., 180, 181
Pöppel, E., 48, 66
Porcherot, C., 113
Porges, S. W., 135, 136
Portella, M. J., 342
Porter, R. H., 291
Posner, J., 56, 57, 58, 131
Posner, M. I., 301, 302, 302 (figure)
Poulton, R., 189
Pourtois, G., 114, 221, 242
Pouthas, V., 254, 255
Pouw, W. T. J. L., 185, 343
Powell, C., 187, 194, 195
Powell, M. C., 129, 251
Powers, M. B., 226
Powers, W. J., 93
Poytress, B. S., 220
Prehn, A., 209
Price, J., 196
Price, T. F., 119, 122
Prickaerts, J., 98, 99, 361
Priester, J. R., 158
Prins, B., 219
Privat, A. M., 191
Proctor, G. B., 84
Proverbio, A. M., 337
Provost, C., 327, 334
Prum, R. O., 308
Przymus, D. E., 380
Ptak, R., 278
Pugh, C. R., 220
Pujol, J., 44, 45
Purkis, H., 223
Puryear, C. B., 121
Putman, P., 220
Putnam, S. K., 348
Puts, D. A., 307

Qi, H., 368, 368 (figure), 369
Qin, S., 216
Qiu, A., 93, 113
Quigley, K. S., 122
Quinn, P. C., 298
Quinn, W. G., 47

Quinton, R. L., 326, 327 (figure)
Quirin, M., 344

Rabie, T., 339
Rabin, B. S., 363
Rademacher, L., 345, 346 (figure)
Radue, E. W., 195, 292
Ragert, P., 317
Raghunathan, T., 363
Ragot, R., 254
Raichle, M. E., 93
Raio, C. M., 211, 226, 227 (figure)
Ramel, W., 268, 276
Ramirez, G., 266, 267 (figure), 268
Ramirez, S., 121
Ramrez, I., 337, 338 (figure), 344
Ramsay, P. T., 84
Ramsey, C. B., 113
Ramsey, N. F., 344
Ramsey, S. E., 335
Ransjö-Arvidson, A.-B., 95
Rao, L.-L., 373, 378
Rapport, M. M., 98
Rauramaa, R., 200
Rauss, K., 372, 377, 378
Ray, R. D., 115, 233, 276
Raye, C. L., 94
Rayner, R., 210, 223
Read, J. D., 247
Read, J. P., 335
Rech, A., 221
Redgrave, P., 170, 172
Redmond, D. E., 218
Redouté, J., 90
Reed, B. R., 368, 369
Rees, G., 239
Reheiser, E. C., 133
Rehme, A. K., 219
Reinisch, J. M., 363
Reis, D. J., 80, 87, 216
Reisenzein, R., 33, 35, 67
Reiss, A. L., 164, 344, 345
Rellini, A. H., 340
Ren, X.-P., 373, 378
Renaud, F. L., 99
Rendall, D., 181, 208
Rendell, L., 356
Ressler, K. J., 121–122, 220, 223, 361

Reynolds, J., 170, 172
Reynolds, J. H., 235, 236 (figure)
Reynolds, V., 356
Rezai, A. R., 27
Rhodes, K., 342
Rhodes, N., 335, 340
Rhudy, J. L., 342
Ribatti, D., 3
Richard, J. M., 172
Richards, J. B., 335
Richards, M. H., 303
Richards, T., 105
Richardson, M. P., 240
Rickman, M., 207
Ridderinkhof, K. R., 142
Riem, M. M. E., 195
Rijpkema, M., 216
Riordan, M. A., 254
Rioux, M., 368
Risch, N., 189
Ritchey, M., 245
Riva, F., 337
Rizzolatti, G., 88, 89
Roberson, D., 134
Robert, P. H., 92
Roberts, N. A., 116
Roberts, S. C., 113
Robertson, G. G., 335, 336 (figure), 340
Robin, L., 339
Robinson, G. F., 161
Robinson, I. C., 292
Robinson, M. D., 339
Robinson, M. J., 197
Robles de Medina, P. G., 361
Röcke, C., 311
Rockland, C., 247, 248
Rodd, J. M., 156
Rodriguez, F., 99
Rodriguez, M. I., 264, 284, 300
Rodriguez Mosquera, P. M., 339
Roeder, U. R., 372
Roelofs, K., 220
Roeper, J., 97
Roesch, E. B., 62–63
Rogers, T. B., 117
Rohr, M., 252
Rohrmann, S., 344
Roiser, J. P., 187

Rolls, E. T., 164
Roman, G., 108
Rombouts, S. A. R. B., 195
Romero-Fernandez, W., 299
Romo, R., 170
Ronai, Z., 299
Rondou, P., 299
Roozendaal, B., 220
Rosch, E., 52–53
Roseman, I. J., 59, 67
Rosen, J. B., 216
Rosen, T. S., 108
Rosenberg, E. L., 127, 208
Rosenthal, L., 361
Ross, H. E., 310
Ross, M. D., 159
Rossell, S. L., 252
Rossetti, M. A., 95
Rostamian, S., 361
Roth, Y., 181, 182, 183
Rothbart, M. K., 301, 302,
    302 (figure)
Rothermund, K., 254
Rothe-Wulf, A., 372, 377, 378
Rottenberg, J., 115, 198
Rouleau, G. A., 189
Rousset, S., 255
Rowland, D., 347 (figure)
Roy, A. K., 205, 268, 269 (figure)
Roy, M., 137
Royet, J. P., 88, 89
Rozenkrantz, L., 181, 182, 183
Rozin, P., 373, 378
Ruan, Y., 96
Rubin, D., 209
Rudebeck, P. H., 194
Rudrauf, D., 317
Rudy, J. W., 220
Rueter, S., 191
Ruhé, H. G., 187, 189
Runge, U., 88
Rushworth, M. F. S., 194
Russell, J. A., 1, 43, 44, 48, 53, 54, 54 (figure),
    55 (figure), 56, 57, 58, 69, 131, 154, 360,
    379, 380
Russo, G. L., 342
Rutten, B. P. F., 361
Rychlowska, M., 231, 233

Rydell, M. T., 324
Rydell, R. J., 324

Sabatinelli, D., 93, 335, 339, 340, 342, 344, 345
Sabini, J., 359
Sacco, K., 48
Sacks, O., 167, 176
Sagarin, B. J., 335
Sagaspe, P., 207
Saj, A., 239
Sakaguchi, A., 80, 87, 216
Sakaki, M., 344
Salvolini, U., 82
Samii, N., 344
Sammer, G., 89, 110
Samson, S., 137, 254
Sananes, C. B., 216
Sanbonmatsu, D. M., 129, 251
Sánchez-Adam, A., 337, 338 (figure), 344
Sánchez-Blázquez, P., 191, 199
Sandberg, S. G., 172
Sander, D., 57, 59, 61–62, 63, 64, 65, 67, 88, 113, 114, 218, 232, 234
Sander, K., 195, 337
Sanders, S. A., 363
Sanford, A. J., 128
Saphier, D., 176
Sapiro, G., 333
Sapolsky, R., 363
Sapolsky, R. M., 363
Sara, S. J., 98
Sarlo, M., 136
Sasvari-Szekely, M., 299
Saucier, J.-F., 361
Sauer, H., 194
Saul, J. P., 135, 136
Saults, J. S., 254
Sauter, D., 154, 157
Sauter, D. A., 154, 382
Savoy, R., 209
Sawyer, A. T., 282
Schachter, S., 32–33, 34 (figure), 115–116
Schacter, D. L., 315, 316, 334
Schaefer, A., 232, 233
Schaefer, H. S., 303
Schafe, G. E., 224, 225 (figure)

Schäfer, A., 342
Schäfer, M., 99
Schaller, M., 342, 366
Schatzberg, A. F., 95
Scheepers, C., 113, 381
Scheeringa, R., 149
Scheich, H., 221, 337
Schell, A. M., 137
Schene, A. H., 187, 189
Scherer, K. R., 43, 45, 47, 59, 61–62, 62–63, 67, 112, 113, 114, 128, 154, 155, 179, 205, 232, 234, 372, 380
Scherer, T., 49
Schettino, A., 242
Schieffelin, E. L., 376
Schienle, A., 89, 342
Schiller, D., 211, 226, 227 (figure)
Schirmer, A., 47, 93, 113, 114, 128, 129 (figure), 137, 159, 181, 184, 233, 252, 253, 255, 256, 352
Schlaepfer, T. E., 219
Schlosberg, H., 50, 51–52, 51 (figure), 53, 57, 138
Schlösser, R., 194, 195
Schmader, T., 324, 325, 325 (figure), 326
Schmeichel, B. J., 276
Schmidt, C., 219
Schmidt, M. H., 298, 299
Schmiedek, F., 311
Schmitt, J. A. J., 189, 201
Schnapp, W., 347
Schneiderman, N., 95
Schnitzer, M. J., 121, 141
Schnülle, J., 279, 280, 282
Schönfelder, S., 276
Schoots, O., 299
Schöpf, V., 128
Schotte, C., 264
Schreder, T., 128
Schroeder, H. W. S., 88
Schroeder, K., 169
Schulkin, J., 220
Schulte, D., 183
Schultheiss, O. C., 340–342, 348
Schultz, W., 170, 174
Schulze, L., 95, 342
Schupp, H. T., 88, 221

Schurtz, D. E., 187, 194, 195
Schütz, E., 200, 201
Schuurmans, C., 361
Schwartz, J. L., 130, 132 (figure)
Schwartz, S., 114, 207, 240
Schwarz, N., 184
Schweckendiek, J., 110, 342
Schweinberger, S. R., 254
Schweinhardt, P., 174
Schweizer, S., 279, 280, 282
Schwenkreis, P., 317
Schwier, C., 194
Schyns, P. G., 113, 381
Scimeca, J. M., 375, 376, 378
Scott, A. C., 361
Scott, S., 154, 157
Scott, S. K., 154, 382
Scoville, W. B., 30, 242
Seal, B. N., 340
Sebastian, C. L., 187
Seebeck, T., 307
Seeley, W. W., 91, 92
Segal, M., 98
Segal, Z. V., 200
Seghier, M. L., 114
Seidl-de-Moura, M. L., 294
Seidlitz, L., 339
Seidman, L. J., 333
Seifert, C. A., 344
Seifritz, E., 195, 292
Seligman, M. E., 200, 211, 212, 212 (figure), 223
Seligman, M. E. P., 152, 156
Seltzer, M., 330
Semendeferi, K., 28, 91–92
Semrud-Clikeman, M., 294
Senécal S., 339, 340
Senoo, A., 292
Seow, C. S., 128, 129 (figure), 181
Sescousse, G., 90
Sessa, P., 375
Seth, A. K., 171 (figure)
Seymour, B., 259
Seymour, T. L., 315, 315 (figure), 316
Shafer, A. T., 242
Shahrokh, D. K., 292
Shakibaei, M., 99
Shamay-Tsoory, S., 295, 297
Shanz, S., 78

Shapiro, J. R., 300, 302
Shapiro, M. L., 30
Sharma, S., 87, 330, 364, 365 (figure)
Sharot, T., 117, 245, 246 (figure), 247
Shaver, P. R., 309
Shaw, M., 363
She, P.-H., 167
Sheeran, P., 265, 266, 270, 273
Sheffield, T. D., 301
Shell, R., 342
Shelton, S. E., 207
Shen, M., 158
Shen, X., 330
Sheppard, L. A., 184
Sheppes, G., 273, 279, 282
Shibasaki, M., 351
Shields, S. A., 37, 339
Shiffrin, R. M., 324
Shih, C. J., 98
Shinkai, T., 199
Shiota, M. N., 154, 163, 379
Shirley, E., 194
Shizgal, P., 164
Shoda, Y., 264, 284, 300
Shryne, J. E., 331
Shu, C., 368
Shuang, M., 96
Shui, G., 48, 128, 209
Shulman, G. L., 93, 235, 237
Shumway, T., 257
Shurick, A. A., 205, 268, 269 (figure)
Shushan, S., 181, 182, 183
Sicking, K., 220
Siddiqui, A., 93
Siegle, G. J., 94, 303
Siemer, M., 67
Siep, N., 276
Sierksma, A. S. R., 361
Silber, B. Y., 189, 201
Silk, J. S., 303
Silva, A. J., 78
Silver, M., 359
Silvers, J. A., 276
Silvestrini, N., 184
Simard, V., 309
Šimeček, P., 181
Simion, F., 293
Simon, R. W., 339, 340

Simons, R. F., 275
Simpson, E., 352
Sims, N., 201
Singer, J., 32–33, 34 (figure), 115–116
Siqueira, J. de O., 294
Sirigu, A., 375
Sitte, N., 99
Siviy, S. M., 154
Skieterska, K., 299
Skorup, V., 47
Skultétyová, I., 349
Skuse, D. H., 331, 337
Slater, A. M., 298
Slattery, D. A., 77
Slifstein, M., 167
Slovic, P., 153, 258
Smeets, T., 349
Smith, C., 59, 67
Smith, C. A., 63, 67, 155, 178, 179
Smith, D. M., 345–346
Smith, G. D., 363
Smith, H. G., 86
Smith, R. H., 106
Smith, S., 342
Smith, S. D., 240
Smith, T. E., 330
Smith, V. G. F., 321
Smith, Y., 310
Smotherman, W. P., 185
Smythies, J., 98
Snowden, J. S., 92
Snyder, A. Z., 93
Soares, J. J., 111, 212
Sobel, N., 181, 182, 183
Soeter, M., 219
Sojka, B., 209
Sokol-Hessner, P., 373
Soler, J., 342
Sollers, J. J., 3rd, 265
Solomon, S., 270
Somayajula, S., 344
Somerville, L. H., 305, 305 (figure)
Sommer, T., 169
Sommers, S. R., 373, 375, 376, 378
Song, A. W., 147, 185
Songer, J. B., 201
Sood, E., 330
Sorabji, R., 3, 6

Sorenson, E. R., 45, 371, 380
Sorge, R. E., 128
Soto, J. A., 380, 382
Sotocinal, S. G., 128
Southgate, E., 85
Søvik, E., 96, 97
Spada, H., 372, 377, 378
Spear, L. P., 304, 304 (figure)
Speckens, A., 344
Spencer, D. D., 88, 211, 216, 247
Spielberger, C. D., 133
Spiess, J., 185
Špinka, M., 181
Sporn, A., 142
Spreckelmeyer, K. N., 345, 346 (figure)
Sprengel, R., 121, 220
Squire, L. R., 243
St. Jacques, P. L., 316
Stadler, M. B., 121, 220
Stamelou, M., 48, 66
Stanley, D. A., 373
Stansfield, K. H., 305
Stanton, A. L., 270
Stanton, M. E., 185
Stanton, S. J., 340–342, 348
Starck, G., 80, 194
Stark, A. K., 77, 78, 85
Stark, R., 89, 110, 216, 342
Steele, C. M., 325
Stegagno, L., 136
Stegbauer, K. C., 105
Steiger, J. H., 53, 55 (figure)
Stein, C., 99
Steinbeis, N., 252, 253
Steinberg, L., 306
Steinbusch, H. W. M., 98, 99, 361
Steinhäuser, N., 372
Stemmler, G., 49
Stenman, H., 88
Stepper, S., 66
Steptoe, A., 174, 340
Sterpenich, V., 98
Stevens, A., 292
Stevens, J. S., 342, 343 (figure), 344
Stewart, S. A., 224
Stillman, T. F., 187, 194, 195
Stiner, M. C., 326, 327, 370
Stohler, C. S., 167

Stokes, J., 242
Stoll, A. L., 191
Stone, P. H., 135, 136
Storey, A. E., 326, 327 (figure)
Stowers, L., 106
Strack, F., 66, 184
Strafella, A. P., 280
Strange, B. A., 105
Strathearn, L., 294
Strey, H. H., 209
Striano, T., 114, 294, 295 (figure), 352
Strick, M., 265
Strigo, I., 80, 194
Strong, D. R., 335
Stroop, J. R., 184
Stroud, L. R., 303
Strout, S., 119
Stuart, G. L., 335
Stumpenhorst, K., 175
Stuss, D., 92
Sugden, K., 189
Sugiyama, Y., 356
Suhara, T., 164
Sullivan, J. M., 292, 293 (figure)
Sullivan, R. M., 291
Summerfield, A. B., 380
Sun, B., 368, 368 (figure), 369
Sung, Y. S., 369, 380, 381 (figure)
Susskind, J. M., 208
Sutherland, M. R., 244
Sutton, G. G., 86
Suveg, C., 330
Suzuki, R., 211
Swaab, D. F., 80–81, 331
Swain, J. E., 195
Swann, A. C., 348
Swanson, C., 116
Swart, M., 344
Swartz, T. S., 67
Swinney, D., 251
Szasz, P. L., 282
Szentagotai, A., 282
Szeto, A., 95
Szyszka, P., 211

Tabaka, J. M., 128
Tabbert, K., 216, 342
Tabibnia, G., 266

Takada, M., 276
Takahashi, H., 164
Takahashi, L. K., 46
Takano, T., 77, 78
Talbot, P. S., 189
Tallet, C., 181
Talmi, D., 240
Tamir, D. I., 117
Tamres, L. K., 348, 349
Tan, G. C. Y., 187
Tan, L., 93, 159, 352
Tanaka, J. W., 298
Tandon, N., 149
Tang, Y., 368, 368 (figure), 369
Tanimoto, H., 211
Tannenbaum, B., 87, 330, 364, 365 (figure)
Tasker, J. G., 222
Tassi, L., 342
Tassinari, C. A., 342
Tassinary, L. G., 339
Tata, P., 238
Tavangar, N. N., 361
Taylor, A., 189
Taylor, S. E., 349
Taylor, S. F., 89, 93, 94, 164, 218
Teasdale, J. D., 244
Tedeschi, G., 195, 292
Tegenthoff, M., 317
Téglás, E., 294, 296 (figure), 297 (figure)
Teh, C., 108, 172, 207, 211
Teh, K. S., 113
Telang, F., 174, 175
Telch, M. J., 226
Tellegen, A., 133, 183, 307
Terkel, J., 356
Terner, J. M., 351
Tetreault, N. A., 28, 91–92
Thaler, R. H., 258
Thayer, J. F., 135, 137, 265
Thibault, P., 381
Thomas, M., 268
Thomas Bigger, J., 135, 136
Thompson, E., 282
Thompson, N., 195
Thompson, P. M., 333
Thomson, J. N., 85
Thorndike, E. L., 152, 162, 212
Thornhill, R., 307, 366, 367 (figure)

Tian, L., 334
Tice, D. M., 187, 194, 195
Tiedens, L. Z., 260
Tierney, P. L., 172
Ting, A., 121, 141
Tiwari, S., 330
Tobin, R. M., 339
Todd, R. M., 282
Toepel, U., 112
Toga, A. W., 333, 368, 368 (figure), 369
Tokutsu, Y., 199
Tolkunov, D., 209
Tolmunen, T., 200
Tomasi, D., 174, 175
Tomkins, S., 42–43, 45
Tonegawa, S., 121
Tong, E. M. W., 184
Toosi, N. R., 373, 375, 376, 378
Tops, M., 195
Torello, M. S., 136, 137
Tost, H., 96
Toth, I., 299
Tovote, P., 185
Townsend, D. W., 145
Tracey, I., 194, 195
Tran, T. P., 340
Tranel, D., 88, 247, 248, 259, 316, 317
Treig, T., 221
Tremblay, D., 220
Trevino, K., 200
Trezza, V., 99
Trinath, T., 149
Trinder, J., 84
Troisi, A., 291
Troje, N. F., 183
Tronick, E., 300
Troy, A. S., 264
Tsai, J. L., 116, 198, 317, 380
Tsai, S. H., 98
Tsuang, M. T., 333
Tunbridge, E. M., 175
Turetsky, B. I., 332–333, 333 (figure)
Turken, A. U., 160
Turner, T. J., 49, 50
Turpin, G., 137
Tuschen-Caffier, B., 279, 280, 282
Tutin, C. E. G., 356
Tversky, A., 153, 257, 258

Uchida, Y., 379
Ueki, S., 211
Ullman, M. T., 251
Umene-Nakano, W., 199
Unal, C. T., 220
Ungerleider, L. G., 241
Uraki, E., 211
Urbach, T. P., 345
Urban, N. B. L., 167
Uvnäs-Moberg, K., 95, 119

Vaca, G. F.-B., 122
Vaitl, D., 89, 110, 216, 342
Valezco, M.-I., 113
Valins, S., 33
Valk, P. E., 145
Vallbo, A. B., 80, 194
Valtonen, M., 200
van Baaren, R. B., 265
Van Craenenbroeck, K., 299
van den Bos, R., 340
van den Hove, D. L. A., 361
van den Maagdenberg, A., 128
van den Wildenberg, W. P. M., 142
Van Der Meer, J., 240
Van der Molen, W. M., 135, 136
van der Veen, R., 220
Van Doesum, N. J., 185, 343
van Donkelaar, E. L., 98, 99
van Honk, J., 344
van Knippenberg, A., 265
Van Leijenhorst, L., 306
van Loon, A. M., 142
Van Schuerbeek, P., 280
van Stegeren, A. H., 142
van Strien, J. W., 316
Van Tol, H. H. M., 299
van Vianen, A. E. M., 339
van Wees, R., 237
Vandekerckhove, M., 264
Vanderhasselt, M.-A., 280
Vanderschuren, L. J. M. J., 99
Vandewalle, G., 98
Vanhoenacker, P., 299
Vanman, E. J., 339
Varendi, H., 291
Varlinskaya, E. I., 304, 304 (figure)
Vasconcellos, A. J., 185

Vasunilashorn, S., 344
Venter, J. C., 86
Ventura, P., 266
Verbraecken, J., 264
Verchinski, B. A., 96, 190
Verkhratsky, A., 77, 78
Vermeiren, R. R. J. M., 195
Vernon, L. L., 272
Verschuere, B., 238
Vertes, R. P., 98
Vick, S. J., 159, 181, 207–208
Vick, S.-J., 284, 285
Viding, E., 187
Viinamäki, H., 200
Vijayakumar, R., 113
Vila, J., 337, 338 (figure), 344
Villafuerte, S., 167
Visser, G. H. A., 361
Vlachos, I., 121, 220
Vogt, B. A., 90
Vogt, L. J., 90
Volkow, N. D., 174, 175
Vollmar, P., 183
Volokhov, R. N., 276
Volz, K. G., 259
von Cramon, D. Y., 253, 259
von Frisch, O., 108, 209
Vroomen, J., 221
Vugt, M. van., 157
Vuilleumier, P., 64, 65, 114, 207, 220, 239,
    240, 241, 242
Vytal, K., 48

Wade, K. A., 247
Waelti, P., 170
Wager, T., 94, 164
Wager, T. D., 58, 89, 93, 94, 218
Wagner, G., 194, 195
Wagner, M., 95, 219
Wagner, T., 221
Wahlqvist, M. L., 361
Walker, D., 303
Walker, E. E., 27–28
Walker-Andrews, A. S., 294, 298
Wall, S., 309
Wallbott, H., 372
Wallbott, H. G., 47, 380
Wallen, K., 88

Waller, B. M., 159, 181, 207–208
Wallin, B. G., 80, 137, 194
Wallius, E., 88
Walsh, C. J., 326, 327 (figure)
Walter, B., 89, 110, 342
Walter, H., 219
Walters, E. E., 222–223
Walters, E. T., 207
Walton, M. E., 175, 194
Wang, A., 56, 57, 58, 131
Wang, F., 78
Wang, G.-J., 174, 175
Wang, H., 167
Wang, J., 334
Wang, L., 185
Wang, S., 78, 113
Wang, X., 375
Wang, X.-J., 334
Wang, Z., 56, 57, 58, 310, 311
Wang, Z.-J., 373, 378
Wani, A., 200
Wardle, J., 174, 340
Warren, J., 376
Wascher, C. A. F., 284, 285
Waser, P. G., 172
Watanabe, K., 46
Waters, E., 309
Watson, C. L., 344
Watson, D., 133, 183
Watson, J. B., 210, 223
Watson, P. J., 196
Watson, R. I., 6
Watts, J. W., 27, 165
Watts, S. W., 98
Weaver, J. M., 295, 298
Webb, T. L., 265, 266, 270, 273
Weber, J., 209
Weber, M., 219
Webster, G. D., 187, 194, 195
Wechsler, D., 138
Wedekind, C., 307
Weibgerber, S. C., 185, 343
Weike, A. I., 88, 221
Weinberger, D. R., 96, 167, 169, 190
Weinberger, N. M., 220
Weisenbach, S. L., 167
Weiskrantz, L., 221
Weisman, M. S., 119

Weiss, R., 264
Weiss, T., 220
Weller, A., 364
Wells, T. T., 190
Wenk, M. R., 48, 128, 209
Wentura, D., 252
Wessa, M., 276
Wessberg, J., 113
Westenberg, P. M., 306
Westerlund, M., 330
Wetzel, W., 221
Weyers, P., 56, 57, 58
Whale, R., 189
Wheeler, K., 299
White, J. G., 85
White, L. A., 335
White, N. M., 172
Whitehead, H., 356
Whiten, A., 356
Wicker, B., 88, 89
Wiebe, S. A., 301
Wiedemann, H.-R., 39
Wiederman, S. D., 235
Wiener, S. G., 179, 180, 181, 185
Wiens, S., 137
Wieser, M. J., 56, 57, 58
Wiesmann, M., 48, 128, 209
Wiest, C., 67
Wildgruber, D., 159
Wilkinson, R. G., 363
Wilkinson, W. W., 335
Williams, C. L., 85, 218, 249, 361
Williams, C. M., 339
Williams, J. R., 310
Williams, K. D., 44, 90, 185, 186,
    187 (figure), 343
Williams, L. M., 45, 221, 342
Willingham, B., 372, 382
Wilson, D. A., 291
Wilson, D. S., 156, 157
Wilson, M. K., 160
Wilson-Mendenhall, C. D., 56–57, 58
Winberg, J., 291
Windrem, M., 78
Wingen, G. A. van, Kooijman, S. C., 351
Wingfield, L. C., 324–326
Winston, J. S., 105
Wirtz, P. H., 342

Wise, R. A., 167, 170, 174
Wise, S., 300
Wittgenstein, L., 52
Wojciulik, E., 239
Wolf, F. W., 207
Wolf, O. T., 216, 342, 349
Wolfe, B. M., 84
Wolff, P. H., 293
Wolff, S. B. E., 121, 220
Wolitzky-Taylor, K. B., 226
Wondergem, T. R., 345
Wong, D., 128
Wong, R., 291
Wood, R., 113
Wood, S., 316
Wood, W., 323, 327, 328
Woodcock, A., 337, 351
Woodworth, R. S., 50, 138
Woodzicka, J. A., 324–326
Worsley, K., 80, 194
Wrangham, R., 342
Wrangham, R. W., 356
Wrase, J., 344
Wright, M. J., 333
Wu, F. C. W., 183, 348
Wu, S., 96
Wulfert, E., 344
Wupperman, P., 265, 279
Wyer, R. S., Jr., 156
Wynne-Edwards, K. E., 326, 327 (figure)

Xi, P., 368
Xiao, Z., 349
Xiong, J., 321
Xu, Q., 78
Xu, X., 167, 375
Xu, Y., 90, 117, 191, 193 (figure)

Yacubian, J., 169
Yagi, K., 218
Yamawaki, S., 194, 195, 343
Yan, C., 334
Yan, M., 332–333, 333 (figure)
Yandell, M., 86
Yang, B.-Z., 190
Yang, X., 96
Yang, Y., 253
Yang, Z., 184

Yazdani, U., 190
Yee, E., 251
Yeh, N.-H., 361
Yeomans, J. S., 126
Yeshurun, Y., 181, 182, 183
Yi, K., 361
Yiend, J., 237, 238
Yik, M., 53, 55 (figure)
Yoshikawa, S., 347 (figure)
Yoshimura, R., 199
Yoshimura, S., 194, 195, 343
Yoshino, A., 194, 195
Young, A. W., 131
Young, E. A., 90, 117, 191, 193 (figure)
Young, E. J., 218
Young, K. A., 190
Young, L. J., 310
Young, S. G., 377, 378 (figure)
Young, W. C., 331, 332 (figure)
Yu, S., 56, 57, 58, 131
Yu, Y. J., 311
Yuan, D., 321
Yücel, M., 44, 45

Zach, U., 293
Zahn-Waxler, C., 329
Zajonc, R. B., 38, 39 (figure), 111
Zak, P. J., 95
Zald, D. H., 233, 240, 276, 334
Zalla, T., 57, 63, 65, 88, 218
Zangen, A., 334
Zani, A., 337
Zatorre, R. J., 380

Zeisel, S. H., 361
Zeiss, A. R., 300
Zeki, S., 307
Zelazo, P. R., 361
Zelman, D. C., 194
Zeman, J., 329, 330
Zernecke, R., 48, 128, 209
Zeyda, T., 185
Zhang, D., 96
Zhang, F., 158
Zhang, J., 330
Zhang, J. X. X., 349
Zhang, M., 158
Zhang, Q., 252
Zhang, T.-Y., 292
Zhang, Y., 96, 330
Zheng, R., 373, 378
Zhong, J., 93, 113
Zhong, S., 96
Zhou, T., 382
Zhou, W., 209
Zhou, Y., 158
Zhu, C., 158
Zhu, H., 56, 57, 58, 131
Zhu, X., 86
Zillmann, D., 33
Zimmermann, E., 159
Zinner, L. R., 115
Zlomke, K. R., 348
Zubieta, J.-K., 90, 117, 167, 191, 193 (figure)
Zuo, X., 375
Zysset, S., 114, 253

Subject Index

Action potentials, 75–77, 76 (figure), 142, 446
Action tendency, 35, 36 (figure), 446
Addiction, 174–176, 446
Adenine variant, 96
Adolescence, 303–306
Adrenaline (epinephrine), 21, 33, 97–98, 446, 450
Affect labeling, 282, 446
Affective judgments, 131
Affective priming, 129–130, 130 (figure), 251–254, 257, 446
Affective Theory of Mind, 297–298
Affects
 defined, 446
 emotion elicitation techniques and, 123
 emotions vs., 43–45, 122
 Tomkins's primary affects, 42–43
Aggression and sex differences, 347–348
Aging, 311–317, 312 (figure)
Agonists, 141, 446
Agranular insula, 89, 89 (figure)
Ainsworth, Mar, 309
American Psychological Association (APA), 102–103, 446
Amino acids, 98, 167, 188–189, 218
Amnesia, 242–243. See also Memory
Amniote evolution, 29 (figure)
Amygdala
 as brain structure, 87–88, 88 (figure)
 decision making and, 259, 260 (figure)
 defined, 446
 dopamine and, 166 (figure)
 emotion regulation and, 276
 fear and, 216–218, 219 (figure), 220–222
 lesion in, 240, 247
 limbic system theory and, 25
 memory and, 245, 247–248, 248 (figure)
 relevance and, 63–64
 sadness and, 185
Anger, 58, 64–65, 64 (figure), 138, 266

Animal models, 142
Animals and emotion
 behavioral activation and inhibition systems, 163
 Darwin on, 13–14
 emotion elicitation and, 104
 learned helplessness and, 191
 nonverbal expressions and, 128, 129 (figure)
 pharmacological manipulations and, 142
 reward conditions and prediction error, 169–172, 171 (figure)
 sham-rage, 21
 smiling and laughter, 159–160, 160 (figure)
 See also Canines; Primates, nonhuman; Rats and rodents
Antagonists, 141, 446
Antecedent-focused emotion regulation, 272–273, 272 (figure), 446
"Anterior," 78, 446
Anterior cingulate, 90–91, 90 (figure), 100, 276
Anterior cingulate cortex (ACC), 186–187, 187 (figure), 195
Anterograde amnesia, 242–243
Anthropology, 355–356, 449, 450
Antithesis, principle of, 13–14
Anxiety, 205, 446. See also Fear
Anxiety disorders, 222–227, 238, 446
Appraisal theory
 appraisals, defined, 446
 Arnold's theory, 35–38, 36 (figure)
 automatic appraisal, 36, 46
 culture and, 372–377
 historical background, 58–59
 limitations of, 65–67
 on positive emotions, 154–155
 Scherer's component process model, 59–62, 61 (figure)
 sex differences and, 334–337, 338 (figure)
 support for, 62–65
 See also Emotion antecedents, appraisal of

Approach, 126

Arginine vasopressin, 310–311, 447

Aristotle, 4–5, 5 (figure), 35, 59

Arnold, Magda, 35–37, 59

Arousal, 56, 58, 154, 216

Astrocytes, 78

Átomos theory (Democritus), 3

Attachment, 107 (figure), 290–298, 303–304

Attachment styles, 309–310, 447

Attention
    behavioral paradigms, 237–238,
        238 (figure)
    brain research insights, 238–240
    fear and, 209–210, 210 (figure)
    mechanisms of, 234–237, 240–242

Attention deployment strategy, 265–268

Attentional blink paradigm, 209–210, 237,
    238 (figure)

Attentional deployment, 300

Autism, 92, 96, 447

Autobiographical memories, 116–117,
    118 (figure), 191

Automatic appraisal, 36, 46

Automatons, 11, 447

Autonomic nervous system
    about, 83–85
    defined, 447
    emotion effects on body physiology
        and, 134
    nonverbal expressions and, 128
    schematic illustration of, 84 (figure)

Autonomic response, 56

Awakenings (Sacks), 167

Axons, 74 (figure), 75, 81

Balloon Analogue Risk Task (BART),
    335, 447

Bard, James, 21, 22

Basal ganglia, 81, 447. *See also* Striatum

Basic emotions
    culture and, 359, 360
    defined, 447
    Descartes and, 10
    Ekman on, 43, 45–47
    positive emotions and, 154

Behavior therapy, 226, 447

Behavioral activation system, 163

Behavioral approach to emotion elicitation,
    118–119

Behavioral correlates of emotions,
    measurement of
    about, 125–126
    explicit explorations, 131–133
    implicit explorations, 126–131
    pros and cons, 133–134

Behavioral inhibition system, 163

Behavioral insights and observations
    attention, 237–238, 238 (figure)
    decision making, 257–258
    language, 251–254
    memory, 243–245
    sex differences, 323, 345–348
    time perception, 254–255

Behavioral tendencies
    fear, 206–209, 206 (figure)
    joy and positive emotions, 158–160
    mental processes and bodily correlates,
        relationship with, 157–158
    sadness, 180–183

Behaviorism, 20, 32, 447. *See also* Skinner box

Benzodiazepines, 224, 447

Beta-endorphins, 99, 191, 447

Bini, Lucio, 199

Biological anthropology, 356

Biological preparedness, 223

Biology as discipline, inception of, 17

Biosocial model, 323–326

Blood oxygen level dependent (BOLD) response,
    147–149

Blood-brain barrier, 85

Bodily correlates and bodily feedback
    Cannon on, 21
    cognitive arousal theory and, 33–34
    Descartes on body and emotion, 10, 11
    James-Lange theory on, 15, 17–18
    joy and positive emotions, 163–169
    mental processes and behavioral tendencies,
        relationship with, 157–158
    sadness, 184–191
    See also Peripheral correlates of emotions,
        measurement of

Body Action and Posture Coding System, 128

Bottom-up processes, 11, 235, 237, 241, 447

Bowerbirds, 307–308

Bradley, Margaret, 56, 57, 111

Brain
    atrophy with aging, 316
    attention and, 238–240

brainstem, diencephalon, cerebrum, and cerebellum, 80–82
Descartes on, 8
emotional elicitation by electrical stimulation of, 66, 120–122
ethnicity and brain variation, 367–369, 368 (figure)
evolution of, 29–30
James on, 16–17
memory and, 245–247
pineal gland, 8 (figure)
sex differences and, 331–334
structures of (overview), 87–94
See also specific structures
Brain correlates of emotions, measurement of
brain metabolism techniques, 145–149
electrical brain activity techniques, 142–145
lesion studies, 138, 140–141
pharmacological approach, 141–142
transcranial magnetic stimulation (TMS), 142
Brain processes theories
Cannon's thalamic theory, 20–21, 22 (figure)
limbic system theory, 24–31, 26 (figure)
Papez circuit, 21–24, 24 (figure), 25
thoughts processes merged with, 39–40
Brainstem, 80, 447
Breast-feeding, 363
Broca, Paul, 25
Brodmann, Korbinian, 82
Brodmann areas, 82, 82 (figure)

CAMP response element binding protein (CREB), 249, 447
Candle task (Duncker), 162, 162 (figure)
Canines
delayed gratification and, 284–285
facial expressions in, 128, 129 (figure), 159, 160, 160 (figure)
novelty appraisals and, 373
Cannibalism in New Guinea, 376
Cannon, Walter, 21, 22, 204, 213, 215, 216
Caparède, Eduard, 242
Catecholamines, 96–98, 249–250, 447
Catechol-O-methyltransferase (COMT) enzyme, 77, 86, 167. *See also* COMT gene
Categorical approach
discrete emotion categories and Tomkins's primary affects, 42–43
Ekman's basic emotions, 43, 45–47

limitations of, 48–50
on positive emotions, 154
support for, 47–48
Categorization, 52–53
Causality appraisals and culture, 377
Central nervous system (CNS)
about, 78–83, 80 (figure)
cell types and architecture, 32
cultural differences and, 380, 381 (figure)
defined, 447
fear, correlates of, 216–220
joy, correlates of, 164–169
sadness, correlates of, 185–191
Cerebellum, 83, 447
Cerebrum, 81–83, 447
Cerletti, Ugo, 199
Chicken game, 306
Childhood. *See* Infancy and childhood
China, 364
Choices, framing of, 257–258
Choline, 361, 447
Chronic pain, 194, 448
Chrysippus, 6
Cingulate gyrus, 22, 23 (figure), 448
Circadian rhythm, 201
Circumplex model, 53–54, 55 (figure), 448
Classical conditioning
attachment and, 291
fear and, 210–211, 212, 213 (figure)
joy and, 162
Pavlov and, 107–108, 109 (figure)
phobias and, 223
See also Unconditioned and conditioned stimuli
Cognition, higher-order
decision making, 257–260, 260 (figure)
defined, 251
language, categorization, and affective priming, 251–254
time perception, 254–257, 256 (figure)
Cognition-emotion polarization, 31, 38–39, 40, 233–234
Cognitive arousal theory, 33–35, 448
Cognitive change strategy, 268–270, 269 (figure)
Cognitive conflict, anterior cingulate and, 91
Cognitive emotion theories
Arnold's appraisal theory, 35–38, 36 (figure)
brain processes merged with, 39–40
historical background, 32

Schachter and Singer's cognitive arousal theory, 32–35, 34 (figure)

Zajonc-Lazarus debate, 38–39

See also Appraisal theory

Cognitive restructuring, 268–269, 269 (figure), 448

Cognitive Theory of Mind, 297–298

Cognitive therapy, 200

Cold-pressor stress task, 244

Component process model, 59–62, 61 (figure), 448

COMT gene, 167, 169 (figure), 175, 448. *See also* Catechol-O-methyltransferase (COMT) enzyme

Concealed Information Test (CIT), 139

Conceptual level of processing, 61–62

Conditioned stimulus. *See* Unconditioned and conditioned stimuli

Confrontation strategies, 266

Congenital adrenal hyperplasia (CAH), 328, 329 (figure), 348, 448

Connectivity, 333–334, 448

Consolidation of memory, 242, 244, 245, 249–250, 448

Constructionist account, 218, 359–360, 448. *See also* Dimensional approach

Contradictory emotions and folk wisdom, 379

Control Question Test (CQT), 139

Controlled appraisal, 36

Convergent evolution, 30, 448

Copernicus, 11

Coping potential, 60

Core affect, 53, 448

Corpus callosum, 81–82, 333

Cortex
in Cannon's thalamic theory, 21, 22 (figure)
defined, 82, 448
Papez circuit and, 22 (figure)

Cortisol and corticosterone (CORT), 176, 220, 222, 291–292

Cranial nerves, 80, 448

Cross-disciplinary approach, 40

Crying, 195

Csikszentmihalyi, Mihaly, 152, 451

Cultural anthropology, 356, 449

Culture and cultural differences
appraisal of emotion antecedents and, 372–377
behavioral responses, 380–382

bodily responses, 380, 381 (figure)

brain differences by ethnicity, 367–369, 368 (figure)

definitions, 355–359, 449

disease prevalence and, 366–367, 367 (figure)

ego-focused vs. other-focused emotions and, 371–372

emergence of, 359 (figure)

emotion regulation and, 274, 382

family size and, 364, 366

independence-interdependence and psychological dimensions of, 369–371

indigenous peoples and emotion outliers, 375–376

mate selection and, 360–361

maternal diet and, 361

mental responses, 378–379

parental care and, 361, 363–364

parental stress and, 361

photographic stimuli and cultural bias, 112–113

research participants and, 355

sex differences and, 337

theoretical positions on, 359–360

wealth-health connection and, 362–363, 362 (figure)

Cumulative learning, 356, 449

Cuthbert, Bruce, 111

Cyberball game, 186

Cytoarchitecture, 82, 449

Cytoplasm, 74

Damasio, Antonio, 259

Darwin, Charles
brain evolution and, 29
chimpanzees and, 159
discrete emotion categories and, 42, 43
Ekman and, 45
The Expression of Emotions in Man and Animals, 12–15
gender stereotypes and, 320
on nonverbal communication, 207
on sadness, 179

Deception, detection of, 139

Deception techniques, 115–116, 449

Decision making, 257–260, 260 (figure)

Declarative (explicit) memory, 30, 243, 449, 451

Default network, 334, 449

Defense cascade, 206–207, 206 (figure), 449

Delayed gratification, 284, 449

Democritus, 3

Dendrites, 74 (figure), 75

Deoxyribonucleic acid (DNA), 74–75,
85–87, 449

Depression
beta-endorphins and, 191
defined, 197, 449
emotion regulation and, 279–281
5-HT, role of, 188–190
sadness and, 197–198
symptoms of, 198
treatment of, 77, 187–188, 198–201

Descartes, René, 8–11, 9 (figure), 15, 42,
43, 263

Desire, Stoics on, 6

Despair, 195–196, 449

Diaries, 266

Diencephalon, 21, 80–81, 449

Diet, 201, 361

Dimensional approach
on fear, 218
limitations of, 57–58
on positive emotions, 154
Russell's circumplex model and core affect,
53–54, 55 (figure)
support for, 55–57
Wittgenstein's categories, 52–53
Woodworth scale and Schlosberg, 50–52

Directed Facial Action Task, 119

Discrete emotion categories, 42–43. *See also*
Categorical approach

Disease prevalence and culture, 366–367,
367 (figure)

Disgust, 89, 343–344

Display rules, 360, 449

Distraction strategies, 265–266, 300, 302

Distractors, 241, 302 (figure)

Distress
beta-endorphins and, 99
defined, 449
dorsal anterior cingulate and, 100
infant crying and, 292
kin bonds and, 366
parenting and, 330
regulation of, 300, 302, 302 (figure)
sex differences and, 342
social, 186–187, 202

as stage of sadness, 180, 180 (figure),
185, 186, 187 (figure)
use of term, 180

Division of labor, sex-based, 326–328

DNA (deoxyribonucleic acid), 74–75, 85–87, 449

Dogs. *See* Canines

Dopamine
addiction and, 174–176
blockage of, 167, 168 (figure)
as catecholamine, 96–98
defined, 449
pathways of, 166 (figure)
PET imaging and, 147
reward, joy, and role of, 165–172

Dopaminergic drugs, 66

"Dorsal," 78–79, 449

Dorsal cortex, 28

Dot-probe task, 238, 238 (figure)

Doyle, Arthur Conan, 287

DRD4, 298–299

Duchenne de Boulogne, Guillaume, 14 (figure)

Duchenne smile, 159, 380, 449

Duncker, Karl, 162, 162 (figure)

Dysgranular insula, 89 (figure)

Eagly, Alice, 323–326

Eccrine sweat glands, 137–138

Eggs and sperm, 321

Ego-focused emotions, 371–372, 449–450

Ekman, Paul, 43, 45–47, 110–111, 119, 154

Electrical brain activity measurement, 142–145

Electrical brain stimulation (EBS)
dopamine blockage and, 168 (figure)
emotional induction by, 66, 120–122
in humans, 165
joy and, 164

Electrocardiogram (ECG), 134–135,
135 (figure), 450

Electroconvulsive therapy (ECT), 199–200, 450

Electrodermal measures, 137–138, 139, 450

Electroencephalography (EEG), 25, 39–40,
143–145, 144 (figure), 450

Elicitation of emotions
autobiographical memories and, 116–117,
118 (figure)
behavioral approach, 118–119
electrical brain stimulation and optogenetics,
120–122
emotion theories and, 122

laboratory constraints on, 102–105
unconditioned and conditioned stimuli, nature of, 105–110
unconditioned and conditioned stimuli, use of, 110–116
"Embodied," 450
Emotion and Personality (Arnold), 35, 37
Emotion antecedents, appraisal of
    causality appraisals and culture, 377
    defined, 372
    goal-conduciveness and in-group/out-group encounters, 376–377, 378 (figure)
    novelty and out-group encounters, 373–375, 374 (figure)
    sex differences and, 334–338, 336 (figure)
Emotion elicitation. *See* Elicitation of emotions
Emotion judgments and explicit explorations of behavior, 131
Emotion prototypes, 54, 450
Emotion regulation
    action and, 263
    attention deployment strategy, 265–268
    brain mechanisms supporting, 276–279, 277 (figure)
    cognitive change strategy, 268–270
    conceptual challenges for, 281–283
    culture and, 274, 382
    defined, 282–283, 450
    Descartes and, 11
    event factors in, 272–274
    functions of, 264–265
    history of interest in, 263–264
    individual factors in, 274–276
    in infants and young children, 300–303
    mental health and, 279–281
    methodological challenges for, 283–285
    response modulation strategies, 270–272
    sex differences and, 348–349, 350 (figure)
Emotion-cognition polarization, 31, 38–39, 40, 233–234
Emotions
    affects and mood vs., 43–45
    definitions of, 31, 37, 69, 450
Emotion-specific physiological and behavioral responses, 46, 48–50
Empathy and social group membership, 373, 375
Encoding of memory, 242, 244, 245, 249–250
Endocrine system, 134

Endogenous opioid system, 200–201
Enzymes, 77, 450
Epigenetic mechanisms, 86, 223, 450
Epilepsy, 25, 450
Epinephrine (adrenaline), 21, 33, 97–98, 446, 450
Epithymētikon, 4
Essential amino acids, 98, 167, 188–189, 450
Estrogen, 349
Ethics standards, 102–103
Ethnicity. *See* Culture and cultural differences
Evaluations
    Arnold's appraisal theory, 35–36
    cognitive arousal theory and, 33–35
    dimensional approach and, 55–56, 57
Event-related heart rate, 135–137, 136 (figure), 450
Event-related potentials (ERPs)
    EEG research and, 143–145, 144 (figure)
    emotion regulation and, 274–275, 275 (figure)
    infants and, 294
    language and, 253
    positive affect and, 161, 161 (figure)
Evolution
    appraisal theory and, 67
    brain evolution, 29–30
    Darwin's theory of, 12–13, 49
    defined, 450
    humor and, 157
    parallel and convergent, 30
    rethinking of, 356–357
Evolutionary anthropology, 356–357, 450
Evolutionary theory, 12–14
Exercise, physical, 200–201
Experience sampling method, 311, 450–451
Explicit emotion processing, 94, 451
Explicit explorations of behavior, 131–134
Explicit (declarative) memories, 30, 243, 449, 451
Exploration in life span, 298–300, 305–306
Exploration methods. *See* Behavioral correlates of emotions, measurement of; Brain correlates of emotions, measurement of; Peripheral correlates of emotions, measurement of
Exploratory behaviors and reward, 173
The Expression of the Emotions in Man and Animals (Darwin), 12–14
Extinction (learning), 108, 226, 227 (figure), 451

Extinction (perception), 240, 451
Extracranial recordings, 143–145
Eye gaze patterns and culture, 380
Eyeblink, 126

Facial Action Coding System, 128, 451
Facial expressions
  as conditioned stimuli, 106, 106 (figure)
  dimensional approach and, 50–51
  Directed Facial Action Task, 119
  Ekman's basic emotions and, 45, 50
  Ekman's Pictures of Facial Affect, 110–111,
    112–113
  exploring emotions with, 127–128,
    129 (figure)
  fear conditioning and, 214–215, 214 (figure)
  pen in teeth and, 66, 66 (figure)
  sex differences and, 345–346, 347 (figure)
  smiles, 158–159, 160 (figure)
Familiarity, 244, 451
Family size and culture, 364, 366
Fear
  amygdala and, 88
  anterior cingulate and, 91
  anxiety disorders and phobias, 222–227
  anxiety vs., 205
  attachment and, 291–292
  behavioral tendencies, 206–209, 206 (figure)
  central nervous system correlates, 216–220
  cognitive restructuring and, 268–269,
    269 (figure)
  conditioning and, 108
  defined, 451
  dimensional approach and, 58
  electrodermal measures and, 138
  elicitation of, 104, 122
  Freud on, 204
  functions of, 222
  in-group/out-group interactions and,
    373, 374 (figure)
  mechanisms, 220–222
  mental processes, 209–213, 210 (figure),
    214–215
  peripheral correlates, 213, 215–216
  physiological changes in, 49
  readiness for, 214–215
  relevance vs. intrinsic pleasantness and,
    64–65, 64 (figure)
  sex differences and, 342
  Stoics on, 6
  triggers for, 204–205
Fear modules, 218, 451
Fear sleep, 376
Fight-or-flight response, 206 (figure), 207, 349
Films, 114–115
5-HT (serotonin) transporter gene, 189–190,
    190 (figure), 451
5-hydroxytryptamine (5-HT or serotonin),
    98–99, 188–189, 451, 458
Flashbulb memories, 117, 118 (figure),
    244–245, 246–247 (figure), 451
Flow, 152, 451
Folk wisdom, 379
Follicular phase, 351, 352 (figure), 451
Forebrain, 164, 451
Freeman, Walter, 27
Freezing, 127, 207, 376, 451
Freud, Sigmund, 25, 204, 279, 320
Frijda, Nico, 37
Frontal lobe, 27, 81 (figure), 276
Frontolobotomies, 27
Frontotemporal dementia, 92, 451
Functional fixedness, 162
Functional magnetic resonance imaging (fMRI),
    63–64, 147–149, 316
Fusiform gyrus, 185

GABAergic activity, 77, 220, 224, 228, 348
Gage, Phineas, 93, 140, 140 (figure)
Galen's theory, 6, 7 (figure)
Galileo, 11
Gametes, 321–323, 322 (figure), 451
Gaming experiments, 344
Gamma-aminobutyric-acid (GABA), 77, 220.
    See also GABAergic activity
Gender, defined, 451–452. *See also*
    Sex differentiation
Gender roles, 323–328
Gendered minds position, 323–326
Gene transcription, 86
Generalized anxiety disorder, 223, 452
Genes, 85–86, 330–331
Genetic regulation of nervous system, 85–87
Gibbon, John, 457
Glial cells, 77–78, 452
Gliotransmitters, 78, 94–95, 452
Globus pallidus, 26, 26 (figure), 452
Glucocorticoid receptors, 364, 365 (figure)

Glucosteroids and memory, 250
Glutamate, 77, 78
Goal conduciveness, 376–377, 378 (figure)
Goal relevance, 65, 155
Goal-conduciveness, 376–377, 378 (figure)
Golgi, Camillo, 32
Go/no-go tasks, 301, 305–306, 452
Goodall, Jane, 159
Granular insula, 89 (figure)
Granule cells, 89, 90, 452
Gray matter, 75, 75 (figure), 316, 332
Greek mythology, 231
Greek philosophy, 2–7, 9, 263, 379
Gross behaviors, 126–127, 127 (figure), 347–348
Guilty Knowledge Test (GKT), 139
Gustatory cortex, 89, 452

H. M., 242–243, 243 (figure)
Habenula, 172
Habits, serviceable associated, 13
Hate crimes, 347
Health-wealth relationship by country,
    362–363, 362 (figure)
Heart, Aristotle on, 5
Heart rate, 134–137, 135 (figure), 136 (figure)
Heart-rate variability (HRV), 135, 452
Heath, Robert, 165
Hebb, Donald, 249
Hebbian learning, 249, 452
Hellenistic period, 5–6
Hemispatial neglect, 239–240, 239 (figure), 452
"Here and now" focus, 312–313, 314 (figure)
Hiding, 127
Higher-order cognitive processes. See Cognition,
    higher-order
Hines, Melissa, 328
Hippocampal glucocorticoid receptors,
    364, 365 (figure)
Hippocampus, 23 (figure)
    defined, 452
    limbic system theory and, 25, 26 (figure), 28
    memory and, 30, 245, 247–248, 248 (figure)
    Papez circuit and, 22
Homer, 231
Homosexuality, 165
Hormones, 94–95, 452
Humanistic psychology, 152
Humor, 156–157
Humors, 6, 452

Hypothalamic-pituitary-adrenal (HPA) axis, 81,
    85, 215–216, 217 (figure), 221
Hypothalamus, 21–22, 23 (figure), 24 (figure),
    80–81, 452

Identity beliefs and Theory of Mind, 297–298
Implication checks, 60
Implicit Association Test (IAT), 130–131,
    132 (figure), 335, 452
Implicit emotion processing, 94, 452
Implicit explorations of behavior
    gross behaviors, 126–127, 127 (figure)
    nonverbal expressions, 127–128, 129 (figure)
    pros and cons of, 133
    psychological tasks, 129–131, 132 (figure)
Implicit (procedural) memories, 243, 452
Imprinting, 290–291, 452–453
Independence, in adolescence, 303–306
Independence-interdependence dimension,
    369–371, 370 (figure)
Indigenous peoples, 375–376
Industrial revolution, 11–12
Industrial revolution, second, 20
Infancy and childhood
    attachment and, 290–298
    crying and, 195
    culture and parental care, 361, 363–364
    Ekman's basic emotions and, 46–47
    emotion regulation and, 300–303
    parental stress and, 361
Inflammatory system, 201
In-group interactions, 373–377, 374 (figure)
Insula, 31, 89–90, 89 (figure), 200, 453
Interaction approach to emotion elicitation, 116
Interdependence and independence,
    369–371, 370 (figure)
Interference tasks, 184
International Affective Picture System (IAPS),
    111, 112–113, 131, 339, 340, 345, 453
Intracranial recordings, 143, 145
Iowa Gambling Task, 259, 340, 342

James, William, 15–18, 20, 34, 118, 119, 259
James-Lange theory, 15, 16 (figure), 17–18,
    21, 32, 34–35
Jokes, 156–157
Joy and positive emotions
    addiction and, 174–176
    behavioral tendencies, 158–160

bodily correlates, 163–169
defined, 155, 453
functions of, 172–174
Maslow's hierarchy of needs and,
    152, 153 (figure)
mechanisms, 169–172
mental processes, 160–163
neglect of and attention to, 152–153
sadness and, 178
theoretical accounts of number of, 154–155
triggers for, 155–157
vocal profile for, 47
Jung, Carl, 138

Kahneman, Daniel, 257–258
Kinship bonds, 366
Korsakoff amnesia, 242
Koskinas, Georg N., 91
Kunst-Wilson, W. R., 38, 39 (figure)

Lamarckian theory, 13, 453
Lang, Peter, 56, 57, 111
Lange, Carl, 15, 16 (figure), 34, 259
Language, 251–254, 378–379
"Lateral," 79, 453
Laughter, 159–160
Lavater, Johann Kaspar, 7 (figure)
Law of effect, 162, 453. *See also* Operant
    conditioning
Lazarus, Richard, 36, 37, 38–39
Learned helplessness, 191, 200, 453
Learning. *See* Behavior therapy; Classical
    conditioning; Operant conditioning;
    Unconditioned and conditioned stimuli;
    Vicarious learning
LeDoux, Joseph, 151, 216, 220
Lesion studies, 138, 140–141, 216, 233
Level of processing, 61–62, 453
Lie detection, 139
Limbic, defined, 453
Limbic system theory
    application of, 27–28
    critique and recent developments, 28–31
    development of, 24–27
Lincoln, Abraham, 246
Locus coeruleus, 218, 453
Logos, 4
Long-term depression (LTD), 172, 453
Long-term potentiation (LTP), 172, 453

Lorenz, Konrad, 107 (figure)
Loss aversion, 258
Luteal phase, 351, 352 (figure), 453

Machines, "intelligent," 32
MacLean, Paul, 24–27, 28, 31, 216
Magnetic resonance imaging (MRI)
    cross-disciplinary approach and,
        39–40
    defined, 453–454
    functional (fMRI), 63–64, 147–149, 316
    sad vs. neutral mood induction study,
        44 (figure)
    technique of, 147, 148 (figure)
Major histocompatibility complex (MHC),
    307, 454
Marcus Aurelius, 266, 268
Marshmallow test, 300, 454
Masks, 111, 454
Maslow, Abraham, 152, 153 (figure)
Mate choice, 306–308, 360–361
Maternal diet, 361
"Medial," 79, 454
Medial forebrain bundle, 164, 166 (figure), 454
Medial prefrontal cortex, 90 (figure),
    93, 316, 334, 454
Medial temporal lobe memory system,
    248 (figure)
Medial temporal lobectomy, 242–243
Membrane potential, 75–76
Memory
    amnesia, 242–243
    autobiographical memories, 116–117,
        118 (figure), 191
    behavioral insights, 243–245
    brain research insights, 245–247
    encoding, consolidation, and retrieval
        processes, 242, 244, 245, 249–250
    fear and, 210–211, 219
    flashbulb memories, 117, 118 (figure),
        244–245, 246–247 (figure), 451
    hormonal changes and, 351
    implicit/procedural vs. explicit/
        declarative, 243
    limbic system theory and, 30
    mechanisms of, 247–251, 248 (figure)
    mental resources underlying, 275–276
    phobias and, 224–225, 225 (figure)
    reward-related information in, 173

sex differences and, 339
thought suppression and, 270–272,
     271 (figure)
Menstrual cycle, 351, 352 (figure)
Mental processes
   behavioral tendencies and bodily correlates,
        relationship with, 157–158
   fear, 209–213, 210 (figure), 214–215
   joy and positive emotions, 160–163
   sadness, 183–184
Mervis, Carolyn, 52–53
Mesocortical pathway, 166 (figure)
Mesostriatal pathway, 166 (figure)
Metabolic changes in the brain, 145–149
Metacognition, 200
Methionine alleles, 167, 169 (figure), 175
Methods for eliciting emotion. *See* Elicitation
     of emotions
Methods for exploring emotions. *See* Behavioral
     correlates of emotions, measurement of;
     Brain correlates of emotions, measurement
     of; Peripheral correlates of emotions,
     measurement of
Methyl groups, 86–87
Mind-body problem, 73, 454
Mindfulness training (MT), 200, 454
Mixed longitudinal design, 454
Moniz, Egas, 27
Monkeys. *See* Primates, nonhuman
Monoamine oxidase (MAO), 77
Monoamineoxidase (MAO) inhibitors,
     77, 187–188, 188 (figure), 454
Monoamines, 96–99, 187–191, 199, 454
Monogamy, 309, 454
Mood disorders. *See* Depression
Moods
   defined, 454
   emotions vs., 44–45
   memory retrieval and, 244
   MRI study, 44 (figure)
Morphine, 141
Mother-infant attachment, 292–298
MRI. *See* Magnetic resonance imaging (MRI)
Multidimensional scaling, 53, 54 (figure), 454
Multidimensional space. *See* Dimensional
     approach
Multiple sclerosis (MS), 78
Mu-opioid system, 191
Music, 113, 114

N400 effect, 253, 253 (figure)
Natural environments, complexity of, 234
Natural selection, 12–13
Needs hierarchy (Maslow), 152, 153 (figure)
Negative affect
   addiction and, 174
   elicitation of, 122
   infant distraction and, 300
   mood, emotion, and, 45
   regulation of, 274, 280
   self-soothing and, 302
   sex differences and, 339–340, 341 (figure),
        342–344, 343 (figure)
   See also Positive and Negative Affect
        Schedule (PANAS)
Negativity bias, 313
Neocortex
   defined, 454
   limbic system theory and, 26 (figure),
        27, 28
   parallel evolution of, 30
Neomammalian brain, 26 (figure), 28, 31
Nervous system
   brain, parts of, 79–83
   cell types and function, 74–78
   central (overview), 78–83, 80 (figure)
   chemical messengers, 94–99
   Darwin on, 14
   defined, 454
   genetic and epigenetic regulation of, 85–87
   microscopic and macroscopic aspects of, 74
   peripheral (overview), 83–85
   schematic illustration of, 80 (figure)
   See also Central nervous system (CNS);
        Peripheral nervous system (PNS)
Neural valuation system, 360
Neurochemicals. *See* Beta-endorphins;
     Dopamine; Monoamines
Neuroimaging
   amygdala and, 88
   appraisal theory and, 63
   cognition-emotion division and, 233
   EEG, 25, 39–40, 143–145, 144 (figure), 450
   limitations of, 40
   on sadness and pain, 195
   valence and arousal and, 56, 58
   See also Magnetic resonance imaging (MRI);
        specific brain structures
Neuronal oscillations, 143

Neurons
  action potential and neurotransmitters, 75–77, 76 (figure)
  defined, 454
  gray and white matter, 75, 75 (figure)
  optogenetics and, 121
  somas, dendrites, and axons, 74–75, 74 (figure)
  transporters, 77
Neuropeptides, 95, 455
Neurotransmitters
  action potential and, 76–77
  chemical messengers and, 94–95
  defined, 75, 455
  See also specific neurotransmitters
New Guinea, 375, 376
9/11 attack and memory, 247
Nociceptors, 193
Noise vs. signal, 103–104
Nonverbal expressions
  implicit exploration of behavior and, 127–128, 129 (figure)
  joy and, 158–159
  suppression of, 270
Norepinephrine (noradrenaline), 97–98, 218–219, 455
Normative significance, 60
Novelty, 298–299, 305–306, 373–375, 374 (figure)
Nucleus accumbens, 293 (figure), 310

Occipital lobe, 81 (figure)
Oddball procedure, 63, 237, 455
Odysseus, 231, 234
Older adults, 311–317
Olds, James, 120, 164
Olfactory perception (smell), 25
Oligodendrocytes, 77–78
On the Soul (Aristotle), 5
Online measures, 59, 455
Operant conditioning
  defined, 455
  fear and, 211, 212 (figure), 213
  joy and reward and, 158, 162–163
  reward-related behaviors and, 173
  Skinner box, 158, 158 (figure), 164
  Thorndike and, 152
Opioids, 99, 455
Optogenetics, 121–122, 121 (figure), 141

Orbicularis occuli, 127, 159, 181, 345, 455
Orbitofrontal cortex, 259, 260 (figure)
Osgood, Charles, 55–56
Other-focused emotions, 371–372, 455
Out-group interactions, 373–377, 374 (figure)
Oxytocin, 95–96, 292, 310–311, 455

Pain
  attachment and, 291
  chronic, 194, 448
  component process model and, 59–60
  sadness and, 192–195
  somatosensory system and, 193–194
  Stoics on, 6
Paleomammalian brain, 26, 26 (figure), 28, 455
Panic disorder, 223, 455
Panksepp, Jaak, 48–49, 154, 160
Papez, James, 21–24, 216
Papez circuit, 21–24, 24 (figure), 25
Parahippocampal gyrus, 56, 245, 455
Parallel evolution, 30, 455
Parasympathetic nervous system, 83–85, 84 (figure), 134, 455
Parental care and culture, 361, 363–364
Parental stress, 361
Parenting and sex differences, 328–330, 329 (figure)
Parietal lobe, 81 (figure), 276–278
Parkinson's disease, 165, 167
The Passions of the Soul (Descartes), 8–11
Pasterski, Vicky, 328
Pathogens, 366–367, 367 (figure), 455
Pavlov, Ivan, 107–108, 173
Peer attachment, 303–304
Peer effect, male, 335
Peer review, 455
Perception. *See* Attention
Perceptual bottlenecks, 235, 455
Peripheral correlates of emotions, measurement of
  about, 134
  electrodermal activity, 137–138, 139
  heart rate, 134–137, 135 (figure), 136 (figure)
Peripheral nervous system (PNS)
  about, 83–85
  aging and, 317
  cultural differences and, 380, 381 (figure)
  defined, 455–456
  fear, correlates of, 213, 215–216

joy, correlates of, 163
sadness, correlates of, 185
Pharmacological approach to influencing brain
    function, 141–142
Phenomenological approach, 35, 456
Pheromones
    categorical approach and, 48
    defined, 456
    fear and, 209
    as nonverbal expressions, 128
    in tears, 181–183
Phobias, 223–226, 456
Photographs
    emotion elicitation via, 110–113
    International Affective Picture System (IAPS),
        111, 112–113, 131, 339, 340, 345, 453
    Pictures of Facial Affect, 110–111,
        112–113, 456
Phylogenetically, defined, 456
Physiological correlates of emotions. *See*
    Peripheral correlates of emotions,
    measurement of
Pictures of Facial Affect, 110–111, 112–113, 456
Pineal gland, 8 (figure), 456
Pituitary, 85
Plato, 3–4, 5 (figure), 6
Plato's Academy, 2–3
Play face, 159
Pleasantness, 59–60, 64–65, 154–155
Pleasure, 6, 59–60
Pleasure center, 120, 164, 165, 166 (figure), 456
Point Subtraction Aggression Paradigm (PSAP),
    347–348, 456
Positive and Negative Affect Schedule (PANAS),
    133, 183, 456
Positive emotions. *See* Joy and positive emotions
Positive psychology, 152, 456
Positivity effect, 313, 315–316, 456
Positron emission tomography (PET), 145–147,
    146 (figure), 149, 191, 192 (figure),
    193 (figure), 456
Postencephalitic Parkinson's, 167
"Posterior," 78, 456
Postsynaptic potentials, 142
Practice, in definition of culture, 358
Prairie voles, 310, 310 (figure)
Precession, 147, 456
Preferential looking paradigm, 298–299,
    299 (figure), 456

Prefrontal cortex
    emotion regulation and, 277 (figure), 280
    medial, 90 (figure), 93, 316, 334, 454
    sadness and ventral prefrontal cortex,
        186–187, 187 (figure)
Pregnancy, 290, 326, 327 (figure), 361
Premotor cortex, 58, 456
Preparedness, 212, 213 (figure), 214–215,
    223, 456
Pride, 372
Primary affects, 42–43, 456
Primary and secondary emotions, 10
Primary social consequences, 178
Primates, nonhuman
    attention and, 236 (figure)
    cumulative learning and, 356, 357 (figure)
    evolution and, 30
    fear and, 208 (figure), 214–215
    infatuation in orangutans, 307
    laughter and, 159
    promiscuity in chimpanzees, 309
    reward-directed behavior and, 170
    sadness and, 185, 194
    silent bared-teeth display,
        159, 160 (figure), 208
    submission and aggression in, 197 (figure)
    von Economo neurons and, 28
Principal component analysis, 62–63,
    456–457
The Principles of Psychology, 17
Problem-based coping, 178–179, 457
Procedural (implicit) memories, 243, 452
Promiscuity, 309
Prospect theory, 258, 457
Prototypes, 53, 457
Psyche, 3, 457. *See also* Soul
Psychoanalytic theory, 25
Psychology
    behaviorism and, 20
    as discipline, inception of, 15, 17
    humanistic, 152
    paradigm shift from behaviorism toward
        cognition, 32
    positive, 152, 456

QRS complexes, 134–135, 457

Radiotracers, 145–147
Ramón y Cajal, Santiago, 32

Rats and rodents
  dopamine blockage and, 167, 168 (figure)
  electrical brain stimulation and optogenetics,
      120–121, 120 (figure), 121 (figure)
  laughter in, 160
  maternal licking and grooming,
      364, 365 (figure)
  reward processing in nucleus accumbens,
      293 (figure)
  sadness and, 185
  social place conditioning, 304, 304 (figure)
Rayner, Rosalie, 210
Readiness potential, 254, 457
Reappraisals, 268–270, 281
Reason in Greek thought, 4, 6–7
Receptive fields, 235, 457
Recollection, 244, 457. *See also* Memory
Reconsolidation, 224, 457
Regulation of emotions. *See* Emotion regulation
Reimer, Bruce, 323
Relaxation, in MRI, 147
Relevance checks, 59–60
Relevance vs. intrinsic pleasantness, 64–65
Remission rates, 199, 200, 457
Renaissance and post-Renaissance
      period, 7–11
Reptilian brain, 26, 26 (figure), 28
Response modulation strategies, 270–272,
      271 (figure), 301–302
Response preparation effects, 254
Response-focused emotion regulation,
      272–273, 272 (figure), 457
Resting periods, 93
Retrieval of memory, 242, 244, 245,
      247, 249–250, 457
Reward
  approach and, 126
  behavioral activation and, 163
  cultural differences and, 380, 381 (figure)
  defined, 156
  dopamine, role of, 165–172
  humor as, 156–157
  joy as unexpected prospect of, 155
  mechanisms and conditions, 169–172
  responses to, 172–174
  sex differences and, 345, 346 (figure)
  ventral striatum and, 48
  See also Joy and positive emotions
Reward prediction error, 170, 171 (figure), 457

Rhinencephalon, 25
Risk
  adolescence and, 305–306
  decision making and, 258
  one-child context and, 366
  preparedness and, 223
  sadness and, 195–196
  sex differences and appraisal of, 334–335,
      342, 344
  stereotype threat and, 325
  uncertainty and, 260
Roman period, 6
Romantic relationships, 306–311
Rosch, Eleanor, 52–53
Russell, James, 53–54, 57, 58

Sacks, Oliver, 167
Sadness
  anterior cingulate and, 90–91
  behavioral tendencies, 180–183
  bodily correlates, 184–191
  defined, 457
  depression, 197–201
  elicitation of, 104
  functions of, 195–197
  joy and, 178
  mechanisms, 191–195
  mental processes, 183–184
  MRI of neutral mood vs., 44 (figure)
  sex differences and, 342–343
  stages of, 179–180, 180 (figure)
  triggers for, 178–179
  vocal profile for, 47
Sanzio, Raffaello, 5 (figure)
Scalar expectancy theory, 255, 457
Schachter, Stanley, 32–33, 37
Schadenfreunde, 164, 379
Schematic level of processing, 61–62
Scherer, Klaus, 47, 59–62
Schlosberg, Harold, 51–52, 57
Schwann cells, 77–78
Sclerosis, 240, 457
Screams, 208
Secondary social consequences, 178–179
Secure and insecure attachments, 309–310
Seeking, 154
Selective serotonin reuptake inhibitors (SSRIs),
      77, 188, 458
Self-actualization, 152, 153 (figure), 458

Self-Assessment Manikin, 111
Self-construal, 369–372, 370 (figure), 377, 458
Self-reference effect, 117, 458
Self-relevance, 117
Seligman, Martin, 152, 453
Semantic processing, 253–254
Sensation seeking, 175
Sensation vs. emotion, Descartes on, 9
Sensory information
    amygdala and, 219 (figure), 228
    in Cannon's thalamic theory, 21, 22 (figure)
    central nervous system and, 100
    Papez circuit and, 22
    thalamus and, 195
Sensory nervous system, 83
Sensory-motor level of processing, 61–62
Sentience, 274–275, 275 (figure), 458
Serotonin. *See* 5-hydroxytryptamine (5-HT
    or serotonin)
Serviceable associated habits, principle of, 13
Sex differentiation
    behavioral responses, 345–348
    bodily responses, 342–345
    brain and, 331–334, 333 (figure)
    elicitation and appraisal of emotion
        antecedents and, 334–338
    emotion regulation and, 348–349, 350 (figure)
    gendered minds position and biosocial model,
        323–326
    genetic factors in, 330–331
    mental responses, 339–342
    origins of, 321–323
    parenting as environmental factor in,
        328–330
    research challenges, 349–352
    sex-typed minds position, 326–328
    Skinner and, 323
    stereotypes and, 320
Sex hormones, changes in, 351, 352 (figure)
Sex-typed minds position, 326–328
Sexual dimorphism, 321, 458
Sham-rage, 21, 458
Shunning of strangers, 375
Signal vs. noise, 103–104
Silent bared-teeth display, 159, 160 (figure), 208
Similarity assessments, 53
Singer, Jerome, 32–33
Single nucleotide polymorphisms (SNPs),
    96, 97 (figure), 458

Skin resistance and skin conductance response,
    137–138
Skinner, B. F., 323
Skinner box, 158, 158 (figure), 164
Sleep and depression, 201
Smell (olfactory perception), 25
Smiling
    across species, 159, 160 (figure)
    culture and, 380–381
    Duchenne smile, 159, 380
    fear and, 208
    in infants, 294
    joy and, 158–159
    pen in teeth and, 66
    sex differences and, 345–346
Social constructionist account,
    218, 359–360, 448
Social distress, 186–187, 202
Social place conditioning, 304, 304 (figure)
Social psychological methods, 115–116
Social status and health, 363
Socioemotional information, sex differences for,
    351–352
Socioemotional selectivity theory (SST),
    312–316, 458
Socratic thinking, 3–4, 458
Somas, 74–75, 74 (figure)
Somatic marker hypothesis, 259, 458
Somatic nervous system, 83, 128
Soul, 3–5, 8–10
Sounds, 113–114. *See also* Vocalizations
Sperm and eggs, 321
Spinal cord, 79
Spontaneous recovery, 226, 458
Startle reflex
    culture and, 380
    defense cascade and, 206–207
    defined, 458
    as gross behavior, 126, 127 (figure)
    sex differences and, 337
Stereotype threat, 324–326,
    325 (figure), 458
Stimulus-dependent emotional processing,
    93–94
Stoic school, 5–6, 263, 458
Streams of thought, movement, and feeling
    (Papez), 22–23
Stress, 176, 361, 363
Striatal beat-frequency model, 255, 458

Striatum
    cerebrum and, 81
    cultural differences and, 380, 381 (figure)
    decision making and, 259, 260 (figure)
    defined, 458–459
    joy and *Schadenfreunde* and, 164
    limbic system theory and, 26, 26 (figure)
    rewarding stimuli and, 48
Stroop, John Ridley, 184, 459
Stroop tasks, 184
    defined, 459
Subcortical nuclei. *See* Basal ganglia
Subliminally, defined, 459
Submission response, 196, 197 (figure)
Suppression, 270–272, 271 (figure), 281
Sympathetic activation
    Cannon on, 21
Sympathetic adrenal medullary system (SAM),
    85, 215–216, 217 (figure)
    fear and, 221
Sympathetic nervous system, 84 (figure)
    autonomic nervous system and, 83–85
    Cannon on, 21
    defined, 459
    emotion effects on body physiology and, 134
Synapses, 75
    defined, 459
Synaptic cleft, 75
Synaptic remodeling, long-term and short-term,
    249, 250 (figure)

Task-dependent emotional processing, 94
Task-relevant and task-irrelevant objects,
    attention and, 235
Taxon
    defined, 459
Tears, 181–183, 182 (figure)
Temporal discounting, 174, 175 (figure)
    defined, 459
Temporal lobe, 81 (figure)
    emotion regulation and, 276
Tend-and-befriend response, 349
    defined, 459
Testosterone, 328, 329 (figure),
    331, 332 (figure), 348
Text anxiety, 267 (figure), 268
Thalamus, 23 (figure)
    Cannon's thalamic theory, 21, 22 (figure)
    defined, 459

    as diencephalon structure, 80
    fear and, 216
    limbic system theory and, 26 (figure)
    pain, sadness, and, 195
    Papez circuit and, 21–22, 24 (figure)
Theories
    defined, 459
    emotion elicitation and, 122
    on positive emotions, 154–155
Theory of Mind (ToM), 295, 297–298
    defined, 459
Thorndike, Edward, 152, 164, 173, 453
Thought suppression, 270–272, 271 (figure)
Thought-based theories. *See* Cognitive emotion
    theories
Threats
    fear and, 204–205, 219
    readiness for, 214–215
    sex differences and, 342
Thymos, 4
Time perception, 254–257, 256 (figure)
Tomkins, Silvan, 37, 42–43, 45
Tonic changes, 172
    defined, 459
Top-down processes
    attention mechanisms, 235, 237, 241–242
    defined, 459
    Descartes on, 11
Total peripheral resistance
    defined, 459
    fear and, 49
Transcranial magnetic stimulation (TMS), 142
    defined, 459
    depression, rTMS for, 280
Transcription factors, 86
Transporters, 77
    defined, 459
Tricyclic antidepressants, 187–188
    defined, 459
Trust game, 364, 366
Tryptamines
    as monoamines, 98–99
Tryptophan
    defined, 460
    serotonin and, 98
Turner syndrome (TS), 331
    defined, 460
Tversky, Amos, 257–258
2-back task, 244

Unconditioned and conditioned stimuli
  defined, 448, 460
  films, 114–115
  nature of conditioned stimuli, 107–110
  nature of unconditioned stimuli, 105–106
  pictures, 110–113
  social psychological methods, 115–116
  sounds, 113–114
Universal antecedents
  defined, 460
  Ekman's basic emotions and, 46
Utku Eskimo, 375–376

Vagus nerve, 80, 85
  defined, 460
Valence
  defined, 460
  dimensional approach and, 56, 58
  novelty appraisals and, 373
  positive emotions and, 154
Valine alleles, 167, 169 (figure), 175
Van Gogh, Vincent, 199 (figure)
Van Karnebeek, Jacques, 7 (figure)
"Ventral," 78–79, 460
Ventral prefrontal cortex (vPFC), 186–187,
  187 (figure)
Ventral striatum. *See* Striatum
Vicarious learning, 108, 460
Violence and sex differences, 347
Viscera, 15, 21, 460
Visual neurons, 235, 236 (figure)
Visual search paradigm, 209, 237,
  238 (figure)

Vocal profiles, 47
Vocalizations
  animals and, 128
  emotion elicitation via, 113–114
  fear and, 208
  laughter, 159–160
  as nonverbal expressions, 128
  sadness and, 180–181
Vomeronasal organ, 48, 460
Von Economo, Constantin, 91
Von Economo neurons, 28, 91–92,
  92 (figure), 460

Watson, John, 210
Watts, James, 27
Wealth-health relationship by country, 362–363,
  362 (figure)
White matter, 75, 75 (figure), 81–82,
  316, 332–333, 460
Wittgenstein, Ludwig, 52
Wood, Wendy, 323–326
Woodworth, Robert, 50–51
Woodworth Emotion Scale, 51, 51 (figure)
World Medical Association, 102–103, 460
Writing for emotion regulation, 266–268
Wundt, William, 15, 20

X chromosome, 330–331

Y chromosome, 330–331

Zajonc, Robert, 38, 39 (figure)
Zygomaticus major, 158–159, 460